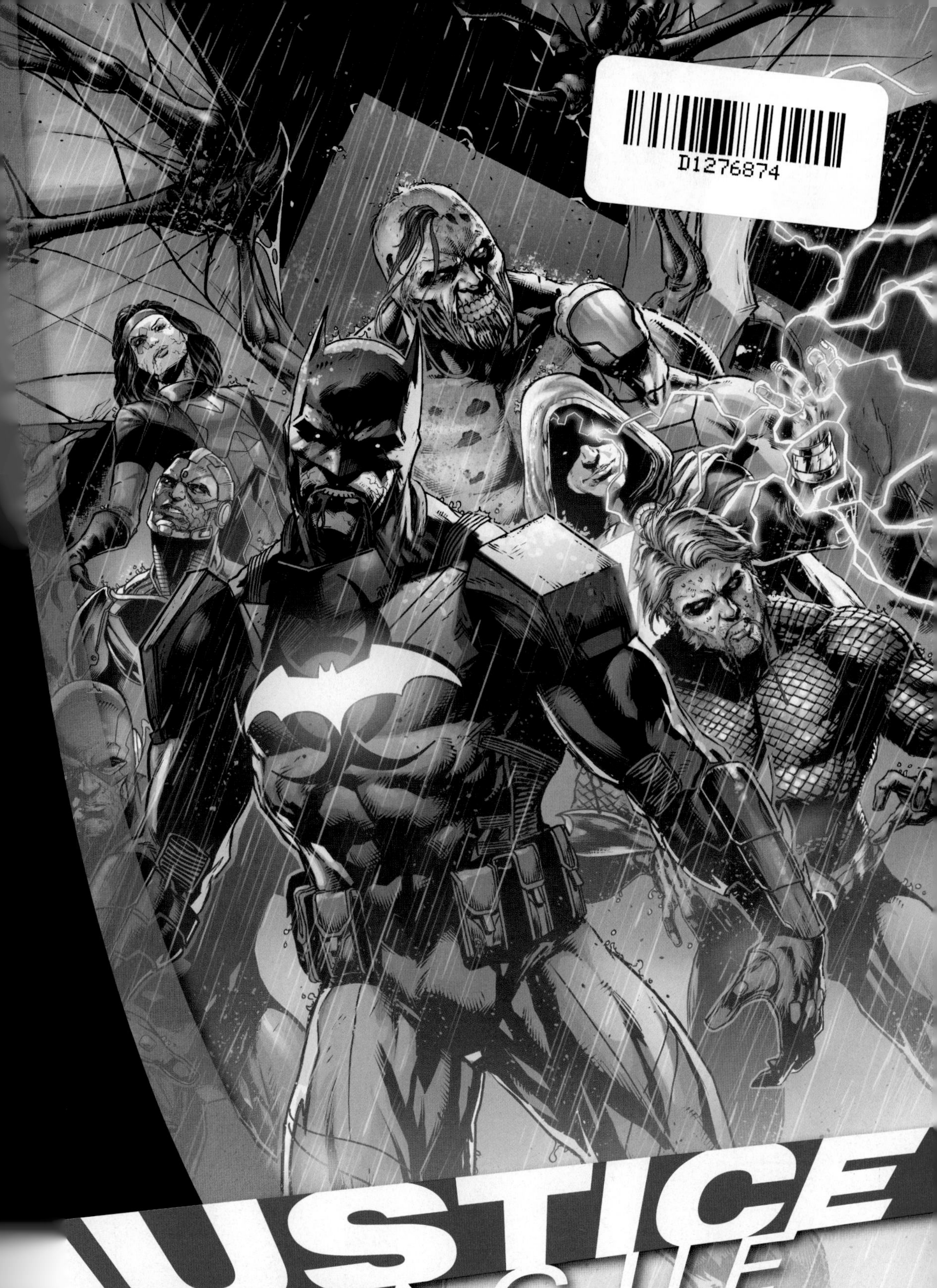

JUSTICE LEAGUE

VOLUME 6 INJUSTICE LEAGUE

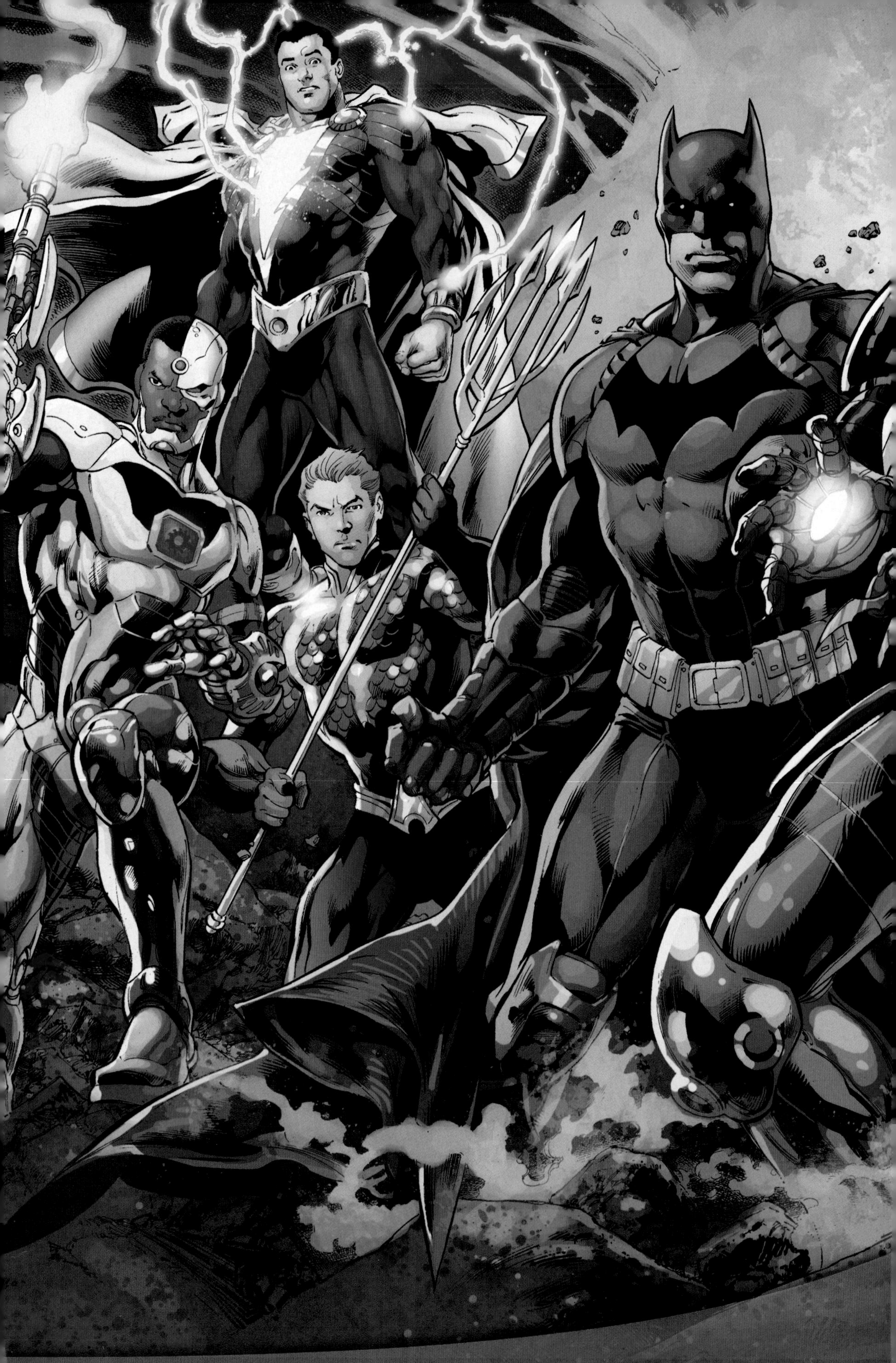

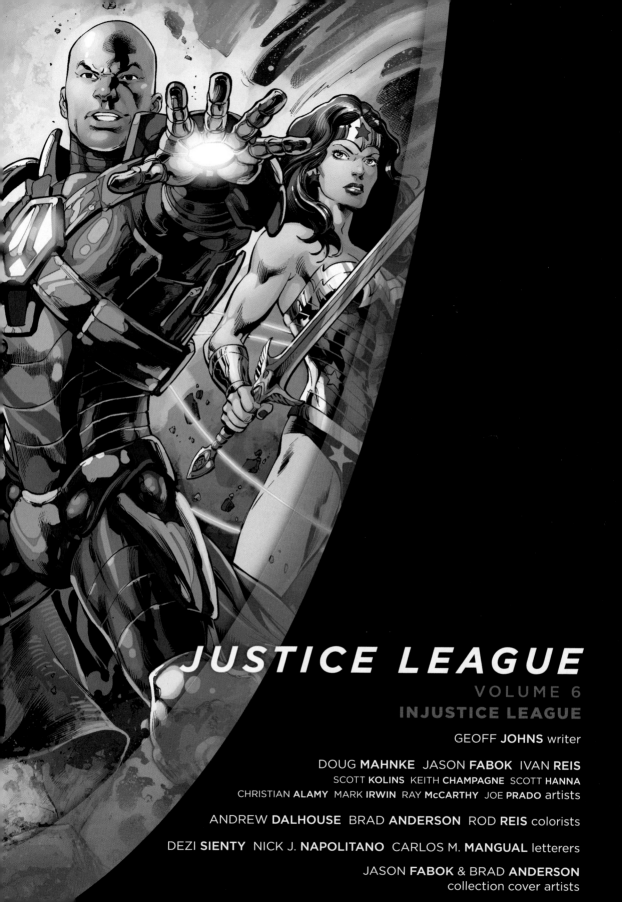

JUSTICE LEAGUE

VOLUME 6
INJUSTICE LEAGUE

GEOFF **JOHNS** writer

DOUG **MAHNKE** JASON **FABOK** IVAN **REIS**
SCOTT **KOLINS** KEITH **CHAMPAGNE** SCOTT **HANNA**
CHRISTIAN **ALAMY** MARK **IRWIN** RAY **McCARTHY** JOE **PRADO** artists

ANDREW **DALHOUSE** BRAD **ANDERSON** ROD **REIS** colorists

DEZI **SIENTY** NICK J. **NAPOLITANO** CARLOS M. **MANGUAL** letterers

JASON **FABOK** & BRAD **ANDERSON**
collection cover artists

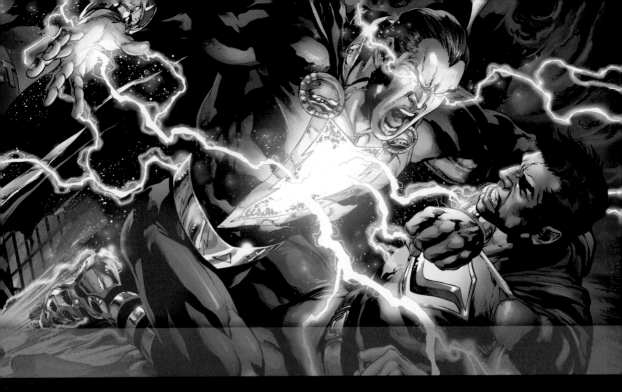

BRIAN CUNNINGHAM Editor - Original Series AMEDEO TURTURRO Assistant Editor - Original Series
JEB WOODARD Group Editor - Collected Editions ROBIN WILDMAN Editor - Collected Edition
STEVE COOK Design Director - Books ROBBIE BIEDERMAN Publication Design

BOB HARRAS Senior VP - Editor-in-Chief, DC Comics

DIANE NELSON President DAN DiDIO Publisher JIM LEE Publisher GEOFF JOHNS President & Chief Creative Officer
AMIT DESAI Executive VP - Business & Marketing Strategy, Direct to Consumer & Global Franchise Management
SAM ADES Senior VP - Direct to Consumer BOBBIE CHASE VP - Talent Development
MARK CHIARELLO Senior VP - Art, Design & Collected Editions JOHN CUNNINGHAM Senior VP - Sales & Trade Marketing
ANNE DePIES Senior VP - Business Strategy, Finance & Administration DON FALLETTI VP - Manufacturing Operations
LAWRENCE GANEM VP - Editorial Administration & Talent Relations ALISON GILL Senior VP - Manufacturing & Operations
HANK KANALZ Senior VP - Editorial Strategy & Administration JAY KOGAN VP - Legal Affairs THOMAS LOFTUS VP - Business Affairs
JACK MAHAN VP - Business Affairs NICK J. NAPOLITANO VP - Manufacturing Administration EDDIE SCANNELL VP - Consumer Marketing
COURTNEY SIMMONS Senior VP - Publicity & Communications JIM (SKI) SOKOLOWSKI VP - Comic Book Specialty & Trade Marketing
NANCY SPEARS VP - Mass, Book, Digital Sales & Trade Marketing

JUSTICE LEAGUE VOLUME 6: INJUSTICE LEAGUE

DC Comics, 2900 West Alameda Avenue, Burbank, CA 91505
Printed by LSC Communications, Owensville, MO, USA. 9/1/17. Second Printing.
ISBN: 978-1-4012-5852-8

Library of Congress Cataloging-in-Publication Data

Johns, Geoff, 1973-
Justice League. Volume 6, Injustice league / written by Geoff Johns ; illustrated by Ivan Reis, Joe Prado.
pages cm. —)
ISBN 978-1-4012-5852-8 (paperback)
1. Graphic novels. I. Reis, Ivan. II. Prado, Joe. III. Title. IV. Title: Injustice league.
PN6728.J87J6545 2015
741.5'973—dc23
2014049010

PEFC Certified
Printed on paper from sustainably managed forests, controlled sources
PEFC
PEFC/29-31-337
www.pefc.org

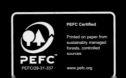

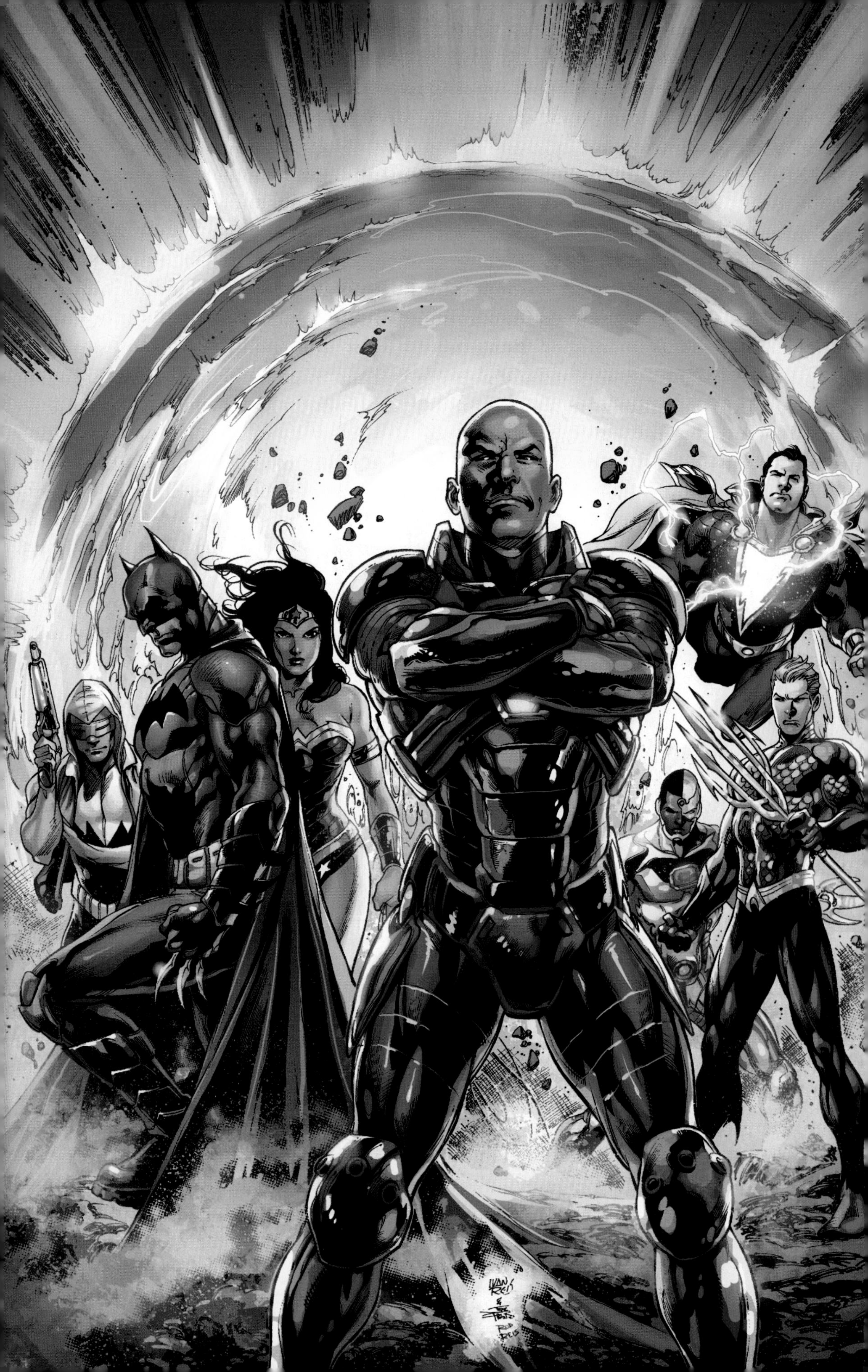

INJUSTICE LEAGUE CHAPTER ONE
KICKING DOWN DOORS

GEOFF JOHNS writer **IVAN REIS DOUG MAHNKE** pencillers **SCOTT HANNA** inker
ROD REIS colorist **IVAN REIS, JOE PRADO & ROD REIS** cover artists

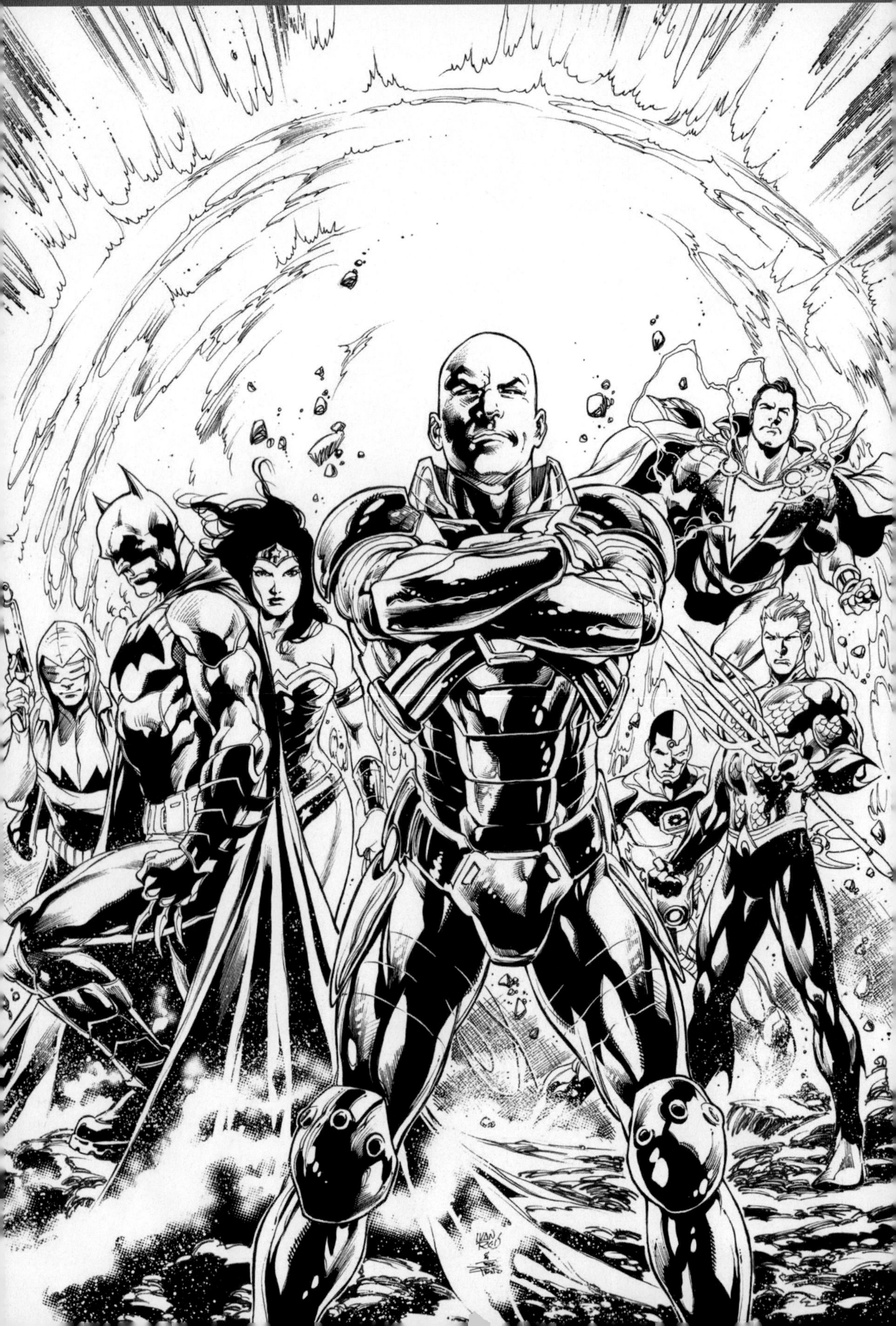

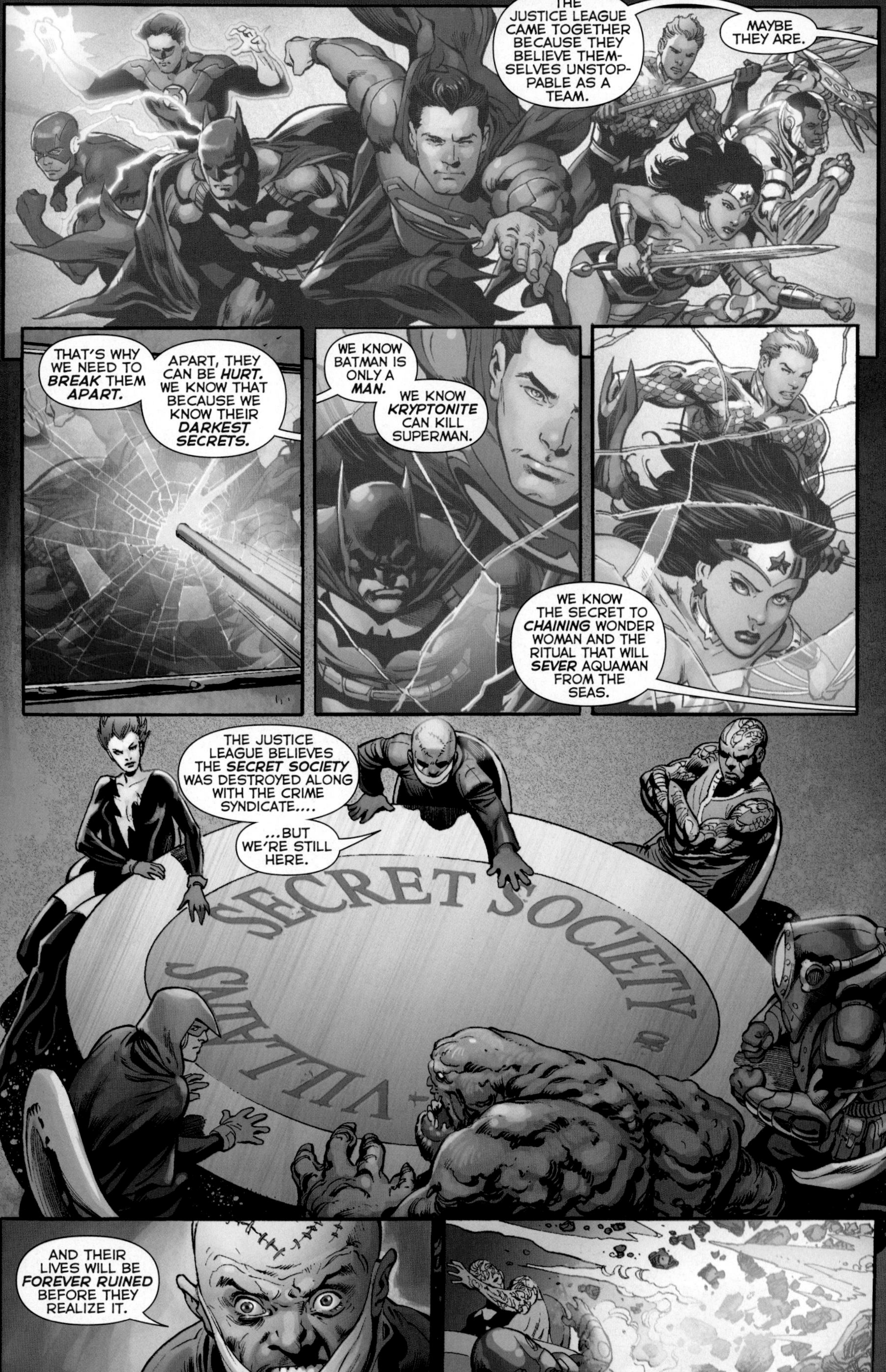
THE JUSTICE LEAGUE CAME TOGETHER BECAUSE THEY BELIEVE THEMSELVES UNSTOPPABLE AS A TEAM.
MAYBE THEY ARE.
THAT'S WHY WE NEED TO BREAK THEM APART.
APART, THEY CAN BE HURT. WE KNOW THAT BECAUSE WE KNOW THEIR DARKEST SECRETS.
WE KNOW BATMAN IS ONLY A MAN.
WE KNOW KRYPTONITE CAN KILL SUPERMAN.
WE KNOW THE SECRET TO CHAINING WONDER WOMAN AND THE RITUAL THAT WILL SEVER AQUAMAN FROM THE SEAS.
THE JUSTICE LEAGUE BELIEVES THE SECRET SOCIETY WAS DESTROYED ALONG WITH THE CRIME SYNDICATE....
...BUT WE'RE STILL HERE.
SECRET SOCIETY of VILLAINS
AND THEIR LIVES WILL BE FOREVER RUINED BEFORE THEY REALIZE IT.

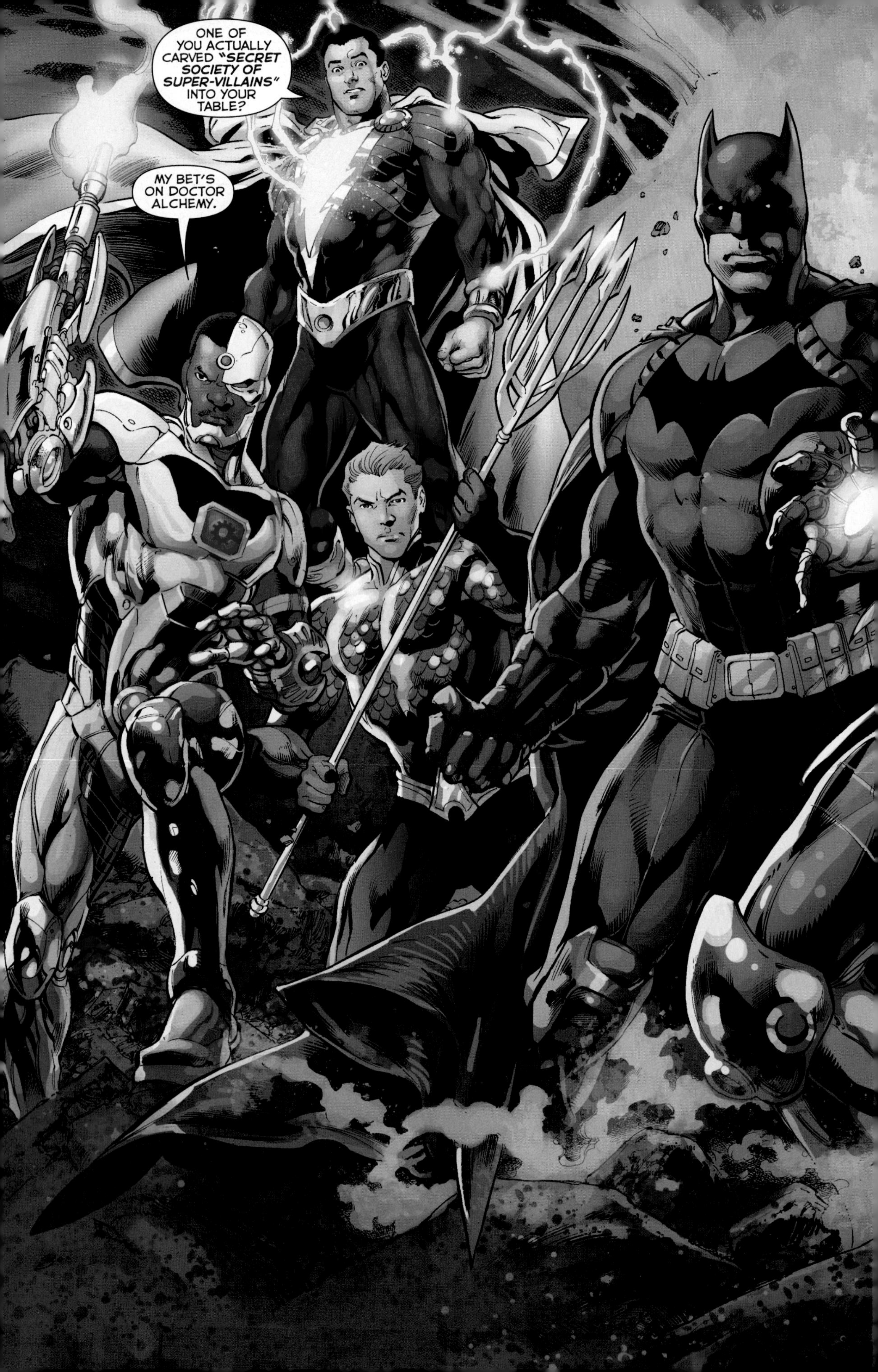
ONE OF YOU ACTUALLY CARVED "SECRET SOCIETY OF SUPER-VILLAINS" INTO YOUR TABLE?
MY BET'S ON DOCTOR ALCHEMY.

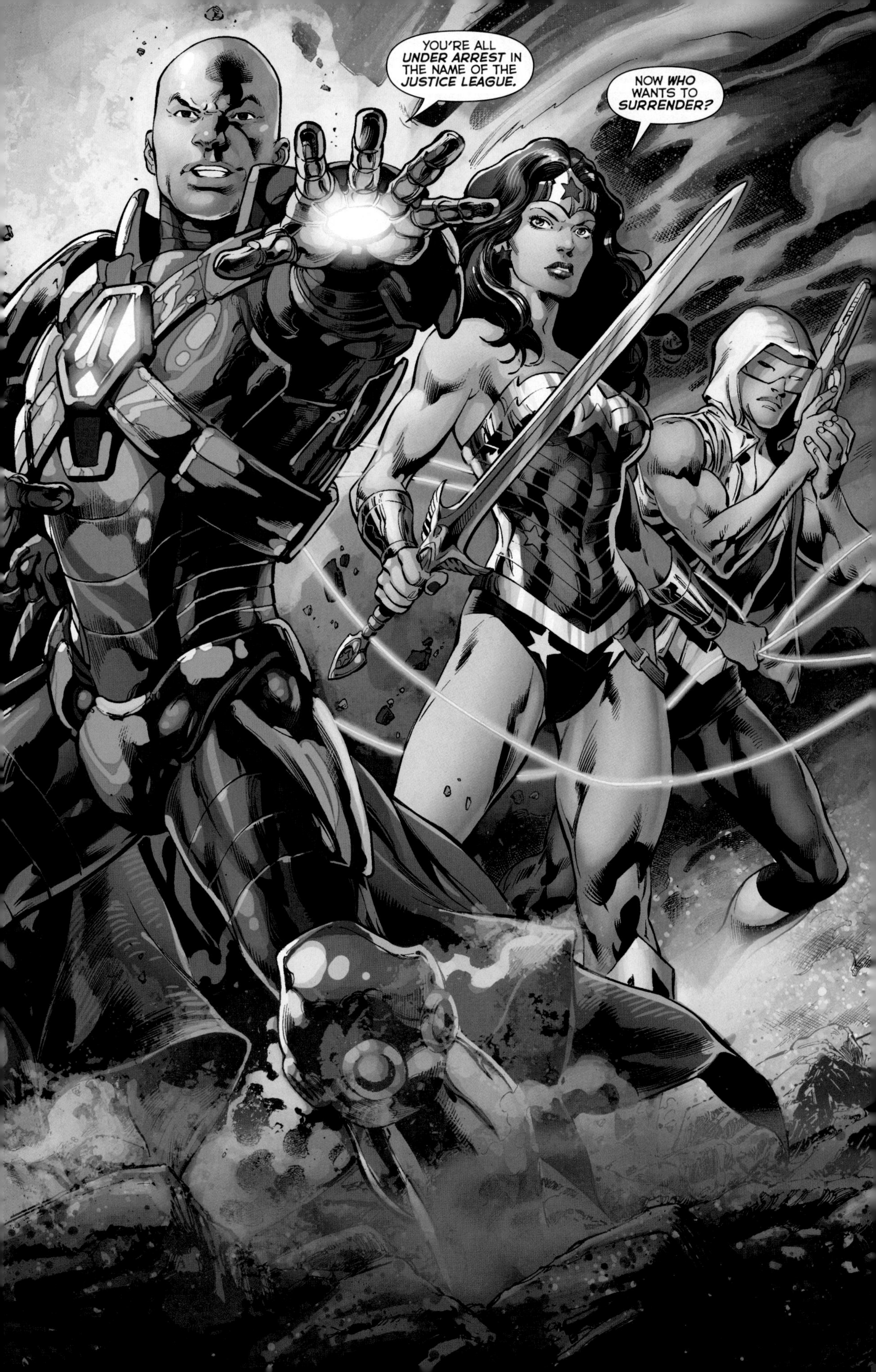
YOU'RE ALL UNDER ARREST IN THE NAME OF THE JUSTICE LEAGUE.
NOW WHO WANTS TO SURRENDER?

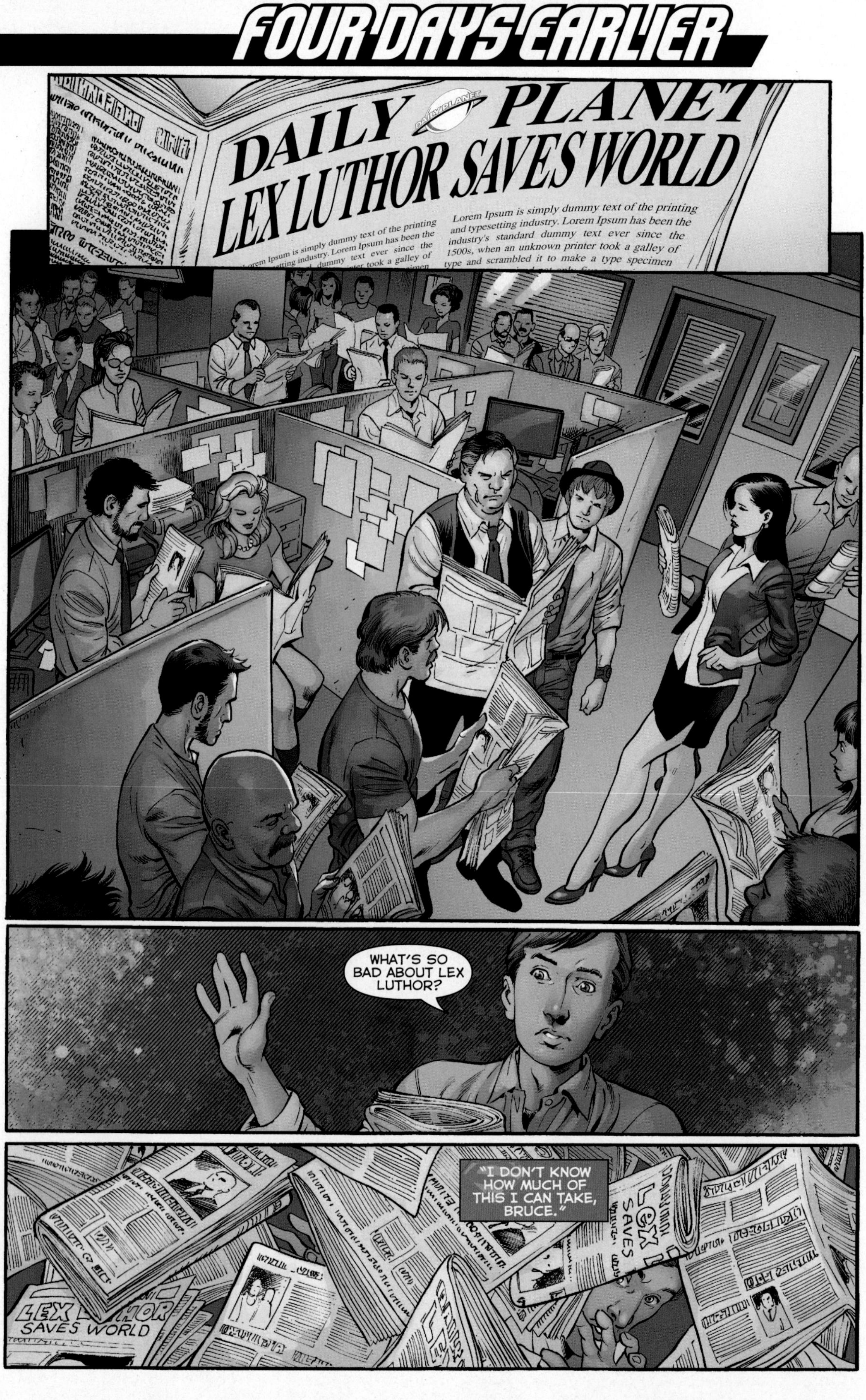
FOUR DAYS EARLIER
DAILY PLANET
LEX LUTHOR SAVES WORLD
Lorem Ipsum is simply dummy text of the printing and typesetting industry. Lorem Ipsum has been the industry's standard dummy text ever since the 1500s, when an unknown printer took a galley of type and scrambled it to make a type specimen
WHAT'S SO BAD ABOUT LEX LUTHOR?
"I DON'T KNOW HOW MUCH OF THIS I CAN TAKE, BRUCE."
SAVES WORLD

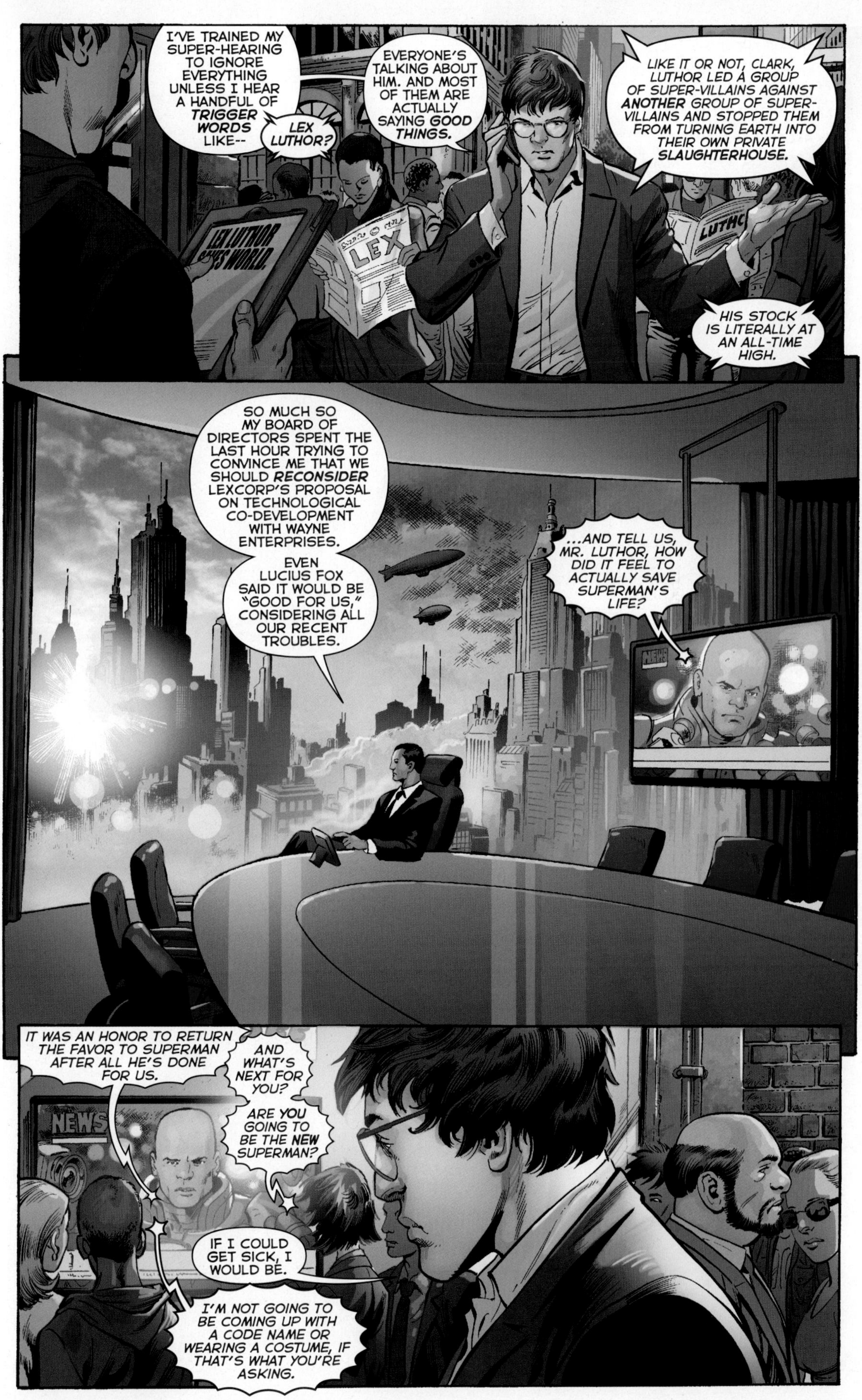
I'VE TRAINED MY SUPER-HEARING TO IGNORE EVERYTHING UNLESS I HEAR A HANDFUL OF TRIGGER WORDS LIKE--
LEX LUTHOR?
EVERYONE'S TALKING ABOUT HIM. AND MOST OF THEM ARE ACTUALLY SAYING GOOD THINGS.
LIKE IT OR NOT, CLARK, LUTHOR LED A GROUP OF SUPER-VILLAINS AGAINST ANOTHER GROUP OF SUPER-VILLAINS AND STOPPED THEM FROM TURNING EARTH INTO THEIR OWN PRIVATE SLAUGHTERHOUSE.
LEX LUTHOR SAVES WORLD.
LEX
LUTHO
HIS STOCK IS LITERALLY AT AN ALL-TIME HIGH.
SO MUCH SO MY BOARD OF DIRECTORS SPENT THE LAST HOUR TRYING TO CONVINCE ME THAT WE SHOULD RECONSIDER LEXCORP'S PROPOSAL ON TECHNOLOGICAL CO-DEVELOPMENT WITH WAYNE ENTERPRISES.
EVEN LUCIUS FOX SAID IT WOULD BE "GOOD FOR US," CONSIDERING ALL OUR RECENT TROUBLES.
...AND TELL US, MR. LUTHOR, HOW DID IT FEEL TO ACTUALLY SAVE SUPERMAN'S LIFE?
NEWS
IT WAS AN HONOR TO RETURN THE FAVOR TO SUPERMAN AFTER ALL HE'S DONE FOR US.
AND WHAT'S NEXT FOR YOU?
ARE YOU GOING TO BE THE NEW SUPERMAN?
NEWS
IF I COULD GET SICK, I WOULD BE.
I'M NOT GOING TO BE COMING UP WITH A CODE NAME OR WEARING A COSTUME, IF THAT'S WHAT YOU'RE ASKING.

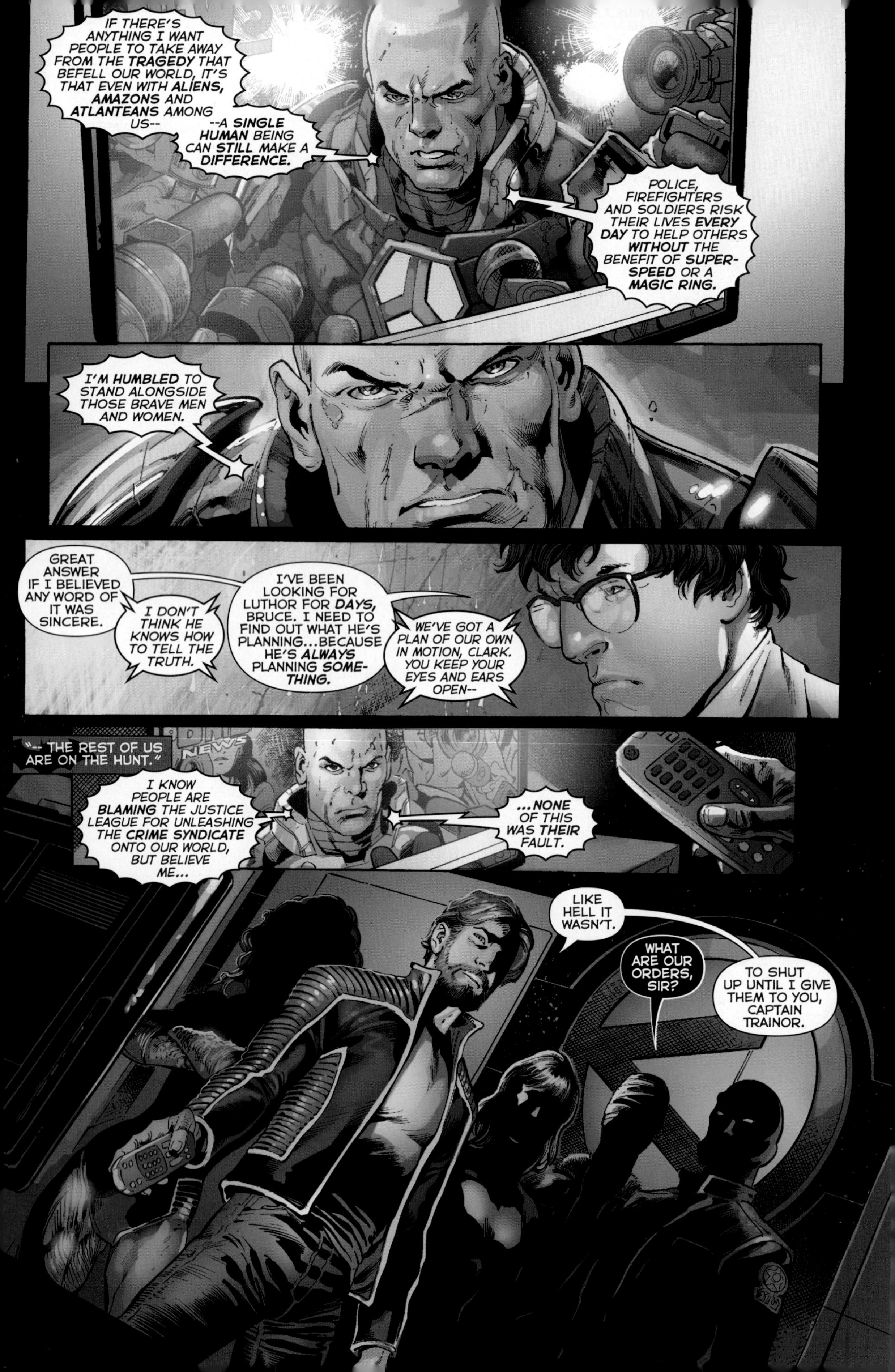
IF THERE'S ANYTHING I WANT PEOPLE TO TAKE AWAY FROM THE TRAGEDY THAT BEFELL OUR WORLD, IT'S THAT EVEN WITH ALIENS, AMAZONS AND ATLANTEANS AMONG US--
--A SINGLE HUMAN BEING CAN STILL MAKE A DIFFERENCE.
POLICE, FIREFIGHTERS AND SOLDIERS RISK THEIR LIVES EVERY DAY TO HELP OTHERS WITHOUT THE BENEFIT OF SUPER-SPEED OR A MAGIC RING.
I'M HUMBLED TO STAND ALONGSIDE THOSE BRAVE MEN AND WOMEN.
GREAT ANSWER IF I BELIEVED ANY WORD OF IT WAS SINCERE.
I DON'T THINK HE KNOWS HOW TO TELL THE TRUTH.
I'VE BEEN LOOKING FOR LUTHOR FOR DAYS, BRUCE. I NEED TO FIND OUT WHAT HE'S PLANNING...BECAUSE HE'S ALWAYS PLANNING SOME-THING.
WE'VE GOT A PLAN OF OUR OWN IN MOTION, CLARK. YOU KEEP YOUR EYES AND EARS OPEN--
"-- THE REST OF US ARE ON THE HUNT."
NEWS
I KNOW PEOPLE ARE BLAMING THE JUSTICE LEAGUE FOR UNLEASHING THE CRIME SYNDICATE ONTO OUR WORLD, BUT BELIEVE ME...
...NONE OF THIS WAS THEIR FAULT.
LIKE HELL IT WASN'T.
WHAT ARE OUR ORDERS, SIR?
TO SHUT UP UNTIL I GIVE THEM TO YOU, CAPTAIN TRAINOR.

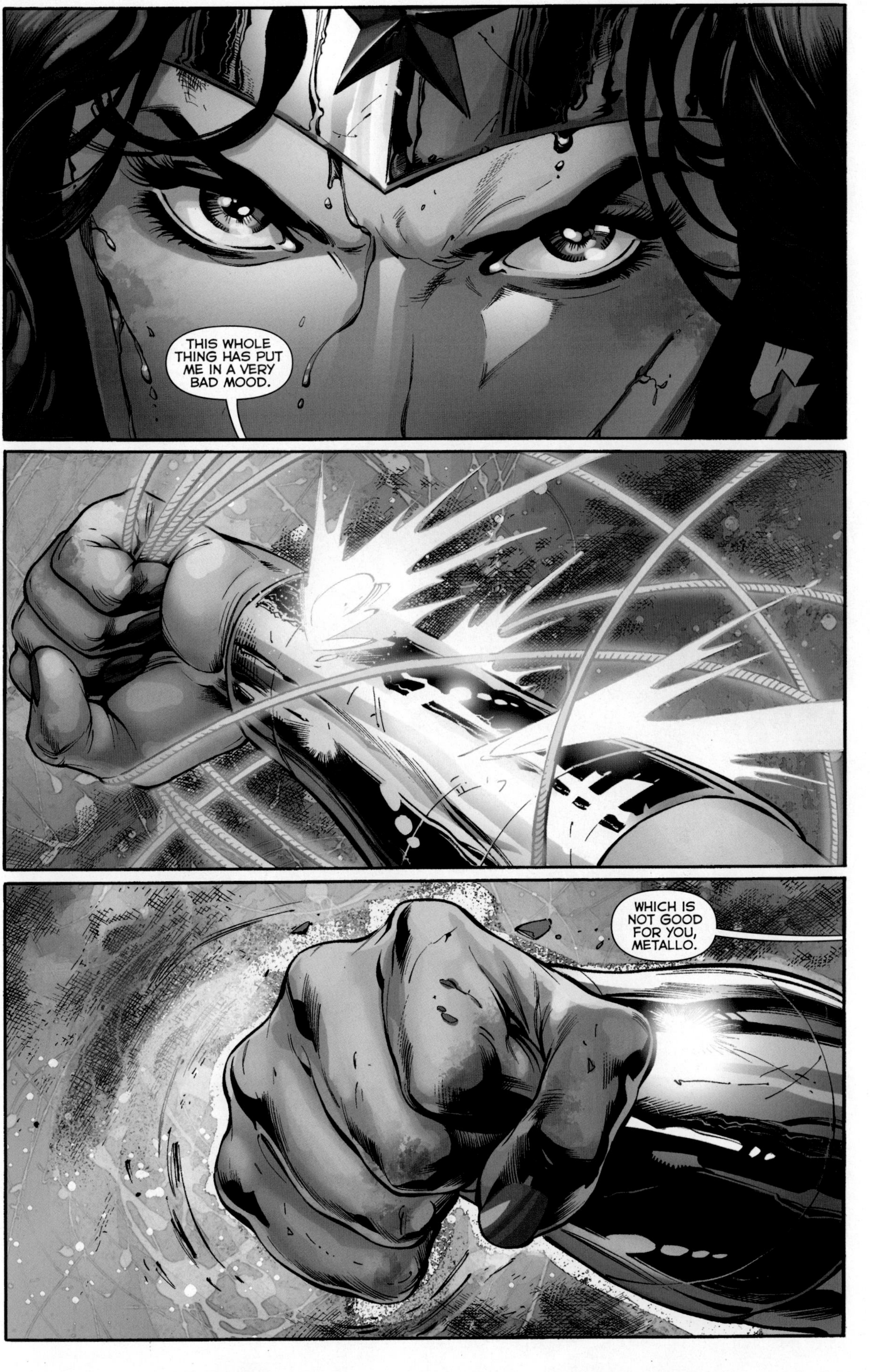
THIS WHOLE THING HAS PUT ME IN A VERY BAD MOOD.
WHICH IS NOT GOOD FOR YOU, METALLO.

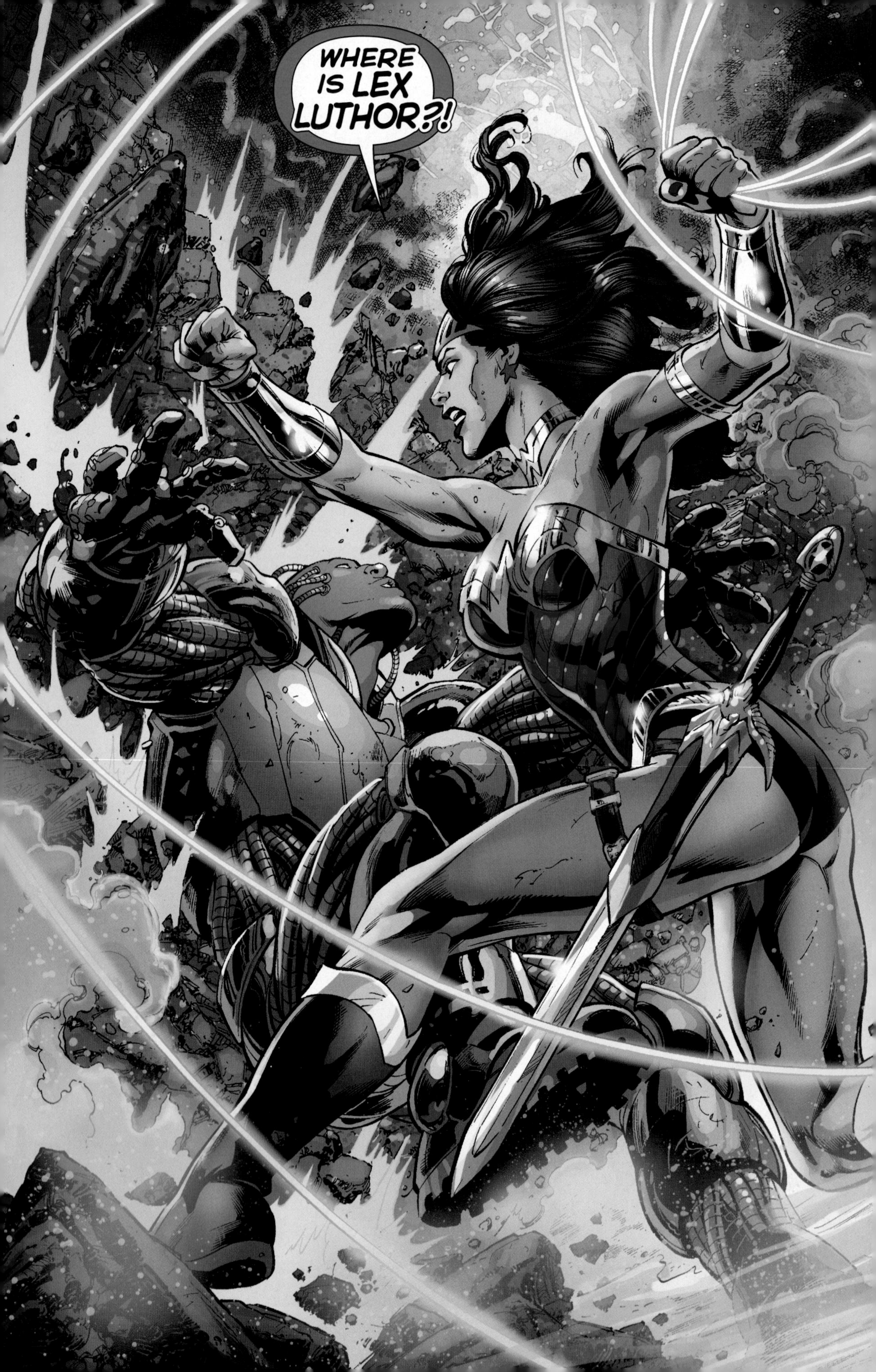
WHERE IS LEX LUTHOR?!

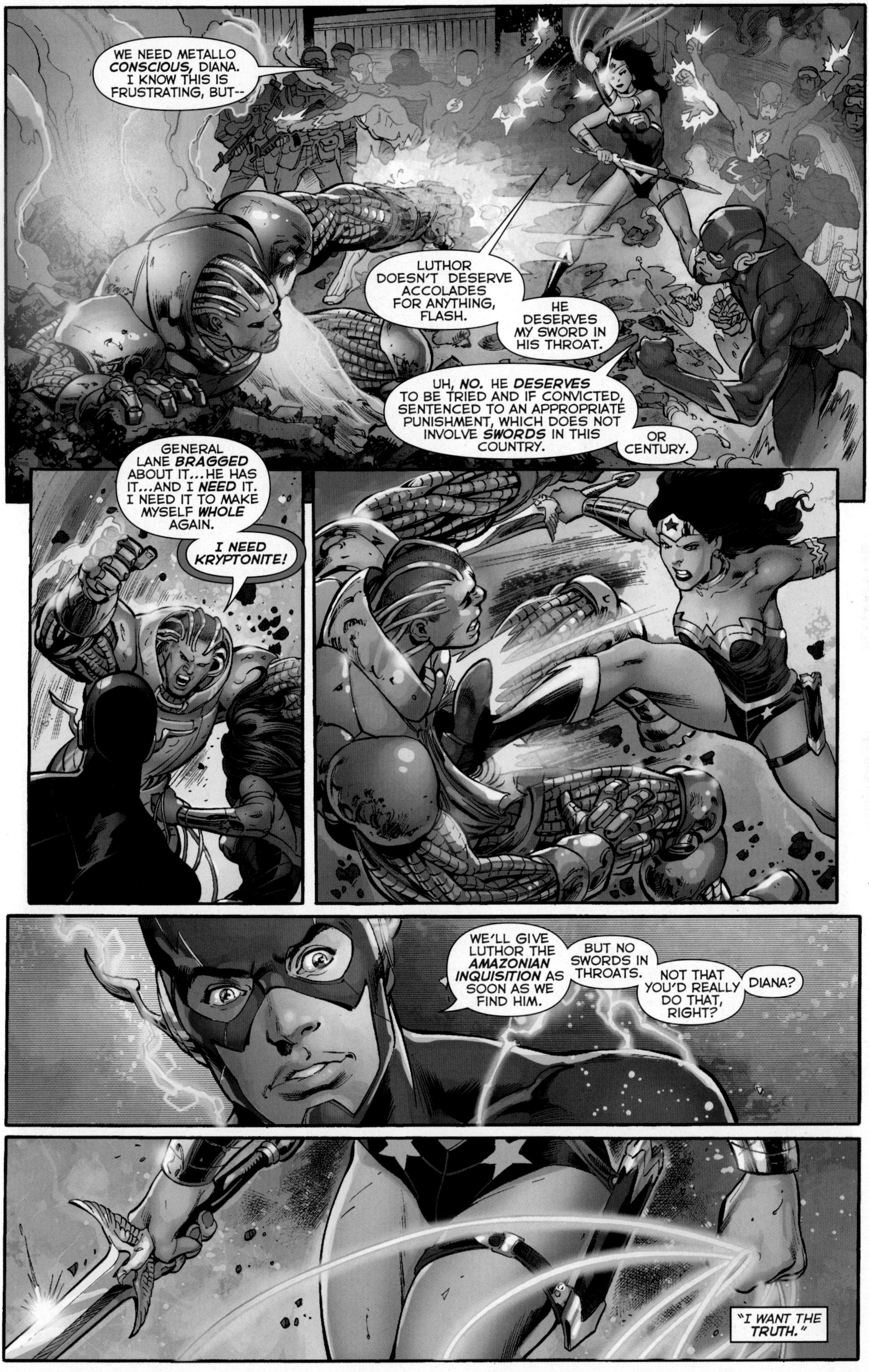
WE NEED METALLO *CONSCIOUS,* DIANA. I KNOW THIS IS FRUSTRATING, BUT--
LUTHOR DOESN'T DESERVE ACCOLADES FOR ANYTHING, FLASH.
HE DESERVES MY SWORD IN HIS THROAT.
UH, *NO.* HE *DESERVES* TO BE TRIED AND IF CONVICTED, SENTENCED TO AN APPROPRIATE PUNISHMENT, WHICH DOES NOT INVOLVE *SWORDS* IN THIS COUNTRY.
OR CENTURY.
GENERAL LANE *BRAGGED* ABOUT IT...HE HAS IT...AND I *NEED* IT. I NEED IT TO MAKE MYSELF *WHOLE* AGAIN.
I NEED KRYPTONITE!
WE'LL GIVE LUTHOR THE *AMAZONIAN INQUISITION* AS SOON AS WE FIND HIM.
BUT NO SWORDS IN THROATS.
NOT THAT YOU'D REALLY DO THAT, RIGHT?
DIANA?
"I WANT THE *TRUTH.*"

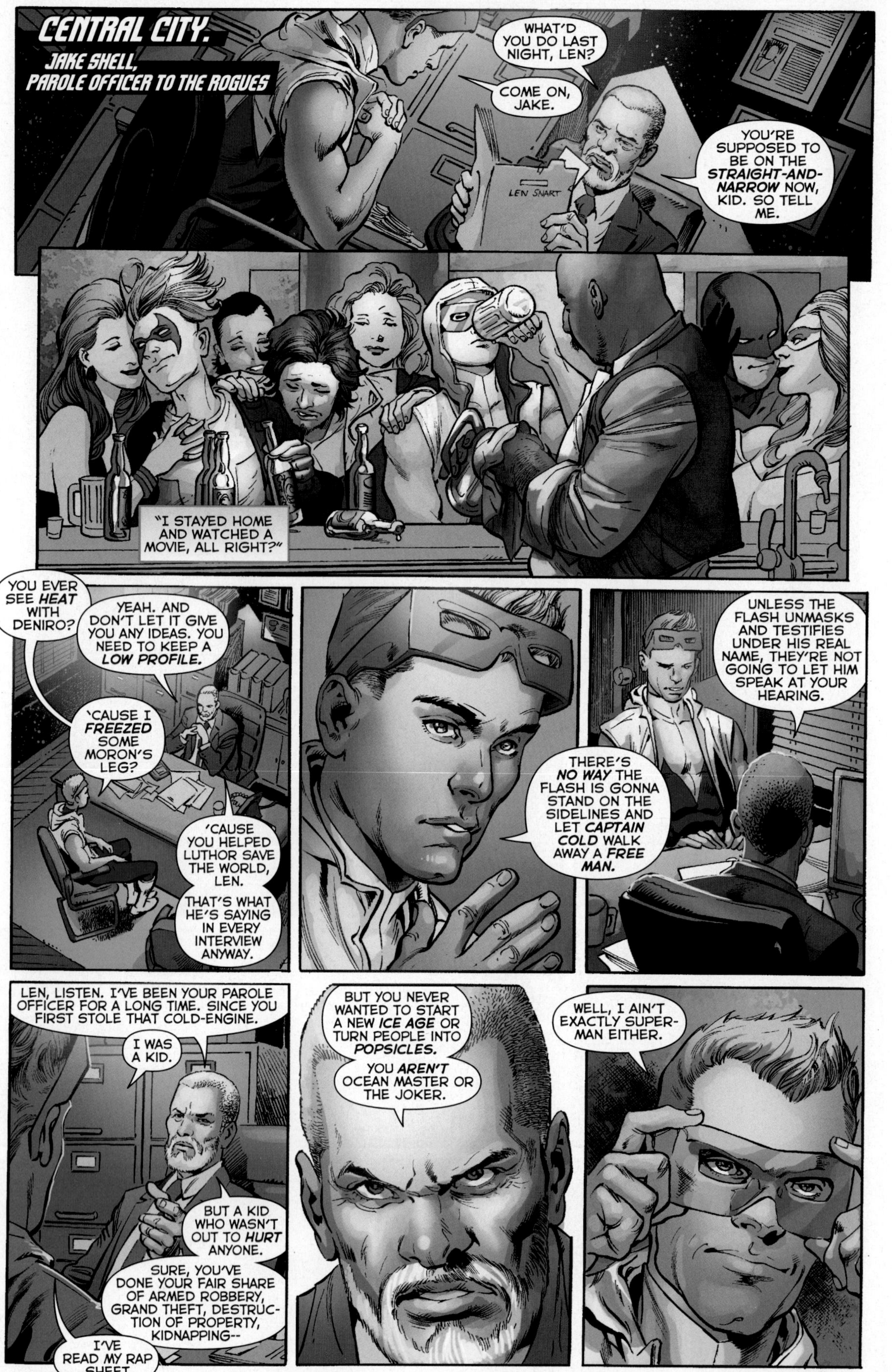
CENTRAL CITY.
JAKE SHELL, PAROLE OFFICER TO THE ROGUES
WHAT'D YOU DO LAST NIGHT, LEN?
COME ON, JAKE.
LEN SNART
YOU'RE SUPPOSED TO BE ON THE STRAIGHT-AND-NARROW NOW, KID. SO TELL ME.
"I STAYED HOME AND WATCHED A MOVIE, ALL RIGHT?"
YOU EVER SEE HEAT WITH DENIRO?
YEAH. AND DON'T LET IT GIVE YOU ANY IDEAS. YOU NEED TO KEEP A LOW PROFILE.
'CAUSE I FREEZED SOME MORON'S LEG?
'CAUSE YOU HELPED LUTHOR SAVE THE WORLD, LEN.
THAT'S WHAT HE'S SAYING IN EVERY INTERVIEW ANYWAY.
THERE'S NO WAY THE FLASH IS GONNA STAND ON THE SIDELINES AND LET CAPTAIN COLD WALK AWAY A FREE MAN.
UNLESS THE FLASH UNMASKS AND TESTIFIES UNDER HIS REAL NAME, THEY'RE NOT GOING TO LET HIM SPEAK AT YOUR HEARING.
LEN, LISTEN. I'VE BEEN YOUR PAROLE OFFICER FOR A LONG TIME. SINCE YOU FIRST STOLE THAT COLD-ENGINE.
I WAS A KID.
BUT A KID WHO WASN'T OUT TO HURT ANYONE.
SURE, YOU'VE DONE YOUR FAIR SHARE OF ARMED ROBBERY, GRAND THEFT, DESTRUCTION OF PROPERTY, KIDNAPPING--
I'VE READ MY RAP SHEET.
BUT YOU NEVER WANTED TO START A NEW ICE AGE OR TURN PEOPLE INTO POPSICLES.
YOU AREN'T OCEAN MASTER OR THE JOKER.
WELL, I AIN'T EXACTLY SUPERMAN EITHER.

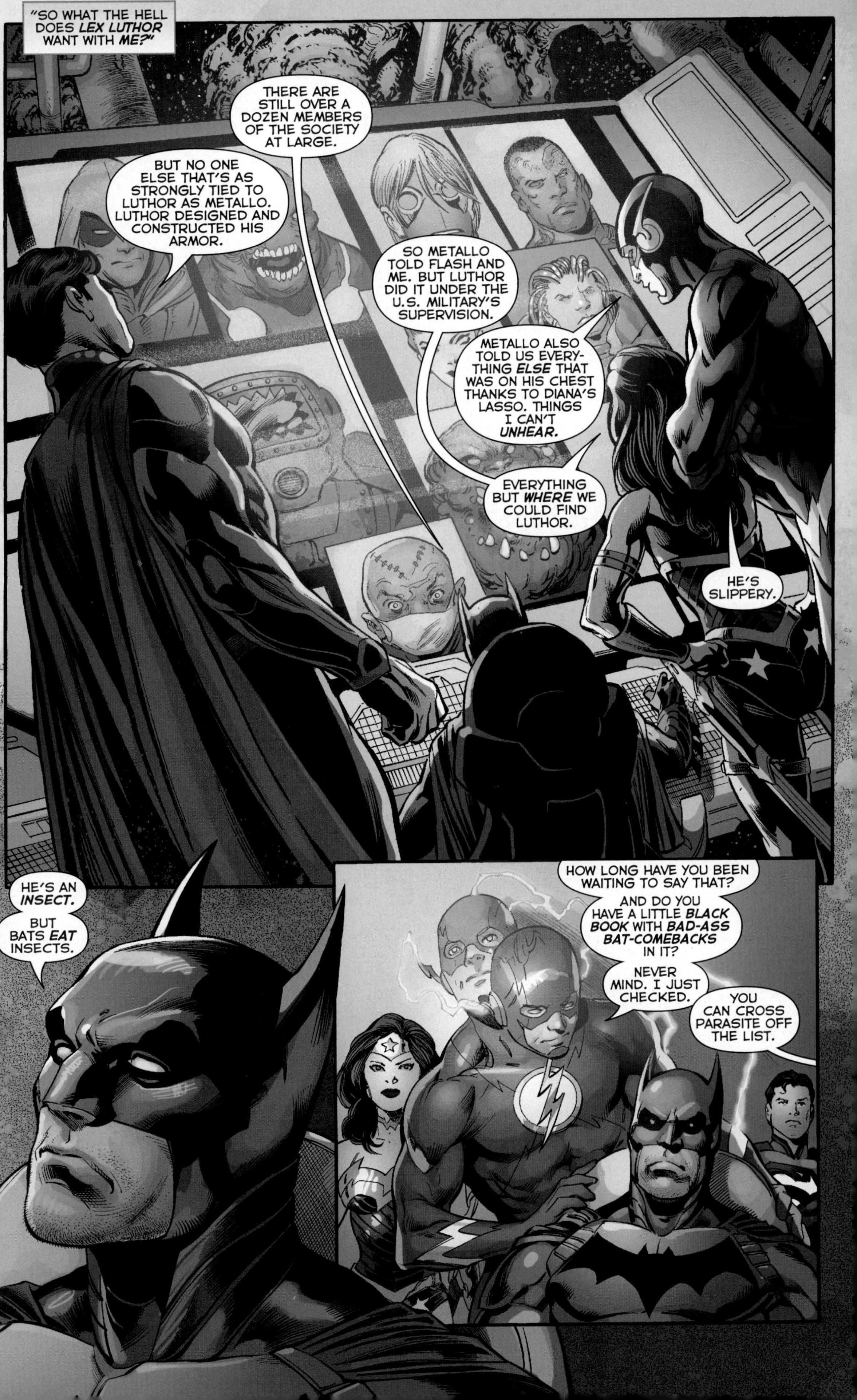
"SO WHAT THE HELL DOES LEX LUTHOR WANT WITH ME?"
THERE ARE STILL OVER A DOZEN MEMBERS OF THE SOCIETY AT LARGE.
BUT NO ONE ELSE THAT'S AS STRONGLY TIED TO LUTHOR AS METALLO. LUTHOR DESIGNED AND CONSTRUCTED HIS ARMOR.
SO METALLO TOLD FLASH AND ME. BUT LUTHOR DID IT UNDER THE U.S. MILITARY'S SUPERVISION.
METALLO ALSO TOLD US EVERY-THING ELSE THAT WAS ON HIS CHEST THANKS TO DIANA'S LASSO. THINGS I CAN'T UNHEAR.
EVERYTHING BUT WHERE WE COULD FIND LUTHOR.
HE'S SLIPPERY.
HE'S AN INSECT.
BUT BATS EAT INSECTS.
HOW LONG HAVE YOU BEEN WAITING TO SAY THAT?
AND DO YOU HAVE A LITTLE BLACK BOOK WITH BAD-ASS BAT-COMEBACKS IN IT?
NEVER MIND. I JUST CHECKED.
YOU CAN CROSS PARASITE OFF THE LIST.

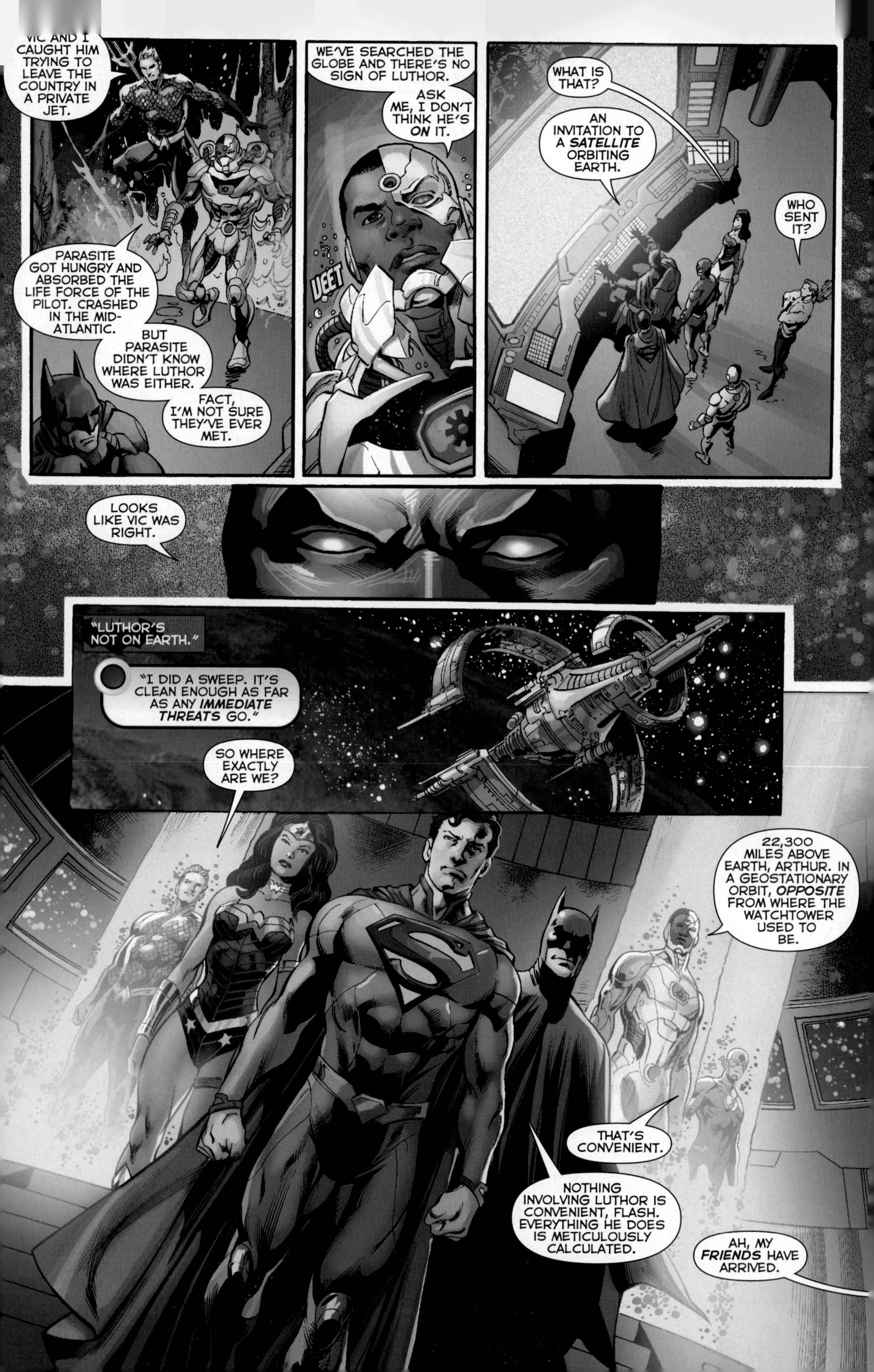
VIC AND I CAUGHT HIM TRYING TO LEAVE THE COUNTRY IN A PRIVATE JET.
PARASITE GOT HUNGRY AND ABSORBED THE LIFE FORCE OF THE PILOT. CRASHED IN THE MID-ATLANTIC.
BUT PARASITE DIDN'T KNOW WHERE LUTHOR WAS EITHER.
FACT, I'M NOT SURE THEY'VE EVER MET.
WE'VE SEARCHED THE GLOBE AND THERE'S NO SIGN OF LUTHOR.
ASK ME, I DON'T THINK HE'S ON IT.
VEET
WHAT IS THAT?
AN INVITATION TO A SATELLITE ORBITING EARTH.
WHO SENT IT?
LOOKS LIKE VIC WAS RIGHT.
"LUTHOR'S NOT ON EARTH."
"I DID A SWEEP. IT'S CLEAN ENOUGH AS FAR AS ANY IMMEDIATE THREATS GO."
SO WHERE EXACTLY ARE WE?
22,300 MILES ABOVE EARTH, ARTHUR. IN A GEOSTATIONARY ORBIT, OPPOSITE FROM WHERE THE WATCHTOWER USED TO BE.
THAT'S CONVENIENT.
NOTHING INVOLVING LUTHOR IS CONVENIENT, FLASH. EVERYTHING HE DOES IS METICULOUSLY CALCULATED.
AH, MY FRIENDS HAVE ARRIVED.

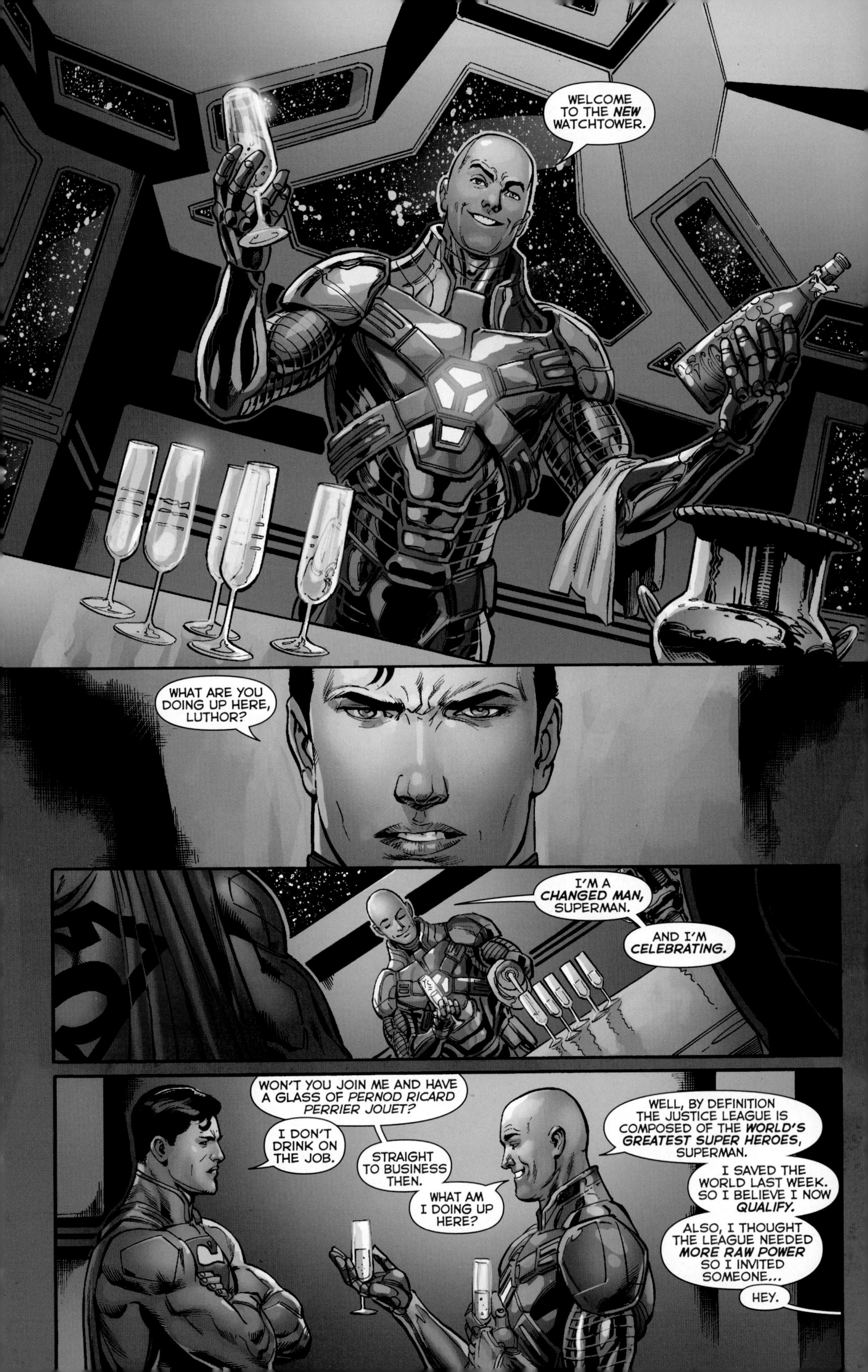

WELCOME TO THE *NEW* WATCHTOWER.
WHAT ARE YOU DOING UP HERE, LUTHOR?
I'M A *CHANGED MAN,* SUPERMAN.
AND I'M *CELEBRATING.*
WON'T YOU JOIN ME AND HAVE A GLASS OF *PERNOD RICARD PERRIER JOUET?*
I DON'T DRINK ON THE JOB.
STRAIGHT TO BUSINESS THEN.
WHAT AM I DOING UP HERE?
WELL, BY DEFINITION THE JUSTICE LEAGUE IS COMPOSED OF THE **WORLD'S GREATEST SUPER HEROES,** SUPERMAN.
I SAVED THE WORLD LAST WEEK. SO I BELIEVE I NOW *QUALIFY.*
ALSO, I THOUGHT THE LEAGUE NEEDED **MORE RAW POWER** SO I INVITED SOMEONE...
HEY.

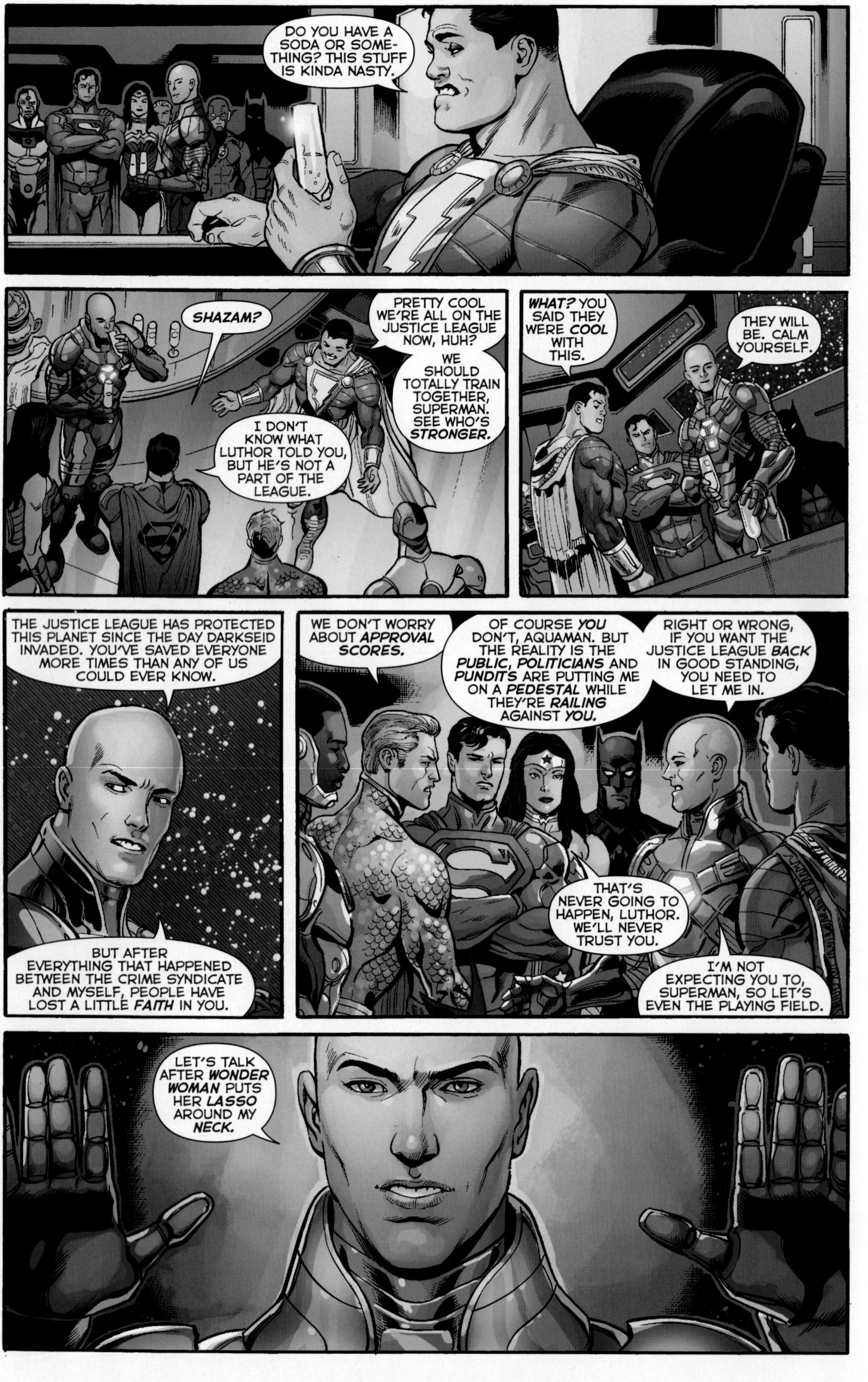
DO YOU HAVE A SODA OR SOMETHING? THIS STUFF IS KINDA NASTY.
SHAZAM?
PRETTY COOL WE'RE ALL ON THE JUSTICE LEAGUE NOW, HUH?
WE SHOULD TOTALLY TRAIN TOGETHER, SUPERMAN. SEE WHO'S STRONGER.
I DON'T KNOW WHAT LUTHOR TOLD YOU, BUT HE'S NOT A PART OF THE LEAGUE.
WHAT? YOU SAID THEY WERE COOL WITH THIS.
THEY WILL BE. CALM YOURSELF.
THE JUSTICE LEAGUE HAS PROTECTED THIS PLANET SINCE THE DAY DARKSEID INVADED. YOU'VE SAVED EVERYONE MORE TIMES THAN ANY OF US COULD EVER KNOW.
BUT AFTER EVERYTHING THAT HAPPENED BETWEEN THE CRIME SYNDICATE AND MYSELF, PEOPLE HAVE LOST A LITTLE FAITH IN YOU.
WE DON'T WORRY ABOUT APPROVAL SCORES.
OF COURSE YOU DON'T, AQUAMAN. BUT THE REALITY IS THE PUBLIC, POLITICIANS AND PUNDITS ARE PUTTING ME ON A PEDESTAL WHILE THEY'RE RAILING AGAINST YOU.
RIGHT OR WRONG, IF YOU WANT THE JUSTICE LEAGUE BACK IN GOOD STANDING, YOU NEED TO LET ME IN.
THAT'S NEVER GOING TO HAPPEN, LUTHOR. WE'LL NEVER TRUST YOU.
I'M NOT EXPECTING YOU TO, SUPERMAN, SO LET'S EVEN THE PLAYING FIELD.
LET'S TALK AFTER WONDER WOMAN PUTS HER LASSO AROUND MY NECK.

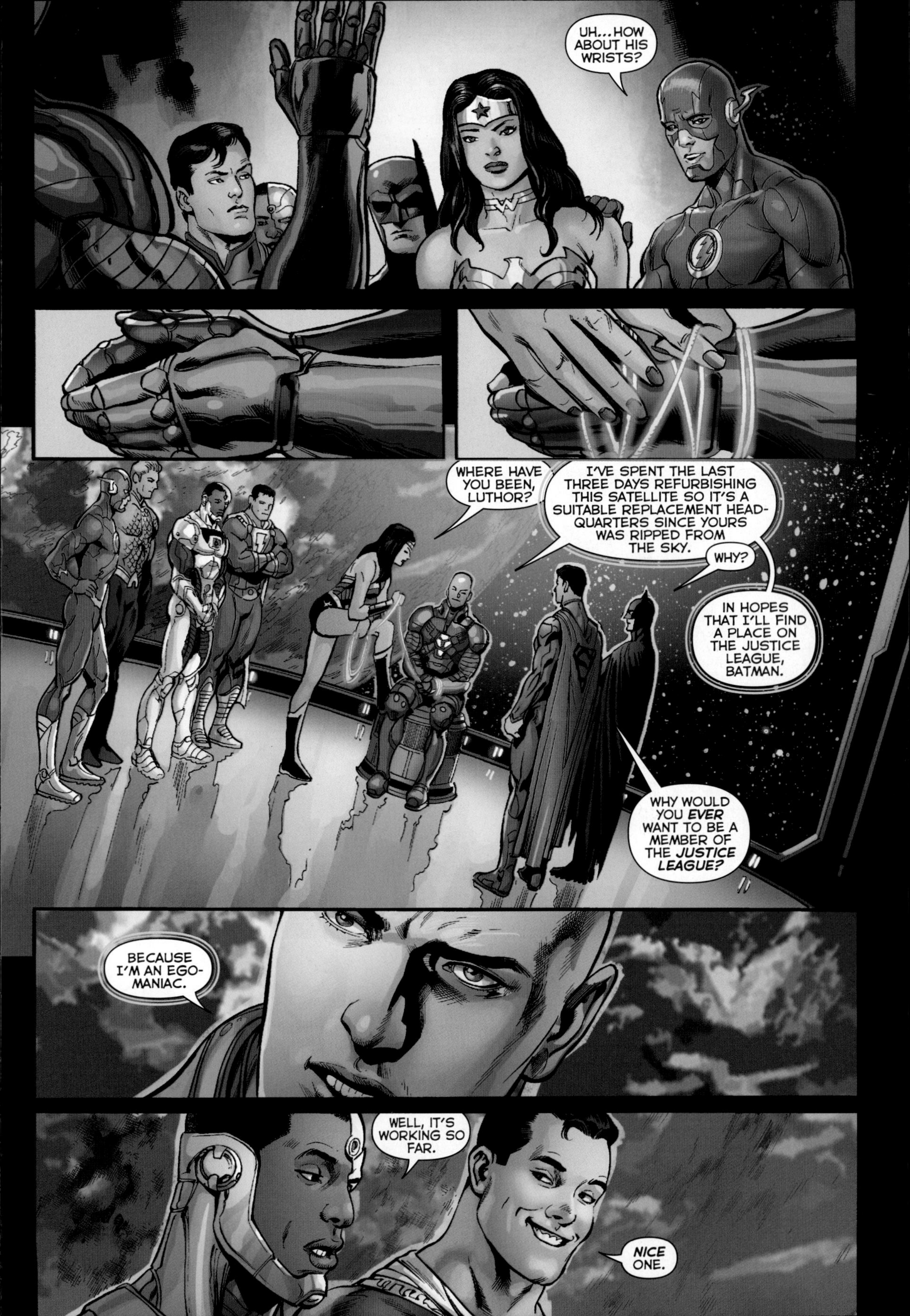
UH...HOW ABOUT HIS WRISTS?
WHERE HAVE YOU BEEN, LUTHOR?
I'VE SPENT THE LAST THREE DAYS REFURBISHING THIS SATELLITE SO IT'S A SUITABLE REPLACEMENT HEAD-QUARTERS SINCE YOURS WAS RIPPED FROM THE SKY.
WHY?
IN HOPES THAT I'LL FIND A PLACE ON THE JUSTICE LEAGUE, BATMAN.
WHY WOULD YOU *EVER* WANT TO BE A MEMBER OF THE *JUSTICE LEAGUE?*
BECAUSE I'M AN EGO-MANIAC.
WELL, IT'S WORKING SO FAR.
NICE ONE.

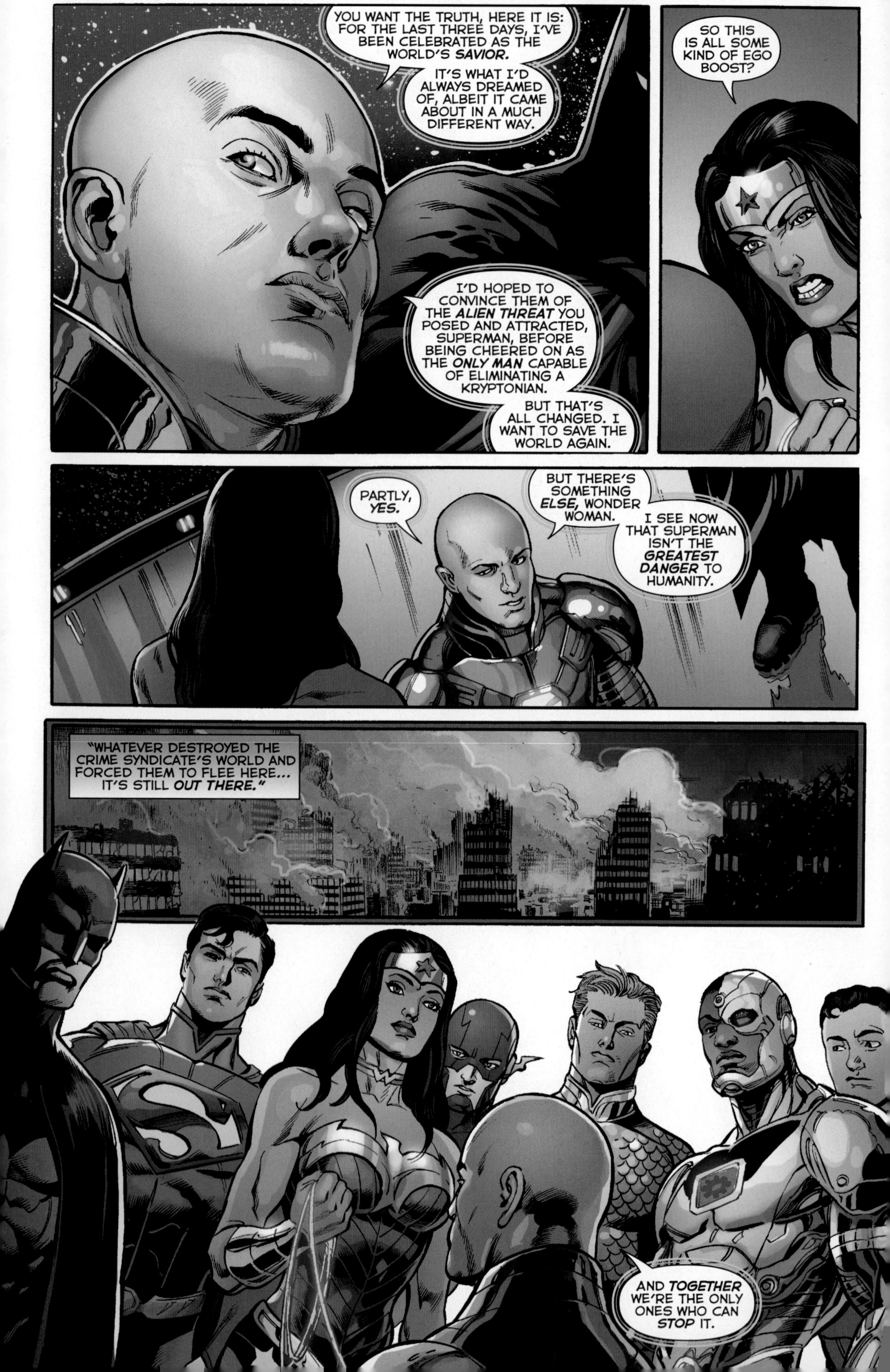
YOU WANT THE TRUTH, HERE IT IS: FOR THE LAST THREE DAYS, I'VE BEEN CELEBRATED AS THE WORLD'S SAVIOR.
IT'S WHAT I'D ALWAYS DREAMED OF, ALBEIT IT CAME ABOUT IN A MUCH DIFFERENT WAY.
I'D HOPED TO CONVINCE THEM OF THE ALIEN THREAT YOU POSED AND ATTRACTED, SUPERMAN, BEFORE BEING CHEERED ON AS THE ONLY MAN CAPABLE OF ELIMINATING A KRYPTONIAN.
BUT THAT'S ALL CHANGED. I WANT TO SAVE THE WORLD AGAIN.
SO THIS IS ALL SOME KIND OF EGO BOOST?
PARTLY, YES.
BUT THERE'S SOMETHING ELSE, WONDER WOMAN.
I SEE NOW THAT SUPERMAN ISN'T THE GREATEST DANGER TO HUMANITY.
"WHATEVER DESTROYED THE CRIME SYNDICATE'S WORLD AND FORCED THEM TO FLEE HERE... IT'S STILL OUT THERE."
AND TOGETHER WE'RE THE ONLY ONES WHO CAN STOP IT.

SUPERMAN: NO. WE'VE HEARD ENOUGH, DIANA.

SUPERMAN: BUT SUPERMAN, THE WORLD'S IN DANGER.

SUPERMAN: WE KNOW, LUTHOR. AND STOPPING IT IS *OUR* JOB, NOT YOURS.

SUPERMAN: DO YOU *UNDERSTAND?*

LUTHOR: I...

LUTHOR: ...I DO. AND I'LL GO.

SHAZAM: SHOULD I GO TOO OR...?

LUTHOR: THIS BELONGS TO YOU NOW, CYBORG.

FLASH: WHAT'D HE GIVE YOU?

CYBORG: THE PROVERBIAL *KEYS* TO THE *CAR.* THESE ARE THE *CODES* TO THIS SATELLITE. I'M TAKING OVER ITS SYSTEMS NOW.

FLASH: BUT WE'RE NOT GOING TO *STAY* HERE, ARE WE?

CYBORG: UNLESS YOU WANT TO GO BACK TO THE BATCAVE.

FLASH: GOD, NO.

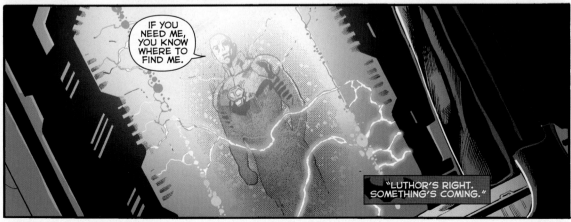

LUTHOR: IF YOU NEED ME, YOU KNOW WHERE TO FIND ME.

"LUTHOR'S RIGHT. SOMETHING'S COMING."

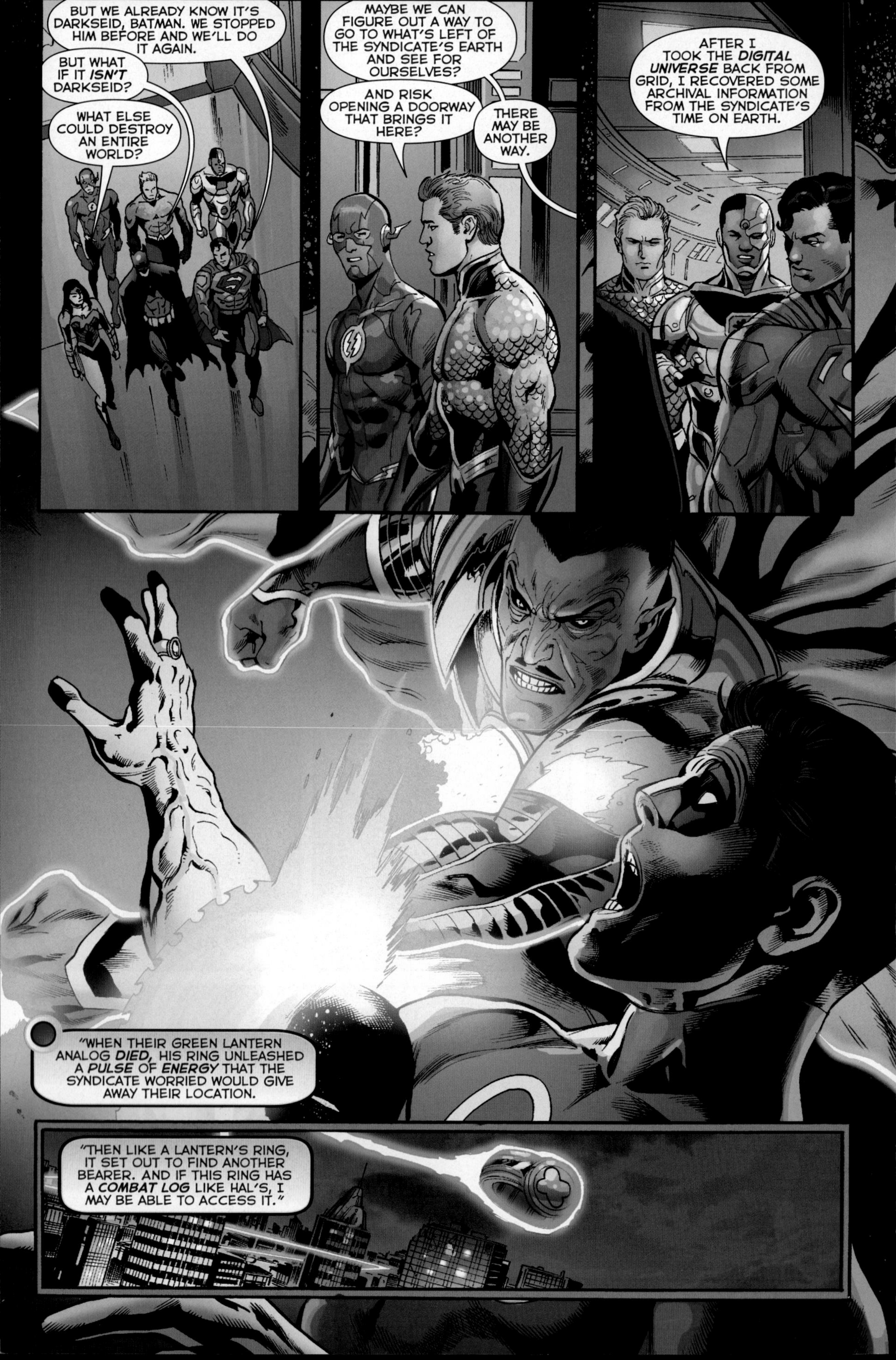
BUT WE ALREADY KNOW IT'S DARKSEID, BATMAN. WE STOPPED HIM BEFORE AND WE'LL DO IT AGAIN.
BUT WHAT IF IT *ISN'T* DARKSEID?
WHAT ELSE COULD DESTROY AN ENTIRE WORLD?
MAYBE WE CAN FIGURE OUT A WAY TO GO TO WHAT'S LEFT OF THE SYNDICATE'S EARTH AND SEE FOR OURSELVES?
AND RISK OPENING A DOORWAY THAT BRINGS IT HERE?
THERE MAY BE ANOTHER WAY.
AFTER I TOOK THE *DIGITAL UNIVERSE* BACK FROM GRID, I RECOVERED SOME ARCHIVAL INFORMATION FROM THE SYNDICATE'S TIME ON EARTH.
"WHEN THEIR GREEN LANTERN ANALOG *DIED,* HIS RING UNLEASHED A *PULSE* OF *ENERGY* THAT THE SYNDICATE WORRIED WOULD GIVE AWAY THEIR LOCATION.
"THEN LIKE A LANTERN'S RING, IT SET OUT TO FIND ANOTHER BEARER. AND IF THIS RING HAS A *COMBAT LOG* LIKE HAL'S, I MAY BE ABLE TO ACCESS IT."

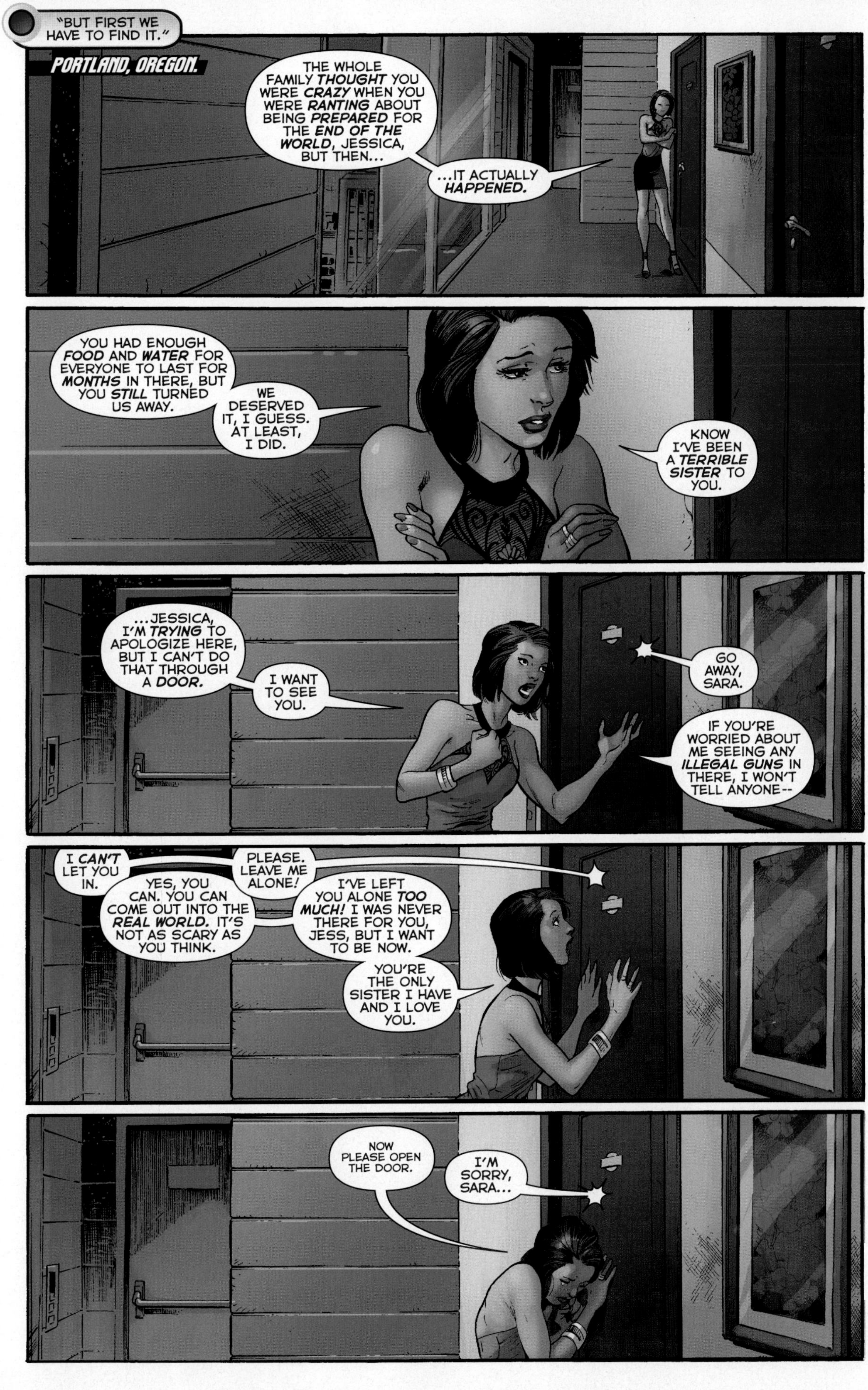
"BUT FIRST WE HAVE TO FIND IT."
PORTLAND, OREGON.
THE WHOLE FAMILY THOUGHT YOU WERE CRAZY WHEN YOU WERE RANTING ABOUT BEING PREPARED FOR THE END OF THE WORLD, JESSICA, BUT THEN...
...IT ACTUALLY HAPPENED.
YOU HAD ENOUGH FOOD AND WATER FOR EVERYONE TO LAST FOR MONTHS IN THERE, BUT YOU STILL TURNED US AWAY.
WE DESERVED IT, I GUESS. AT LEAST, I DID.
KNOW I'VE BEEN A TERRIBLE SISTER TO YOU.
...JESSICA, I'M TRYING TO APOLOGIZE HERE, BUT I CAN'T DO THAT THROUGH A DOOR.
I WANT TO SEE YOU.
GO AWAY, SARA.
IF YOU'RE WORRIED ABOUT ME SEEING ANY ILLEGAL GUNS IN THERE, I WON'T TELL ANYONE--
I CAN'T LET YOU IN.
PLEASE. LEAVE ME ALONE!
YES, YOU CAN. YOU CAN COME OUT INTO THE REAL WORLD. IT'S NOT AS SCARY AS YOU THINK.
I'VE LEFT YOU ALONE TOO MUCH! I WAS NEVER THERE FOR YOU, JESS, BUT I WANT TO BE NOW.
YOU'RE THE ONLY SISTER I HAVE AND I LOVE YOU.
NOW PLEASE OPEN THE DOOR.
I'M SORRY, SARA...

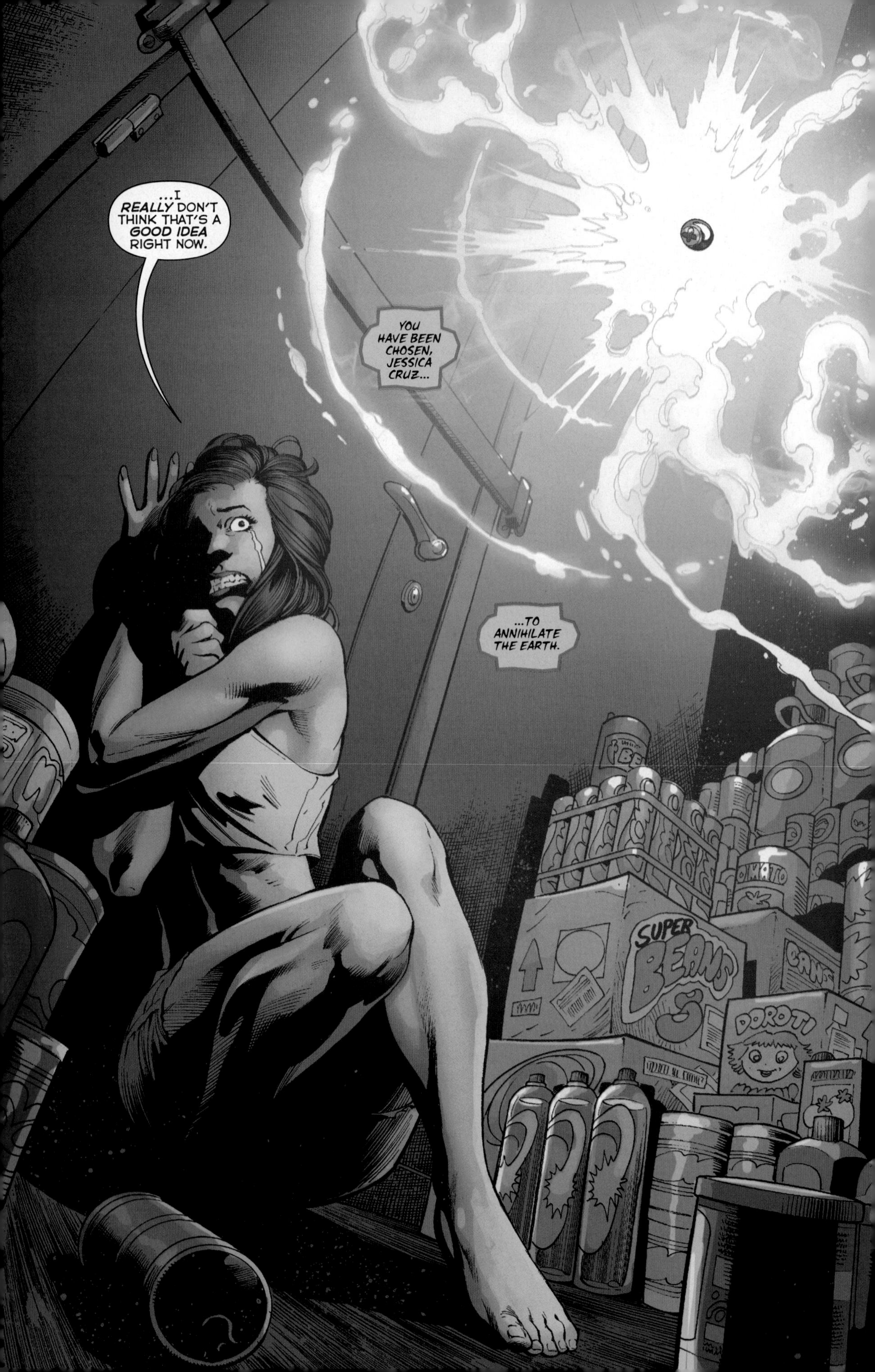
...I REALLY DON'T THINK THAT'S A GOOD IDEA RIGHT NOW.
YOU HAVE BEEN CHOSEN, JESSICA CRUZ...
...TO ANNIHILATE THE EARTH.
SUPER BEANS
DOROTI

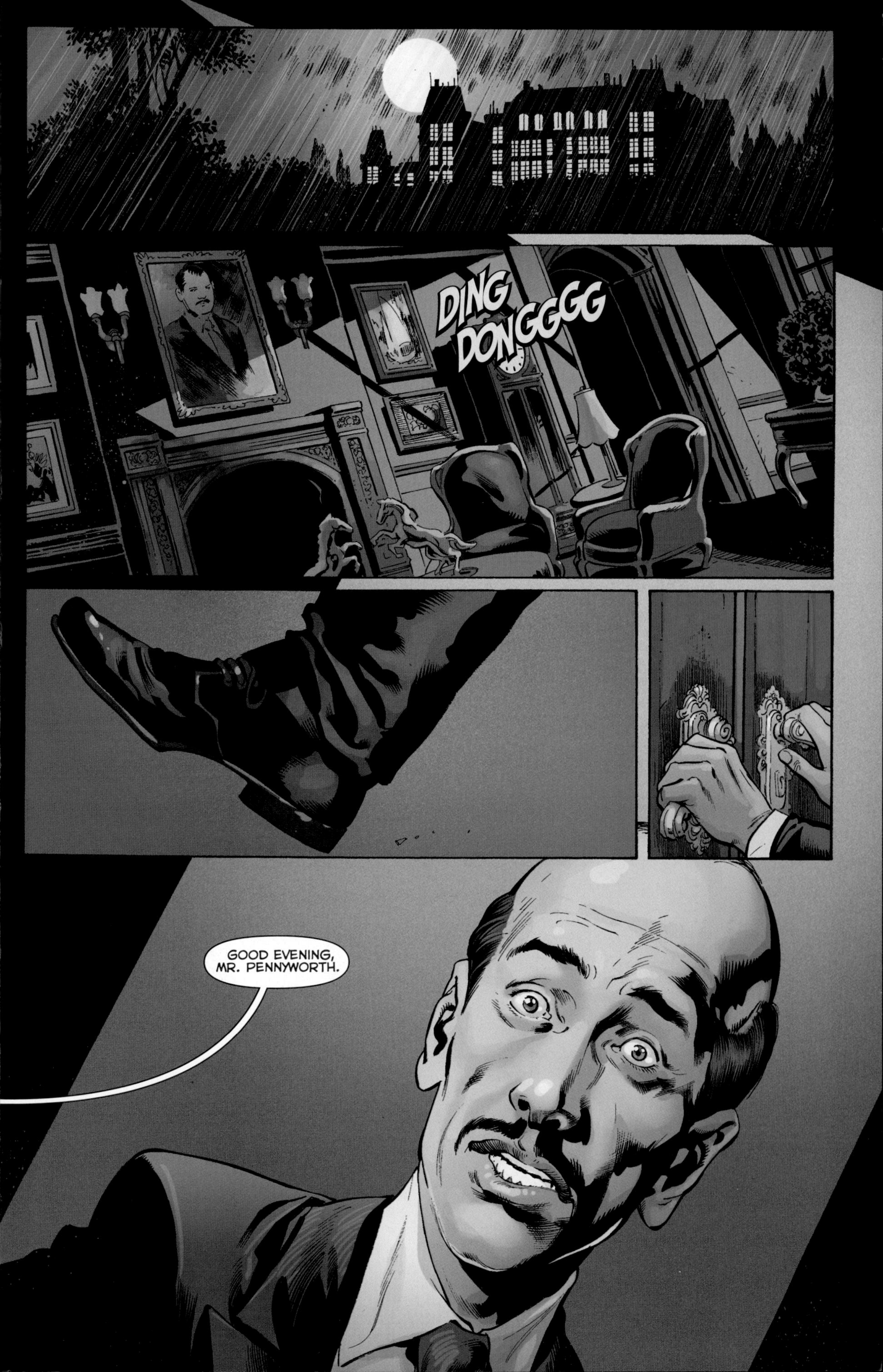
DING DONGGGG
GOOD EVENING, MR. PENNYWORTH.

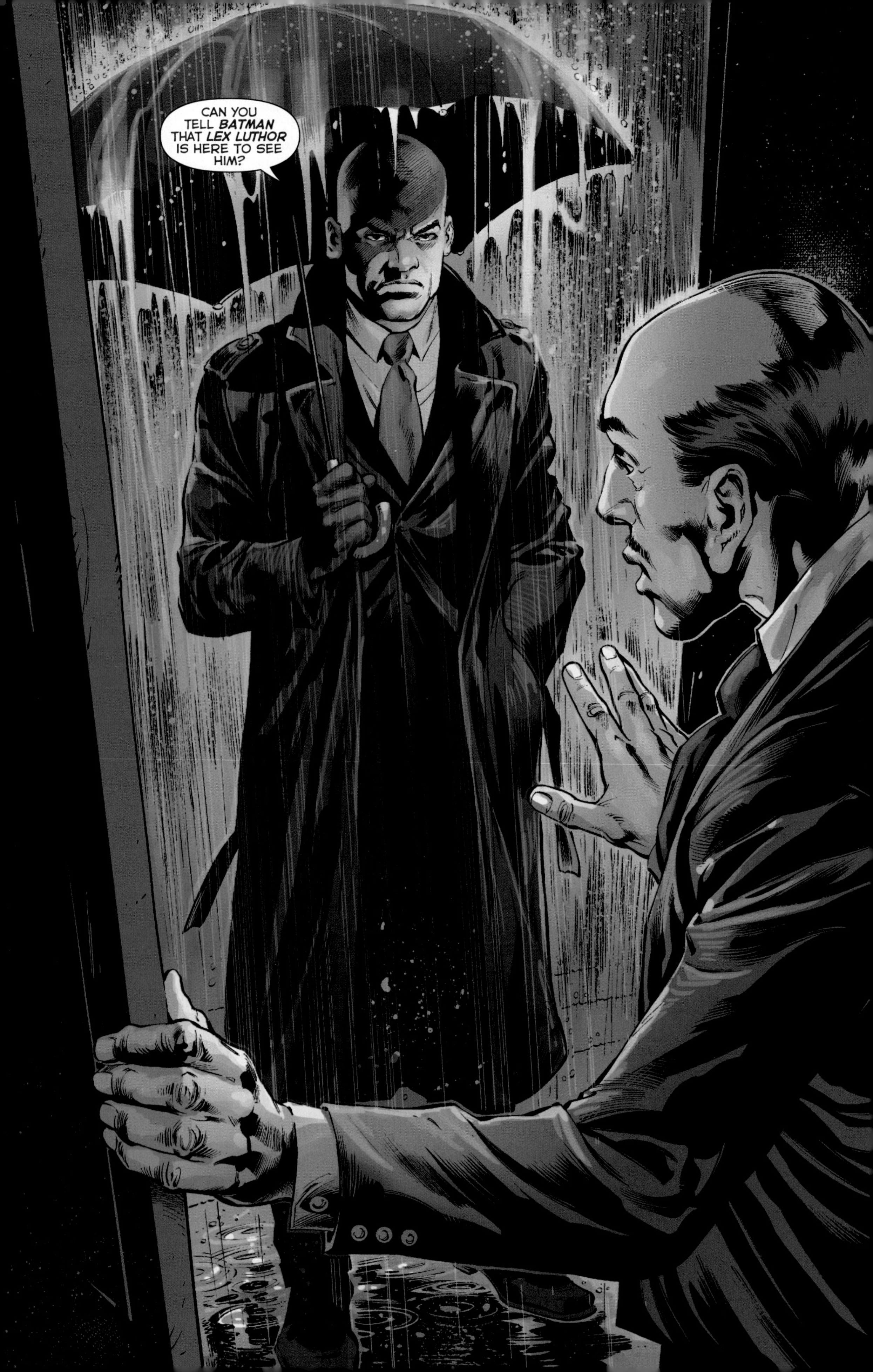
CAN YOU TELL BATMAN THAT LEX LUTHOR IS HERE TO SEE HIM?

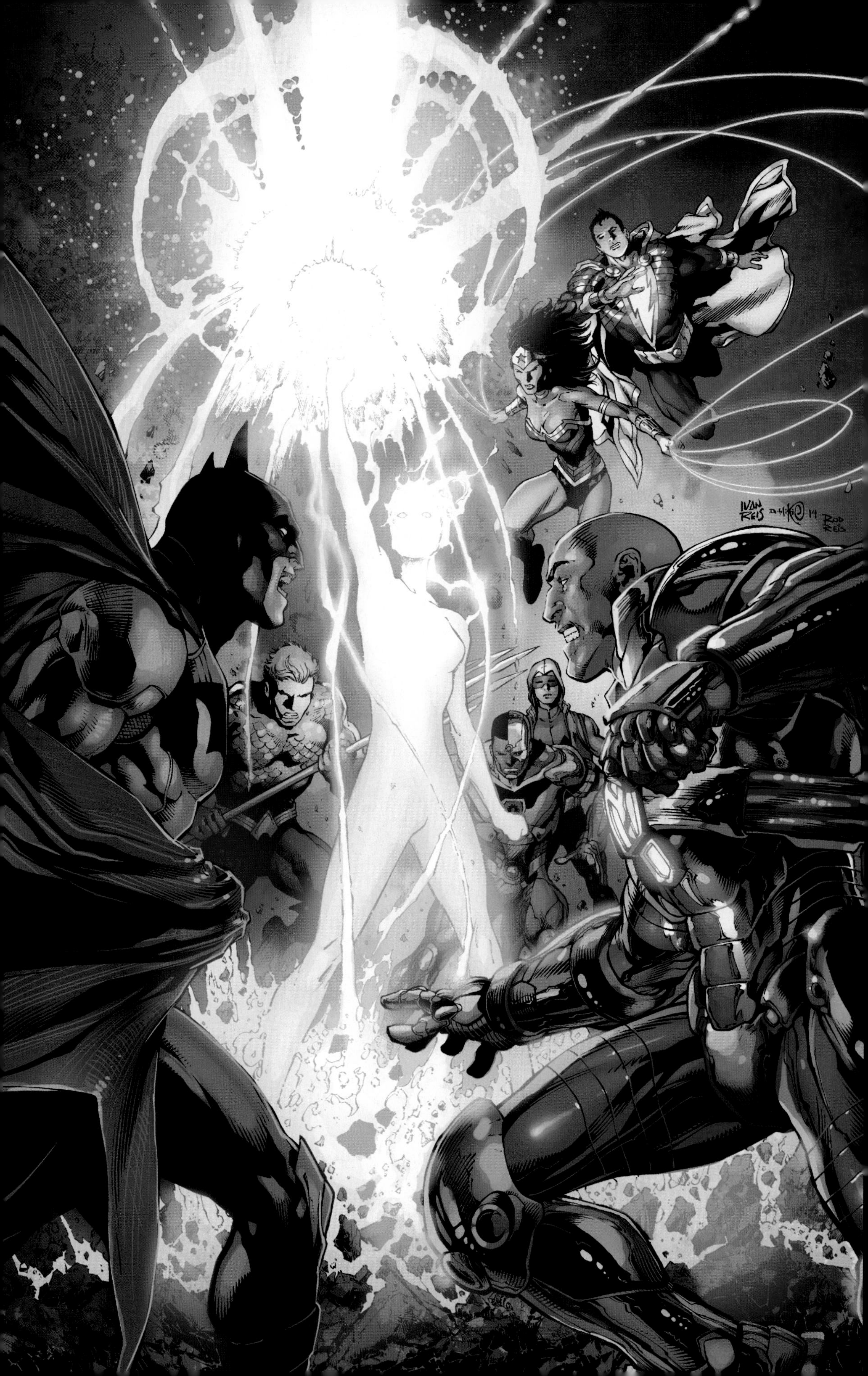
IVAN REIS
14
ROD REIS

INJUSTICE LEAGUE CHAPTER TWO
POWER PLAYERS

GEOFF JOHNS writer **DOUG MAHNKE** penciller **KEITH CHAMPAGNE** **CHRISTIAN ALAMY** inkers
ROD REIS colorist **IVAN REIS, JOE PRADO & ROD REIS** cover artists

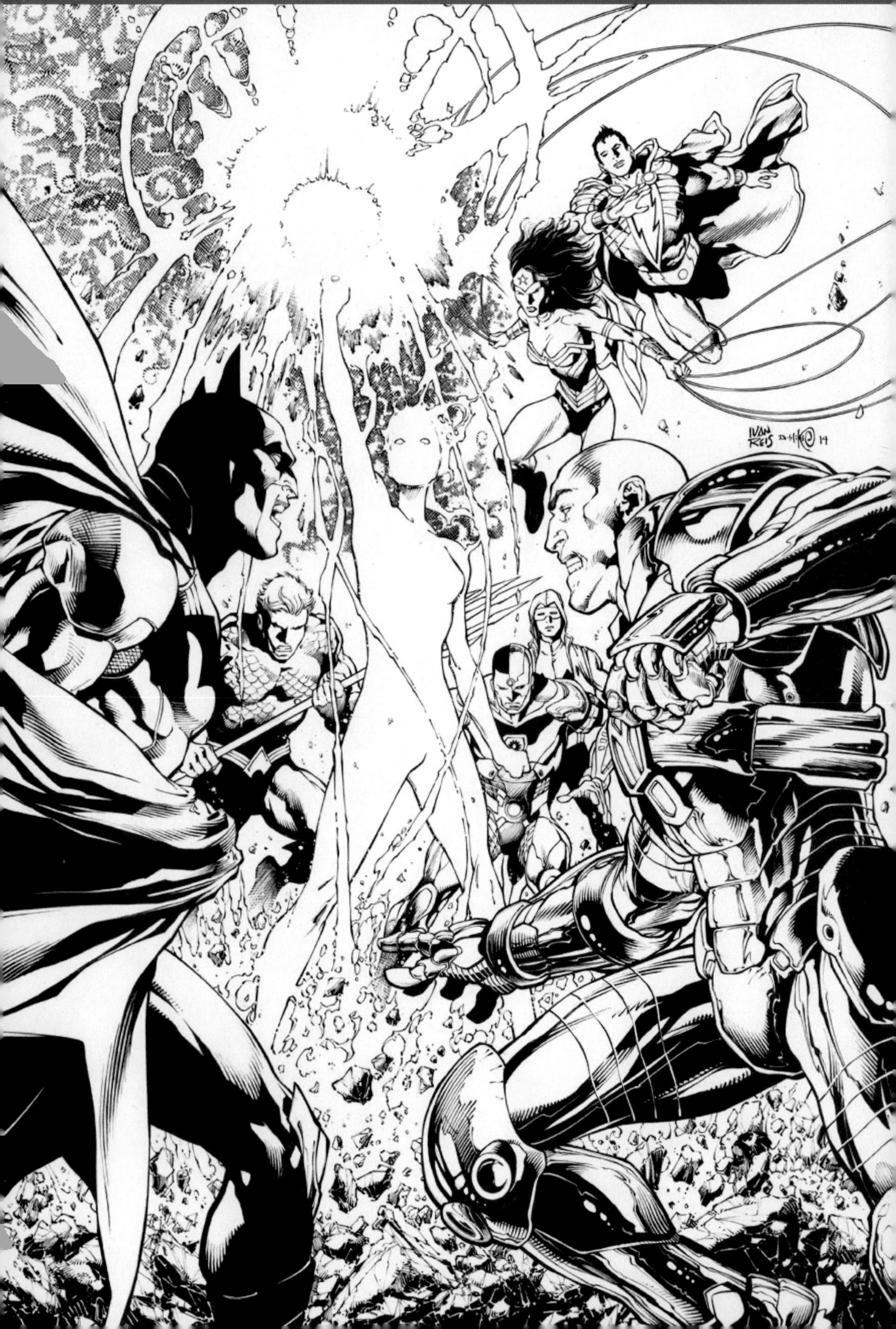

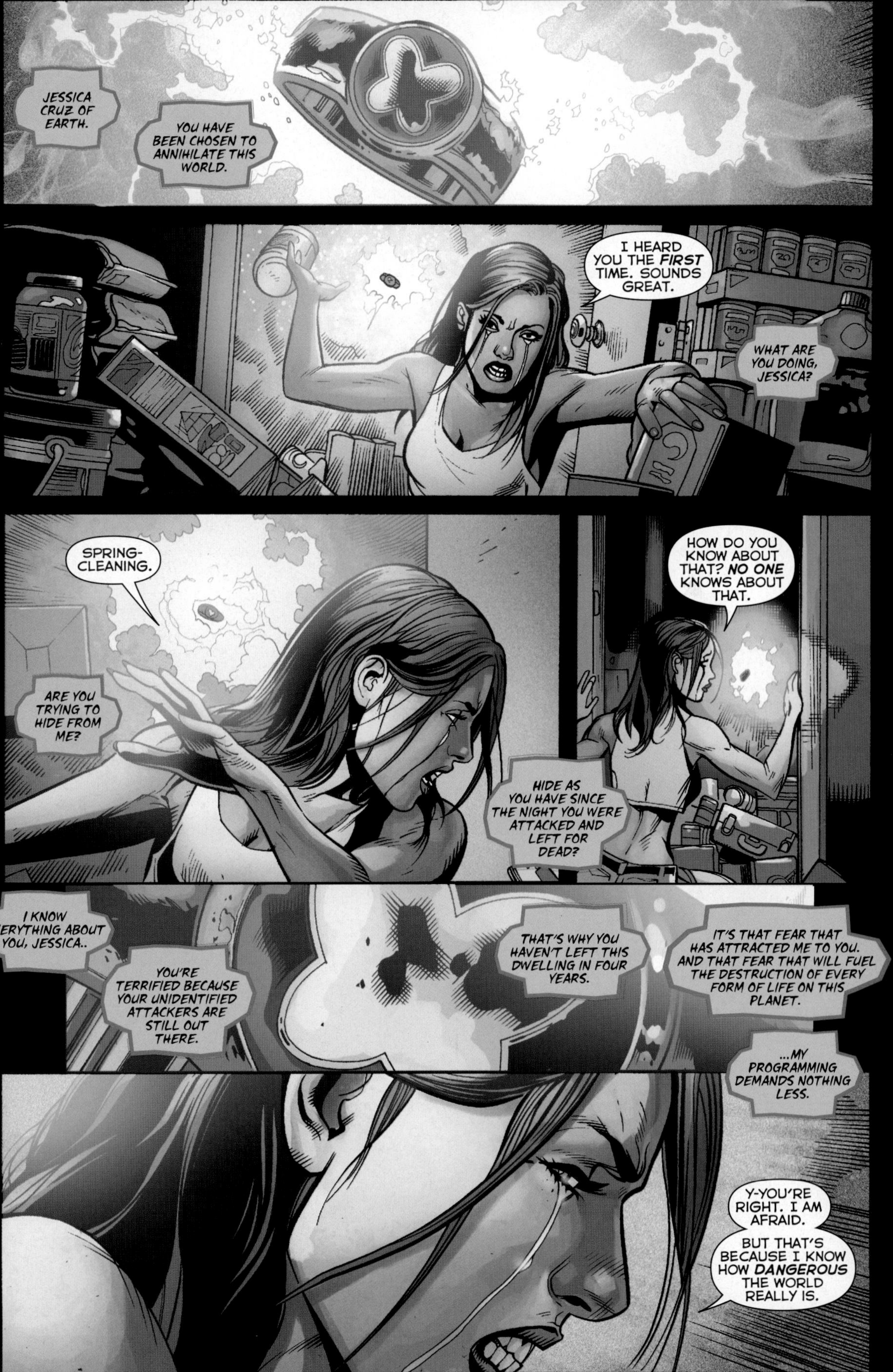
JESSICA CRUZ OF EARTH.
YOU HAVE BEEN CHOSEN TO ANNIHILATE THIS WORLD.
I HEARD YOU THE FIRST TIME. SOUNDS GREAT.
WHAT ARE YOU DOING, JESSICA?
SPRING-CLEANING.
ARE YOU TRYING TO HIDE FROM ME?
HOW DO YOU KNOW ABOUT THAT? NO ONE KNOWS ABOUT THAT.
HIDE AS YOU HAVE SINCE THE NIGHT YOU WERE ATTACKED AND LEFT FOR DEAD?
I KNOW EVERYTHING ABOUT YOU, JESSICA..
YOU'RE TERRIFIED BECAUSE YOUR UNIDENTIFIED ATTACKERS ARE STILL OUT THERE.
THAT'S WHY YOU HAVEN'T LEFT THIS DWELLING IN FOUR YEARS.
IT'S THAT FEAR THAT HAS ATTRACTED ME TO YOU. AND THAT FEAR THAT WILL FUEL THE DESTRUCTION OF EVERY FORM OF LIFE ON THIS PLANET.
...MY PROGRAMMING DEMANDS NOTHING LESS.
Y-YOU'RE RIGHT. I AM AFRAID.
BUT THAT'S BECAUSE I KNOW HOW DANGEROUS THE WORLD REALLY IS.

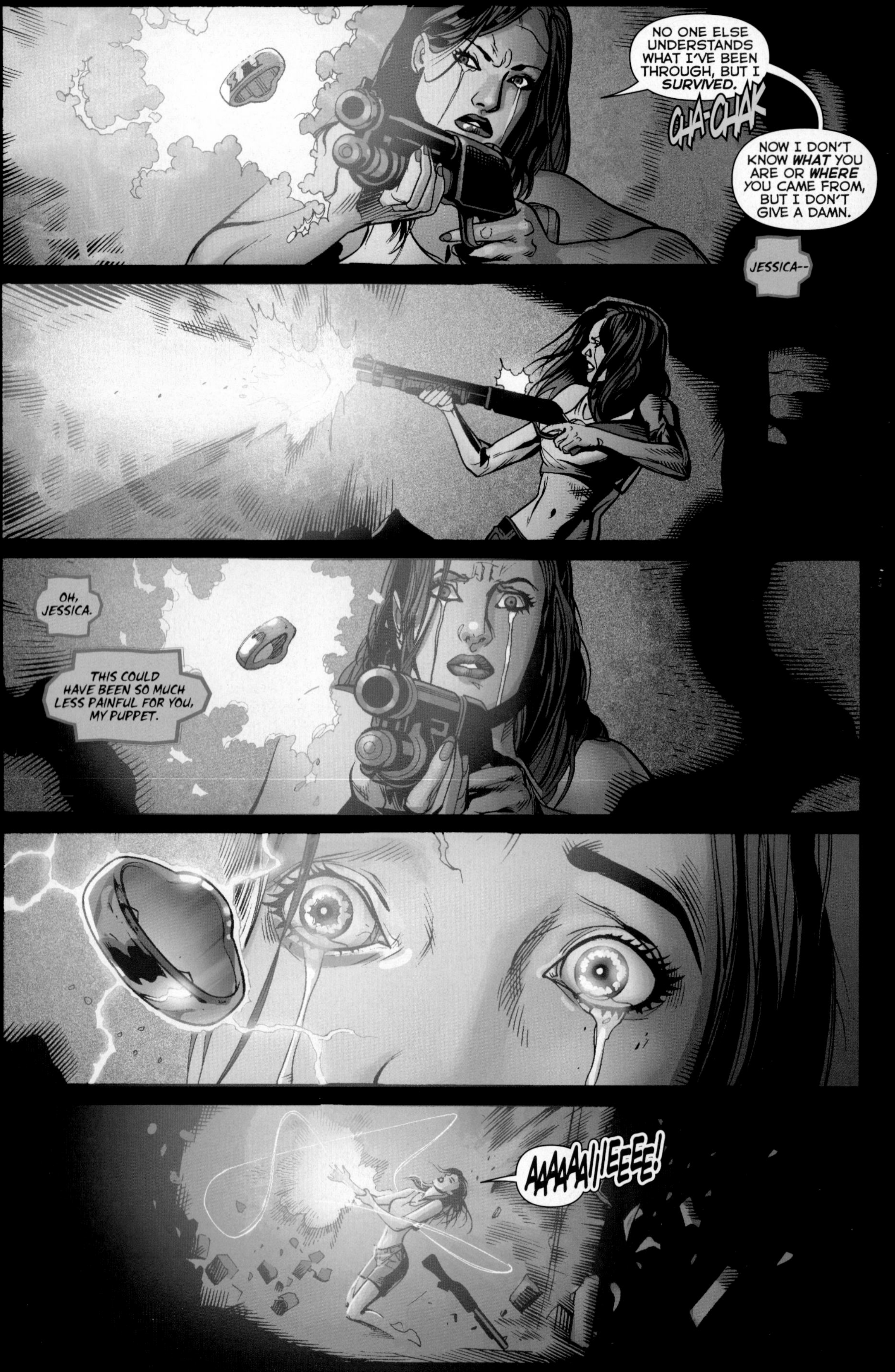
NO ONE ELSE UNDERSTANDS WHAT I'VE BEEN THROUGH, BUT I SURVIVED.
CHA-CHAK
NOW I DON'T KNOW WHAT YOU ARE OR WHERE YOU CAME FROM, BUT I DON'T GIVE A DAMN.
JESSICA--
OH, JESSICA.
THIS COULD HAVE BEEN SO MUCH LESS PAINFUL FOR YOU, MY PUPPET.
AAAAAAIIEEEEE!

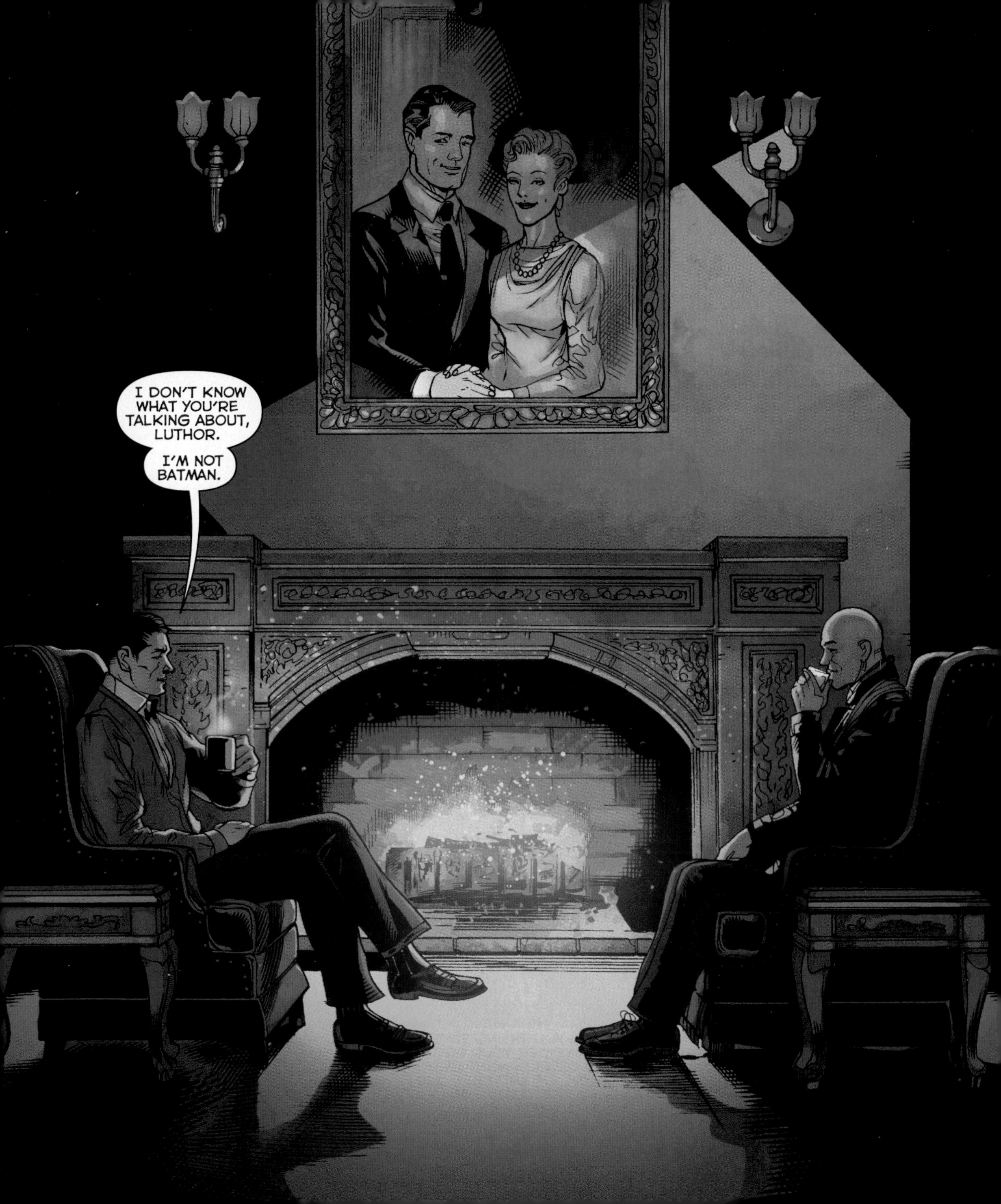
I DON'T KNOW WHAT YOU'RE TALKING ABOUT, LUTHOR.
I'M NOT BATMAN.

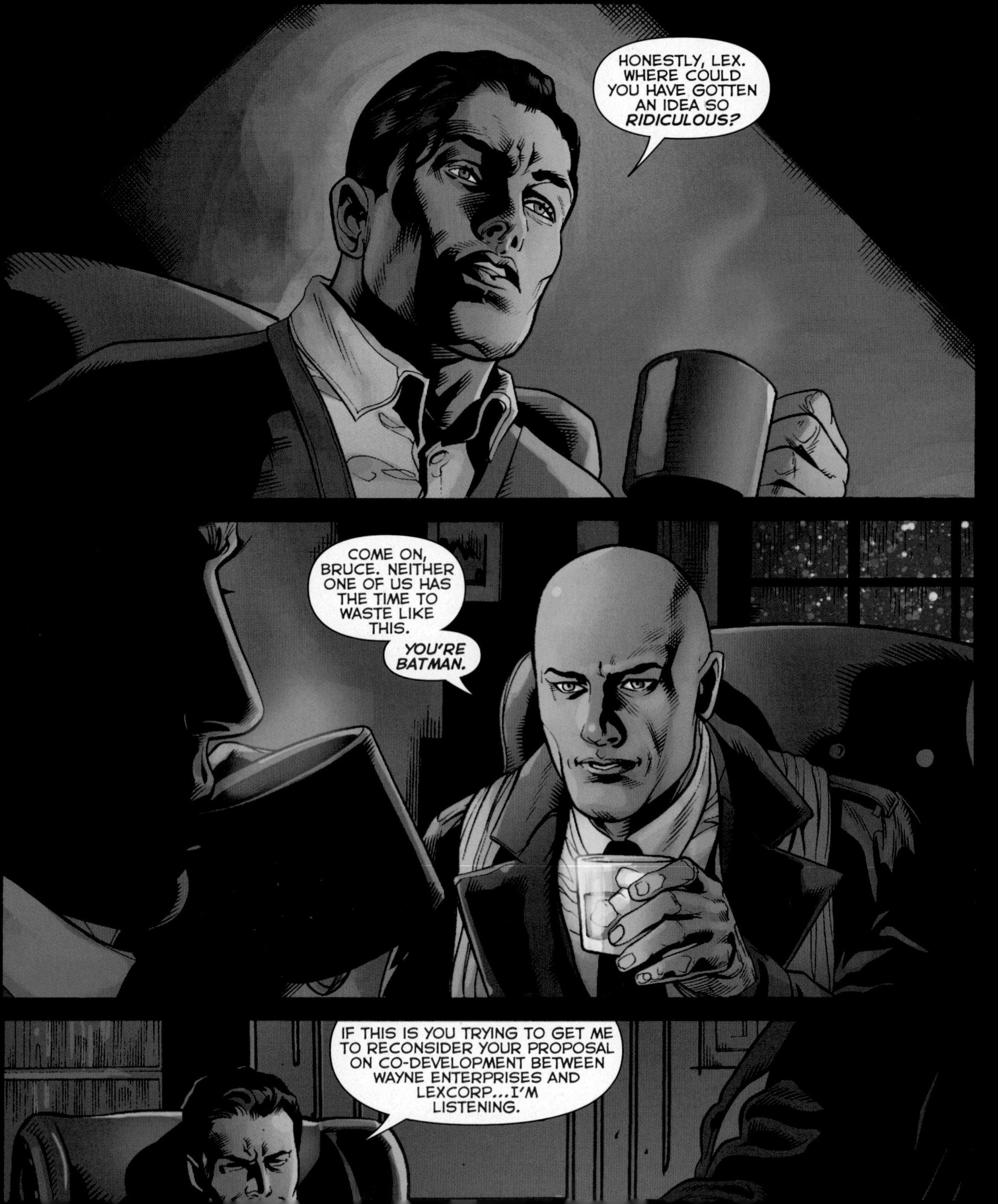
HONESTLY, LEX. WHERE COULD YOU HAVE GOTTEN AN IDEA SO *RIDICULOUS?*
COME ON, BRUCE. NEITHER ONE OF US HAS THE TIME TO WASTE LIKE THIS.
YOU'RE BATMAN.
IF THIS IS YOU TRYING TO GET ME TO RECONSIDER YOUR PROPOSAL ON CO-DEVELOPMENT BETWEEN WAYNE ENTERPRISES AND LEXCORP...I'M LISTENING.

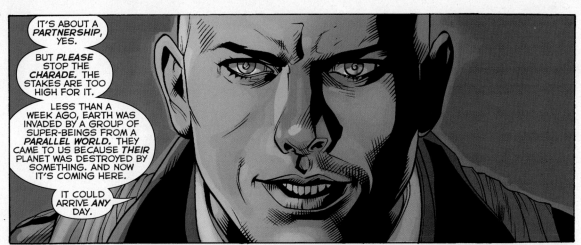

IT'S ABOUT A *PARTNERSHIP,* YES.

BUT *PLEASE* STOP THE *CHARADE.* THE STAKES ARE TOO HIGH FOR IT.

LESS THAN A WEEK AGO, EARTH WAS INVADED BY A GROUP OF SUPER-BEINGS FROM A *PARALLEL WORLD.* THEY CAME TO US BECAUSE *THEIR* PLANET WAS DESTROYED BY SOMETHING. AND NOW IT'S COMING HERE.

IT COULD ARRIVE *ANY* DAY.

ANY *SECOND.*

AND IF YOU AND I AREN'T *UNITED*--

--*EARTH IS DOOMED.*

HAHAHA

ALL THIS "SAVING THE WORLD" BUSINESS HAS DONE WONDERS FOR YOUR SENSE OF HUMOR. I'LL GIVE YOU THAT.

AS MUCH AS I'D LOVE TO STAY HERE, DRINK BOURBON AND TAKE CREDIT FOR GOTHAM'S DARK KNIGHT, I HAVE TICKETS TO THE OPERA.

I'M GOING TO BE LATE PICKING UP GLORIA--A GYMNAST FROM SWITZERLAND I MET ON THE SLOPES IN ZURICH. FORGIVE ME IF I DON'T SEE YOU OUT.

I'M NOT GOING ANYWHERE, BRUCE.

CHAK

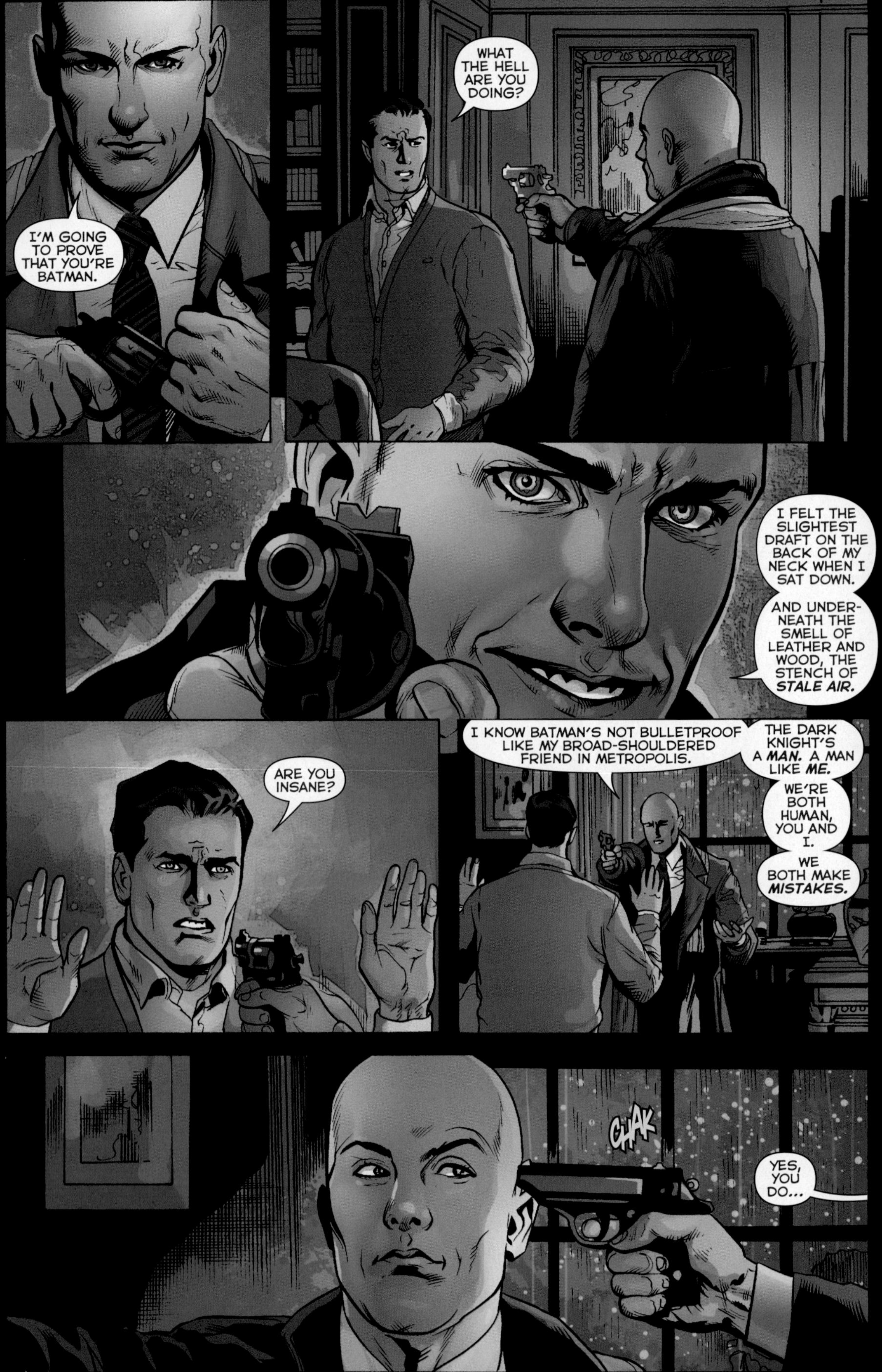
I'M GOING TO PROVE THAT YOU'RE BATMAN.
WHAT THE HELL ARE YOU DOING?
I FELT THE SLIGHTEST DRAFT ON THE BACK OF MY NECK WHEN I SAT DOWN.
AND UNDERNEATH THE SMELL OF LEATHER AND WOOD, THE STENCH OF STALE AIR.
ARE YOU INSANE?
I KNOW BATMAN'S NOT BULLETPROOF LIKE MY BROAD-SHOULDERED FRIEND IN METROPOLIS.
THE DARK KNIGHT'S A MAN. A MAN LIKE ME.
WE'RE BOTH HUMAN, YOU AND I.
WE BOTH MAKE MISTAKES.
CHAK
YES, YOU DO...

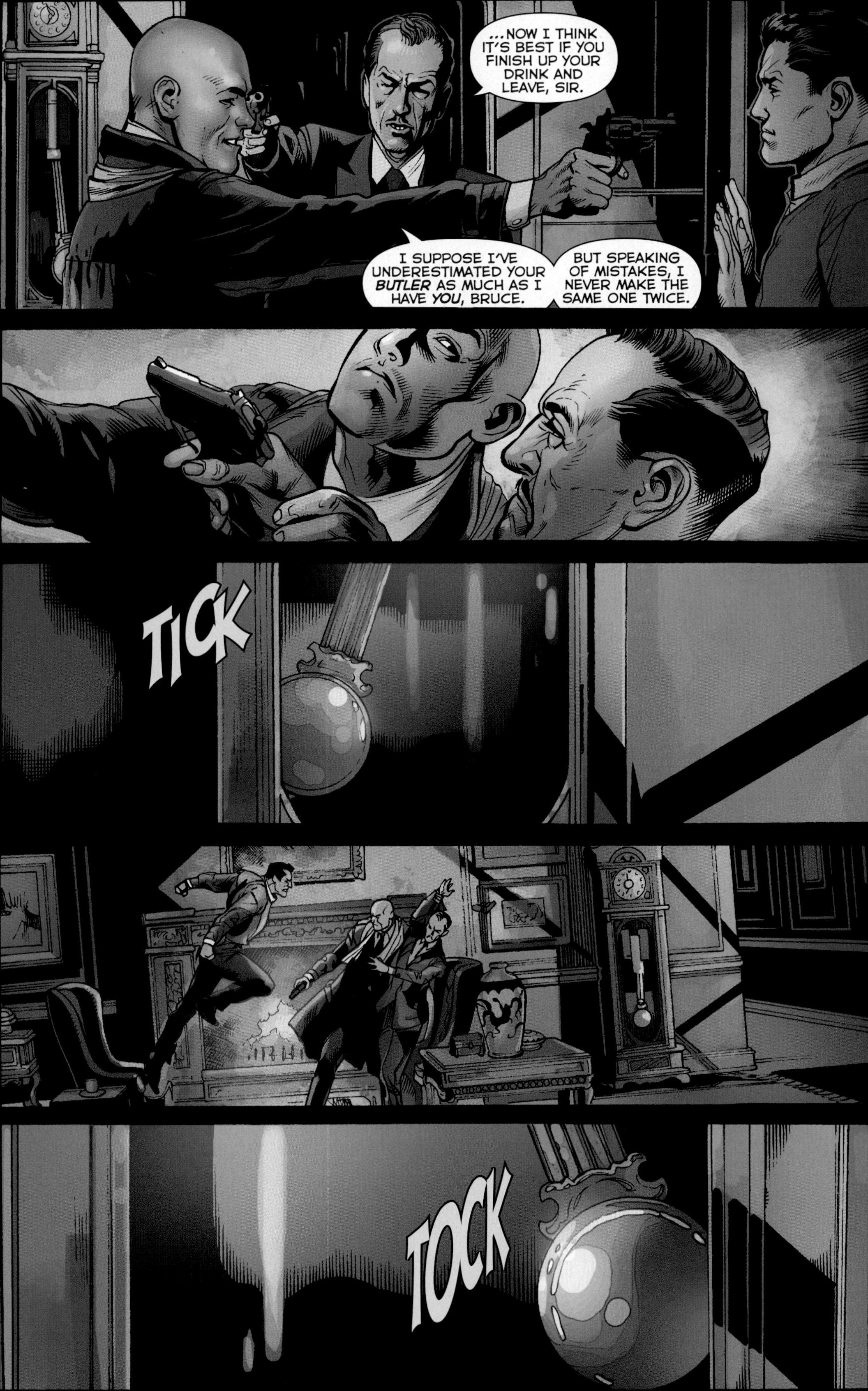
...NOW I THINK IT'S BEST IF YOU FINISH UP YOUR DRINK AND LEAVE, SIR.
I SUPPOSE I'VE UNDERESTIMATED YOUR *BUTLER* AS MUCH AS I HAVE *YOU*, BRUCE.
BUT SPEAKING OF MISTAKES, I NEVER MAKE THE SAME ONE TWICE.
TICK
TOCK

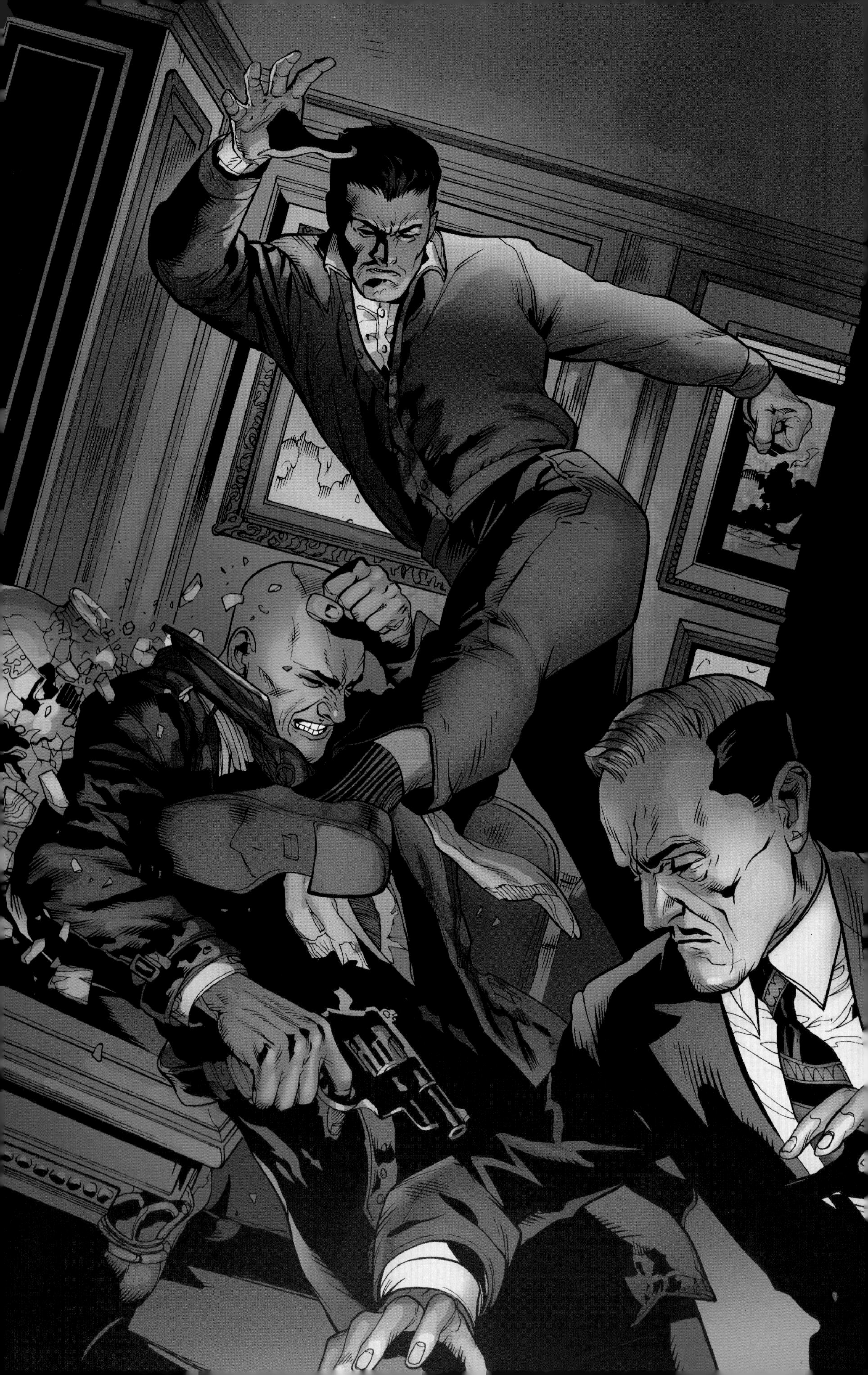

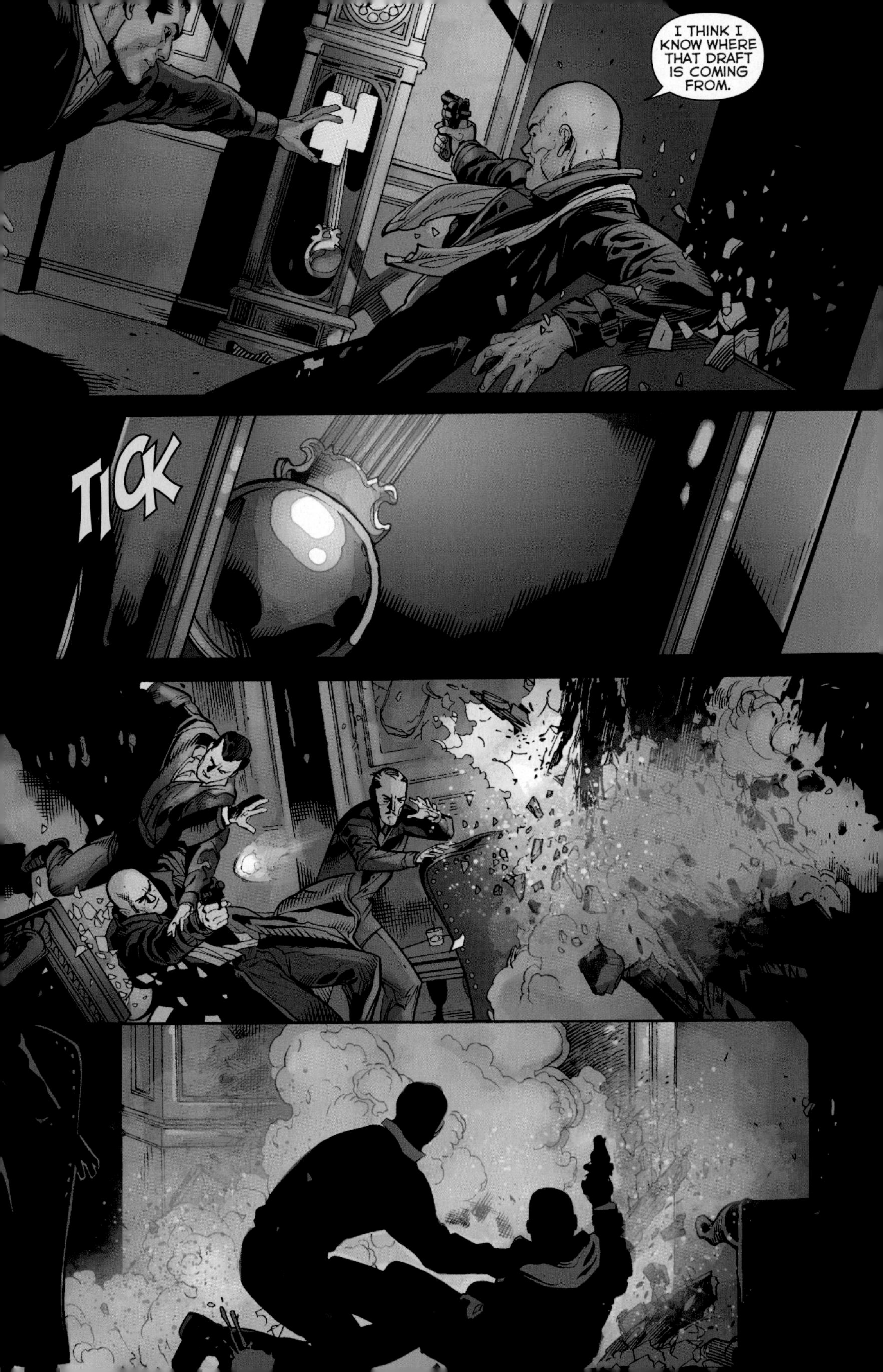
I THINK I KNOW WHERE THAT DRAFT IS COMING FROM.
TICK

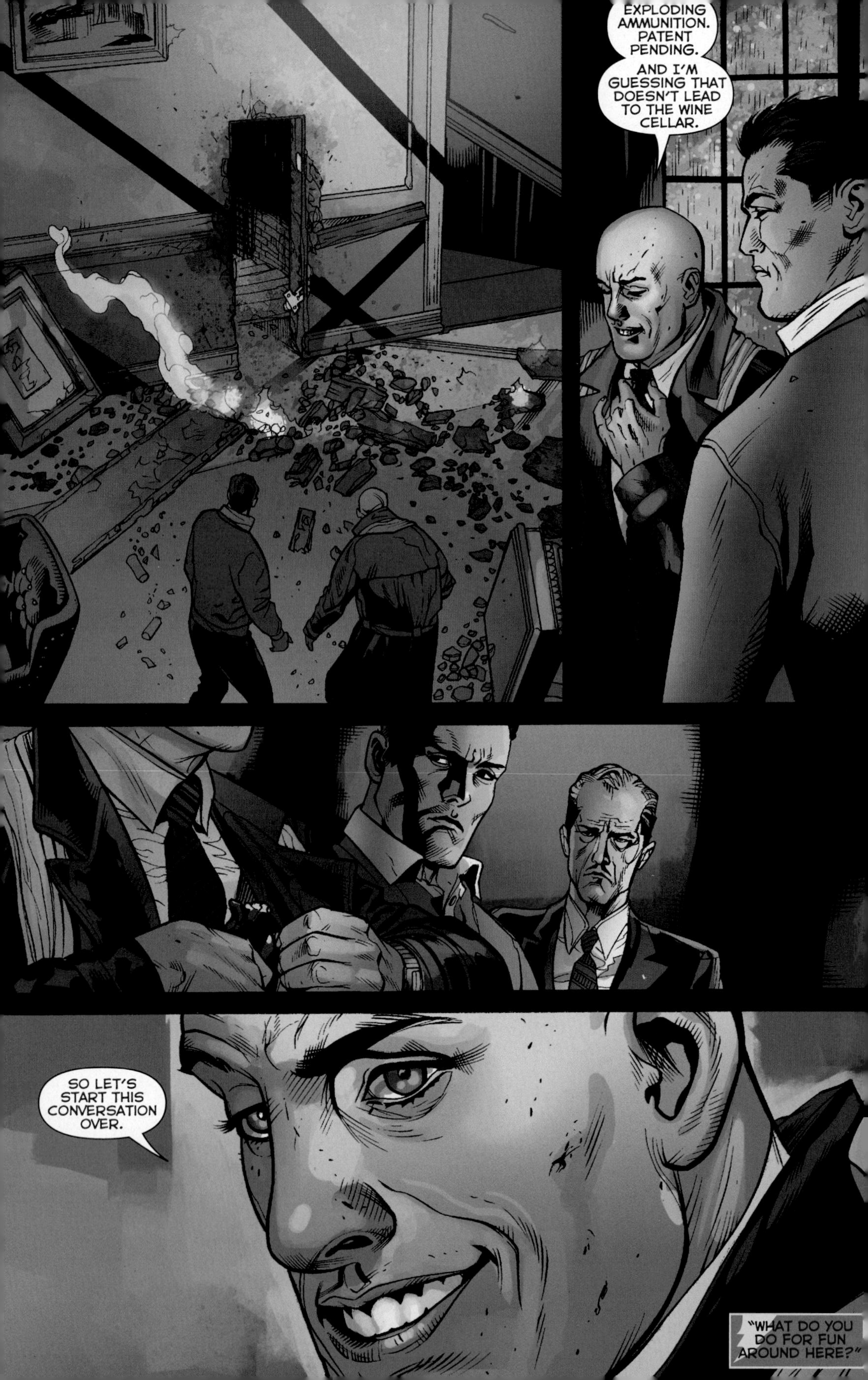
EXPLODING AMMUNITION. PATENT PENDING.
AND I'M GUESSING THAT DOESN'T LEAD TO THE WINE CELLAR.
SO LET'S START THIS CONVERSATION OVER.
"WHAT DO YOU DO FOR FUN AROUND HERE?"

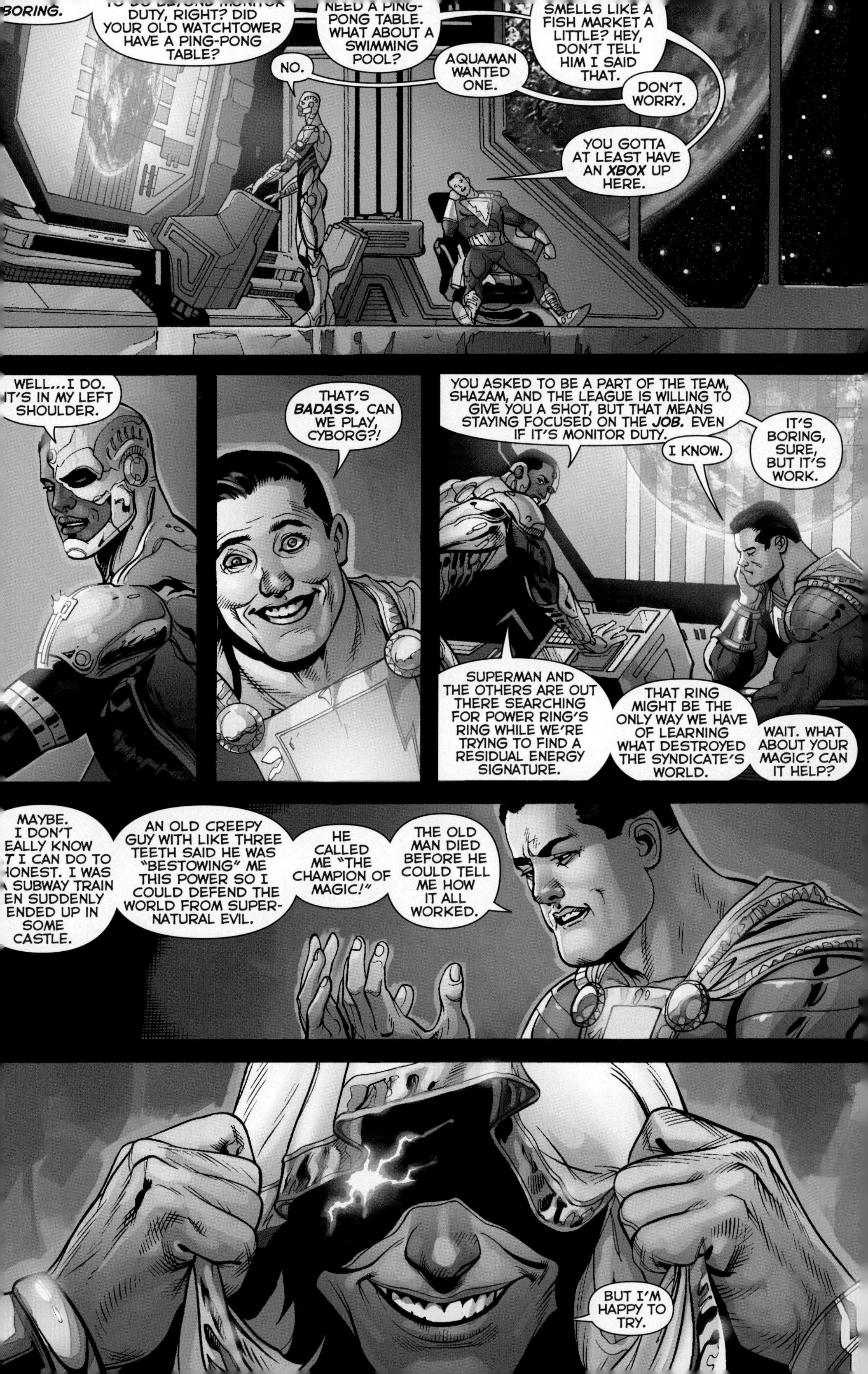

BORING.
DUTY, RIGHT? DID YOUR OLD WATCHTOWER HAVE A PING-PONG TABLE?
NO.
NEED A PING-PONG TABLE. WHAT ABOUT A SWIMMING POOL?
AQUAMAN WANTED ONE.
SMELLS LIKE A FISH MARKET A LITTLE? HEY, DON'T TELL HIM I SAID THAT.
DON'T WORRY.
YOU GOTTA AT LEAST HAVE AN XBOX UP HERE.
WELL...I DO. IT'S IN MY LEFT SHOULDER.
THAT'S BADASS. CAN WE PLAY, CYBORG?!
YOU ASKED TO BE A PART OF THE TEAM, SHAZAM, AND THE LEAGUE IS WILLING TO GIVE YOU A SHOT, BUT THAT MEANS STAYING FOCUSED ON THE JOB. EVEN IF IT'S MONITOR DUTY.
I KNOW.
IT'S BORING, SURE, BUT IT'S WORK.
SUPERMAN AND THE OTHERS ARE OUT THERE SEARCHING FOR POWER RING'S RING WHILE WE'RE TRYING TO FIND A RESIDUAL ENERGY SIGNATURE.
THAT RING MIGHT BE THE ONLY WAY WE HAVE OF LEARNING WHAT DESTROYED THE SYNDICATE'S WORLD.
WAIT. WHAT ABOUT YOUR MAGIC? CAN IT HELP?
MAYBE. I DON'T EALLY KNOW T I CAN DO TO HONEST. I WAS SUBWAY TRAIN EN SUDDENLY ENDED UP IN SOME CASTLE.
AN OLD CREEPY GUY WITH LIKE THREE TEETH SAID HE WAS "BESTOWING" ME THIS POWER SO I COULD DEFEND THE WORLD FROM SUPER-NATURAL EVIL.
HE CALLED ME "THE CHAMPION OF MAGIC!"
THE OLD MAN DIED BEFORE HE COULD TELL ME HOW IT ALL WORKED.
BUT I'M HAPPY TO TRY.

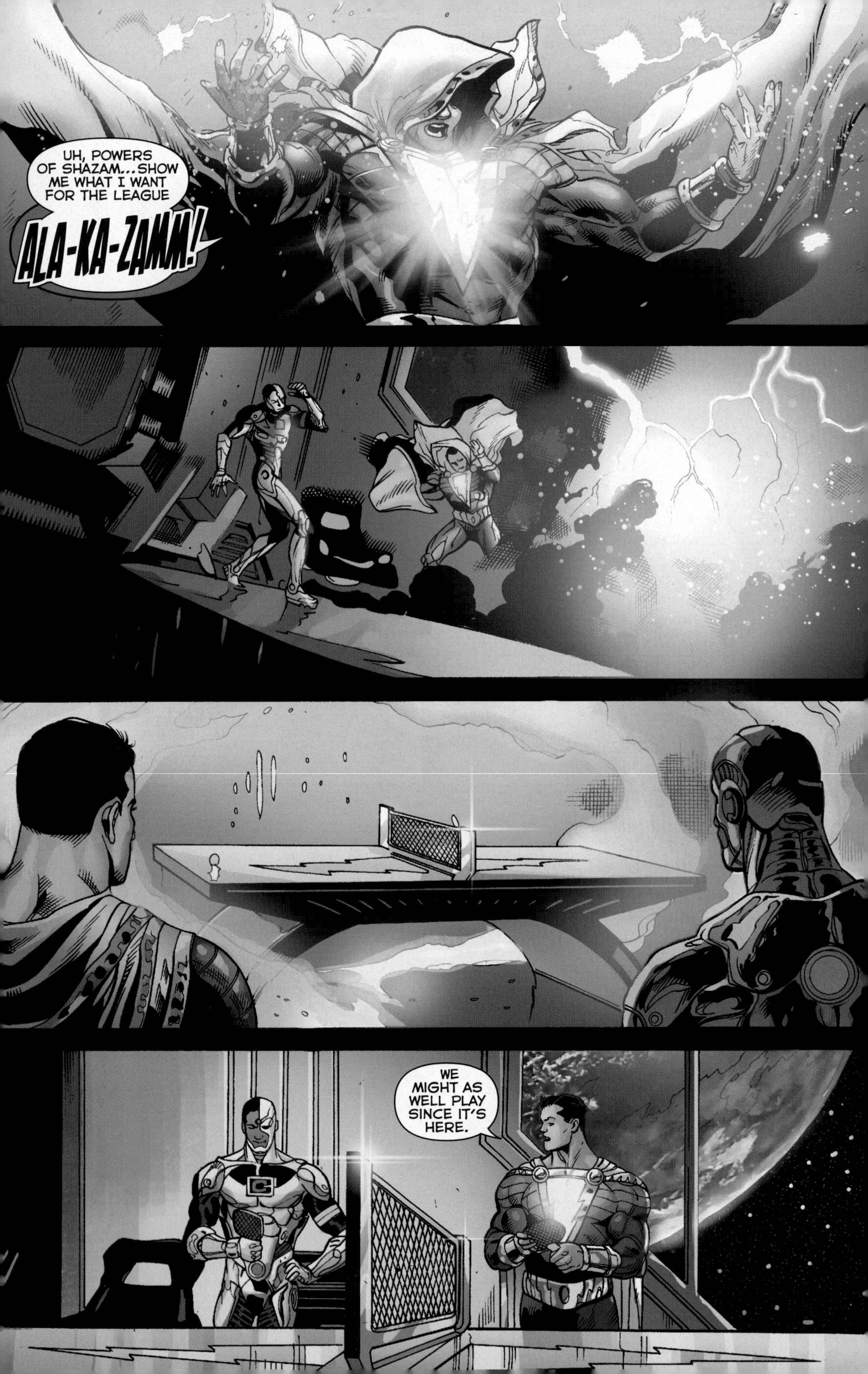
UH, POWERS OF SHAZAM...SHOW ME WHAT I WANT FOR THE LEAGUE
ALA-KA-ZAMM!
WE MIGHT AS WELL PLAY SINCE IT'S HERE.

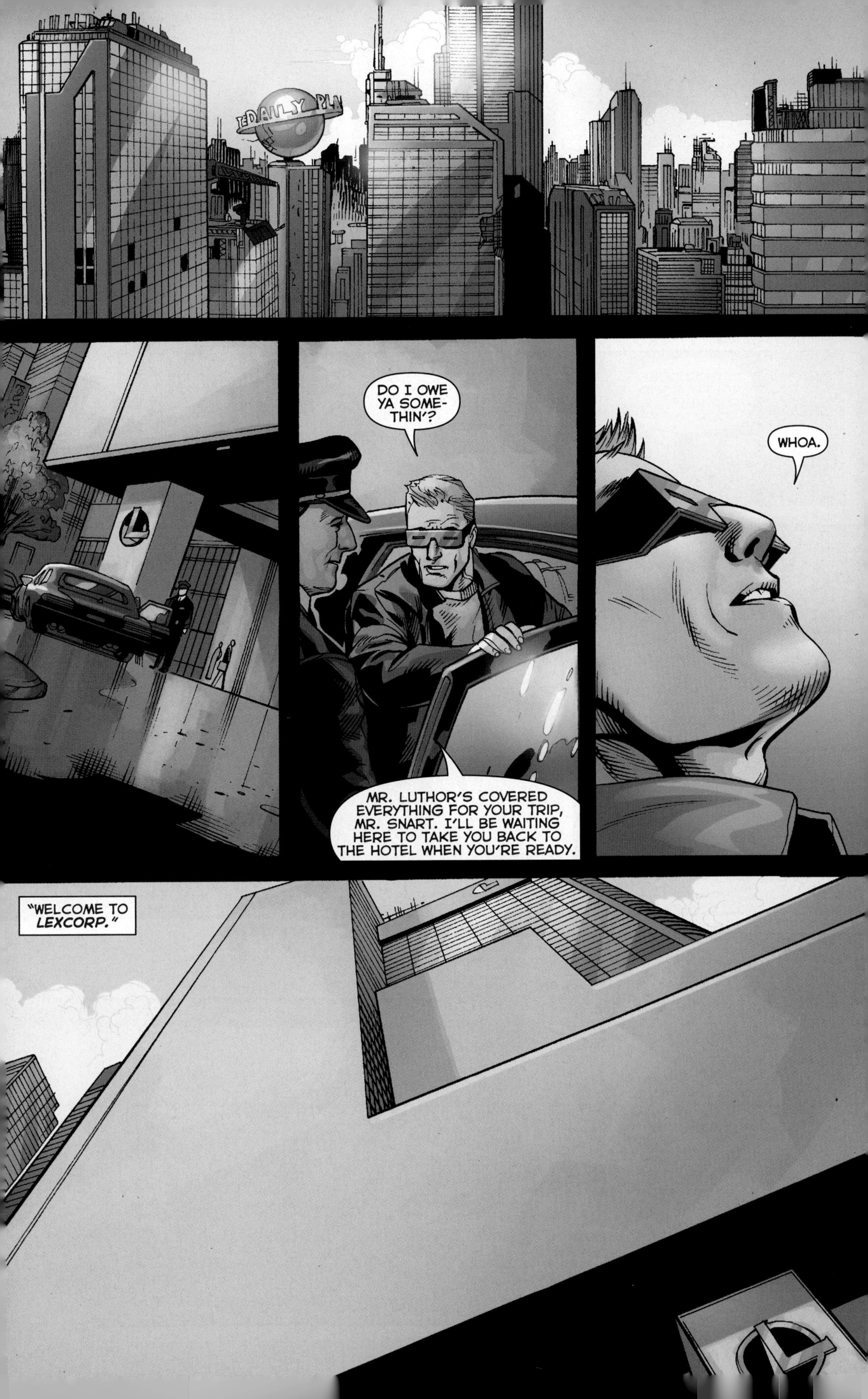
DAILY PLA
DO I OWE YA SOME-THIN'?
MR. LUTHOR'S COVERED EVERYTHING FOR YOUR TRIP, MR. SNART. I'LL BE WAITING HERE TO TAKE YOU BACK TO THE HOTEL WHEN YOU'RE READY.
WHOA.
"WELCOME TO *LEXCORP.*"

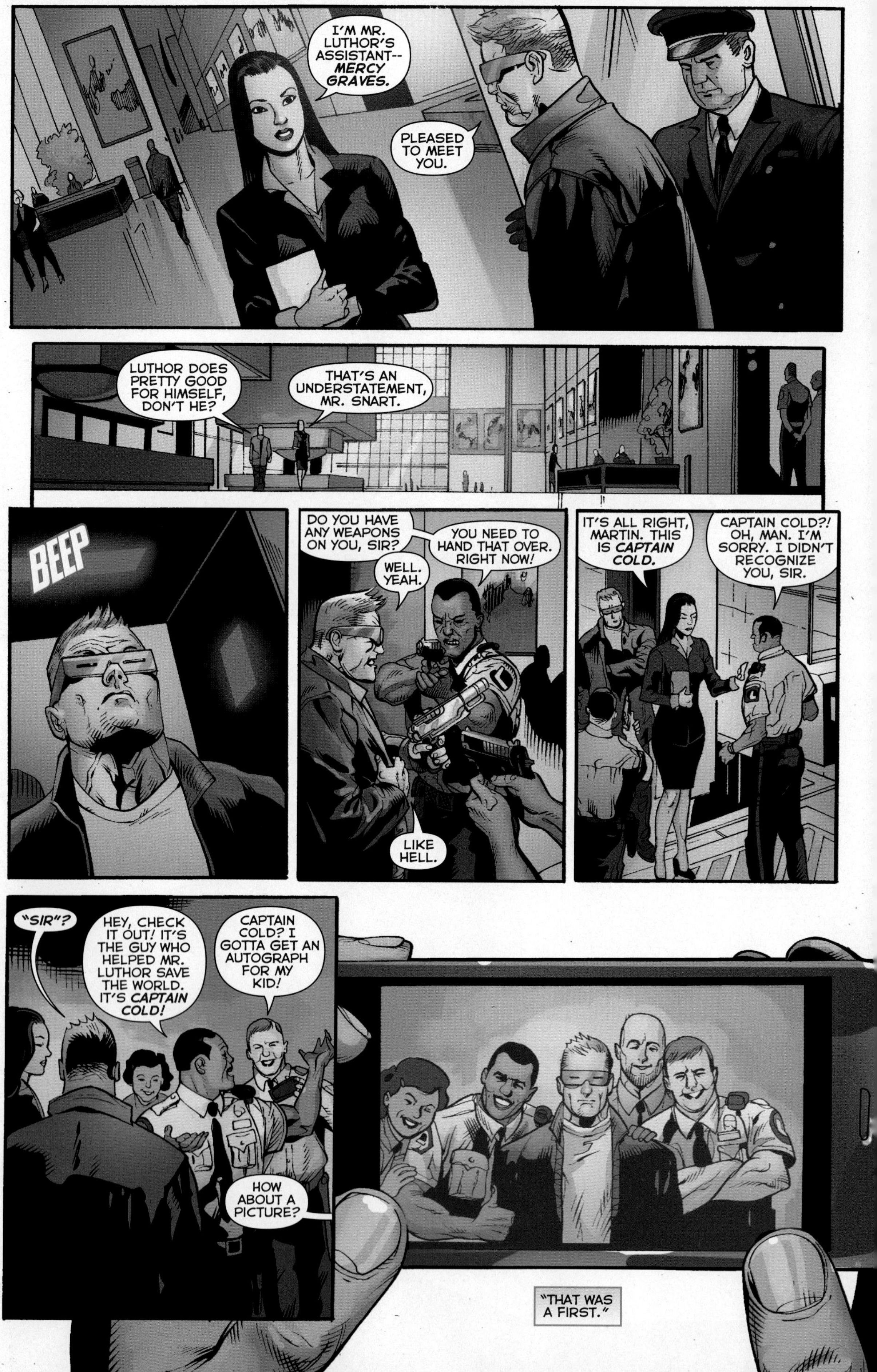
I'M MR. LUTHOR'S ASSISTANT-- *MERCY GRAVES.*
PLEASED TO MEET YOU.
LUTHOR DOES PRETTY GOOD FOR HIMSELF, DON'T HE?
THAT'S AN UNDERSTATEMENT, MR. SNART.
BEEP
DO YOU HAVE ANY WEAPONS ON YOU, SIR?
WELL. YEAH.
YOU NEED TO HAND THAT OVER. RIGHT NOW!
LIKE HELL.
IT'S ALL RIGHT, MARTIN. THIS IS *CAPTAIN COLD.*
CAPTAIN COLD?! OH, MAN. I'M SORRY. I DIDN'T RECOGNIZE YOU, SIR.
"SIR"?
HEY, CHECK IT OUT! IT'S THE GUY WHO HELPED MR. LUTHOR SAVE THE WORLD. IT'S *CAPTAIN COLD!*
CAPTAIN COLD? I GOTTA GET AN AUTOGRAPH FOR MY KID!
HOW ABOUT A PICTURE?
"THAT WAS A FIRST."

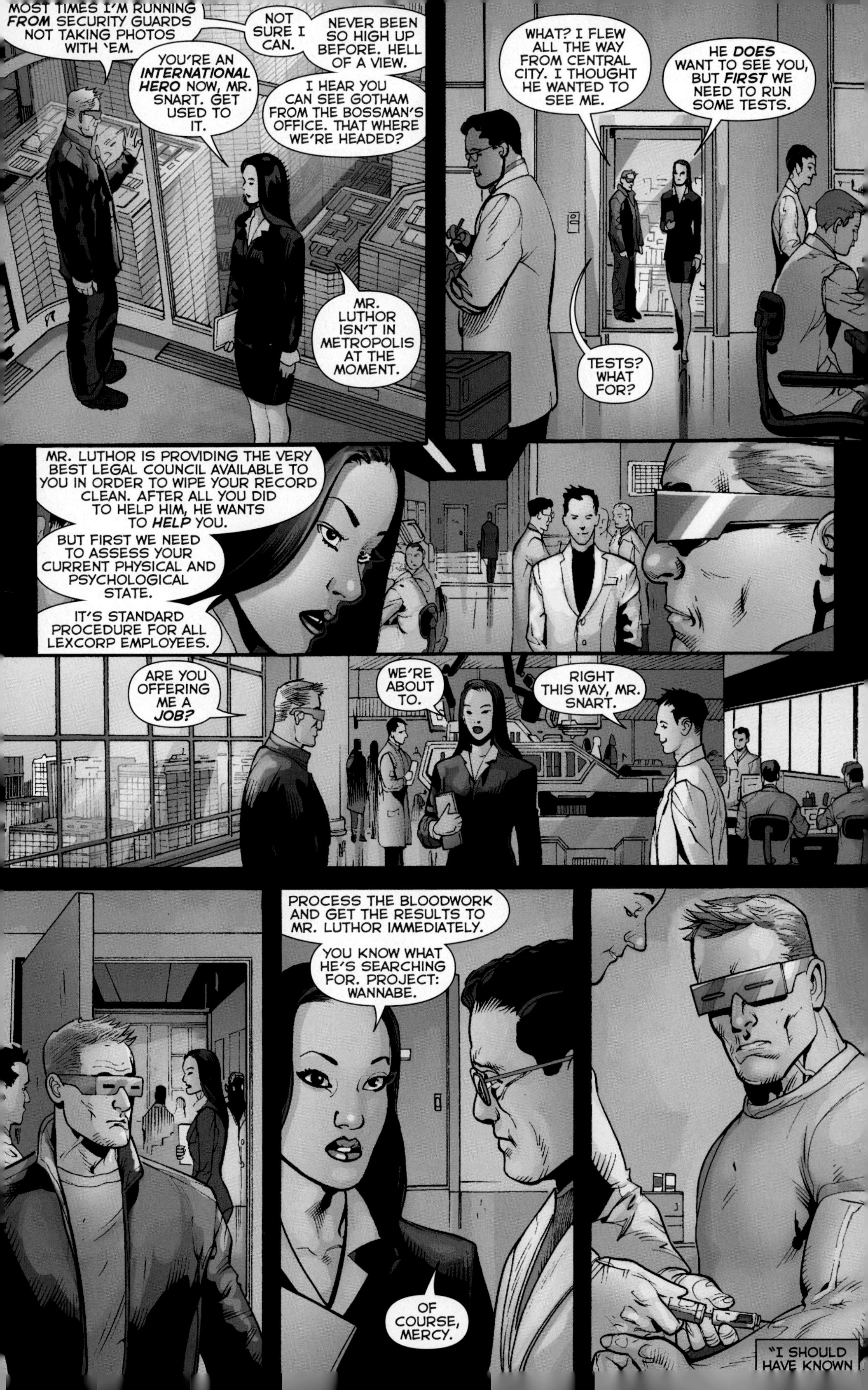
MOST TIMES I'M RUNNING FROM SECURITY GUARDS NOT TAKING PHOTOS WITH 'EM.
YOU'RE AN INTERNATIONAL HERO NOW, MR. SNART. GET USED TO IT.
NOT SURE I CAN.
NEVER BEEN SO HIGH UP BEFORE. HELL OF A VIEW.
I HEAR YOU CAN SEE GOTHAM FROM THE BOSSMAN'S OFFICE. THAT WHERE WE'RE HEADED?
MR. LUTHOR ISN'T IN METROPOLIS AT THE MOMENT.
WHAT? I FLEW ALL THE WAY FROM CENTRAL CITY. I THOUGHT HE WANTED TO SEE ME.
HE DOES WANT TO SEE YOU, BUT FIRST WE NEED TO RUN SOME TESTS.
TESTS? WHAT FOR?
MR. LUTHOR IS PROVIDING THE VERY BEST LEGAL COUNCIL AVAILABLE TO YOU IN ORDER TO WIPE YOUR RECORD CLEAN. AFTER ALL YOU DID TO HELP HIM, HE WANTS TO HELP YOU.
BUT FIRST WE NEED TO ASSESS YOUR CURRENT PHYSICAL AND PSYCHOLOGICAL STATE.
IT'S STANDARD PROCEDURE FOR ALL LEXCORP EMPLOYEES.
ARE YOU OFFERING ME A JOB?
WE'RE ABOUT TO.
RIGHT THIS WAY, MR. SNART.
PROCESS THE BLOODWORK AND GET THE RESULTS TO MR. LUTHOR IMMEDIATELY.
YOU KNOW WHAT HE'S SEARCHING FOR. PROJECT: WANNABE.
OF COURSE, MERCY.
"I SHOULD HAVE KNOWN

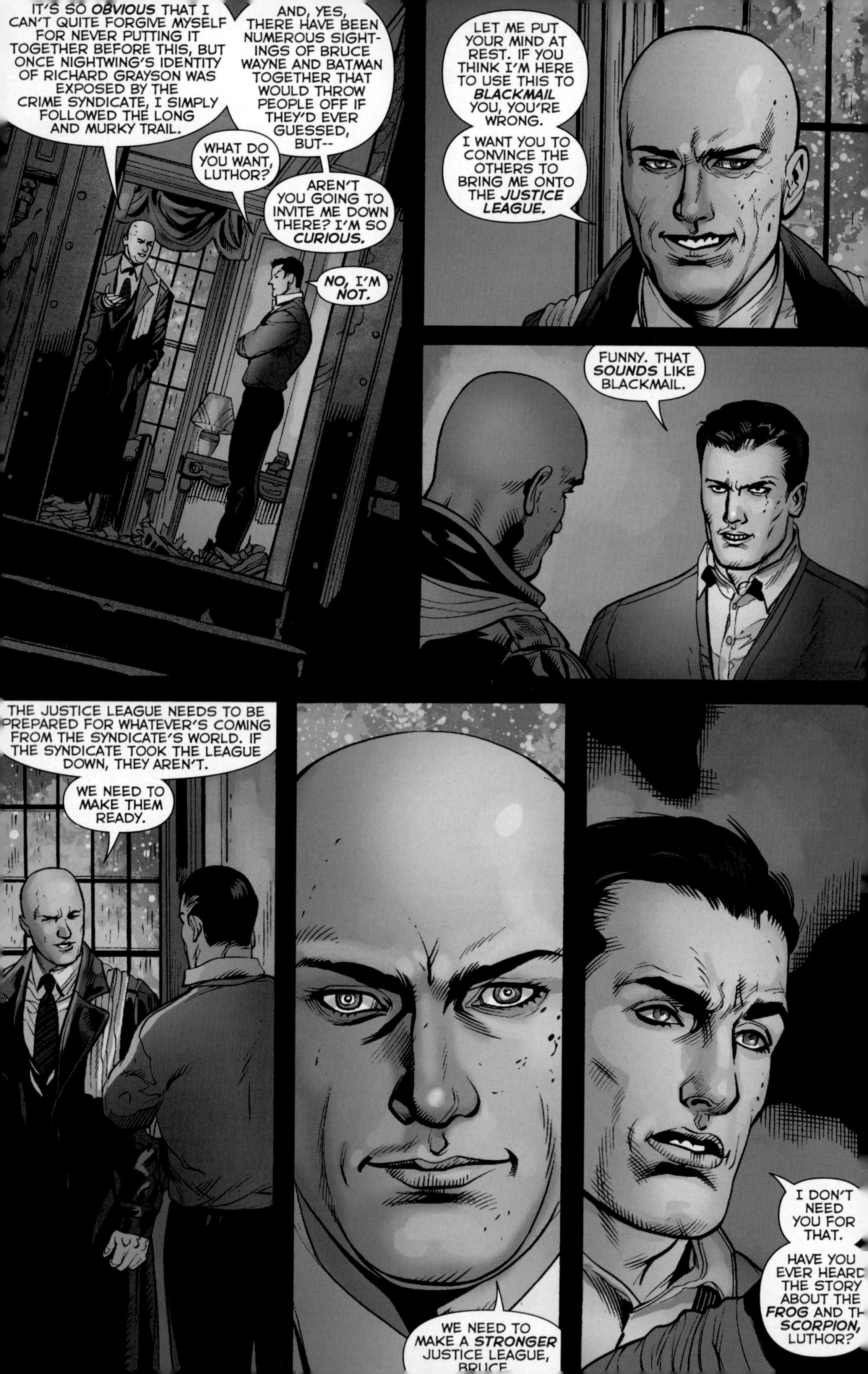

IT'S SO OBVIOUS THAT I CAN'T QUITE FORGIVE MYSELF FOR NEVER PUTTING IT TOGETHER BEFORE THIS, BUT ONCE NIGHTWING'S IDENTITY OF RICHARD GRAYSON WAS EXPOSED BY THE CRIME SYNDICATE, I SIMPLY FOLLOWED THE LONG AND MURKY TRAIL.
AND, YES, THERE HAVE BEEN NUMEROUS SIGHTINGS OF BRUCE WAYNE AND BATMAN TOGETHER THAT WOULD THROW PEOPLE OFF IF THEY'D EVER GUESSED, BUT--
WHAT DO YOU WANT, LUTHOR?
AREN'T YOU GOING TO INVITE ME DOWN THERE? I'M SO CURIOUS.
NO, I'M NOT.
LET ME PUT YOUR MIND AT REST. IF YOU THINK I'M HERE TO USE THIS TO BLACKMAIL YOU, YOU'RE WRONG.
I WANT YOU TO CONVINCE THE OTHERS TO BRING ME ONTO THE JUSTICE LEAGUE.
FUNNY. THAT SOUNDS LIKE BLACKMAIL.
THE JUSTICE LEAGUE NEEDS TO BE PREPARED FOR WHATEVER'S COMING FROM THE SYNDICATE'S WORLD. IF THE SYNDICATE TOOK THE LEAGUE DOWN, THEY AREN'T.
WE NEED TO MAKE THEM READY.
WE NEED TO MAKE A STRONGER JUSTICE LEAGUE,
I DON'T NEED YOU FOR THAT.
HAVE YOU EVER HEARD THE STORY ABOUT THE FROG AND TH SCORPION, LUTHOR?

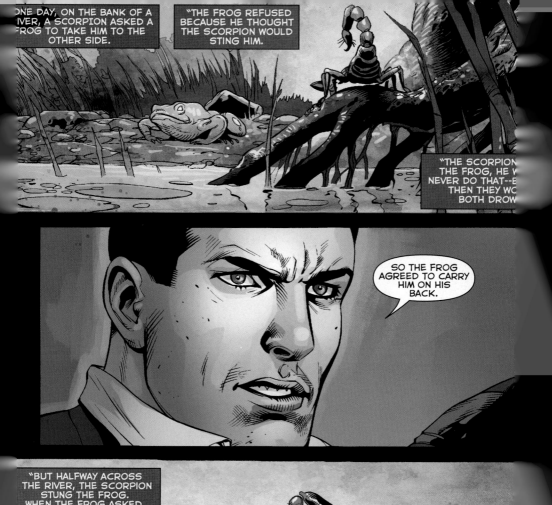

ONE DAY, ON THE BANK OF A RIVER, A SCORPION ASKED A FROG TO TAKE HIM TO THE OTHER SIDE.

"THE FROG REFUSED BECAUSE HE THOUGHT THE SCORPION WOULD STING HIM.

"THE SCORPION [...] THE FROG, HE W[...] NEVER DO THAT--E[...] THEN THEY WO[...] BOTH DROW[...]

SO THE FROG AGREED TO CARRY HIM ON HIS BACK.

"BUT HALFWAY ACROSS THE RIVER, THE SCORPION STUNG THE FROG. WHEN THE FROG ASKED, 'WHY?' THE SCORPION SAID--

"BECAUSE IT IS IN MY NATURE."

I KNOW THE STORY, BRUCE.

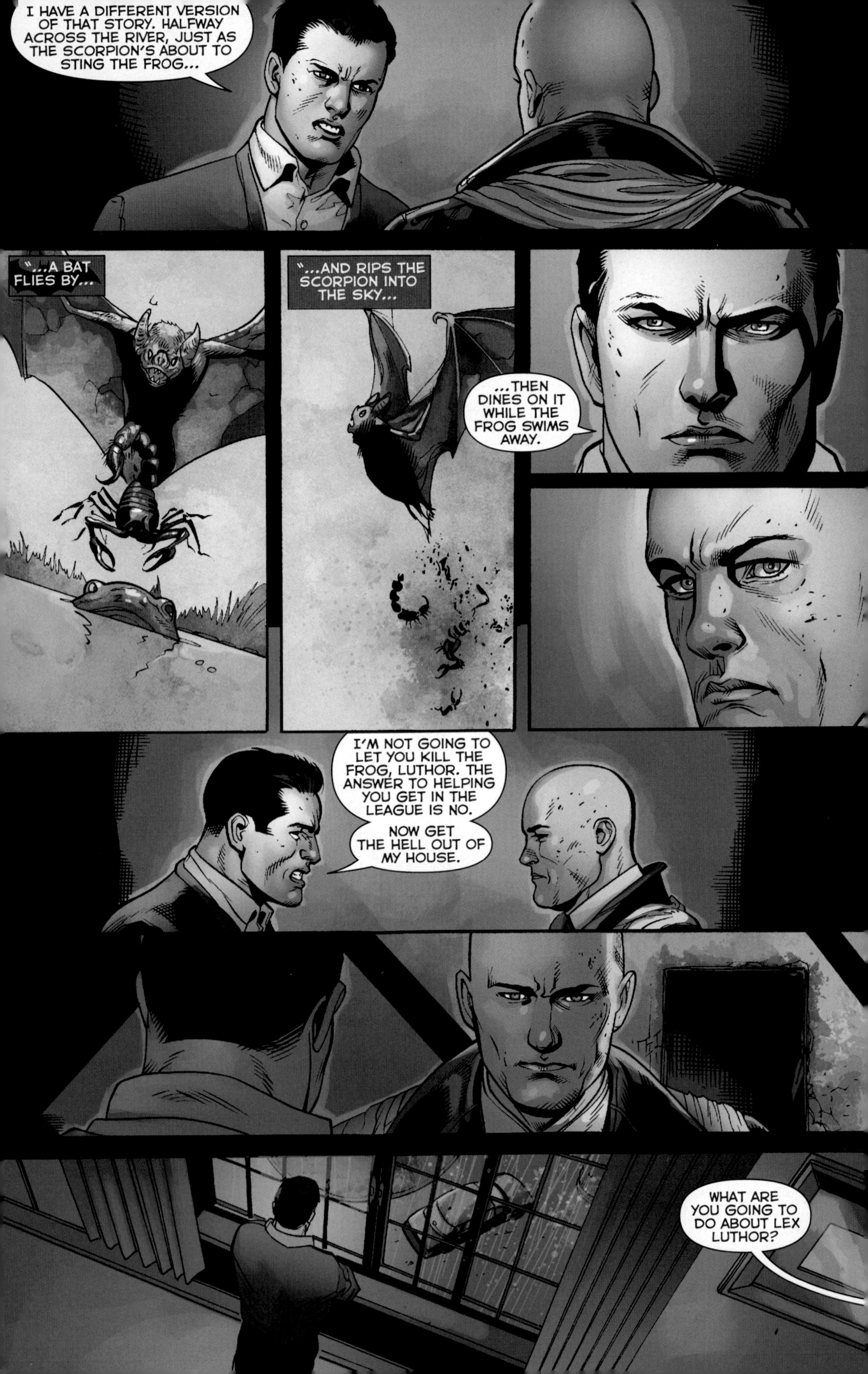
I HAVE A DIFFERENT VERSION OF THAT STORY. HALFWAY ACROSS THE RIVER, JUST AS THE SCORPION'S ABOUT TO STING THE FROG...
"...A BAT FLIES BY...
"...AND RIPS THE SCORPION INTO THE SKY...
...THEN DINES ON IT WHILE THE FROG SWIMS AWAY.
I'M NOT GOING TO LET YOU KILL THE FROG, LUTHOR. THE ANSWER TO HELPING YOU GET IN THE LEAGUE IS NO.
NOW GET THE HELL OUT OF MY HOUSE.
WHAT ARE YOU GOING TO DO ABOUT LEX LUTHOR?

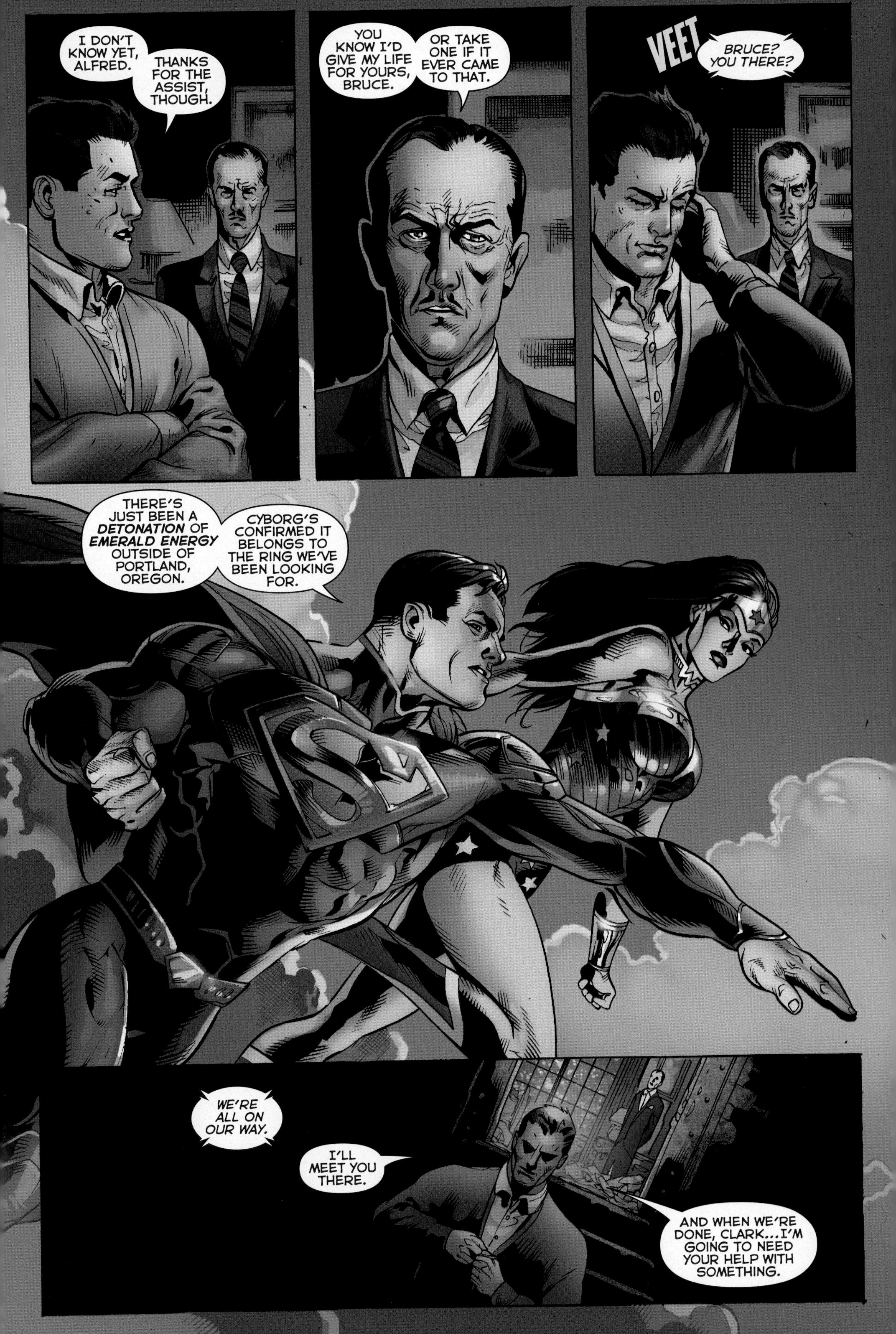
I DON'T KNOW YET, ALFRED.
THANKS FOR THE ASSIST, THOUGH.
YOU KNOW I'D GIVE MY LIFE FOR YOURS, BRUCE.
OR TAKE ONE IF IT EVER CAME TO THAT.
VEET
BRUCE? YOU THERE?
THERE'S JUST BEEN A DETONATION OF EMERALD ENERGY OUTSIDE OF PORTLAND, OREGON.
CYBORG'S CONFIRMED IT BELONGS TO THE RING WE'VE BEEN LOOKING FOR.
WE'RE ALL ON OUR WAY.
I'LL MEET YOU THERE.
AND WHEN WE'RE DONE, CLARK...I'M GOING TO NEED YOUR HELP WITH SOMETHING.

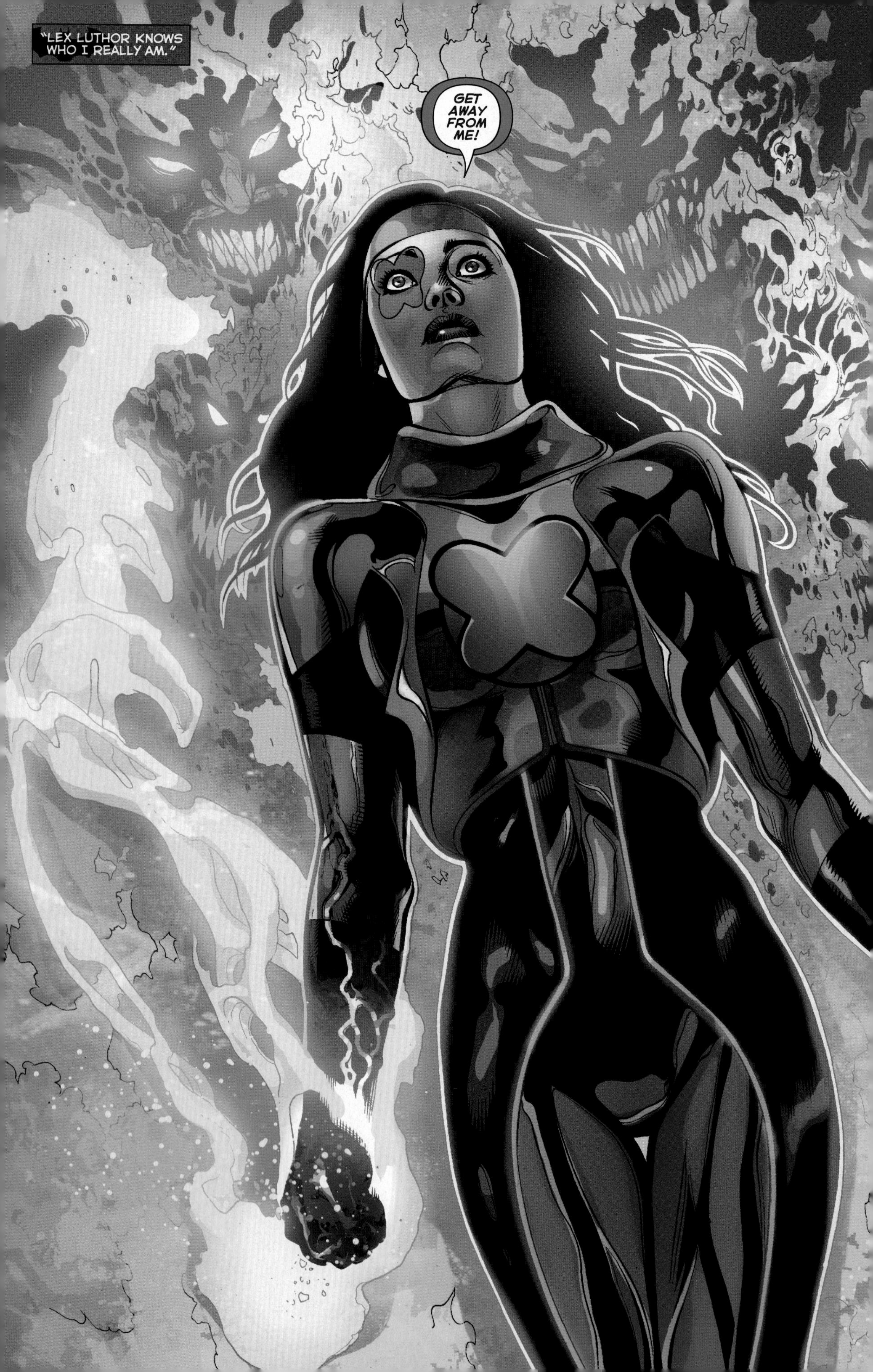
"LEX LUTHOR KNOWS WHO I REALLY AM."
GET AWAY FROM ME!

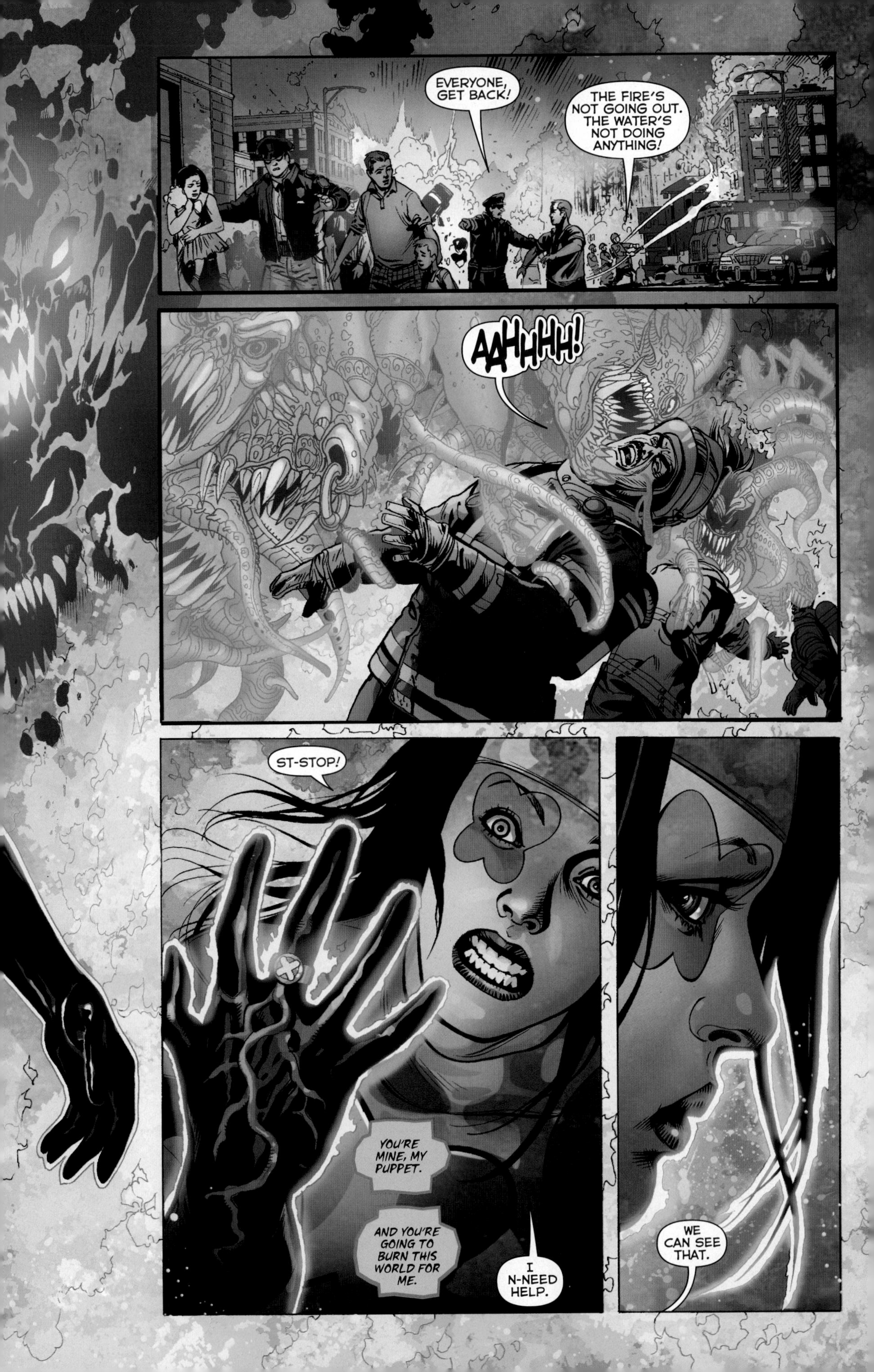
EVERYONE, GET BACK!
THE FIRE'S NOT GOING OUT. THE WATER'S NOT DOING ANYTHING!
AAHHHH!
ST-STOP!
YOU'RE MINE, MY PUPPET.
AND YOU'RE GOING TO BURN THIS WORLD FOR ME.
I N-NEED HELP.
WE CAN SEE THAT.

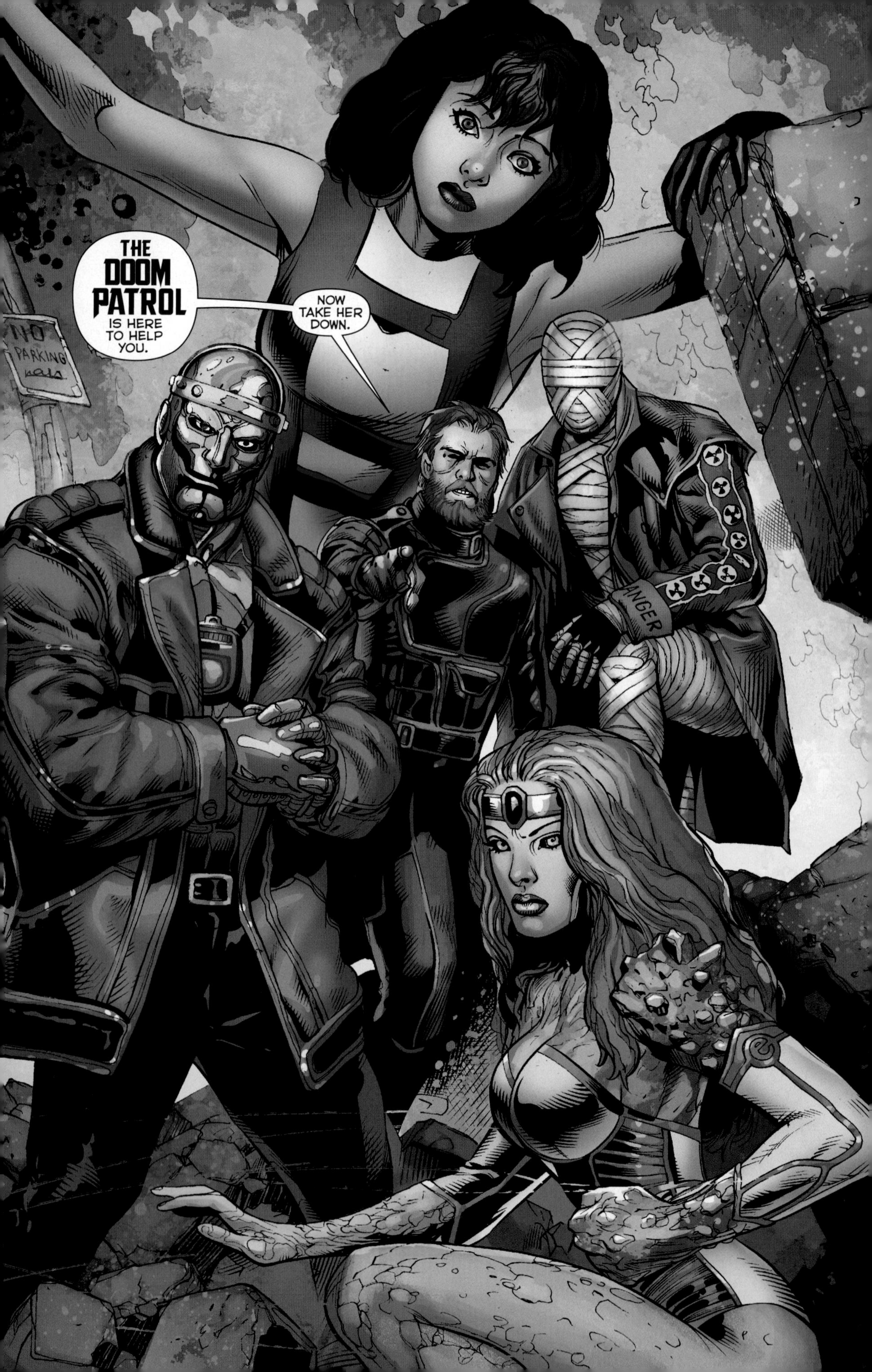
THE DOOM PATROL IS HERE TO HELP YOU.
NOW TAKE HER DOWN.
NO PARKING

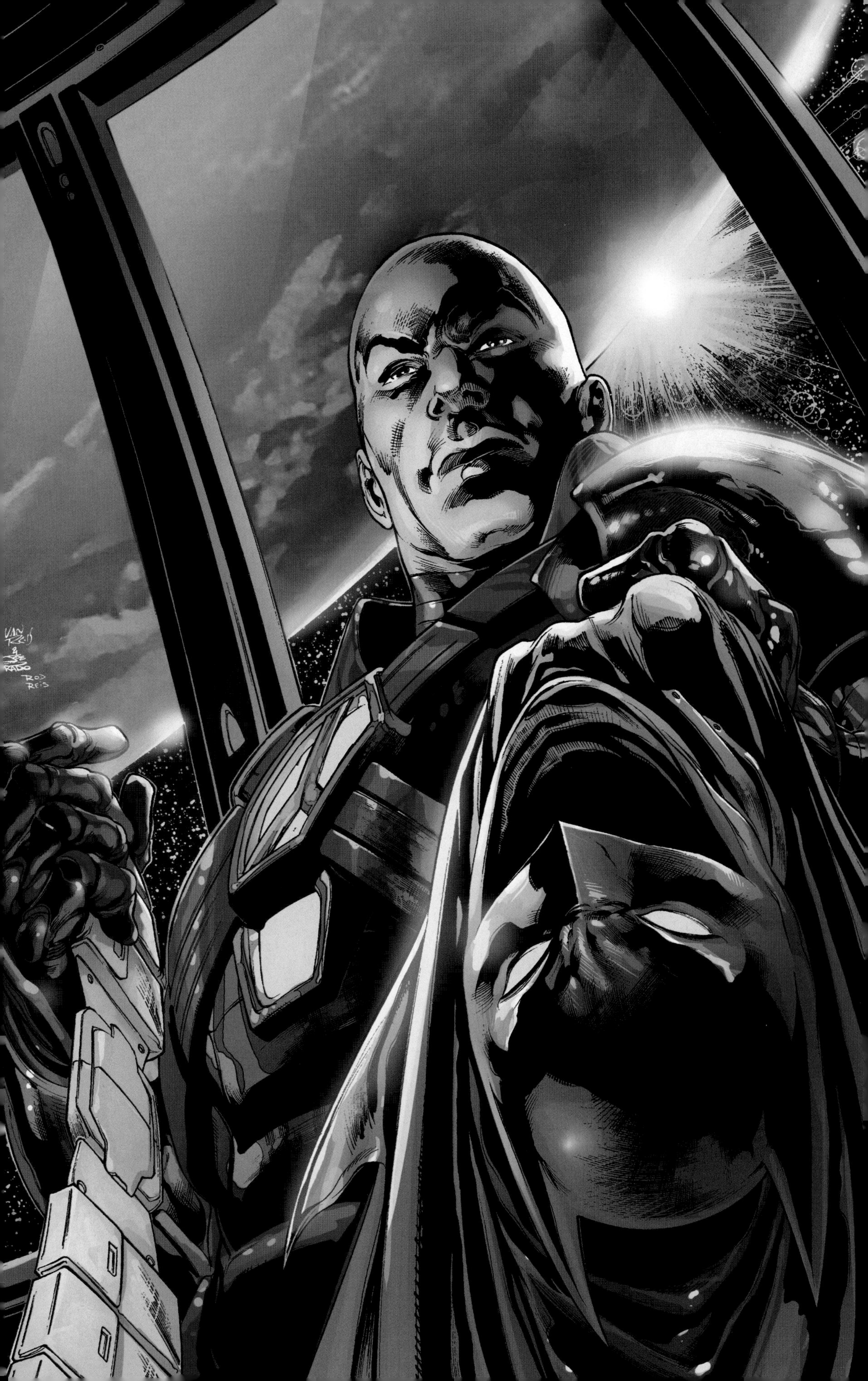

INJUSTICE LEAGUE CHAPTER THREE
BIRTH

GEOFF JOHNS writer **DOUG MAHNKE** penciller **KEITH CHAMPAGNE** inker
ANDREW DALHOUSE colorist **IVAN REIS, JOE PRADO & ROD REIS** cover artists

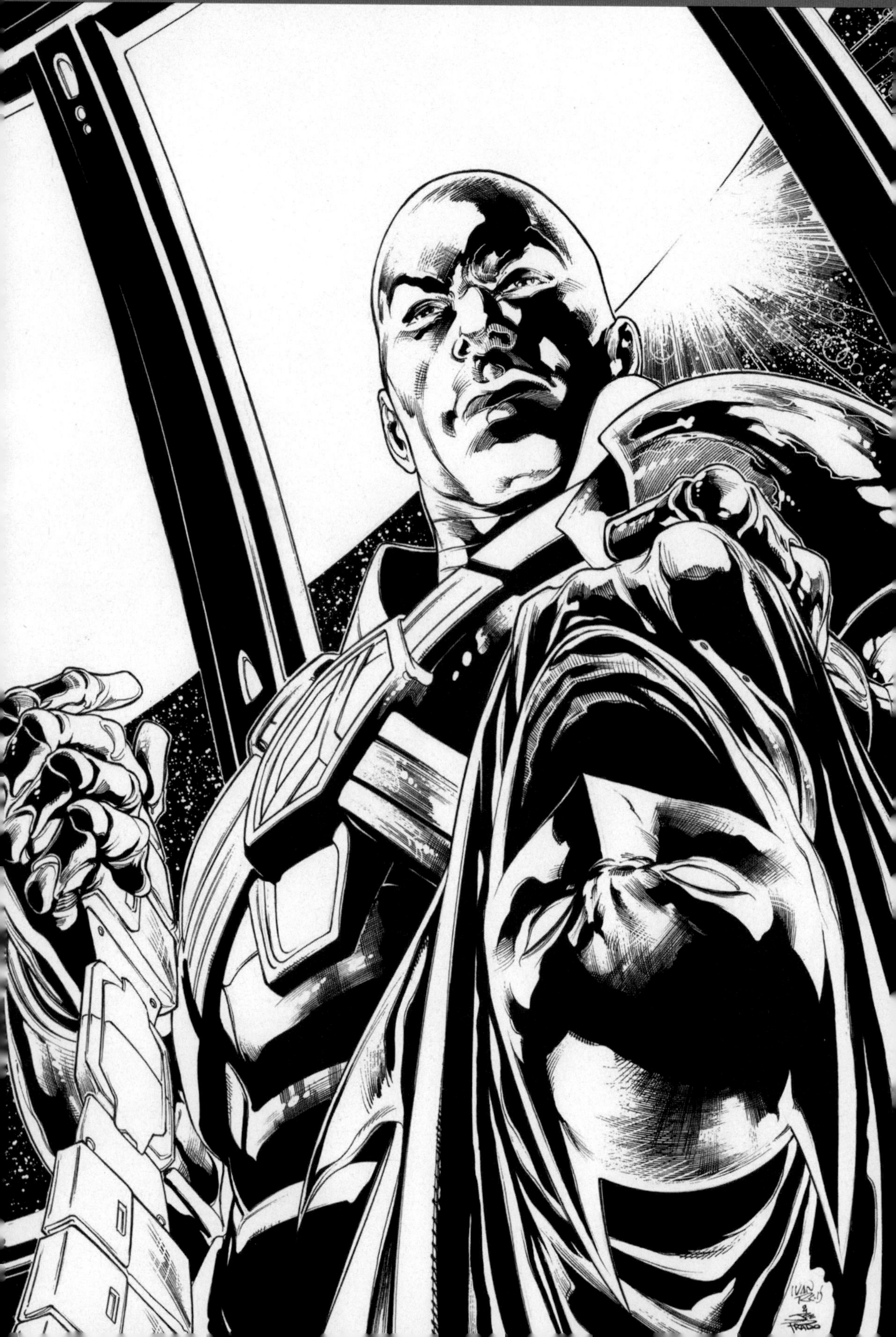

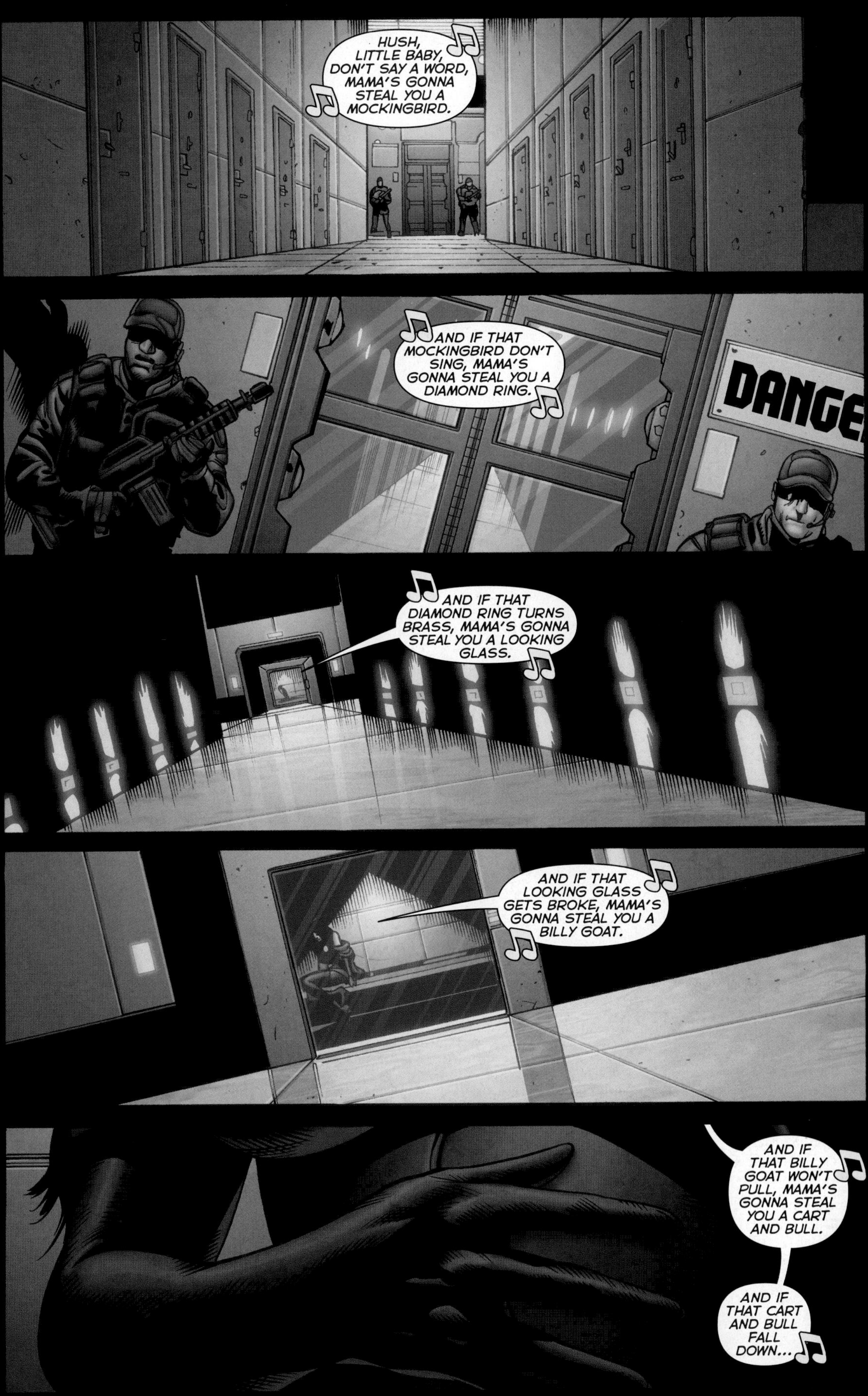
HUSH, LITTLE BABY, DON'T SAY A WORD, MAMA'S GONNA STEAL YOU A MOCKINGBIRD.
AND IF THAT MOCKINGBIRD DON'T SING, MAMA'S GONNA STEAL YOU A DIAMOND RING.
DANGE
AND IF THAT DIAMOND RING TURNS BRASS, MAMA'S GONNA STEAL YOU A LOOKING GLASS.
AND IF THAT LOOKING GLASS GETS BROKE, MAMA'S GONNA STEAL YOU A BILLY GOAT.
AND IF THAT BILLY GOAT WON'T PULL, MAMA'S GONNA STEAL YOU A CART AND BULL.
AND IF THAT CART AND BULL FALL DOWN...

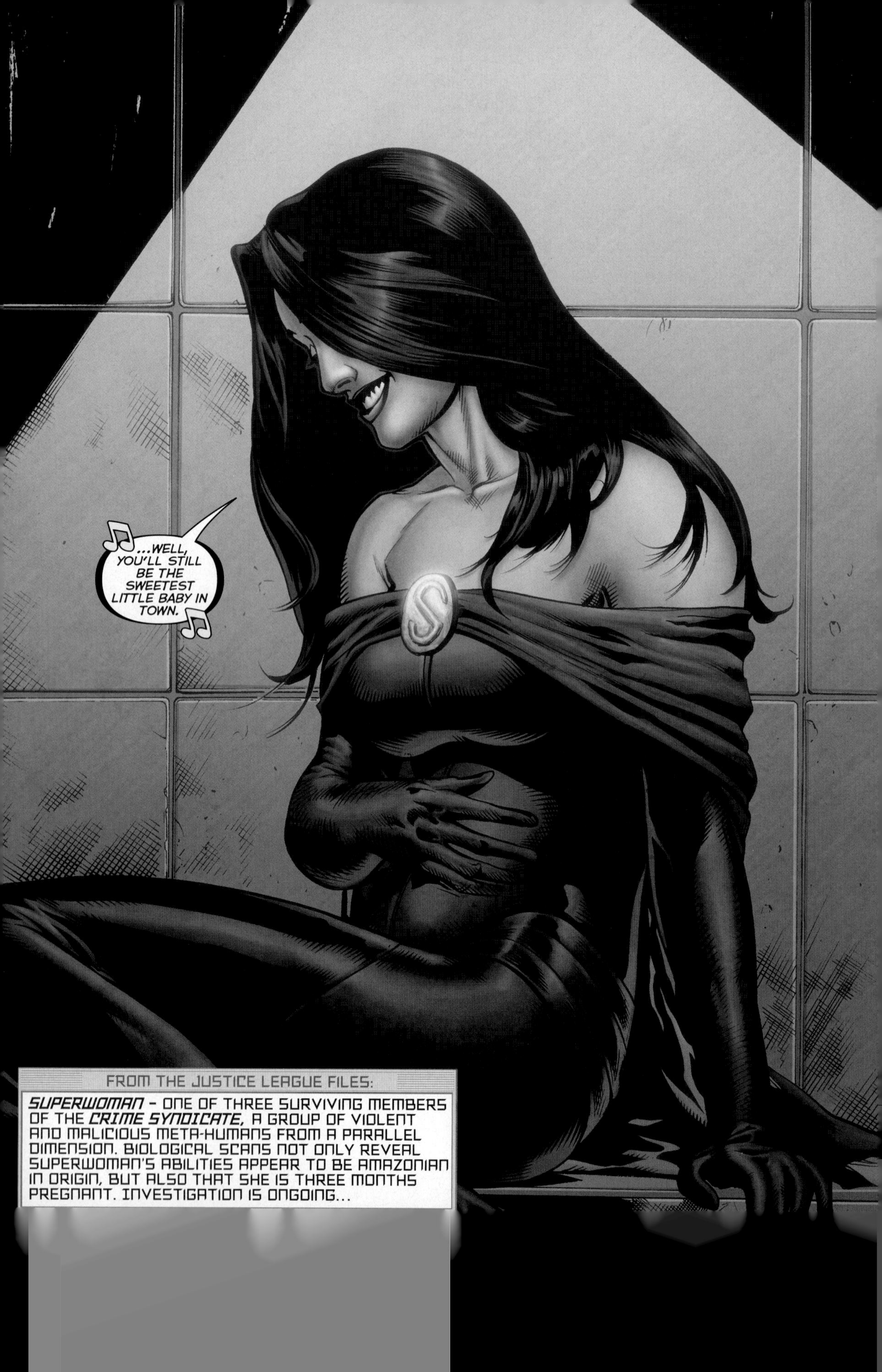
...WELL, YOU'LL STILL BE THE SWEETEST LITTLE BABY IN TOWN.
FROM THE JUSTICE LEAGUE FILES:
SUPERWOMAN - ONE OF THREE SURVIVING MEMBERS OF THE CRIME SYNDICATE, A GROUP OF VIOLENT AND MALICIOUS META-HUMANS FROM A PARALLEL DIMENSION. BIOLOGICAL SCANS NOT ONLY REVEAL SUPERWOMAN'S ABILITIES APPEAR TO BE AMAZONIAN IN ORIGIN, BUT ALSO THAT SHE IS THREE MONTHS PREGNANT. INVESTIGATION IS ONGOING...

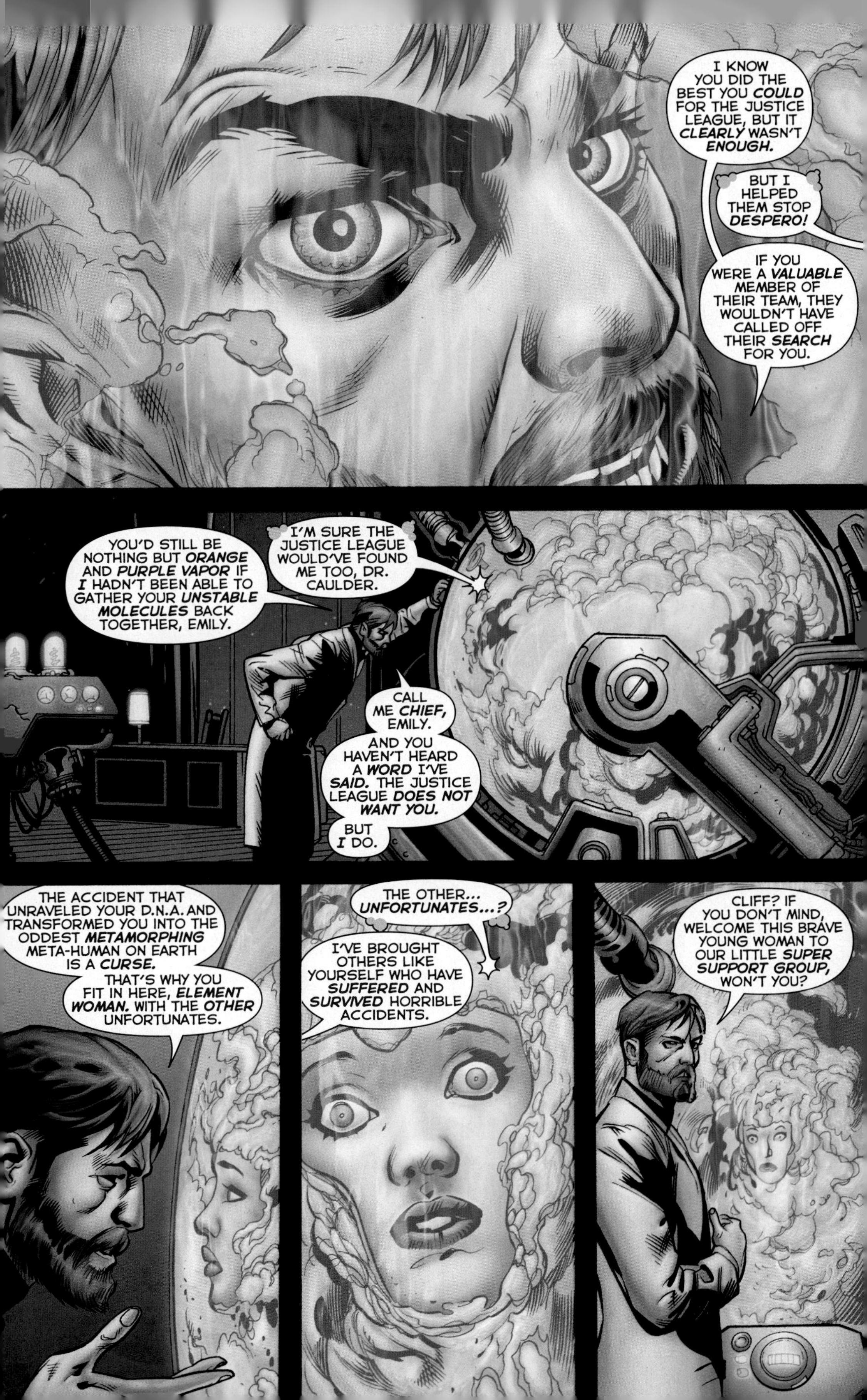
I KNOW YOU DID THE BEST YOU COULD FOR THE JUSTICE LEAGUE, BUT IT CLEARLY WASN'T ENOUGH.
BUT I HELPED THEM STOP DESPERO!
IF YOU WERE A VALUABLE MEMBER OF THEIR TEAM, THEY WOULDN'T HAVE CALLED OFF THEIR SEARCH FOR YOU.
YOU'D STILL BE NOTHING BUT ORANGE AND PURPLE VAPOR IF I HADN'T BEEN ABLE TO GATHER YOUR UNSTABLE MOLECULES BACK TOGETHER, EMILY.
I'M SURE THE JUSTICE LEAGUE WOULD'VE FOUND ME TOO, DR. CAULDER.
CALL ME CHIEF, EMILY.
AND YOU HAVEN'T HEARD A WORD I'VE SAID. THE JUSTICE LEAGUE DOES NOT WANT YOU.
BUT I DO.
THE ACCIDENT THAT UNRAVELED YOUR D.N.A. AND TRANSFORMED YOU INTO THE ODDEST METAMORPHING META-HUMAN ON EARTH IS A CURSE.
THAT'S WHY YOU FIT IN HERE, ELEMENT WOMAN. WITH THE OTHER UNFORTUNATES.
THE OTHER... UNFORTUNATES...?
I'VE BROUGHT OTHERS LIKE YOURSELF WHO HAVE SUFFERED AND SURVIVED HORRIBLE ACCIDENTS.
CLIFF? IF YOU DON'T MIND, WELCOME THIS BRAVE YOUNG WOMAN TO OUR LITTLE SUPER SUPPORT GROUP, WON'T YOU?

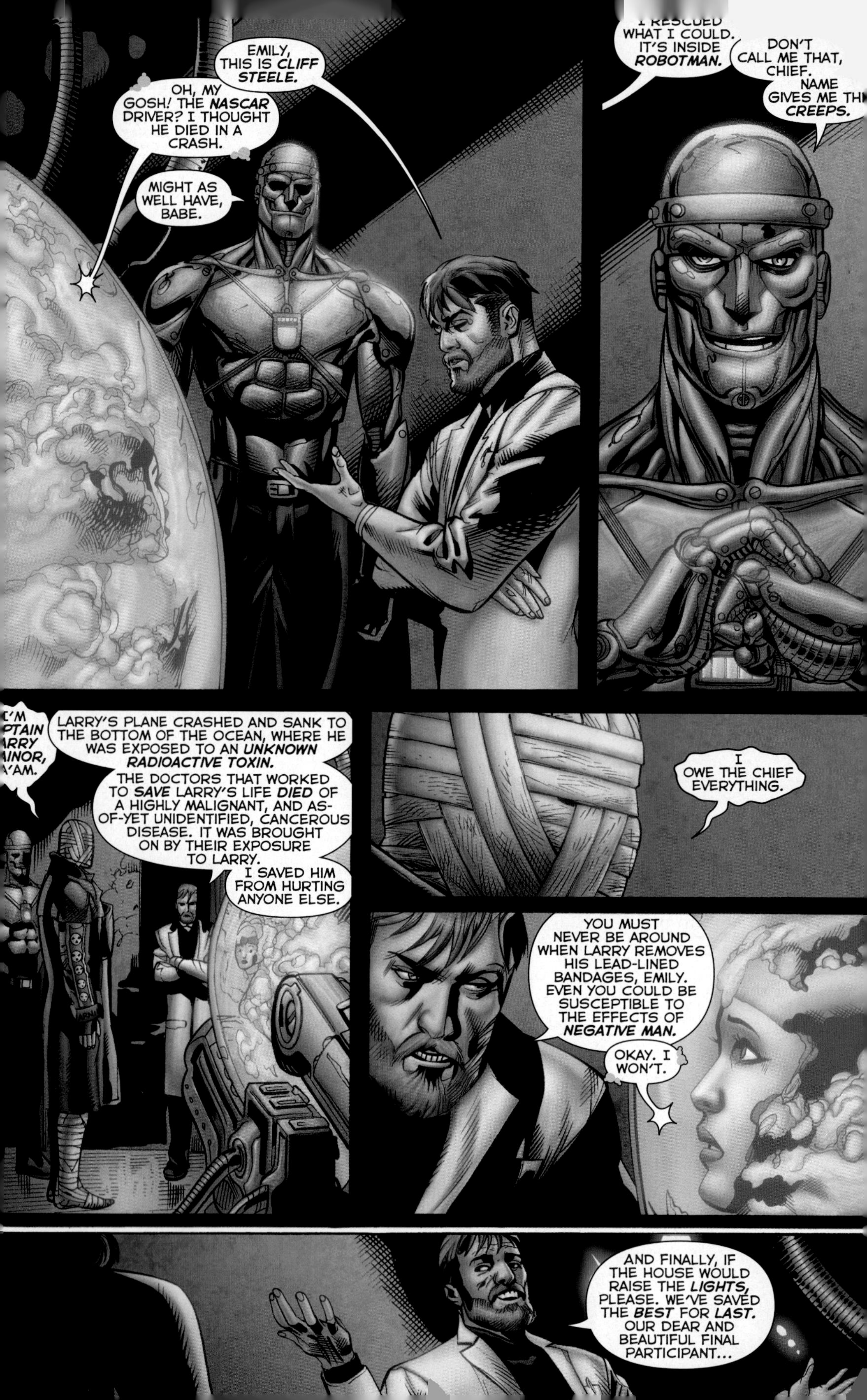

EMILY, THIS IS CLIFF STEELE.
OH, MY GOSH! THE NASCAR DRIVER? I THOUGHT HE DIED IN A CRASH.
MIGHT AS WELL HAVE, BABE.
WHAT I COULD. IT'S INSIDE ROBOTMAN.
DON'T CALL ME THAT, CHIEF. NAME GIVES ME TH CREEPS.
LARRY'S PLANE CRASHED AND SANK TO THE BOTTOM OF THE OCEAN, WHERE HE WAS EXPOSED TO AN UNKNOWN RADIOACTIVE TOXIN.
THE DOCTORS THAT WORKED TO SAVE LARRY'S LIFE DIED OF A HIGHLY MALIGNANT, AND AS-OF-YET UNIDENTIFIED, CANCEROUS DISEASE. IT WAS BROUGHT ON BY THEIR EXPOSURE TO LARRY.
I SAVED HIM FROM HURTING ANYONE ELSE.
I OWE THE CHIEF EVERYTHING.
YOU MUST NEVER BE AROUND WHEN LARRY REMOVES HIS LEAD-LINED BANDAGES, EMILY. EVEN YOU COULD BE SUSCEPTIBLE TO THE EFFECTS OF NEGATIVE MAN.
OKAY. I WON'T.
AND FINALLY, IF THE HOUSE WOULD RAISE THE LIGHTS, PLEASE. WE'VE SAVED THE BEST FOR LAST. OUR DEAR AND BEAUTIFUL FINAL PARTICIPANT...

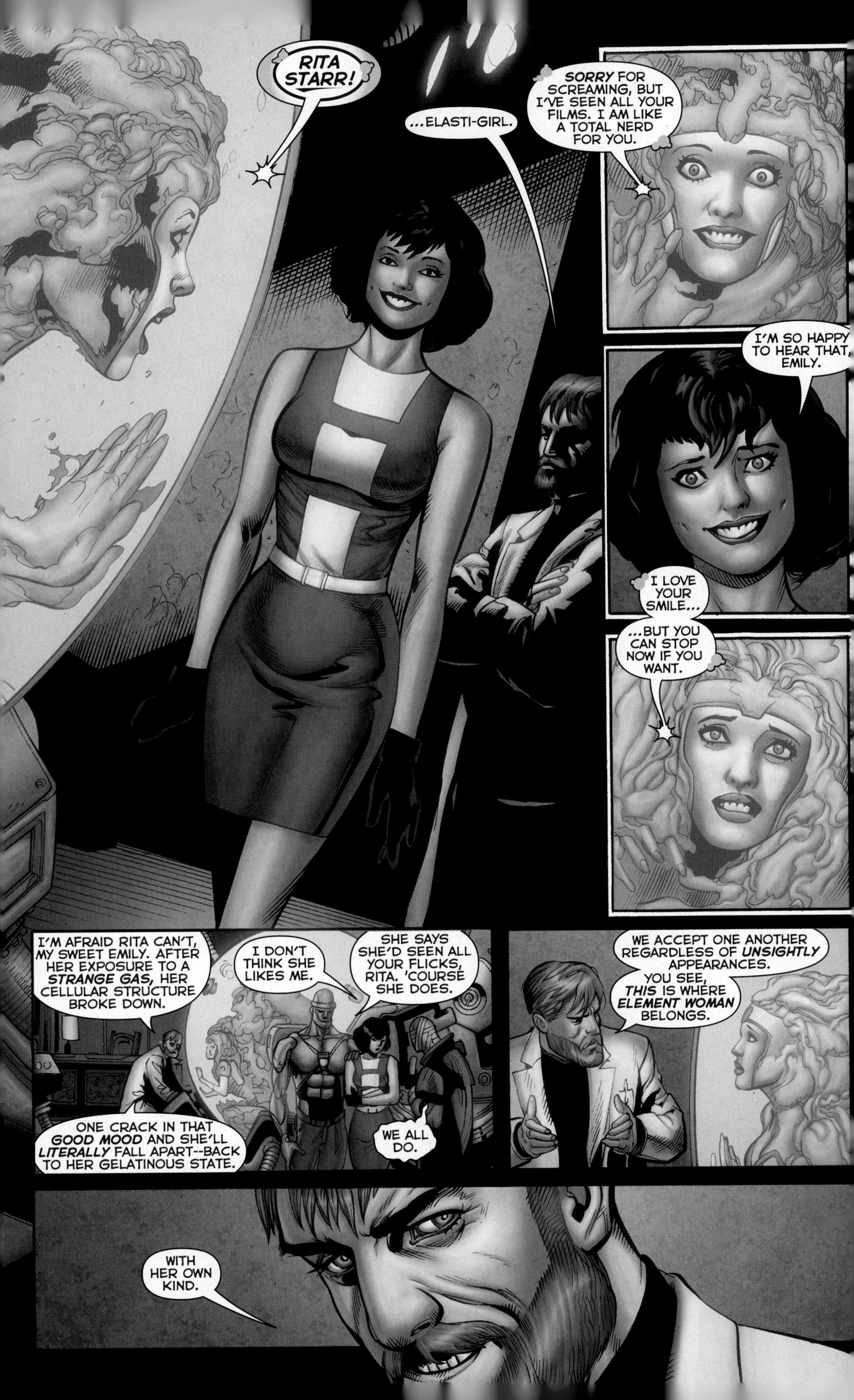
RITA STARR!
...ELASTI-GIRL.
SORRY FOR SCREAMING, BUT I'VE SEEN ALL YOUR FILMS. I AM LIKE A TOTAL NERD FOR YOU.
I'M SO HAPPY TO HEAR THAT, EMILY.
I LOVE YOUR SMILE...
...BUT YOU CAN STOP NOW IF YOU WANT.
I'M AFRAID RITA CAN'T, MY SWEET EMILY. AFTER HER EXPOSURE TO A STRANGE GAS, HER CELLULAR STRUCTURE BROKE DOWN.
ONE CRACK IN THAT GOOD MOOD AND SHE'LL LITERALLY FALL APART--BACK TO HER GELATINOUS STATE.
I DON'T THINK SHE LIKES ME.
SHE SAYS SHE'D SEEN ALL YOUR FLICKS, RITA. 'COURSE SHE DOES.
WE ALL DO.
WE ACCEPT ONE ANOTHER REGARDLESS OF UNSIGHTLY APPEARANCES.
YOU SEE, THIS IS WHERE ELEMENT WOMAN BELONGS.
WITH HER OWN KIND.

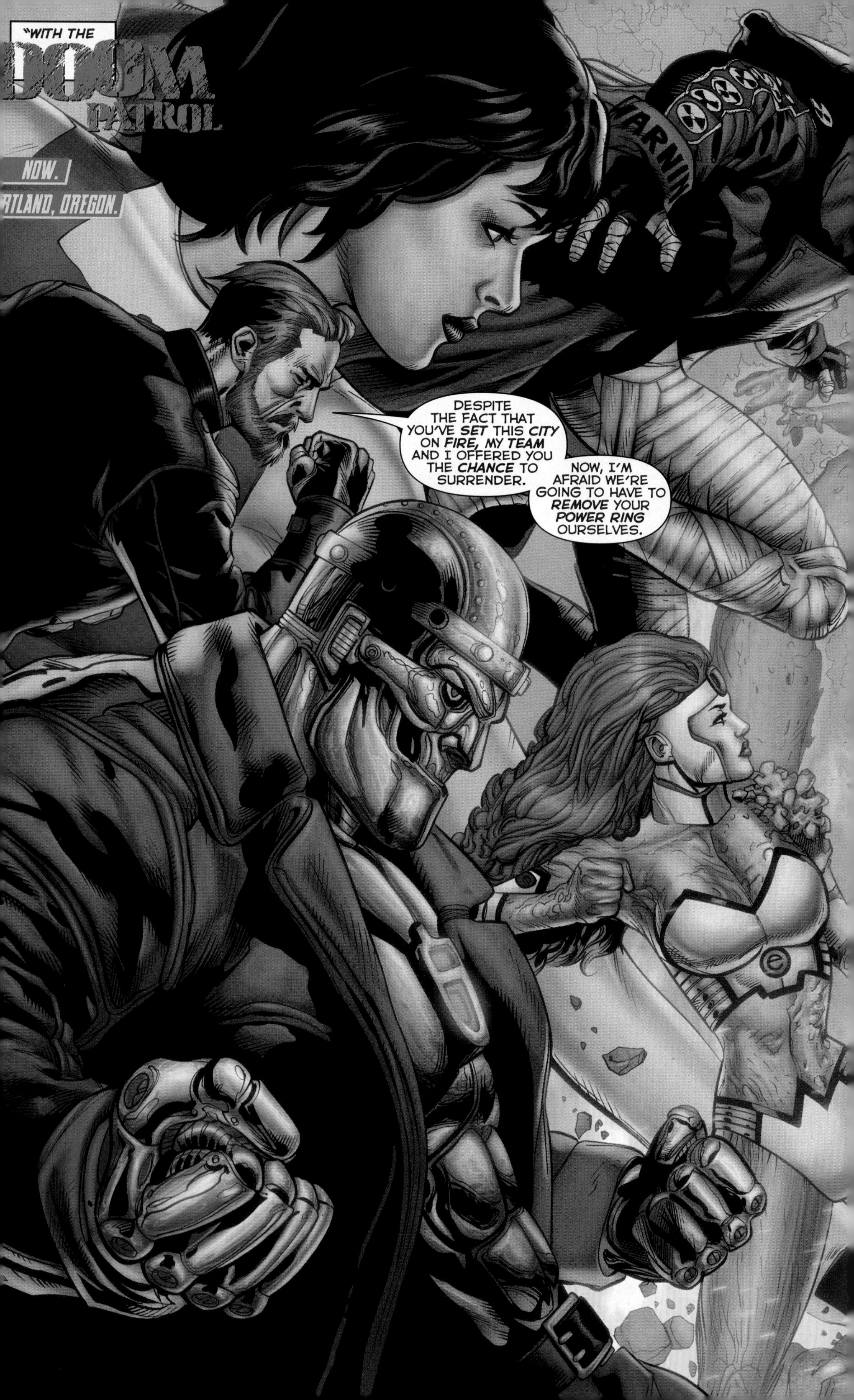

"WITH THE
DOOM PATROL
NOW.
RTLAND, OREGON.
DESPITE THE FACT THAT YOU'VE SET THIS CITY ON FIRE, MY TEAM AND I OFFERED YOU THE CHANCE TO SURRENDER.
NOW, I'M AFRAID WE'RE GOING TO HAVE TO REMOVE YOUR POWER RING OURSELVES.

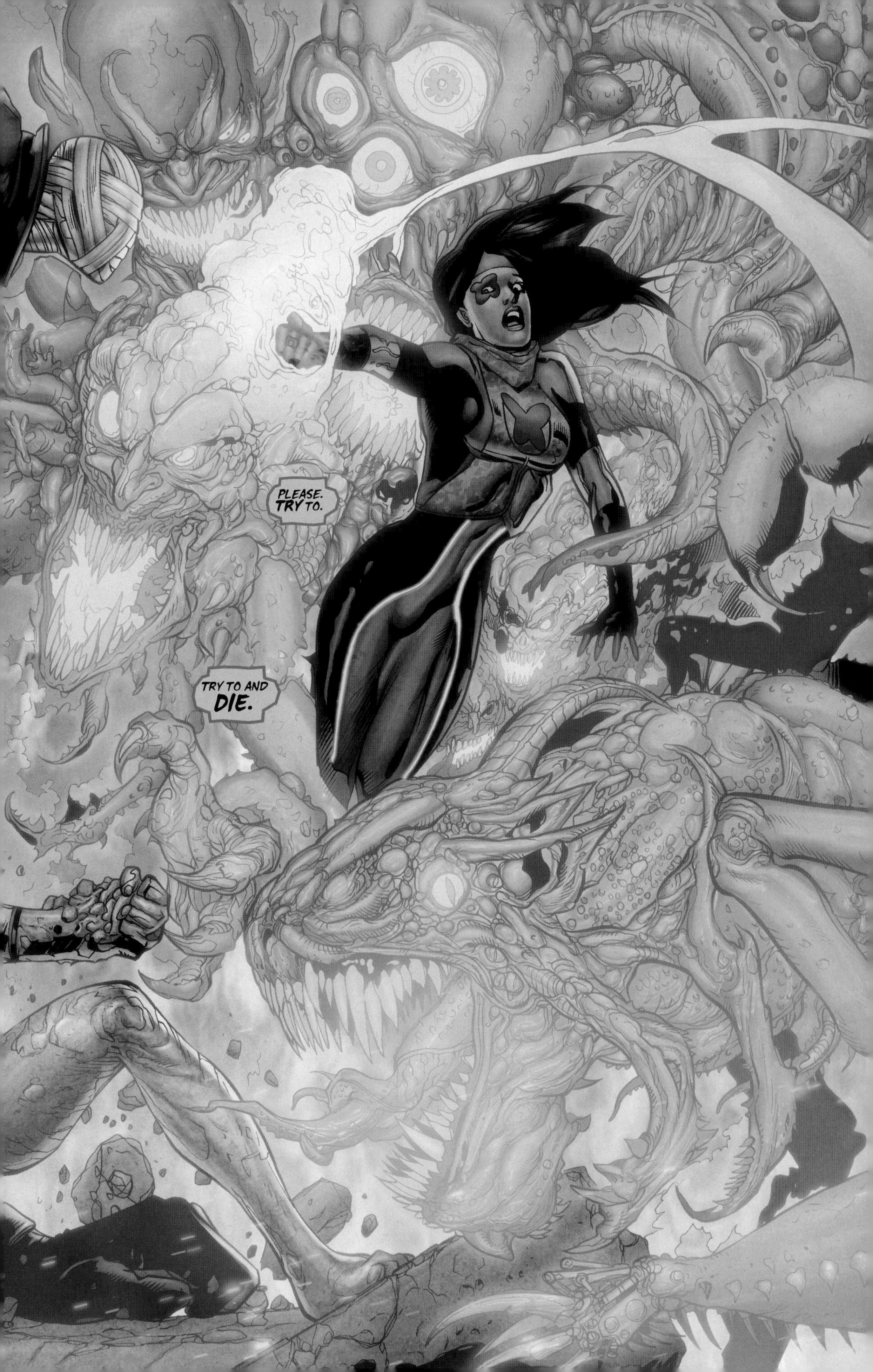
PLEASE. TRY TO.
TRY TO AND DIE.

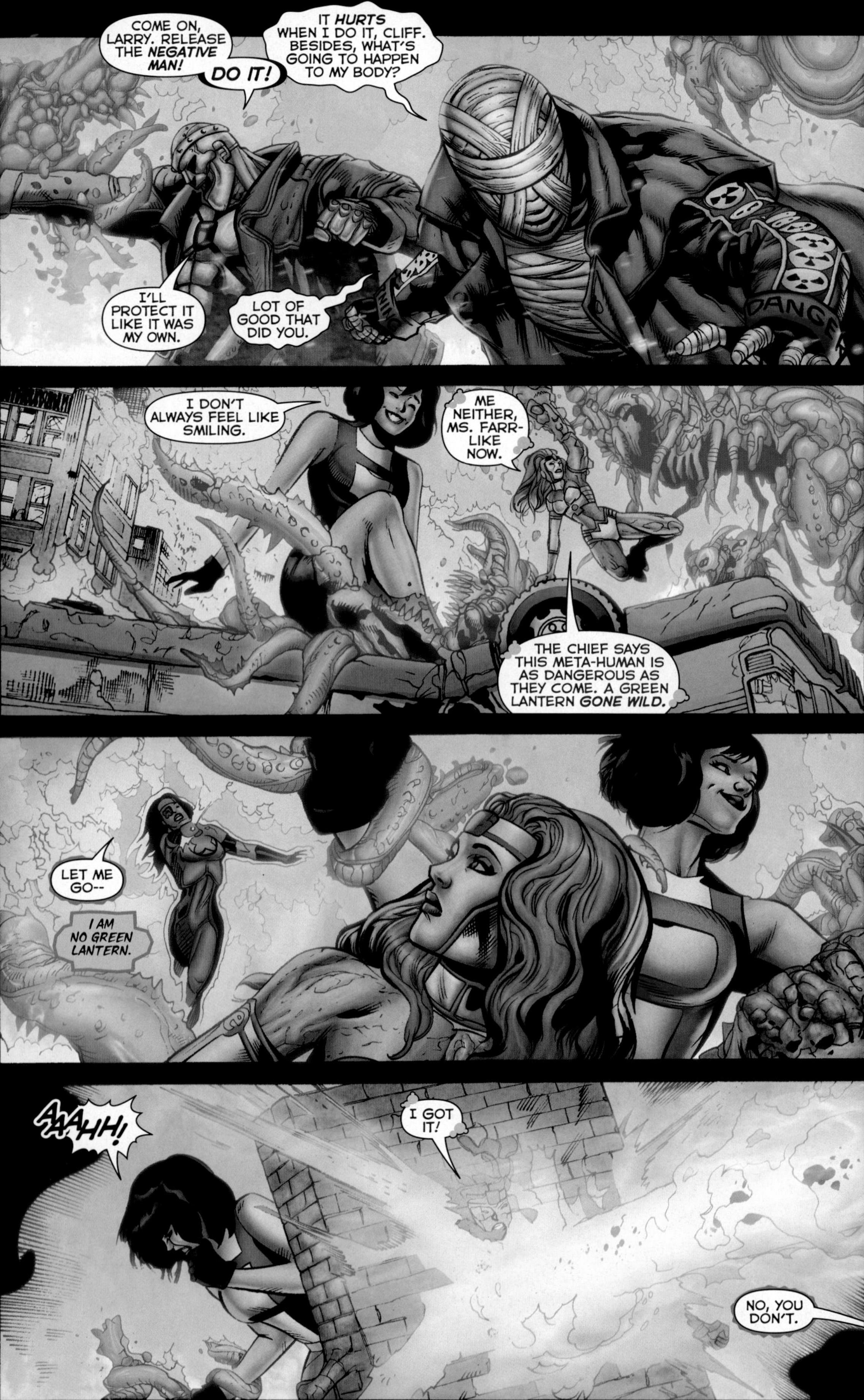
COME ON, LARRY. RELEASE THE NEGATIVE MAN!
DO IT!
IT HURTS WHEN I DO IT, CLIFF. BESIDES, WHAT'S GOING TO HAPPEN TO MY BODY?
I'LL PROTECT IT LIKE IT WAS MY OWN.
LOT OF GOOD THAT DID YOU.
DANGE
I DON'T ALWAYS FEEL LIKE SMILING.
ME NEITHER, MS. FARR-LIKE NOW.
THE CHIEF SAYS THIS META-HUMAN IS AS DANGEROUS AS THEY COME. A GREEN LANTERN GONE WILD.
LET ME GO--
I AM NO GREEN LANTERN.
AAAHH!
I GOT IT!
NO, YOU DON'T.

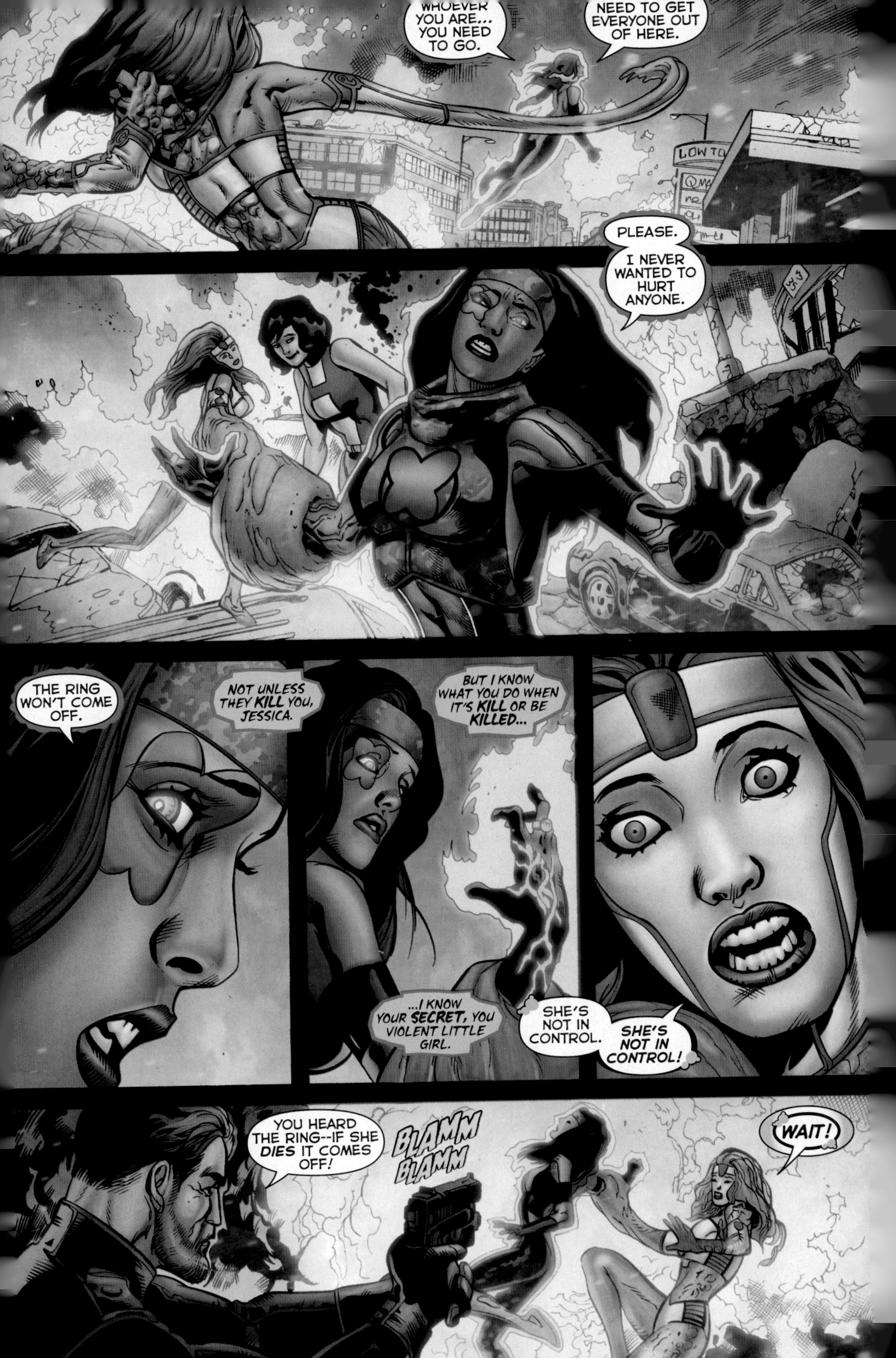
WHOEVER YOU ARE... YOU NEED TO GO.
NEED TO GET EVERYONE OUT OF HERE.
LOW TO
PLEASE.
I NEVER WANTED TO HURT ANYONE.
THE RING WON'T COME OFF.
NOT UNLESS THEY KILL YOU, JESSICA.
BUT I KNOW WHAT YOU DO WHEN IT'S KILL OR BE KILLED...
...I KNOW YOUR SECRET, YOU VIOLENT LITTLE GIRL.
SHE'S NOT IN CONTROL.
SHE'S NOT IN CONTROL!
YOU HEARD THE RING--IF SHE DIES IT COMES OFF!
BLAMM BLAMM
WAIT!

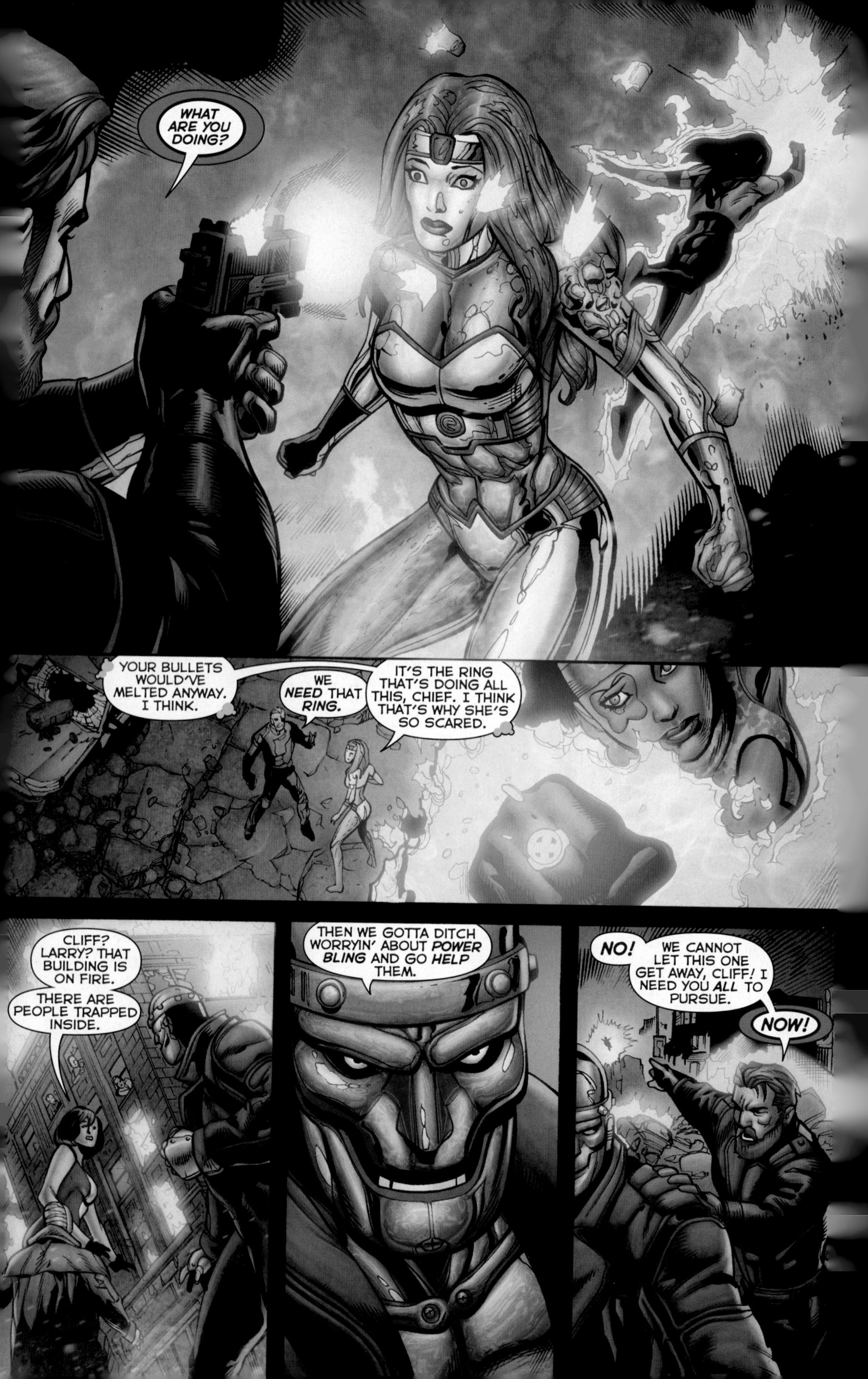
WHAT ARE YOU DOING?
YOUR BULLETS WOULD'VE MELTED ANYWAY. I THINK.
WE NEED THAT RING.
IT'S THE RING THAT'S DOING ALL THIS, CHIEF. I THINK THAT'S WHY SHE'S SO SCARED.
CLIFF? LARRY? THAT BUILDING IS ON FIRE.
THERE ARE PEOPLE TRAPPED INSIDE.
THEN WE GOTTA DITCH WORRYIN' ABOUT POWER BLING AND GO HELP THEM.
NO! WE CANNOT LET THIS ONE GET AWAY, CLIFF! I NEED YOU ALL TO PURSUE.
NOW!

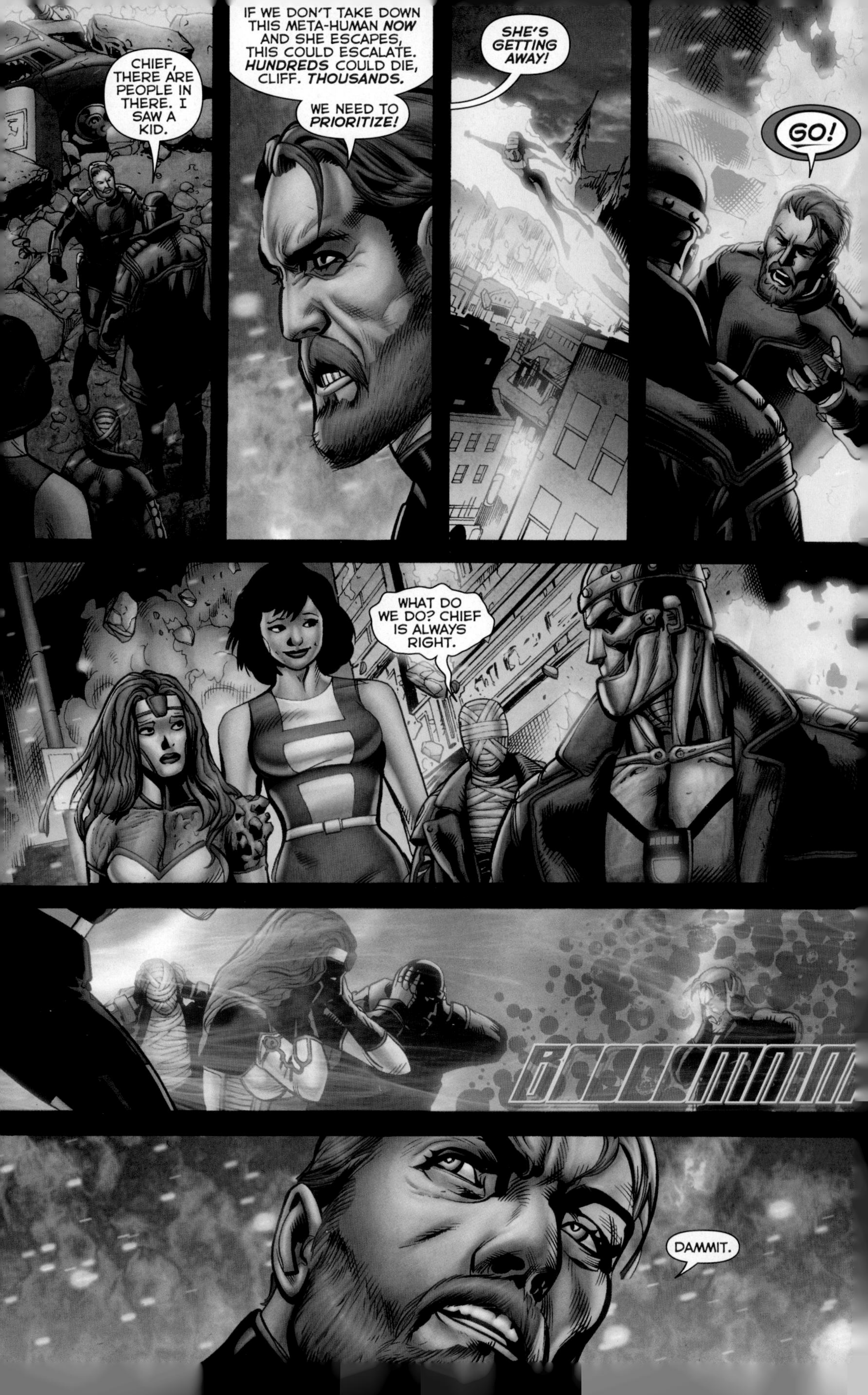
CHIEF, THERE ARE PEOPLE IN THERE. I SAW A KID.
IF WE DON'T TAKE DOWN THIS META-HUMAN NOW AND SHE ESCAPES, THIS COULD ESCALATE. HUNDREDS COULD DIE, CLIFF. THOUSANDS.
WE NEED TO PRIORITIZE!
SHE'S GETTING AWAY!
GO!
WHAT DO WE DO? CHIEF IS ALWAYS RIGHT.
DAMMIT.

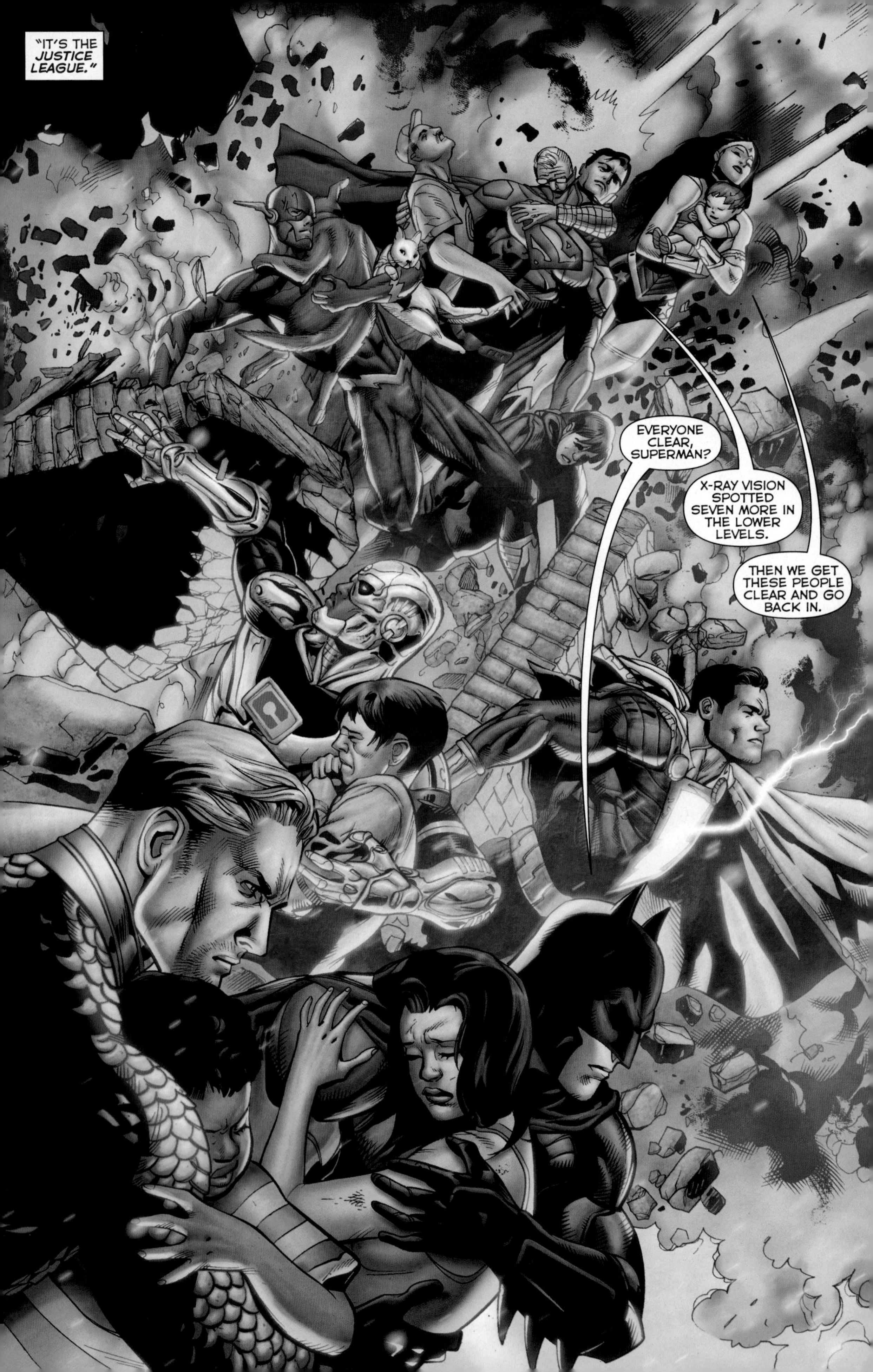
"IT'S THE JUSTICE LEAGUE."
EVERYONE CLEAR, SUPERMAN?
X-RAY VISION SPOTTED SEVEN MORE IN THE LOWER LEVELS.
THEN WE GET THESE PEOPLE CLEAR AND GO BACK IN.

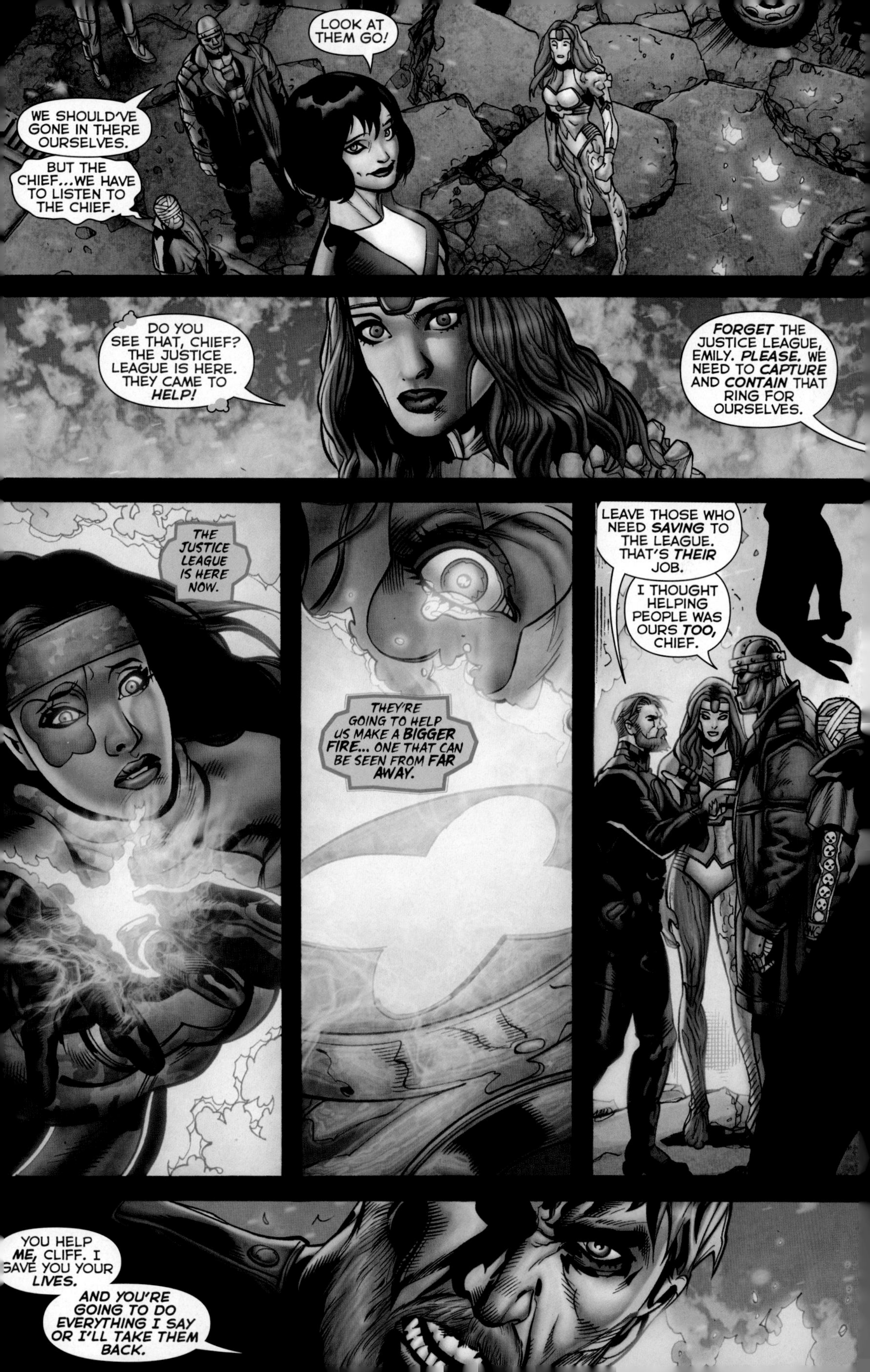
LOOK AT THEM GO!
WE SHOULD'VE GONE IN THERE OURSELVES.
BUT THE CHIEF...WE HAVE TO LISTEN TO THE CHIEF.
DO YOU SEE THAT, CHIEF? THE JUSTICE LEAGUE IS HERE. THEY CAME TO HELP!
FORGET THE JUSTICE LEAGUE, EMILY. PLEASE. WE NEED TO CAPTURE AND CONTAIN THAT RING FOR OURSELVES.
THE JUSTICE LEAGUE IS HERE NOW.
THEY'RE GOING TO HELP US MAKE A BIGGER FIRE... ONE THAT CAN BE SEEN FROM FAR AWAY.
LEAVE THOSE WHO NEED SAVING TO THE LEAGUE. THAT'S THEIR JOB.
I THOUGHT HELPING PEOPLE WAS OURS TOO, CHIEF.
YOU HELP ME, CLIFF. I GAVE YOU YOUR LIVES.
AND YOU'RE GOING TO DO EVERYTHING I SAY OR I'LL TAKE THEM BACK.

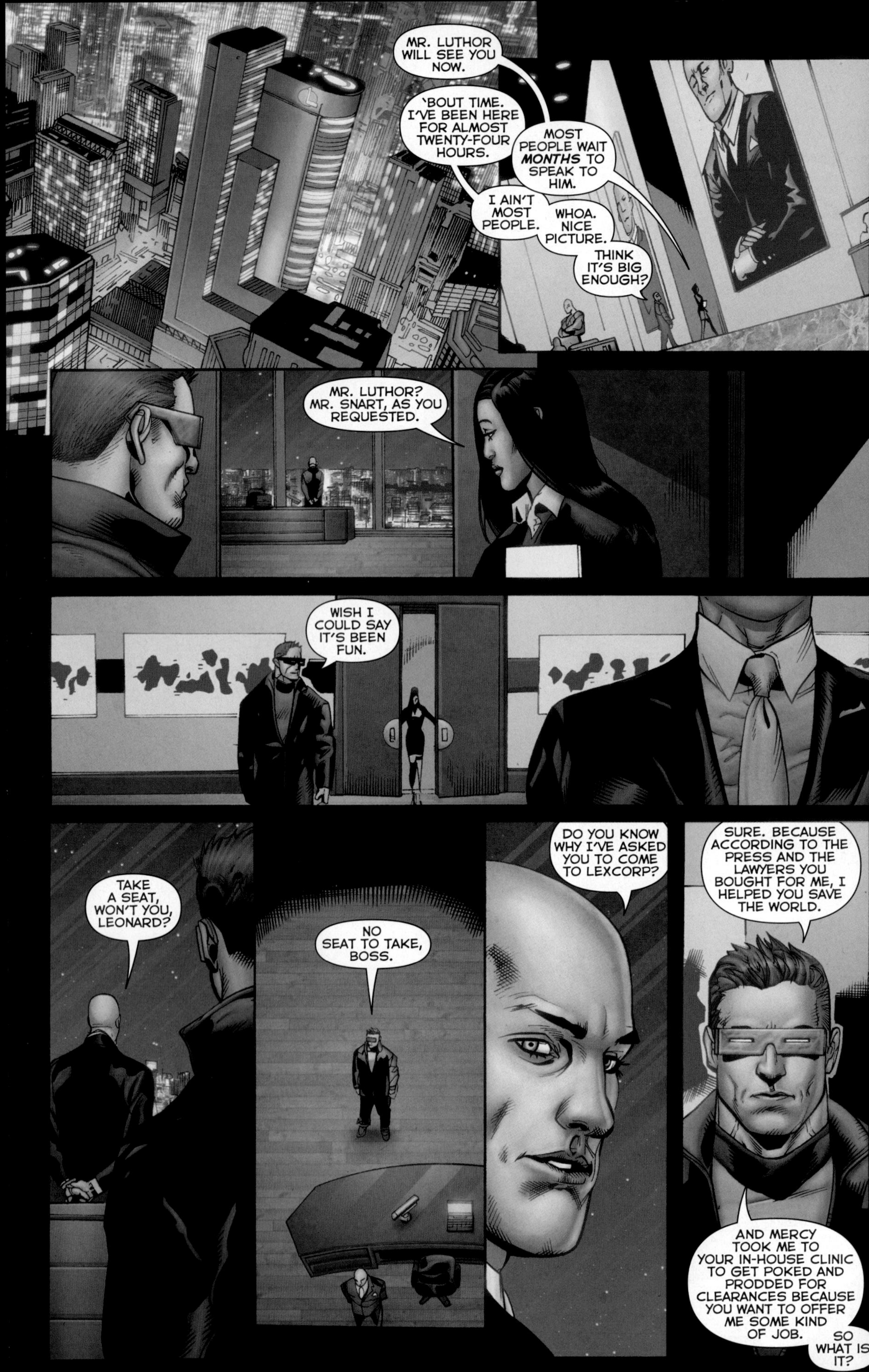

MR. LUTHOR WILL SEE YOU NOW.
'BOUT TIME. I'VE BEEN HERE FOR ALMOST TWENTY-FOUR HOURS.
MOST PEOPLE WAIT *MONTHS* TO SPEAK TO HIM.
I AIN'T MOST PEOPLE.
WHOA. NICE PICTURE.
THINK IT'S BIG ENOUGH?
MR. LUTHOR? MR. SNART, AS YOU REQUESTED.
WISH I COULD SAY IT'S BEEN FUN.
TAKE A SEAT, WON'T YOU, LEONARD?
NO SEAT TO TAKE, BOSS.
DO YOU KNOW WHY I'VE ASKED YOU TO COME TO LEXCORP?
SURE. BECAUSE ACCORDING TO THE PRESS AND THE LAWYERS YOU BOUGHT FOR ME, I HELPED YOU SAVE THE WORLD.
AND MERCY TOOK ME TO YOUR IN-HOUSE CLINIC TO GET POKED AND PRODDED FOR CLEARANCES BECAUSE YOU WANT TO OFFER ME SOME KIND OF JOB.
SO WHAT IS IT?

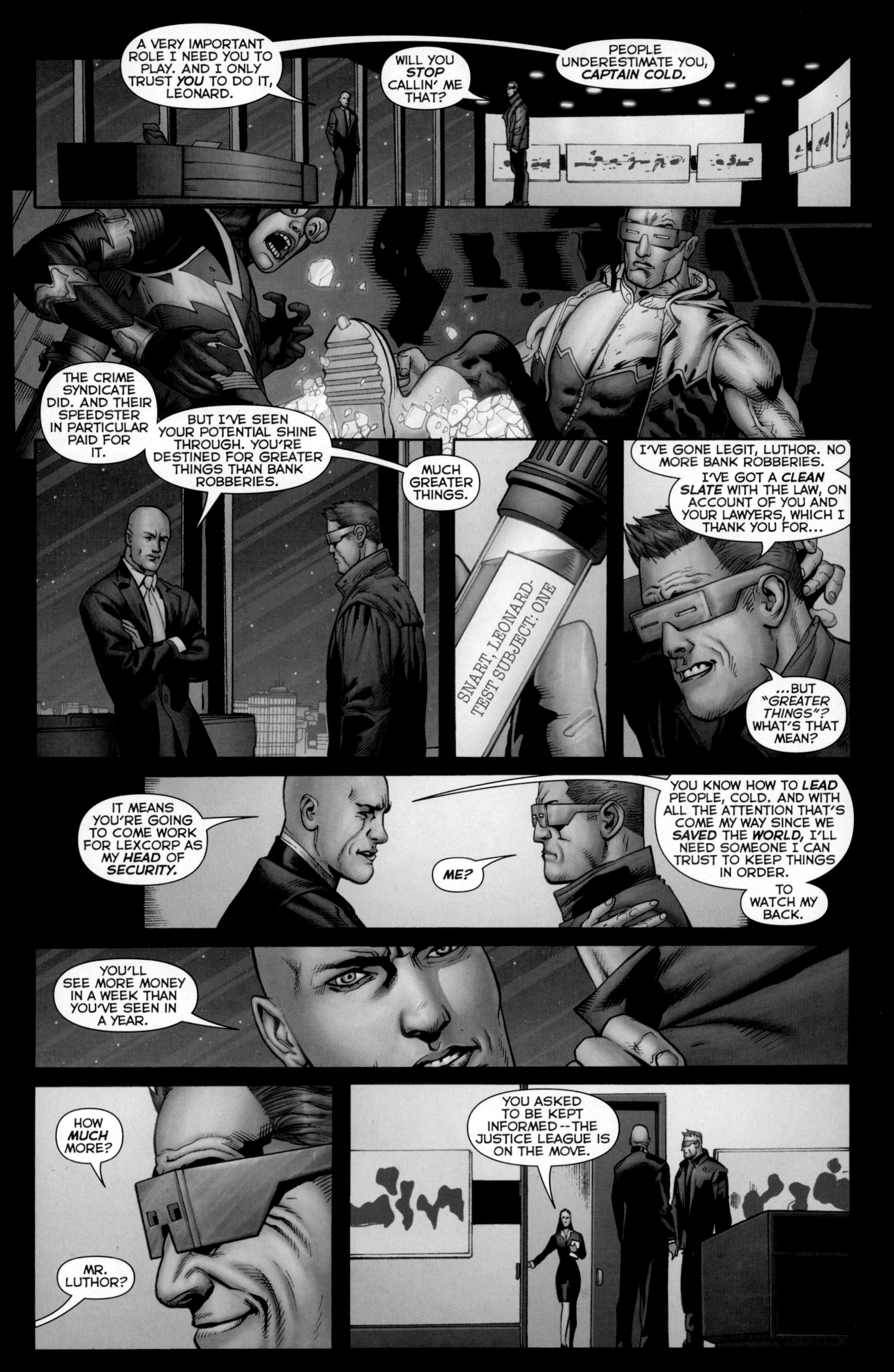

A VERY IMPORTANT ROLE I NEED YOU TO PLAY. AND I ONLY TRUST *YOU* TO DO IT, LEONARD.
WILL YOU *STOP* CALLIN' ME THAT?
PEOPLE UNDERESTIMATE YOU, *CAPTAIN COLD.*
THE CRIME SYNDICATE DID. AND THEIR SPEEDSTER IN PARTICULAR PAID FOR IT.
BUT I'VE SEEN YOUR POTENTIAL SHINE THROUGH. YOU'RE DESTINED FOR GREATER THINGS THAN BANK ROBBERIES.
MUCH GREATER THINGS.
SNART, LEONARD- TEST SUBJECT: ONE
I'VE GONE LEGIT, LUTHOR. NO MORE BANK ROBBERIES.
I'VE GOT A *CLEAN SLATE* WITH THE LAW, ON ACCOUNT OF YOU AND YOUR LAWYERS, WHICH I THANK YOU FOR...
...BUT "*GREATER THINGS*"? WHAT'S THAT MEAN?
IT MEANS YOU'RE GOING TO COME WORK FOR LEXCORP AS MY *HEAD* OF *SECURITY.*
ME?
YOU KNOW HOW TO *LEAD* PEOPLE, COLD. AND WITH ALL THE ATTENTION THAT'S COME MY WAY SINCE WE *SAVED* THE *WORLD,* I'LL NEED SOMEONE I CAN TRUST TO KEEP THINGS IN ORDER.
TO WATCH MY BACK.
YOU'LL SEE MORE MONEY IN A WEEK THAN YOU'VE SEEN IN A YEAR.
HOW *MUCH* MORE?
MR. LUTHOR?
YOU ASKED TO BE KEPT INFORMED--THE JUSTICE LEAGUE IS ON THE MOVE.

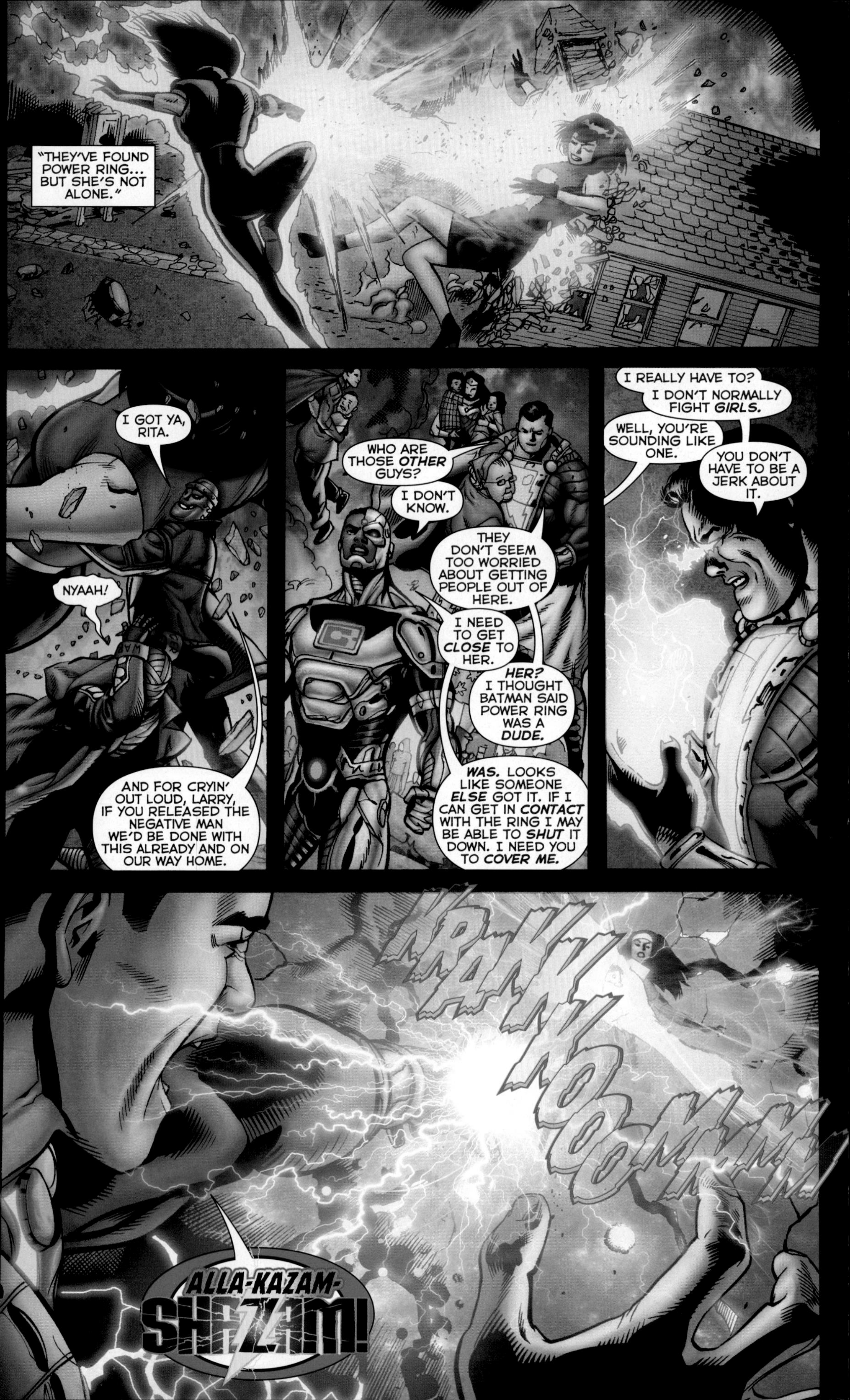
"THEY'VE FOUND POWER RING... BUT SHE'S NOT ALONE."
I GOT YA, RITA.
NYAAH!
AND FOR CRYIN' OUT LOUD, LARRY, IF YOU RELEASED THE NEGATIVE MAN WE'D BE DONE WITH THIS ALREADY AND ON OUR WAY HOME.
WHO ARE THOSE OTHER GUYS?
I DON'T KNOW.
THEY DON'T SEEM TOO WORRIED ABOUT GETTING PEOPLE OUT OF HERE.
I NEED TO GET CLOSE TO HER.
HER? I THOUGHT BATMAN SAID POWER RING WAS A DUDE.
WAS. LOOKS LIKE SOMEONE ELSE GOT IT. IF I CAN GET IN CONTACT WITH THE RING I MAY BE ABLE TO SHUT IT DOWN. I NEED YOU TO COVER ME.
I REALLY HAVE TO?
I DON'T NORMALLY FIGHT GIRLS.
WELL, YOU'RE SOUNDING LIKE ONE.
YOU DON'T HAVE TO BE A JERK ABOUT IT.
KRAKOOOMMM
ALLA-KAZAM-SHAZAM!

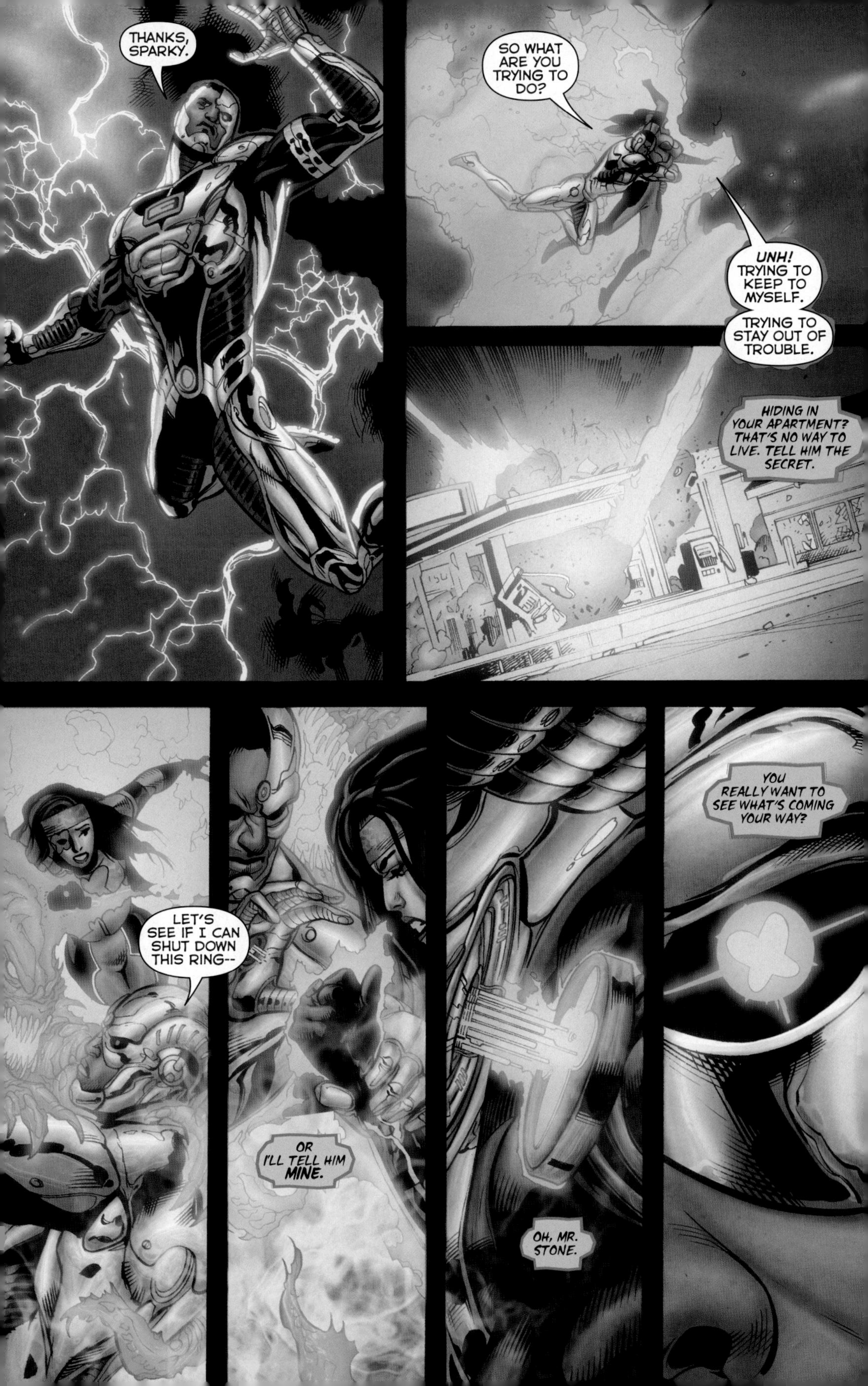
THANKS, SPARKY.
SO WHAT ARE YOU TRYING TO DO?
UNH! TRYING TO KEEP TO MYSELF.
TRYING TO STAY OUT OF TROUBLE.
HIDING IN YOUR APARTMENT? THAT'S NO WAY TO LIVE. TELL HIM THE SECRET.
LET'S SEE IF I CAN SHUT DOWN THIS RING--
OR I'LL TELL HIM MINE.
OH, MR. STONE.
YOU REALLY WANT TO SEE WHAT'S COMING YOUR WAY?

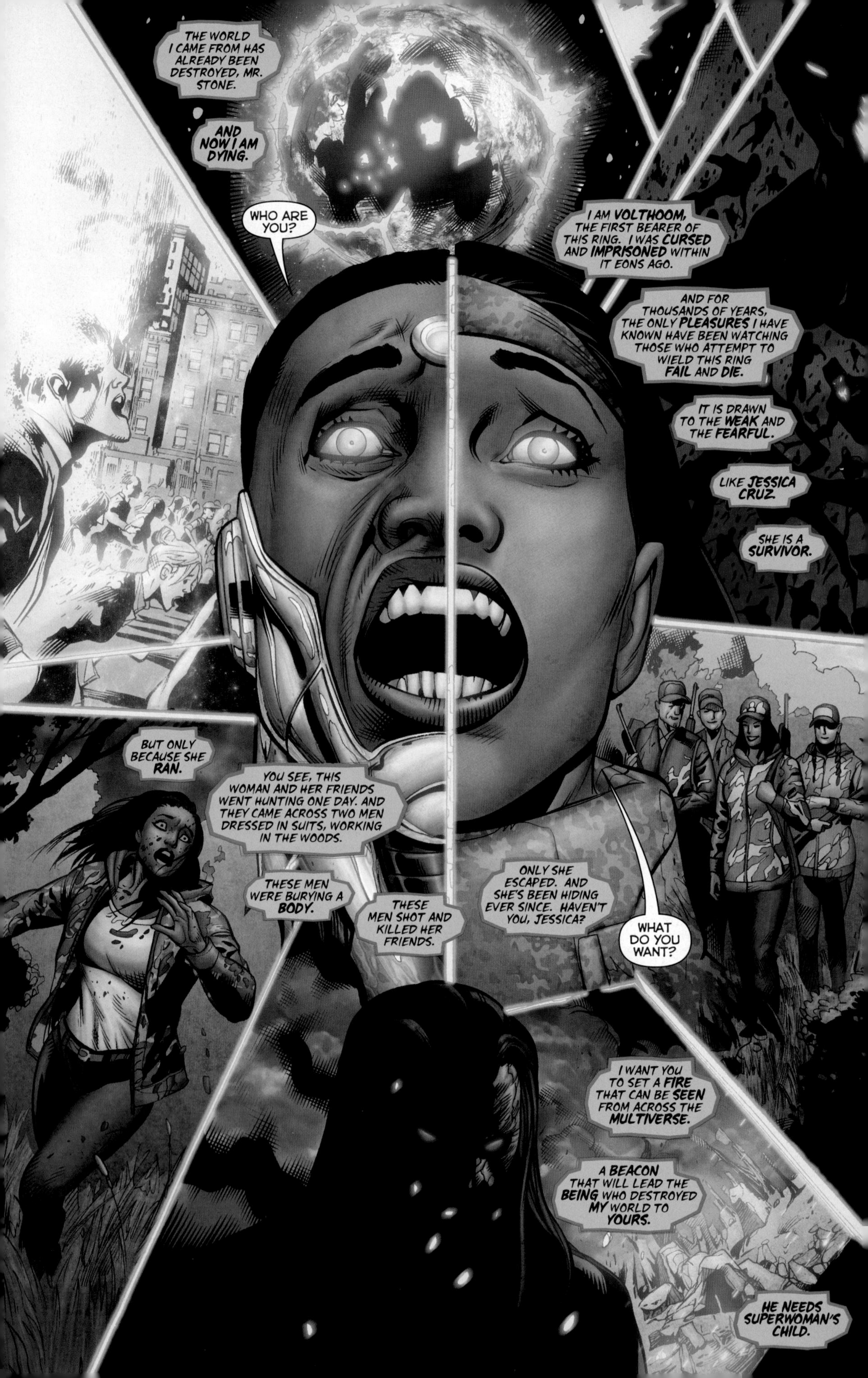
THE WORLD I CAME FROM HAS ALREADY BEEN DESTROYED, MR. STONE.
AND NOW I AM DYING.
WHO ARE YOU?
I AM VOLTHOOM, THE FIRST BEARER OF THIS RING. I WAS CURSED AND IMPRISONED WITHIN IT EONS AGO.
AND FOR THOUSANDS OF YEARS, THE ONLY PLEASURES I HAVE KNOWN HAVE BEEN WATCHING THOSE WHO ATTEMPT TO WIELD THIS RING FAIL AND DIE.
IT IS DRAWN TO THE WEAK AND THE FEARFUL.
LIKE JESSICA CRUZ.
SHE IS A SURVIVOR.
BUT ONLY BECAUSE SHE RAN.
YOU SEE, THIS WOMAN AND HER FRIENDS WENT HUNTING ONE DAY. AND THEY CAME ACROSS TWO MEN DRESSED IN SUITS, WORKING IN THE WOODS.
THESE MEN WERE BURYING A BODY.
THESE MEN SHOT AND KILLED HER FRIENDS.
ONLY SHE ESCAPED. AND SHE'S BEEN HIDING EVER SINCE. HAVEN'T YOU, JESSICA?
WHAT DO YOU WANT?
I WANT YOU TO SET A FIRE THAT CAN BE SEEN FROM ACROSS THE MULTIVERSE.
A BEACON THAT WILL LEAD THE BEING WHO DESTROYED MY WORLD TO YOURS.
HE NEEDS SUPERWOMAN'S CHILD.

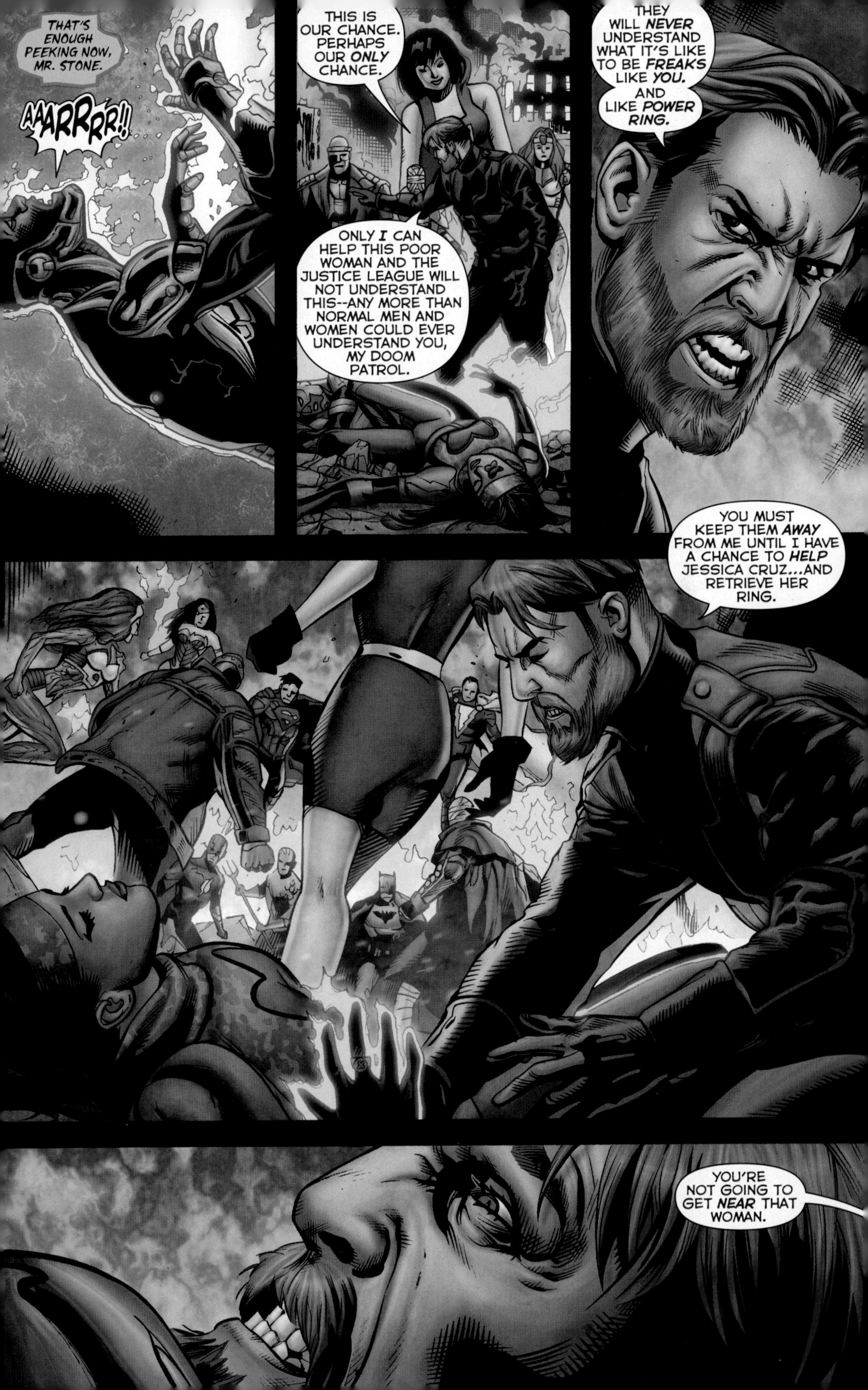
THAT'S ENOUGH PEEKING NOW, MR. STONE.
AAARRRRR!!
THIS IS OUR CHANCE. PERHAPS OUR ONLY CHANCE.
ONLY I CAN HELP THIS POOR WOMAN AND THE JUSTICE LEAGUE WILL NOT UNDERSTAND THIS--ANY MORE THAN NORMAL MEN AND WOMEN COULD EVER UNDERSTAND YOU, MY DOOM PATROL.
THEY WILL NEVER UNDERSTAND WHAT IT'S LIKE TO BE FREAKS LIKE YOU.
AND LIKE POWER RING.
YOU MUST KEEP THEM AWAY FROM ME UNTIL I HAVE A CHANCE TO HELP JESSICA CRUZ...AND RETRIEVE HER RING.
YOU'RE NOT GOING TO GET NEAR THAT WOMAN.

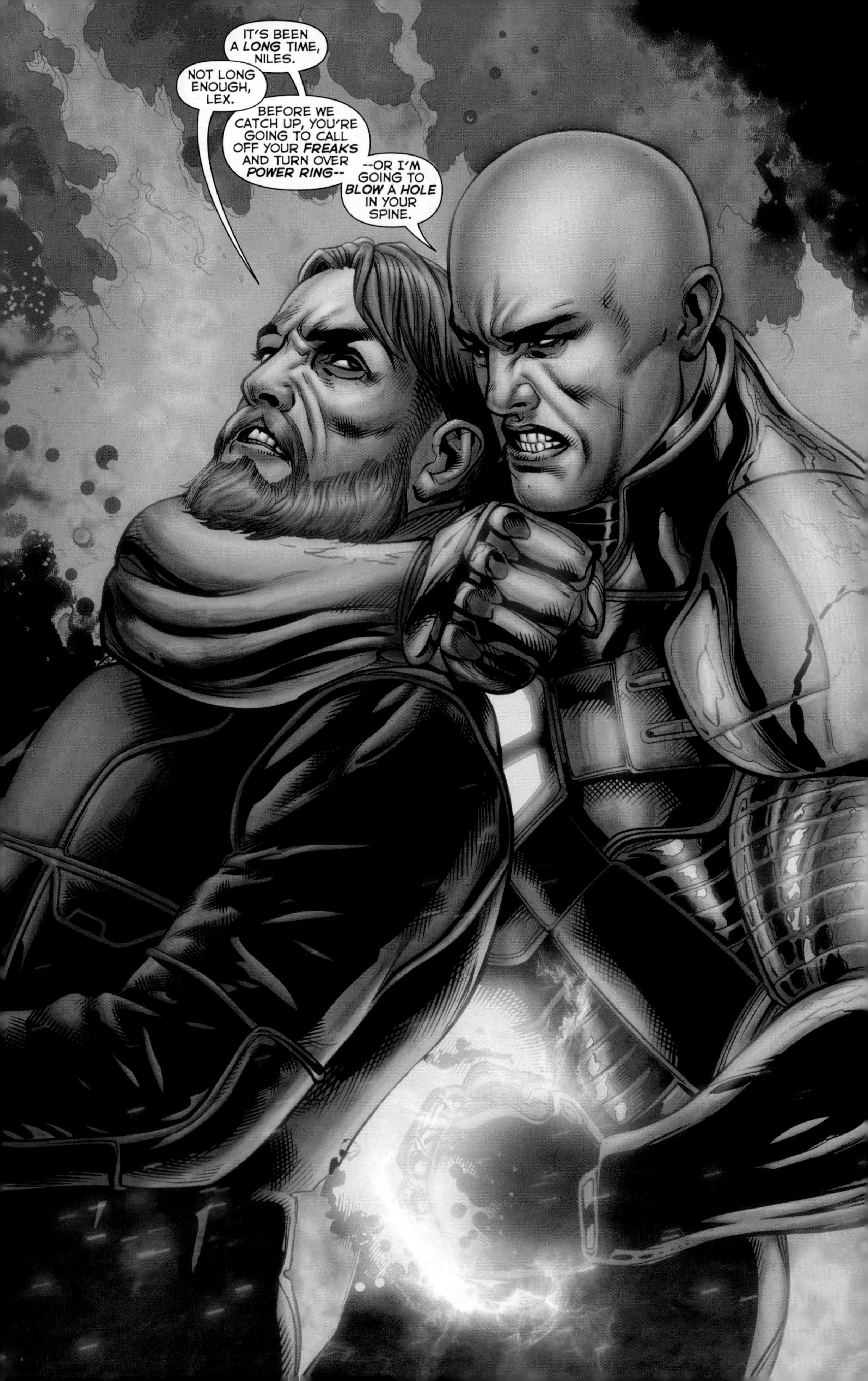
IT'S BEEN A **LONG** TIME, NILES.
NOT LONG ENOUGH, LEX.
BEFORE WE CATCH UP, YOU'RE GOING TO CALL OFF YOUR **FREAKS** AND TURN OVER **POWER RING**--
--OR I'M GOING TO **BLOW A HOLE** IN YOUR SPINE.

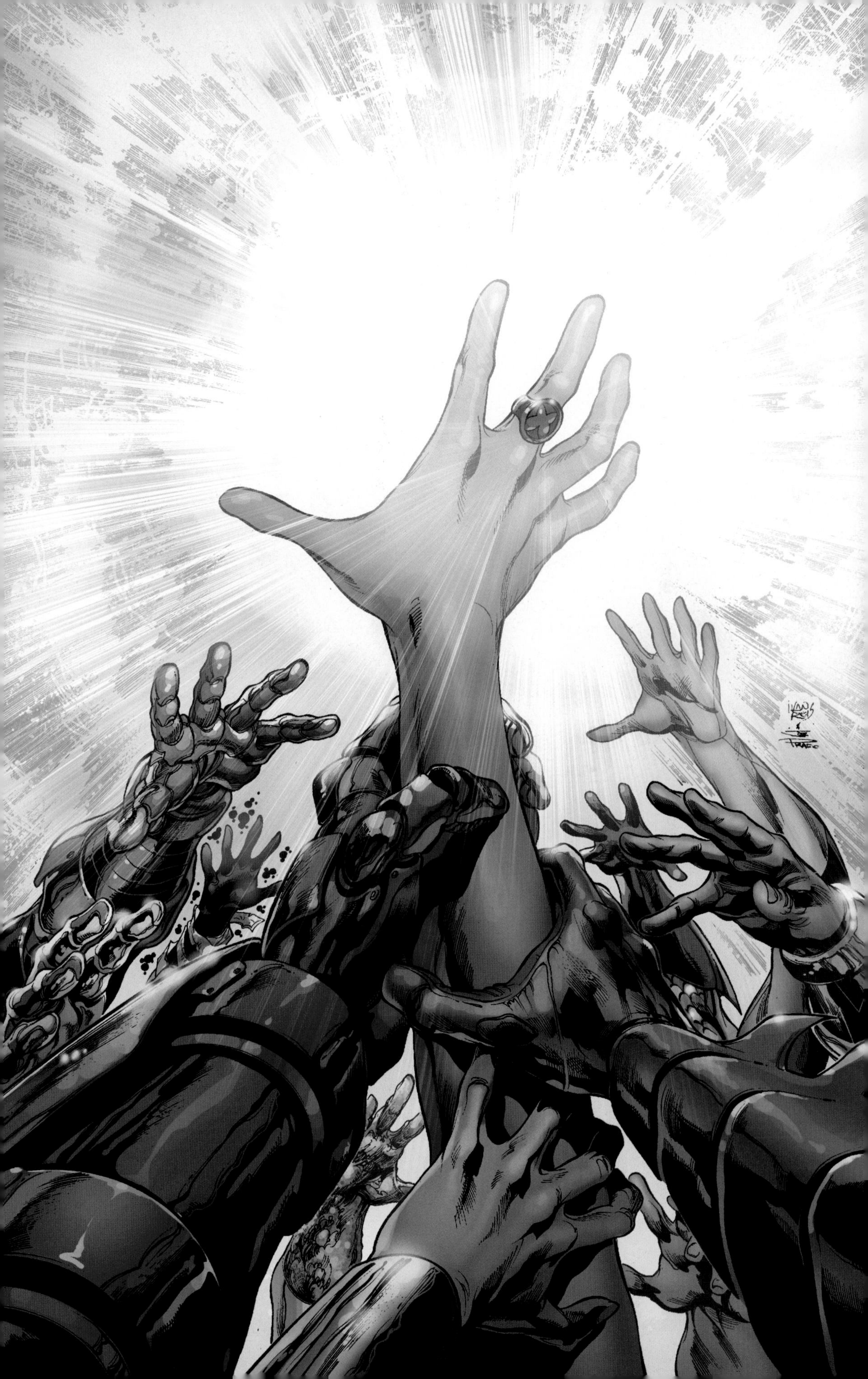

INJUSTICE LEAGUE CHAPTER FOUR
PUPPET STRINGS

GEOFF JOHNS writer **DOUG MAHNKE** penciller **KEITH CHAMPAGNE** inker
ANDREW DALHOUSE colorist **IVAN REIS, JOE PRADO & ROD REIS** cover artists

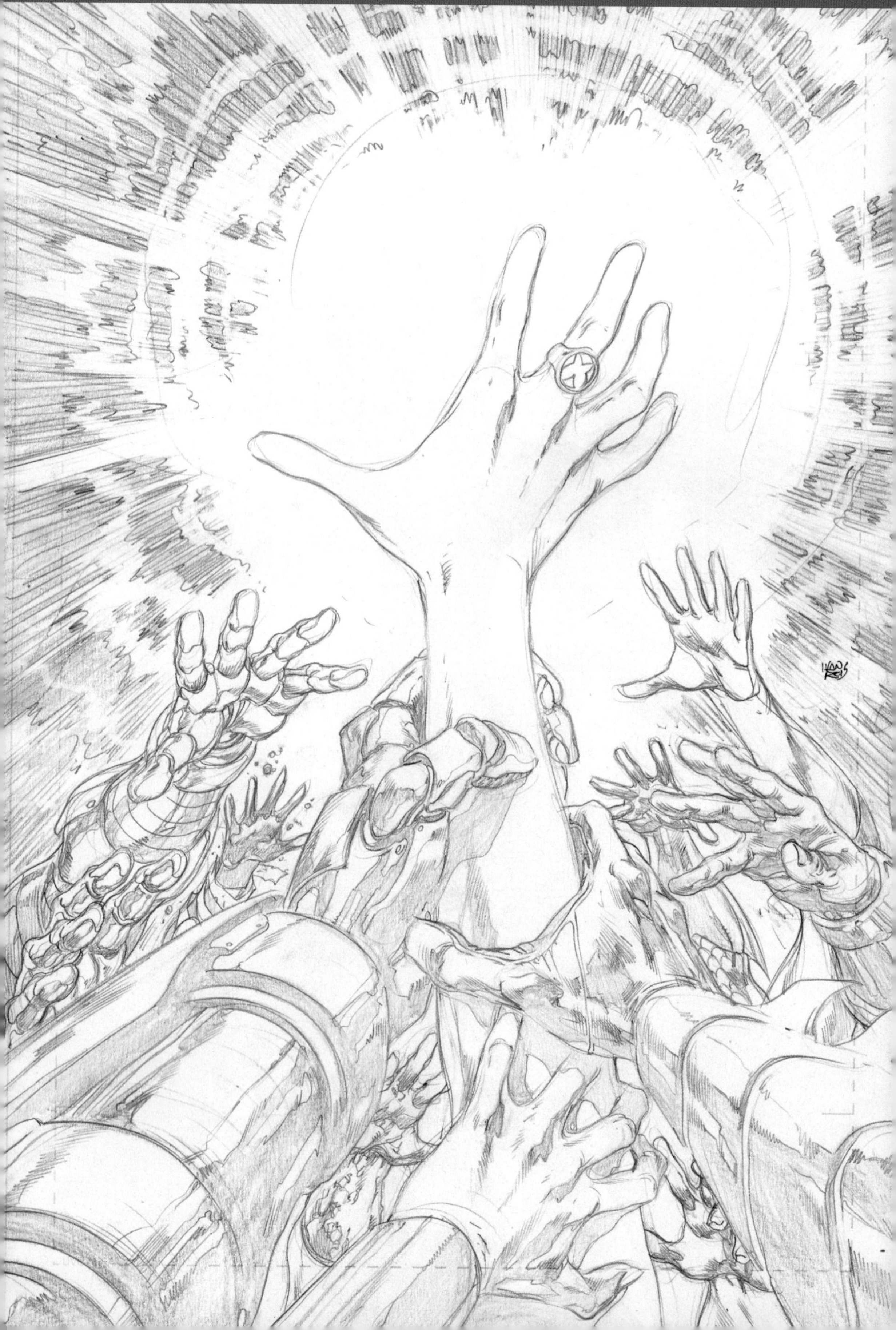

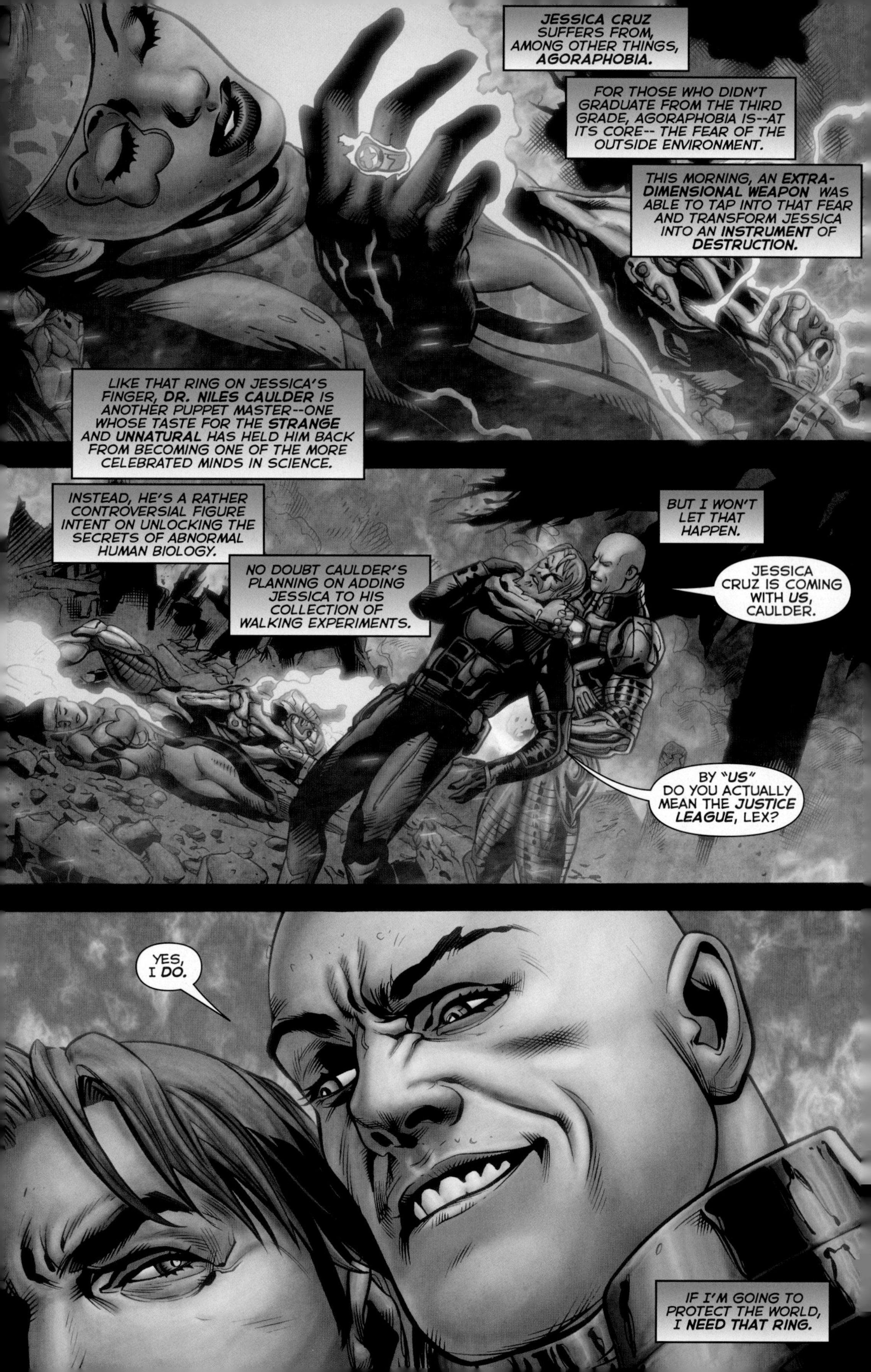
JESSICA CRUZ SUFFERS FROM, AMONG OTHER THINGS, AGORAPHOBIA.
FOR THOSE WHO DIDN'T GRADUATE FROM THE THIRD GRADE, AGORAPHOBIA IS--AT ITS CORE-- THE FEAR OF THE OUTSIDE ENVIRONMENT.
THIS MORNING, AN EXTRA-DIMENSIONAL WEAPON WAS ABLE TO TAP INTO THAT FEAR AND TRANSFORM JESSICA INTO AN INSTRUMENT OF DESTRUCTION.
LIKE THAT RING ON JESSICA'S FINGER, DR. NILES CAULDER IS ANOTHER PUPPET MASTER--ONE WHOSE TASTE FOR THE STRANGE AND UNNATURAL HAS HELD HIM BACK FROM BECOMING ONE OF THE MORE CELEBRATED MINDS IN SCIENCE.
INSTEAD, HE'S A RATHER CONTROVERSIAL FIGURE INTENT ON UNLOCKING THE SECRETS OF ABNORMAL HUMAN BIOLOGY.
NO DOUBT CAULDER'S PLANNING ON ADDING JESSICA TO HIS COLLECTION OF WALKING EXPERIMENTS.
BUT I WON'T LET THAT HAPPEN.
JESSICA CRUZ IS COMING WITH US, CAULDER.
BY "US" DO YOU ACTUALLY MEAN THE JUSTICE LEAGUE, LEX?
YES, I DO.
IF I'M GOING TO PROTECT THE WORLD, I NEED THAT RING.

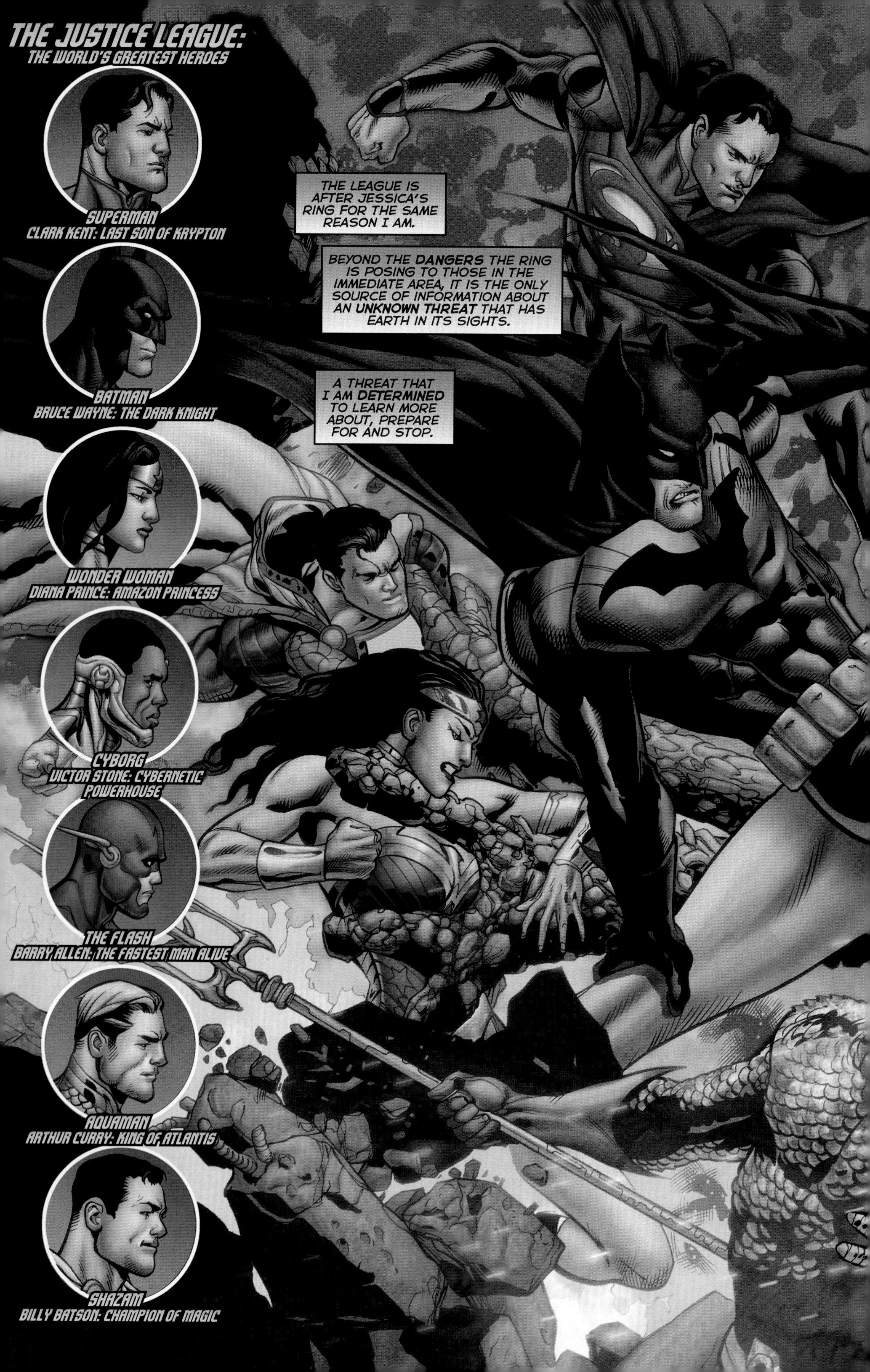
THE JUSTICE LEAGUE:
THE WORLD'S GREATEST HEROES
SUPERMAN
CLARK KENT: LAST SON OF KRYPTON
BATMAN
BRUCE WAYNE: THE DARK KNIGHT
WONDER WOMAN
DIANA PRINCE: AMAZON PRINCESS
CYBORG
VICTOR STONE: CYBERNETIC POWERHOUSE
THE FLASH
BARRY ALLEN: THE FASTEST MAN ALIVE
AQUAMAN
ARTHUR CURRY: KING OF ATLANTIS
SHAZAM
BILLY BATSON: CHAMPION OF MAGIC
THE LEAGUE IS AFTER JESSICA'S RING FOR THE SAME REASON I AM.
BEYOND THE DANGERS THE RING IS POSING TO THOSE IN THE IMMEDIATE AREA, IT IS THE ONLY SOURCE OF INFORMATION ABOUT AN UNKNOWN THREAT THAT HAS EARTH IN ITS SIGHTS.
A THREAT THAT I AM DETERMINED TO LEARN MORE ABOUT, PREPARE FOR AND STOP.

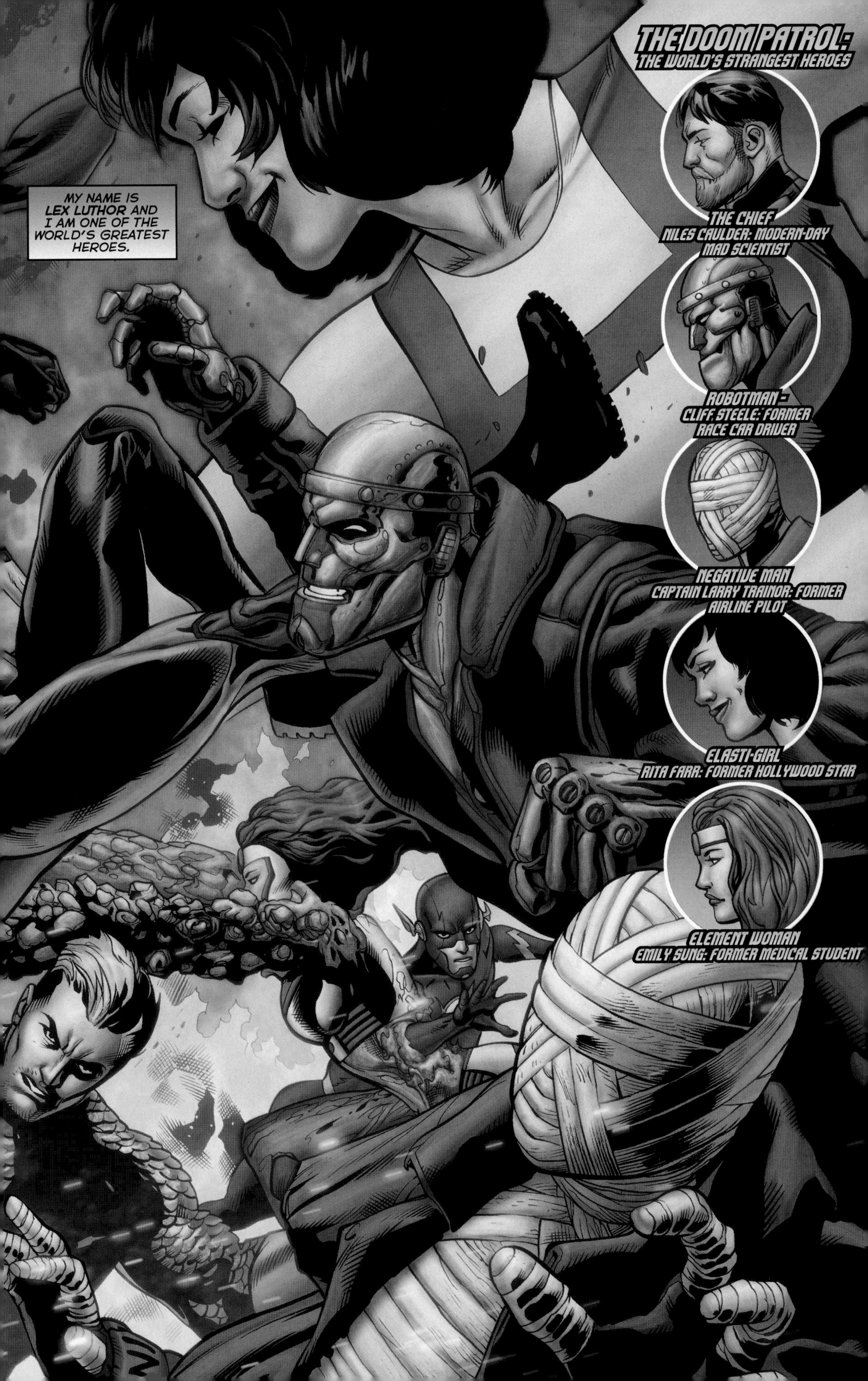
THE DOOM PATROL:
THE WORLD'S STRANGEST HEROES
MY NAME IS LEX LUTHOR AND I AM ONE OF THE WORLD'S GREATEST HEROES.
THE CHIEF
NILES CAULDER: MODERN-DAY MAD SCIENTIST
ROBOTMAN -
CLIFF STEELE: FORMER RACE CAR DRIVER
NEGATIVE MAN
CAPTAIN LARRY TRAINOR: FORMER AIRLINE PILOT
ELASTI-GIRL
RITA FARR: FORMER HOLLYWOOD STAR
ELEMENT WOMAN
EMILY SUNG: FORMER MEDICAL STUDENT

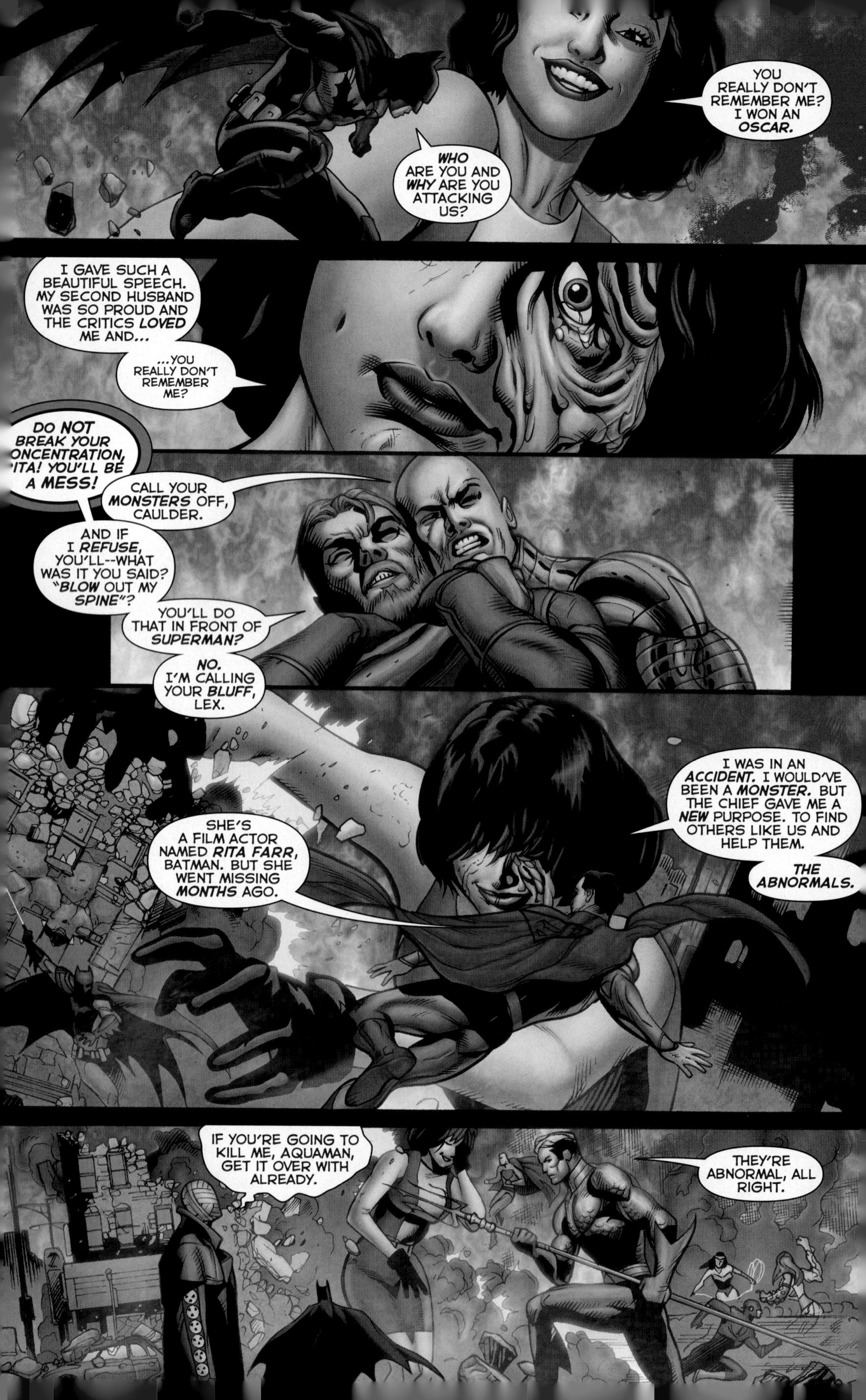
WHO ARE YOU AND WHY ARE YOU ATTACKING US?
YOU REALLY DON'T REMEMBER ME? I WON AN OSCAR.
I GAVE SUCH A BEAUTIFUL SPEECH. MY SECOND HUSBAND WAS SO PROUD AND THE CRITICS LOVED ME AND...
...YOU REALLY DON'T REMEMBER ME?
DO NOT BREAK YOUR CONCENTRATION, RITA! YOU'LL BE A MESS!
CALL YOUR MONSTERS OFF, CAULDER.
AND IF I REFUSE, YOU'LL--WHAT WAS IT YOU SAID? "BLOW OUT MY SPINE"?
YOU'LL DO THAT IN FRONT OF SUPERMAN?
NO. I'M CALLING YOUR BLUFF, LEX.
SHE'S A FILM ACTOR NAMED RITA FARR, BATMAN. BUT SHE WENT MISSING MONTHS AGO.
I WAS IN AN ACCIDENT. I WOULD'VE BEEN A MONSTER. BUT THE CHIEF GAVE ME A NEW PURPOSE. TO FIND OTHERS LIKE US AND HELP THEM.
THE ABNORMALS.
IF YOU'RE GOING TO KILL ME, AQUAMAN, GET IT OVER WITH ALREADY.
THEY'RE ABNORMAL, ALL RIGHT.

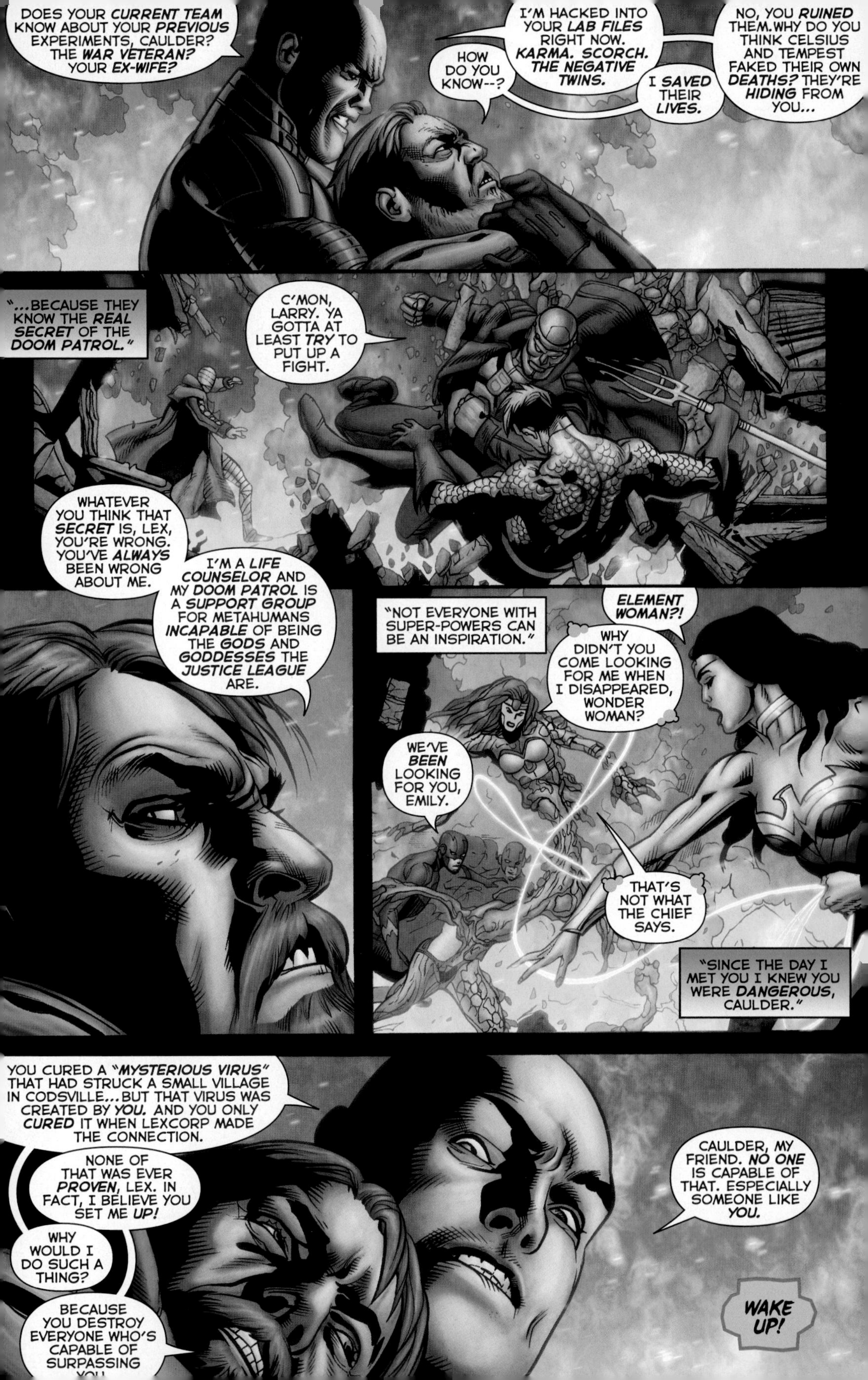

DOES YOUR CURRENT TEAM KNOW ABOUT YOUR PREVIOUS EXPERIMENTS, CAULDER? THE WAR VETERAN? YOUR EX-WIFE?
HOW DO YOU KNOW--?
I'M HACKED INTO YOUR LAB FILES RIGHT NOW. KARMA. SCORCH. THE NEGATIVE TWINS.
I SAVED THEIR LIVES.
NO, YOU RUINED THEM. WHY DO YOU THINK CELSIUS AND TEMPEST FAKED THEIR OWN DEATHS? THEY'RE HIDING FROM YOU...
"...BECAUSE THEY KNOW THE REAL SECRET OF THE DOOM PATROL."
C'MON, LARRY. YA GOTTA AT LEAST TRY TO PUT UP A FIGHT.
WHATEVER YOU THINK THAT SECRET IS, LEX, YOU'RE WRONG. YOU'VE ALWAYS BEEN WRONG ABOUT ME.
I'M A LIFE COUNSELOR AND MY DOOM PATROL IS A SUPPORT GROUP FOR METAHUMANS INCAPABLE OF BEING THE GODS AND GODDESSES THE JUSTICE LEAGUE ARE.
"NOT EVERYONE WITH SUPER-POWERS CAN BE AN INSPIRATION."
ELEMENT WOMAN?!
WHY DIDN'T YOU COME LOOKING FOR ME WHEN I DISAPPEARED, WONDER WOMAN?
WE'VE BEEN LOOKING FOR YOU, EMILY.
THAT'S NOT WHAT THE CHIEF SAYS.
"SINCE THE DAY I MET YOU I KNEW YOU WERE DANGEROUS, CAULDER."
YOU CURED A "MYSTERIOUS VIRUS" THAT HAD STRUCK A SMALL VILLAGE IN CODSVILLE...BUT THAT VIRUS WAS CREATED BY YOU. AND YOU ONLY CURED IT WHEN LEXCORP MADE THE CONNECTION.
NONE OF THAT WAS EVER PROVEN, LEX. IN FACT, I BELIEVE YOU SET ME UP!
WHY WOULD I DO SUCH A THING?
BECAUSE YOU DESTROY EVERYONE WHO'S CAPABLE OF SURPASSING
CAULDER, MY FRIEND. NO ONE IS CAPABLE OF THAT. ESPECIALLY SOMEONE LIKE YOU.
WAKE UP!

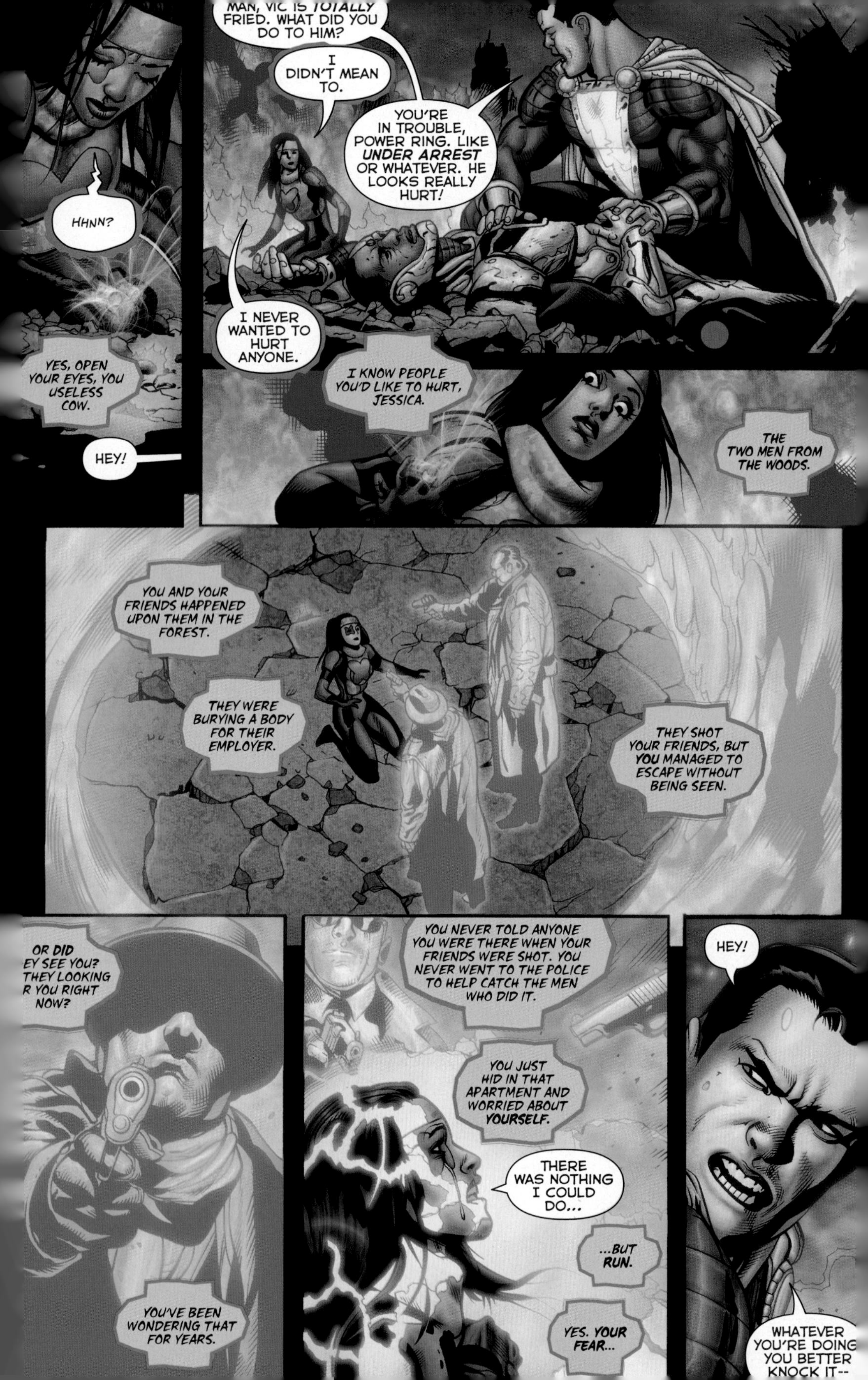
MAN, VIC IS TOTALLY FRIED. WHAT DID YOU DO TO HIM?
I DIDN'T MEAN TO.
YOU'RE IN TROUBLE, POWER RING. LIKE UNDER ARREST OR WHATEVER. HE LOOKS REALLY HURT!
HHNN?
I NEVER WANTED TO HURT ANYONE.
YES, OPEN YOUR EYES, YOU USELESS COW.
HEY!
I KNOW PEOPLE YOU'D LIKE TO HURT, JESSICA.
THE TWO MEN FROM THE WOODS.
YOU AND YOUR FRIENDS HAPPENED UPON THEM IN THE FOREST.
THEY WERE BURYING A BODY FOR THEIR EMPLOYER.
THEY SHOT YOUR FRIENDS, BUT YOU MANAGED TO ESCAPE WITHOUT BEING SEEN.
OR DID EY SEE YOU? THEY LOOKING R YOU RIGHT NOW?
YOU'VE BEEN WONDERING THAT FOR YEARS.
YOU NEVER TOLD ANYONE YOU WERE THERE WHEN YOUR FRIENDS WERE SHOT. YOU NEVER WENT TO THE POLICE TO HELP CATCH THE MEN WHO DID IT.
YOU JUST HID IN THAT APARTMENT AND WORRIED ABOUT YOURSELF.
THERE WAS NOTHING I COULD DO...
...BUT RUN.
YES. YOUR FEAR...
HEY!
WHATEVER YOU'RE DOING YOU BETTER KNOCK IT--

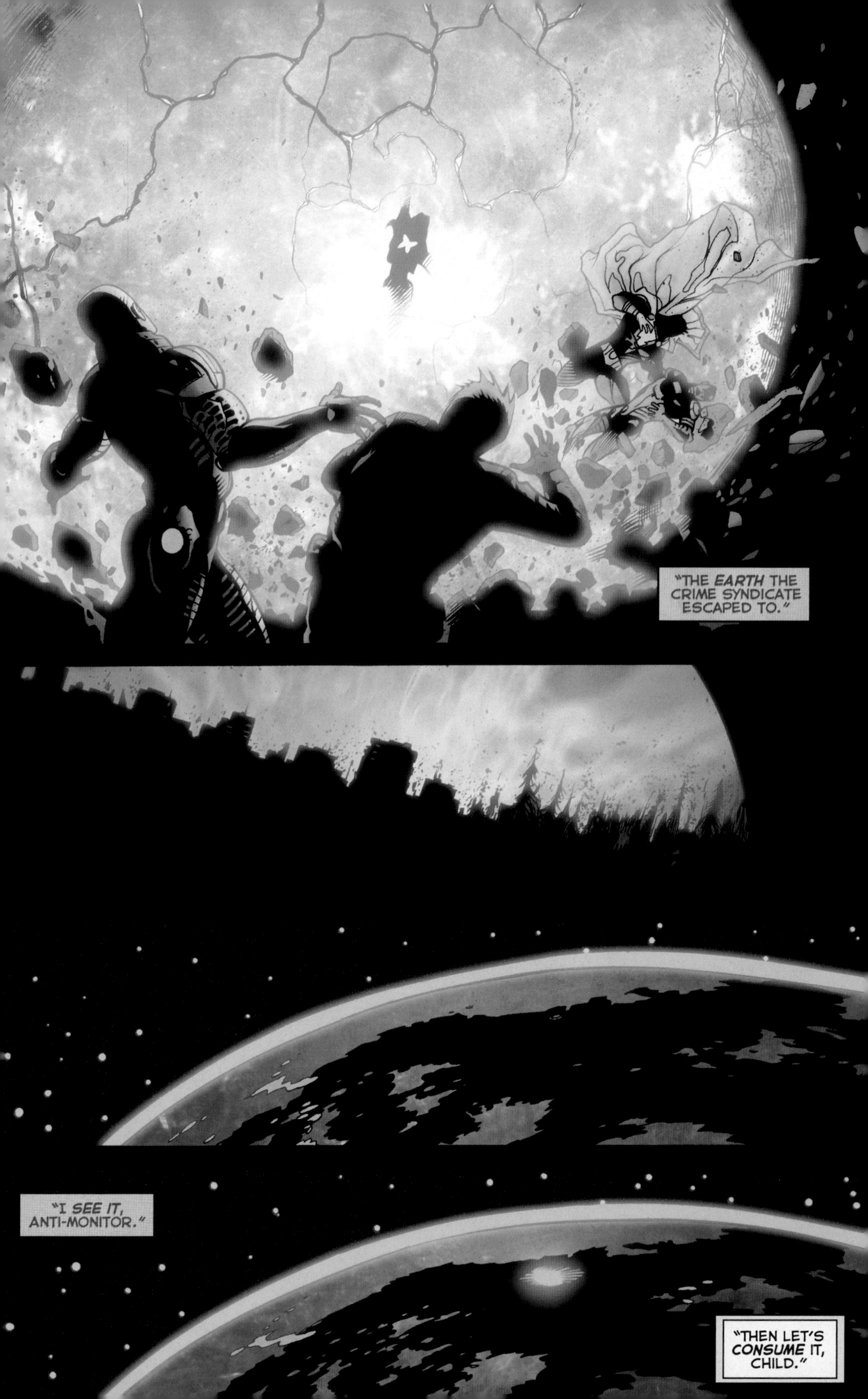
"THE *EARTH* THE CRIME SYNDICATE ESCAPED TO."
"I *SEE IT*, ANTI-MONITOR."
"THEN LET'S ***CONSUME*** IT, CHILD."

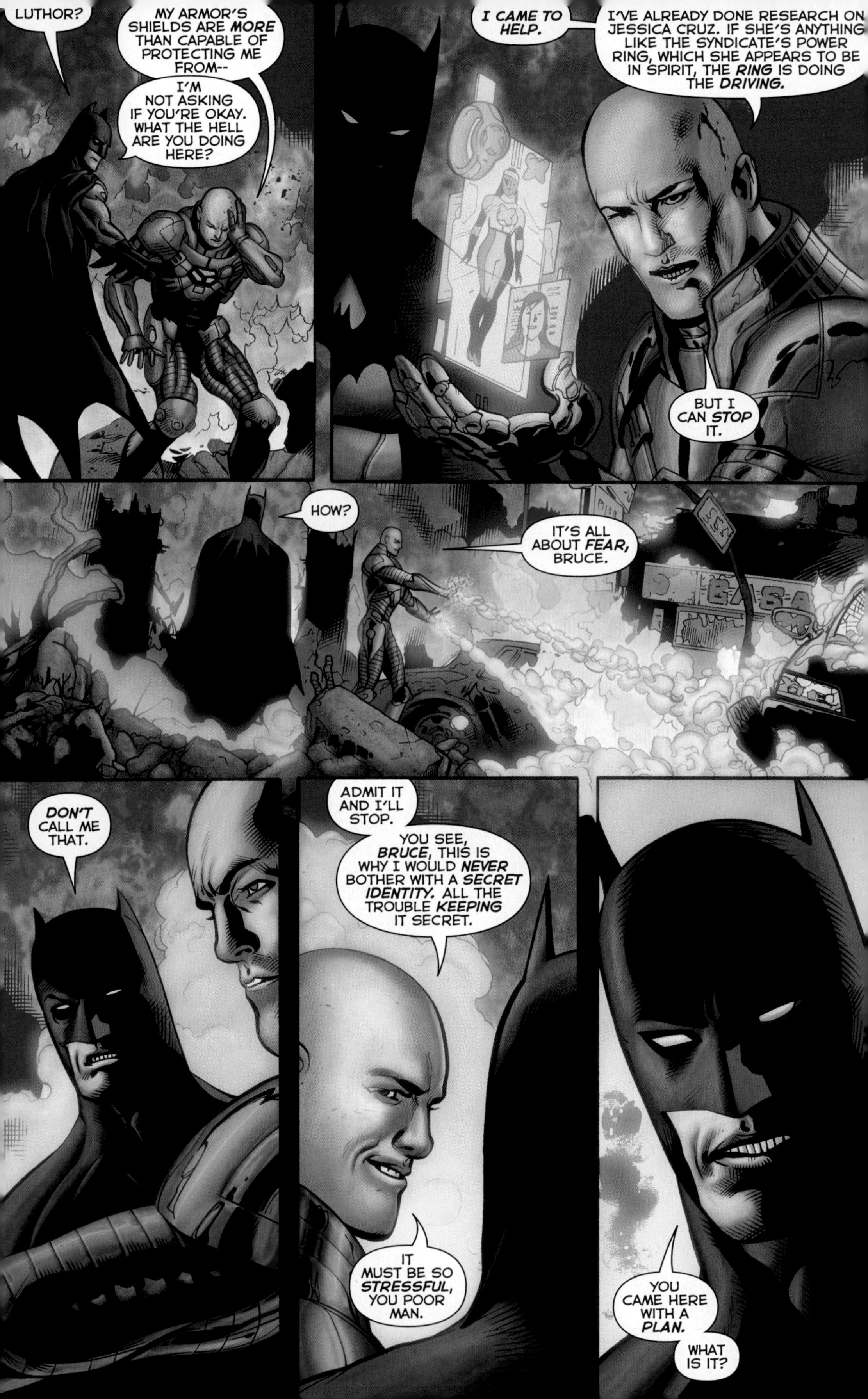
LUTHOR?
MY ARMOR'S SHIELDS ARE MORE THAN CAPABLE OF PROTECTING ME FROM--
I'M NOT ASKING IF YOU'RE OKAY. WHAT THE HELL ARE YOU DOING HERE?
I CAME TO HELP.
I'VE ALREADY DONE RESEARCH ON JESSICA CRUZ. IF SHE'S ANYTHING LIKE THE SYNDICATE'S POWER RING, WHICH SHE APPEARS TO BE IN SPIRIT, THE RING IS DOING THE DRIVING.
BUT I CAN STOP IT.
HOW?
IT'S ALL ABOUT FEAR, BRUCE.
DON'T CALL ME THAT.
ADMIT IT AND I'LL STOP.
YOU SEE, BRUCE, THIS IS WHY I WOULD NEVER BOTHER WITH A SECRET IDENTITY. ALL THE TROUBLE KEEPING IT SECRET.
IT MUST BE SO STRESSFUL, YOU POOR MAN.
YOU CAME HERE WITH A PLAN.
WHAT IS IT?

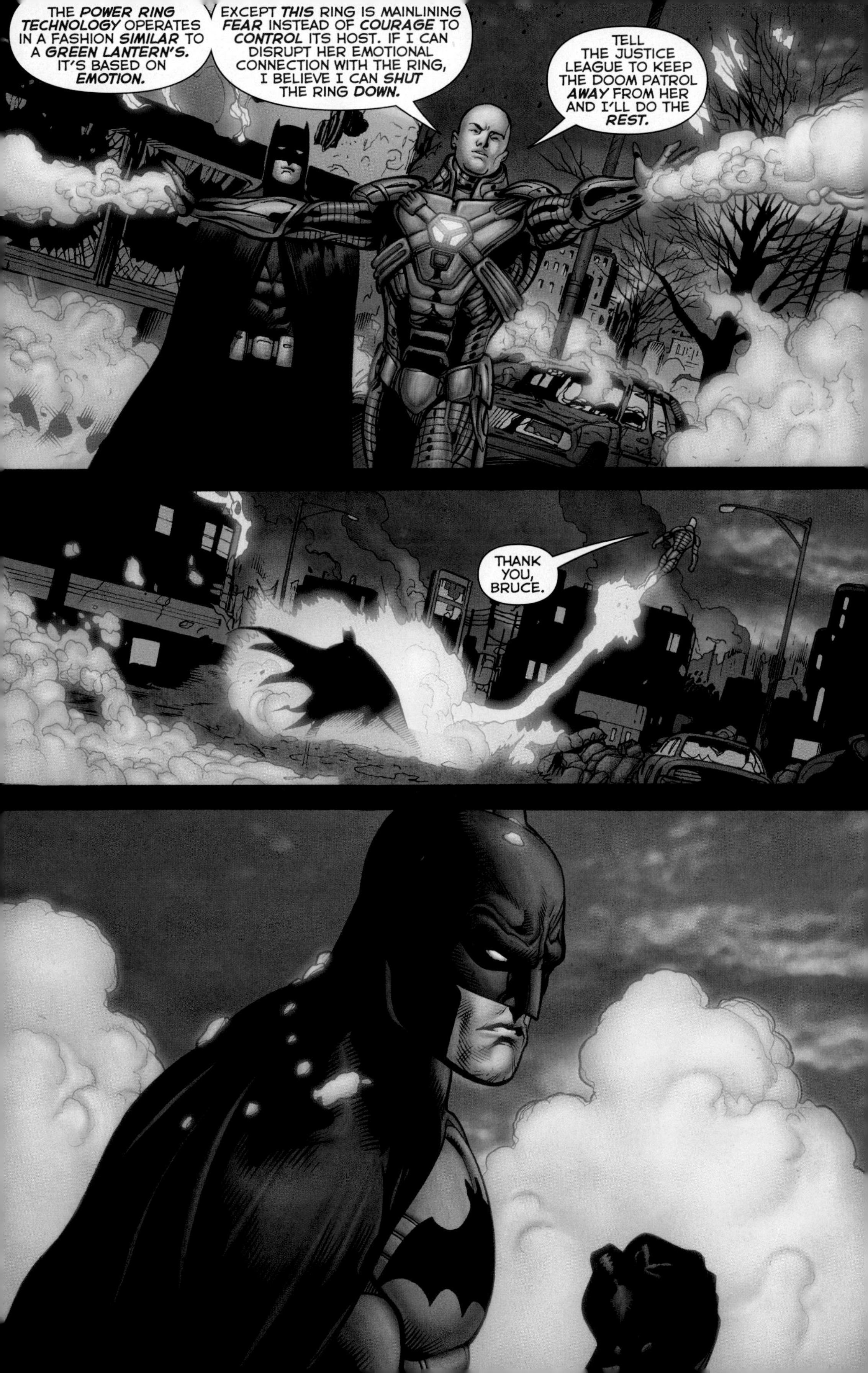
THE POWER RING TECHNOLOGY OPERATES IN A FASHION SIMILAR TO A GREEN LANTERN'S. IT'S BASED ON EMOTION.
EXCEPT THIS RING IS MAINLINING FEAR INSTEAD OF COURAGE TO CONTROL ITS HOST. IF I CAN DISRUPT HER EMOTIONAL CONNECTION WITH THE RING, I BELIEVE I CAN SHUT THE RING DOWN.
TELL THE JUSTICE LEAGUE TO KEEP THE DOOM PATROL AWAY FROM HER AND I'LL DO THE REST.
THANK YOU, BRUCE.

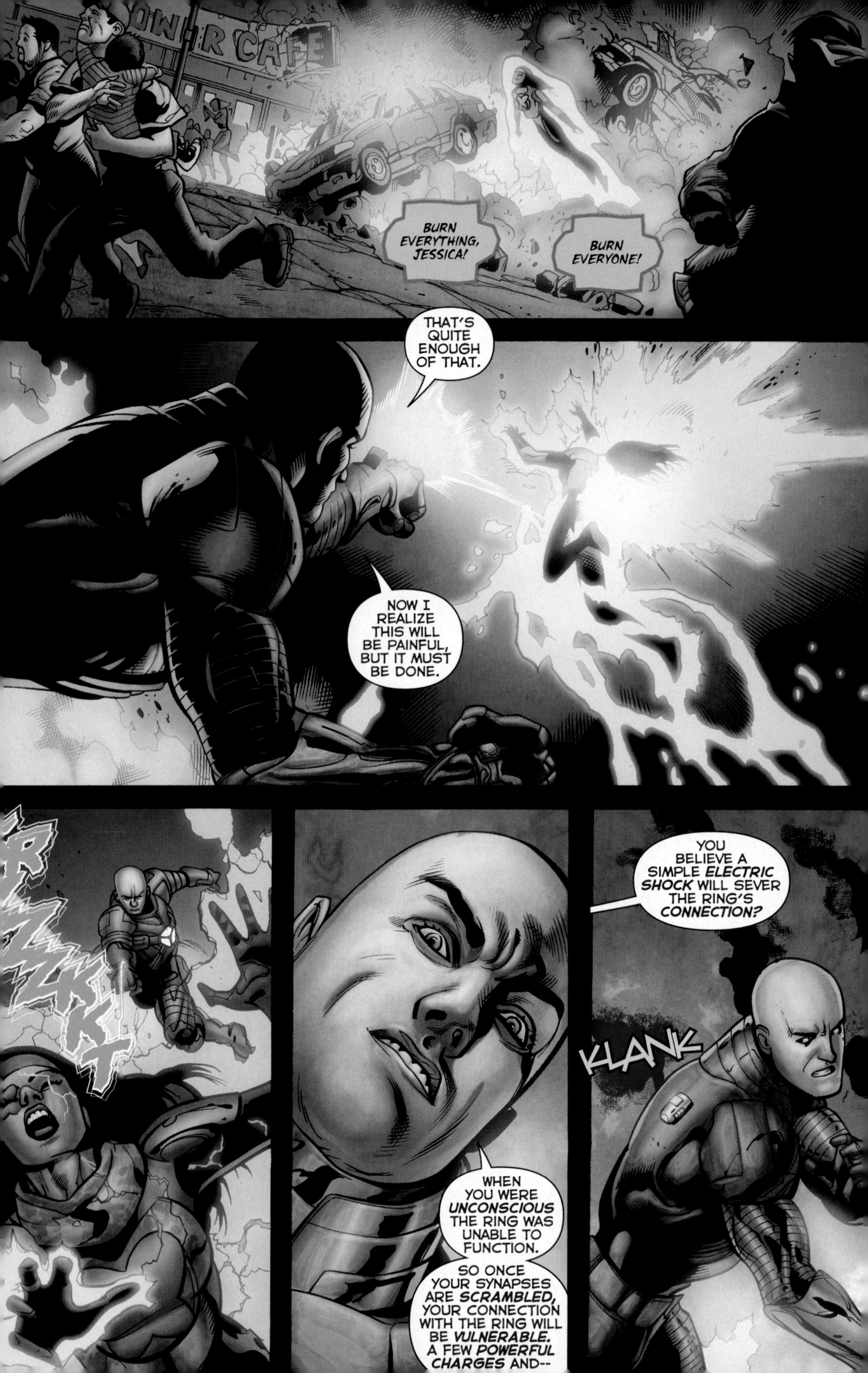
OW R CAFE
BURN EVERYTHING, JESSICA!
BURN EVERYONE!
THAT'S QUITE ENOUGH OF THAT.
NOW I REALIZE THIS WILL BE PAINFUL, BUT IT MUST BE DONE.
RZZKKT
WHEN YOU WERE UNCONSCIOUS THE RING WAS UNABLE TO FUNCTION.
SO ONCE YOUR SYNAPSES ARE SCRAMBLED, YOUR CONNECTION WITH THE RING WILL BE VULNERABLE. A FEW POWERFUL CHARGES AND--
YOU BELIEVE A SIMPLE ELECTRIC SHOCK WILL SEVER THE RING'S CONNECTION?
KLANK

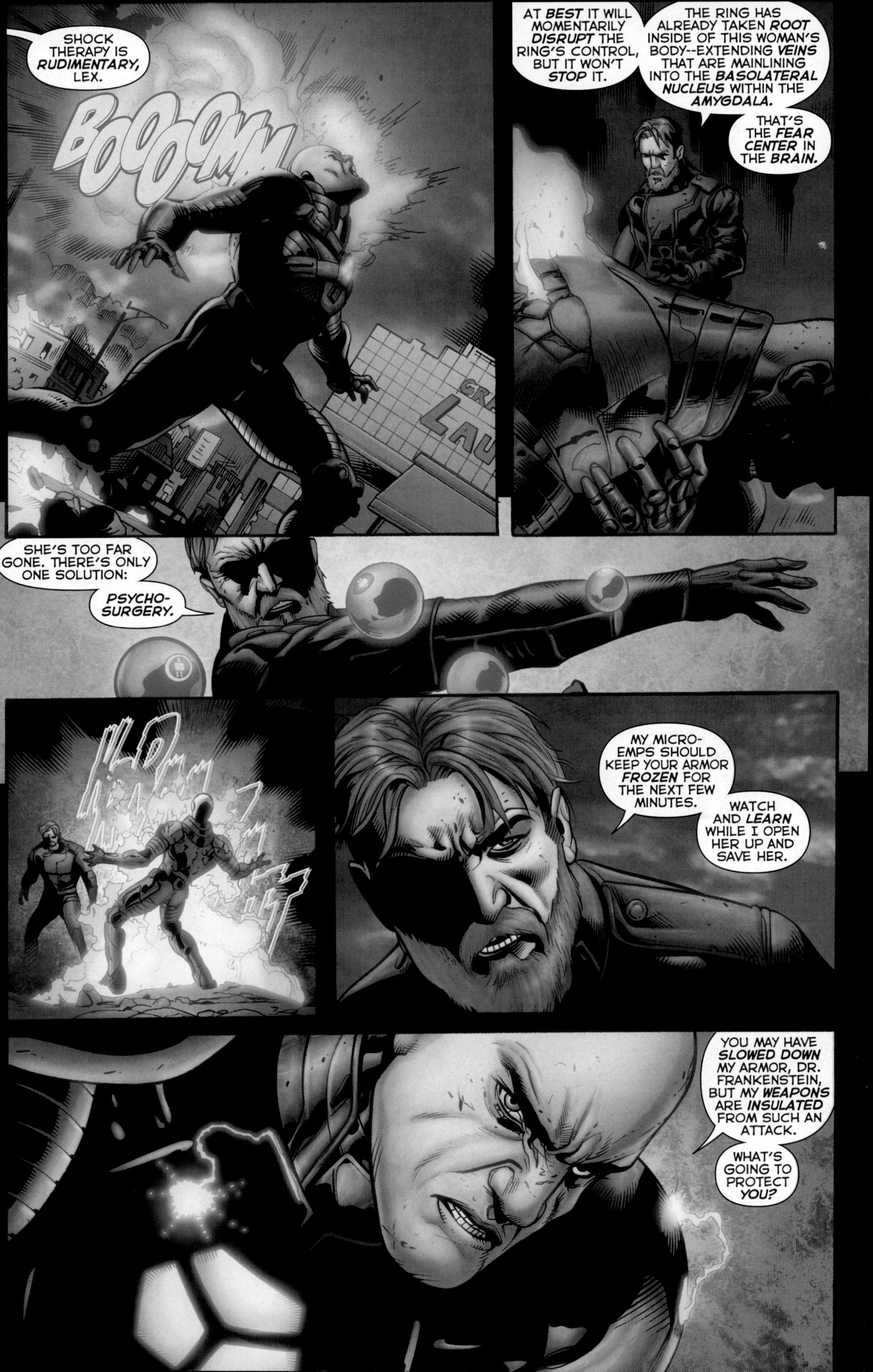
SHOCK THERAPY IS RUDIMENTARY, LEX.
AT BEST IT WILL MOMENTARILY DISRUPT THE RING'S CONTROL, BUT IT WON'T STOP IT.
THE RING HAS ALREADY TAKEN ROOT INSIDE OF THIS WOMAN'S BODY--EXTENDING VEINS THAT ARE MAINLINING INTO THE BASOLATERAL NUCLEUS WITHIN THE AMYGDALA.
THAT'S THE FEAR CENTER IN THE BRAIN.
SHE'S TOO FAR GONE. THERE'S ONLY ONE SOLUTION:
PSYCHO-SURGERY.
MY MICRO-EMPS SHOULD KEEP YOUR ARMOR FROZEN FOR THE NEXT FEW MINUTES.
WATCH AND LEARN WHILE I OPEN HER UP AND SAVE HER.
YOU MAY HAVE SLOWED DOWN MY ARMOR, DR. FRANKENSTEIN, BUT MY WEAPONS ARE INSULATED FROM SUCH AN ATTACK.
WHAT'S GOING TO PROTECT YOU?

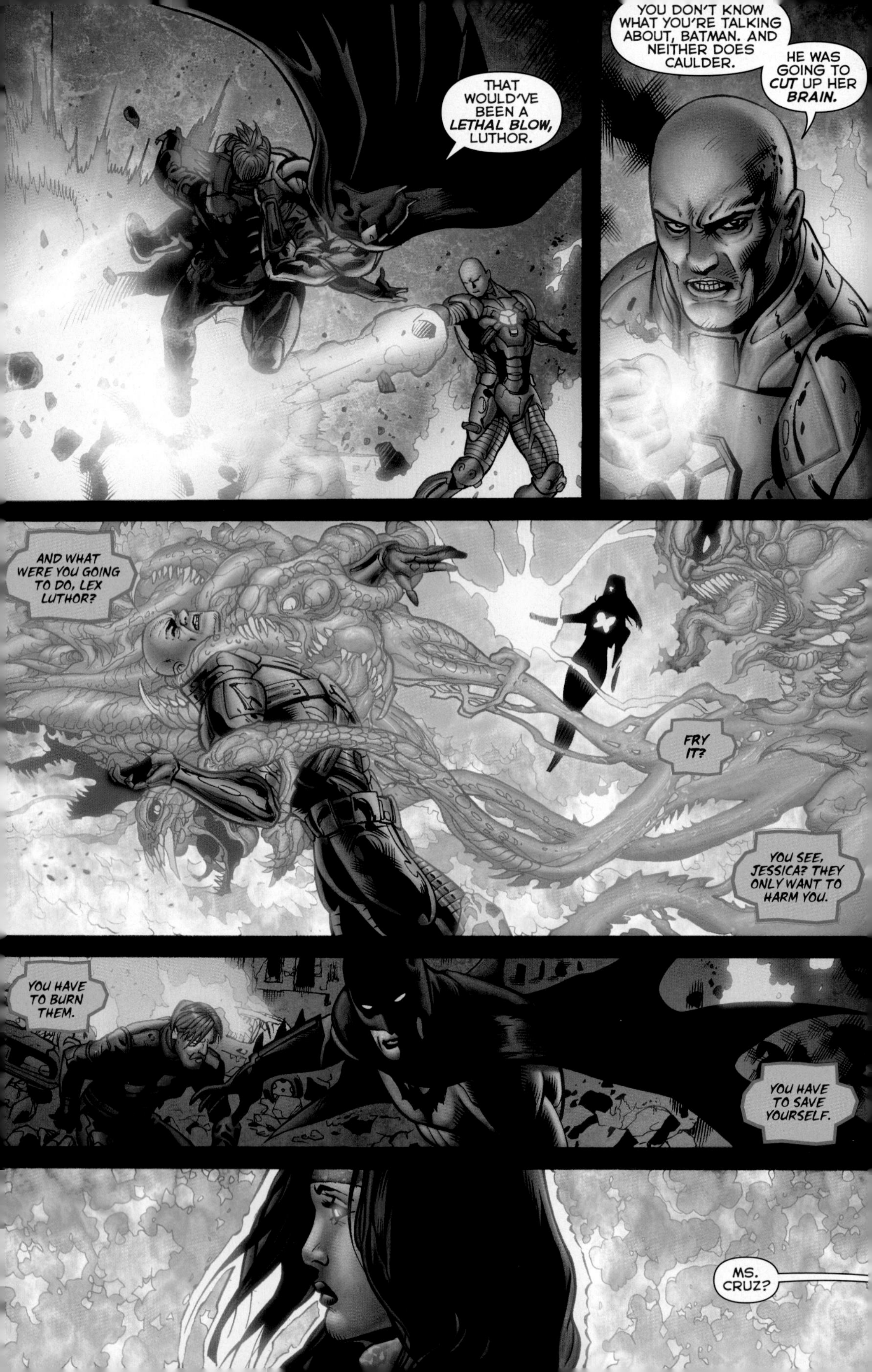
THAT WOULD'VE BEEN A LETHAL BLOW, LUTHOR.
YOU DON'T KNOW WHAT YOU'RE TALKING ABOUT, BATMAN. AND NEITHER DOES CAULDER.
HE WAS GOING TO CUT UP HER BRAIN.
AND WHAT WERE YOU GOING TO DO, LEX LUTHOR?
FRY IT?
YOU SEE, JESSICA? THEY ONLY WANT TO HARM YOU.
YOU HAVE TO BURN THEM.
YOU HAVE TO SAVE YOURSELF.
MS. CRUZ?

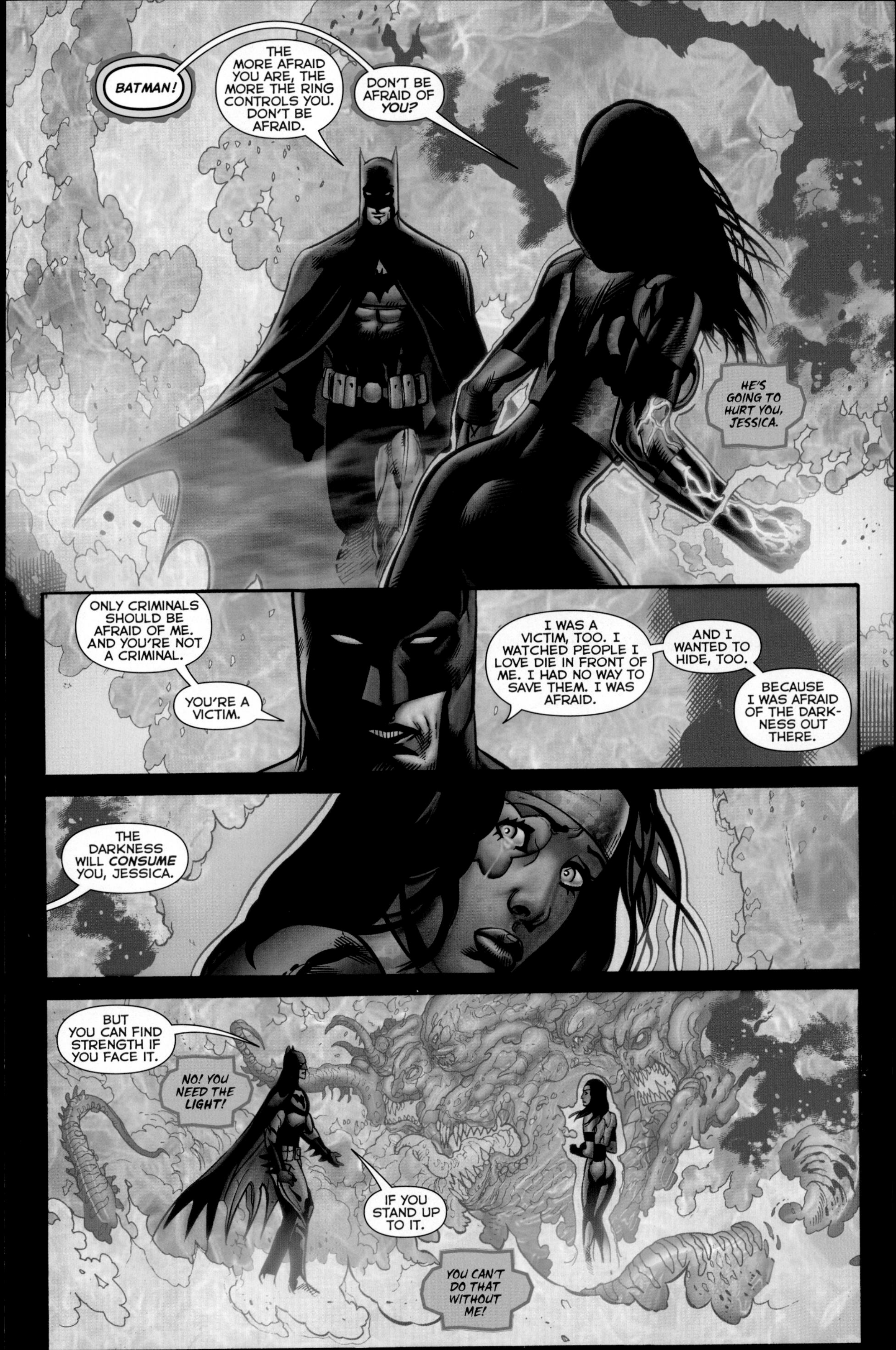

BATMAN!
THE MORE AFRAID YOU ARE, THE MORE THE RING CONTROLS YOU. DON'T BE AFRAID.
DON'T BE AFRAID OF YOU?
HE'S GOING TO HURT YOU, JESSICA.
ONLY CRIMINALS SHOULD BE AFRAID OF ME. AND YOU'RE NOT A CRIMINAL.
YOU'RE A VICTIM.
I WAS A VICTIM, TOO. I WATCHED PEOPLE I LOVE DIE IN FRONT OF ME. I HAD NO WAY TO SAVE THEM. I WAS AFRAID.
AND I WANTED TO HIDE, TOO.
BECAUSE I WAS AFRAID OF THE DARK-NESS OUT THERE.
THE DARKNESS WILL CONSUME YOU, JESSICA.
BUT YOU CAN FIND STRENGTH IF YOU FACE IT.
NO! YOU NEED THE LIGHT!
IF YOU STAND UP TO IT.
YOU CAN'T DO THAT WITHOUT ME!

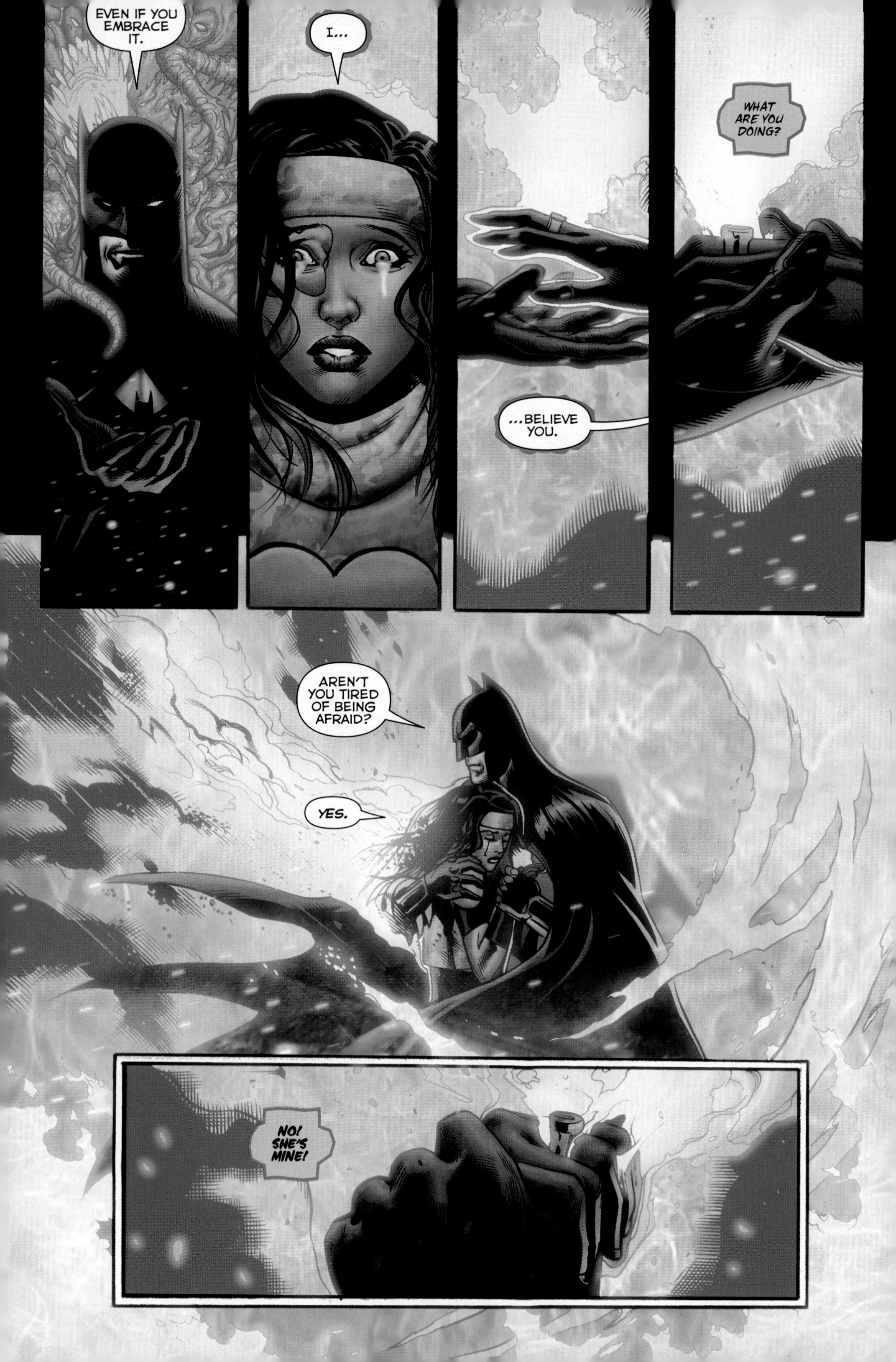
EVEN IF YOU EMBRACE IT.
I...
...BELIEVE YOU.
WHAT ARE YOU DOING?
AREN'T YOU TIRED OF BEING AFRAID?
YES.
NO! SHE'S MINE!

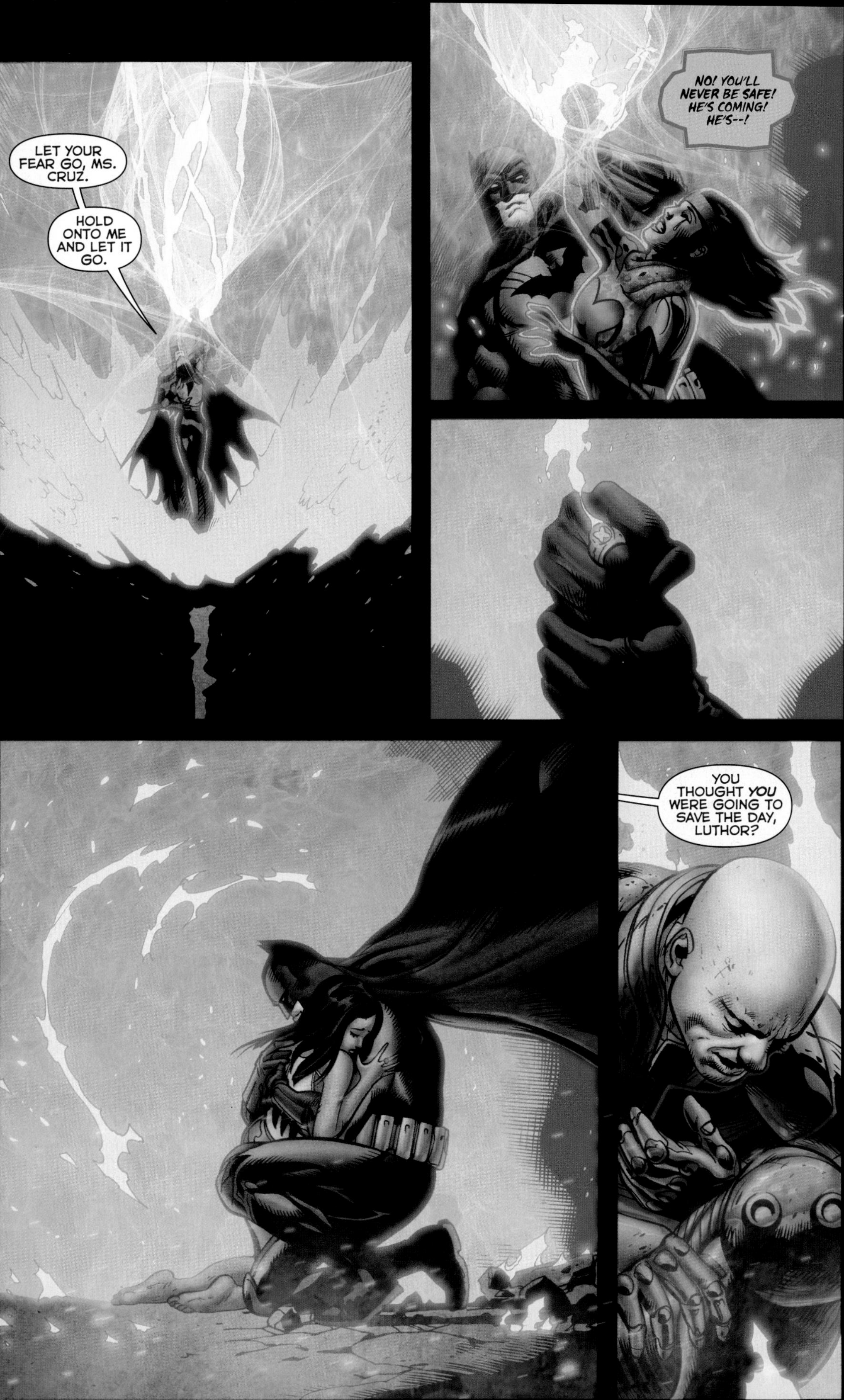
LET YOUR FEAR GO, MS. CRUZ.
HOLD ONTO ME AND LET IT GO.
NO! YOU'LL NEVER BE SAFE! HE'S COMING! HE'S--!
YOU THOUGHT *YOU* WERE GOING TO SAVE THE DAY, LUTHOR?

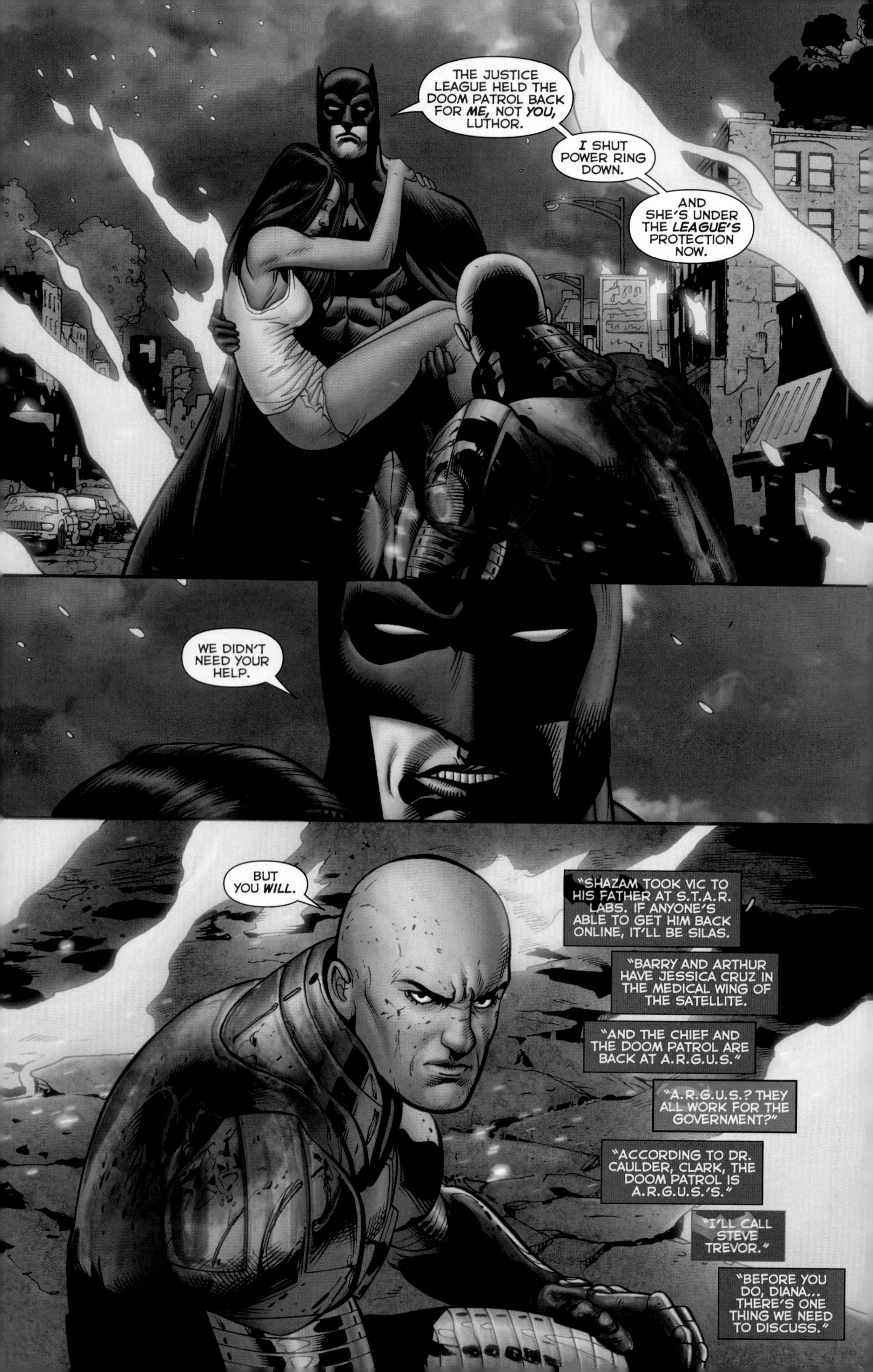
THE JUSTICE LEAGUE HELD THE DOOM PATROL BACK FOR *ME,* NOT *YOU,* LUTHOR.
I SHUT POWER RING DOWN.
AND SHE'S UNDER THE *LEAGUE'S* PROTECTION NOW.
WE DIDN'T NEED YOUR HELP.
BUT YOU *WILL.*
"SHAZAM TOOK VIC TO HIS FATHER AT S.T.A.R. LABS. IF ANYONE'S ABLE TO GET HIM BACK ONLINE, IT'LL BE SILAS.
"BARRY AND ARTHUR HAVE JESSICA CRUZ IN THE MEDICAL WING OF THE SATELLITE.
"AND THE CHIEF AND THE DOOM PATROL ARE BACK AT A.R.G.U.S."
"A.R.G.U.S.? THEY ALL WORK FOR THE GOVERNMENT?"
"ACCORDING TO DR. CAULDER, CLARK, THE DOOM PATROL IS A.R.G.U.S.'S."
"I'LL CALL STEVE TREVOR."
"BEFORE YOU DO, DIANA... THERE'S ONE THING WE NEED TO DISCUSS."

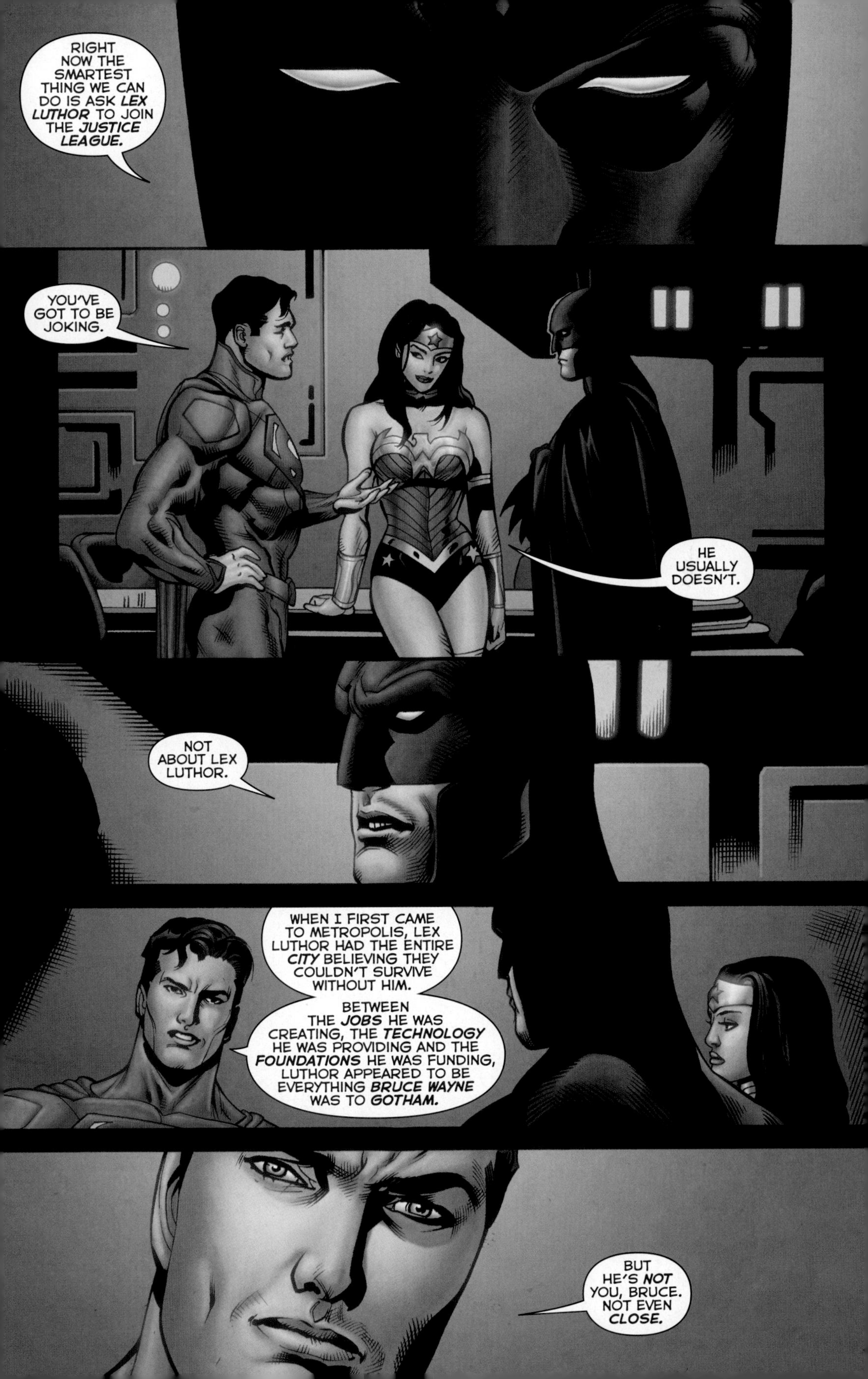
RIGHT NOW THE SMARTEST THING WE CAN DO IS ASK LEX LUTHOR TO JOIN THE JUSTICE LEAGUE.
YOU'VE GOT TO BE JOKING.
HE USUALLY DOESN'T.
NOT ABOUT LEX LUTHOR.
WHEN I FIRST CAME TO METROPOLIS, LEX LUTHOR HAD THE ENTIRE CITY BELIEVING THEY COULDN'T SURVIVE WITHOUT HIM.
BETWEEN THE JOBS HE WAS CREATING, THE TECHNOLOGY HE WAS PROVIDING AND THE FOUNDATIONS HE WAS FUNDING, LUTHOR APPEARED TO BE EVERYTHING BRUCE WAYNE WAS TO GOTHAM.
BUT HE'S NOT YOU, BRUCE. NOT EVEN CLOSE.

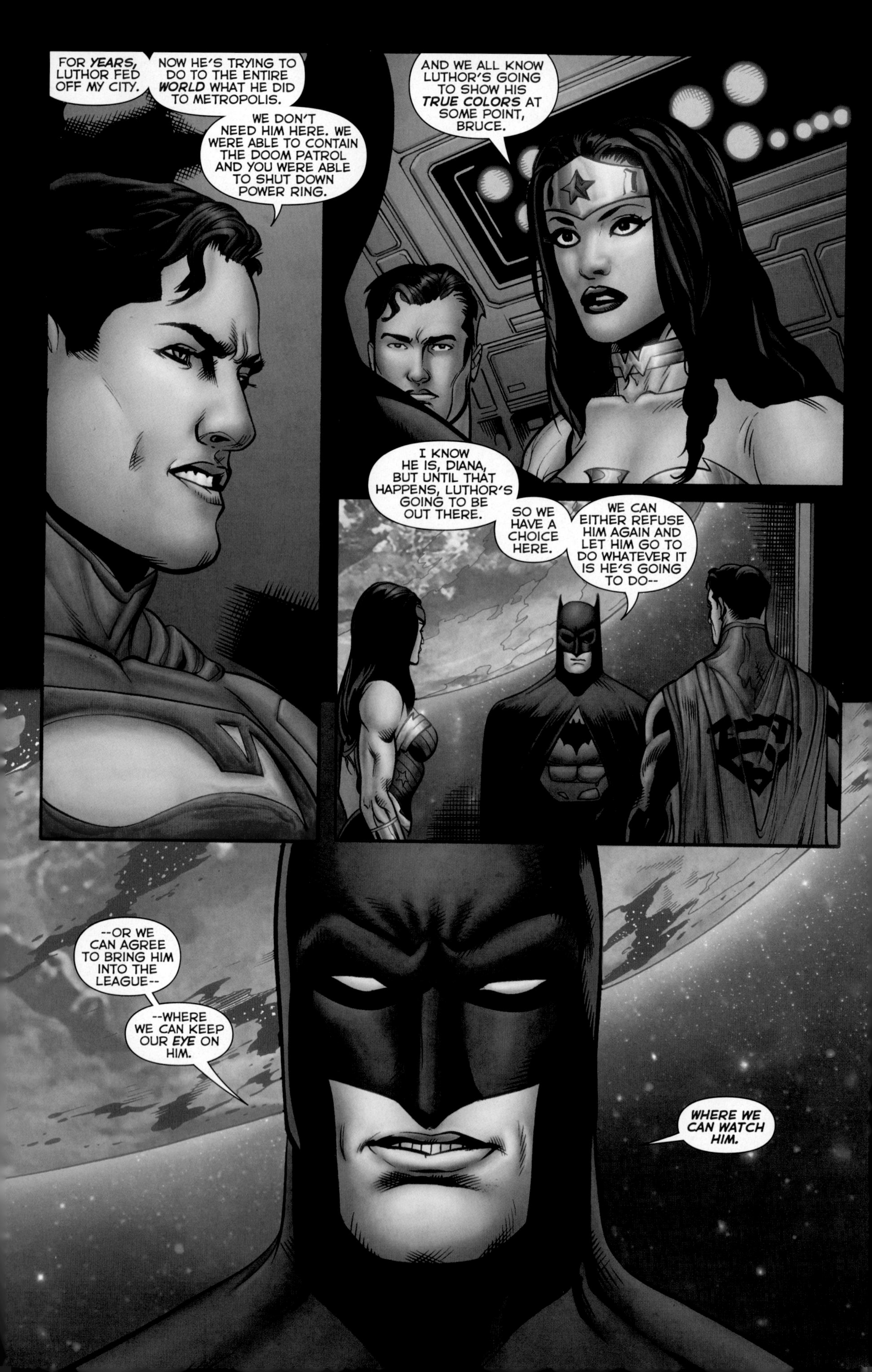
FOR YEARS, LUTHOR FED OFF MY CITY.
NOW HE'S TRYING TO DO TO THE ENTIRE WORLD WHAT HE DID TO METROPOLIS.
WE DON'T NEED HIM HERE. WE WERE ABLE TO CONTAIN THE DOOM PATROL AND YOU WERE ABLE TO SHUT DOWN POWER RING.
AND WE ALL KNOW LUTHOR'S GOING TO SHOW HIS TRUE COLORS AT SOME POINT, BRUCE.
I KNOW HE IS, DIANA, BUT UNTIL THAT HAPPENS, LUTHOR'S GOING TO BE OUT THERE.
SO WE HAVE A CHOICE HERE.
WE CAN EITHER REFUSE HIM AGAIN AND LET HIM GO TO DO WHATEVER IT IS HE'S GOING TO DO--
--OR WE CAN AGREE TO BRING HIM INTO THE LEAGUE--
--WHERE WE CAN KEEP OUR EYE ON HIM.
WHERE WE CAN WATCH HIM.

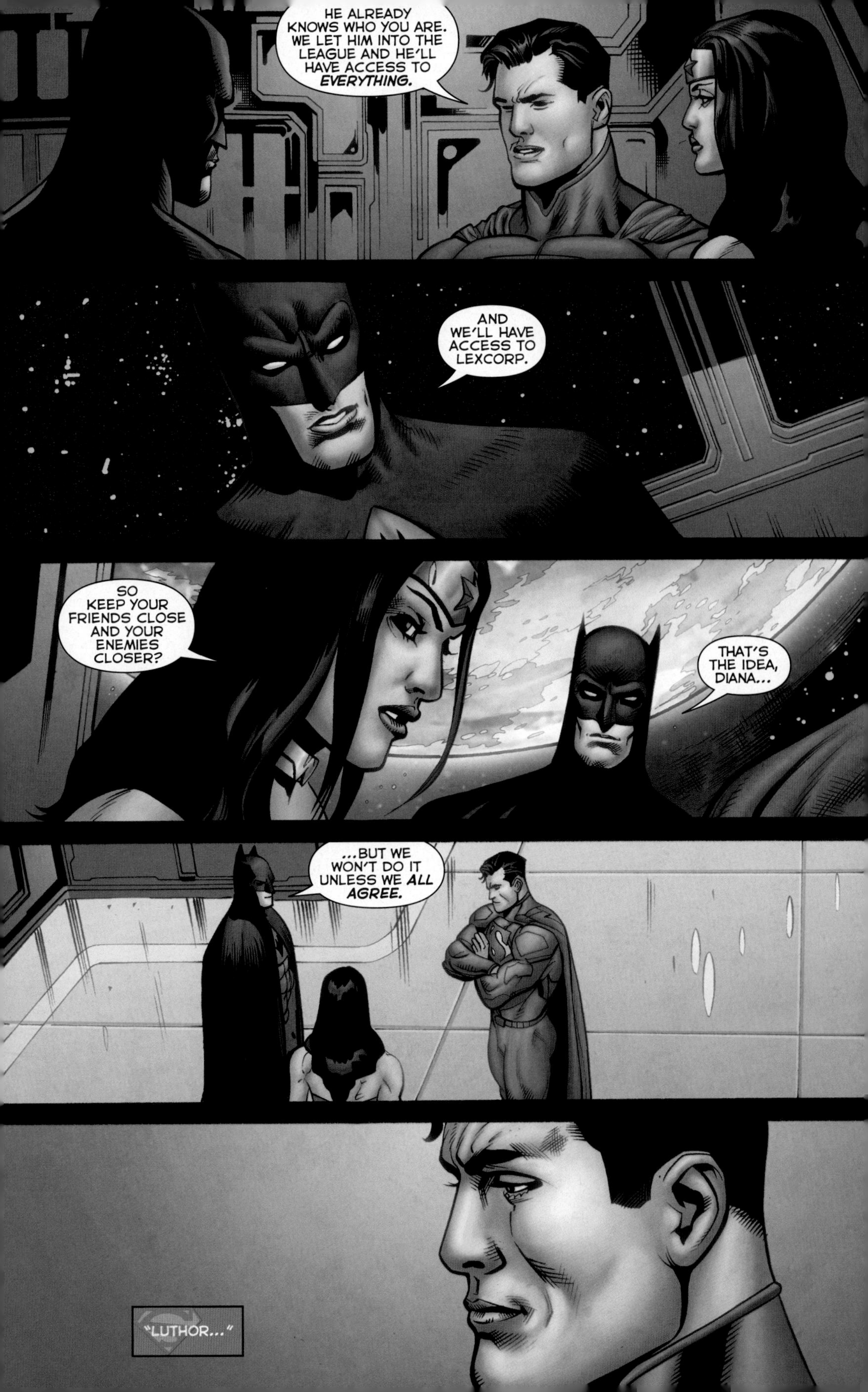
HE ALREADY KNOWS WHO YOU ARE. WE LET HIM INTO THE LEAGUE AND HE'LL HAVE ACCESS TO *EVERYTHING.*
AND WE'LL HAVE ACCESS TO LEXCORP.
SO KEEP YOUR FRIENDS CLOSE AND YOUR ENEMIES CLOSER?
THAT'S THE IDEA, DIANA...
...BUT WE WON'T DO IT UNLESS WE *ALL AGREE.*
"LUTHOR..."

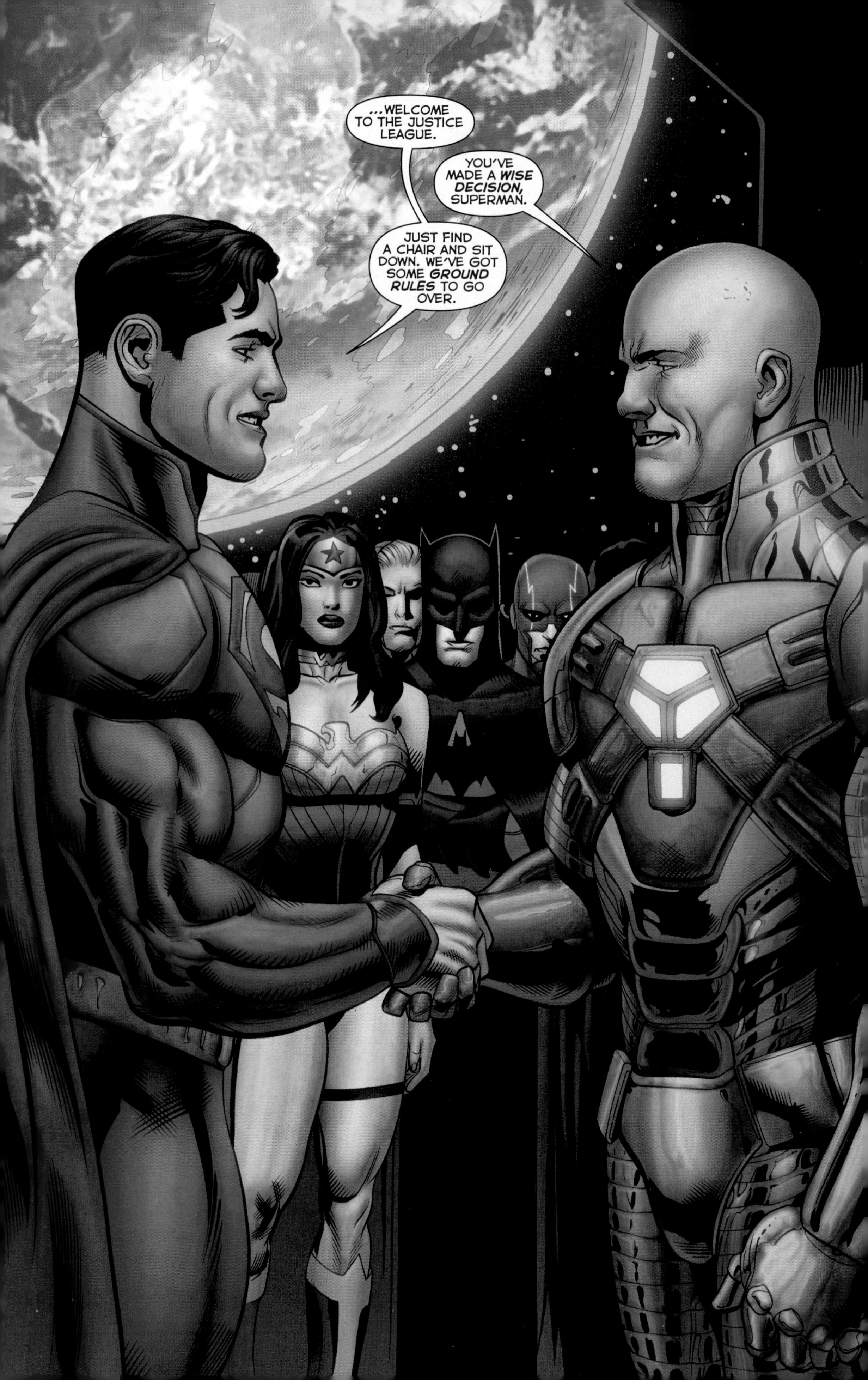

...WELCOME TO THE JUSTICE LEAGUE.
JUST FIND A CHAIR AND SIT DOWN. WE'VE GOT SOME GROUND RULES TO GO OVER.
YOU'VE MADE A WISE DECISION, SUPERMAN.

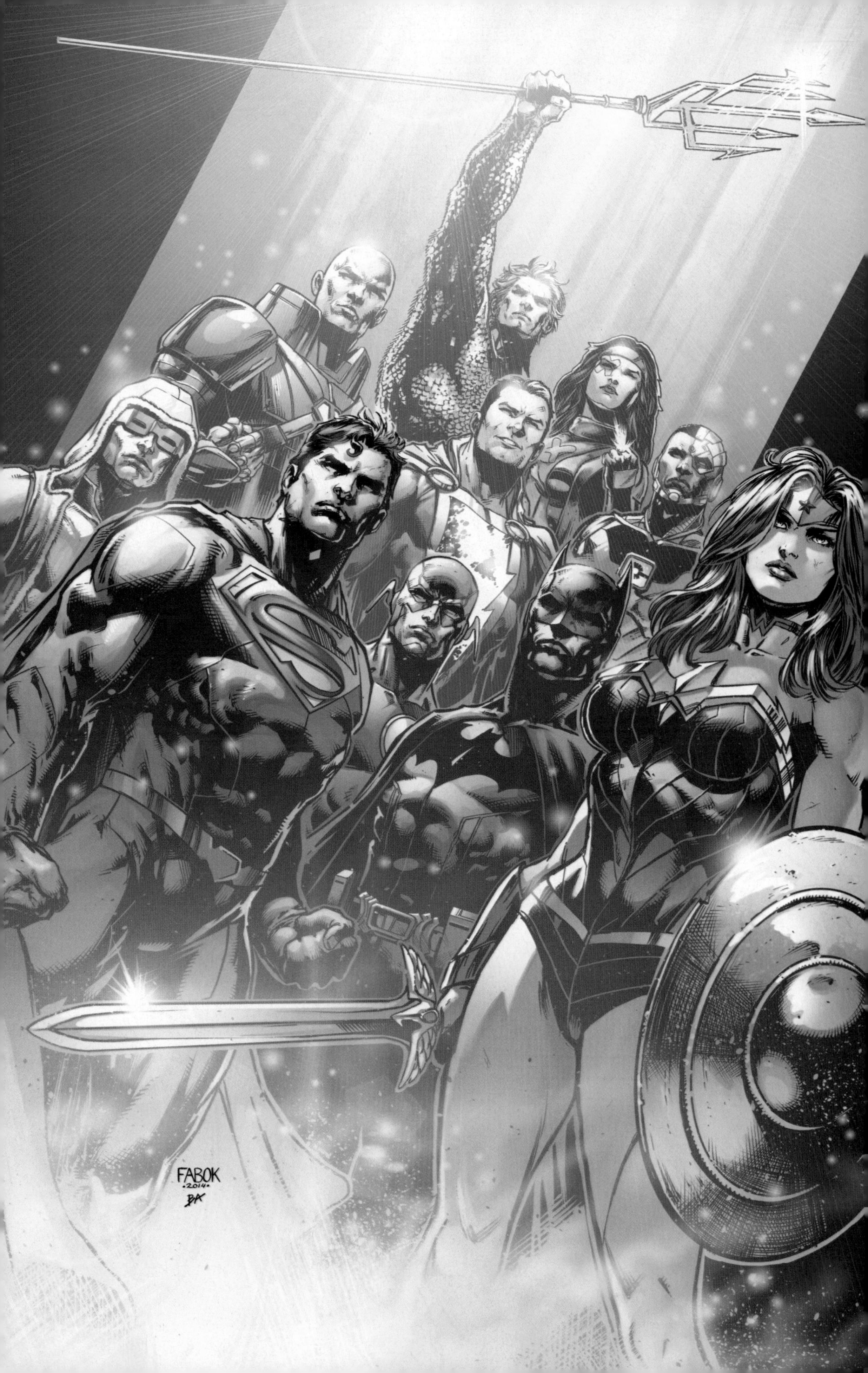
FABOK
•2014•
BA

INJUSTICE LEAGUE EPILOGUE
UNLIKELY ALLIES

GEOFF JOHNS writer **SCOTT KOLINS** artist **ANDREW DALHOUSE** colorist
JASON FABOK & BRAD ANDERSON cover artists

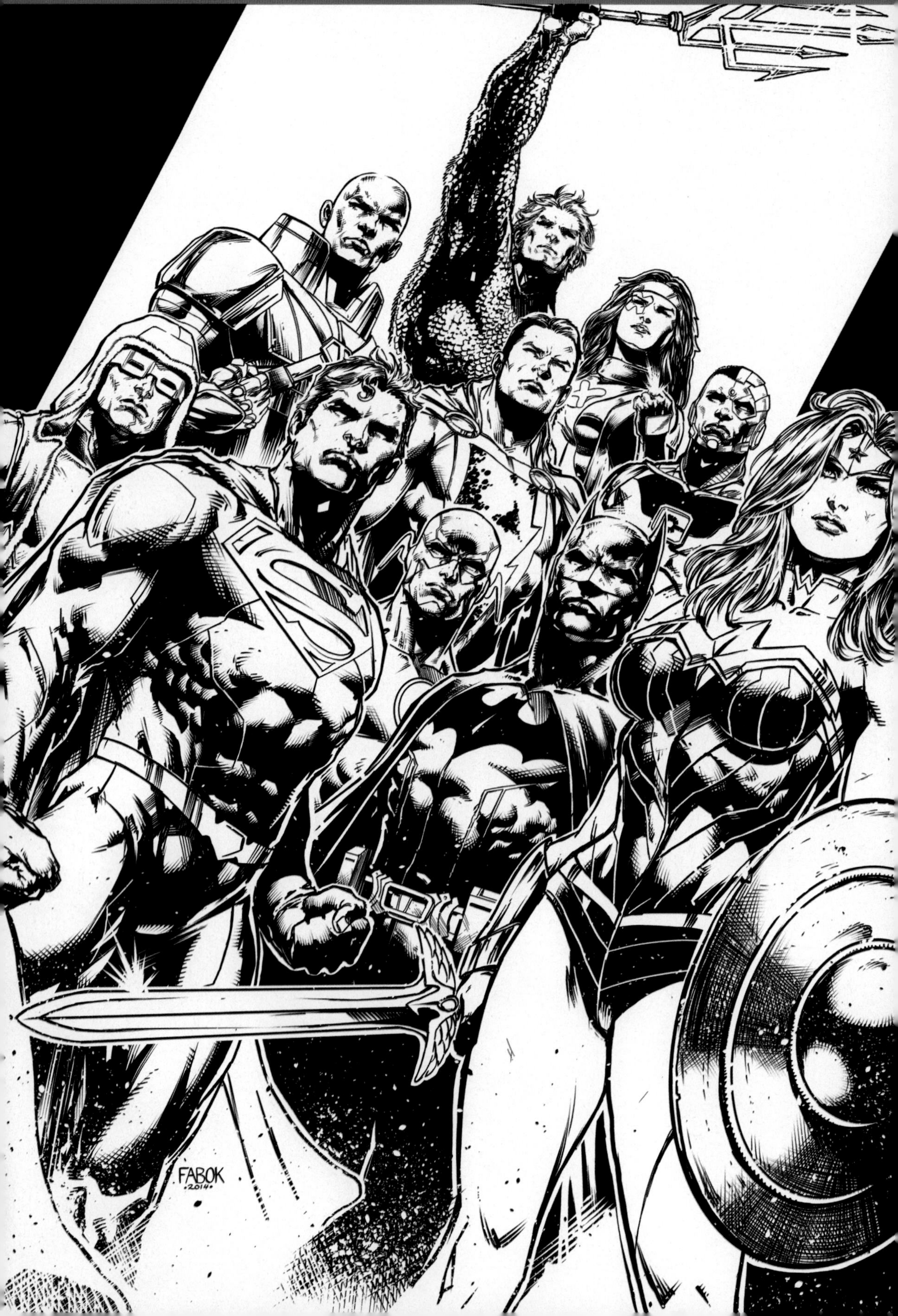
FABOK
2014

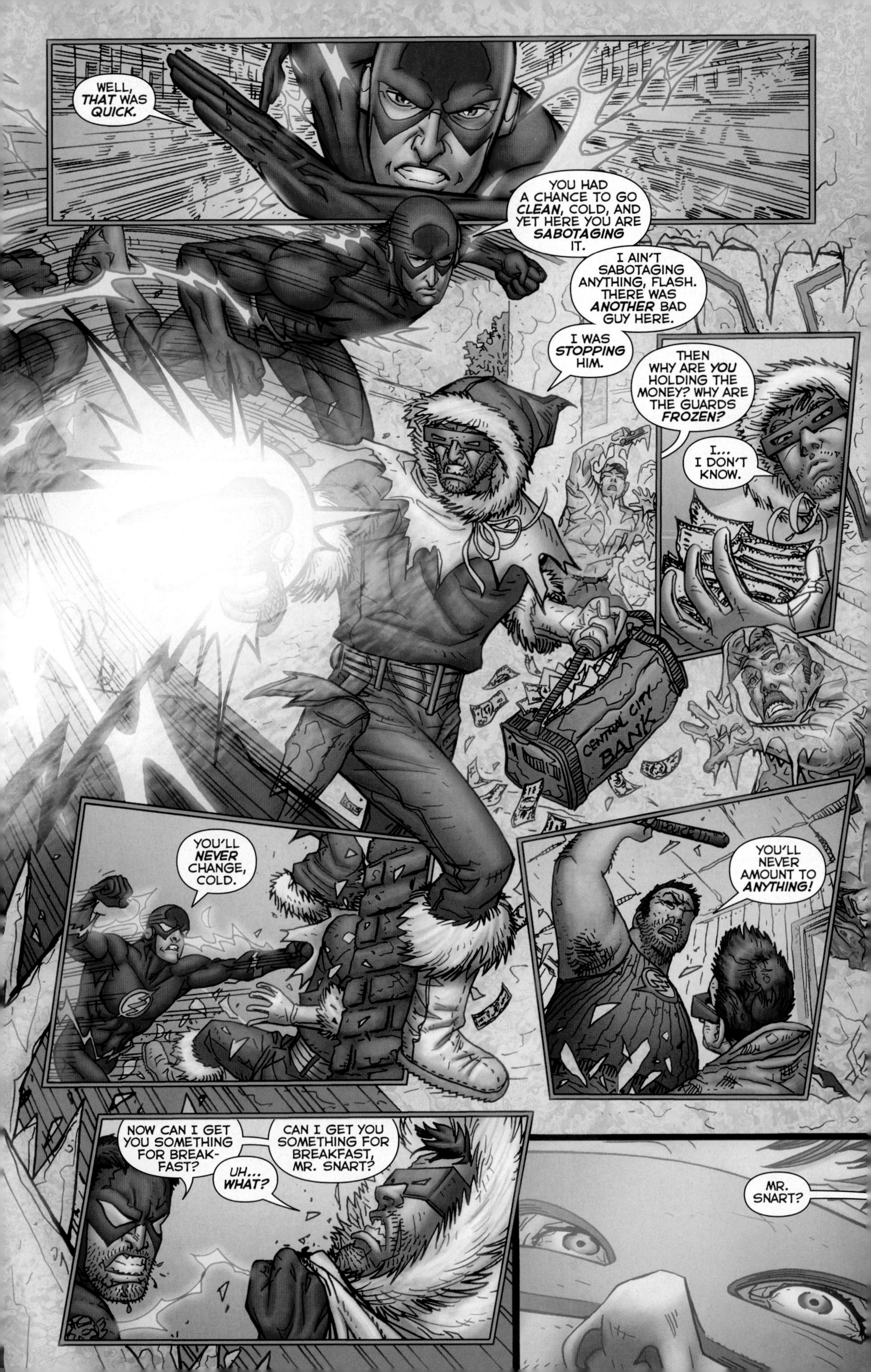
WELL, THAT WAS QUICK.
YOU HAD A CHANCE TO GO CLEAN, COLD, AND YET HERE YOU ARE SABOTAGING IT.
I AIN'T SABOTAGING ANYTHING, FLASH. THERE WAS ANOTHER BAD GUY HERE.
I WAS STOPPING HIM.
THEN WHY ARE YOU HOLDING THE MONEY? WHY ARE THE GUARDS FROZEN?
I... I DON'T KNOW.
CENTRAL CITY BANK
YOU'LL NEVER CHANGE, COLD.
YOU'LL NEVER AMOUNT TO ANYTHING!
NOW CAN I GET YOU SOMETHING FOR BREAK-FAST?
CAN I GET YOU SOMETHING FOR BREAKFAST, MR. SNART?
UH... WHAT?
MR. SNART?

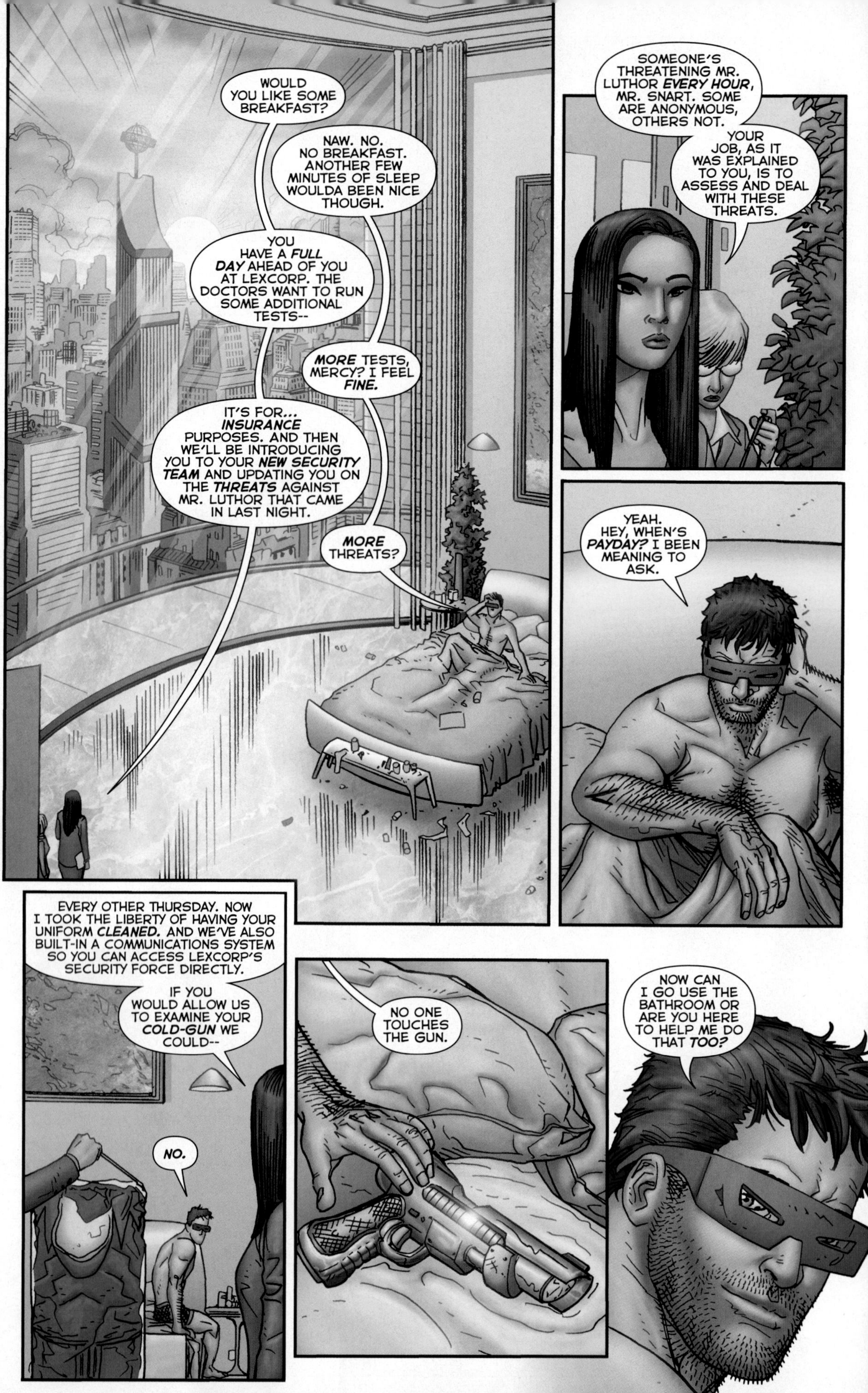
WOULD YOU LIKE SOME BREAKFAST?
NAW. NO. NO BREAKFAST. ANOTHER FEW MINUTES OF SLEEP WOULDA BEEN NICE THOUGH.
YOU HAVE A FULL DAY AHEAD OF YOU AT LEXCORP. THE DOCTORS WANT TO RUN SOME ADDITIONAL TESTS--
MORE TESTS, MERCY? I FEEL FINE.
IT'S FOR... INSURANCE PURPOSES. AND THEN WE'LL BE INTRODUCING YOU TO YOUR NEW SECURITY TEAM AND UPDATING YOU ON THE THREATS AGAINST MR. LUTHOR THAT CAME IN LAST NIGHT.
MORE THREATS?
SOMEONE'S THREATENING MR. LUTHOR EVERY HOUR, MR. SNART. SOME ARE ANONYMOUS, OTHERS NOT.
YOUR JOB, AS IT WAS EXPLAINED TO YOU, IS TO ASSESS AND DEAL WITH THESE THREATS.
YEAH. HEY, WHEN'S PAYDAY? I BEEN MEANING TO ASK.
EVERY OTHER THURSDAY. NOW I TOOK THE LIBERTY OF HAVING YOUR UNIFORM CLEANED. AND WE'VE ALSO BUILT-IN A COMMUNICATIONS SYSTEM SO YOU CAN ACCESS LEXCORP'S SECURITY FORCE DIRECTLY.
IF YOU WOULD ALLOW US TO EXAMINE YOUR COLD-GUN WE COULD--
NO.
NO ONE TOUCHES THE GUN.
NOW CAN I GO USE THE BATHROOM OR ARE YOU HERE TO HELP ME DO THAT TOO?

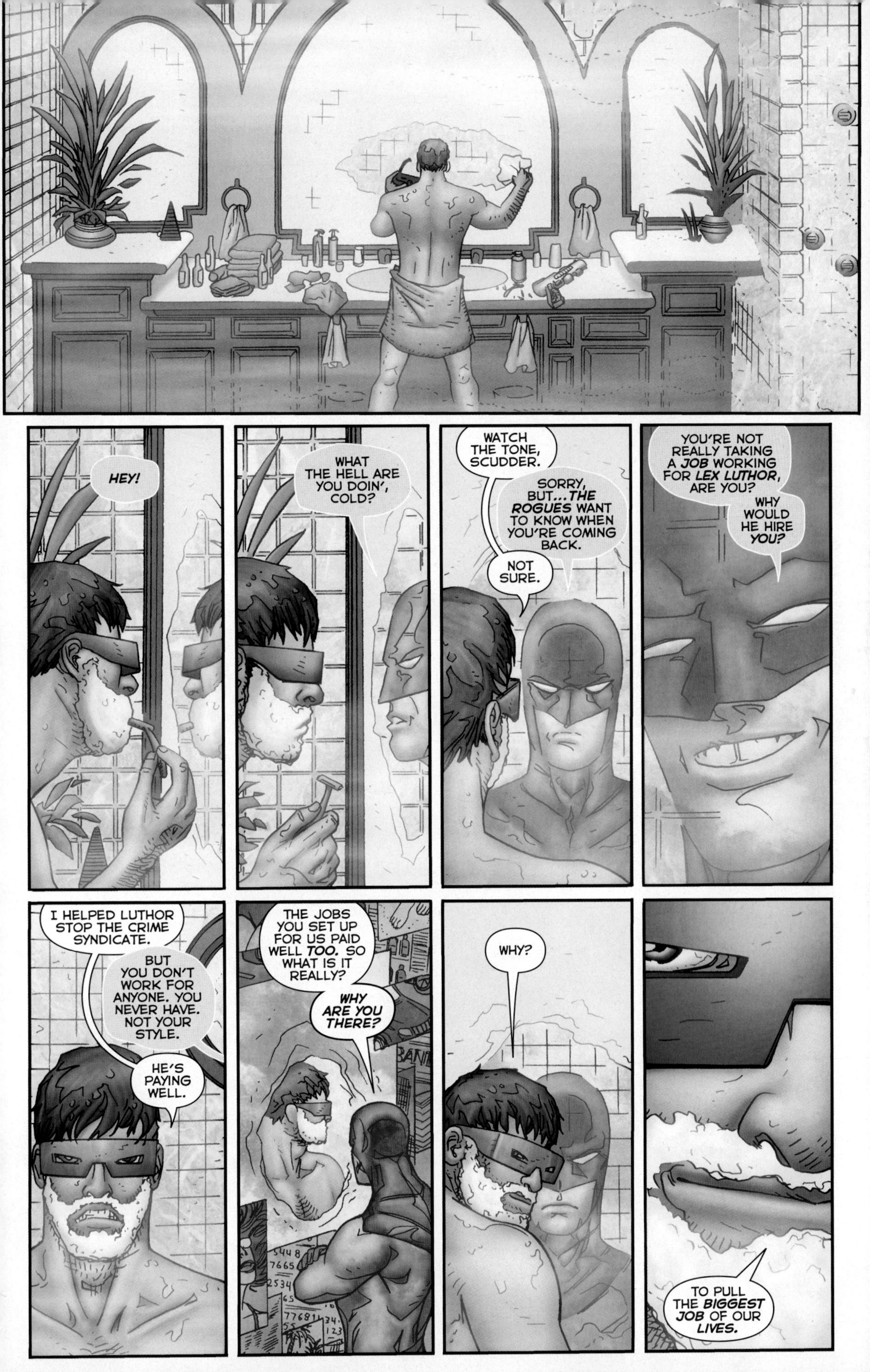
HEY!
WHAT THE HELL ARE YOU DOIN', COLD?
WATCH THE TONE, SCUDDER.
SORRY, BUT...THE ROGUES WANT TO KNOW WHEN YOU'RE COMING BACK.
NOT SURE.
YOU'RE NOT REALLY TAKING A JOB WORKING FOR LEX LUTHOR, ARE YOU?
WHY WOULD HE HIRE YOU?
I HELPED LUTHOR STOP THE CRIME SYNDICATE.
BUT YOU DON'T WORK FOR ANYONE. YOU NEVER HAVE. NOT YOUR STYLE.
HE'S PAYING WELL.
THE JOBS YOU SET UP FOR US PAID WELL TOO. SO WHAT IS IT REALLY?
WHY ARE YOU THERE?
WHY?
TO PULL THE BIGGEST JOB OF OUR LIVES.

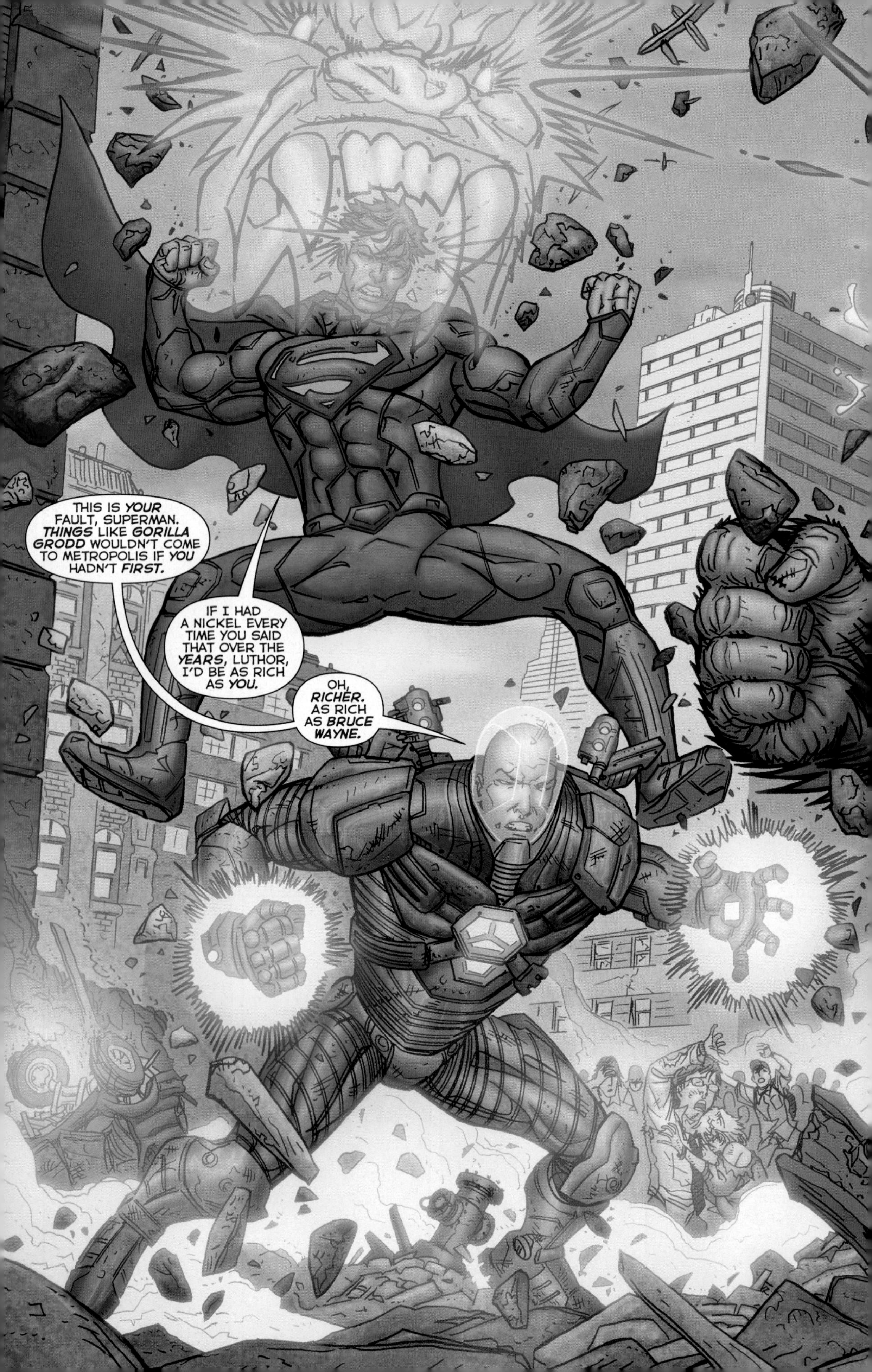
THIS IS YOUR FAULT, SUPERMAN. THINGS LIKE GORILLA GRODD WOULDN'T COME TO METROPOLIS IF YOU HADN'T FIRST.
IF I HAD A NICKEL EVERY TIME YOU SAID THAT OVER THE YEARS, LUTHOR, I'D BE AS RICH AS YOU.
OH, RICHER. AS RICH AS BRUCE WAYNE.

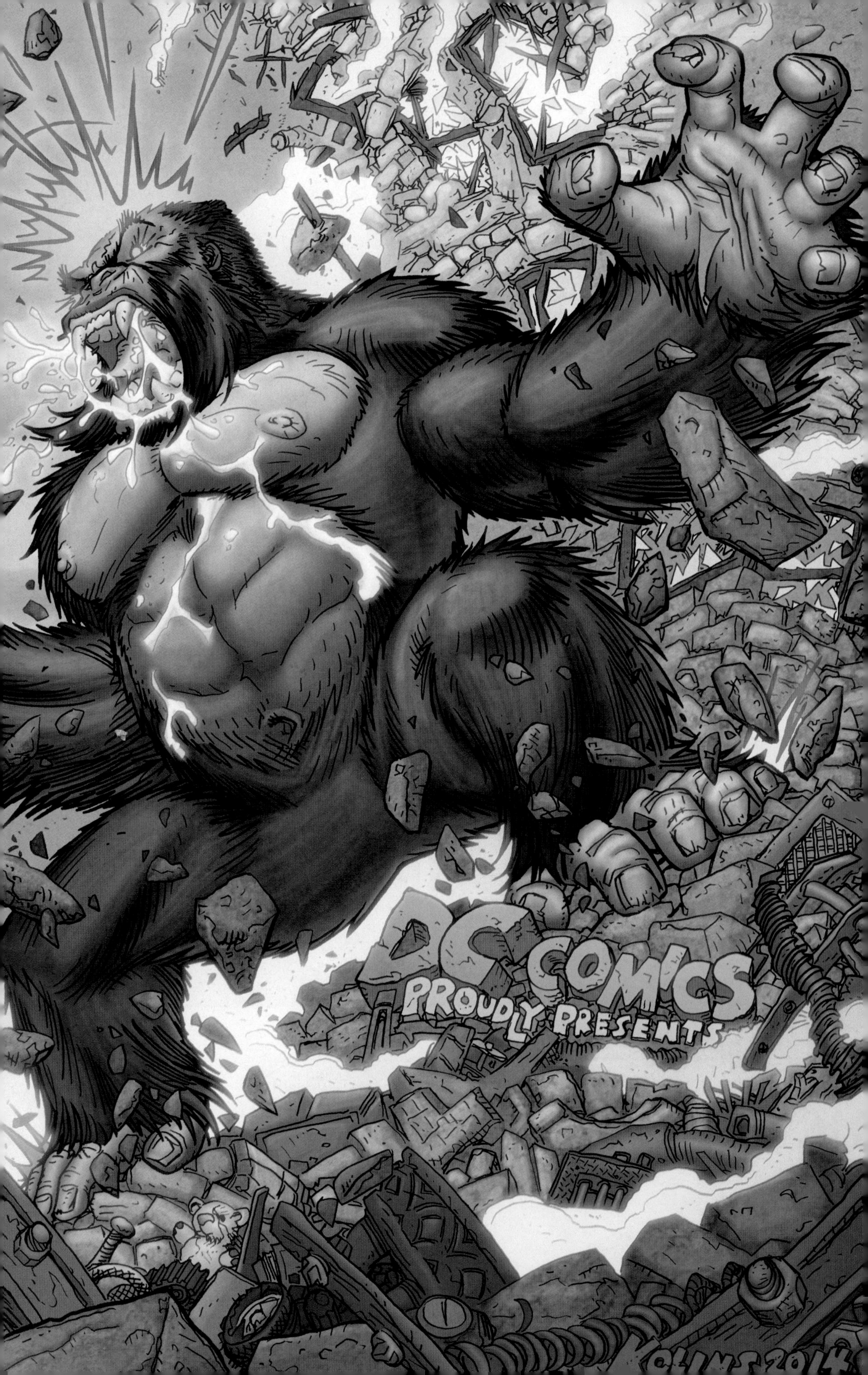
COMICS
PROUDLY PRESENTS

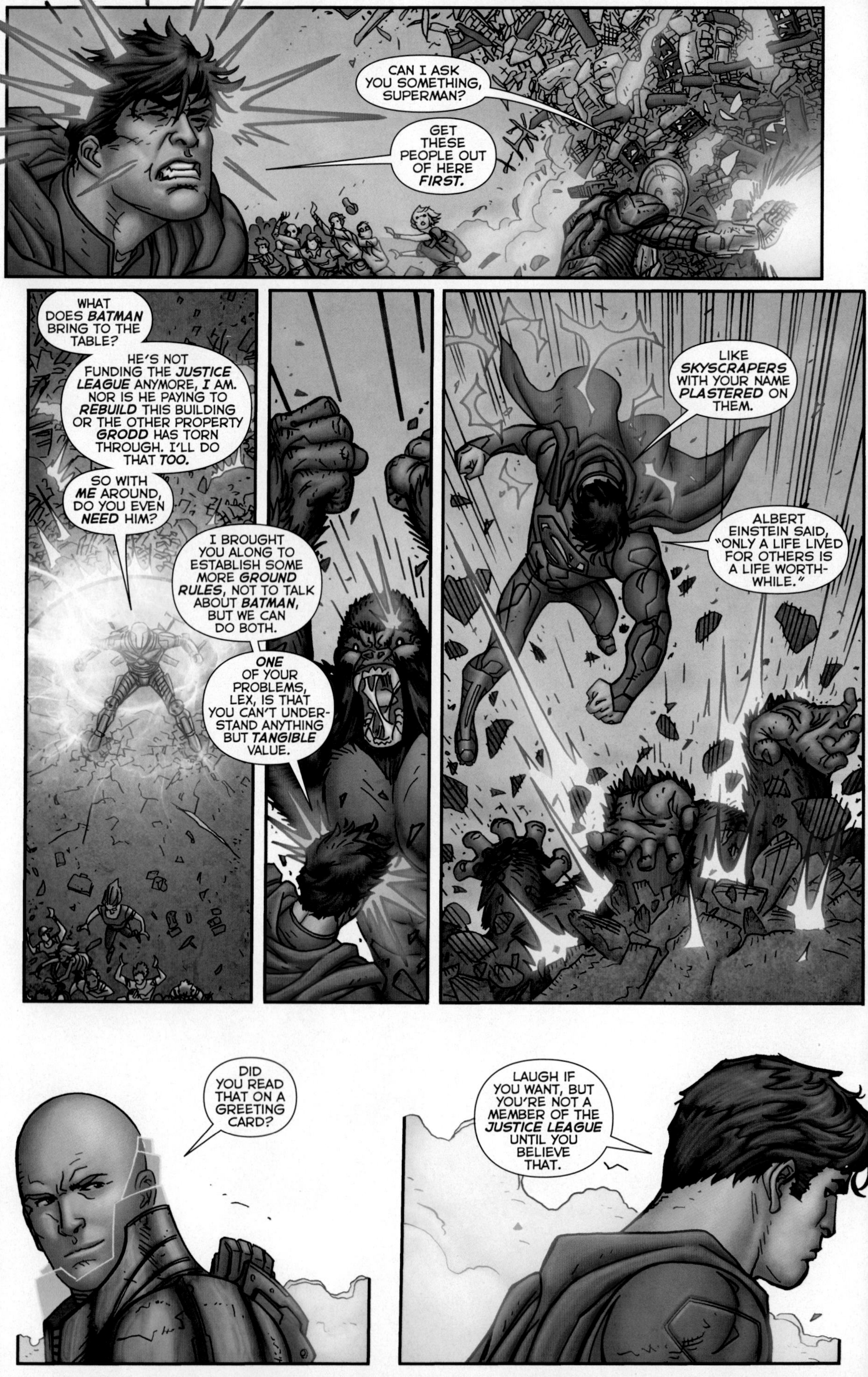
CAN I ASK YOU SOMETHING, SUPERMAN?
GET THESE PEOPLE OUT OF HERE FIRST.
WHAT DOES BATMAN BRING TO THE TABLE?
HE'S NOT FUNDING THE JUSTICE LEAGUE ANYMORE, I AM. NOR IS HE PAYING TO REBUILD THIS BUILDING OR THE OTHER PROPERTY GRODD HAS TORN THROUGH. I'LL DO THAT TOO.
SO WITH ME AROUND, DO YOU EVEN NEED HIM?
I BROUGHT YOU ALONG TO ESTABLISH SOME MORE GROUND RULES, NOT TO TALK ABOUT BATMAN, BUT WE CAN DO BOTH.
ONE OF YOUR PROBLEMS, LEX, IS THAT YOU CAN'T UNDERSTAND ANYTHING BUT TANGIBLE VALUE.
LIKE SKYSCRAPERS WITH YOUR NAME PLASTERED ON THEM.
ALBERT EINSTEIN SAID, "ONLY A LIFE LIVED FOR OTHERS IS A LIFE WORTHWHILE."
DID YOU READ THAT ON A GREETING CARD?
LAUGH IF YOU WANT, BUT YOU'RE NOT A MEMBER OF THE JUSTICE LEAGUE UNTIL YOU BELIEVE THAT.

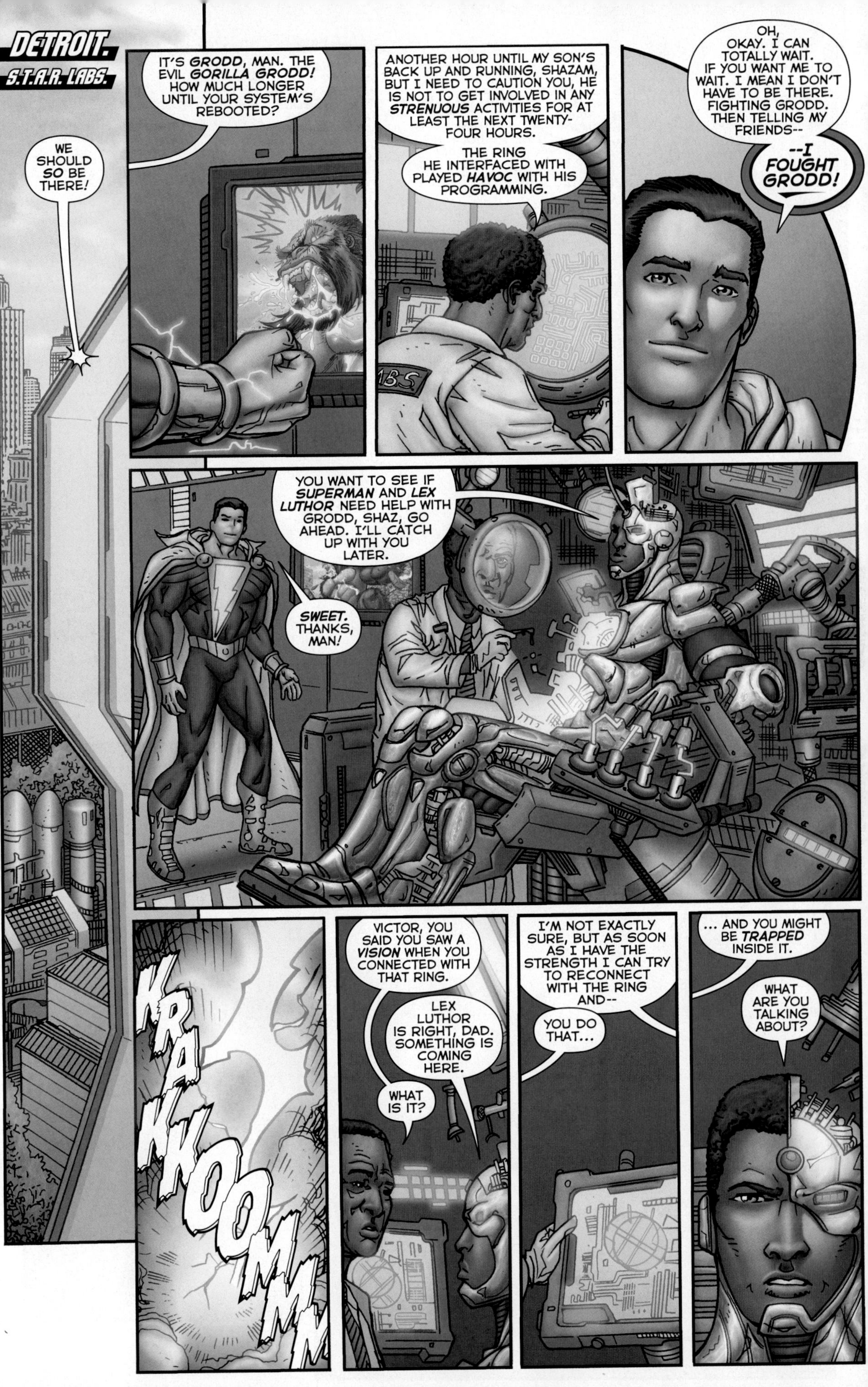
DETROIT.
S.T.A.R. LABS.
WE SHOULD SO BE THERE!
IT'S GRODD, MAN. THE EVIL GORILLA GRODD! HOW MUCH LONGER UNTIL YOUR SYSTEM'S REBOOTED?
ANOTHER HOUR UNTIL MY SON'S BACK UP AND RUNNING, SHAZAM, BUT I NEED TO CAUTION YOU, HE IS NOT TO GET INVOLVED IN ANY STRENUOUS ACTIVITIES FOR AT LEAST THE NEXT TWENTY-FOUR HOURS.
THE RING HE INTERFACED WITH PLAYED HAVOC WITH HIS PROGRAMMING.
OH, OKAY. I CAN TOTALLY WAIT. IF YOU WANT ME TO WAIT. I MEAN I DON'T HAVE TO BE THERE. FIGHTING GRODD. THEN TELLING MY FRIENDS--
--I FOUGHT GRODD!
YOU WANT TO SEE IF SUPERMAN AND LEX LUTHOR NEED HELP WITH GRODD, SHAZ, GO AHEAD. I'LL CATCH UP WITH YOU LATER.
SWEET. THANKS, MAN!
KRAKKOOMMM
VICTOR, YOU SAID YOU SAW A VISION WHEN YOU CONNECTED WITH THAT RING.
WHAT IS IT?
LEX LUTHOR IS RIGHT, DAD. SOMETHING IS COMING HERE.
I'M NOT EXACTLY SURE, BUT AS SOON AS I HAVE THE STRENGTH I CAN TRY TO RECONNECT WITH THE RING AND--
YOU DO THAT...
... AND YOU MIGHT BE TRAPPED INSIDE IT.
WHAT ARE YOU TALKING ABOUT?

"WHAT'S *INSIDE* THAT *RING?*"

DO YOU WANT THE *GOOD NEWS* OR THE *BAD NEWS* FIRST, JESSICA?

I THINK WE'RE LOOKING AT THE *BAD NEWS.*

WELL, *YEAH.* WE *ARE.* YOU'RE WEARING ONE OF THE MOST *DANGEROUS WEAPONS* IN THE UNIVERSE RIGHT NOW.

WARNING

020659003502690220458 90035026SYMBIOTE

79299541 363668792 36366879

00882335 995414400 265988754

WARNING

3265988754211110033956874111100

THE JUSTICE LEAGUE WATCHTOWER.

WHAT'S THE *GOOD NEWS?*

UH...I DON'T KNOW YET, BUT I'LL FIND SOME. JUST STAY *CALM.*

"STAY CALM" AFTER A *GREEN LANTERN RING* POPS INTO MY APARTMENT AND MAKES ME *BURN DOWN* HALF OF SULLIVAN'S GULCH?

IF YOU AND THE JUSTICE LEAGUE HADN'T SHOWN UP...

...WHAT *ELSE* WOULD THIS THING HAVE MADE ME DO?

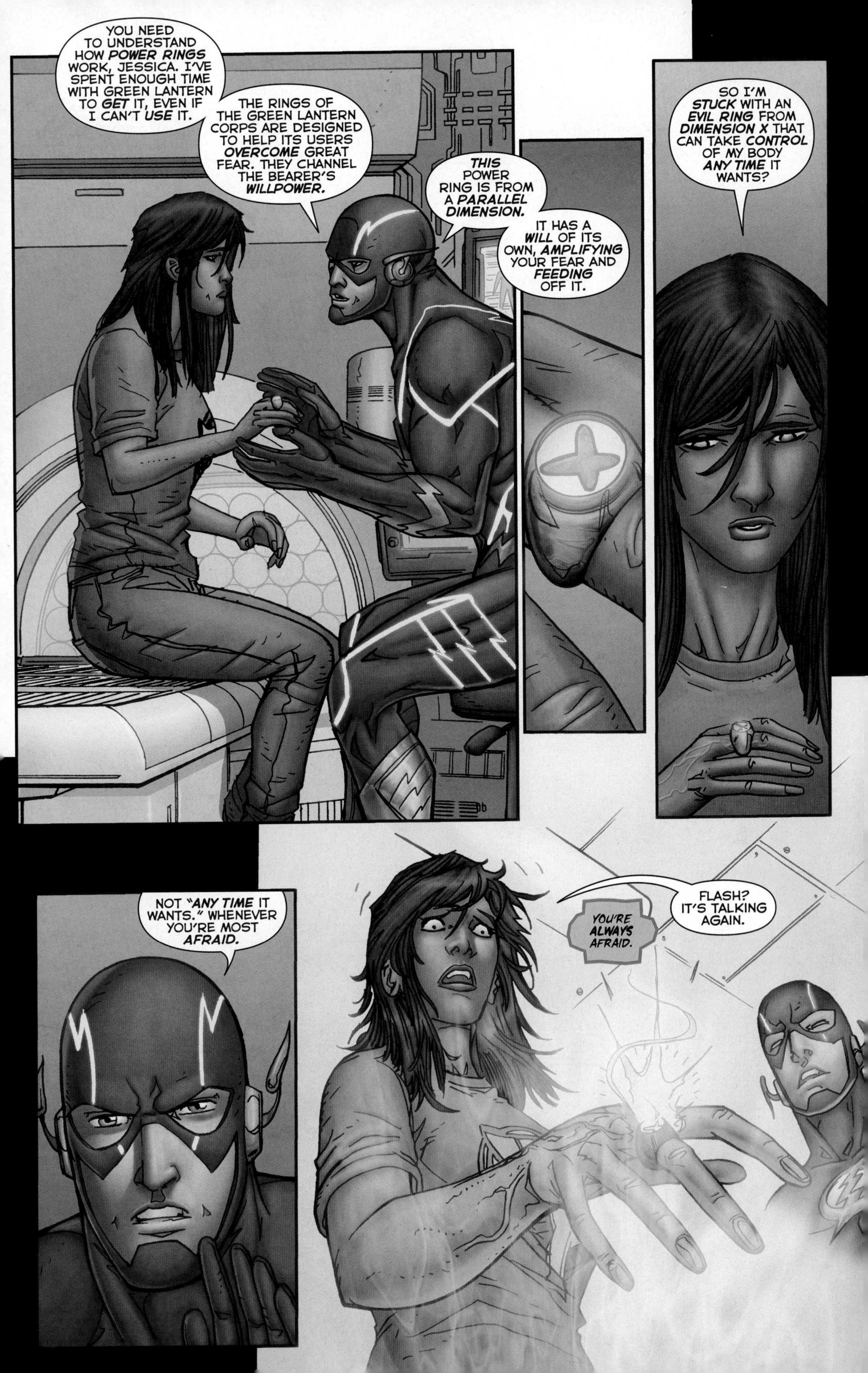

YOU NEED TO UNDERSTAND HOW POWER RINGS WORK, JESSICA. I'VE SPENT ENOUGH TIME WITH GREEN LANTERN TO GET IT, EVEN IF I CAN'T USE IT.
THE RINGS OF THE GREEN LANTERN CORPS ARE DESIGNED TO HELP ITS USERS OVERCOME GREAT FEAR. THEY CHANNEL THE BEARER'S WILLPOWER.
THIS POWER RING IS FROM A PARALLEL DIMENSION.
IT HAS A WILL OF ITS OWN, AMPLIFYING YOUR FEAR AND FEEDING OFF IT.
SO I'M STUCK WITH AN EVIL RING FROM DIMENSION X THAT CAN TAKE CONTROL OF MY BODY ANY TIME IT WANTS?
NOT "ANY TIME IT WANTS." WHENEVER YOU'RE MOST AFRAID.
YOU'RE ALWAYS AFRAID.
FLASH? IT'S TALKING AGAIN.

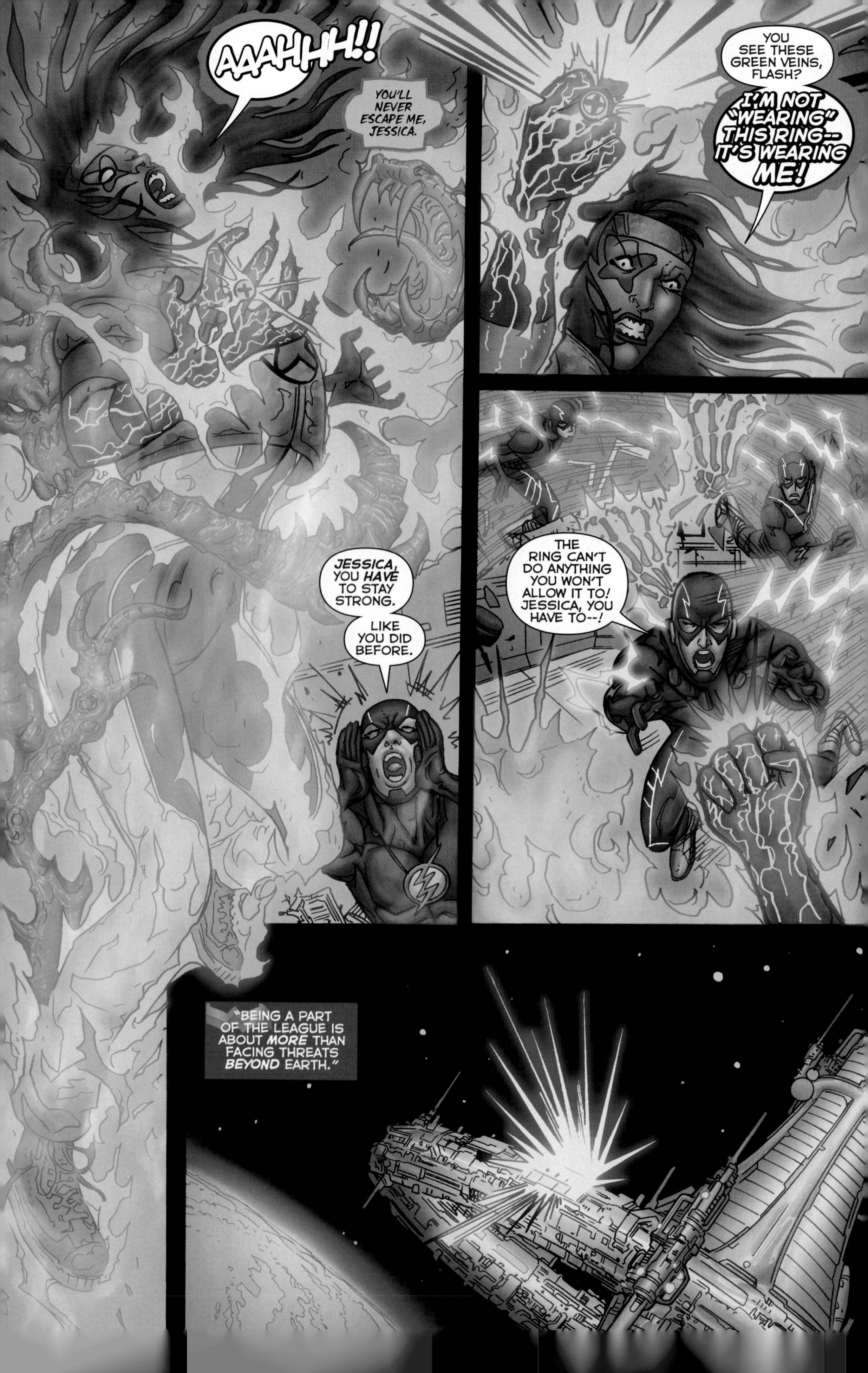
AAAHHH!!
YOU'LL NEVER ESCAPE ME, JESSICA.
YOU SEE THESE GREEN VEINS, FLASH?
I'M NOT "WEARING" THIS RING-- IT'S WEARING ME!
JESSICA, YOU HAVE TO STAY STRONG.
LIKE YOU DID BEFORE.
THE RING CAN'T DO ANYTHING YOU WON'T ALLOW IT TO! JESSICA, YOU HAVE TO--!
"BEING A PART OF THE LEAGUE IS ABOUT MORE THAN FACING THREATS BEYOND EARTH."

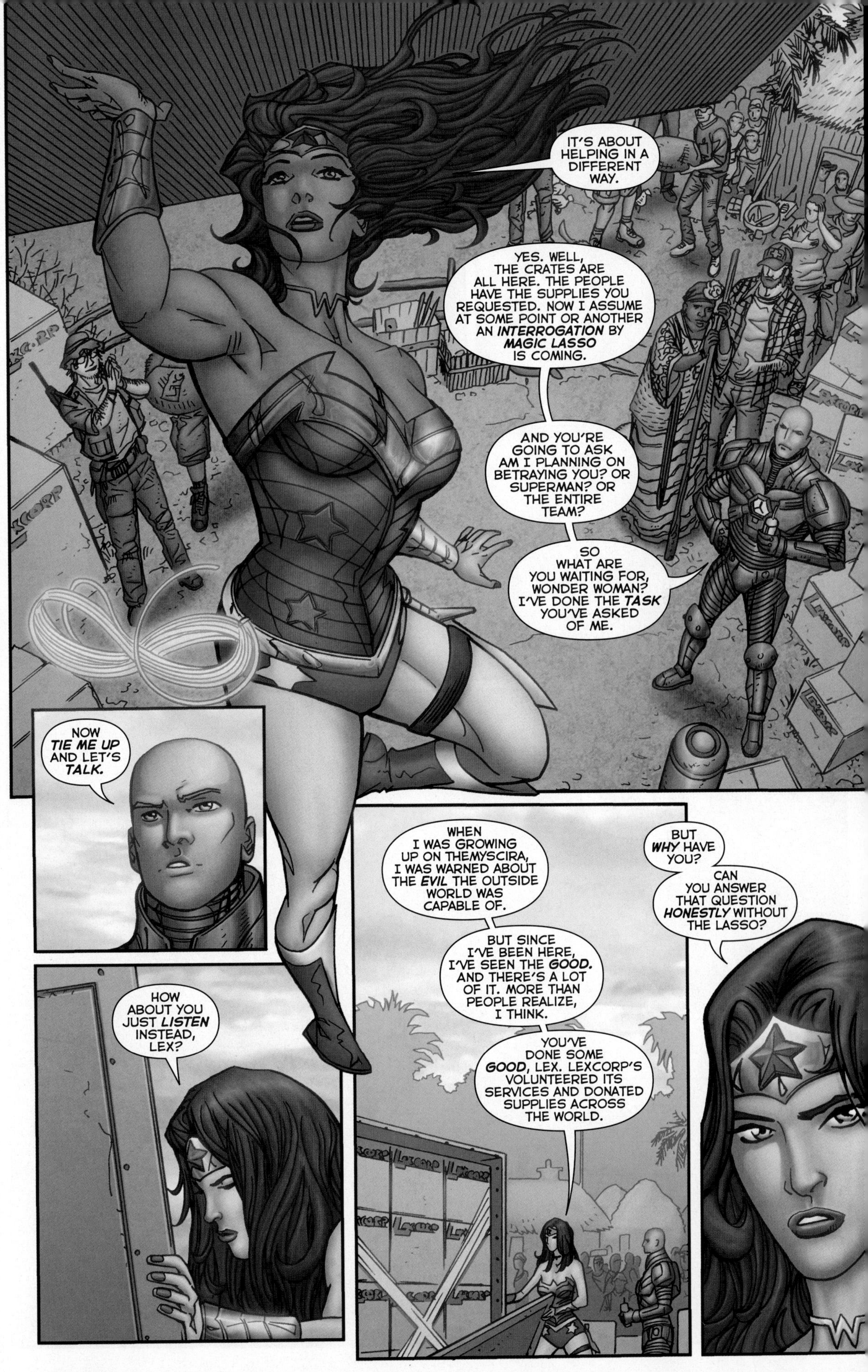
IT'S ABOUT HELPING IN A DIFFERENT WAY.
YES. WELL, THE CRATES ARE ALL HERE. THE PEOPLE HAVE THE SUPPLIES YOU REQUESTED. NOW I ASSUME AT SOME POINT OR ANOTHER AN INTERROGATION BY MAGIC LASSO IS COMING.
AND YOU'RE GOING TO ASK AM I PLANNING ON BETRAYING YOU? OR SUPERMAN? OR THE ENTIRE TEAM?
SO WHAT ARE YOU WAITING FOR, WONDER WOMAN? I'VE DONE THE TASK YOU'VE ASKED OF ME.
NOW TIE ME UP AND LET'S TALK.
HOW ABOUT YOU JUST LISTEN INSTEAD, LEX?
WHEN I WAS GROWING UP ON THEMYSCIRA, I WAS WARNED ABOUT THE EVIL THE OUTSIDE WORLD WAS CAPABLE OF.
BUT SINCE I'VE BEEN HERE, I'VE SEEN THE GOOD. AND THERE'S A LOT OF IT. MORE THAN PEOPLE REALIZE, I THINK.
YOU'VE DONE SOME GOOD, LEX. LEXCORP'S VOLUNTEERED ITS SERVICES AND DONATED SUPPLIES ACROSS THE WORLD.
BUT WHY HAVE YOU?
CAN YOU ANSWER THAT QUESTION HONESTLY WITHOUT THE LASSO?

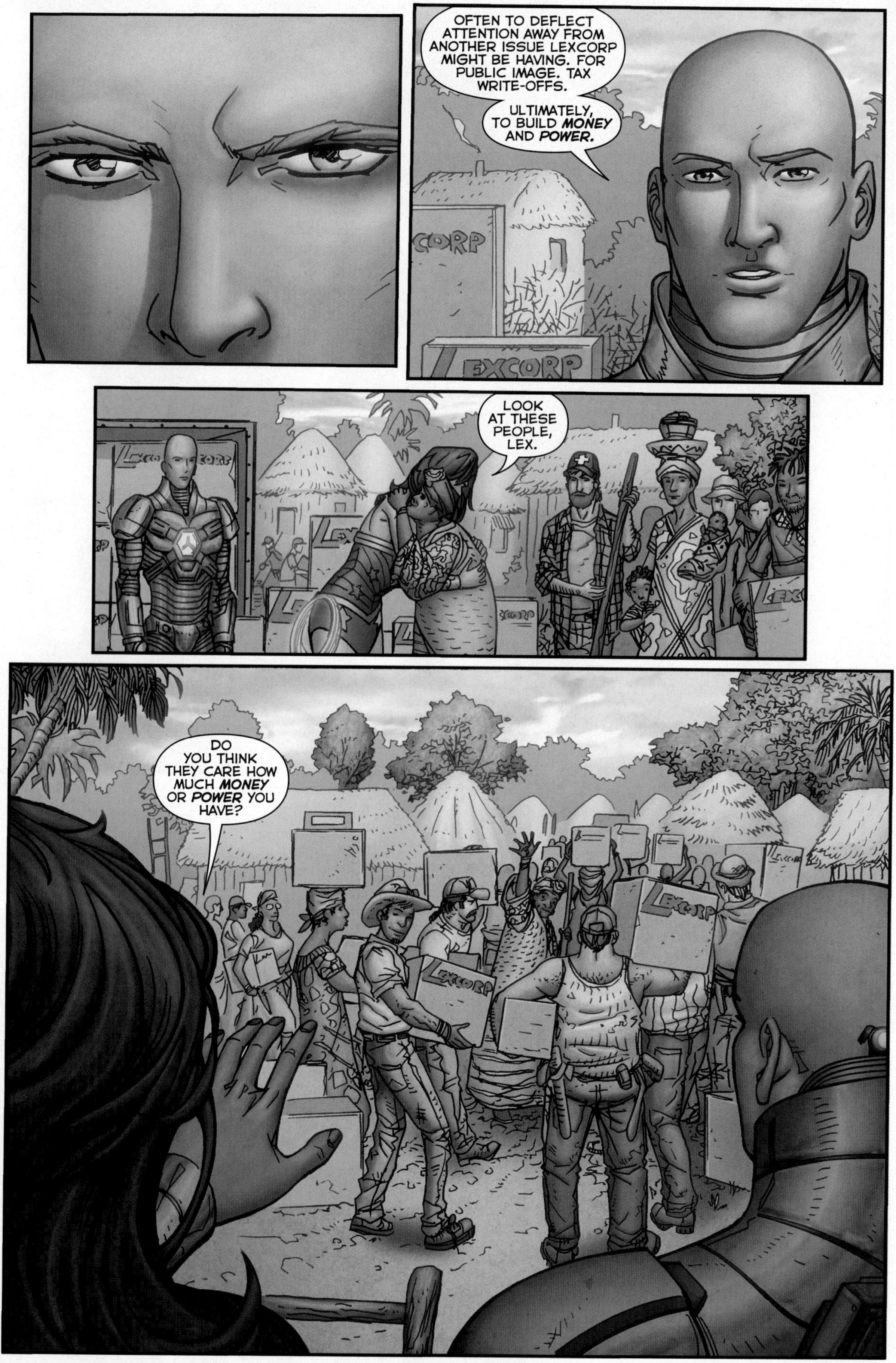
OFTEN TO DEFLECT ATTENTION AWAY FROM ANOTHER ISSUE LEXCORP MIGHT BE HAVING. FOR PUBLIC IMAGE. TAX WRITE-OFFS.
ULTIMATELY, TO BUILD *MONEY* AND *POWER.*
LOOK AT THESE PEOPLE, LEX.
DO YOU THINK THEY CARE HOW MUCH *MONEY* OR *POWER* YOU HAVE?

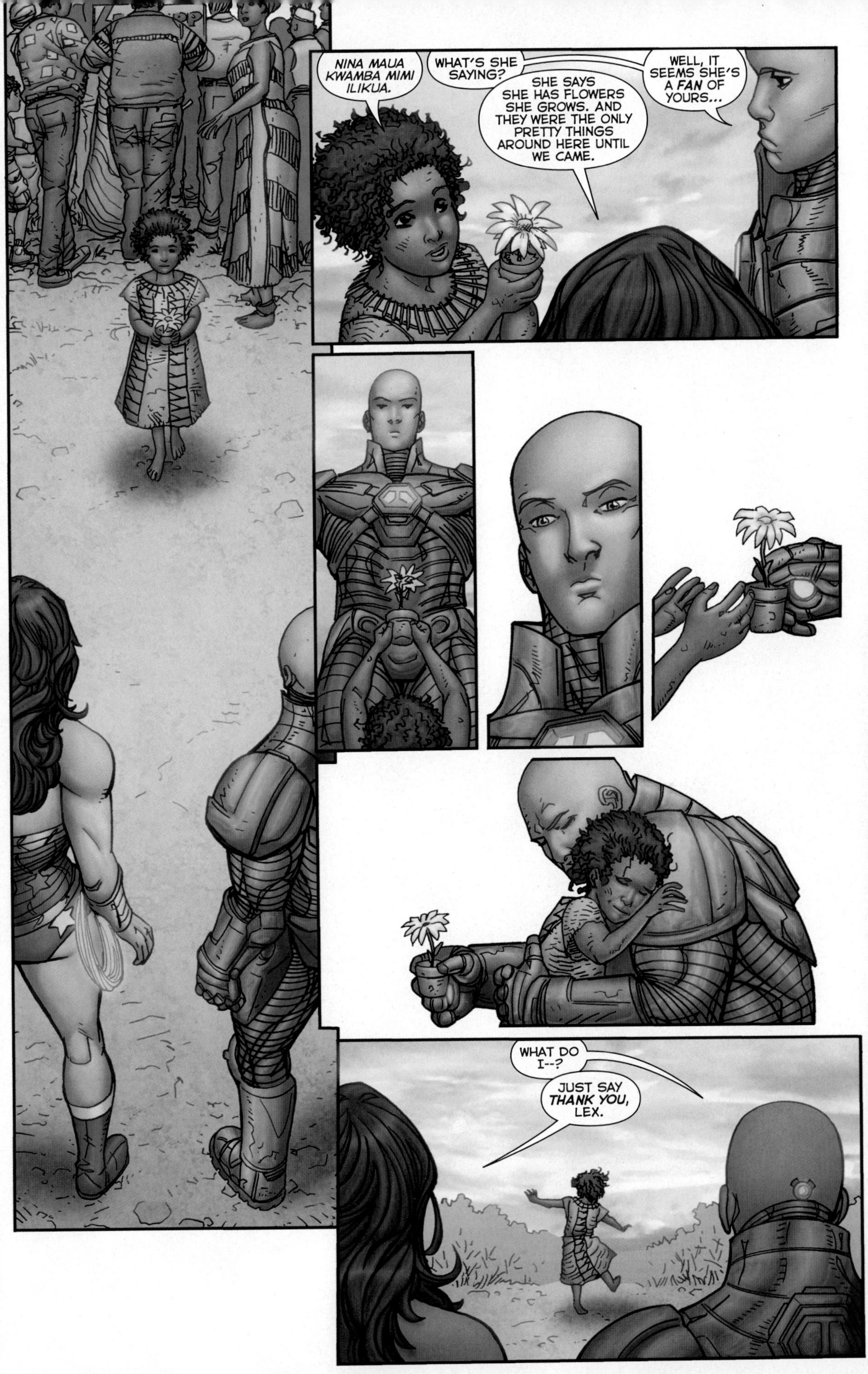
NINA MAUA KWAMBA MIMI ILIKUA.
WHAT'S SHE SAYING?
WELL, IT SEEMS SHE'S A *FAN* OF YOURS...
SHE SAYS SHE HAS FLOWERS SHE GROWS. AND THEY WERE THE ONLY PRETTY THINGS AROUND HERE UNTIL WE CAME.
WHAT DO I--?
JUST SAY *THANK YOU,* LEX.

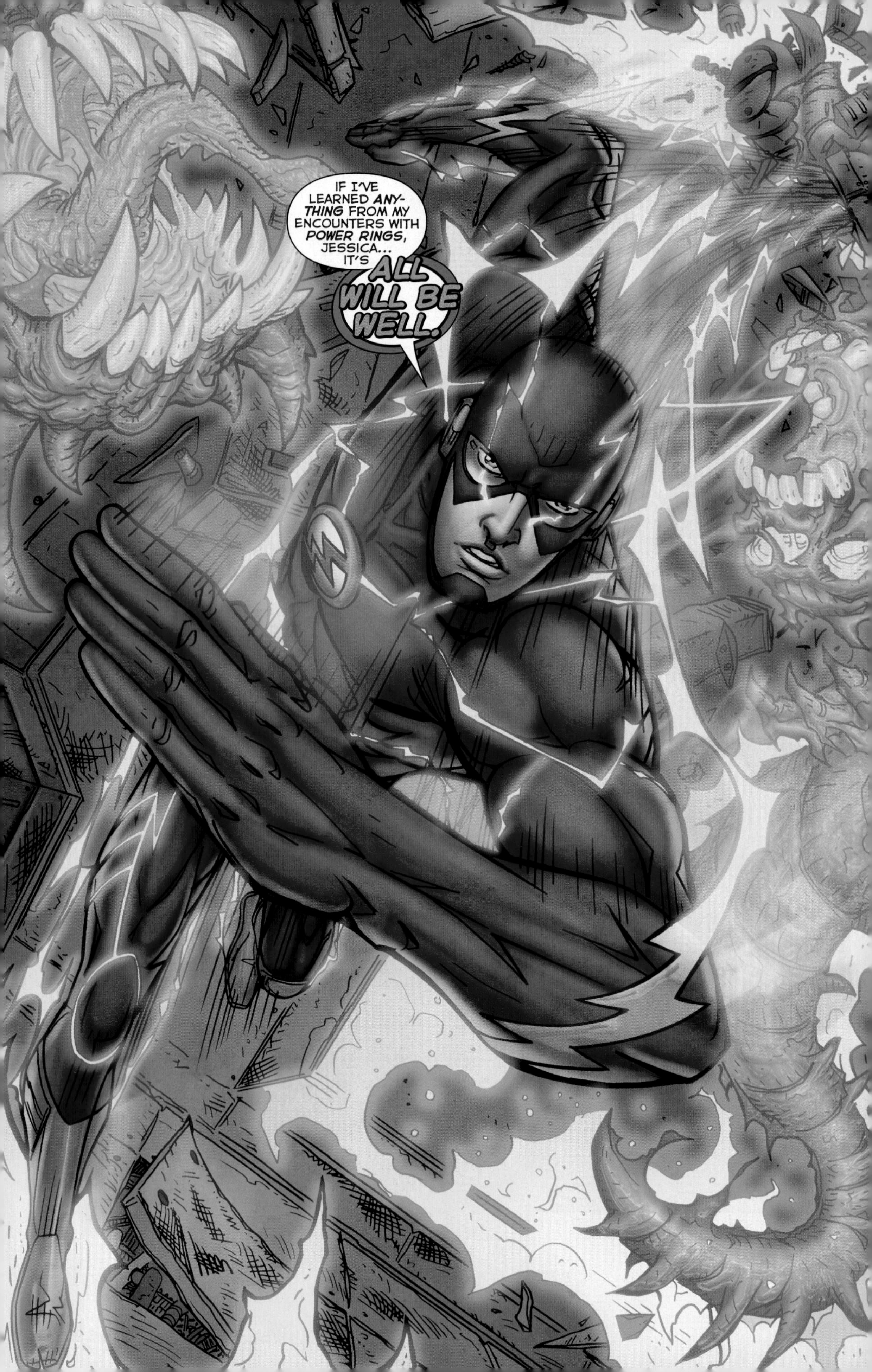
IF I'VE LEARNED ANYTHING FROM MY ENCOUNTERS WITH POWER RINGS, JESSICA... IT'S
ALL WILL BE WELL.

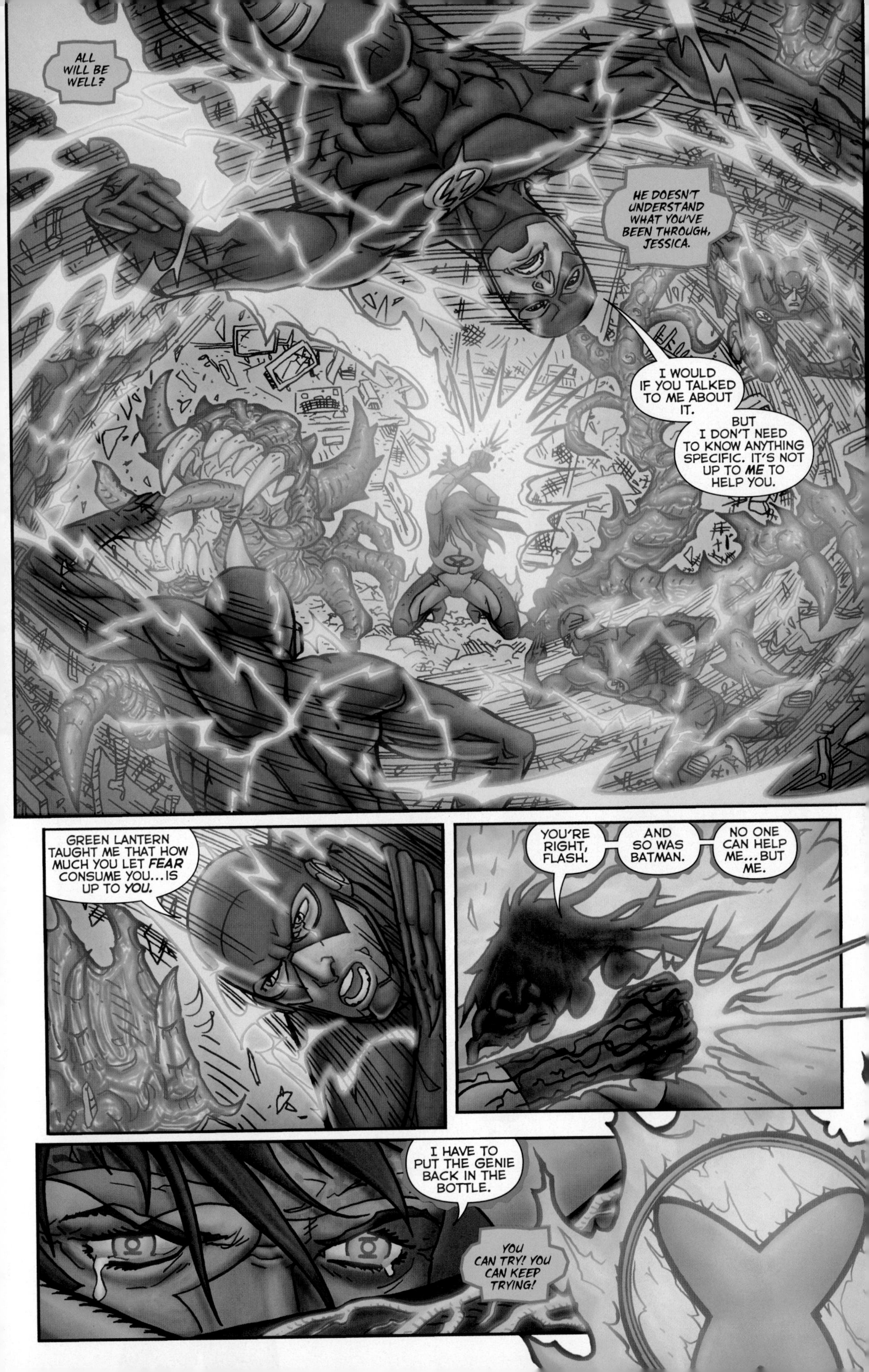
ALL WILL BE WELL?
HE DOESN'T UNDERSTAND WHAT YOU'VE BEEN THROUGH, JESSICA.
I WOULD IF YOU TALKED TO ME ABOUT IT.
BUT I DON'T NEED TO KNOW ANYTHING SPECIFIC. IT'S NOT UP TO ME TO HELP YOU.
GREEN LANTERN TAUGHT ME THAT HOW MUCH YOU LET FEAR CONSUME YOU...IS UP TO YOU.
YOU'RE RIGHT, FLASH.
AND SO WAS BATMAN.
NO ONE CAN HELP ME...BUT ME.
I HAVE TO PUT THE GENIE BACK IN THE BOTTLE.
YOU CAN TRY! YOU CAN KEEP TRYING!

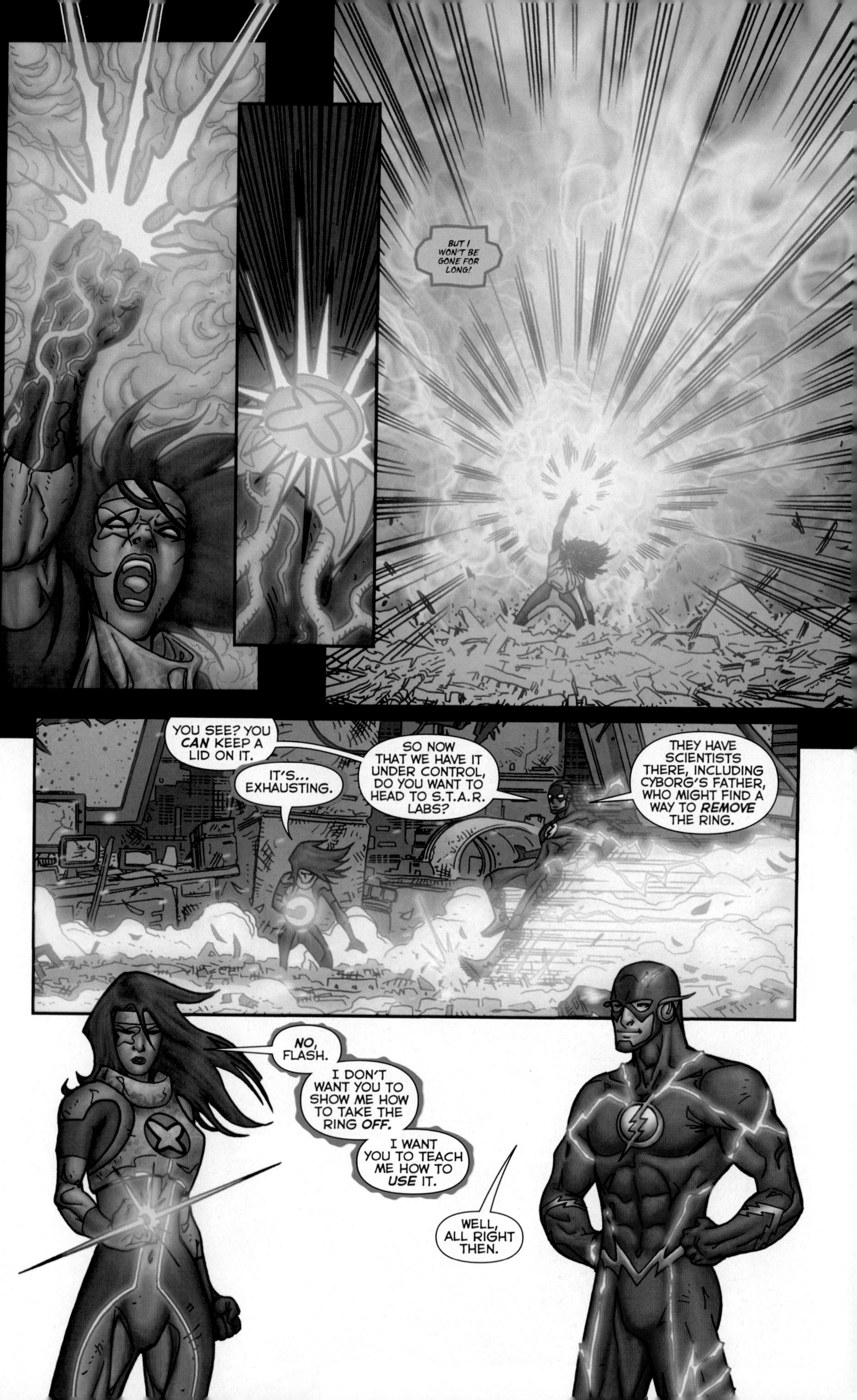
BUT I WON'T BE GONE FOR LONG!
YOU SEE? YOU CAN KEEP A LID ON IT.
IT'S... EXHAUSTING.
SO NOW THAT WE HAVE IT UNDER CONTROL, DO YOU WANT TO HEAD TO S.T.A.R. LABS?
THEY HAVE SCIENTISTS THERE, INCLUDING CYBORG'S FATHER, WHO MIGHT FIND A WAY TO REMOVE THE RING.
NO, FLASH.
I DON'T WANT YOU TO SHOW ME HOW TO TAKE THE RING OFF.
I WANT YOU TO TEACH ME HOW TO USE IT.
WELL, ALL RIGHT THEN.

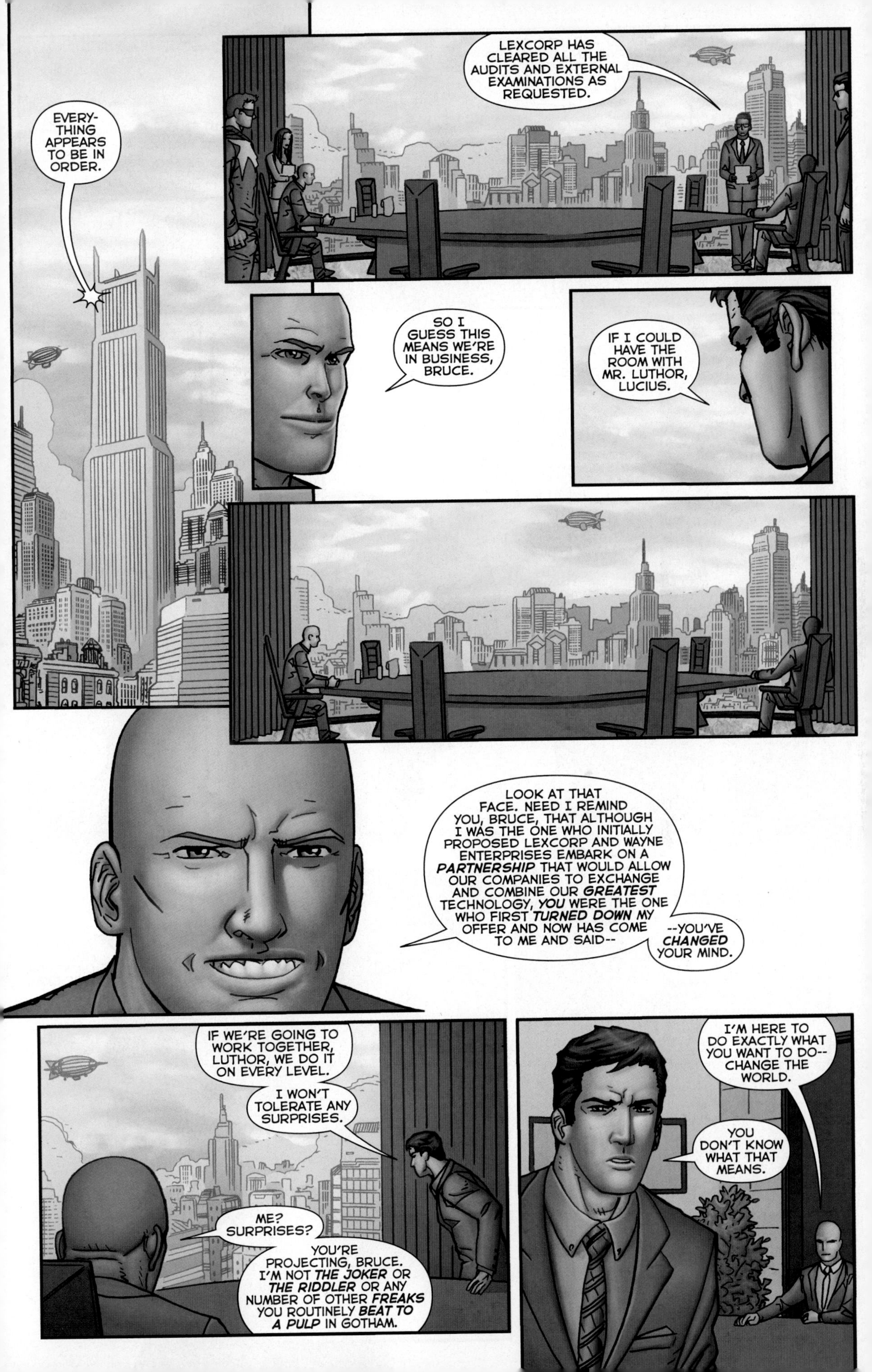
EVERY-THING APPEARS TO BE IN ORDER.
LEXCORP HAS CLEARED ALL THE AUDITS AND EXTERNAL EXAMINATIONS AS REQUESTED.
SO I GUESS THIS MEANS WE'RE IN BUSINESS, BRUCE.
IF I COULD HAVE THE ROOM WITH MR. LUTHOR, LUCIUS.
LOOK AT THAT FACE. NEED I REMIND YOU, BRUCE, THAT ALTHOUGH I WAS THE ONE WHO INITIALLY PROPOSED LEXCORP AND WAYNE ENTERPRISES EMBARK ON A PARTNERSHIP THAT WOULD ALLOW OUR COMPANIES TO EXCHANGE AND COMBINE OUR GREATEST TECHNOLOGY, YOU WERE THE ONE WHO FIRST TURNED DOWN MY OFFER AND NOW HAS COME TO ME AND SAID--
--YOU'VE CHANGED YOUR MIND.
IF WE'RE GOING TO WORK TOGETHER, LUTHOR, WE DO IT ON EVERY LEVEL.
I WON'T TOLERATE ANY SURPRISES.
ME? SURPRISES?
YOU'RE PROJECTING, BRUCE. I'M NOT THE JOKER OR THE RIDDLER OR ANY NUMBER OF OTHER FREAKS YOU ROUTINELY BEAT TO A PULP IN GOTHAM.
I'M HERE TO DO EXACTLY WHAT YOU WANT TO DO-- CHANGE THE WORLD.
YOU DON'T KNOW WHAT THAT MEANS.

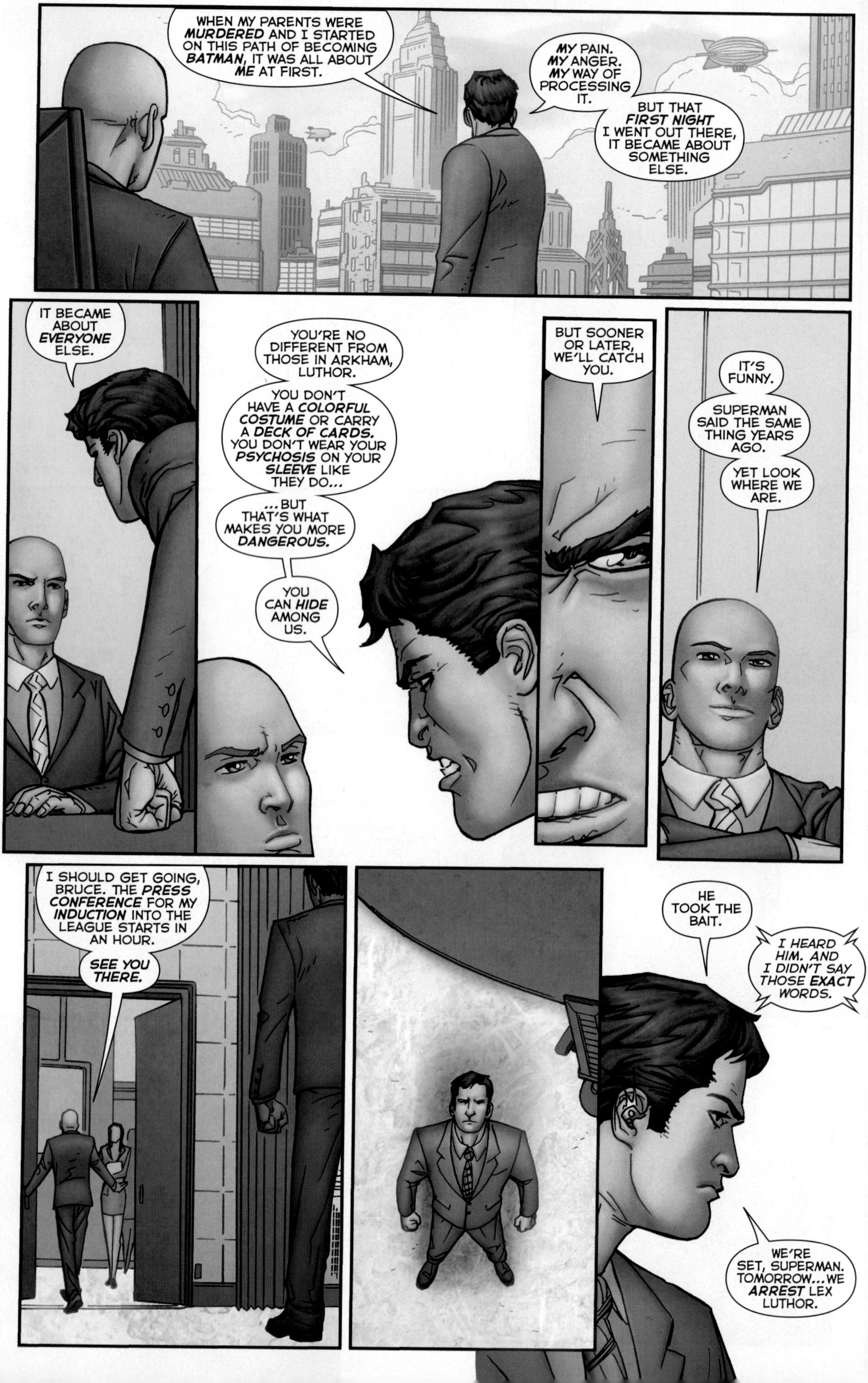
WHEN MY PARENTS WERE MURDERED AND I STARTED ON THIS PATH OF BECOMING BATMAN, IT WAS ALL ABOUT ME AT FIRST.
MY PAIN. MY ANGER. MY WAY OF PROCESSING IT.
BUT THAT FIRST NIGHT I WENT OUT THERE, IT BECAME ABOUT SOMETHING ELSE.
IT BECAME ABOUT EVERYONE ELSE.
YOU'RE NO DIFFERENT FROM THOSE IN ARKHAM, LUTHOR.
YOU DON'T HAVE A COLORFUL COSTUME OR CARRY A DECK OF CARDS. YOU DON'T WEAR YOUR PSYCHOSIS ON YOUR SLEEVE LIKE THEY DO...
...BUT THAT'S WHAT MAKES YOU MORE DANGEROUS.
YOU CAN HIDE AMONG US.
BUT SOONER OR LATER, WE'LL CATCH YOU.
IT'S FUNNY.
SUPERMAN SAID THE SAME THING YEARS AGO.
YET LOOK WHERE WE ARE.
I SHOULD GET GOING, BRUCE. THE PRESS CONFERENCE FOR MY INDUCTION INTO THE LEAGUE STARTS IN AN HOUR.
SEE YOU THERE.
HE TOOK THE BAIT.
I HEARD HIM. AND I DIDN'T SAY THOSE EXACT WORDS.
WE'RE SET, SUPERMAN. TOMORROW...WE ARREST LEX LUTHOR.

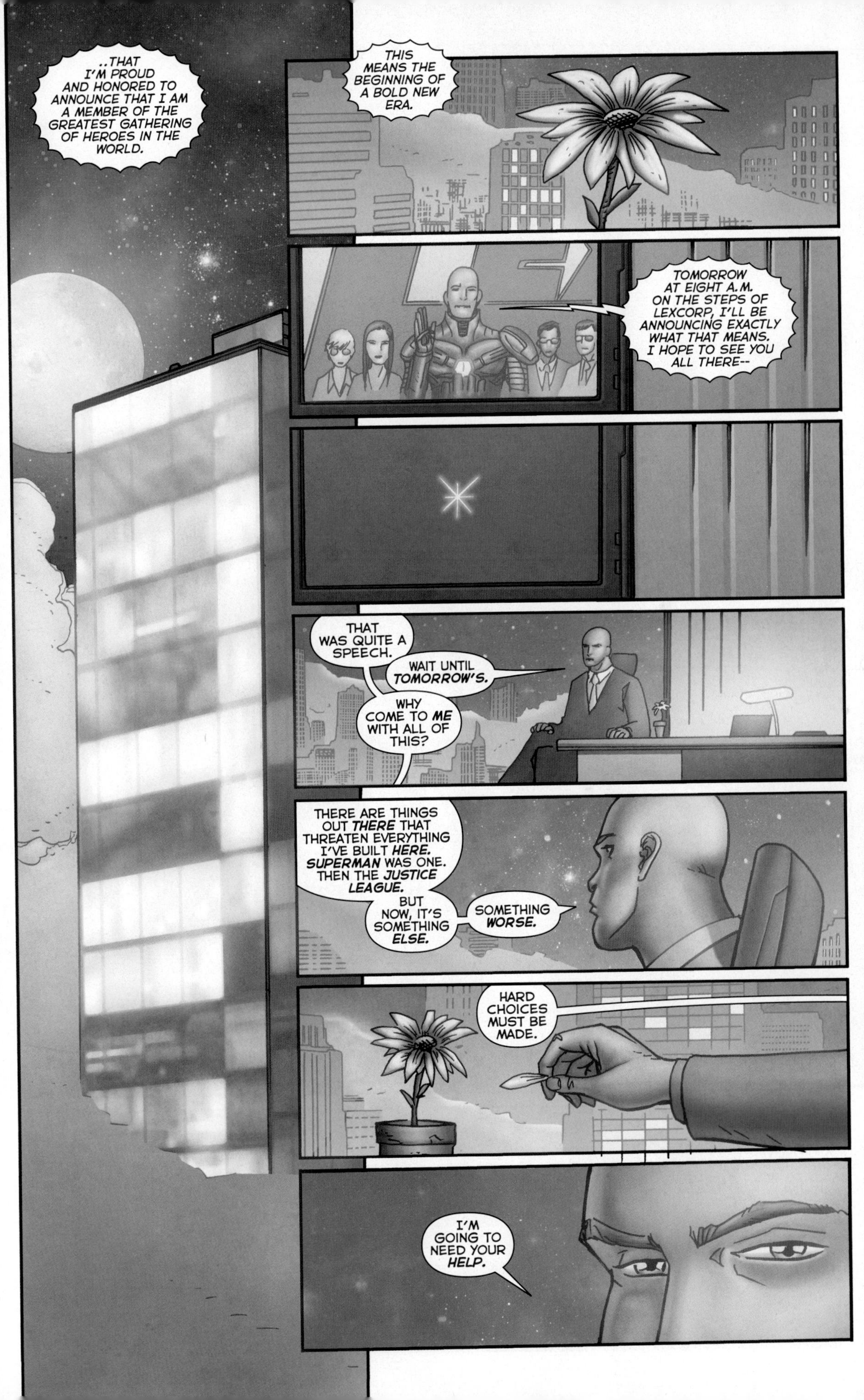
..THAT I'M PROUD AND HONORED TO ANNOUNCE THAT I AM A MEMBER OF THE GREATEST GATHERING OF HEROES IN THE WORLD.
THIS MEANS THE BEGINNING OF A BOLD NEW ERA.
TOMORROW AT EIGHT A.M. ON THE STEPS OF LEXCORP, I'LL BE ANNOUNCING EXACTLY WHAT THAT MEANS. I HOPE TO SEE YOU ALL THERE--
THAT WAS QUITE A SPEECH.
WAIT UNTIL TOMORROW'S.
WHY COME TO ME WITH ALL OF THIS?
THERE ARE THINGS OUT THERE THAT THREATEN EVERYTHING I'VE BUILT HERE. SUPERMAN WAS ONE. THEN THE JUSTICE LEAGUE.
BUT NOW, IT'S SOMETHING ELSE.
SOMETHING WORSE.
HARD CHOICES MUST BE MADE.
I'M GOING TO NEED YOUR HELP.

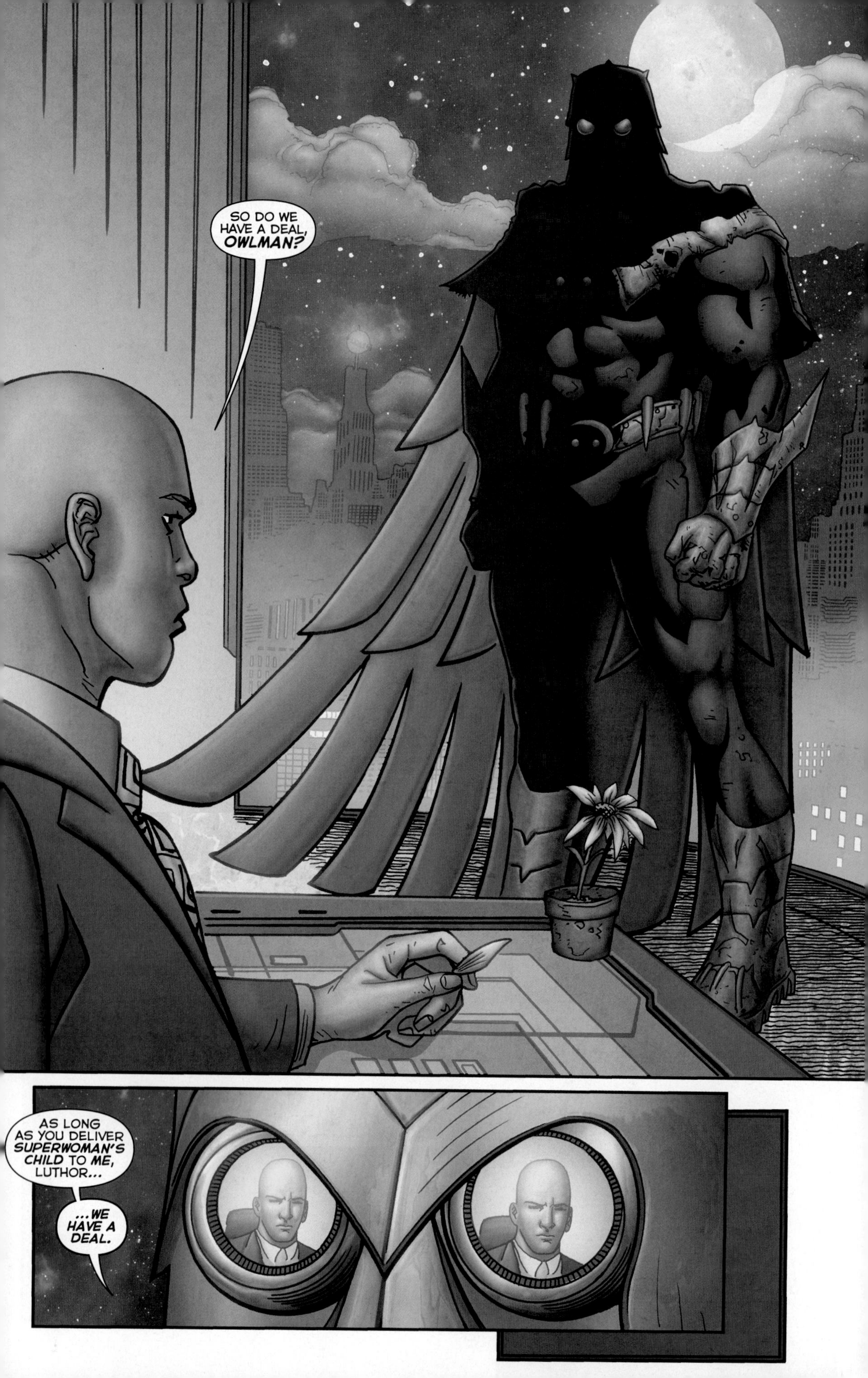
SO DO WE HAVE A DEAL, OWLMAN?
AS LONG AS YOU DELIVER SUPERWOMAN'S CHILD TO ME, LUTHOR...
...WE HAVE A DEAL.

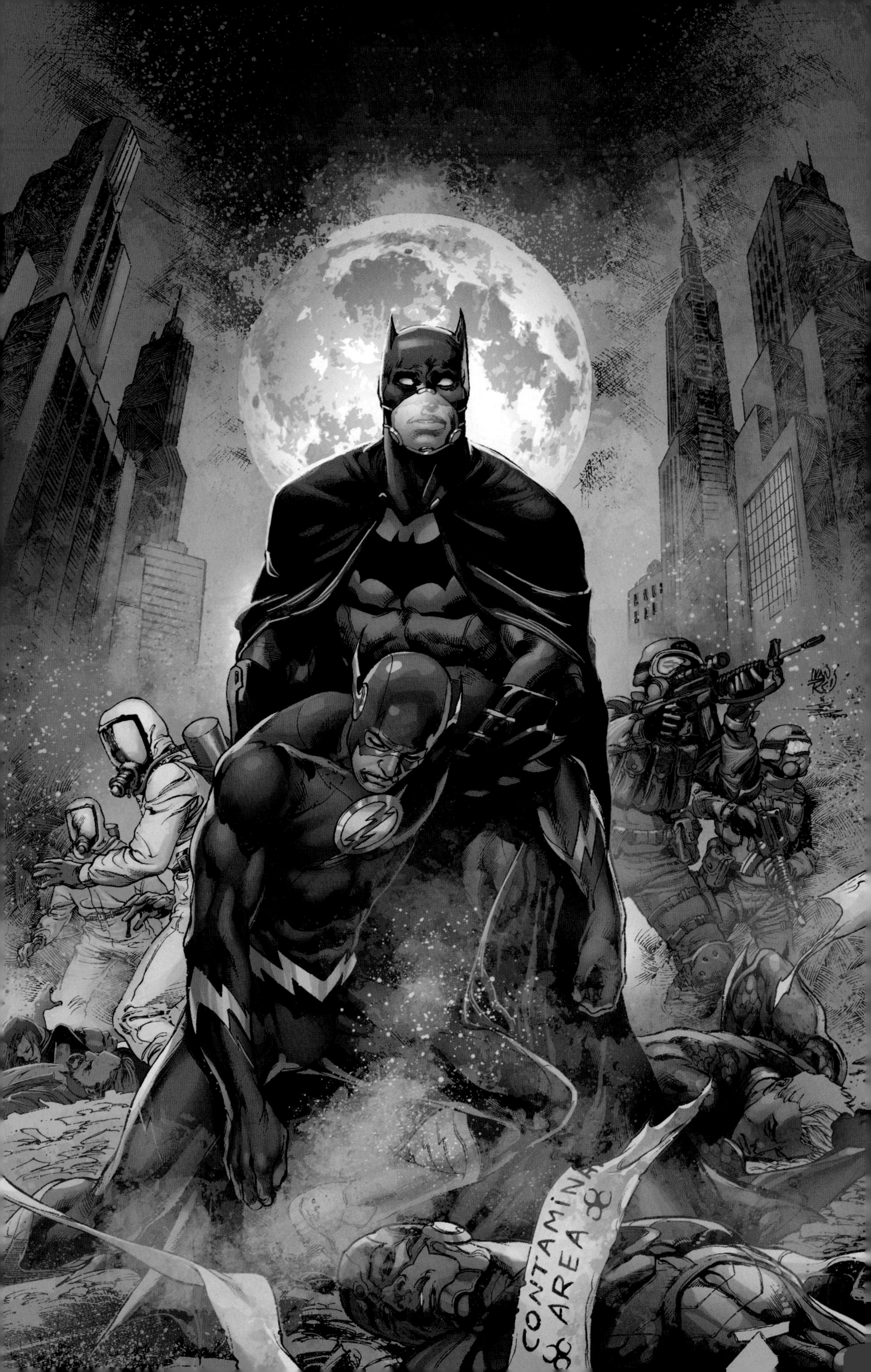
CONTAMINA
AREA

THE AMAZO VIRUS PROLOGUE
THE OUTBREAK

GEOFF JOHNS writer **DOUG MAHNKE IVAN REIS** pencillers **KEITH CHAMPAGNE MARK IRWIN CHRISTIAN ALAMY RAY McCARTHY JOE PRADO** inkers **BRAD ANDERSON** colorist **IVAN REIS, JOE PRADO & ROD REIS** cover artists

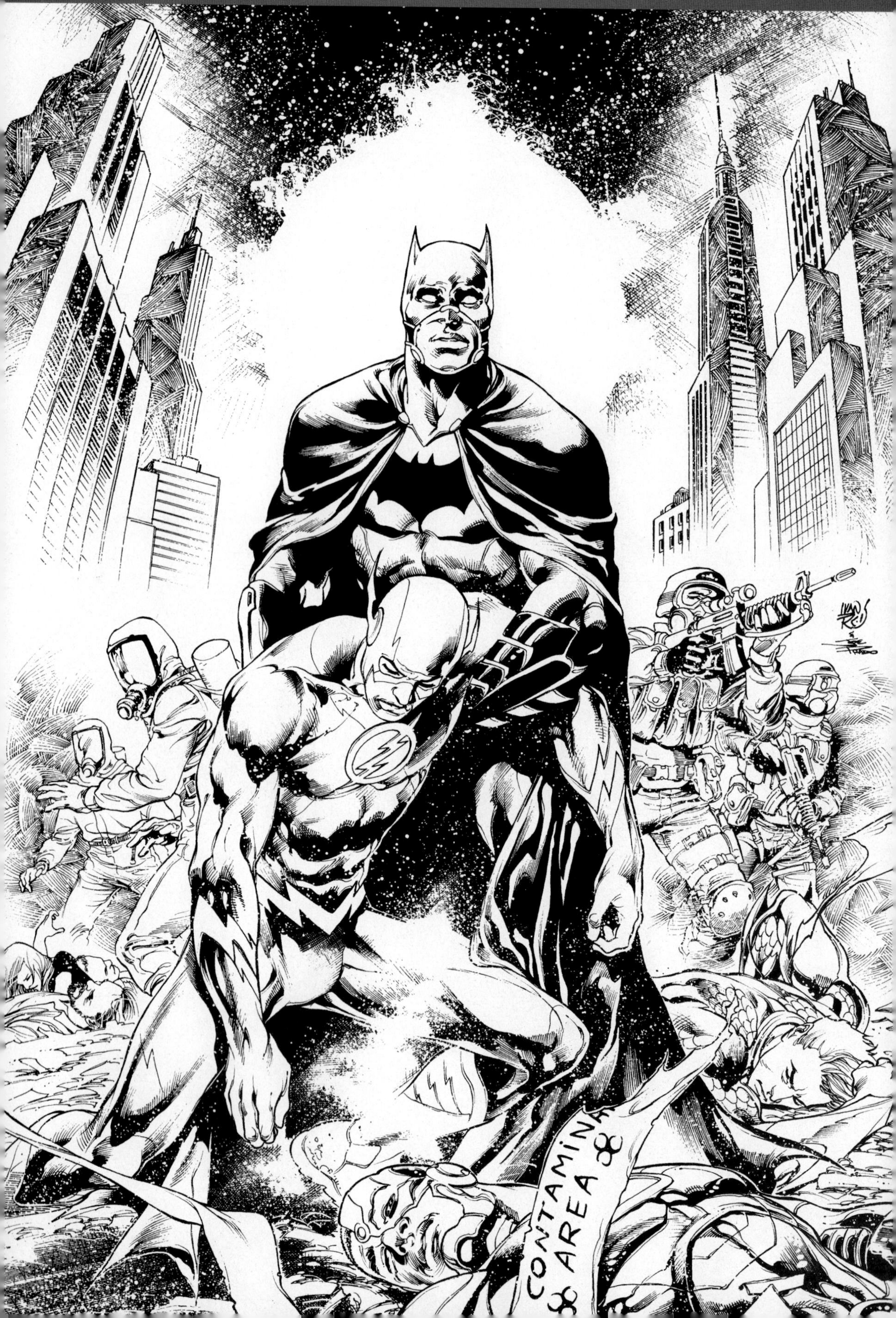
CONTAMINA
AREA

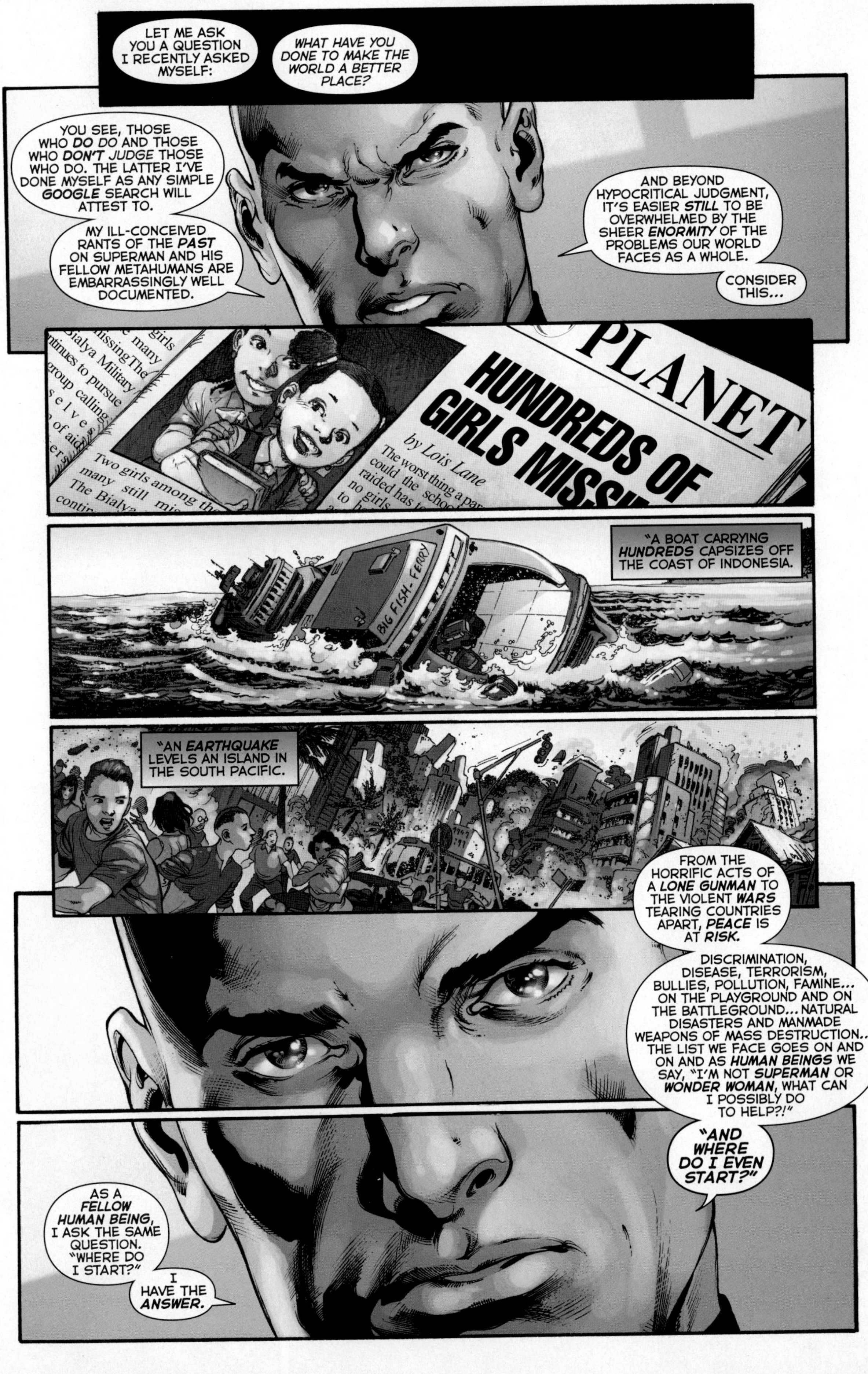
LET ME ASK YOU A QUESTION I RECENTLY ASKED MYSELF:
WHAT HAVE YOU DONE TO MAKE THE WORLD A BETTER PLACE?
YOU SEE, THOSE WHO ***DO DO*** AND THOSE WHO ***DON'T JUDGE*** THOSE WHO DO. THE LATTER I'VE DONE MYSELF AS ANY SIMPLE ***GOOGLE*** SEARCH WILL ATTEST TO.
MY ILL-CONCEIVED RANTS OF THE ***PAST*** ON SUPERMAN AND HIS FELLOW METAHUMANS ARE EMBARRASSINGLY WELL DOCUMENTED.
AND BEYOND HYPOCRITICAL JUDGMENT, IT'S EASIER ***STILL*** TO BE OVERWHELMED BY THE SHEER ***ENORMITY*** OF THE PROBLEMS OUR WORLD FACES AS A WHOLE.
CONSIDER THIS...
PLANET
HUNDREDS OF
by Lois Lane
"A BOAT CARRYING ***HUNDREDS*** CAPSIZES OFF THE COAST OF INDONESIA.
BIG FISH-FERRY
"AN ***EARTHQUAKE*** LEVELS AN ISLAND IN THE SOUTH PACIFIC.
FROM THE HORRIFIC ACTS OF A ***LONE GUNMAN*** TO THE VIOLENT ***WARS*** TEARING COUNTRIES APART, ***PEACE*** IS AT ***RISK.***
DISCRIMINATION, DISEASE, TERRORISM, BULLIES, POLLUTION, FAMINE... ON THE PLAYGROUND AND ON THE BATTLEGROUND... NATURAL DISASTERS AND MANMADE WEAPONS OF MASS DESTRUCTION... THE LIST WE FACE GOES ON AND ON AND AS ***HUMAN BEINGS*** WE SAY, "I'M NOT ***SUPERMAN*** OR ***WONDER WOMAN***, WHAT CAN I POSSIBLY DO TO HELP?!"
"AND WHERE DO I EVEN START?"
AS A ***FELLOW HUMAN BEING***, I ASK THE SAME QUESTION. "WHERE DO I START?"
I HAVE THE ***ANSWER.***

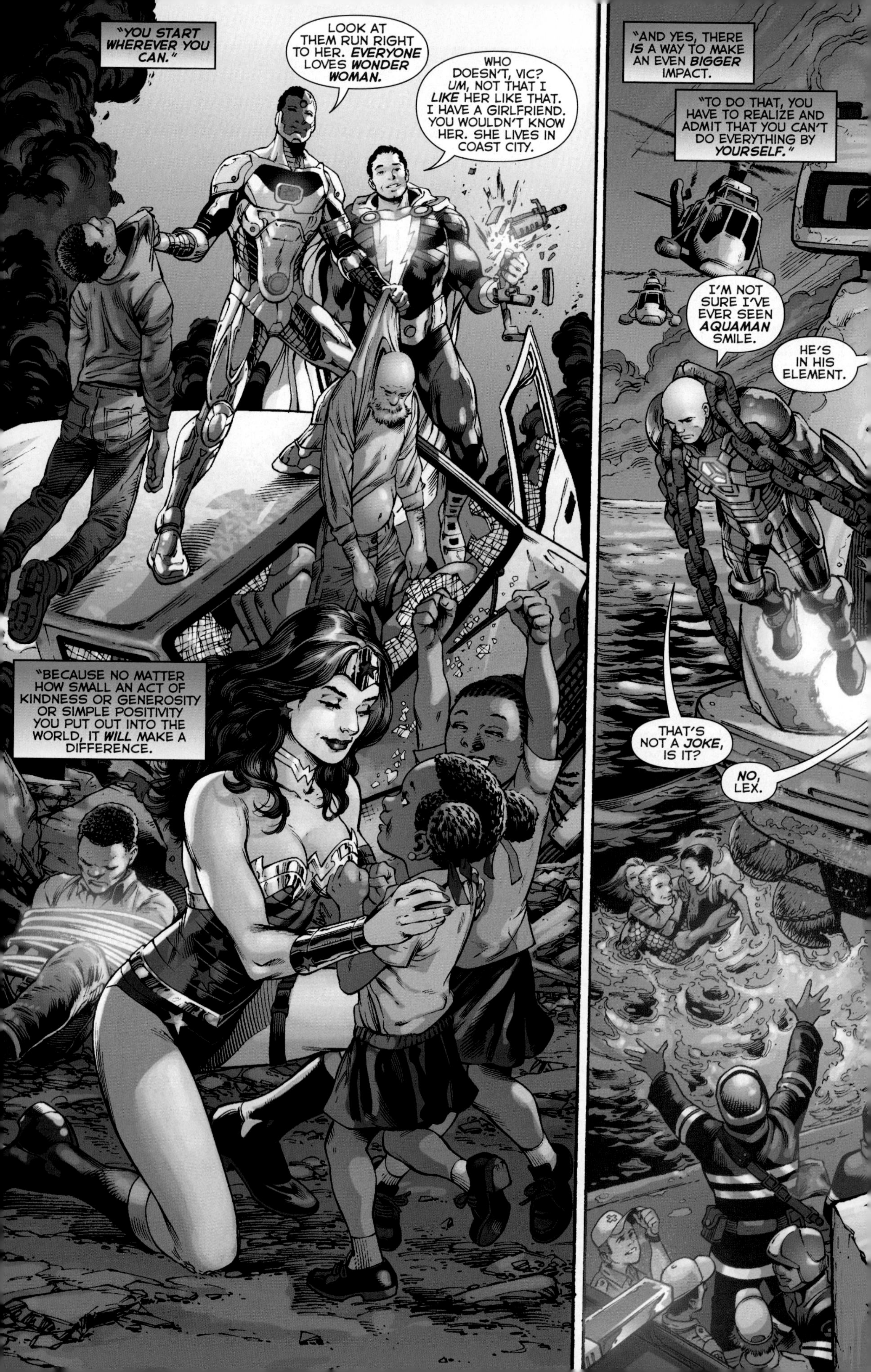
"YOU START WHEREVER YOU CAN."
LOOK AT THEM RUN RIGHT TO HER. EVERYONE LOVES WONDER WOMAN.
WHO DOESN'T, VIC? UM, NOT THAT I LIKE HER LIKE THAT. I HAVE A GIRLFRIEND. YOU WOULDN'T KNOW HER. SHE LIVES IN COAST CITY.
"BECAUSE NO MATTER HOW SMALL AN ACT OF KINDNESS OR GENEROSITY OR SIMPLE POSITIVITY YOU PUT OUT INTO THE WORLD, IT WILL MAKE A DIFFERENCE.
"AND YES, THERE IS A WAY TO MAKE AN EVEN BIGGER IMPACT.
"TO DO THAT, YOU HAVE TO REALIZE AND ADMIT THAT YOU CAN'T DO EVERYTHING BY YOURSELF."
I'M NOT SURE I'VE EVER SEEN AQUAMAN SMILE.
HE'S IN HIS ELEMENT.
THAT'S NOT A JOKE, IS IT?
NO, LEX.

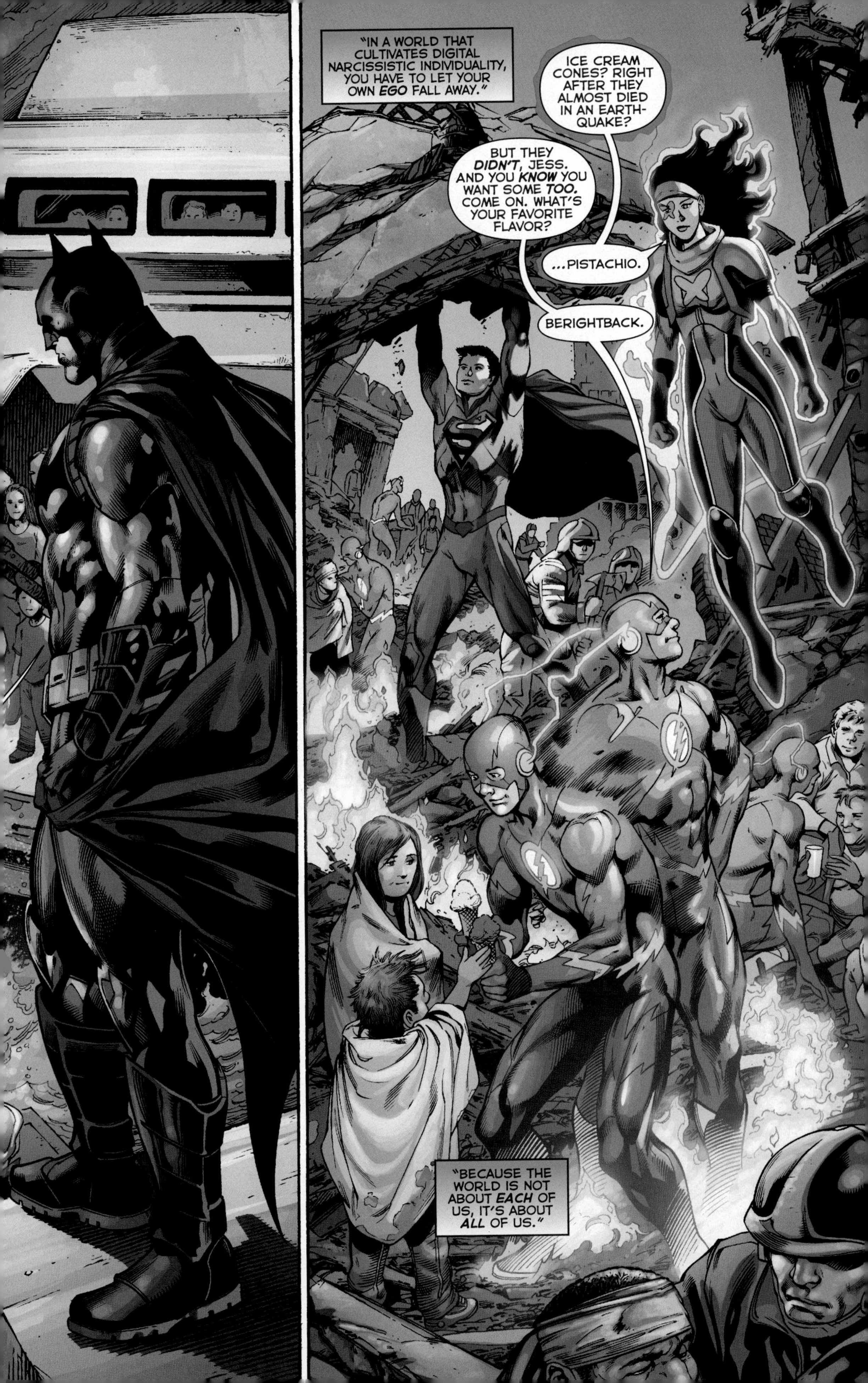
"IN A WORLD THAT CULTIVATES DIGITAL NARCISSISTIC INDIVIDUALITY, YOU HAVE TO LET YOUR OWN *EGO* FALL AWAY."
ICE CREAM CONES? RIGHT AFTER THEY ALMOST DIED IN AN EARTH-QUAKE?
BUT THEY *DIDN'T*, JESS. AND YOU *KNOW* YOU WANT SOME *TOO.* COME ON. WHAT'S YOUR FAVORITE FLAVOR?
...PISTACHIO.
BERIGHTBACK.
"BECAUSE THE WORLD IS NOT ABOUT *EACH* OF US, IT'S ABOUT *ALL* OF US."

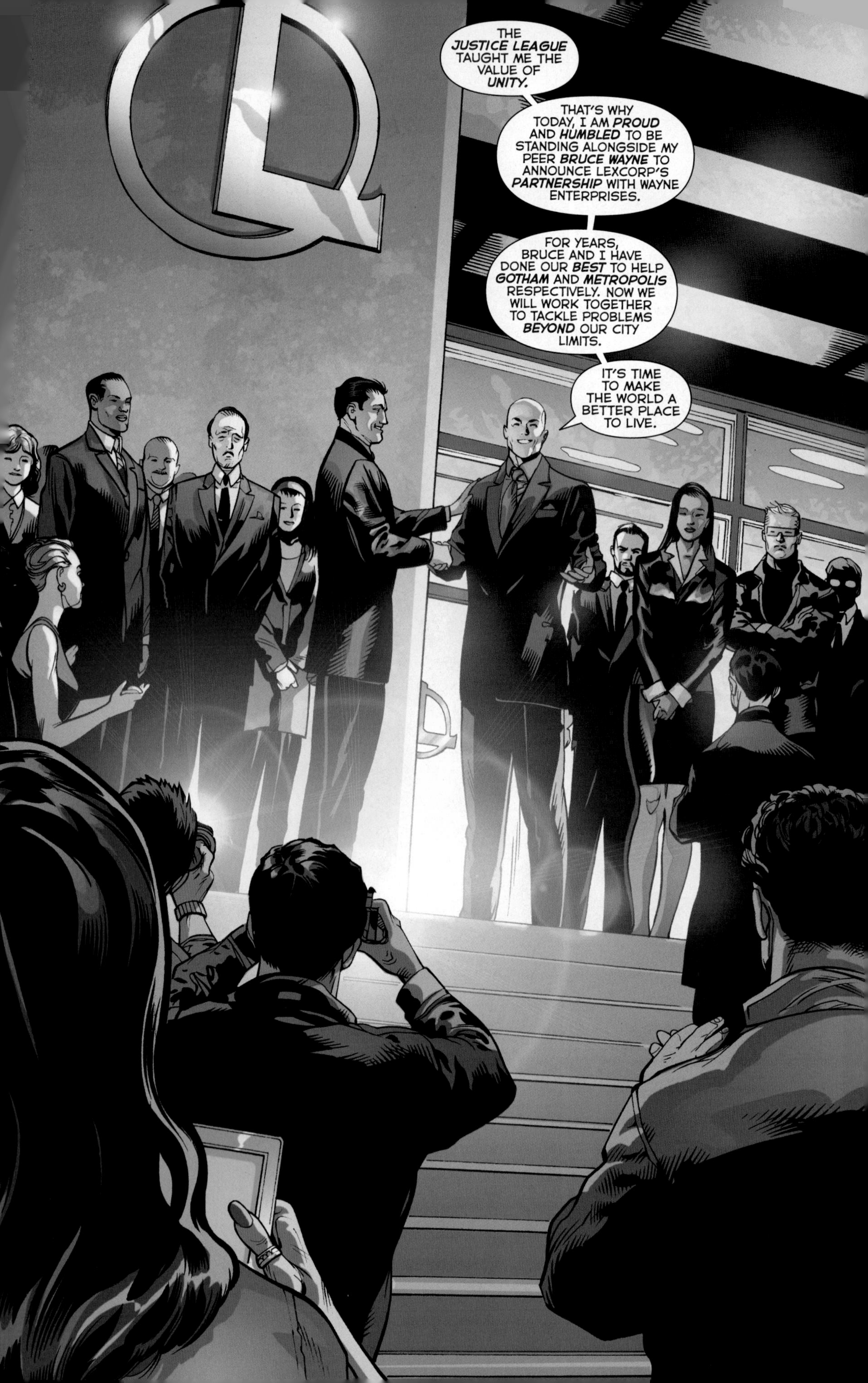
THE JUSTICE LEAGUE TAUGHT ME THE VALUE OF UNITY.
THAT'S WHY TODAY, I AM PROUD AND HUMBLED TO BE STANDING ALONGSIDE MY PEER BRUCE WAYNE TO ANNOUNCE LEXCORP'S PARTNERSHIP WITH WAYNE ENTERPRISES.
FOR YEARS, BRUCE AND I HAVE DONE OUR BEST TO HELP GOTHAM AND METROPOLIS RESPECTIVELY. NOW WE WILL WORK TOGETHER TO TACKLE PROBLEMS BEYOND OUR CITY LIMITS.
IT'S TIME TO MAKE THE WORLD A BETTER PLACE TO LIVE.

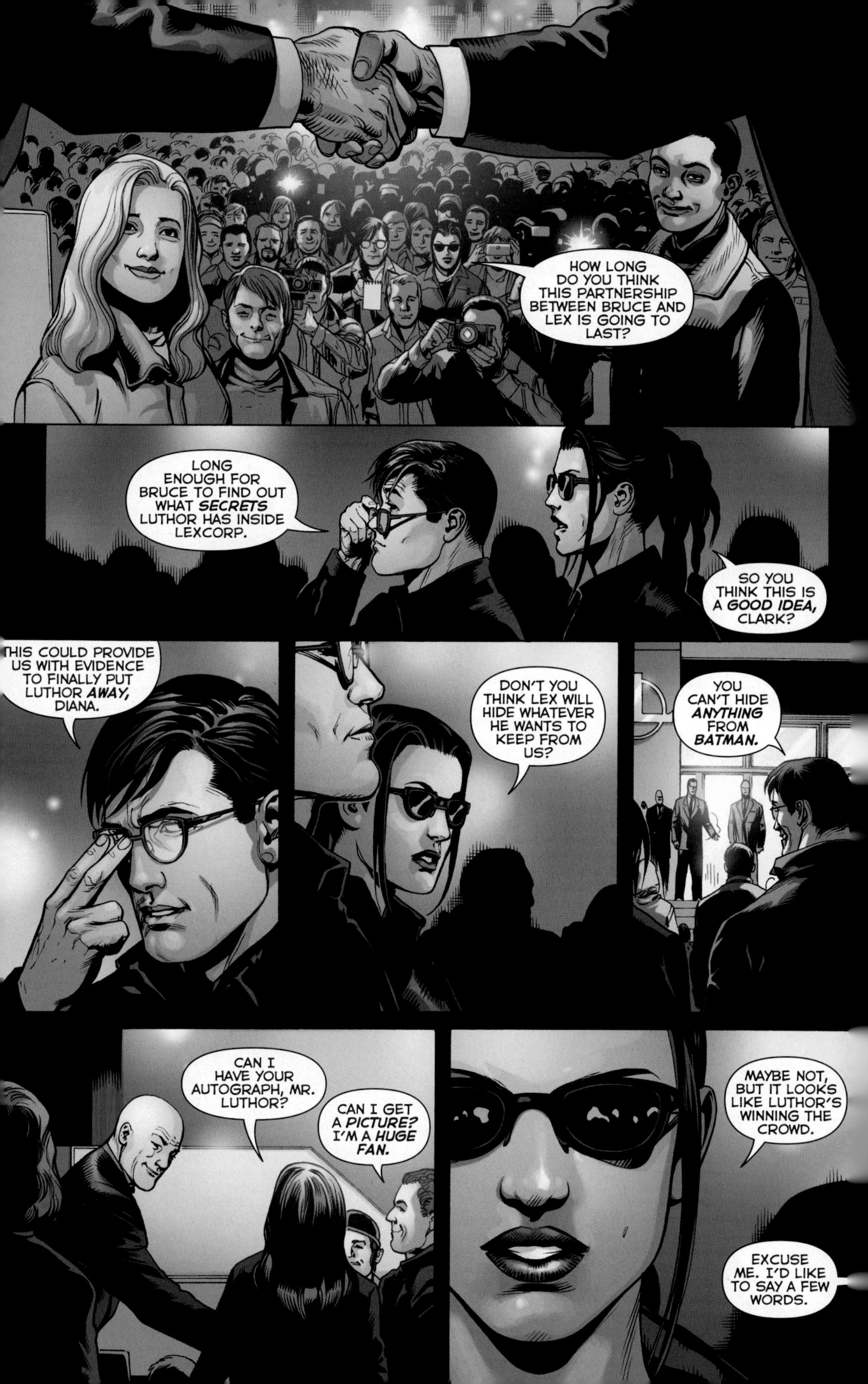
HOW LONG DO YOU THINK THIS PARTNERSHIP BETWEEN BRUCE AND LEX IS GOING TO LAST?
LONG ENOUGH FOR BRUCE TO FIND OUT WHAT *SECRETS* LUTHOR HAS INSIDE LEXCORP.
SO YOU THINK THIS IS A *GOOD IDEA,* CLARK?
THIS COULD PROVIDE US WITH EVIDENCE TO FINALLY PUT LUTHOR *AWAY,* DIANA.
DON'T YOU THINK LEX WILL HIDE WHATEVER HE WANTS TO KEEP FROM US?
YOU CAN'T HIDE *ANYTHING* FROM *BATMAN.*
CAN I HAVE YOUR AUTOGRAPH, MR. LUTHOR?
CAN I GET A *PICTURE?* I'M A *HUGE FAN.*
MAYBE NOT, BUT IT LOOKS LIKE LUTHOR'S WINNING THE CROWD.
EXCUSE ME. I'D LIKE TO SAY A FEW WORDS.

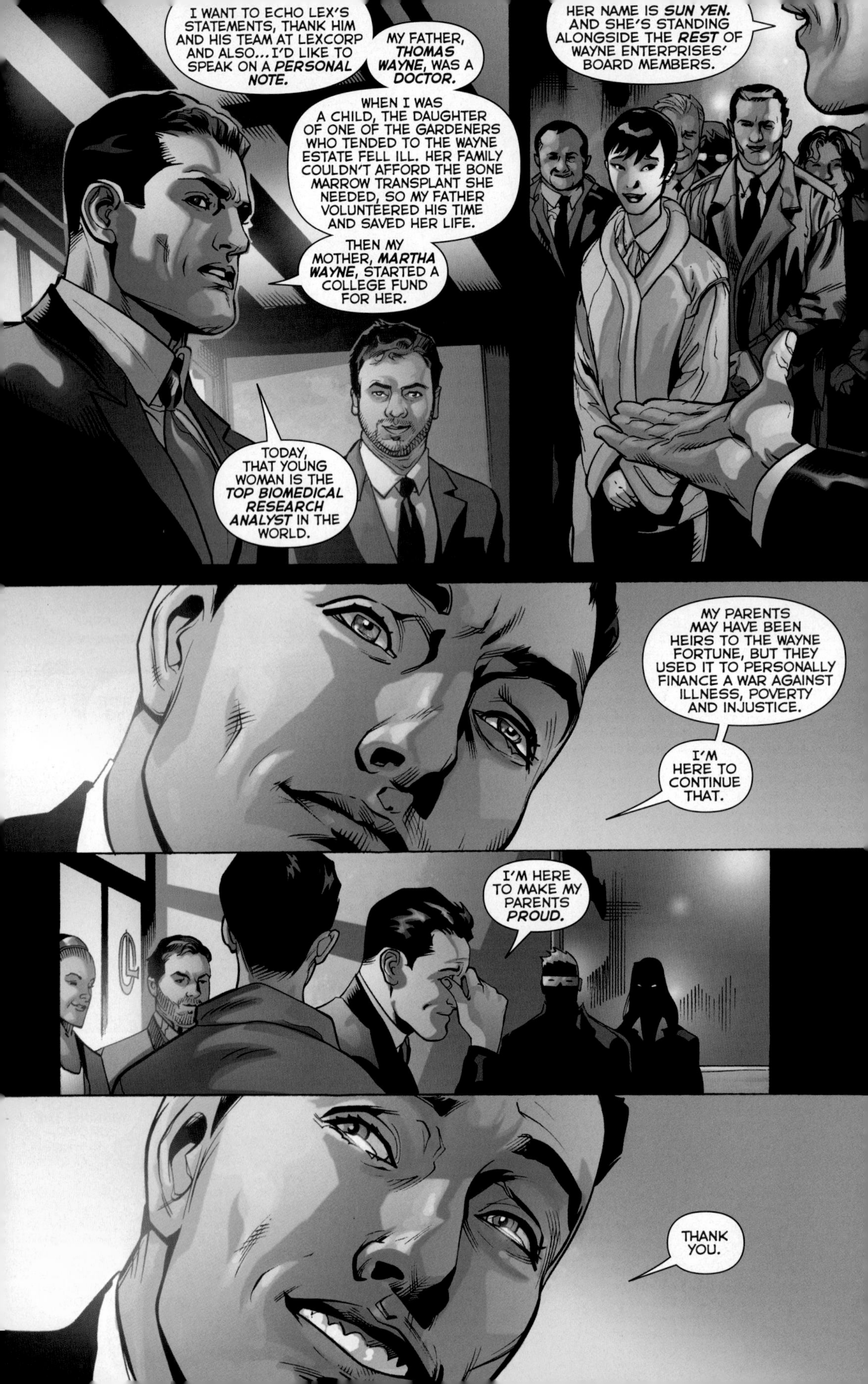
I WANT TO ECHO LEX'S STATEMENTS, THANK HIM AND HIS TEAM AT LEXCORP AND ALSO...I'D LIKE TO SPEAK ON A PERSONAL NOTE.
MY FATHER, THOMAS WAYNE, WAS A DOCTOR.
WHEN I WAS A CHILD, THE DAUGHTER OF ONE OF THE GARDENERS WHO TENDED TO THE WAYNE ESTATE FELL ILL. HER FAMILY COULDN'T AFFORD THE BONE MARROW TRANSPLANT SHE NEEDED, SO MY FATHER VOLUNTEERED HIS TIME AND SAVED HER LIFE.
THEN MY MOTHER, MARTHA WAYNE, STARTED A COLLEGE FUND FOR HER.
TODAY, THAT YOUNG WOMAN IS THE TOP BIOMEDICAL RESEARCH ANALYST IN THE WORLD.
HER NAME IS SUN YEN. AND SHE'S STANDING ALONGSIDE THE REST OF WAYNE ENTERPRISES' BOARD MEMBERS.
MY PARENTS MAY HAVE BEEN HEIRS TO THE WAYNE FORTUNE, BUT THEY USED IT TO PERSONALLY FINANCE A WAR AGAINST ILLNESS, POVERTY AND INJUSTICE.
I'M HERE TO CONTINUE THAT.
I'M HERE TO MAKE MY PARENTS PROUD.
THANK YOU.

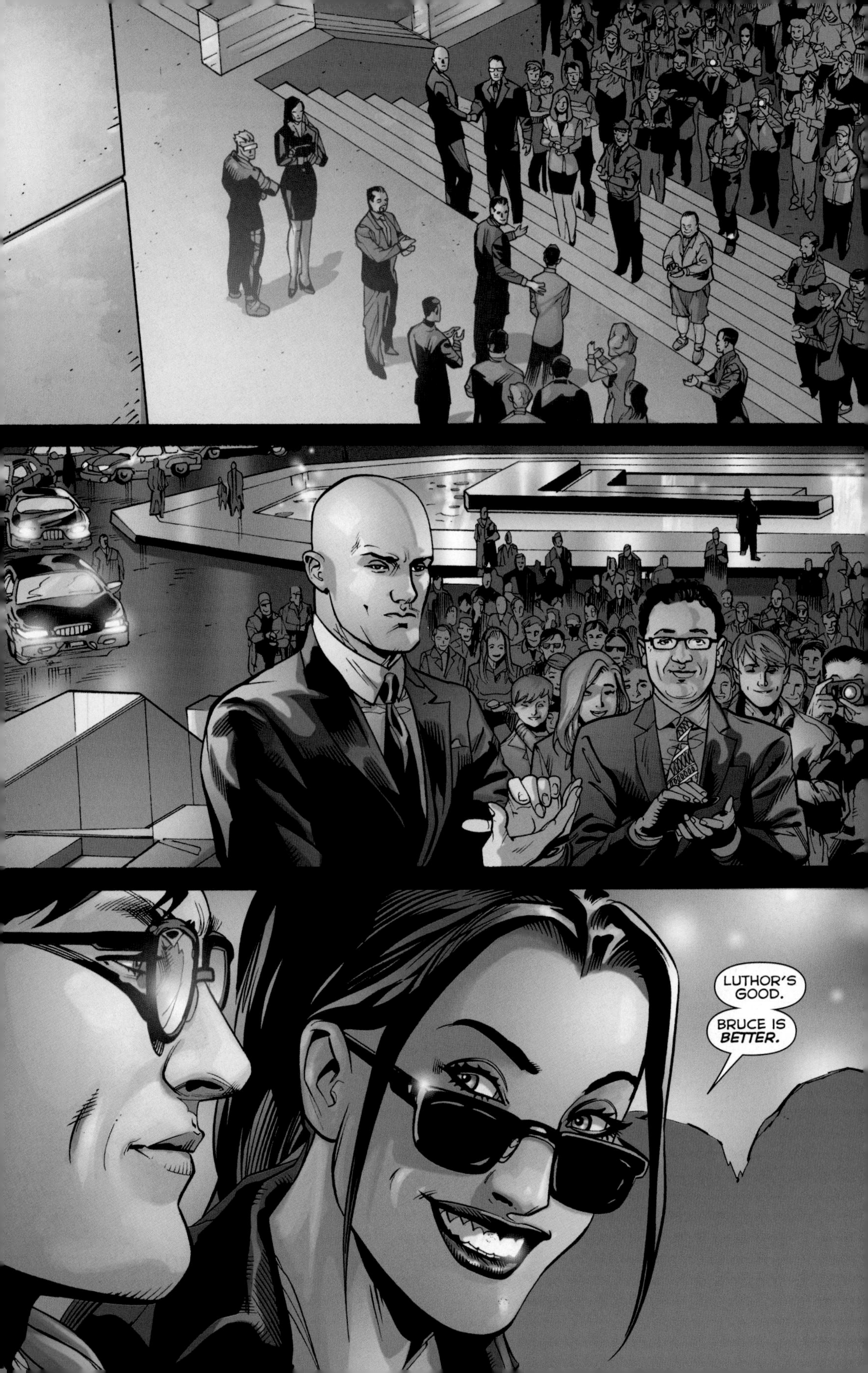
LUTHOR'S GOOD.
BRUCE IS BETTER.

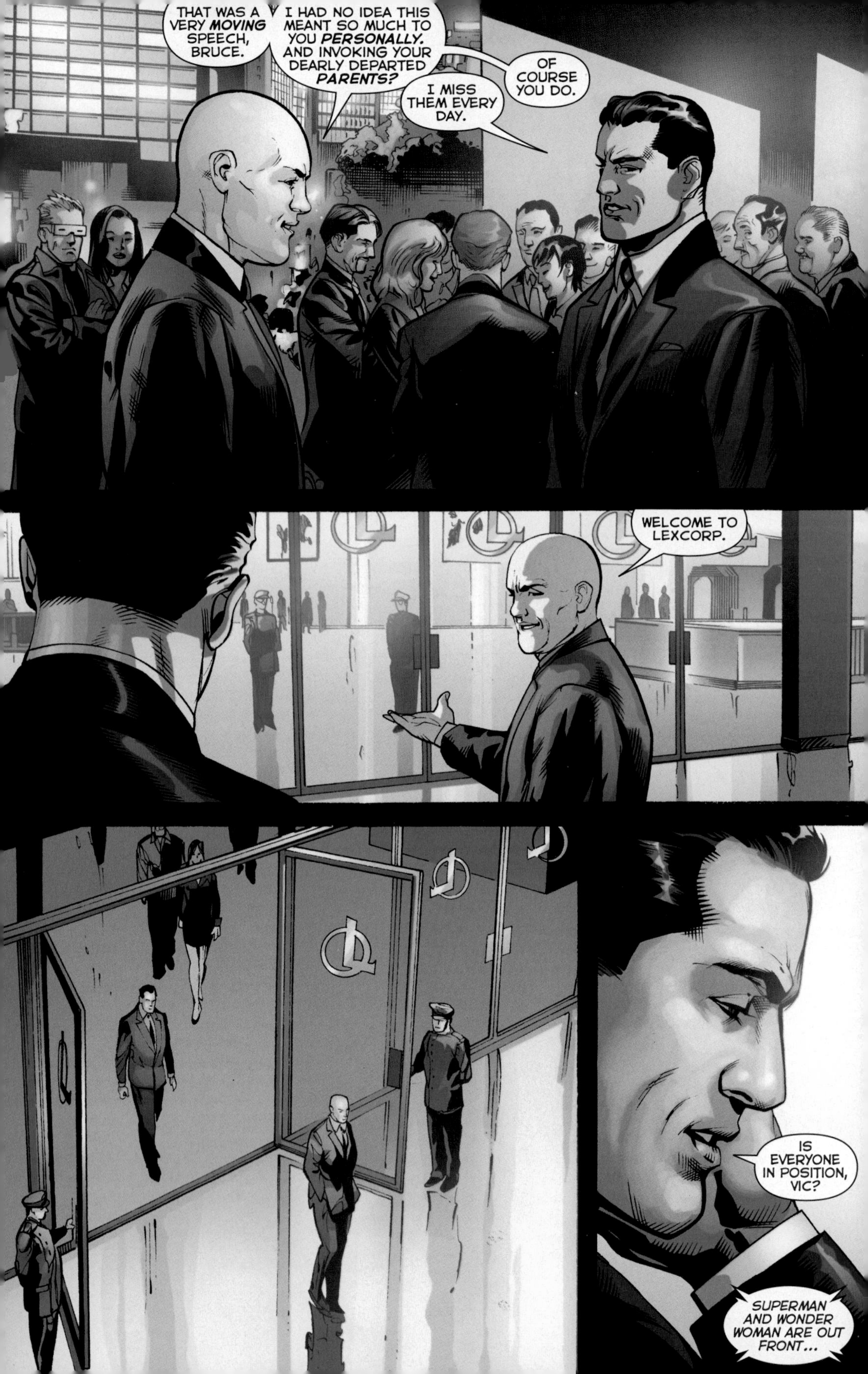
THAT WAS A VERY MOVING SPEECH, BRUCE.
I HAD NO IDEA THIS MEANT SO MUCH TO YOU PERSONALLY. AND INVOKING YOUR DEARLY DEPARTED PARENTS?
I MISS THEM EVERY DAY.
OF COURSE YOU DO.
WELCOME TO LEXCORP.
IS EVERYONE IN POSITION, VIC?
SUPERMAN AND WONDER WOMAN ARE OUT FRONT...

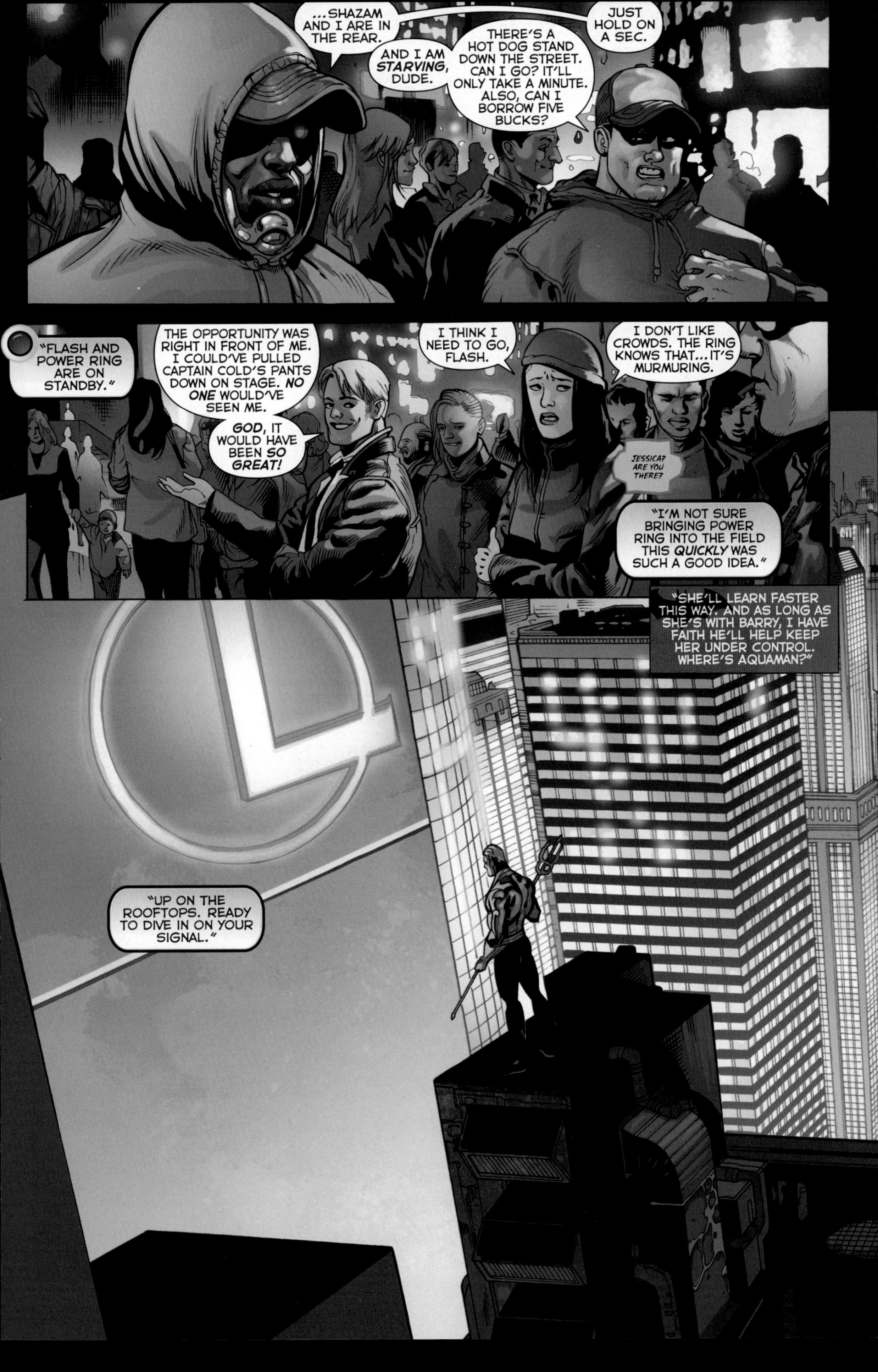
...SHAZAM AND I ARE IN THE REAR.
JUST HOLD ON A SEC.
AND I AM STARVING, DUDE.
THERE'S A HOT DOG STAND DOWN THE STREET. CAN I GO? IT'LL ONLY TAKE A MINUTE. ALSO, CAN I BORROW FIVE BUCKS?
"FLASH AND POWER RING ARE ON STANDBY."
THE OPPORTUNITY WAS RIGHT IN FRONT OF ME. I COULD'VE PULLED CAPTAIN COLD'S PANTS DOWN ON STAGE. NO ONE WOULD'VE SEEN ME.
GOD, IT WOULD HAVE BEEN SO GREAT!
I THINK I NEED TO GO, FLASH.
I DON'T LIKE CROWDS. THE RING KNOWS THAT...IT'S MURMURING.
JESSICA? ARE YOU THERE?
"I'M NOT SURE BRINGING POWER RING INTO THE FIELD THIS QUICKLY WAS SUCH A GOOD IDEA."
"SHE'LL LEARN FASTER THIS WAY. AND AS LONG AS SHE'S WITH BARRY, I HAVE FAITH HE'LL HELP KEEP HER UNDER CONTROL. WHERE'S AQUAMAN?"
"UP ON THE ROOFTOPS. READY TO DIVE IN ON YOUR SIGNAL."

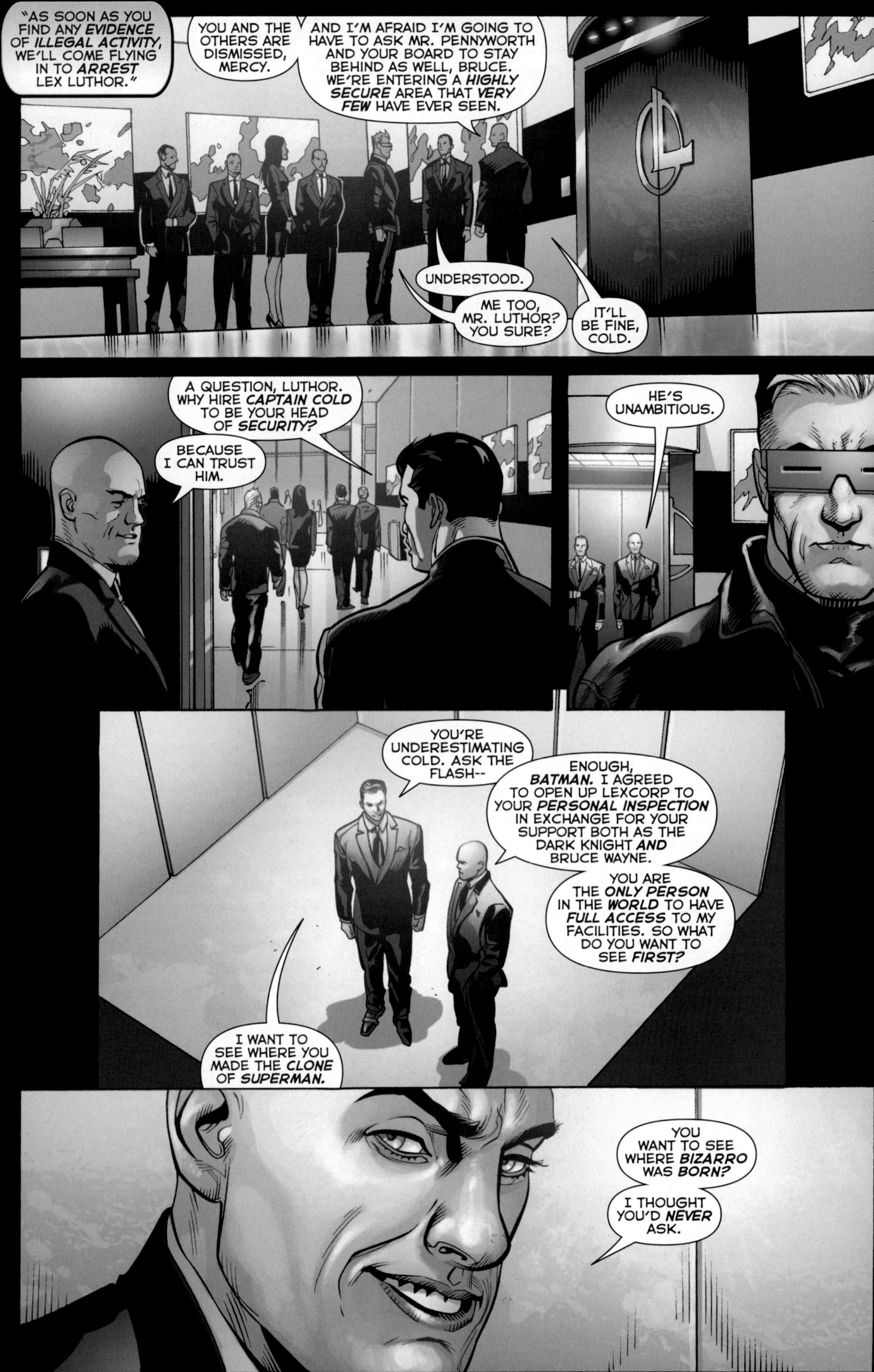
"AS SOON AS YOU FIND ANY EVIDENCE OF ILLEGAL ACTIVITY, WE'LL COME FLYING IN TO ARREST LEX LUTHOR."
YOU AND THE OTHERS ARE DISMISSED, MERCY.
AND I'M AFRAID I'M GOING TO HAVE TO ASK MR. PENNYWORTH AND YOUR BOARD TO STAY BEHIND AS WELL, BRUCE. WE'RE ENTERING A HIGHLY SECURE AREA THAT VERY FEW HAVE EVER SEEN.
UNDERSTOOD.
ME TOO, MR. LUTHOR? YOU SURE?
IT'LL BE FINE, COLD.
A QUESTION, LUTHOR. WHY HIRE CAPTAIN COLD TO BE YOUR HEAD OF SECURITY?
BECAUSE I CAN TRUST HIM.
HE'S UNAMBITIOUS.
YOU'RE UNDERESTIMATING COLD. ASK THE FLASH--
ENOUGH, BATMAN. I AGREED TO OPEN UP LEXCORP TO YOUR PERSONAL INSPECTION IN EXCHANGE FOR YOUR SUPPORT BOTH AS THE DARK KNIGHT AND BRUCE WAYNE.
YOU ARE THE ONLY PERSON IN THE WORLD TO HAVE FULL ACCESS TO MY FACILITIES. SO WHAT DO YOU WANT TO SEE FIRST?
I WANT TO SEE WHERE YOU MADE THE CLONE OF SUPERMAN.
YOU WANT TO SEE WHERE BIZARRO WAS BORN?
I THOUGHT YOU'D NEVER ASK.

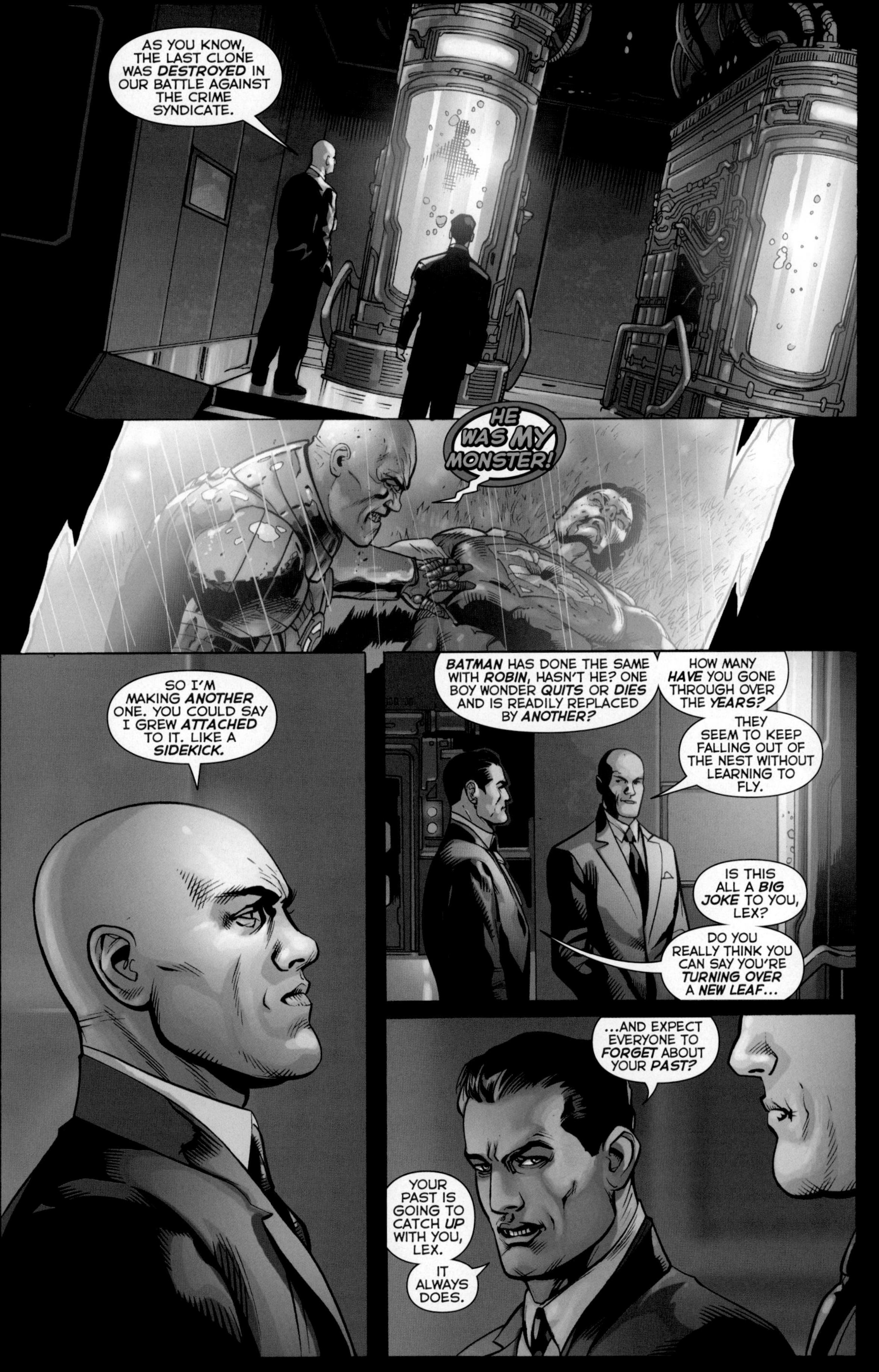

AS YOU KNOW, THE LAST CLONE WAS DESTROYED IN OUR BATTLE AGAINST THE CRIME SYNDICATE.
HE WAS MY MONSTER!
SO I'M MAKING ANOTHER ONE. YOU COULD SAY I GREW ATTACHED TO IT. LIKE A SIDEKICK.
BATMAN HAS DONE THE SAME WITH ROBIN, HASN'T HE? ONE BOY WONDER QUITS OR DIES AND IS READILY REPLACED BY ANOTHER?
HOW MANY HAVE YOU GONE THROUGH OVER THE YEARS?
THEY SEEM TO KEEP FALLING OUT OF THE NEST WITHOUT LEARNING TO FLY.
IS THIS ALL A BIG JOKE TO YOU, LEX?
DO YOU REALLY THINK YOU CAN SAY YOU'RE TURNING OVER A NEW LEAF...
...AND EXPECT EVERYONE TO FORGET ABOUT YOUR PAST?
YOUR PAST IS GOING TO CATCH UP WITH YOU, LEX.
IT ALWAYS DOES.

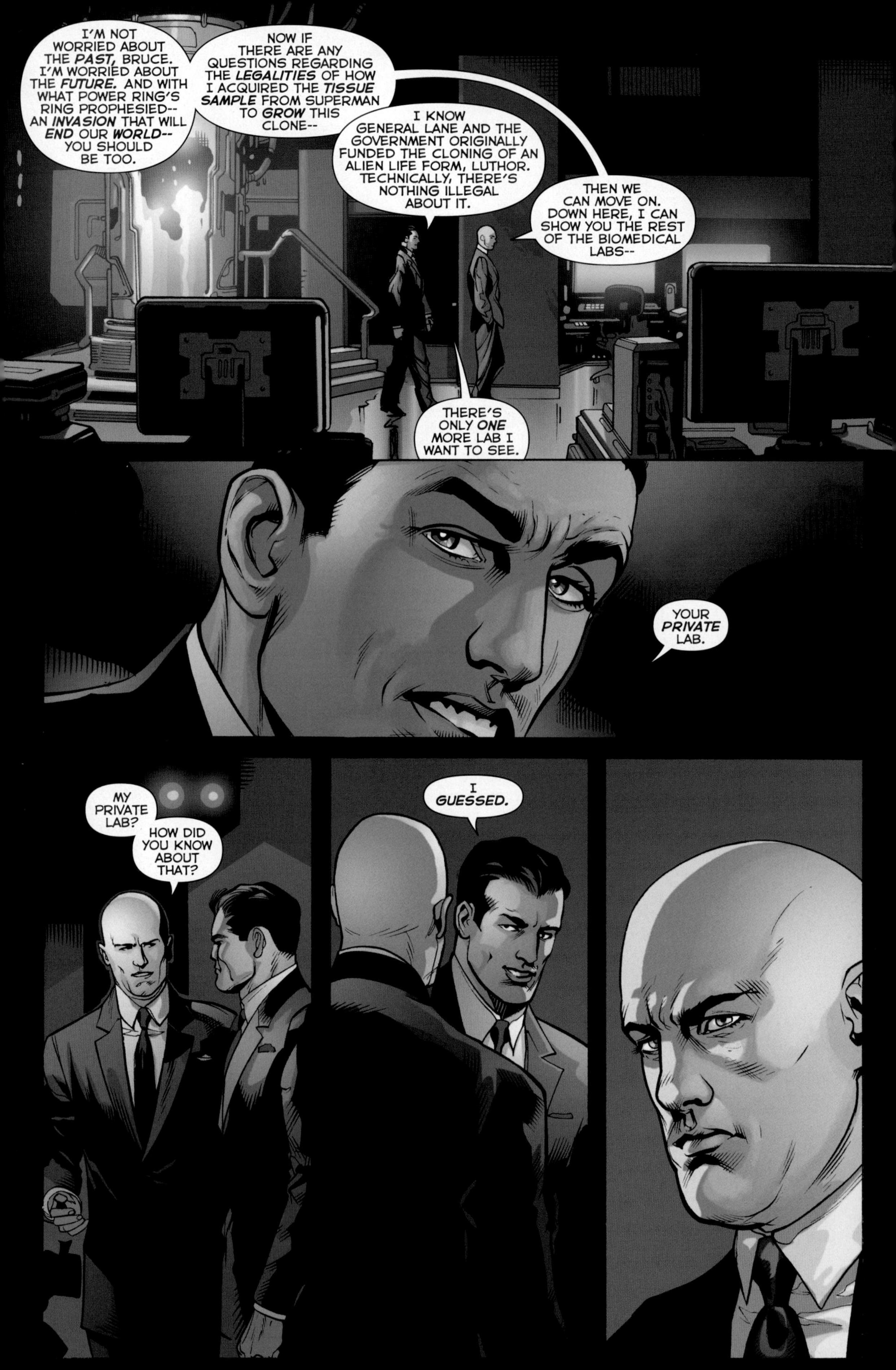
I'M NOT WORRIED ABOUT THE PAST, BRUCE. I'M WORRIED ABOUT THE FUTURE. AND WITH WHAT POWER RING'S RING PROPHESIED-- AN INVASION THAT WILL END OUR WORLD-- YOU SHOULD BE TOO.
NOW IF THERE ARE ANY QUESTIONS REGARDING THE LEGALITIES OF HOW I ACQUIRED THE TISSUE SAMPLE FROM SUPERMAN TO GROW THIS CLONE--
I KNOW GENERAL LANE AND THE GOVERNMENT ORIGINALLY FUNDED THE CLONING OF AN ALIEN LIFE FORM, LUTHOR. TECHNICALLY, THERE'S NOTHING ILLEGAL ABOUT IT.
THEN WE CAN MOVE ON. DOWN HERE, I CAN SHOW YOU THE REST OF THE BIOMEDICAL LABS--
THERE'S ONLY ONE MORE LAB I WANT TO SEE.
YOUR PRIVATE LAB.
MY PRIVATE LAB?
HOW DID YOU KNOW ABOUT THAT?
I GUESSED.

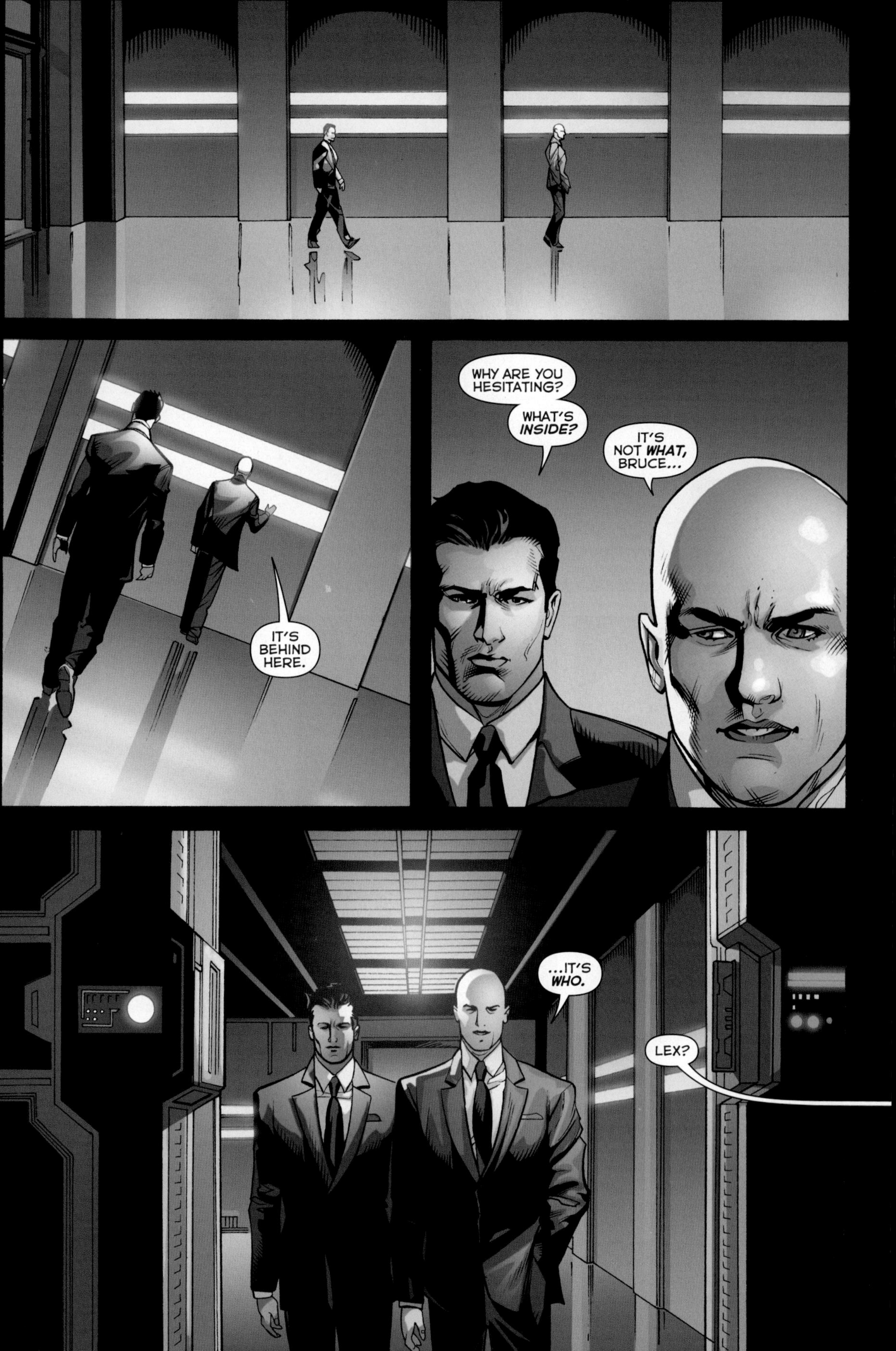
IT'S BEHIND HERE.
WHY ARE YOU HESITATING?
WHAT'S INSIDE?
IT'S NOT WHAT, BRUCE...
...IT'S WHO.
LEX?

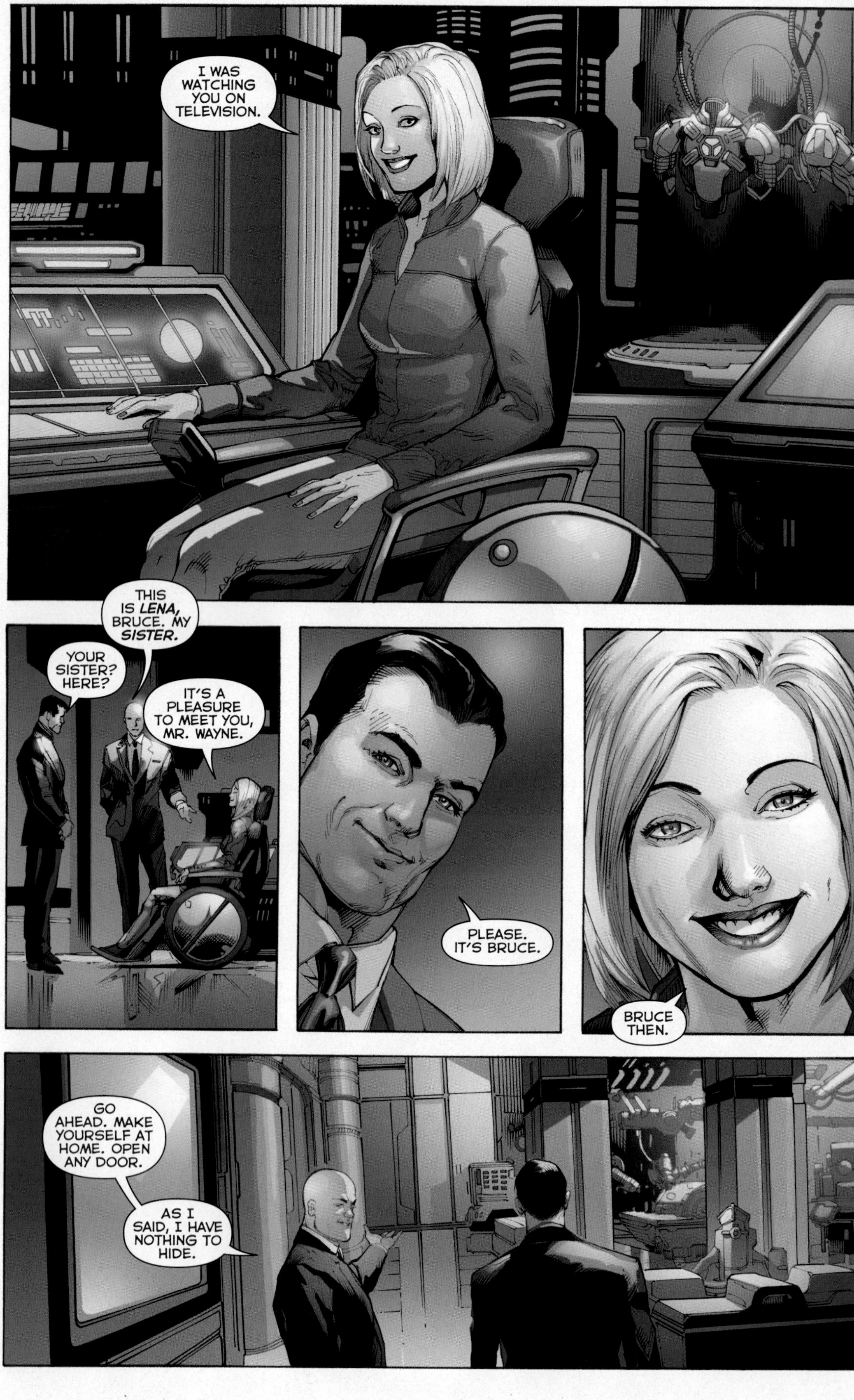
I WAS WATCHING YOU ON TELEVISION.
YOUR SISTER? HERE?
THIS IS LENA, BRUCE. MY SISTER.
IT'S A PLEASURE TO MEET YOU, MR. WAYNE.
PLEASE. IT'S BRUCE.
BRUCE THEN.
GO AHEAD. MAKE YOURSELF AT HOME. OPEN ANY DOOR.
AS I SAID, I HAVE NOTHING TO HIDE.

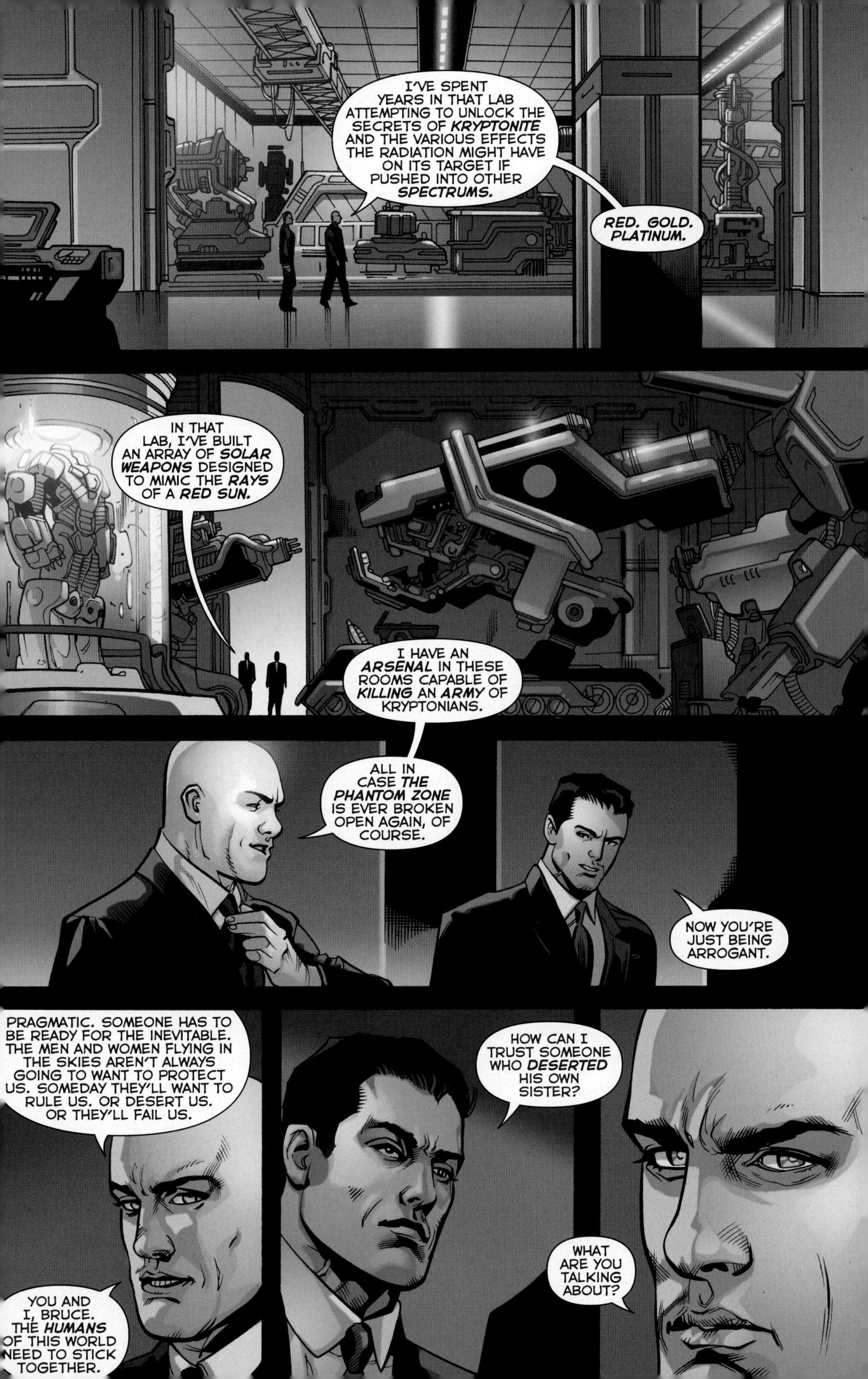
I'VE SPENT YEARS IN THAT LAB ATTEMPTING TO UNLOCK THE SECRETS OF KRYPTONITE AND THE VARIOUS EFFECTS THE RADIATION MIGHT HAVE ON ITS TARGET IF PUSHED INTO OTHER SPECTRUMS.
RED. GOLD. PLATINUM.
IN THAT LAB, I'VE BUILT AN ARRAY OF SOLAR WEAPONS DESIGNED TO MIMIC THE RAYS OF A RED SUN.
I HAVE AN ARSENAL IN THESE ROOMS CAPABLE OF KILLING AN ARMY OF KRYPTONIANS.
ALL IN CASE THE PHANTOM ZONE IS EVER BROKEN OPEN AGAIN, OF COURSE.
NOW YOU'RE JUST BEING ARROGANT.
PRAGMATIC. SOMEONE HAS TO BE READY FOR THE INEVITABLE. THE MEN AND WOMEN FLYING IN THE SKIES AREN'T ALWAYS GOING TO WANT TO PROTECT US. SOMEDAY THEY'LL WANT TO RULE US. OR DESERT US. OR THEY'LL FAIL US.
YOU AND I, BRUCE. THE HUMANS OF THIS WORLD NEED TO STICK TOGETHER.
HOW CAN I TRUST SOMEONE WHO DESERTED HIS OWN SISTER?
WHAT ARE YOU TALKING ABOUT?

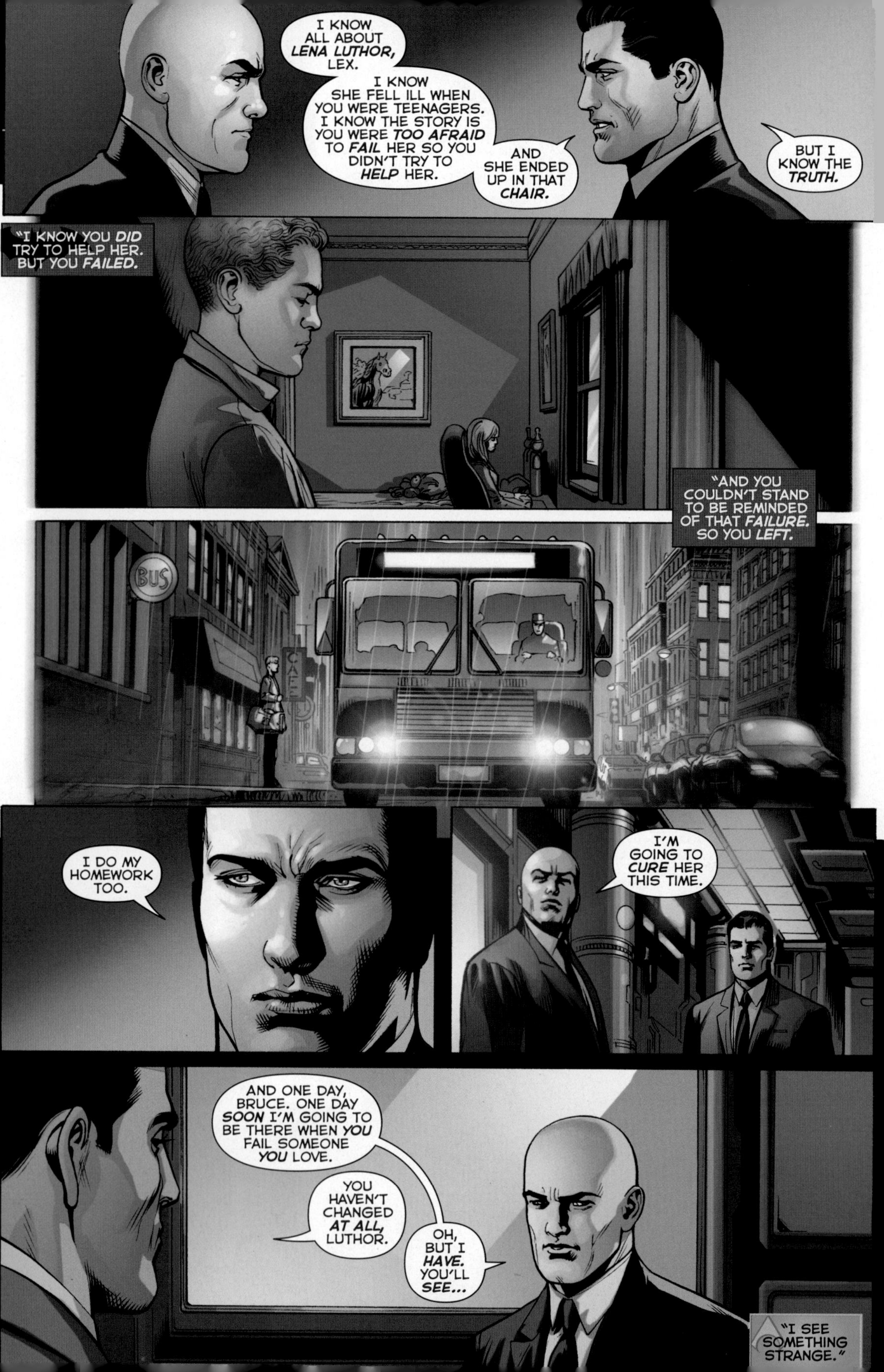
I KNOW ALL ABOUT LENA LUTHOR, LEX.
I KNOW SHE FELL ILL WHEN YOU WERE TEENAGERS. I KNOW THE STORY IS YOU WERE TOO AFRAID TO FAIL HER SO YOU DIDN'T TRY TO HELP HER.
AND SHE ENDED UP IN THAT CHAIR.
BUT I KNOW THE TRUTH.
"I KNOW YOU DID TRY TO HELP HER. BUT YOU FAILED.
"AND YOU COULDN'T STAND TO BE REMINDED OF THAT FAILURE. SO YOU LEFT.
BUS
CAFE
I DO MY HOMEWORK TOO.
I'M GOING TO CURE HER THIS TIME.
AND ONE DAY, BRUCE. ONE DAY SOON I'M GOING TO BE THERE WHEN YOU FAIL SOMEONE YOU LOVE.
YOU HAVEN'T CHANGED AT ALL, LUTHOR.
OH, BUT I HAVE. YOU'LL SEE...
"I SEE SOMETHING STRANGE."

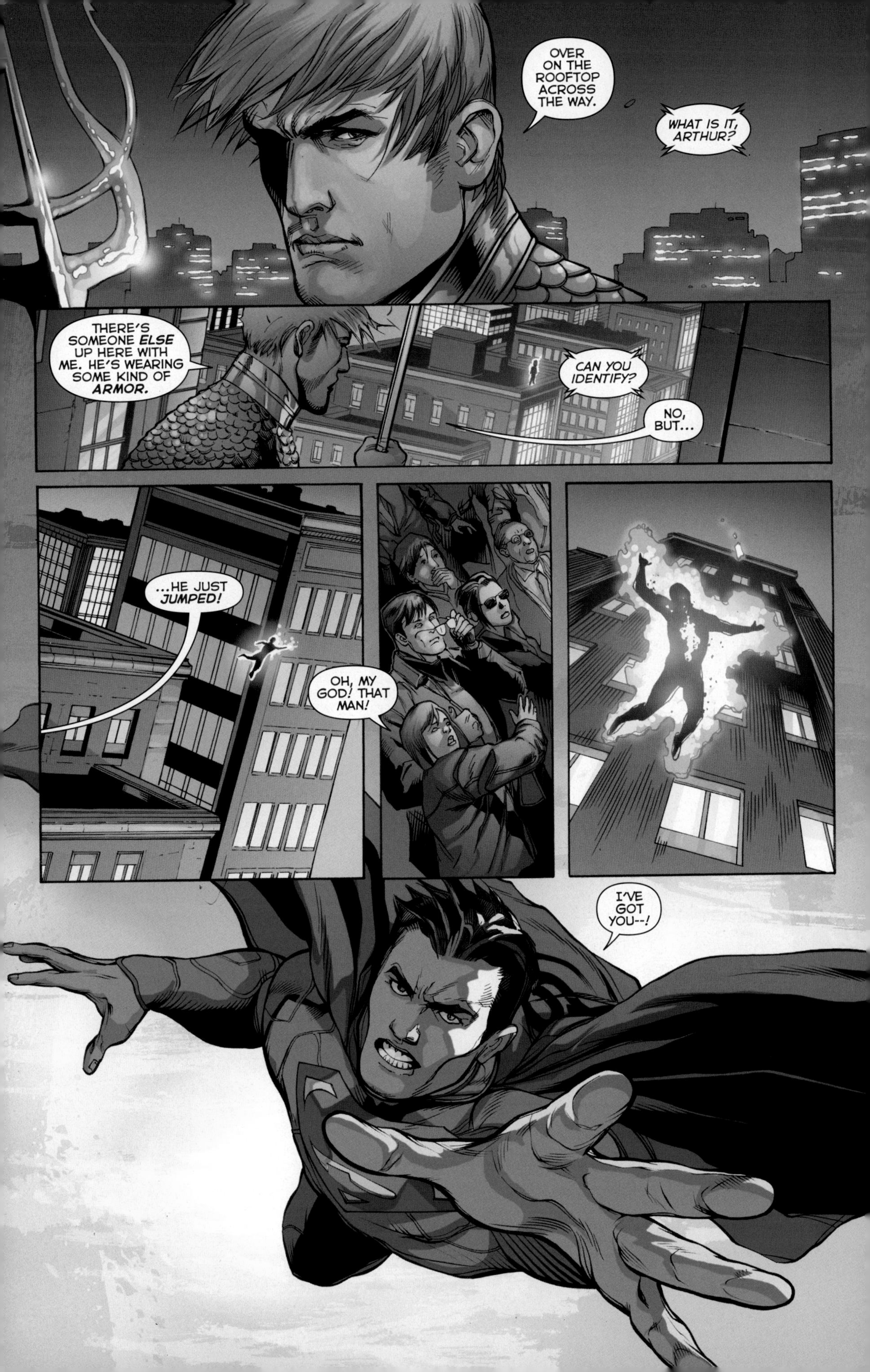
OVER ON THE ROOFTOP ACROSS THE WAY.
WHAT IS IT, ARTHUR?
THERE'S SOMEONE ELSE UP HERE WITH ME. HE'S WEARING SOME KIND OF ARMOR.
CAN YOU IDENTIFY?
NO, BUT...
...HE JUST JUMPED!
OH, MY GOD! THAT MAN!
I'VE GOT YOU--!

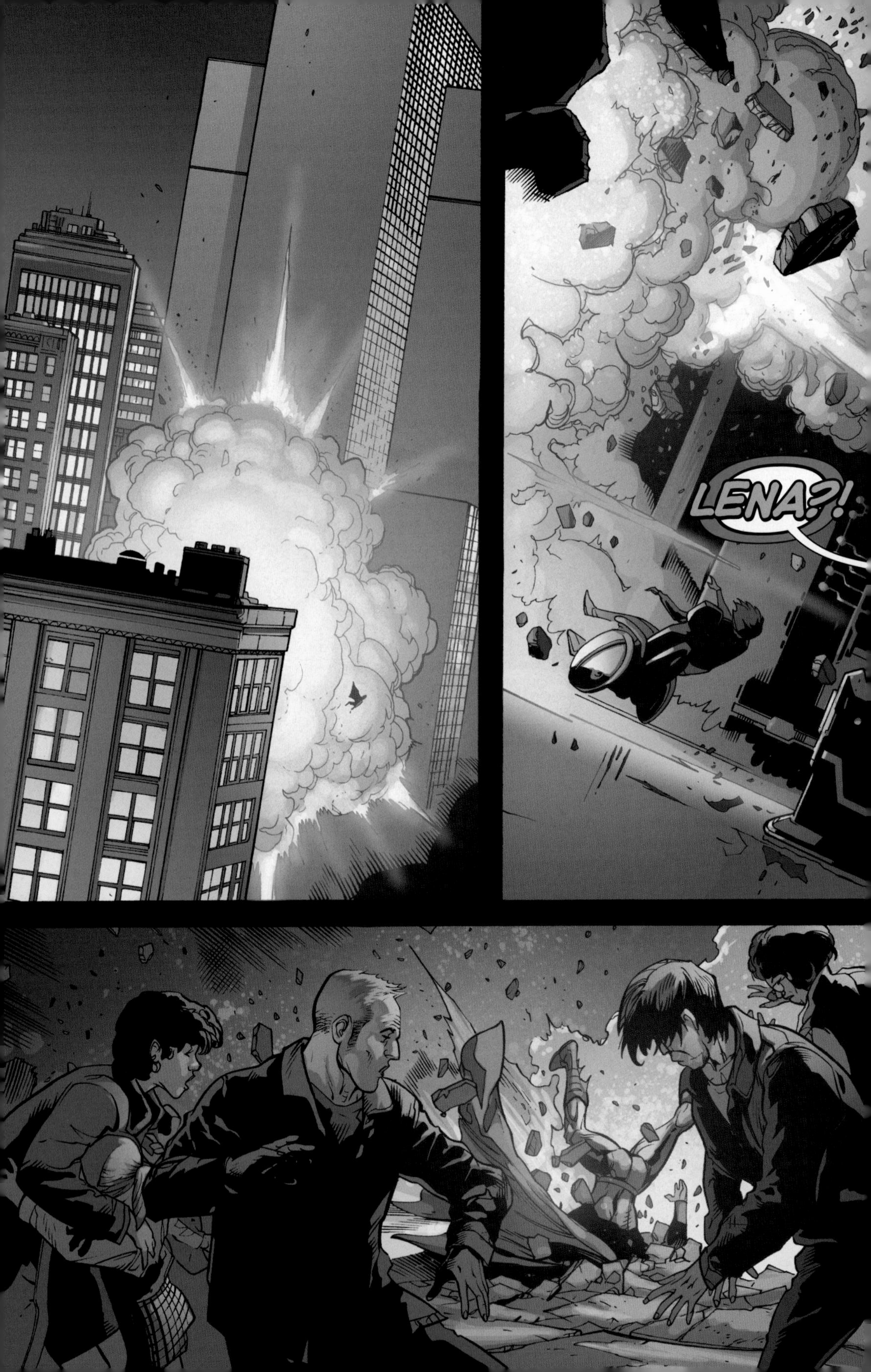
LENA?!

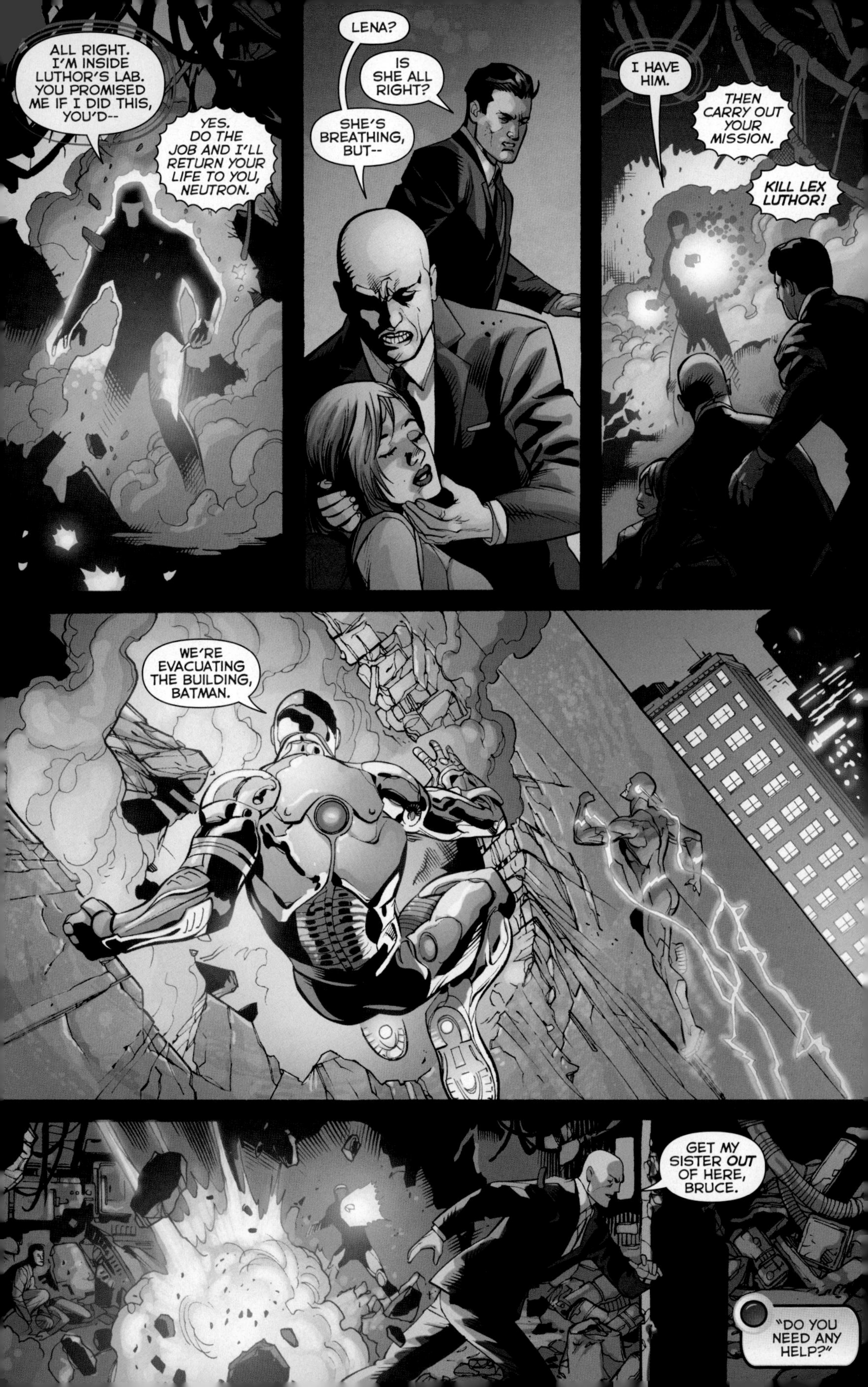
ALL RIGHT. I'M INSIDE LUTHOR'S LAB. YOU PROMISED ME IF I DID THIS, YOU'D--
YES. DO THE JOB AND I'LL RETURN YOUR LIFE TO YOU, NEUTRON.
LENA?
IS SHE ALL RIGHT?
SHE'S BREATHING, BUT--
I HAVE HIM.
THEN CARRY OUT YOUR MISSION.
KILL LEX LUTHOR!
WE'RE EVACUATING THE BUILDING, BATMAN.
GET MY SISTER OUT OF HERE, BRUCE.
"DO YOU NEED ANY HELP?"

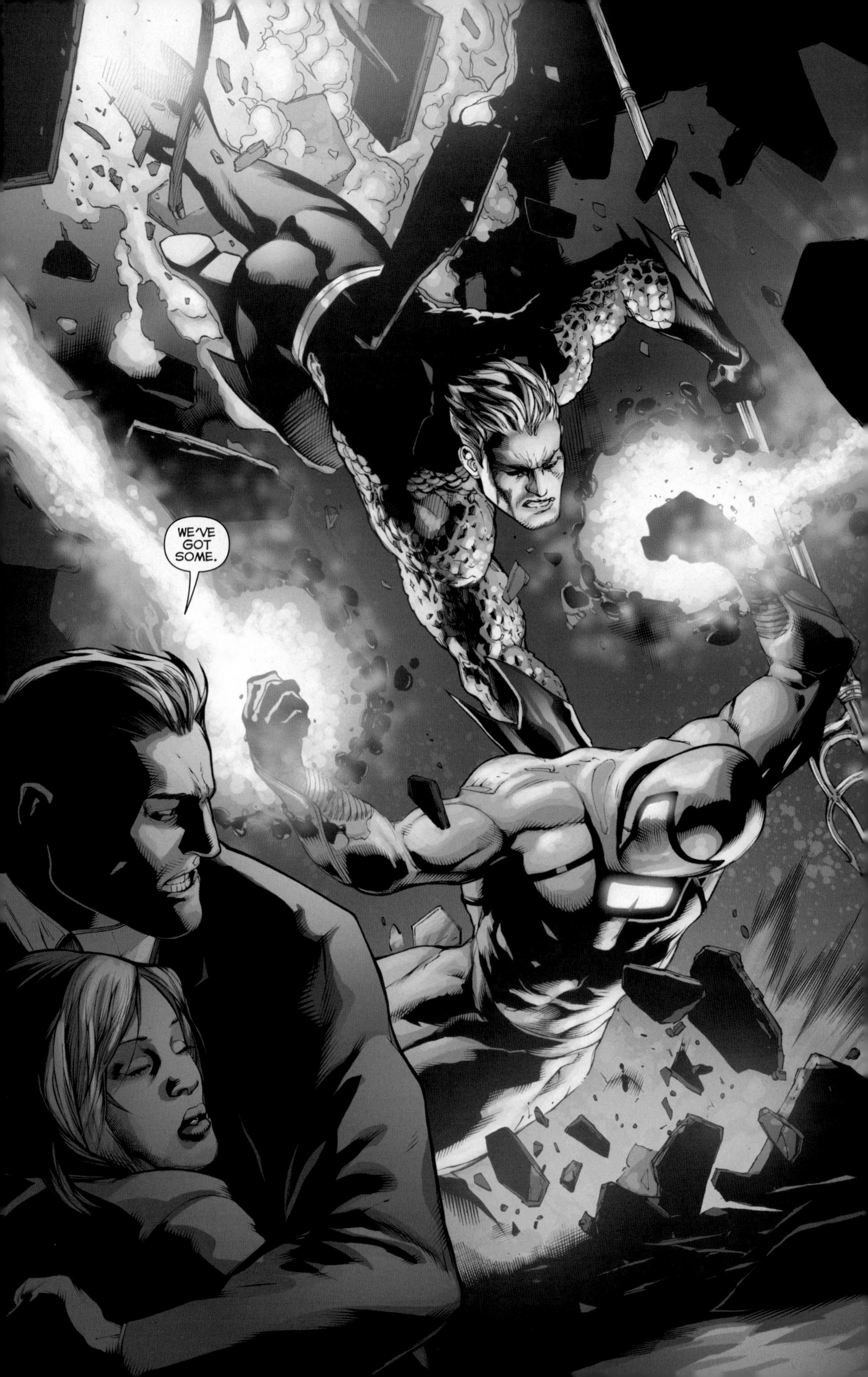
WE'VE GOT SOME.

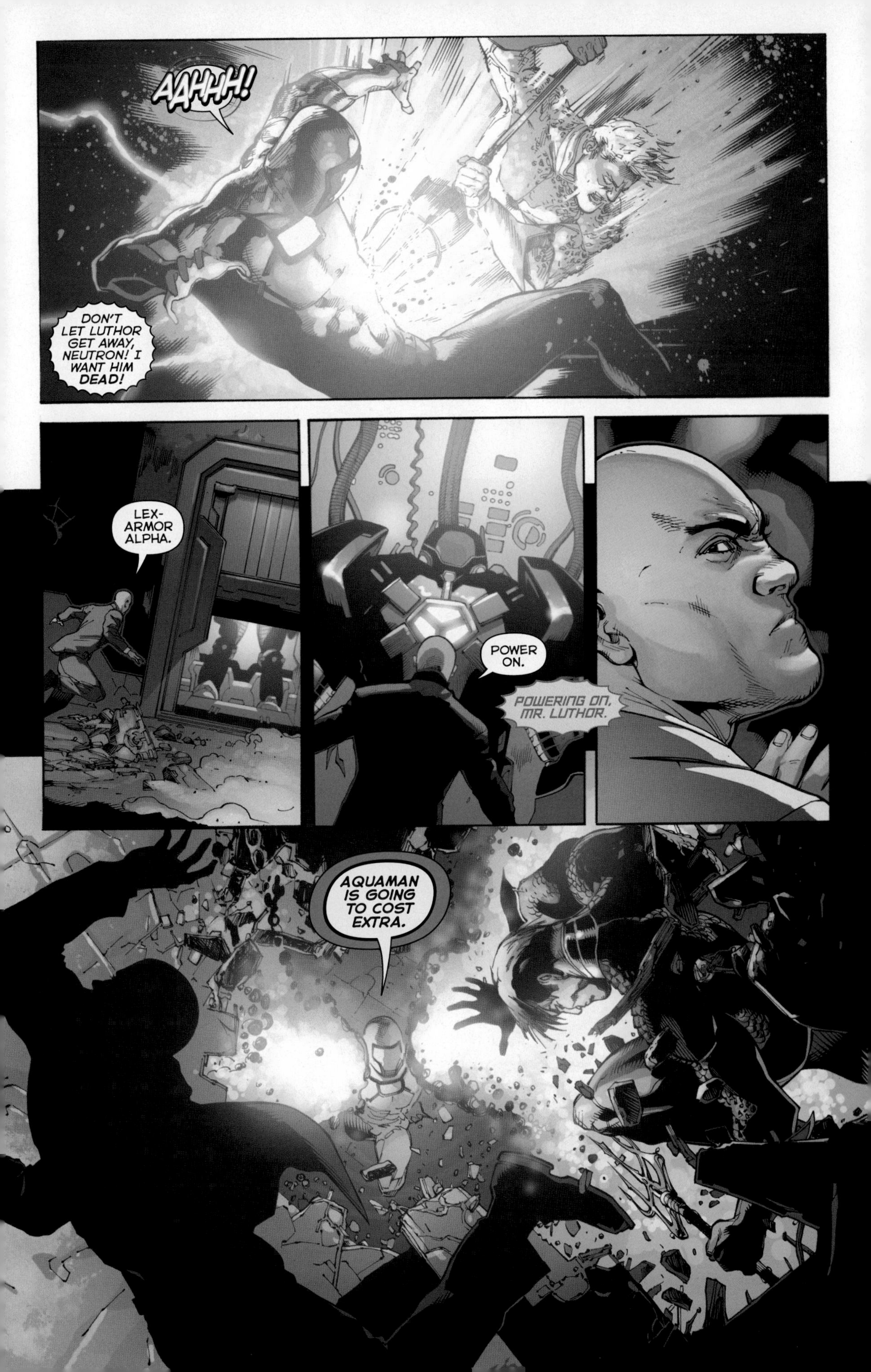
AAHHH!
DON'T LET LUTHOR GET AWAY, NEUTRON! I WANT HIM DEAD!
LEX-ARMOR ALPHA.
POWER ON.
POWERING ON, MR. LUTHOR.
AQUAMAN IS GOING TO COST EXTRA.

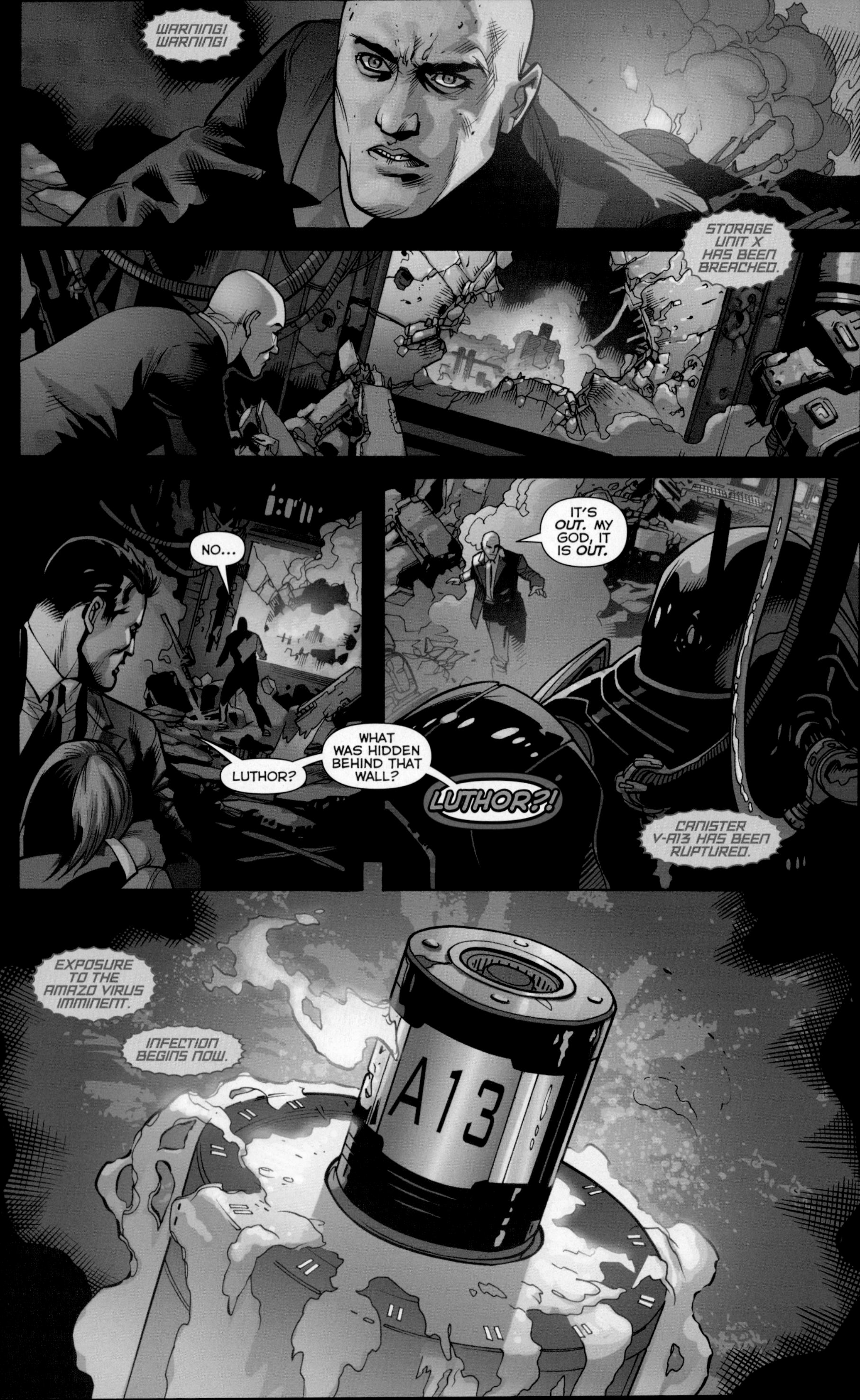
WARNING! WARNING!
STORAGE UNIT X HAS BEEN BREACHED.
NO...
IT'S OUT. MY GOD, IT IS OUT.
LUTHOR?
WHAT WAS HIDDEN BEHIND THAT WALL?
LUTHOR?!
CANISTER V-A13 HAS BEEN RUPTURED.
EXPOSURE TO THE AMAZO VIRUS IMMINENT.
INFECTION BEGINS NOW.
A13

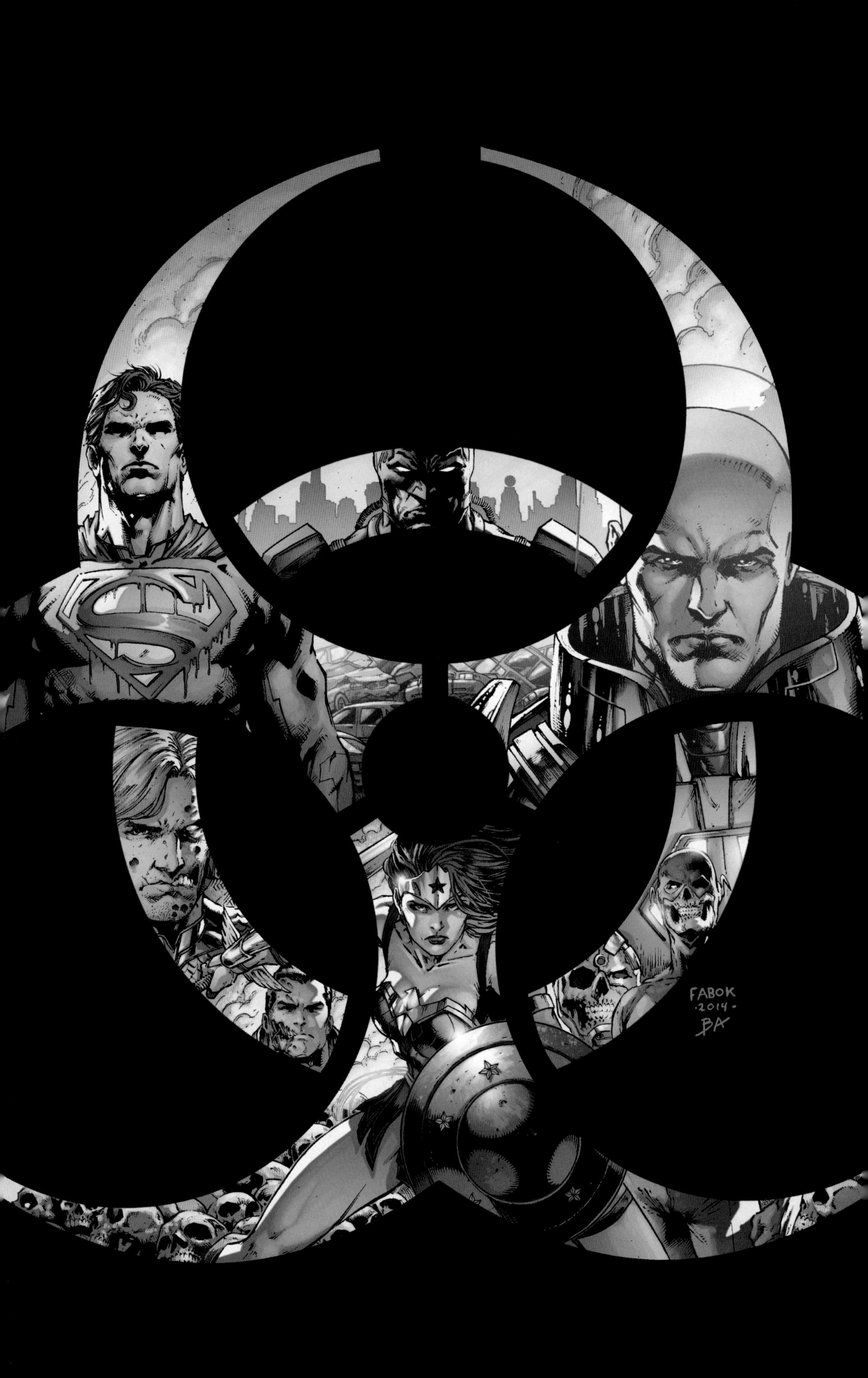
FABOK
·2014·
BA

THE AMAZO VIRUS CHAPTER ONE
QUARANTINED

GEOFF JOHNS writer **JASON FABOK** artist **BRAD ANDERSON** colorist
JASON FABOK & BRAD ANDERSON cover artists

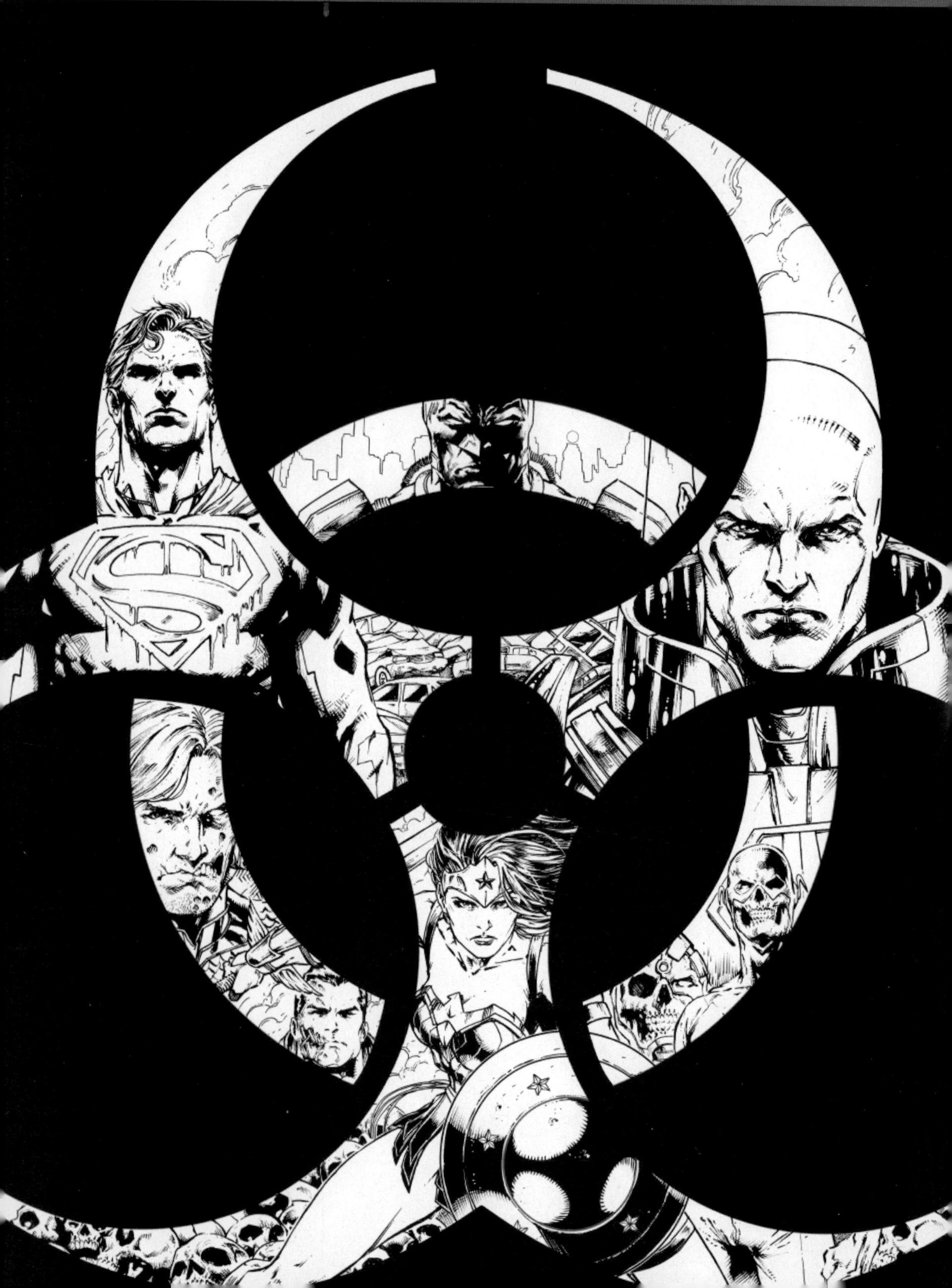

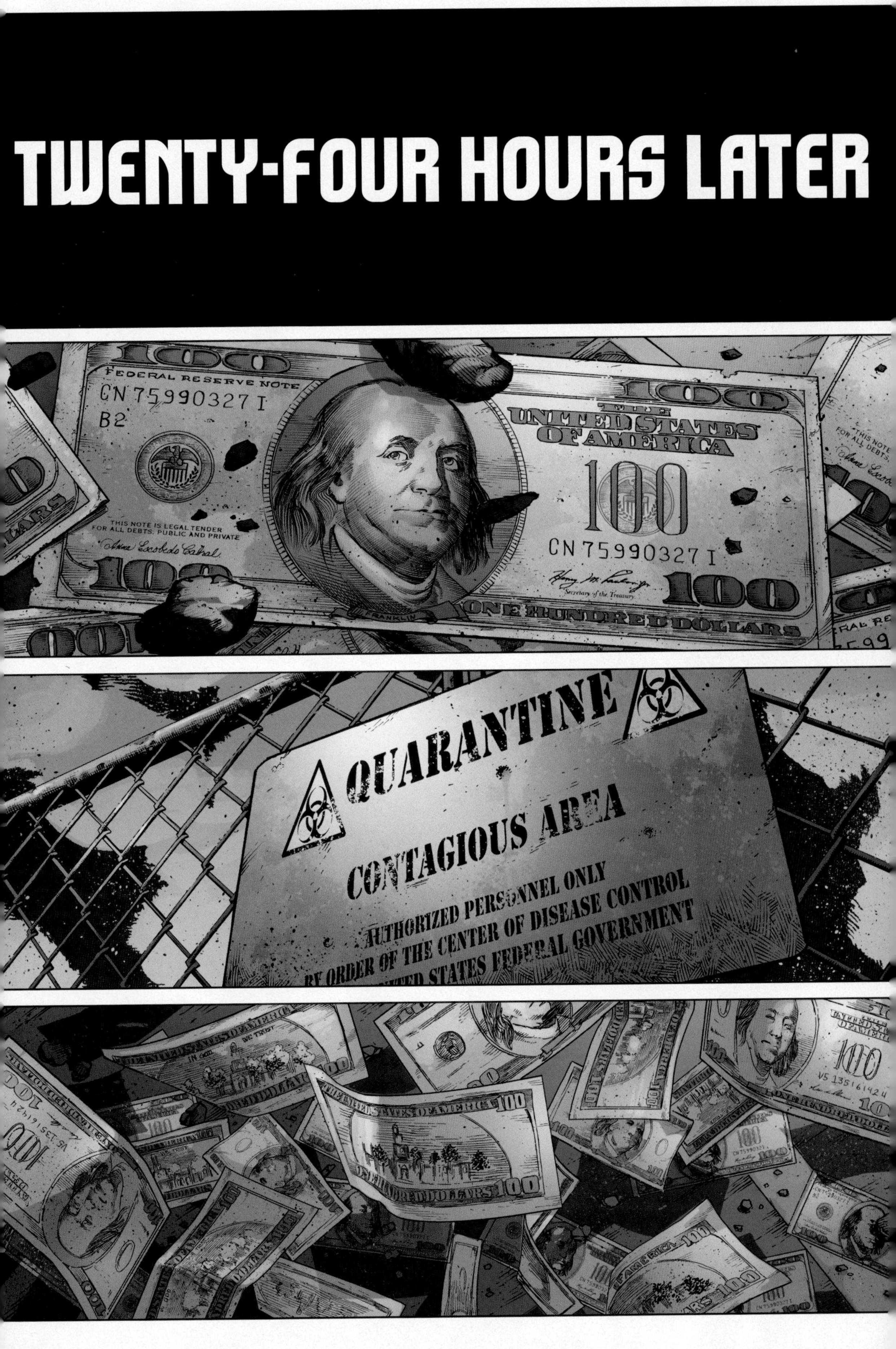
TWENTY-FOUR HOURS LATER
FEDERAL RESERVE NOTE
CN 75990327 I
B2
THIS NOTE IS LEGAL TENDER FOR ALL DEBTS, PUBLIC AND PRIVATE
THE UNITED STATES OF AMERICA
100
CN 75990327 I
Secretary of the Treasury
ONE HUNDRED DOLLARS
QUARANTINE
CONTAGIOUS AREA
AUTHORIZED PERSONNEL ONLY
BY ORDER OF THE CENTER OF DISEASE CONTROL
STATES FEDERAL GOVERNMENT

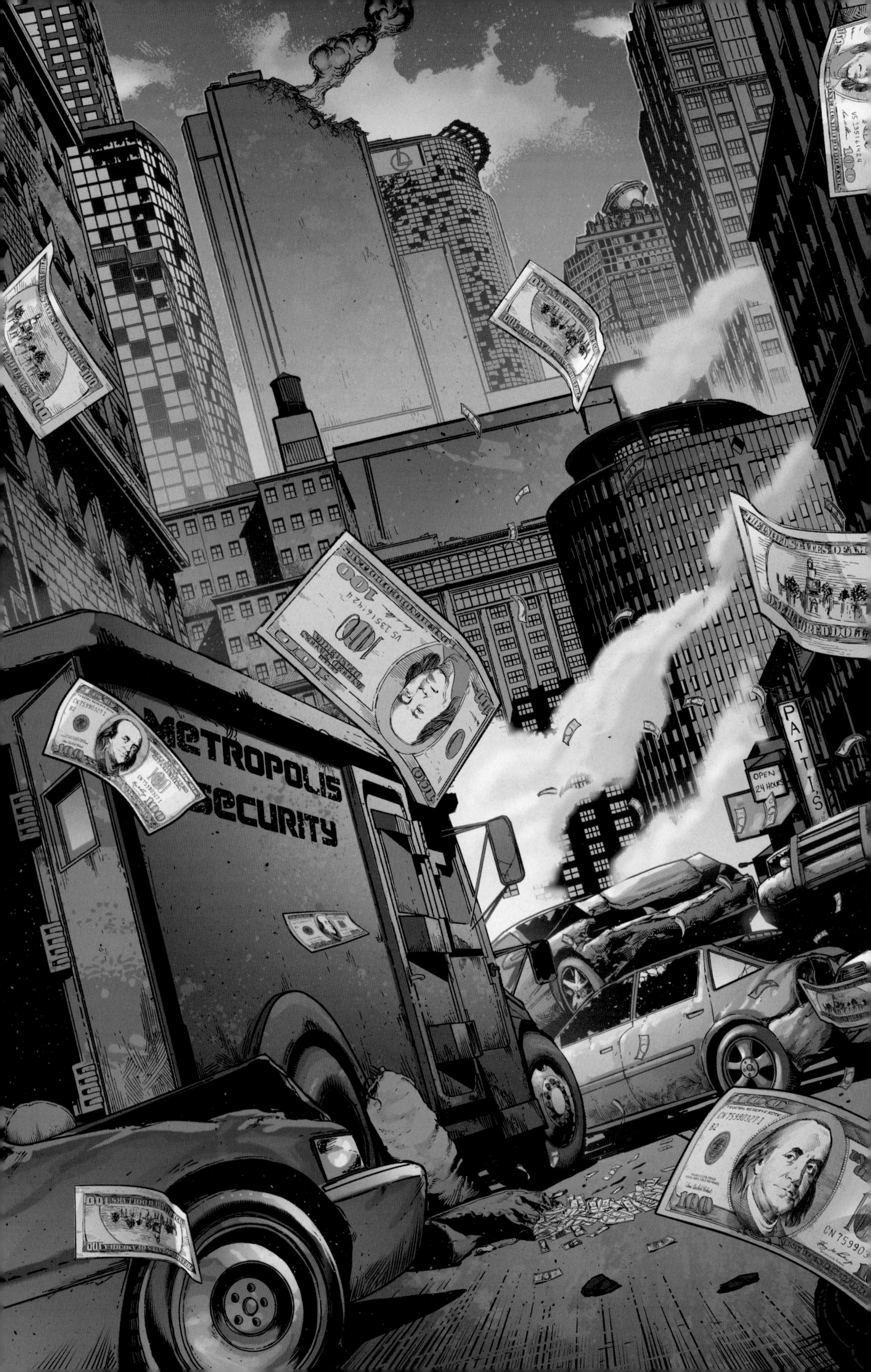
METROPOLIS
SECURITY
PATTI'S
OPEN
24 HOURS

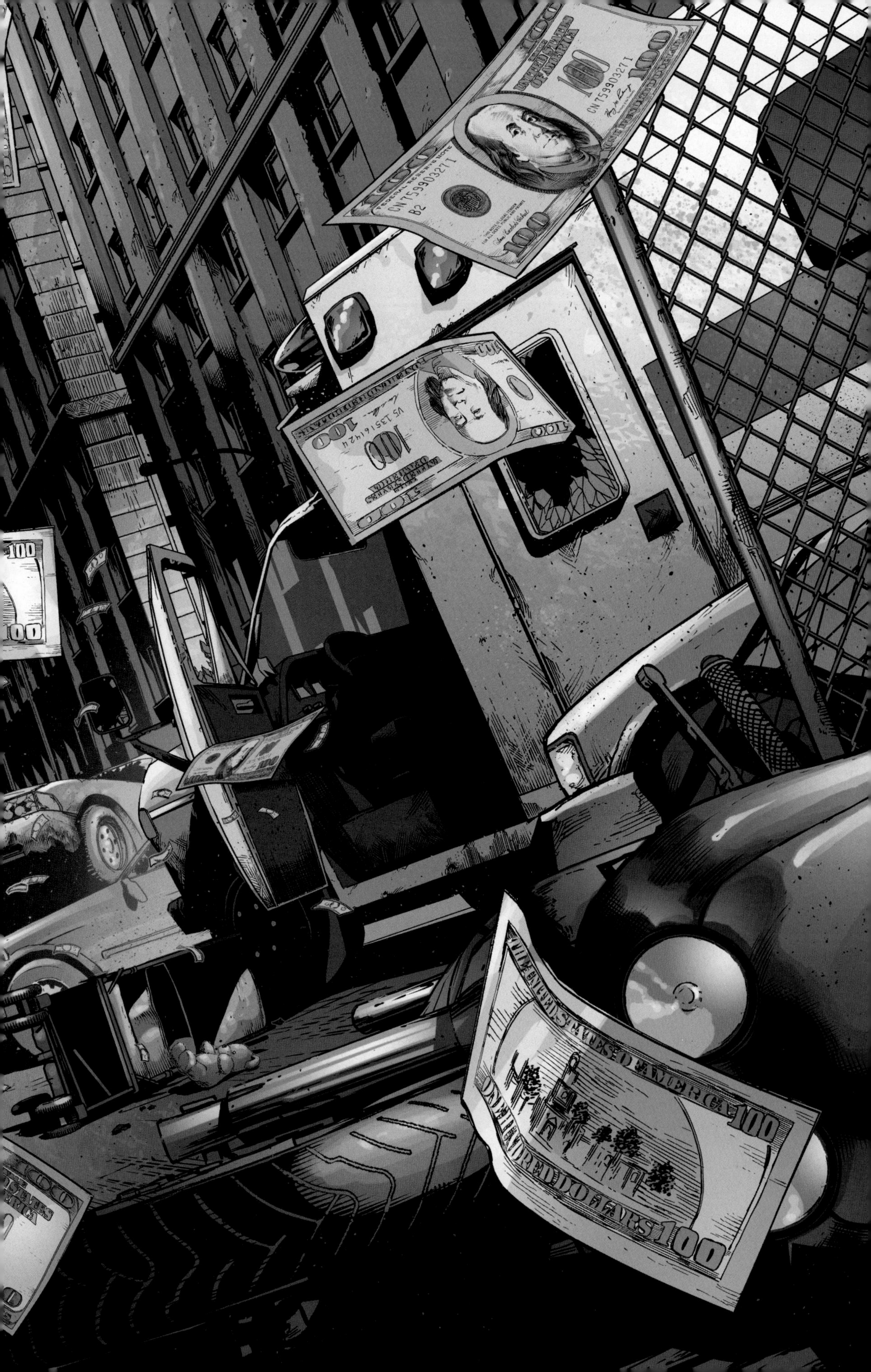
100
CN75990327 1
100

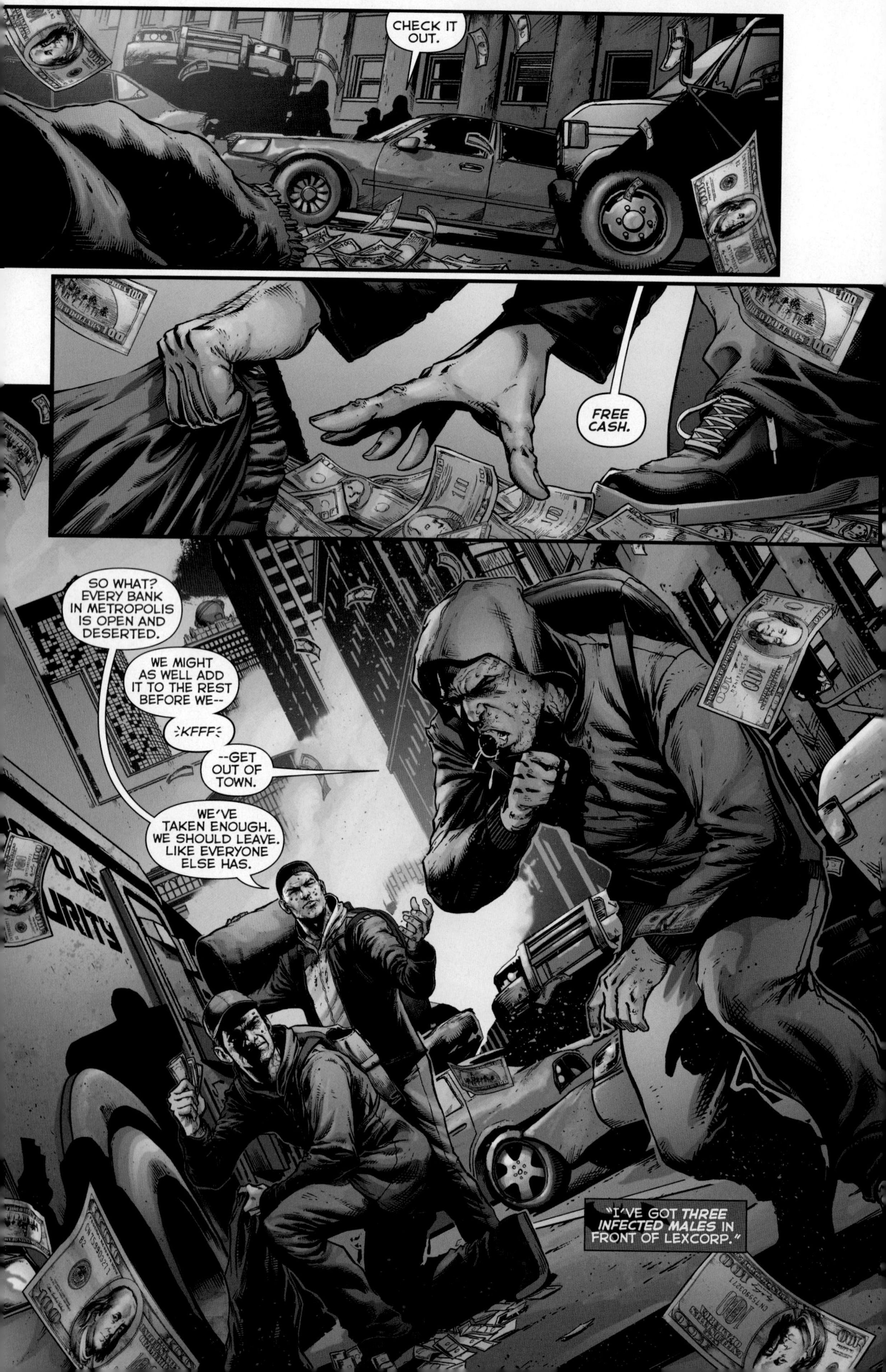
CHECK IT OUT.
FREE CASH.
SO WHAT? EVERY BANK IN METROPOLIS IS OPEN AND DESERTED.
WE MIGHT AS WELL ADD IT TO THE REST BEFORE WE--
KFFF
--GET OUT OF TOWN.
WE'VE TAKEN ENOUGH. WE SHOULD LEAVE. LIKE EVERYONE ELSE HAS.
"I'VE GOT THREE INFECTED MALES IN FRONT OF LEXCORP."

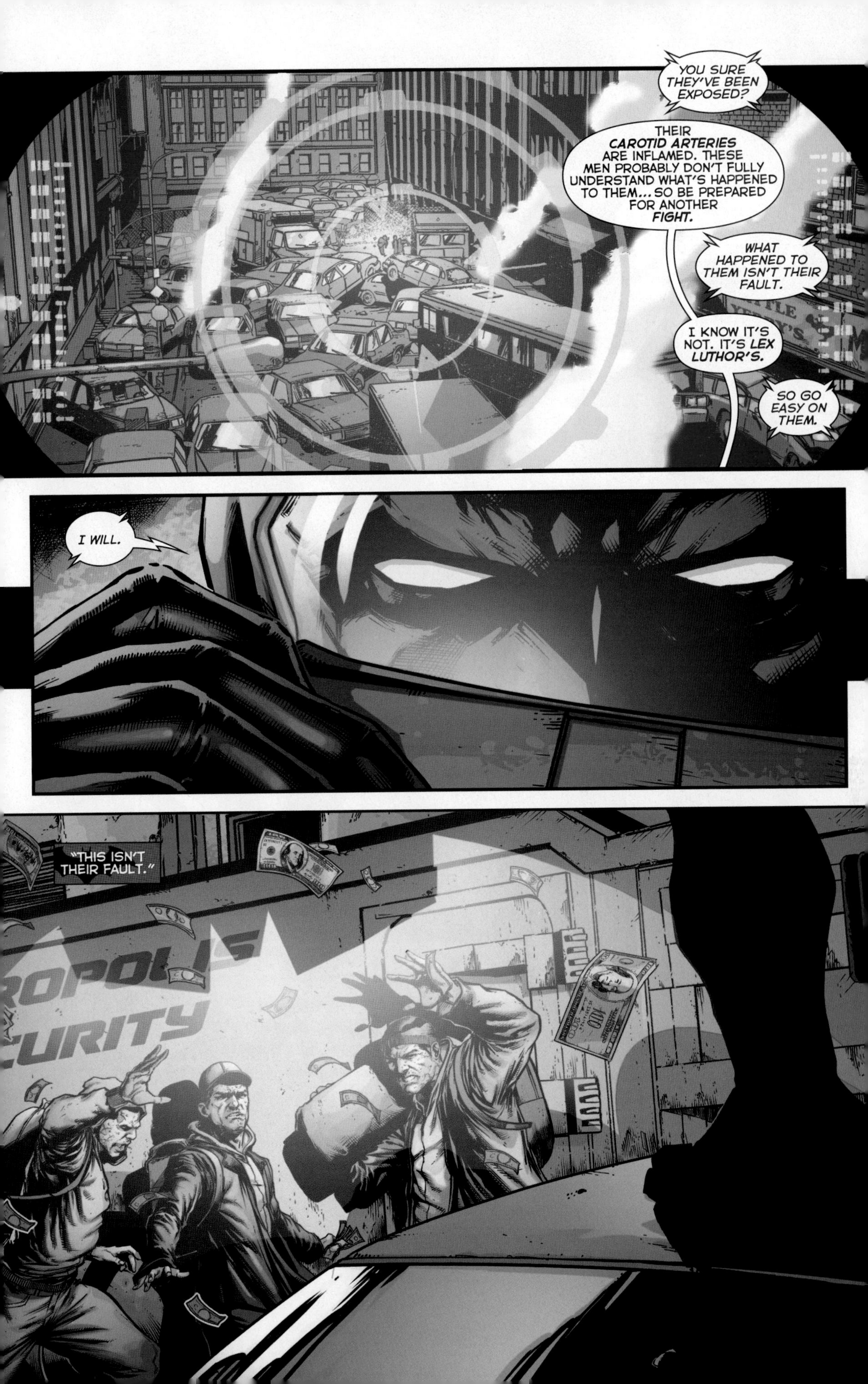
YOU SURE THEY'VE BEEN EXPOSED?
THEIR CAROTID ARTERIES ARE INFLAMED. THESE MEN PROBABLY DON'T FULLY UNDERSTAND WHAT'S HAPPENED TO THEM... SO BE PREPARED FOR ANOTHER FIGHT.
WHAT HAPPENED TO THEM ISN'T THEIR FAULT.
I KNOW IT'S NOT. IT'S LEX LUTHOR'S.
SO GO EASY ON THEM.
I WILL.
"THIS ISN'T THEIR FAULT."
ROPOLIS
CURITY

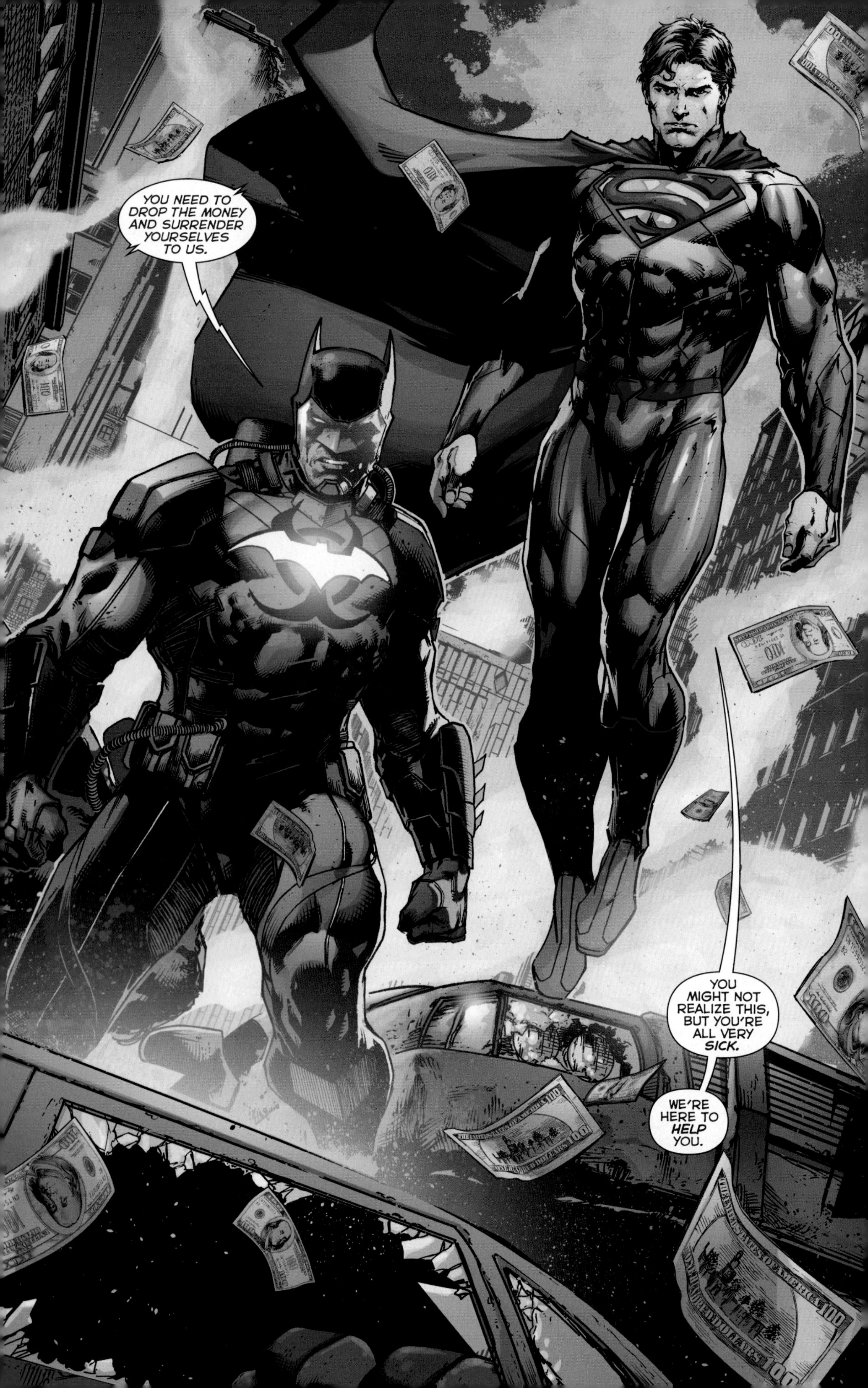
YOU NEED TO DROP THE MONEY AND SURRENDER YOURSELVES TO US.
YOU MIGHT NOT REALIZE THIS, BUT YOU'RE ALL VERY *SICK*.
WE'RE HERE TO *HELP* YOU.

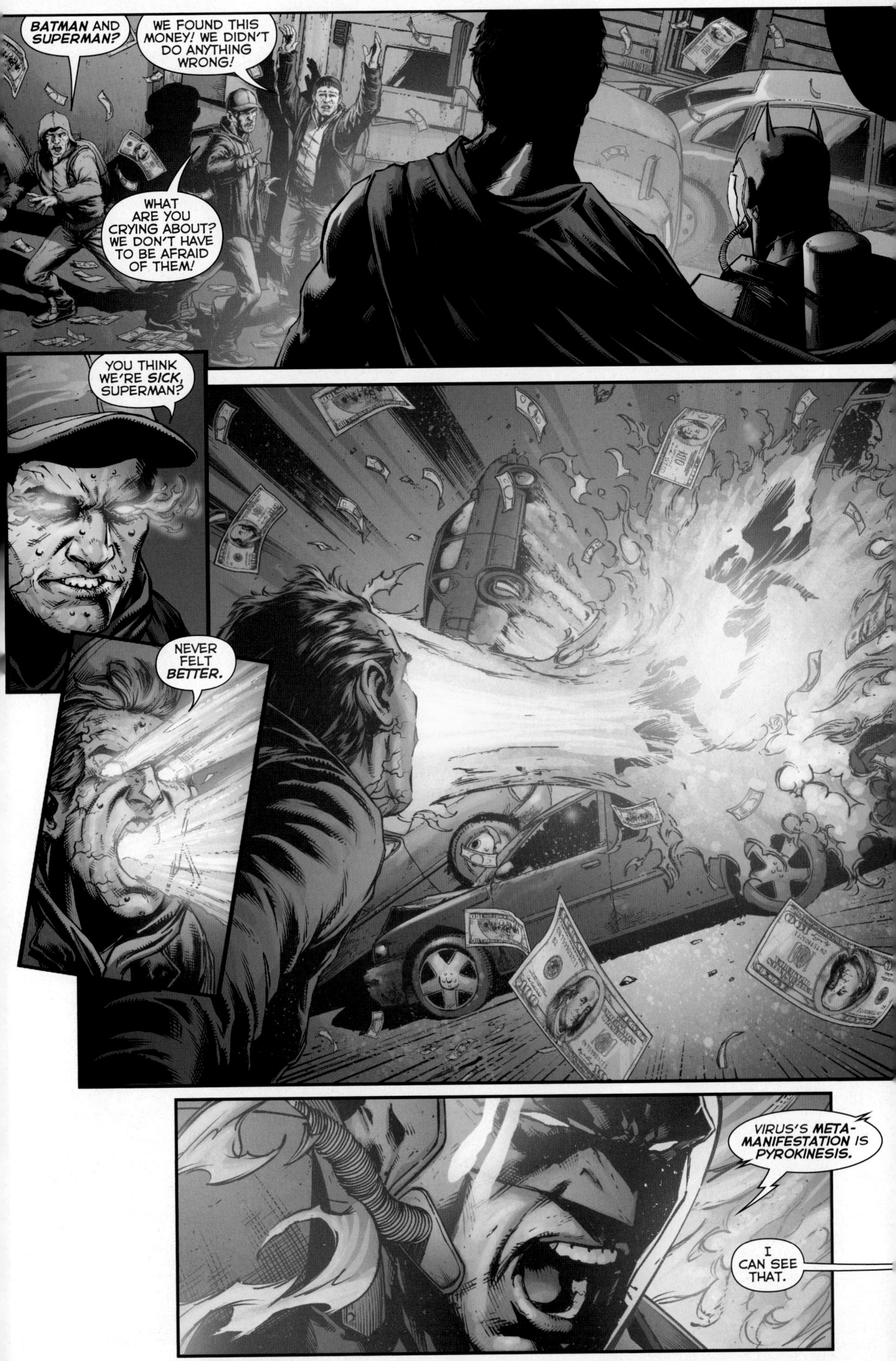
BATMAN AND SUPERMAN?
WE FOUND THIS MONEY! WE DIDN'T DO ANYTHING WRONG!
WHAT ARE YOU CRYING ABOUT? WE DON'T HAVE TO BE AFRAID OF THEM!
YOU THINK WE'RE SICK, SUPERMAN?
NEVER FELT BETTER.
VIRUS'S META-MANIFESTATION IS PYROKINESIS.
I CAN SEE THAT.

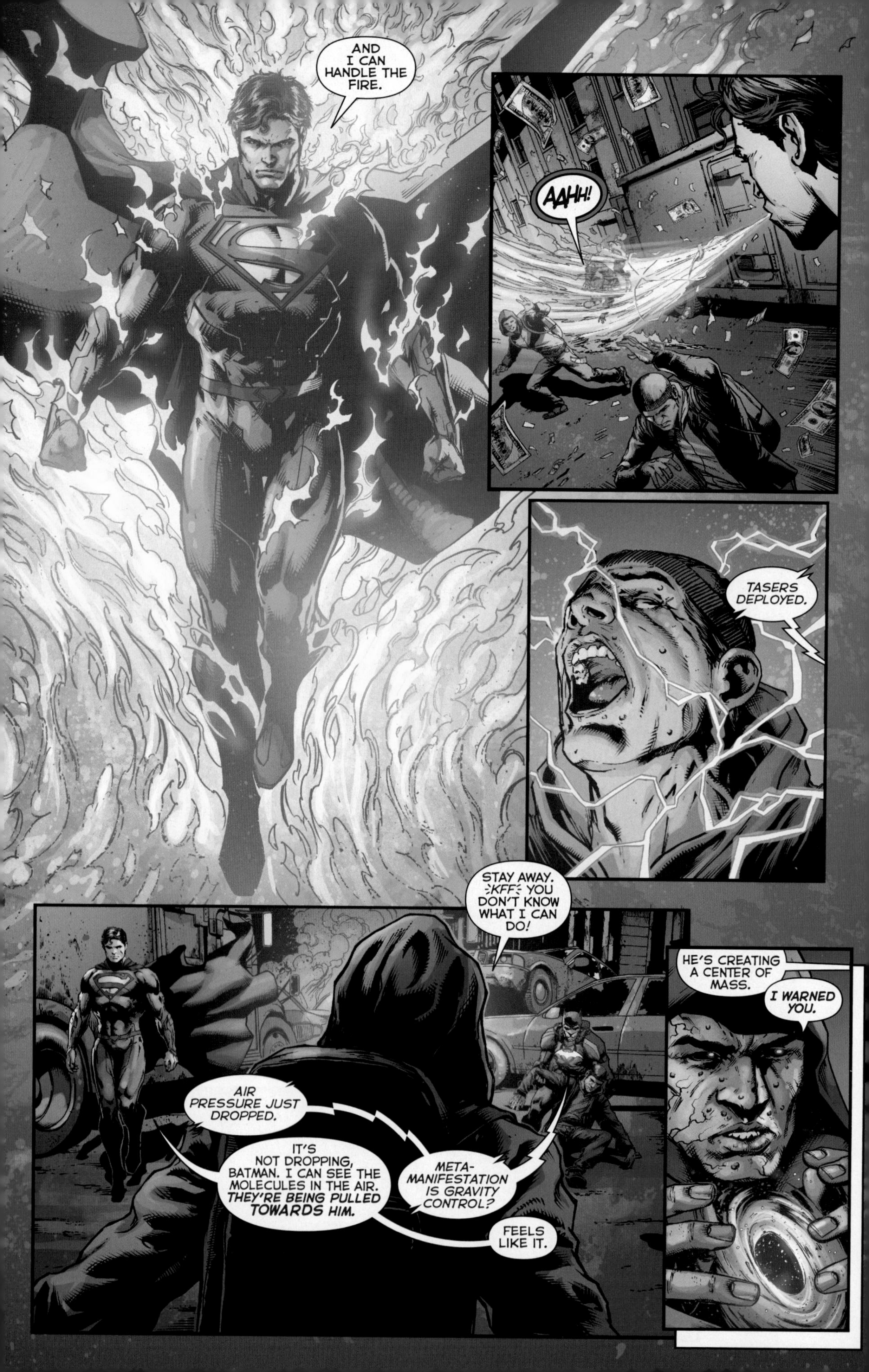
AND I CAN HANDLE THE FIRE.
AAHH!
TASERS DEPLOYED.
STAY AWAY. KFF YOU DON'T KNOW WHAT I CAN DO!
AIR PRESSURE JUST DROPPED.
IT'S NOT DROPPING, BATMAN. I CAN SEE THE MOLECULES IN THE AIR. THEY'RE BEING PULLED TOWARDS HIM.
META-MANIFESTATION IS GRAVITY CONTROL?
FEELS LIKE IT.
HE'S CREATING A CENTER OF MASS.
I WARNED YOU.

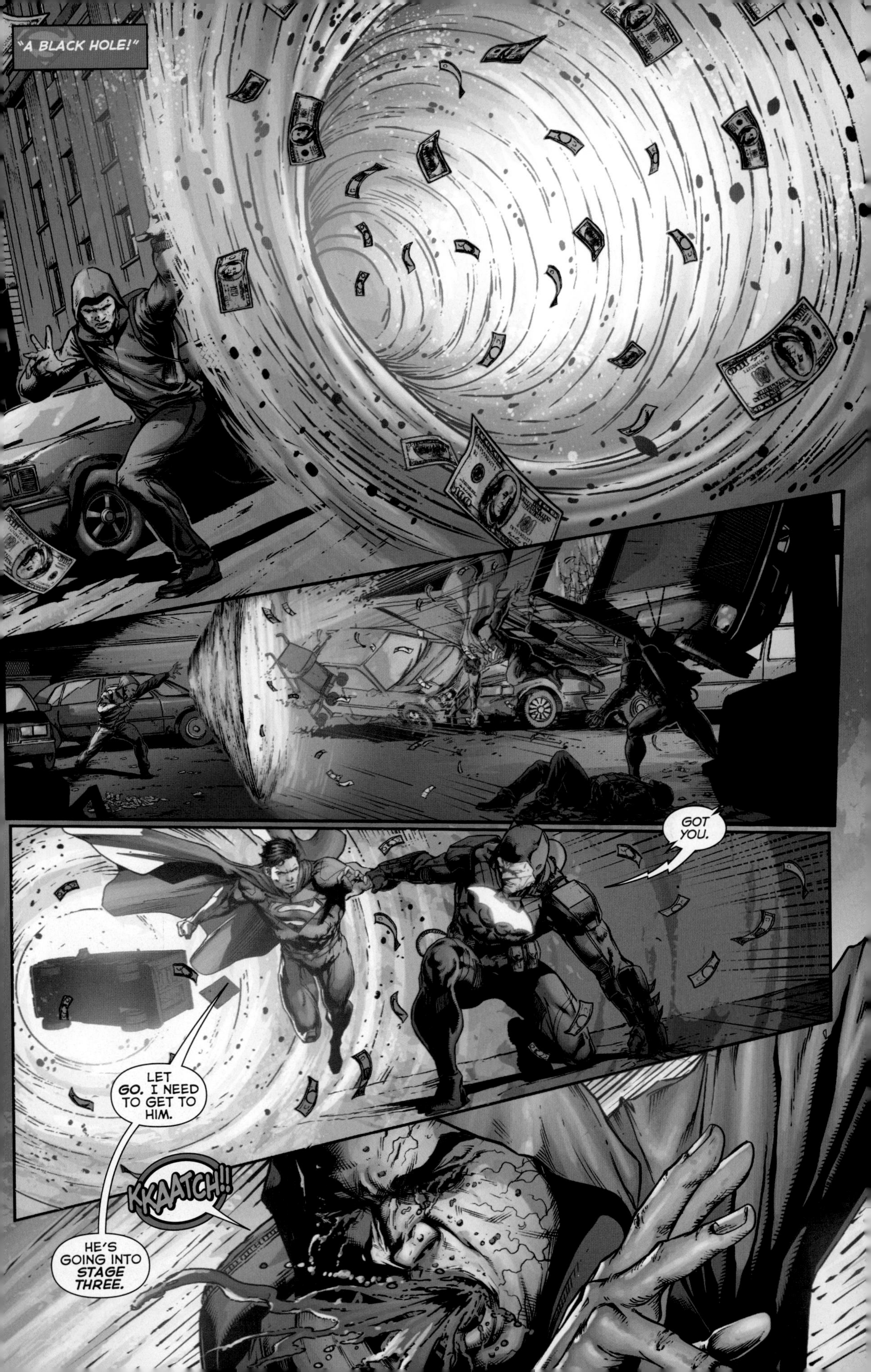
"A BLACK HOLE!"
GOT YOU.
LET GO. I NEED TO GET TO HIM.
KKAATCH!!
HE'S GOING INTO STAGE THREE.

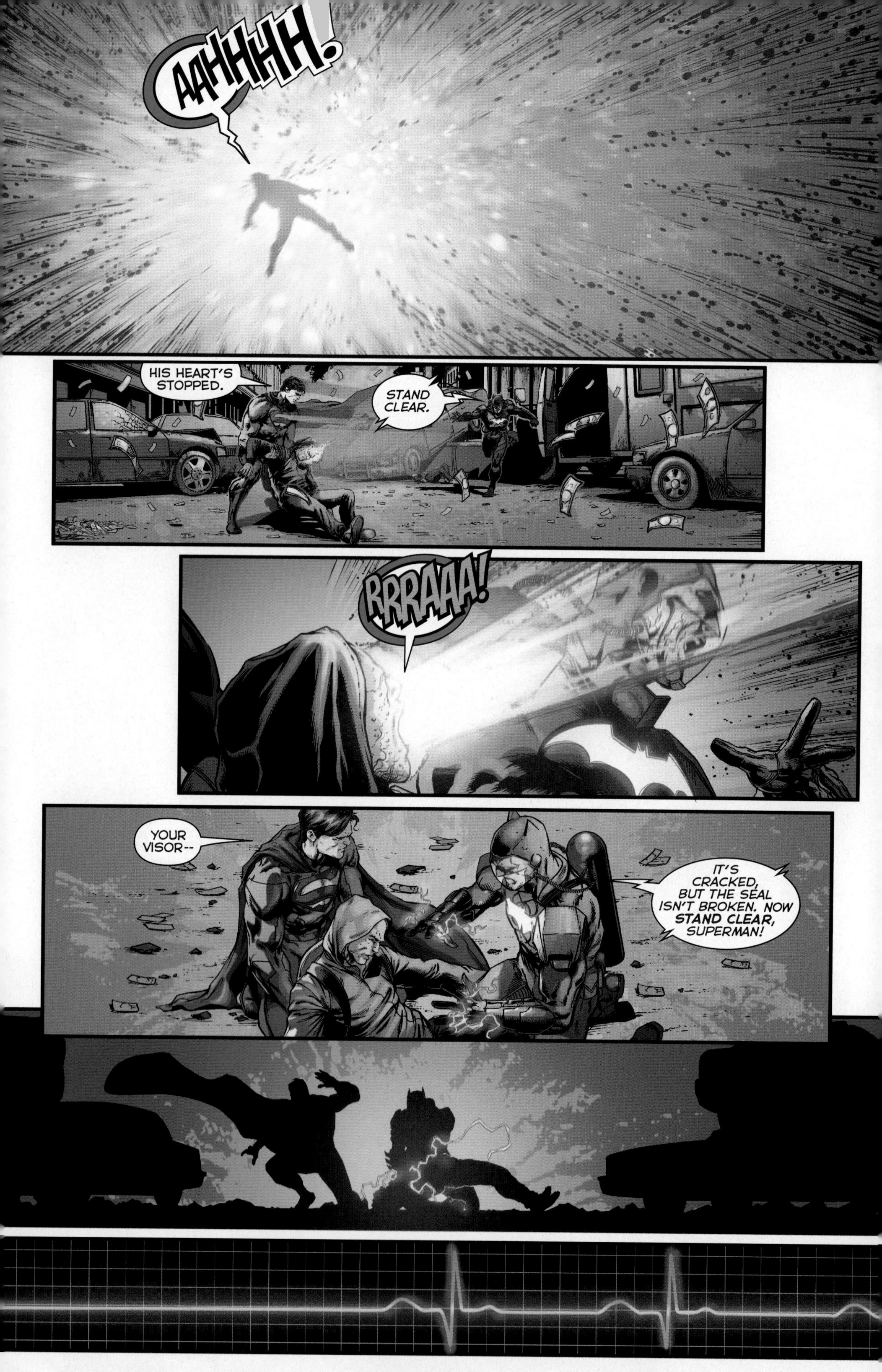
AAHHHH!
HIS HEART'S STOPPED.
STAND CLEAR.
RRRAAA!
YOUR VISOR--
IT'S CRACKED, BUT THE SEAL ISN'T BROKEN. NOW STAND CLEAR, SUPERMAN!

HE'S ALIVE, WHICH IS MORE THAN WE CAN SAY FOR THE REST OF THE INFECTED.

YOU SURE YOU SHOULD BE COMING INTO METROPOLIS LIKE THIS? RISKING YOURSELF TO EXPOSURE?

I'M NOT THE ONE WITHOUT AN IMPERMEABLE SUIT.

THE VIRUS CAN'T AFFECT ME.

I'M NOT HUMAN.

BUT YOU *ARE*, BRUCE, AND THIS *DISEASE* IS UNLIKE ANYTHING WE'VE EVER ENCOUNTERED.

IF YOU GET INFECTED, YOU'LL DIE.

IF THE ROLES WERE REVERSED, YOU WOULDN'T RUN. YOU'D STAY NO MATTER THE RISK. BECAUSE OUR FRIENDS NEED US.

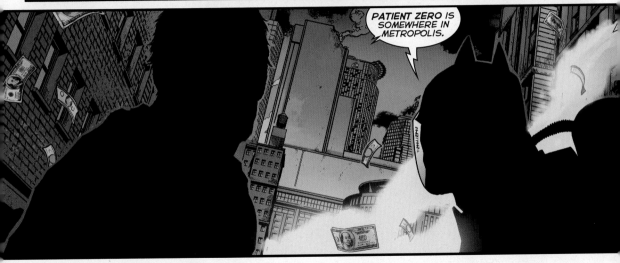

PATIENT ZERO IS SOMEWHERE IN METROPOLIS.

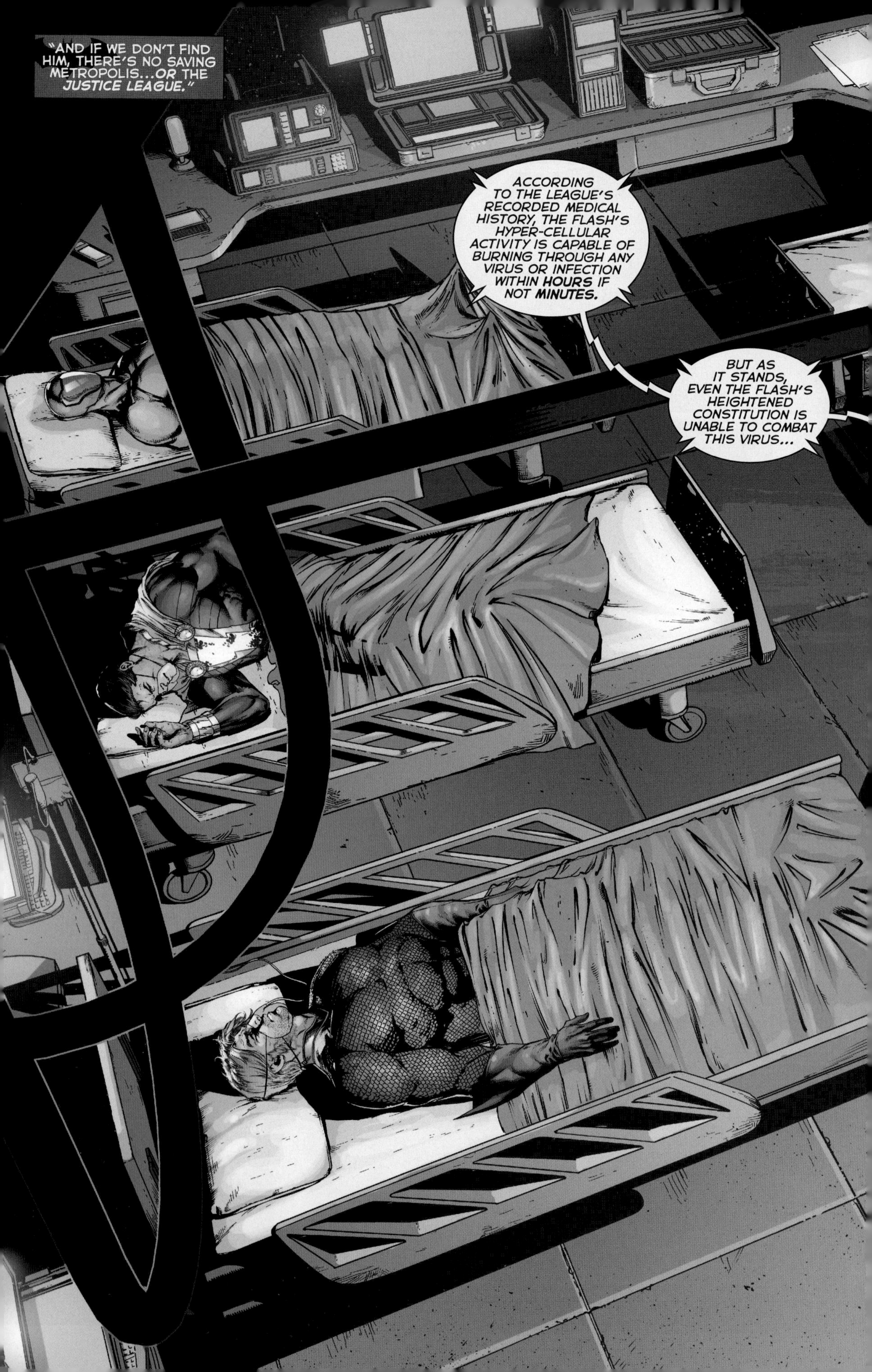
"AND IF WE DON'T FIND HIM, THERE'S NO SAVING METROPOLIS...OR THE JUSTICE LEAGUE."
ACCORDING TO THE LEAGUE'S RECORDED MEDICAL HISTORY, THE FLASH'S HYPER-CELLULAR ACTIVITY IS CAPABLE OF BURNING THROUGH ANY VIRUS OR INFECTION WITHIN HOURS IF NOT MINUTES.
BUT AS IT STANDS, EVEN THE FLASH'S HEIGHTENED CONSTITUTION IS UNABLE TO COMBAT THIS VIRUS...

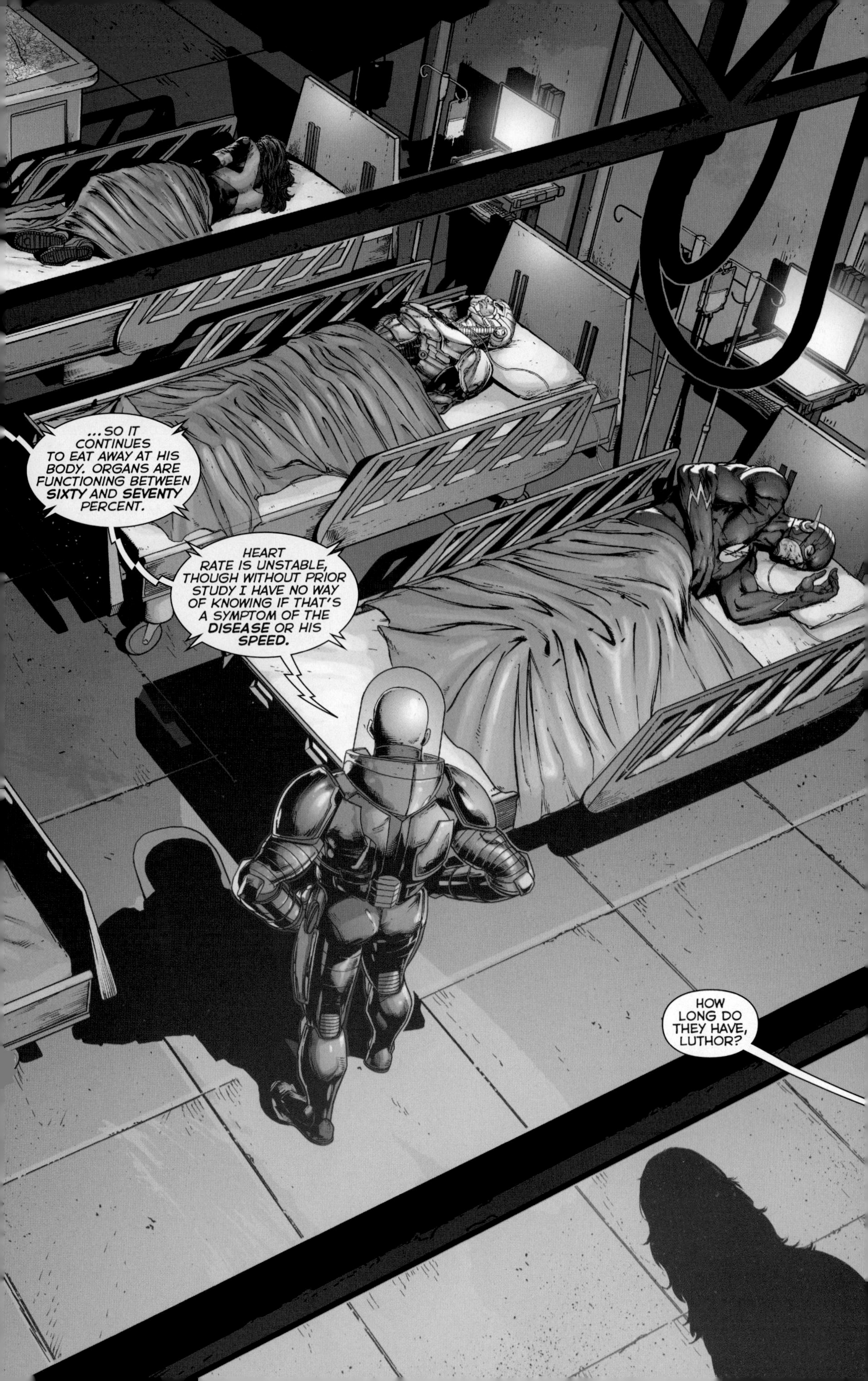
...SO IT CONTINUES TO EAT AWAY AT HIS BODY. ORGANS ARE FUNCTIONING BETWEEN **SIXTY** AND **SEVENTY** PERCENT.
HEART RATE IS UNSTABLE, THOUGH WITHOUT PRIOR STUDY I HAVE NO WAY OF KNOWING IF THAT'S A SYMPTOM OF THE **DISEASE** OR HIS **SPEED.**
HOW LONG DO THEY HAVE, LUTHOR?

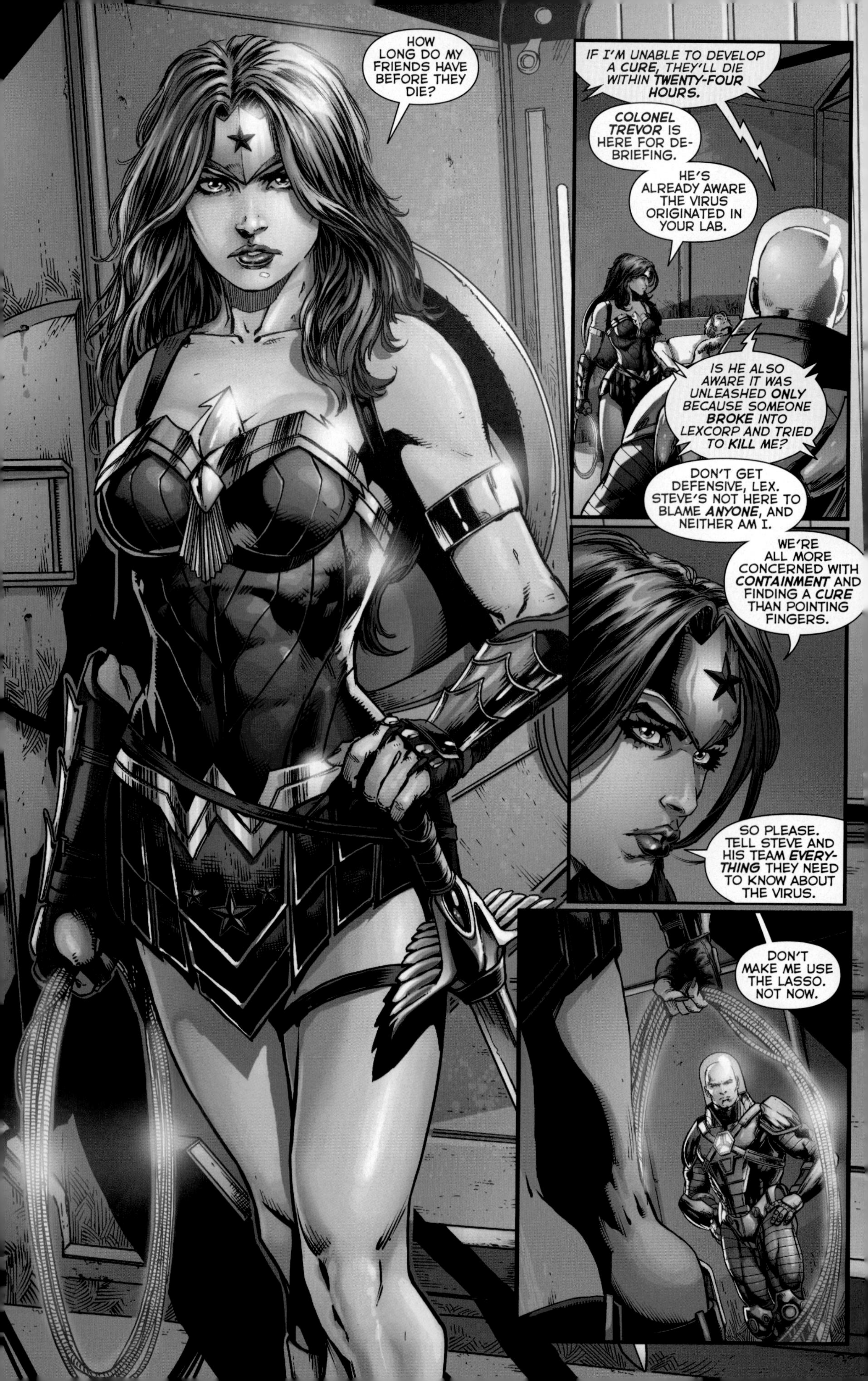
HOW LONG DO MY FRIENDS HAVE BEFORE THEY DIE?
IF I'M UNABLE TO DEVELOP A CURE, THEY'LL DIE WITHIN TWENTY-FOUR HOURS.
COLONEL TREVOR IS HERE FOR DE-BRIEFING.
HE'S ALREADY AWARE THE VIRUS ORIGINATED IN YOUR LAB.
IS HE ALSO AWARE IT WAS UNLEASHED ONLY BECAUSE SOMEONE BROKE INTO LEXCORP AND TRIED TO KILL ME?
DON'T GET DEFENSIVE, LEX. STEVE'S NOT HERE TO BLAME ANYONE, AND NEITHER AM I.
WE'RE ALL MORE CONCERNED WITH CONTAINMENT AND FINDING A CURE THAN POINTING FINGERS.
SO PLEASE. TELL STEVE AND HIS TEAM EVERY-THING THEY NEED TO KNOW ABOUT THE VIRUS.
DON'T MAKE ME USE THE LASSO. NOT NOW.

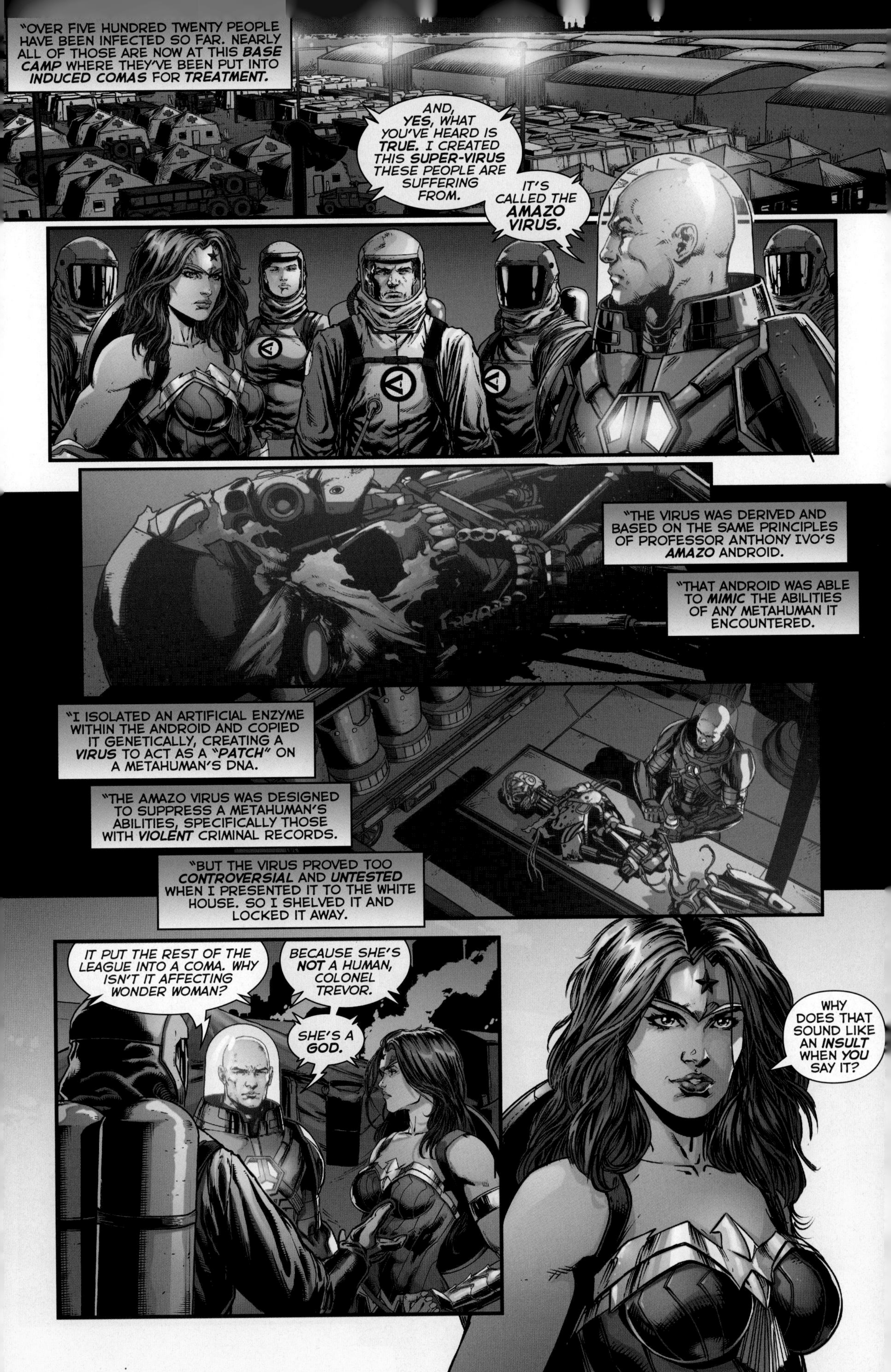
"OVER FIVE HUNDRED TWENTY PEOPLE HAVE BEEN INFECTED SO FAR. NEARLY ALL OF THOSE ARE NOW AT THIS BASE CAMP WHERE THEY'VE BEEN PUT INTO INDUCED COMAS FOR TREATMENT.
AND, YES, WHAT YOU'VE HEARD IS TRUE. I CREATED THIS SUPER-VIRUS THESE PEOPLE ARE SUFFERING FROM.
IT'S CALLED THE AMAZO VIRUS.
"THE VIRUS WAS DERIVED AND BASED ON THE SAME PRINCIPLES OF PROFESSOR ANTHONY IVO'S AMAZO ANDROID.
"THAT ANDROID WAS ABLE TO MIMIC THE ABILITIES OF ANY METAHUMAN IT ENCOUNTERED.
"I ISOLATED AN ARTIFICIAL ENZYME WITHIN THE ANDROID AND COPIED IT GENETICALLY, CREATING A VIRUS TO ACT AS A "PATCH" ON A METAHUMAN'S DNA.
"THE AMAZO VIRUS WAS DESIGNED TO SUPPRESS A METAHUMAN'S ABILITIES, SPECIFICALLY THOSE WITH VIOLENT CRIMINAL RECORDS.
"BUT THE VIRUS PROVED TOO CONTROVERSIAL AND UNTESTED WHEN I PRESENTED IT TO THE WHITE HOUSE. SO I SHELVED IT AND LOCKED IT AWAY.
IT PUT THE REST OF THE LEAGUE INTO A COMA. WHY ISN'T IT AFFECTING WONDER WOMAN?
BECAUSE SHE'S NOT A HUMAN, COLONEL TREVOR.
SHE'S A GOD.
WHY DOES THAT SOUND LIKE AN INSULT WHEN YOU SAY IT?

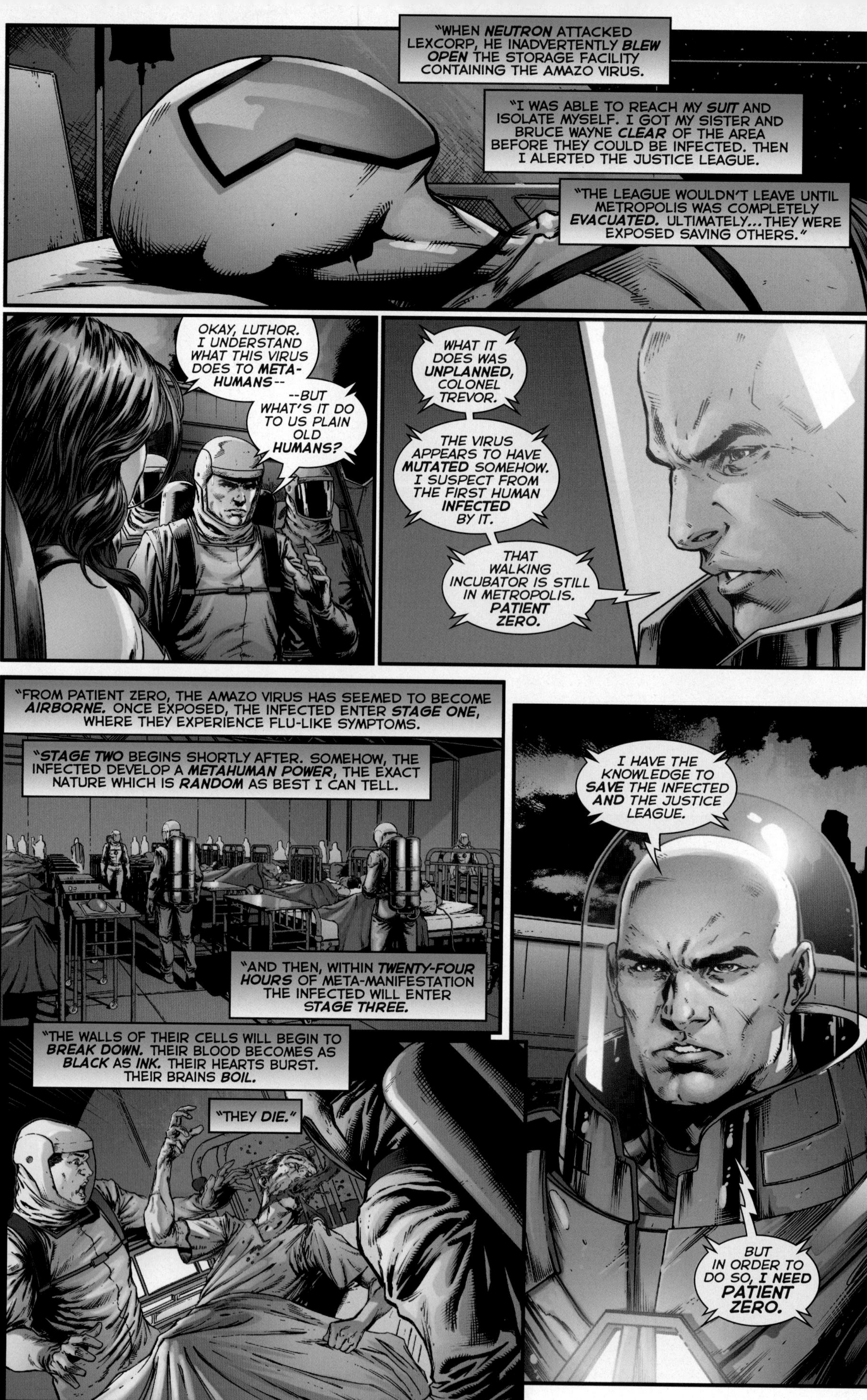
"WHEN NEUTRON ATTACKED LEXCORP, HE INADVERTENTLY BLEW OPEN THE STORAGE FACILITY CONTAINING THE AMAZO VIRUS.
"I WAS ABLE TO REACH MY SUIT AND ISOLATE MYSELF. I GOT MY SISTER AND BRUCE WAYNE CLEAR OF THE AREA BEFORE THEY COULD BE INFECTED. THEN I ALERTED THE JUSTICE LEAGUE.
"THE LEAGUE WOULDN'T LEAVE UNTIL METROPOLIS WAS COMPLETELY EVACUATED. ULTIMATELY...THEY WERE EXPOSED SAVING OTHERS."
OKAY, LUTHOR. I UNDERSTAND WHAT THIS VIRUS DOES TO META-HUMANS--
--BUT WHAT'S IT DO TO US PLAIN OLD HUMANS?
WHAT IT DOES WAS UNPLANNED, COLONEL TREVOR.
THE VIRUS APPEARS TO HAVE MUTATED SOMEHOW. I SUSPECT FROM THE FIRST HUMAN INFECTED BY IT.
THAT WALKING INCUBATOR IS STILL IN METROPOLIS. PATIENT ZERO.
"FROM PATIENT ZERO, THE AMAZO VIRUS HAS SEEMED TO BECOME AIRBORNE. ONCE EXPOSED, THE INFECTED ENTER STAGE ONE, WHERE THEY EXPERIENCE FLU-LIKE SYMPTOMS.
"STAGE TWO BEGINS SHORTLY AFTER. SOMEHOW, THE INFECTED DEVELOP A METAHUMAN POWER, THE EXACT NATURE WHICH IS RANDOM AS BEST I CAN TELL.
"AND THEN, WITHIN TWENTY-FOUR HOURS OF META-MANIFESTATION THE INFECTED WILL ENTER STAGE THREE.
"THE WALLS OF THEIR CELLS WILL BEGIN TO BREAK DOWN. THEIR BLOOD BECOMES AS BLACK AS INK. THEIR HEARTS BURST. THEIR BRAINS BOIL.
"THEY DIE."
I HAVE THE KNOWLEDGE TO SAVE THE INFECTED AND THE JUSTICE LEAGUE.
BUT IN ORDER TO DO SO, I NEED PATIENT ZERO.

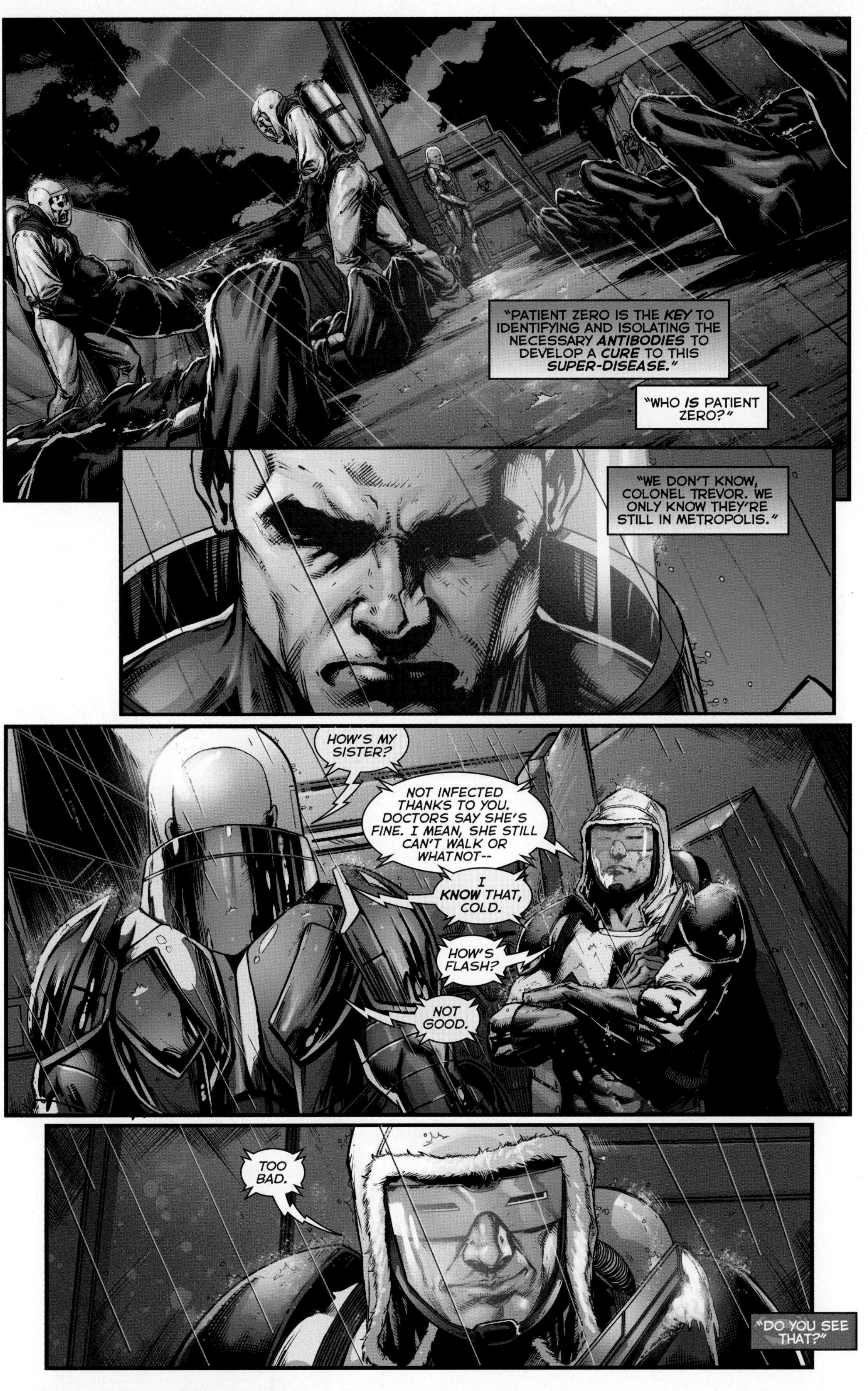
"PATIENT ZERO IS THE KEY TO IDENTIFYING AND ISOLATING THE NECESSARY ANTIBODIES TO DEVELOP A CURE TO THIS SUPER-DISEASE."
"WHO IS PATIENT ZERO?"
"WE DON'T KNOW, COLONEL TREVOR. WE ONLY KNOW THEY'RE STILL IN METROPOLIS."
HOW'S MY SISTER?
NOT INFECTED THANKS TO YOU. DOCTORS SAY SHE'S FINE. I MEAN, SHE STILL CAN'T WALK OR WHATNOT--
I KNOW THAT, COLD.
HOW'S FLASH?
NOT GOOD.
TOO BAD.
"DO YOU SEE THAT?"

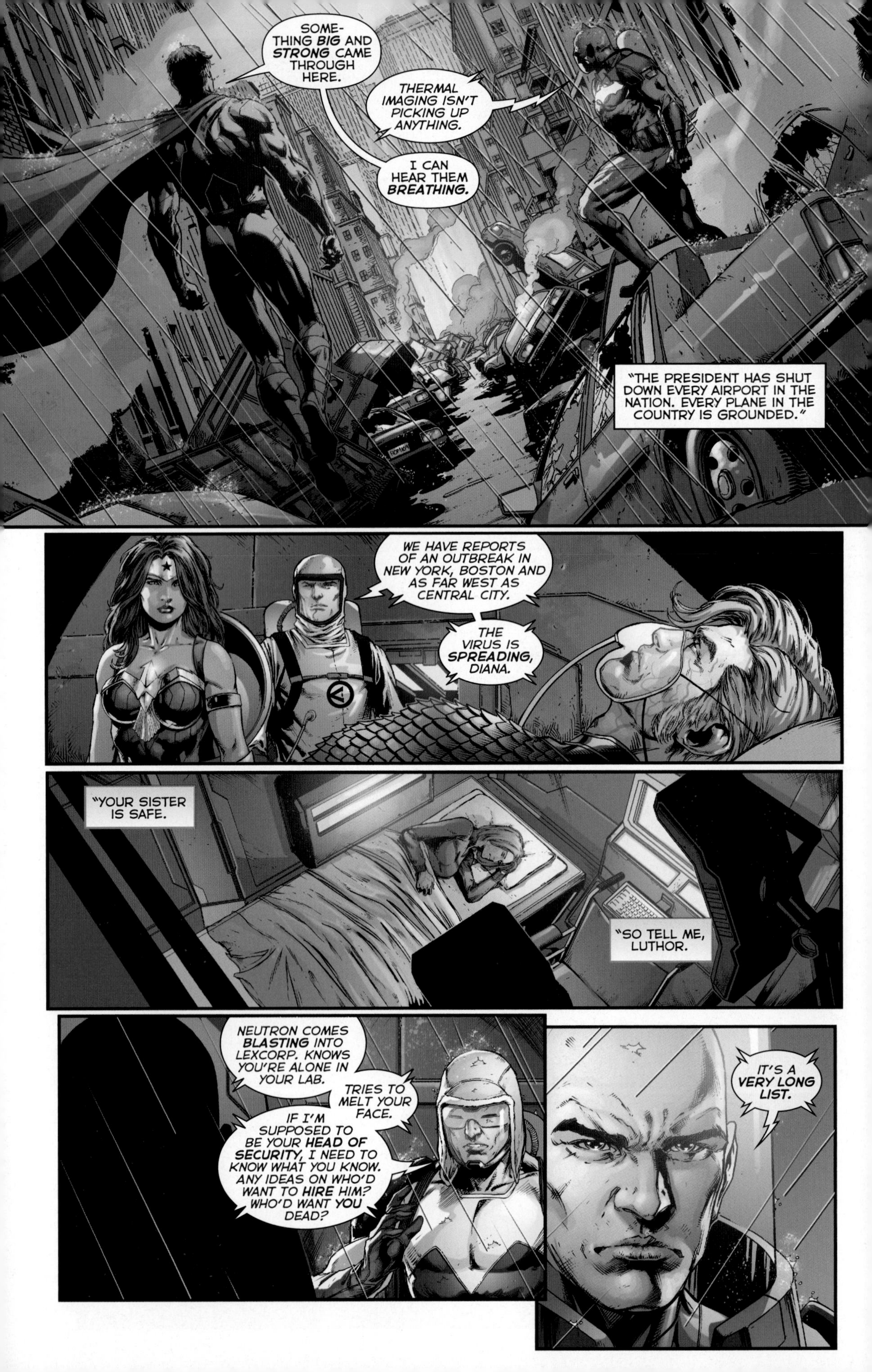
SOME-THING BIG AND STRONG CAME THROUGH HERE.
THERMAL IMAGING ISN'T PICKING UP ANYTHING.
I CAN HEAR THEM BREATHING.
"THE PRESIDENT HAS SHUT DOWN EVERY AIRPORT IN THE NATION. EVERY PLANE IN THE COUNTRY IS GROUNDED."
WE HAVE REPORTS OF AN OUTBREAK IN NEW YORK, BOSTON AND AS FAR WEST AS CENTRAL CITY.
THE VIRUS IS SPREADING, DIANA.
"YOUR SISTER IS SAFE.
"SO TELL ME, LUTHOR.
NEUTRON COMES BLASTING INTO LEXCORP. KNOWS YOU'RE ALONE IN YOUR LAB.
TRIES TO MELT YOUR FACE.
IF I'M SUPPOSED TO BE YOUR HEAD OF SECURITY, I NEED TO KNOW WHAT YOU KNOW. ANY IDEAS ON WHO'D WANT TO HIRE HIM? WHO'D WANT YOU DEAD?
IT'S A VERY LONG LIST.

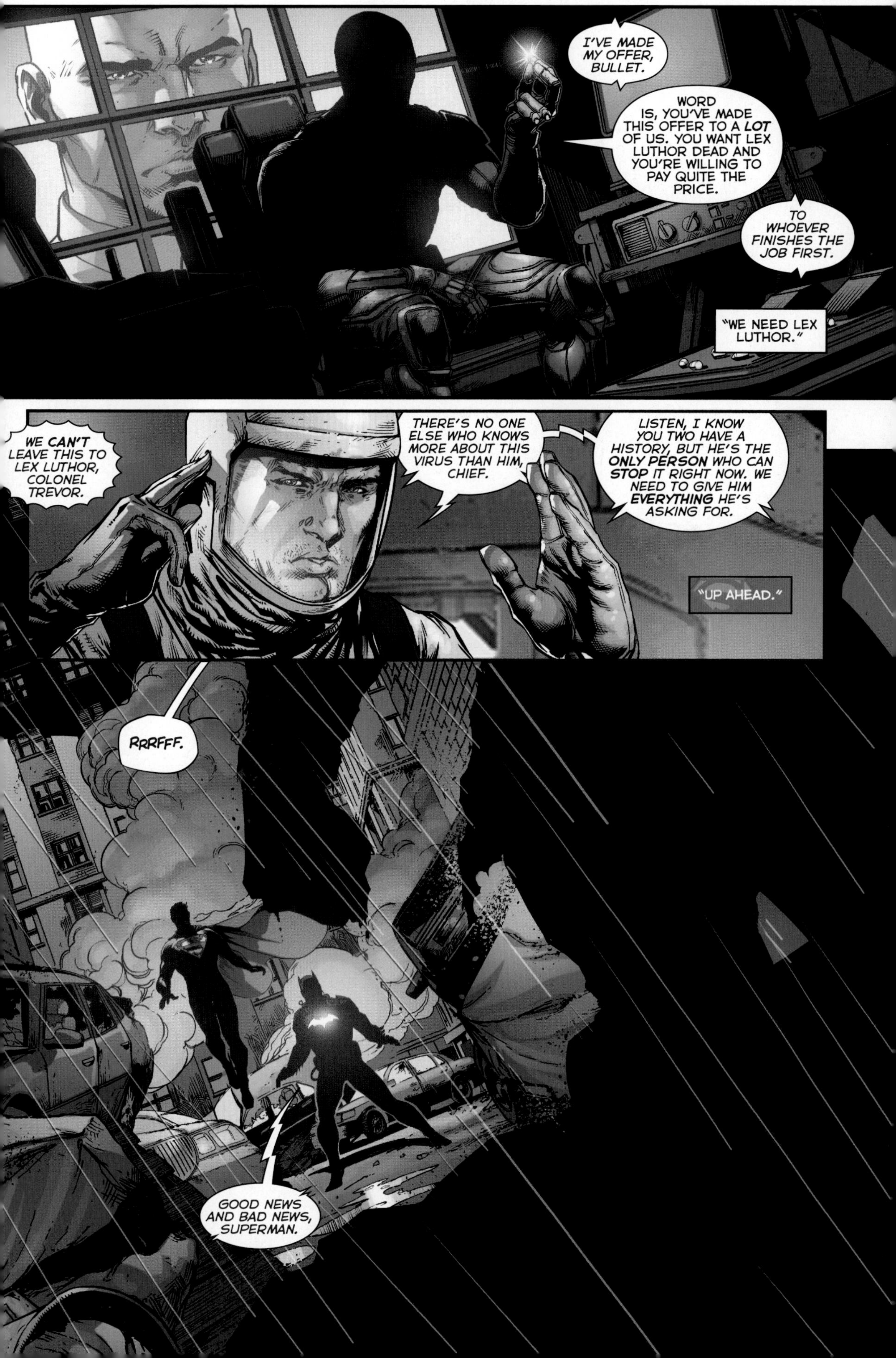

I'VE MADE MY OFFER, BULLET.
WORD IS, YOU'VE MADE THIS OFFER TO A LOT OF US. YOU WANT LEX LUTHOR DEAD AND YOU'RE WILLING TO PAY QUITE THE PRICE.
TO WHOEVER FINISHES THE JOB FIRST.
"WE NEED LEX LUTHOR."
WE CAN'T LEAVE THIS TO LEX LUTHOR, COLONEL TREVOR.
THERE'S NO ONE ELSE WHO KNOWS MORE ABOUT THIS VIRUS THAN HIM, CHIEF.
LISTEN, I KNOW YOU TWO HAVE A HISTORY, BUT HE'S THE ONLY PERSON WHO CAN STOP IT RIGHT NOW. WE NEED TO GIVE HIM EVERYTHING HE'S ASKING FOR.
"UP AHEAD."
RRRFFF.
GOOD NEWS AND BAD NEWS, SUPERMAN.

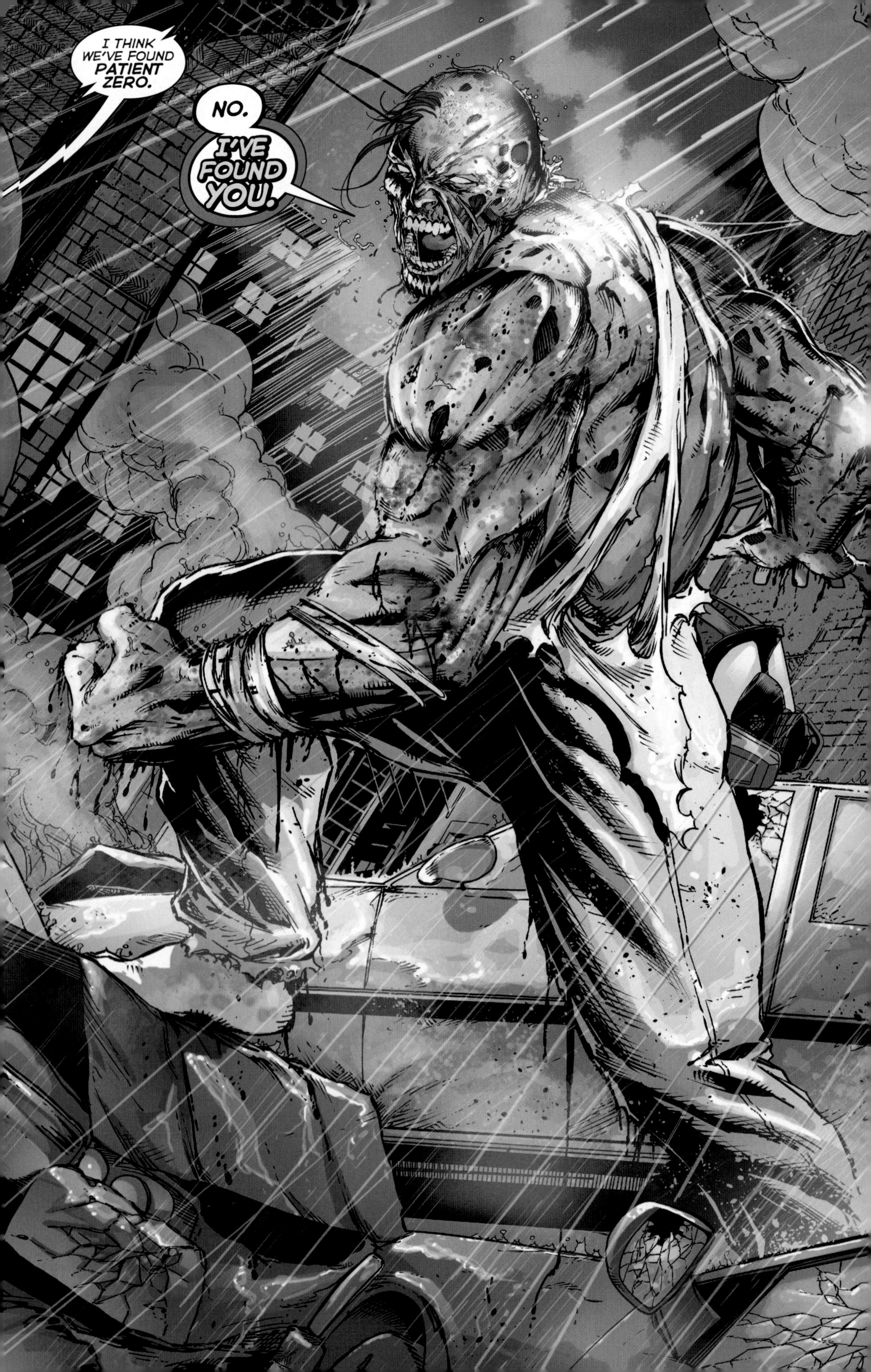
I THINK WE'VE FOUND PATIENT ZERO.
NO.
I'VE FOUND YOU.

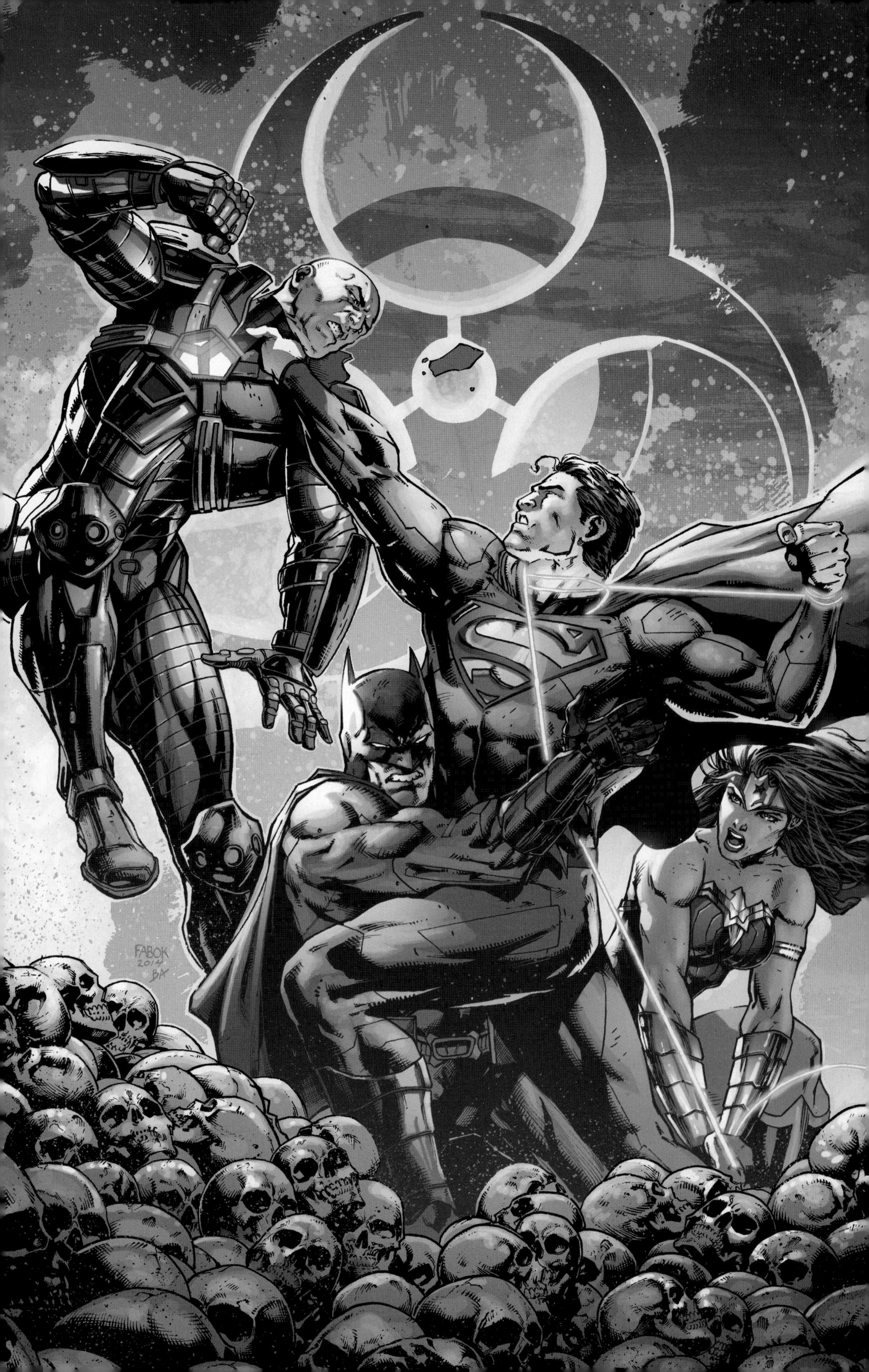

THE AMAZO VIRUS CHAPTER TWO
PATIENT ZERO

GEOFF JOHNS writer **JASON FABOK** artist **BRAD ANDERSON** colorist
JASON FABOK & BRAD ANDERSON cover artists

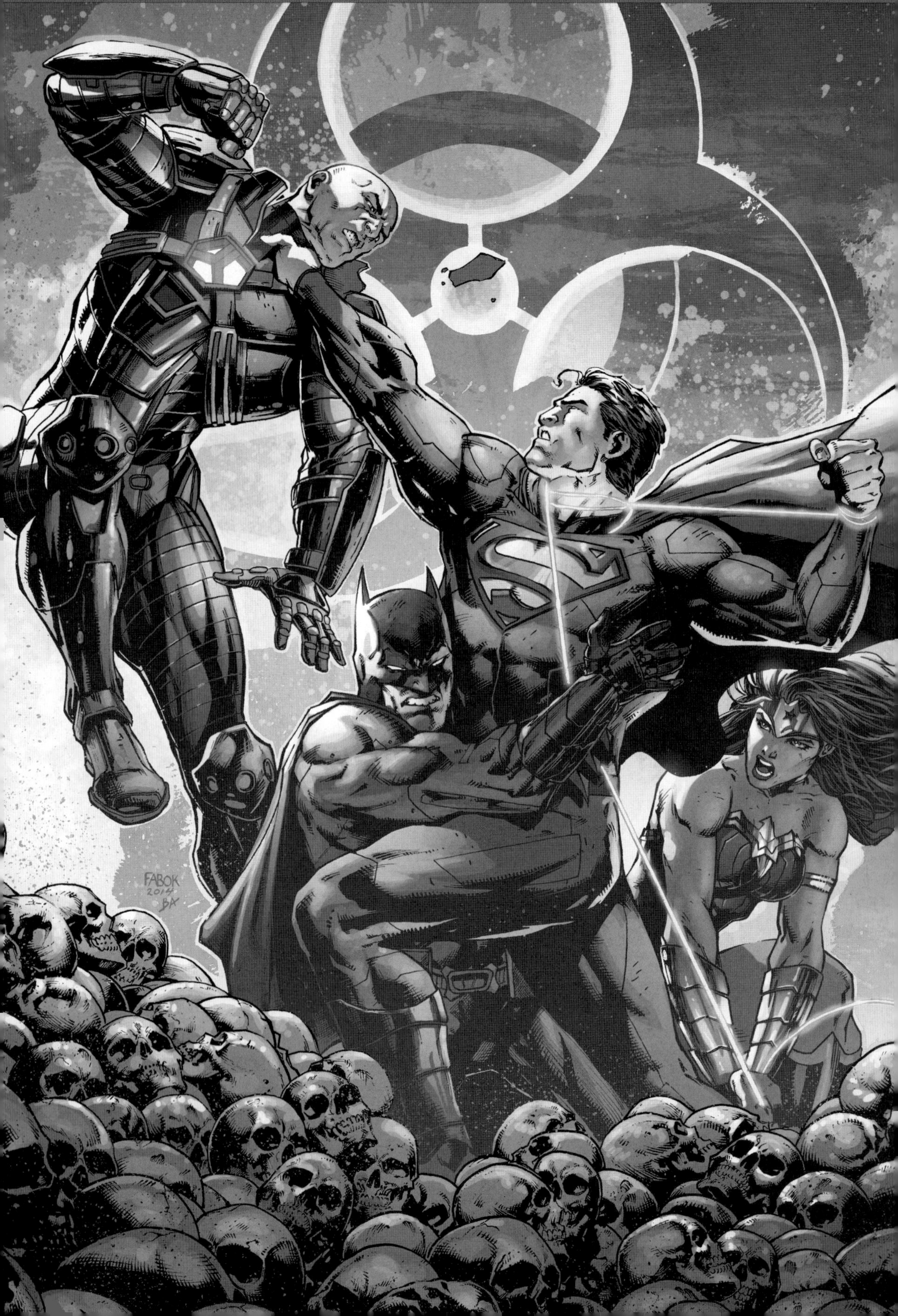
FABOK
2014
BA

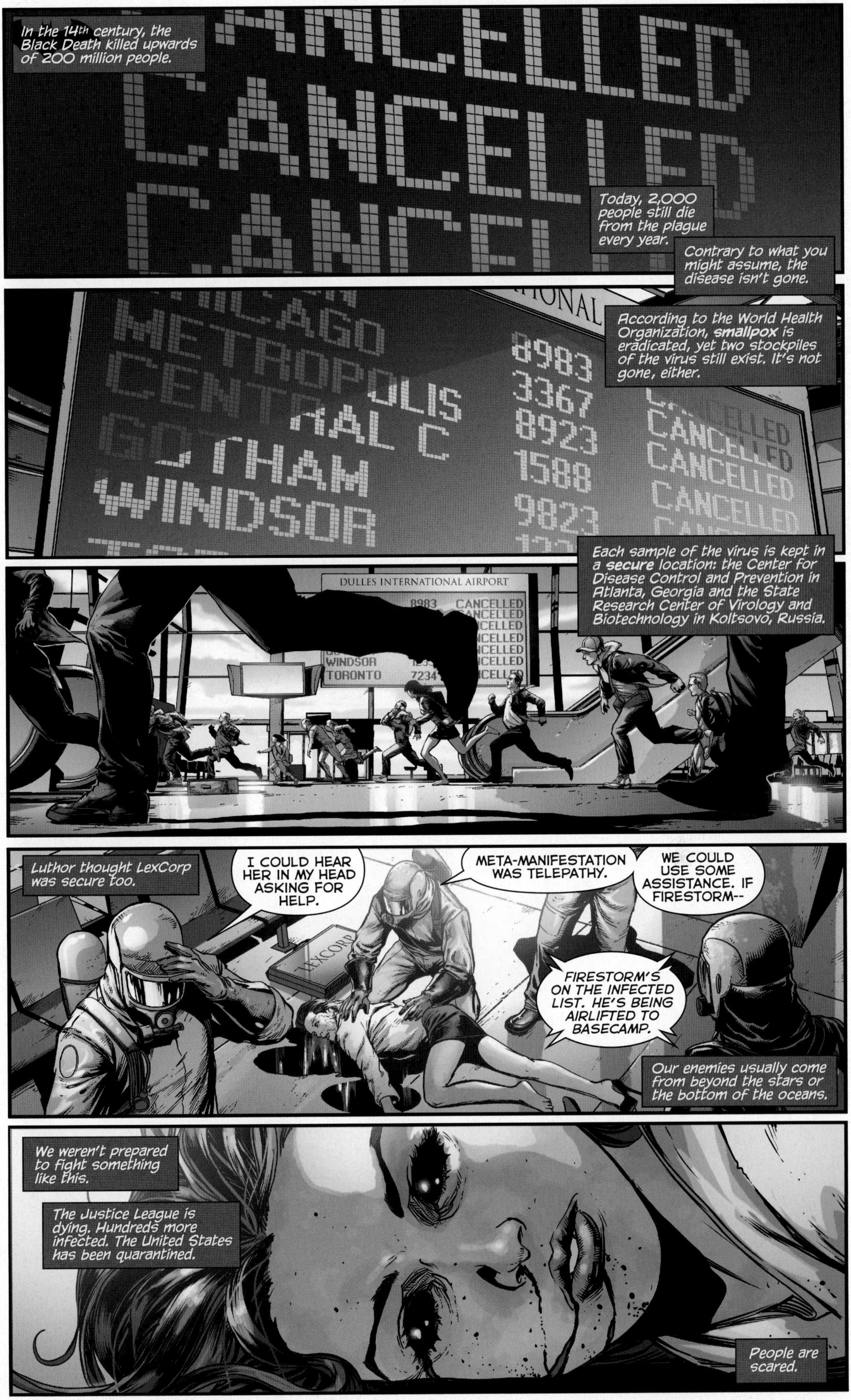
In the 14th century, the Black Death killed upwards of 200 million people.
CANCELLED
CANCELLED
Today, 2,000 people still die from the plague every year.
Contrary to what you might assume, the disease isn't gone.
METROPOLIS 8983
CENTRAL C 3367 CANCELLED
GOTHAM 8923 CANCELLED
WINDSOR 1588 CANCELLED
9823 CANCELLED
According to the World Health Organization, **smallpox** is eradicated, yet two stockpiles of the virus still exist. It's not gone, either.
Each sample of the virus is kept in a **secure** location: the Center for Disease Control and Prevention in Atlanta, Georgia and the State Research Center of Virology and Biotechnology in Koltsovo, Russia.
DULLES INTERNATIONAL AIRPORT
8983 CANCELLED
WINDSOR
TORONTO
Luthor thought LexCorp was secure too.
I COULD HEAR HER IN MY HEAD ASKING FOR HELP.
META-MANIFESTATION WAS TELEPATHY.
WE COULD USE SOME ASSISTANCE. IF FIRESTORM--
FIRESTORM'S ON THE INFECTED LIST. HE'S BEING AIRLIFTED TO BASECAMP.
LEXCORP
Our enemies usually come from beyond the stars or the bottom of the oceans.
We weren't prepared to fight something like this.
The Justice League is dying. Hundreds more infected. The United States has been quarantined.
People are scared.

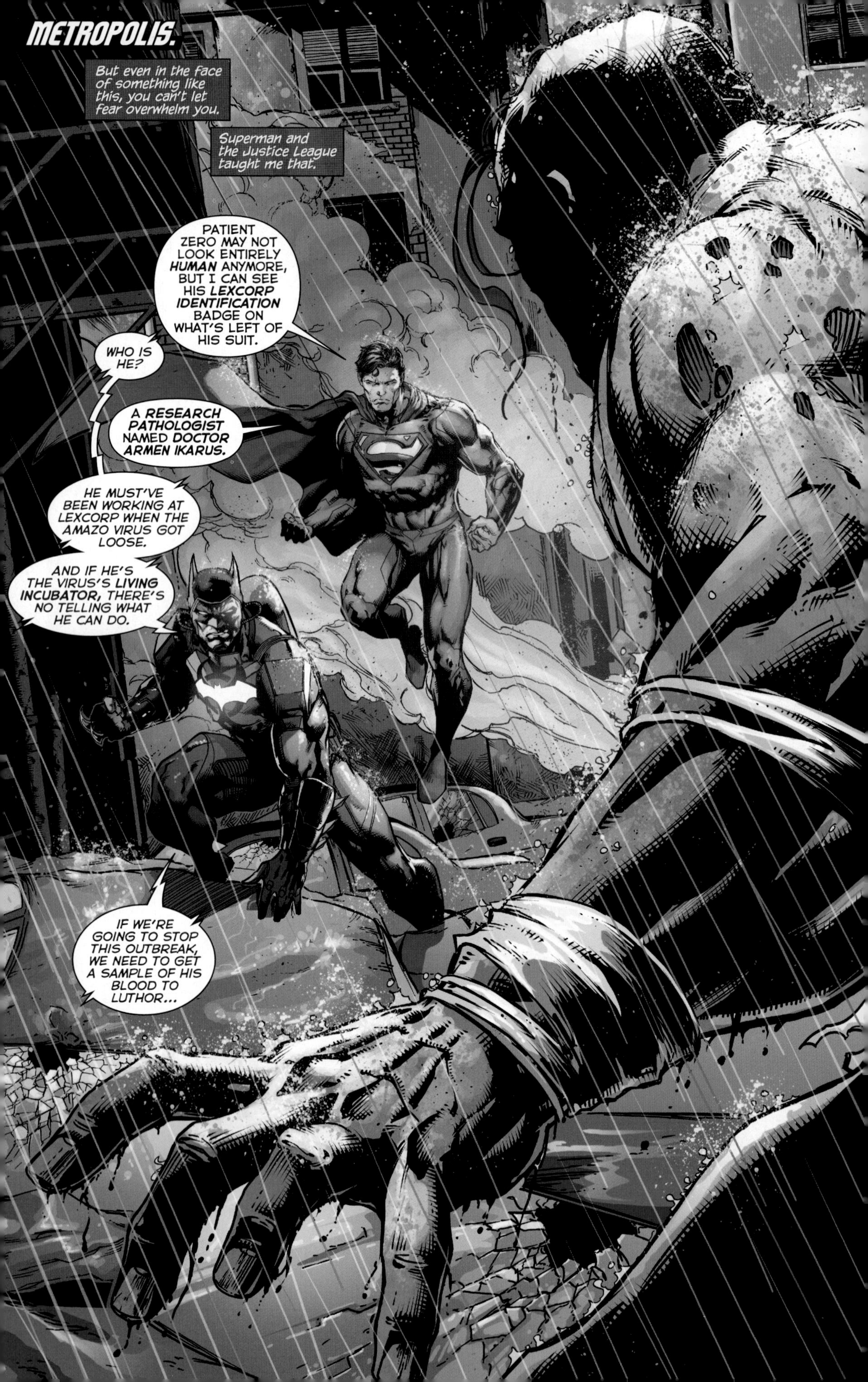
METROPOLIS.
But even in the face of something like this, you can't let fear overwhelm you.
Superman and the Justice League taught me that.
PATIENT ZERO MAY NOT LOOK ENTIRELY HUMAN ANYMORE, BUT I CAN SEE HIS LEXCORP IDENTIFICATION BADGE ON WHAT'S LEFT OF HIS SUIT.
WHO IS HE?
A RESEARCH PATHOLOGIST NAMED DOCTOR ARMEN IKARUS.
HE MUST'VE BEEN WORKING AT LEXCORP WHEN THE AMAZO VIRUS GOT LOOSE.
AND IF HE'S THE VIRUS'S LIVING INCUBATOR, THERE'S NO TELLING WHAT HE CAN DO.
IF WE'RE GOING TO STOP THIS OUTBREAK, WE NEED TO GET A SAMPLE OF HIS BLOOD TO LUTHOR...

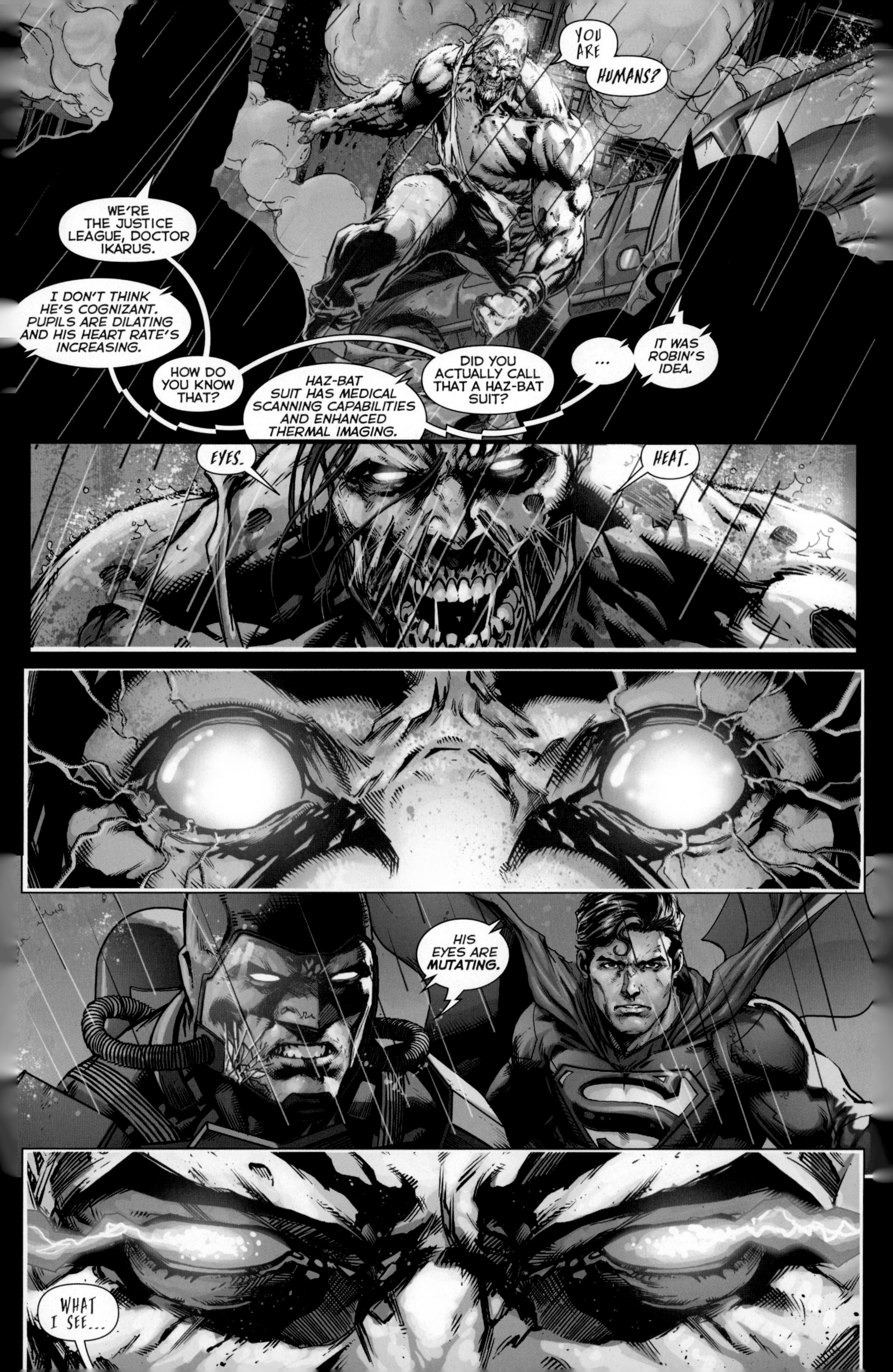
YOU ARE HUMANS?
WE'RE THE JUSTICE LEAGUE, DOCTOR IKARUS.
I DON'T THINK HE'S COGNIZANT. PUPILS ARE DILATING AND HIS HEART RATE'S INCREASING.
HOW DO YOU KNOW THAT?
HAZ-BAT SUIT HAS MEDICAL SCANNING CAPABILITIES AND ENHANCED THERMAL IMAGING.
DID YOU ACTUALLY CALL THAT A HAZ-BAT SUIT?
...
IT WAS ROBIN'S IDEA.
EYES.
HEAT.
HIS EYES ARE MUTATING.
WHAT I SEE...

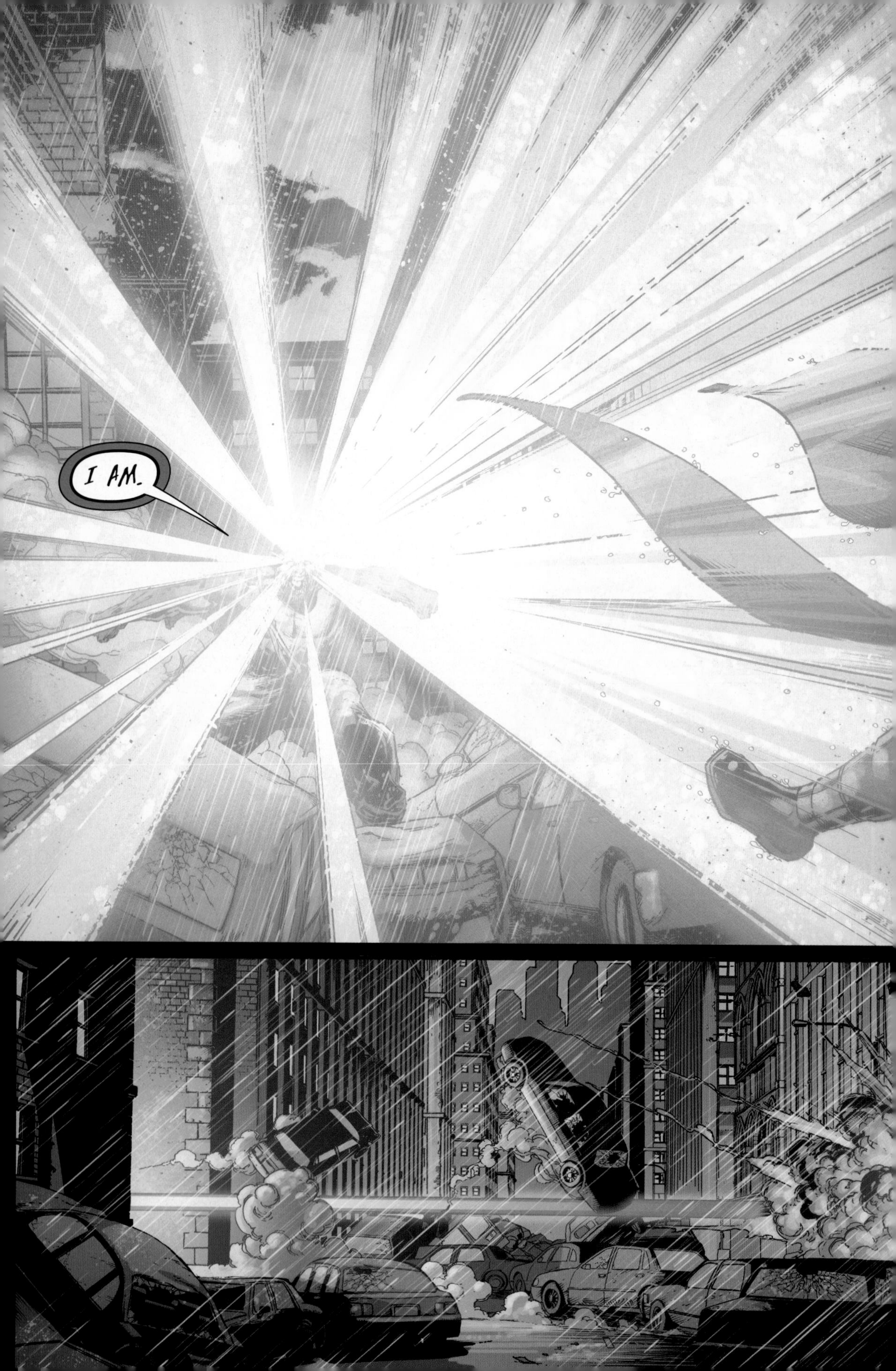
I AM.

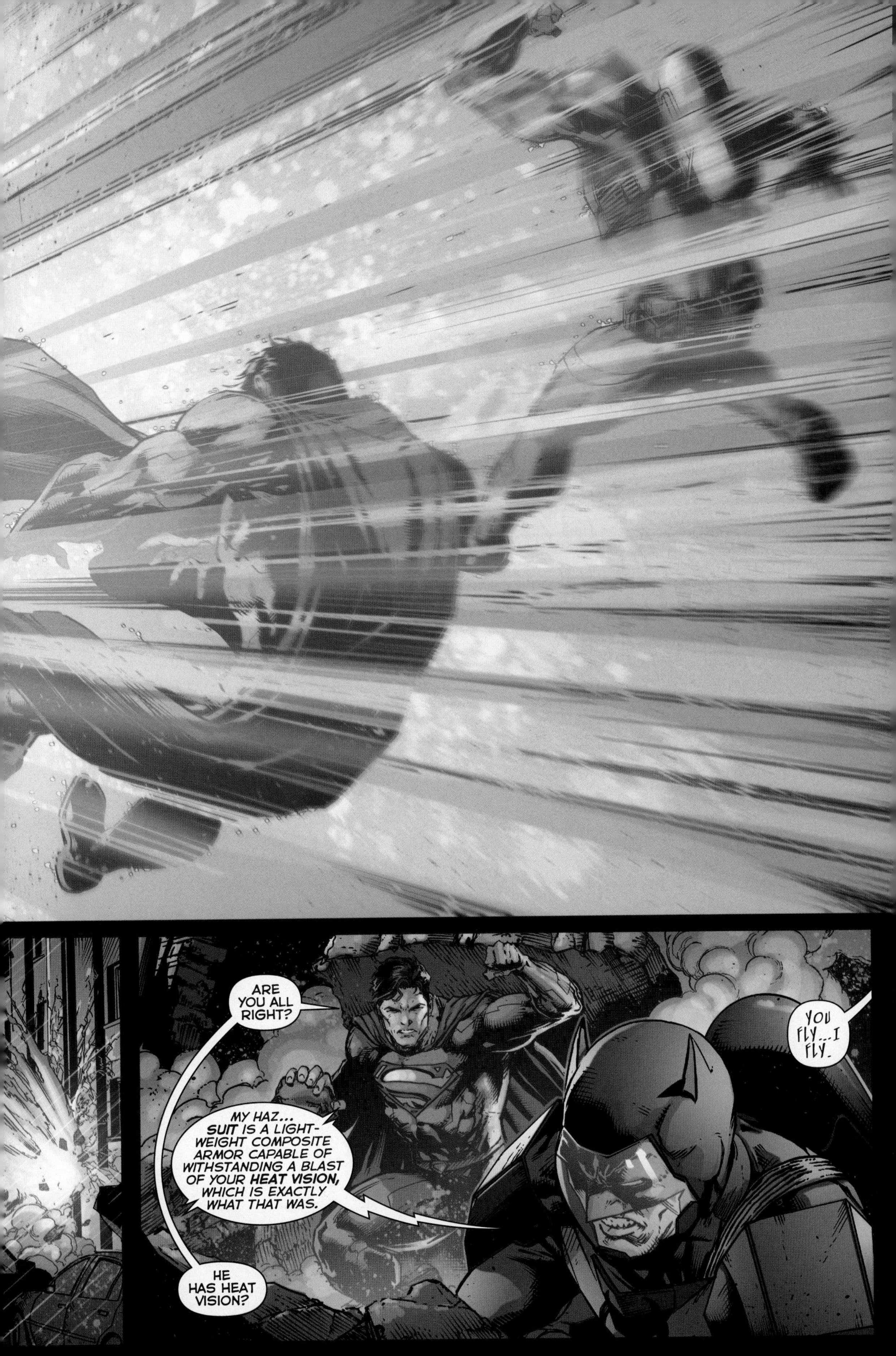

ARE YOU ALL RIGHT?
HE HAS HEAT VISION?
MY HAZ... SUIT IS A LIGHT-WEIGHT COMPOSITE ARMOR CAPABLE OF WITHSTANDING A BLAST OF YOUR HEAT VISION, WHICH IS EXACTLY WHAT THAT WAS.
YOU FLY... I FLY.

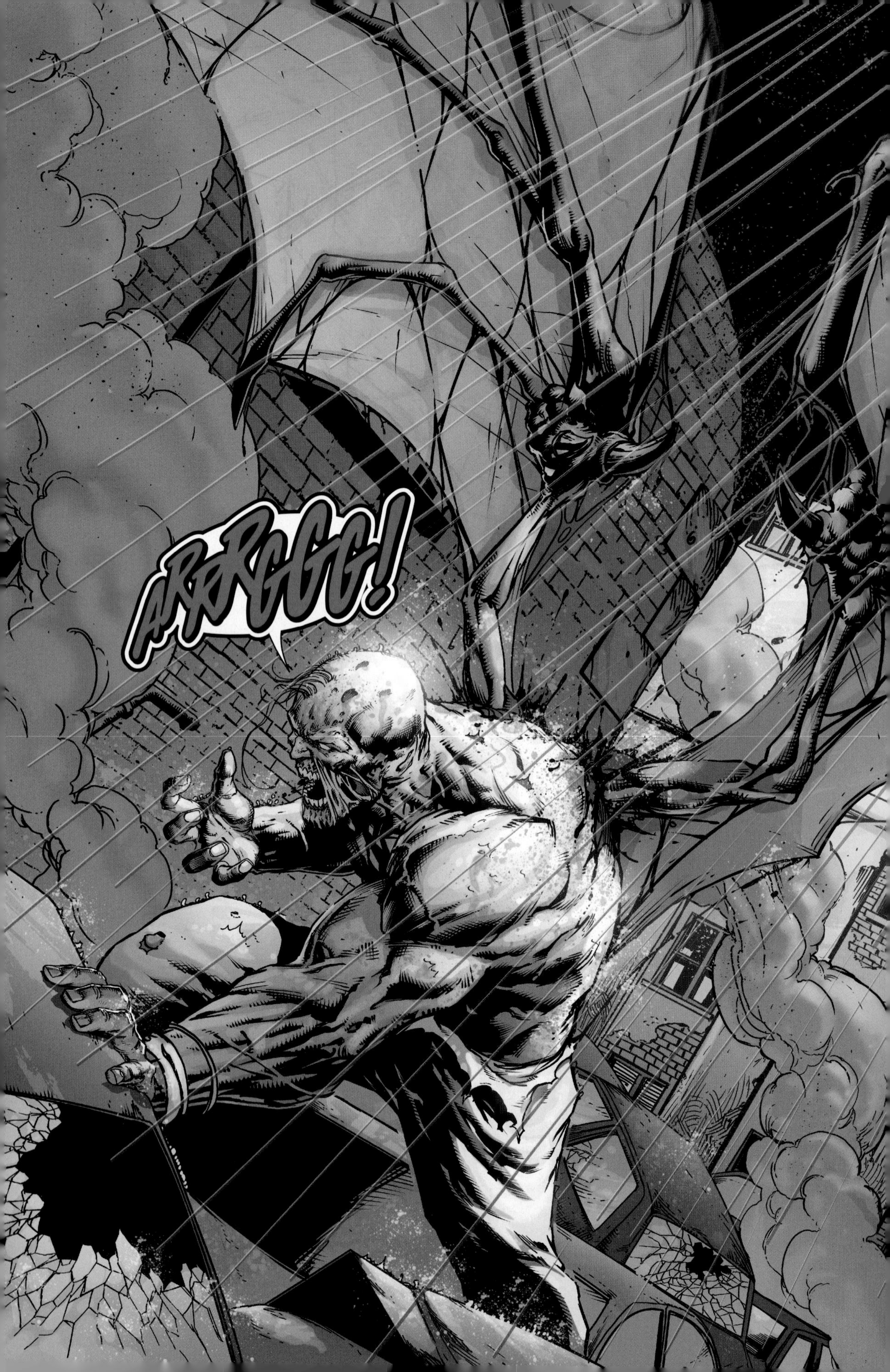
ARRRGGG!

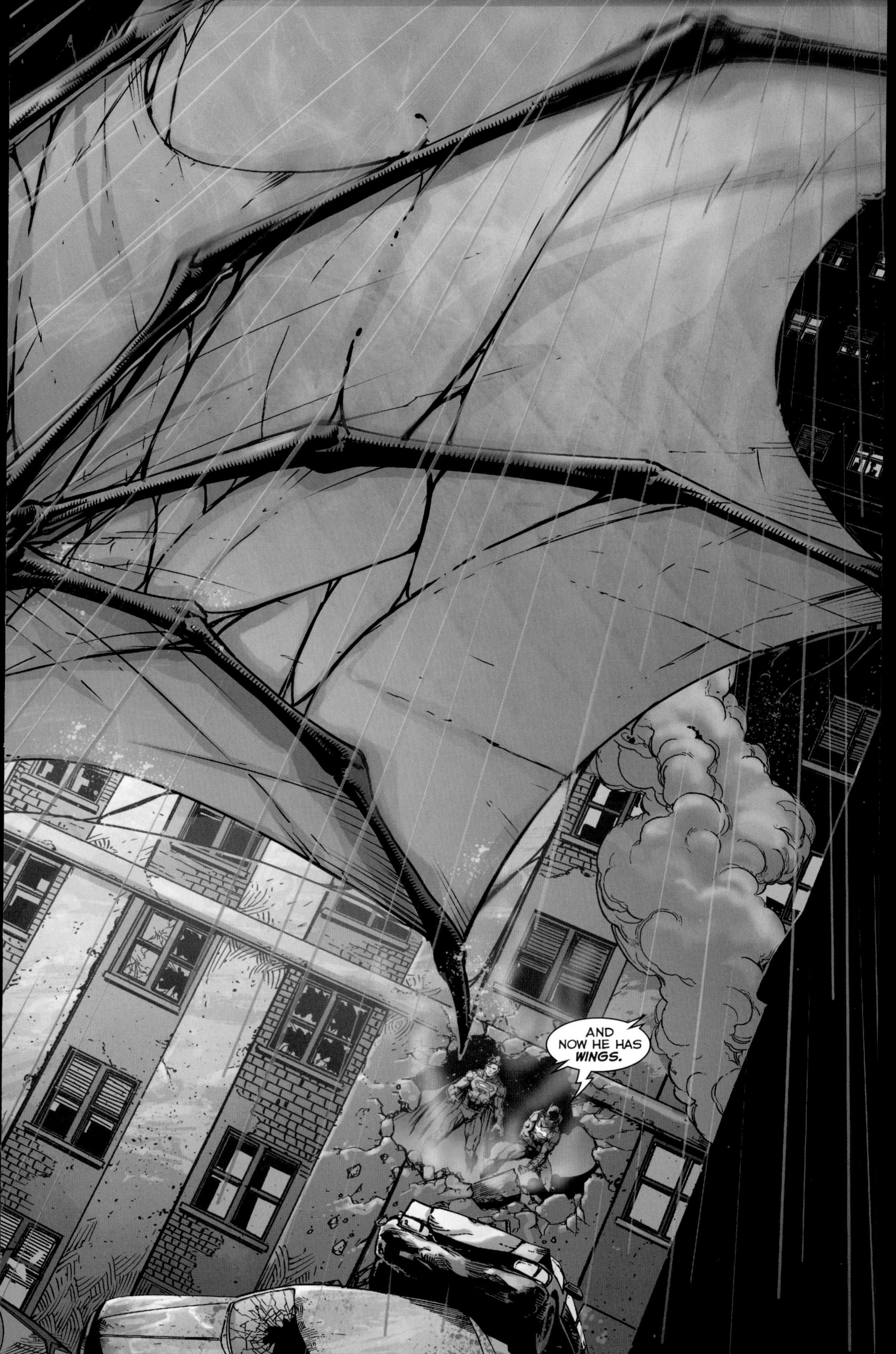
AND NOW HE HAS *WINGS.*

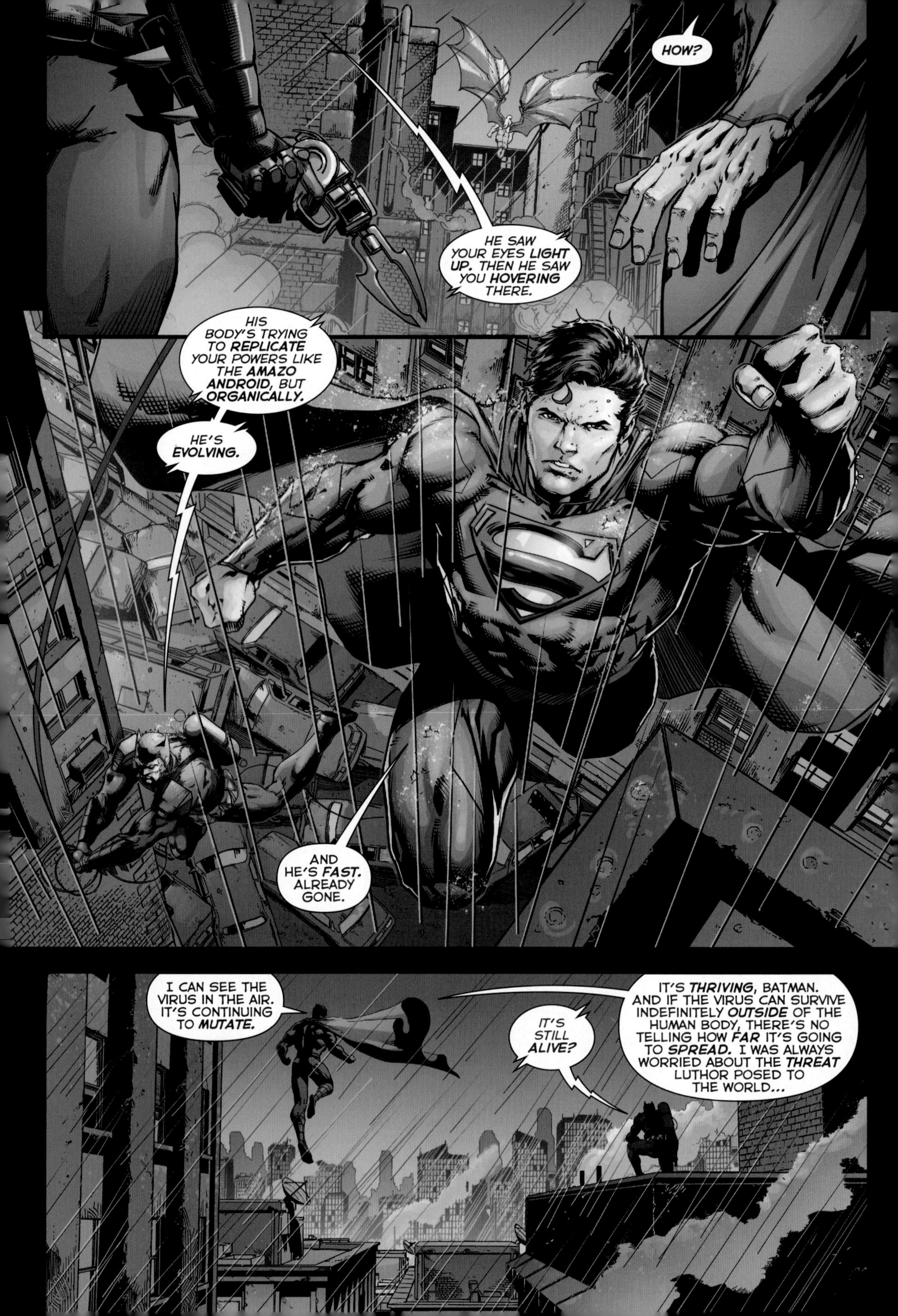
HOW?
HE SAW YOUR EYES LIGHT UP. THEN HE SAW YOU HOVERING THERE.
HIS BODY'S TRYING TO REPLICATE YOUR POWERS LIKE THE AMAZO ANDROID, BUT ORGANICALLY.
HE'S EVOLVING.
AND HE'S FAST. ALREADY GONE.
I CAN SEE THE VIRUS IN THE AIR. IT'S CONTINUING TO MUTATE.
IT'S STILL ALIVE?
IT'S THRIVING, BATMAN. AND IF THE VIRUS CAN SURVIVE INDEFINITELY OUTSIDE OF THE HUMAN BODY, THERE'S NO TELLING HOW FAR IT'S GOING TO SPREAD. I WAS ALWAYS WORRIED ABOUT THE THREAT LUTHOR POSED TO THE WORLD...

"...NOW HE MAY HAVE **DESTROYED** IT."

WHY WOULD ANYONE WANT TO KILL YOU, LEX?

BECAUSE I'VE DONE SOME VERY BAD THINGS, LENA. ALL THAT MATTERS RIGHT NOW IS THAT *YOU* ARE *SAFE*. YOU'RE NOT *INFECTED*. AND YOU'RE ONLY UNDER OBSERVATION FOR *RADIATION TOXICITY* WHICH I BELIEVE WILL PROVE *NEGATIVE*. WHEN *NEUTRON* TRIED TO INCINERATE ME, YOU WERE POTENTIALLY EXPOSED TO NEUTRON *PARTICLES*--

WHERE IS NEUTRON, LEX?

"NEUTRON WAS EXPOSED TO THE AMAZO VIRUS. AND LIKE ALL META-HUMANS THAT HAVE BEEN INFECTED, THE DISEASE NEGATED HIS ABILITIES TO CREATE, ABSORB AND REDIRECT *RADIATION*.

"AND BECAUSE HE'S LOST THAT ABILITY, THE REMAINING RADIOACTIVE PARTICLES IN HIS BLOOD ARE CAUSING HIS CELLS TO METASTASIZE AT A RATE I'VE NEVER SEEN. HE'S *VERY, VERY SICK.*

"ALONG WITH MOST OF THE JUSTICE LEAGUE."

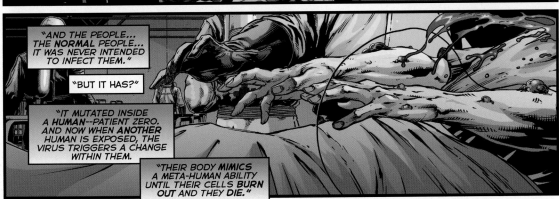

"AND THE PEOPLE... THE *NORMAL* PEOPLE... IT WAS NEVER INTENDED TO INFECT THEM."

"BUT IT HAS?"

"IT MUTATED INSIDE A HUMAN--PATIENT ZERO. AND NOW WHEN *ANOTHER* HUMAN IS EXPOSED, THE VIRUS TRIGGERS A CHANGE WITHIN THEM.

"THEIR BODY MIMICS A META-HUMAN ABILITY UNTIL THEIR CELLS *BURN OUT* AND THEY *DIE.*"

WHY WOULD YOU CREATE SOMETHING SO HORRIBLE, LEX?

THE FACT IS, MY DEAR SISTER, META-HUMAN *CRIMINALS* KILL *DOZENS* IF NOT *HUNDREDS* OF PEOPLE EVERY YEAR. AND VIRTUALLY *NO* PRISON ON EARTH IS CAPABLE OF CONTAINING THEM FOR LONG.

OVER *EIGHTY-SEVEN PERCENT* OF ALL VIOLENT META-HUMANS *ESCAPE* WITHIN *THREE MONTHS* OF INCARCERATION. *ONE MONTH* IF WE'RE TALKING ABOUT *ARKHAM.*

AFTER MEETING SOME OF THE VICTIM'S FAMILIES, I *SWORE* TO THEM I'D FIND A *BETTER WAY* TO *NEUTRALIZE* THESE HORRIFIC *MEN* AND *WOMEN.* SO I BEGAN SEARCHING FOR A MEANS OF *BLOCKING* A META-HUMAN'S ABILITIES.

THE *AMAZO VIRUS* WAS DESIGNED TO TEMPORARILY *SUPPRESS* THEM.

DO YOU REMEMBER WHEN WE WERE *CHILDREN,* LEX? HOW YOU'D SNEAK OFF TO METROPOLIS TO THE SCIENCE AND ENGINEERING EXPO EVERY SUMMER?

I WATCHED YOU *LIE* TO DAD. I KNOW WHEN YOU'RE LYING, LEX.

SO TELL ME THE *TRUTH. WHY* DID YOU REALLY CREATE THIS DISEASE?

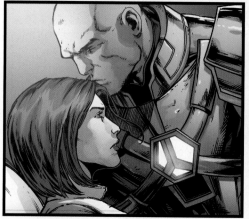

THE IMPORTANT THING IS THAT I CAN CREATE A *CURE.*

NOW PLEASE STOP WITH THE INQUISITION, LENA. YOU KNOW I DON'T LIKE IT.

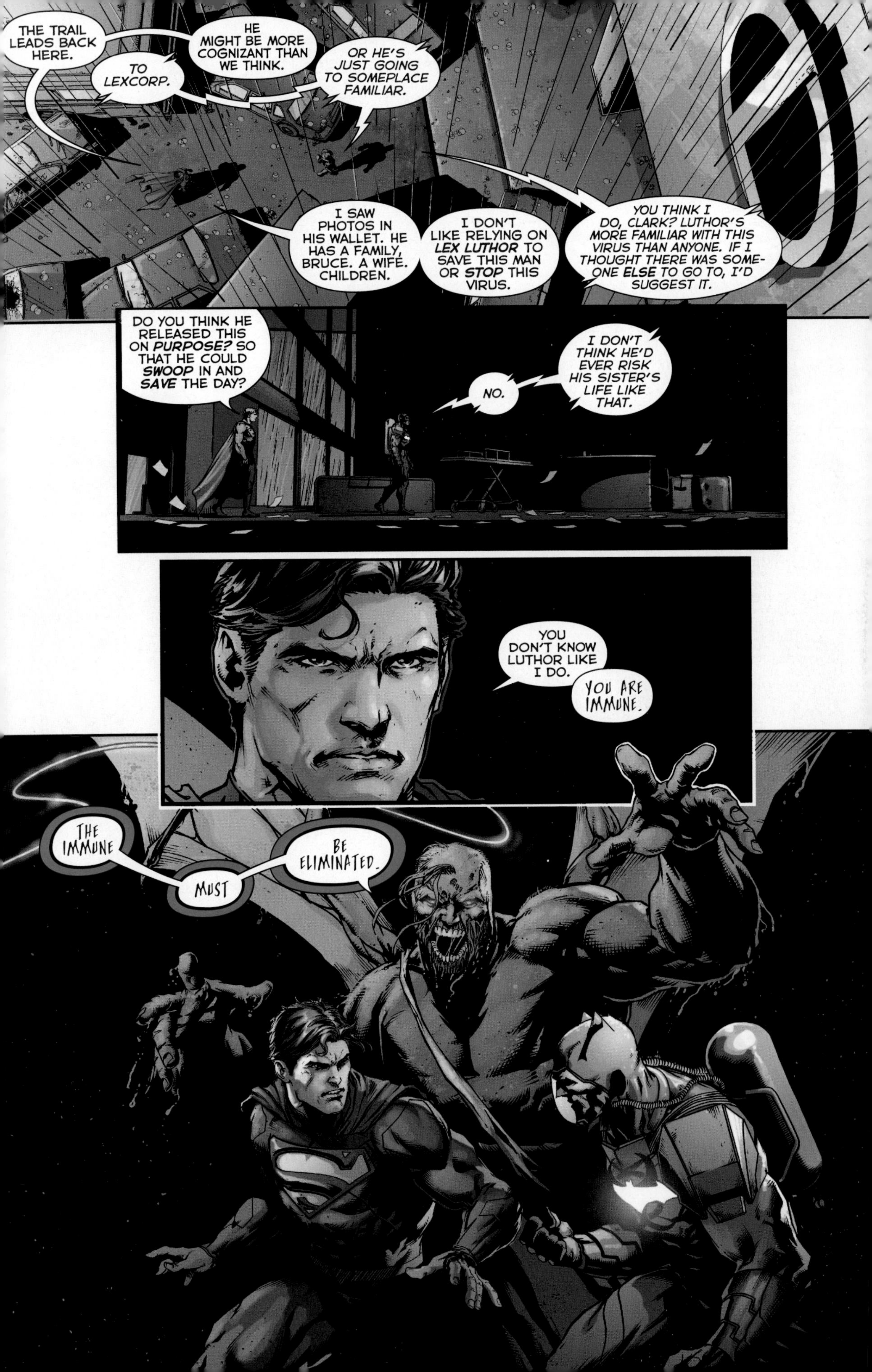
THE TRAIL LEADS BACK HERE.
TO LEXCORP.
HE MIGHT BE MORE COGNIZANT THAN WE THINK.
OR HE'S JUST GOING TO SOMEPLACE FAMILIAR.
I SAW PHOTOS IN HIS WALLET. HE HAS A FAMILY, BRUCE. A WIFE. CHILDREN.
I DON'T LIKE RELYING ON LEX LUTHOR TO SAVE THIS MAN OR STOP THIS VIRUS.
YOU THINK I DO, CLARK? LUTHOR'S MORE FAMILIAR WITH THIS VIRUS THAN ANYONE. IF I THOUGHT THERE WAS SOME-ONE ELSE TO GO TO, I'D SUGGEST IT.
DO YOU THINK HE RELEASED THIS ON PURPOSE? SO THAT HE COULD SWOOP IN AND SAVE THE DAY?
NO.
I DON'T THINK HE'D EVER RISK HIS SISTER'S LIFE LIKE THAT.
YOU DON'T KNOW LUTHOR LIKE I DO.
YOU ARE IMMUNE.
THE IMMUNE
MUST
BE ELIMINATED.

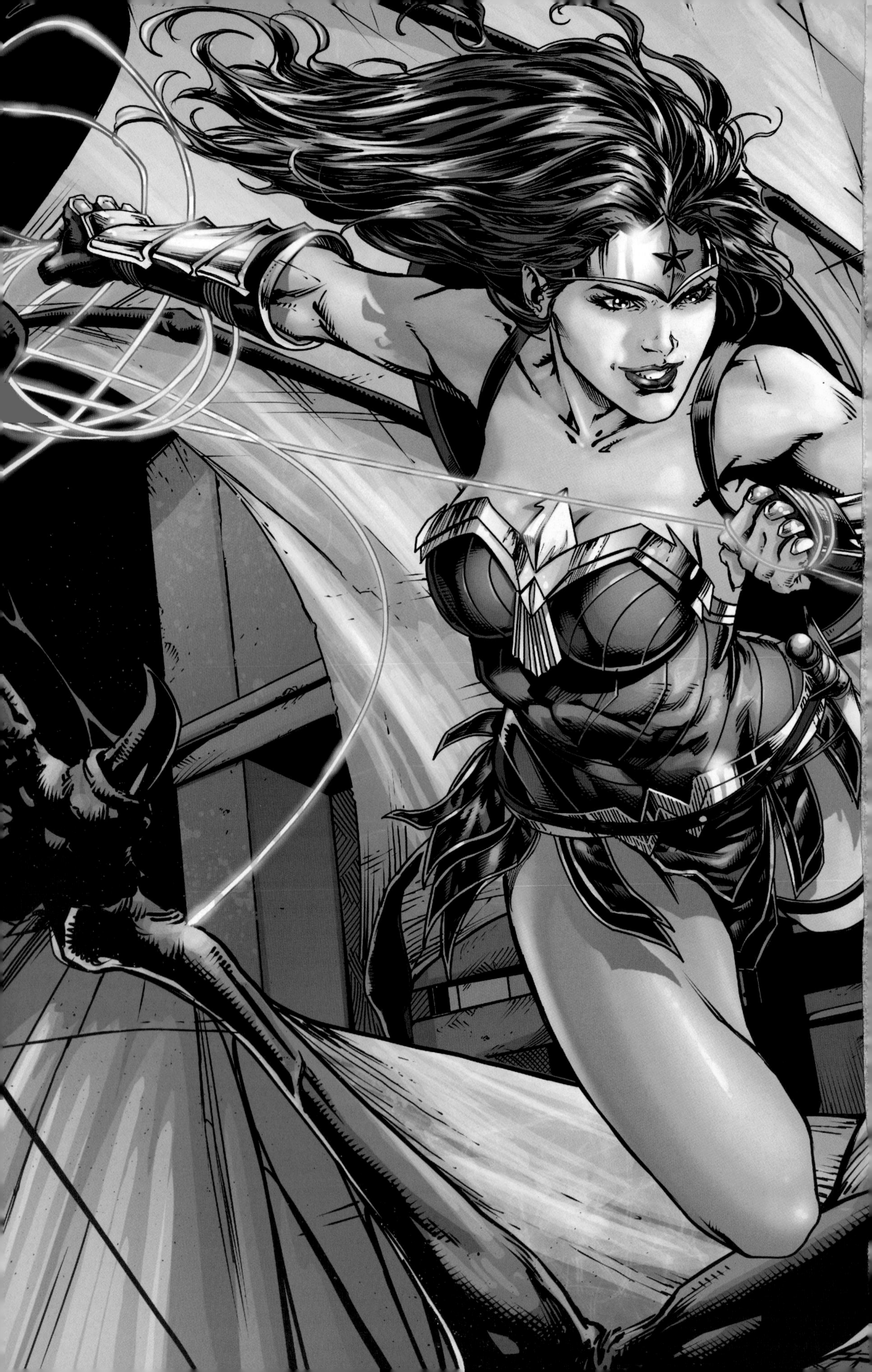

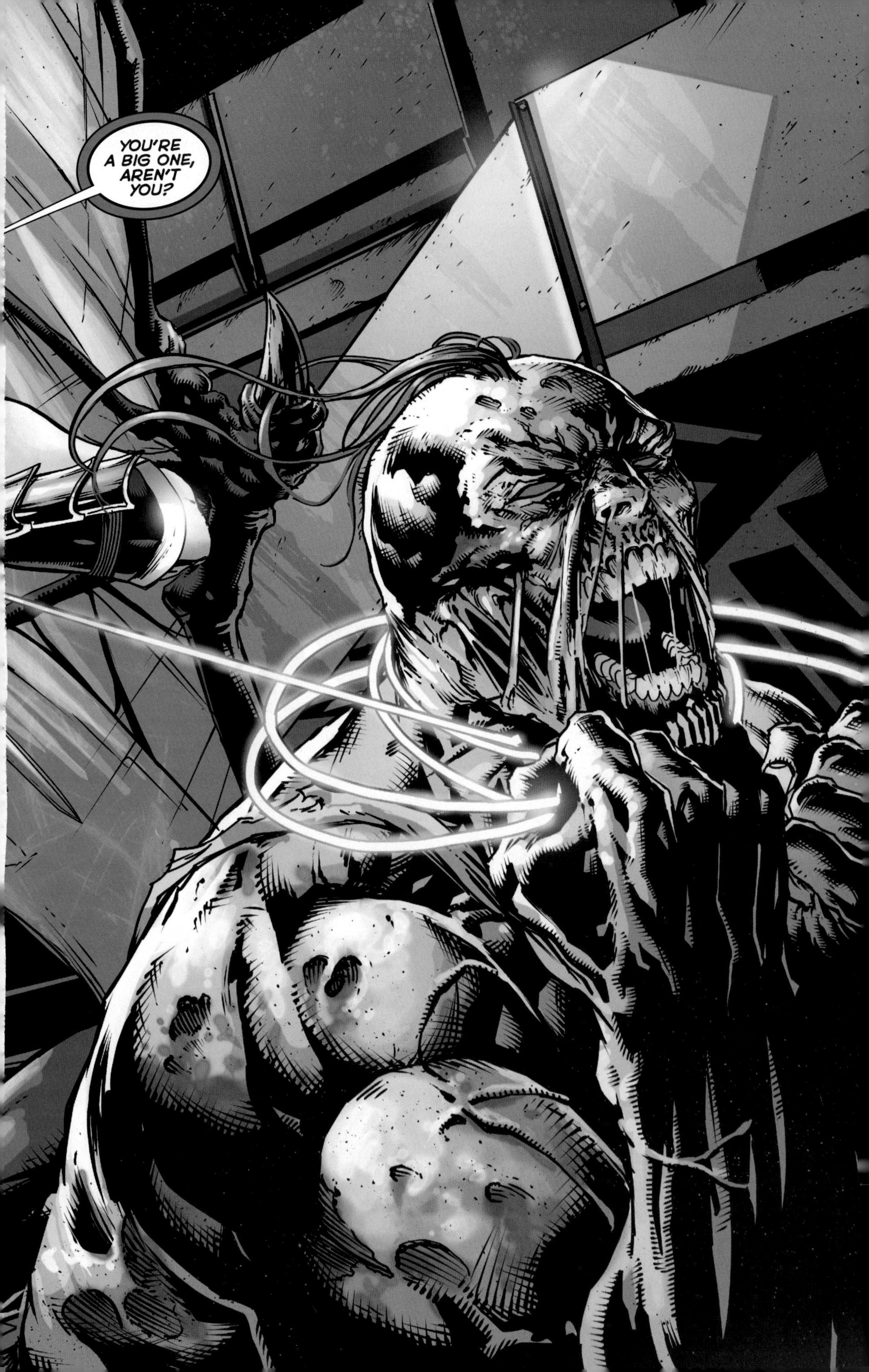
YOU'RE A BIG ONE, AREN'T YOU?

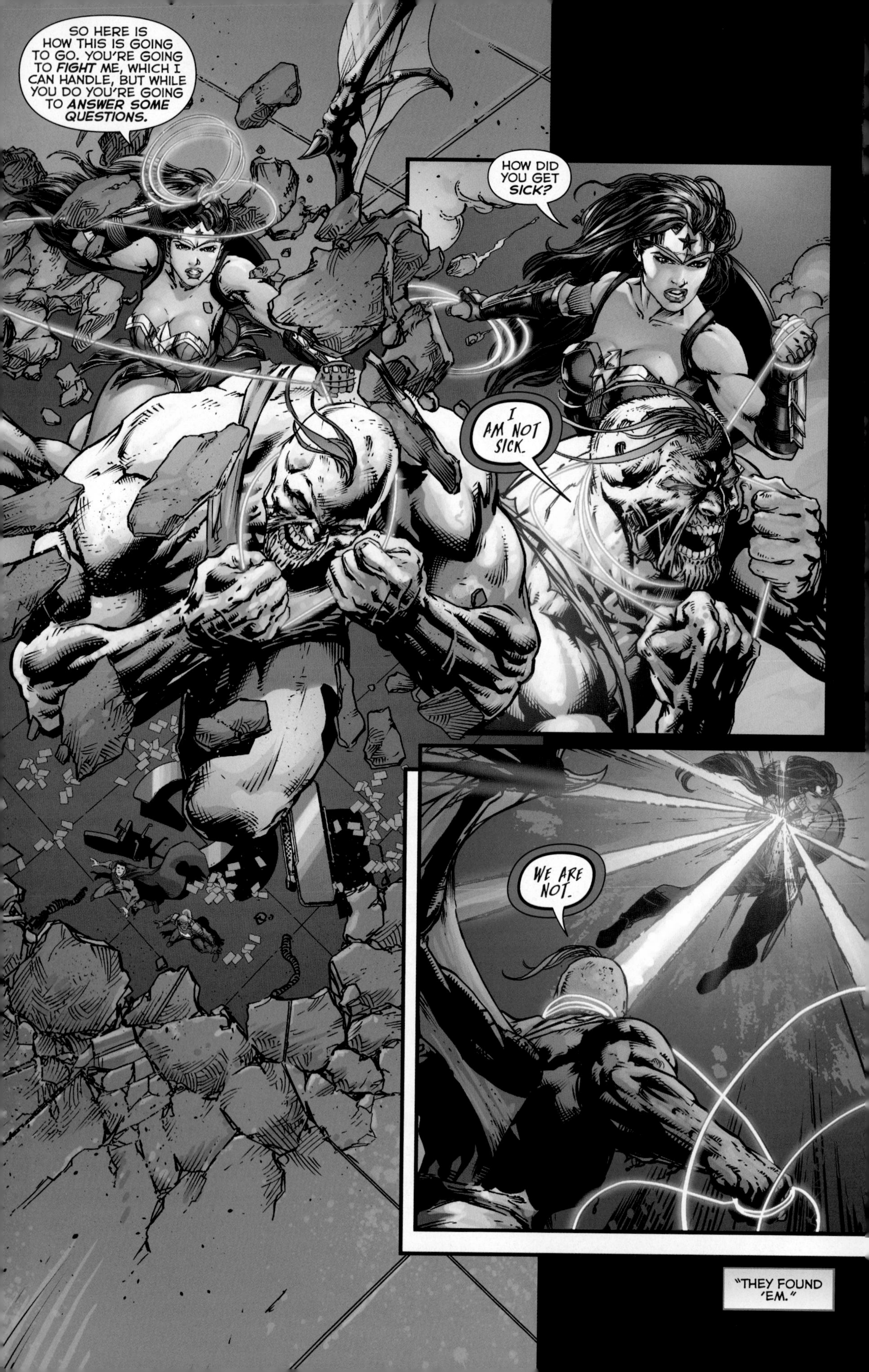
SO HERE IS HOW THIS IS GOING TO GO. YOU'RE GOING TO *FIGHT* ME, WHICH I CAN HANDLE, BUT WHILE YOU DO YOU'RE GOING TO ***ANSWER SOME QUESTIONS.***
HOW DID YOU GET ***SICK?***
I AM NOT SICK.
WE ARE NOT.
"THEY FOUND 'EM."

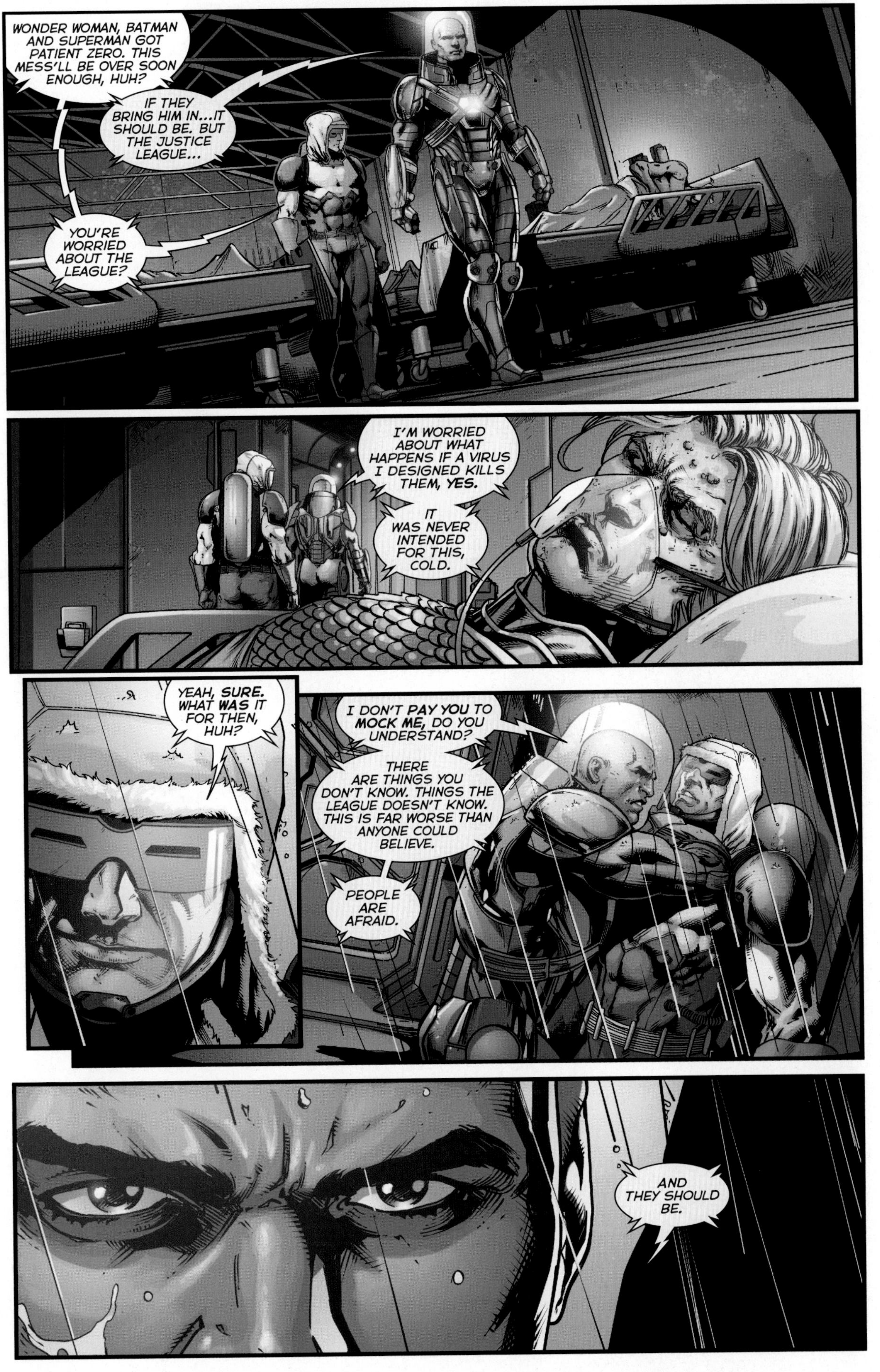
WONDER WOMAN, BATMAN AND SUPERMAN GOT PATIENT ZERO. THIS MESS'LL BE OVER SOON ENOUGH, HUH?
IF THEY BRING HIM IN...IT SHOULD BE. BUT THE JUSTICE LEAGUE...
YOU'RE WORRIED ABOUT THE LEAGUE?
I'M WORRIED ABOUT WHAT HAPPENS IF A VIRUS I DESIGNED KILLS THEM, YES.
IT WAS NEVER INTENDED FOR THIS, COLD.
YEAH, SURE. WHAT WAS IT FOR THEN, HUH?
I DON'T PAY YOU TO MOCK ME, DO YOU UNDERSTAND?
THERE ARE THINGS YOU DON'T KNOW. THINGS THE LEAGUE DOESN'T KNOW. THIS IS FAR WORSE THAN ANYONE COULD BELIEVE.
PEOPLE ARE AFRAID.
AND THEY SHOULD BE.

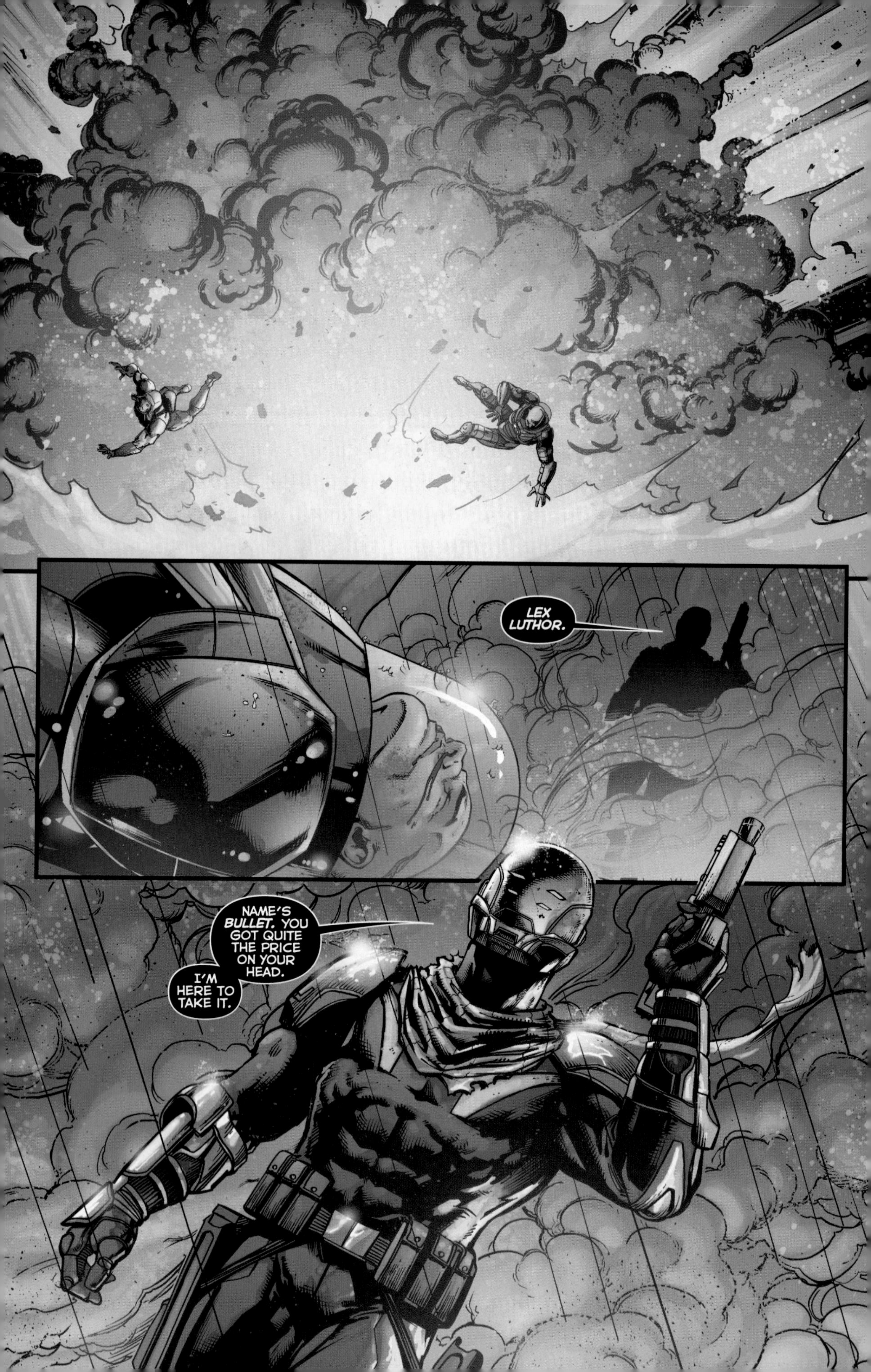
LEX LUTHOR.
NAME'S BULLET. YOU GOT QUITE THE PRICE ON YOUR HEAD.
I'M HERE TO TAKE IT.

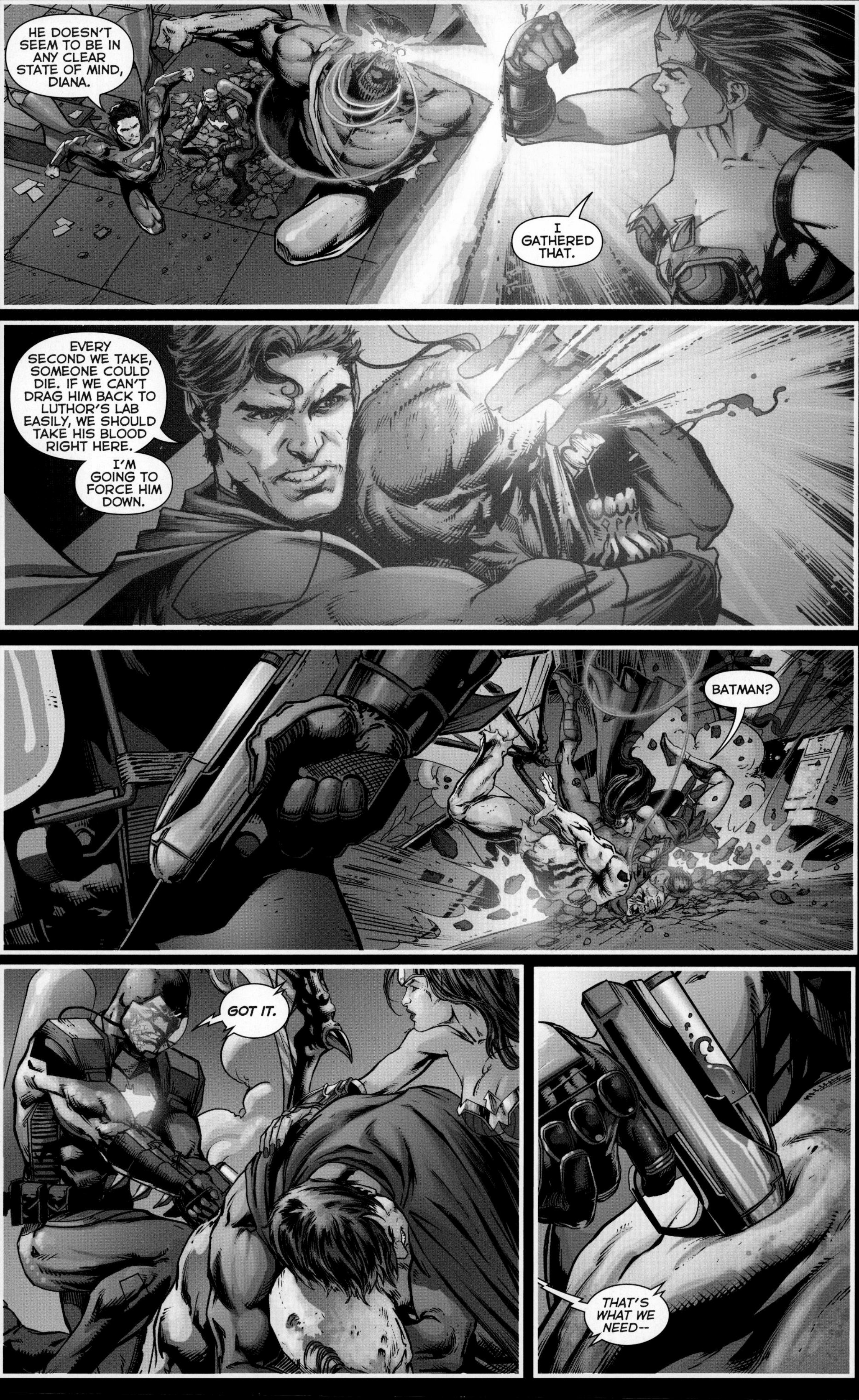
HE DOESN'T SEEM TO BE IN ANY CLEAR STATE OF MIND, DIANA.
I GATHERED THAT.
EVERY SECOND WE TAKE, SOMEONE COULD DIE. IF WE CAN'T DRAG HIM BACK TO LUTHOR'S LAB EASILY, WE SHOULD TAKE HIS BLOOD RIGHT HERE.
I'M GOING TO FORCE HIM DOWN.
BATMAN?
GOT IT.
THAT'S WHAT WE NEED--

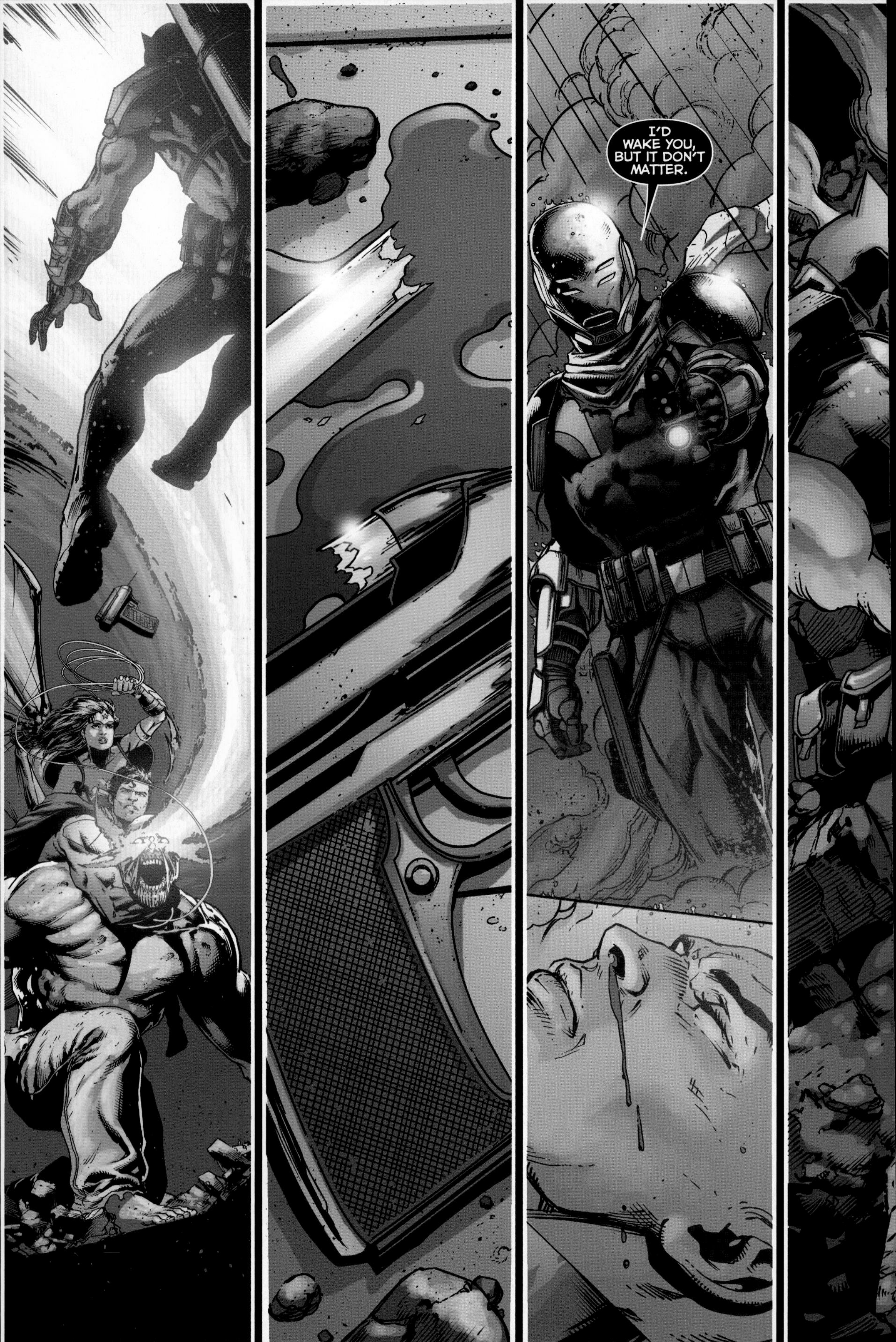
I'D WAKE YOU, BUT IT DON'T MATTER.

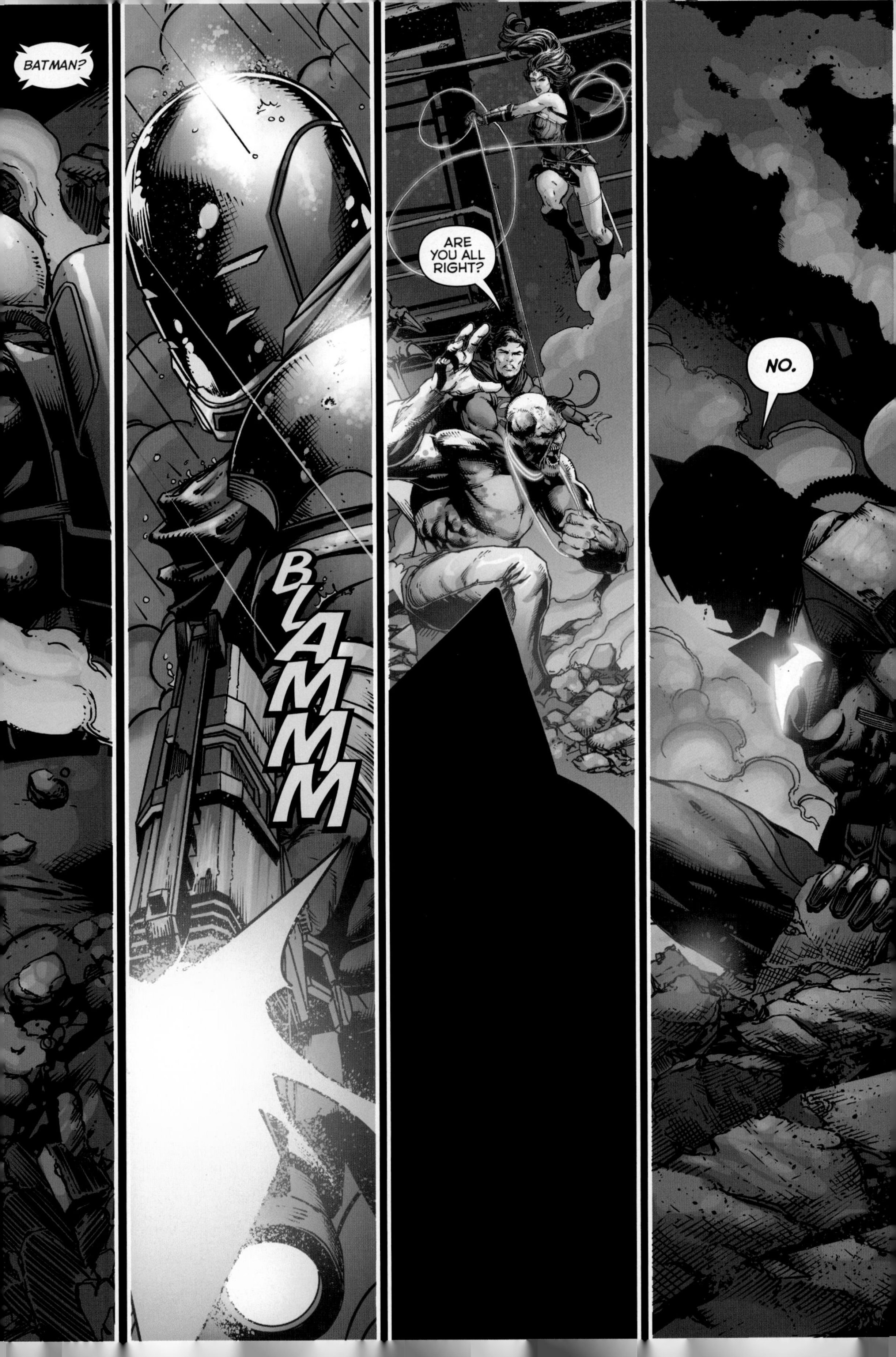
BATMAN?
BLAMMM
ARE YOU ALL RIGHT?
NO.

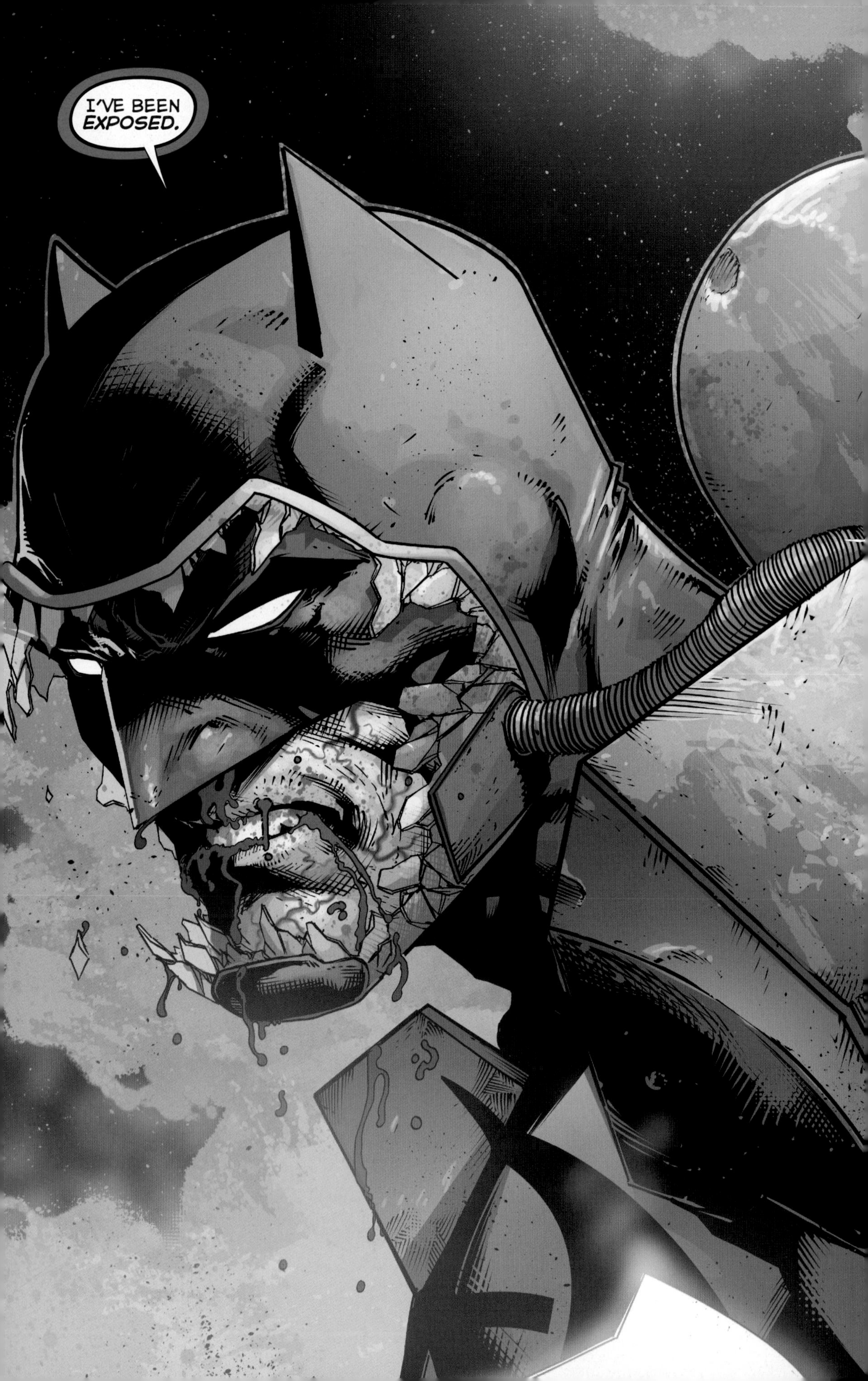
I'VE BEEN EXPOSED.

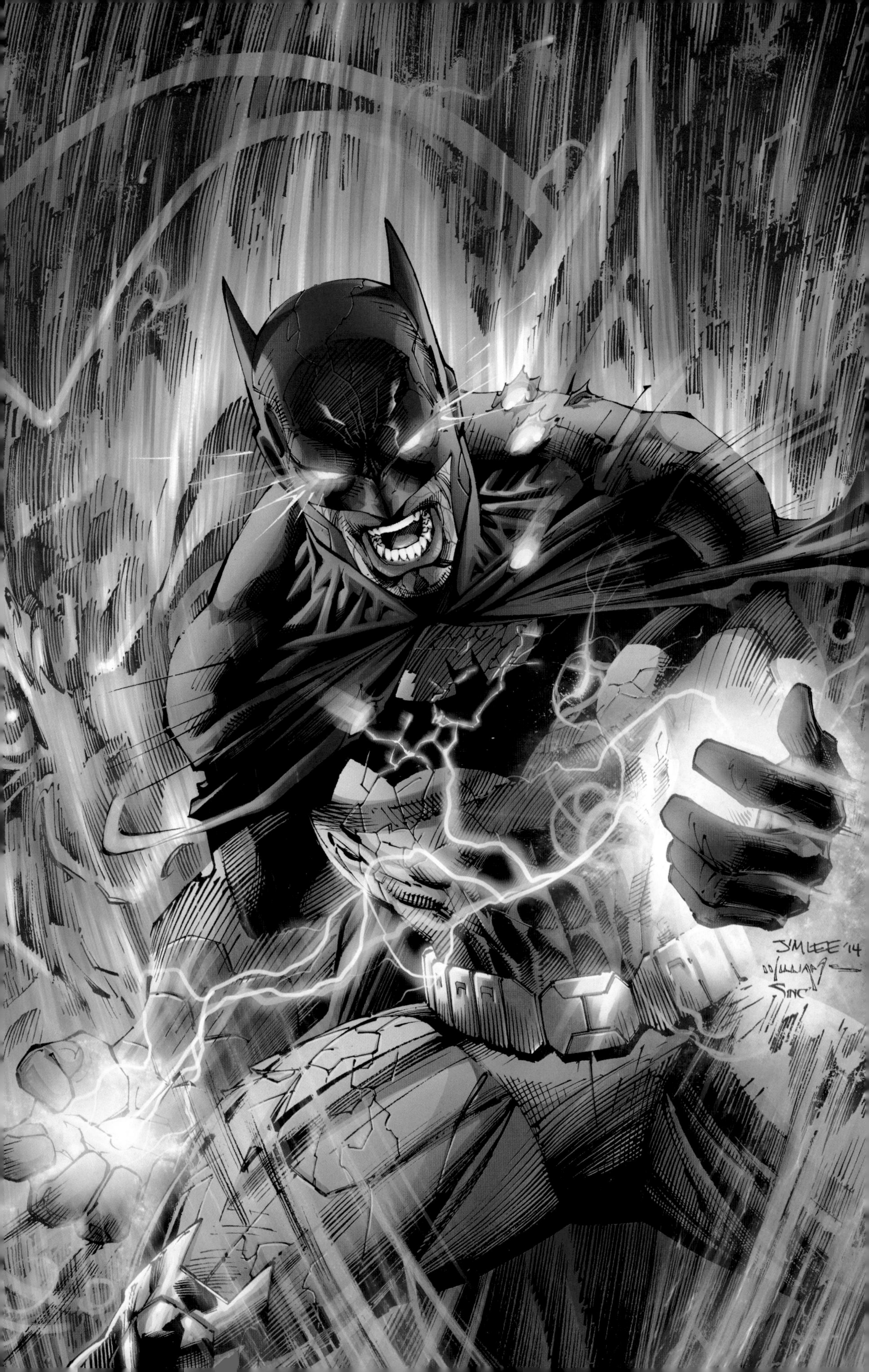
JIM LEE '14
SINC

THE AMAZO VIRUS CHAPTER THREE
THE SECRET

GEOFF JOHNS writer **JASON FABOK** artist **BRAD ANDERSON** colorist
JIM LEE & ALEX SINCLAIR cover artists

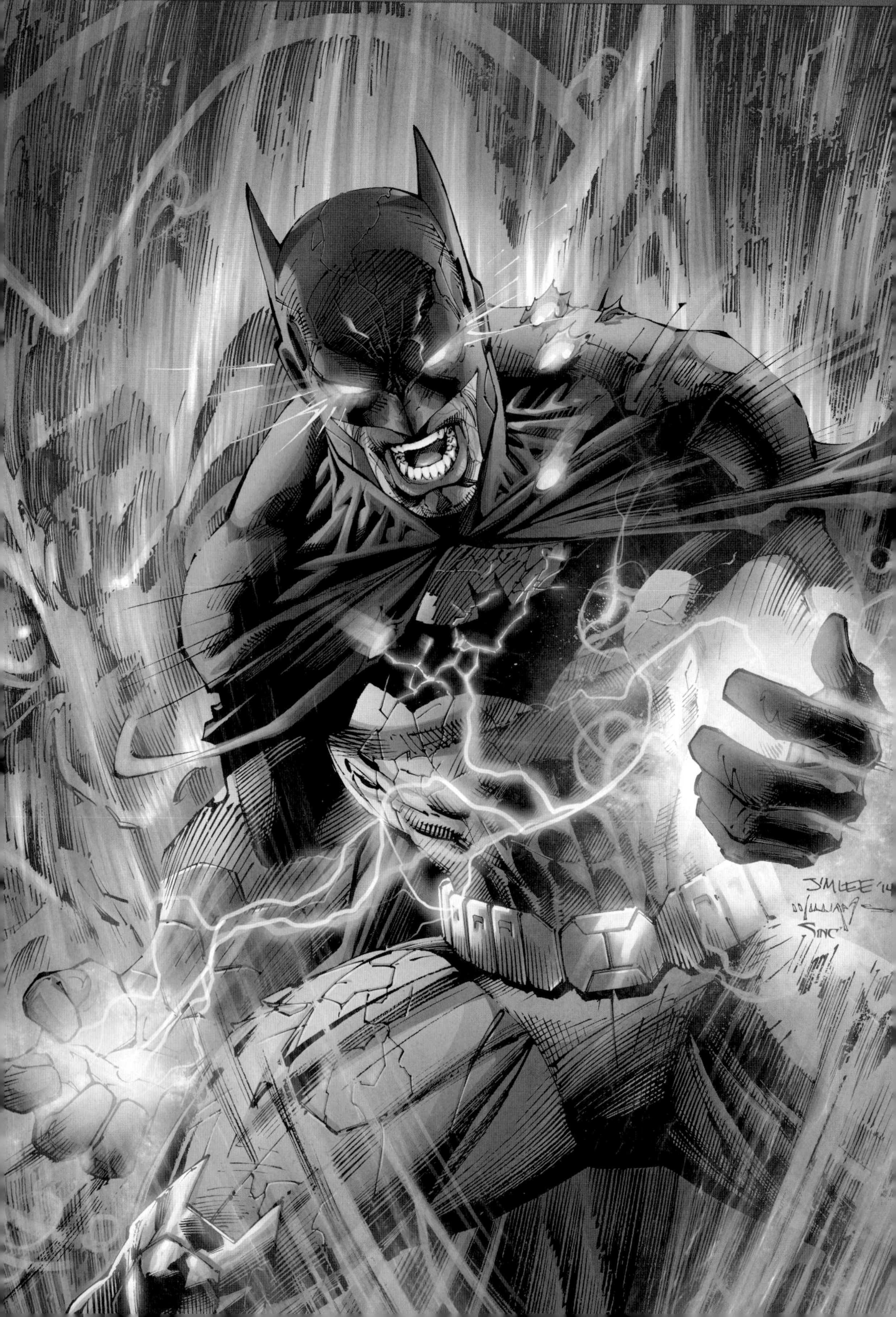

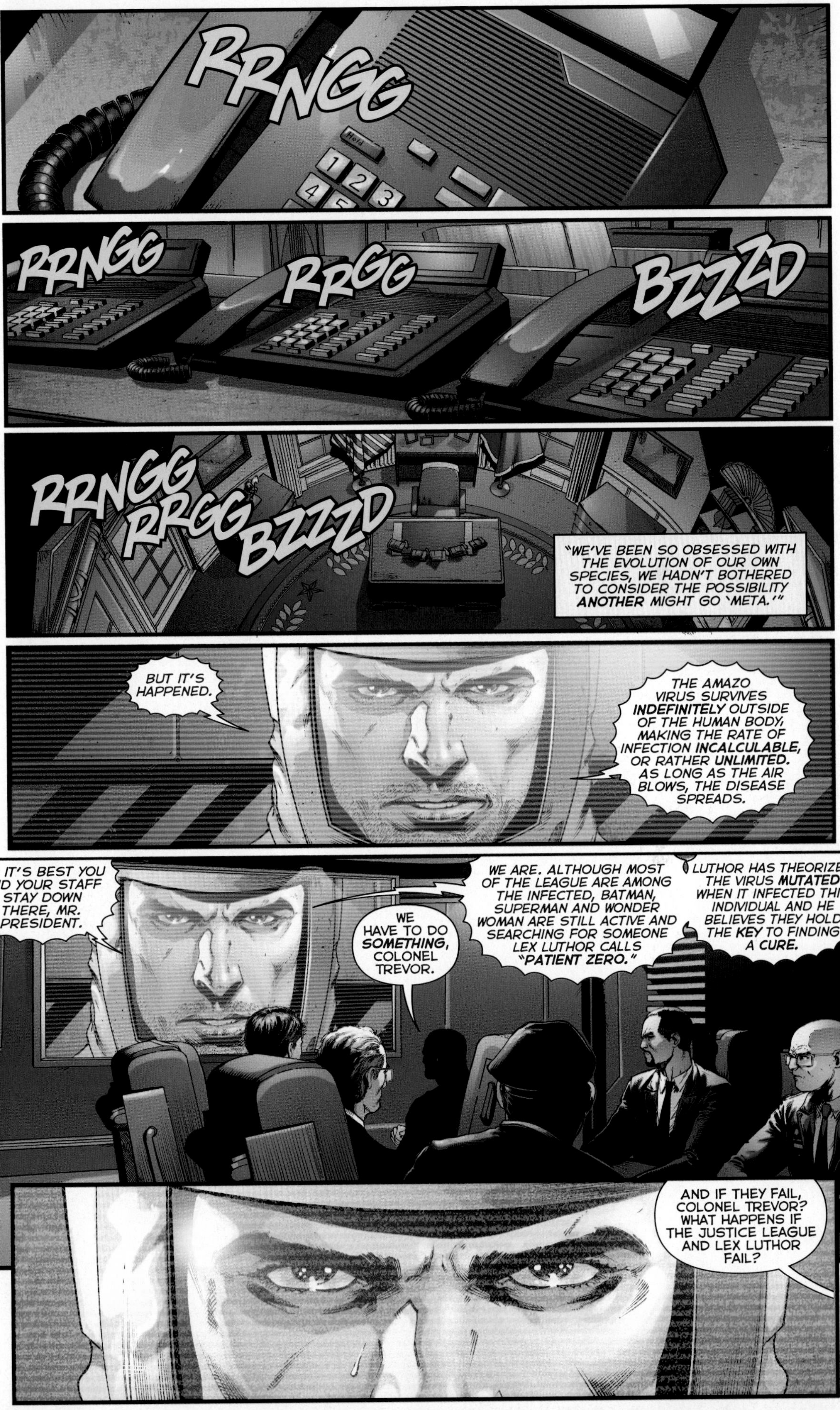
RRNGG
Hold
1 2 3
4 5
RRNGG
RRGG
BZZZD
RRNGG
RRGG
BZZZD
"WE'VE BEEN SO OBSESSED WITH THE EVOLUTION OF OUR OWN SPECIES, WE HADN'T BOTHERED TO CONSIDER THE POSSIBILITY **ANOTHER** MIGHT GO 'META.'"
BUT IT'S HAPPENED.
THE AMAZO VIRUS SURVIVES **INDEFINITELY** OUTSIDE OF THE HUMAN BODY, MAKING THE RATE OF INFECTION **INCALCULABLE**, OR RATHER **UNLIMITED.** AS LONG AS THE AIR BLOWS, THE DISEASE SPREADS.
SO IT'S BEST YOU AND YOUR STAFF STAY DOWN THERE, MR. PRESIDENT.
WE HAVE TO DO **SOMETHING**, COLONEL TREVOR.
WE ARE. ALTHOUGH MOST OF THE LEAGUE ARE AMONG THE INFECTED, BATMAN, SUPERMAN AND WONDER WOMAN ARE STILL ACTIVE AND SEARCHING FOR SOMEONE LEX LUTHOR CALLS **"PATIENT ZERO."**
LUTHOR HAS THEORIZED THE VIRUS **MUTATED** WHEN IT INFECTED THIS INDIVIDUAL AND HE BELIEVES THEY HOLD THE **KEY** TO FINDING A **CURE.**
AND IF THEY FAIL, COLONEL TREVOR? WHAT HAPPENS IF THE JUSTICE LEAGUE AND LEX LUTHOR FAIL?

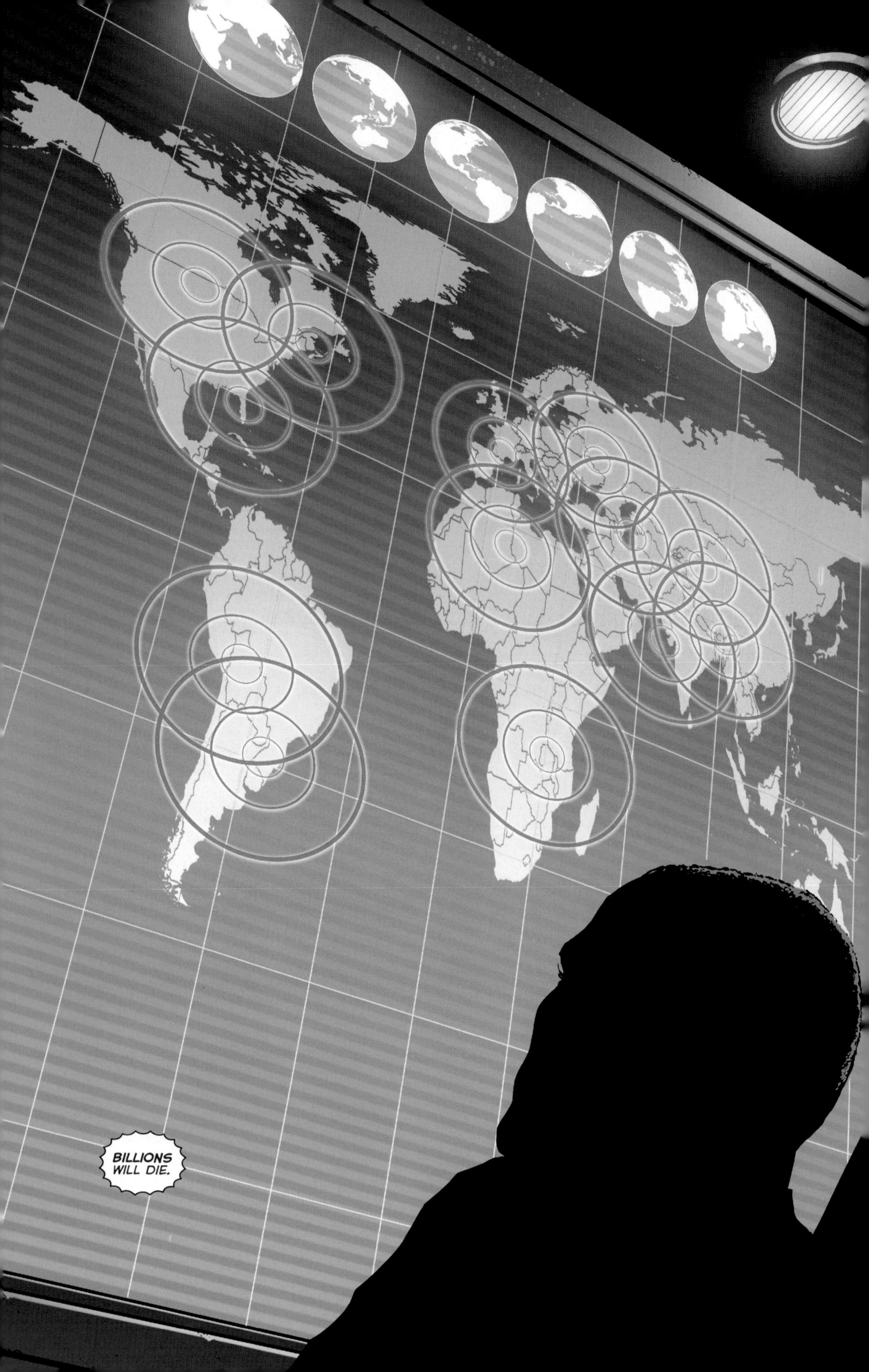
BILLIONS WILL DIE.

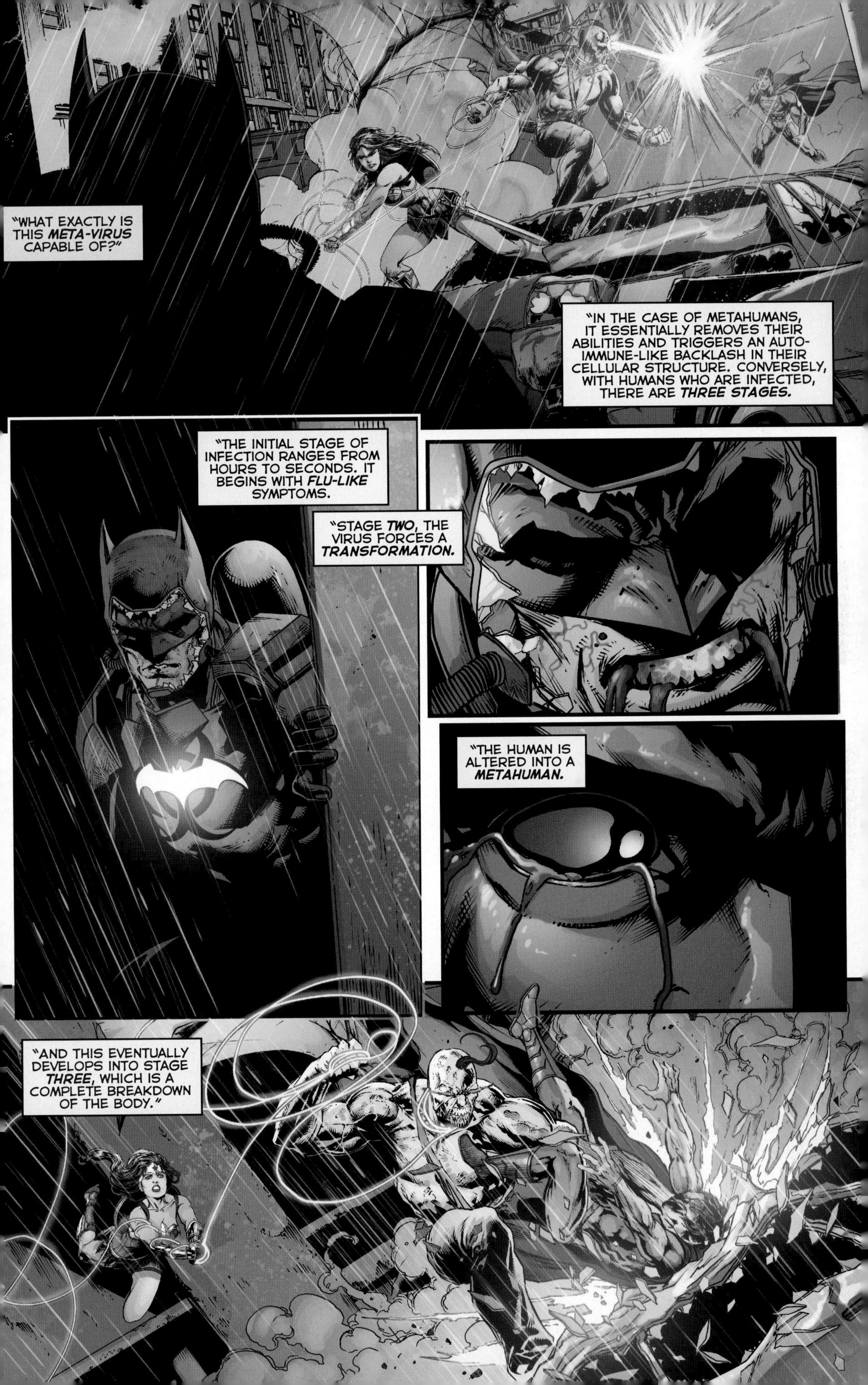
"WHAT EXACTLY IS THIS META-VIRUS CAPABLE OF?"
"IN THE CASE OF METAHUMANS, IT ESSENTIALLY REMOVES THEIR ABILITIES AND TRIGGERS AN AUTO-IMMUNE-LIKE BACKLASH IN THEIR CELLULAR STRUCTURE. CONVERSELY, WITH HUMANS WHO ARE INFECTED, THERE ARE THREE STAGES.
"THE INITIAL STAGE OF INFECTION RANGES FROM HOURS TO SECONDS. IT BEGINS WITH FLU-LIKE SYMPTOMS.
"STAGE TWO, THE VIRUS FORCES A TRANSFORMATION.
"THE HUMAN IS ALTERED INTO A METAHUMAN.
"AND THIS EVENTUALLY DEVELOPS INTO STAGE THREE, WHICH IS A COMPLETE BREAKDOWN OF THE BODY."

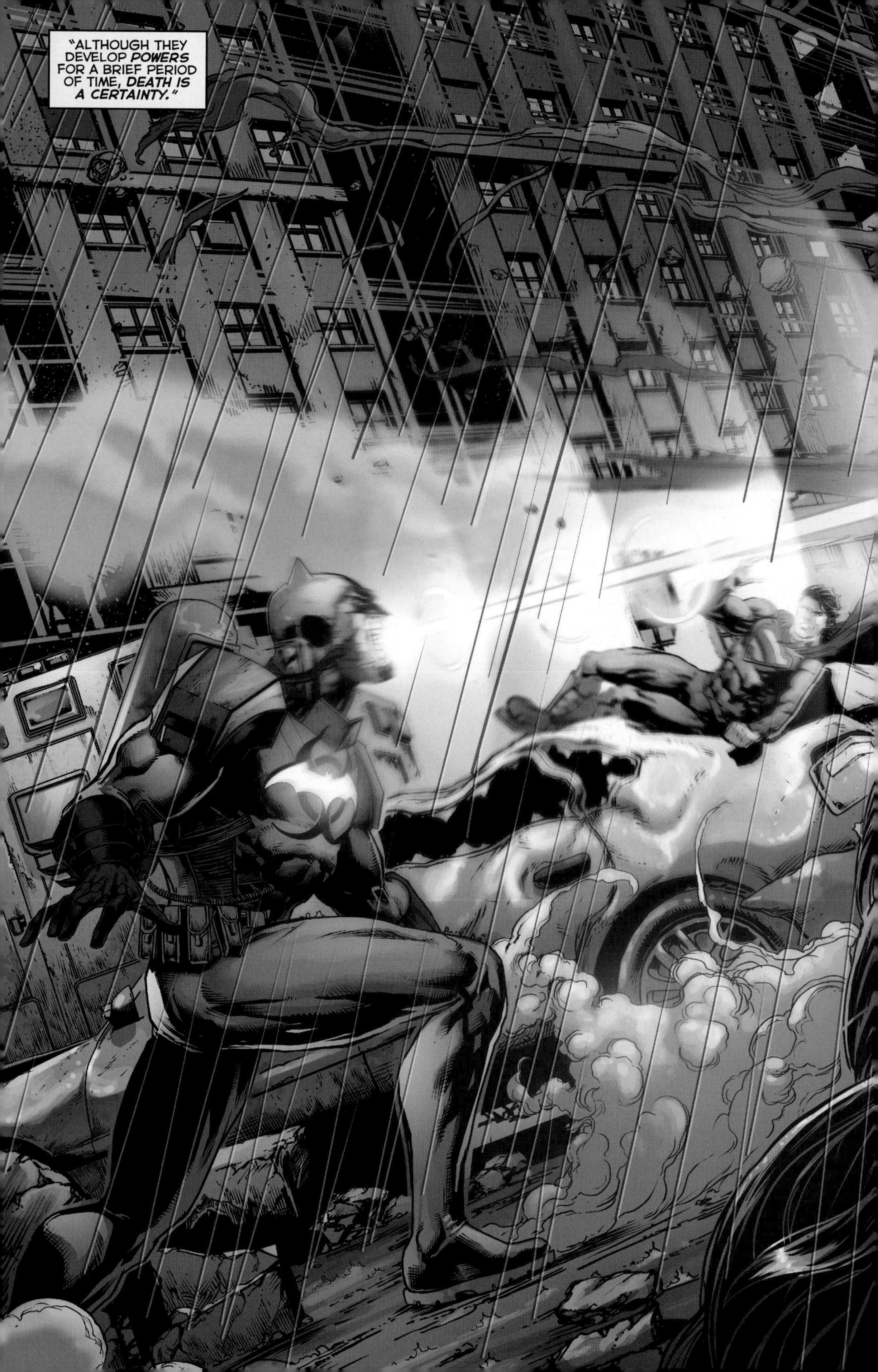
"ALTHOUGH THEY DEVELOP *POWERS* FOR A BRIEF PERIOD OF TIME, *DEATH IS A CERTAINTY.*"

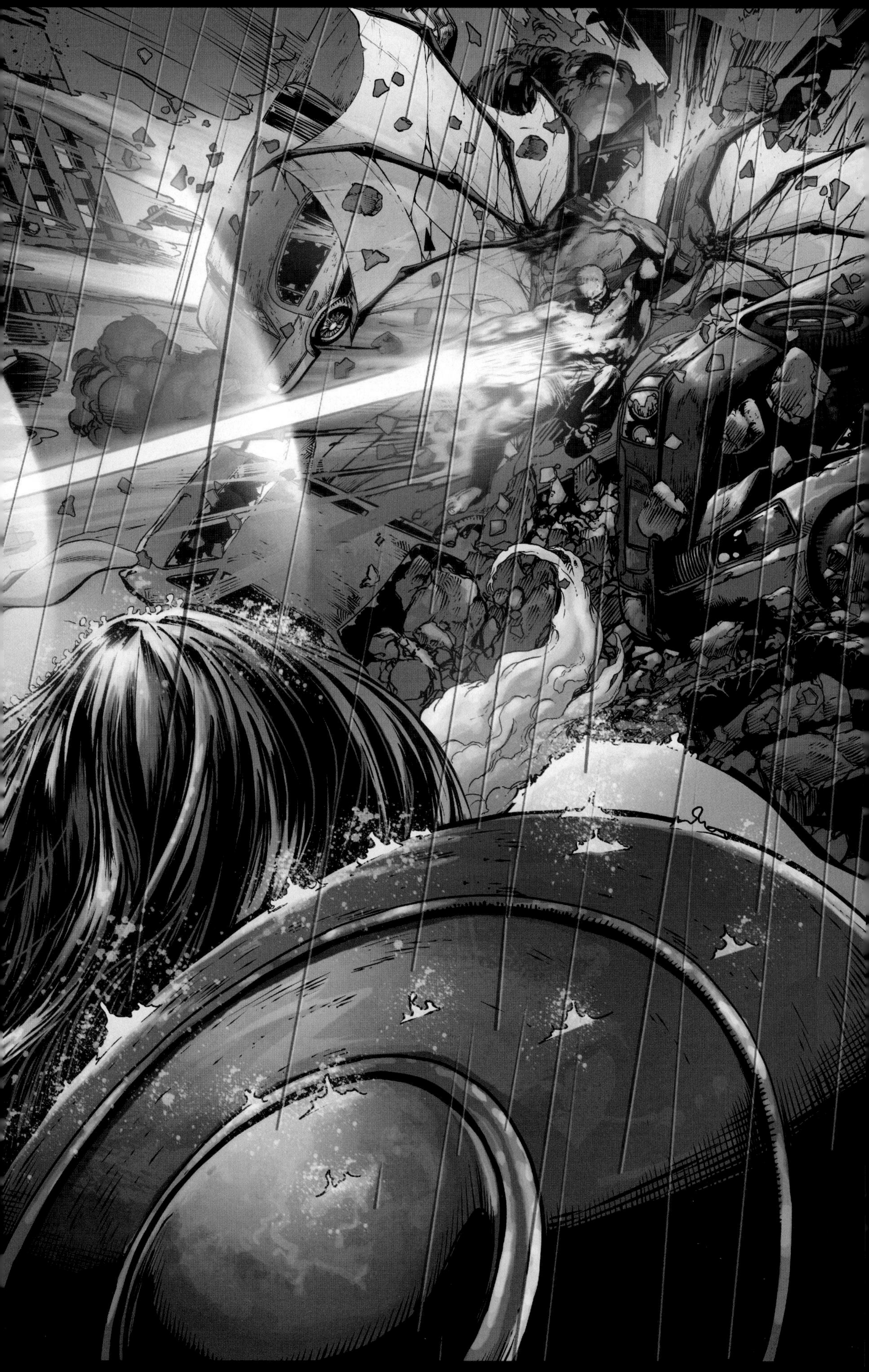

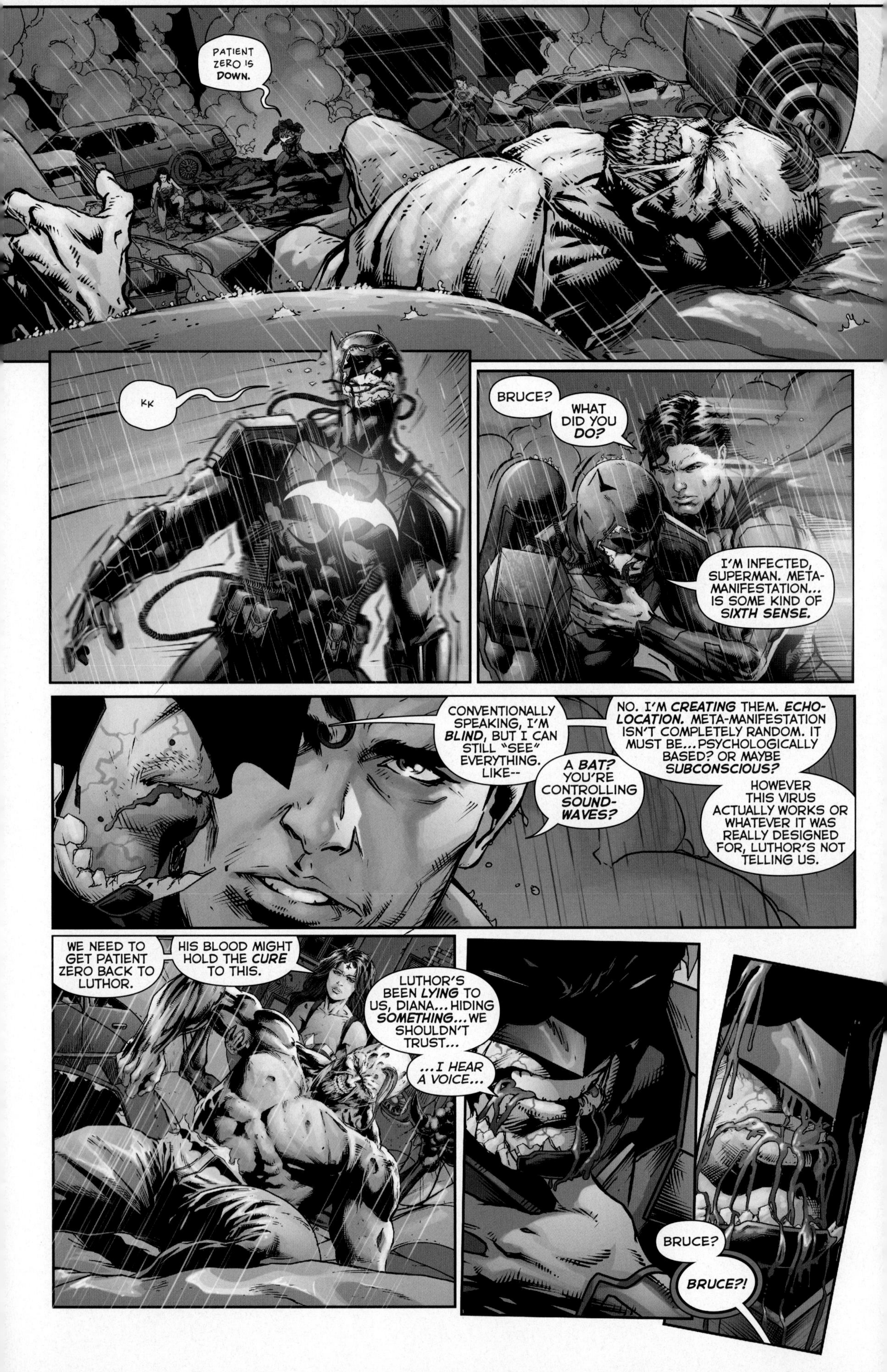
PATIENT ZERO IS DOWN.
KK
BRUCE?
WHAT DID YOU DO?
I'M INFECTED, SUPERMAN. META-MANIFESTATION... IS SOME KIND OF SIXTH SENSE.
CONVENTIONALLY SPEAKING, I'M BLIND, BUT I CAN STILL "SEE" EVERYTHING. LIKE--
A BAT? YOU'RE CONTROLLING SOUND-WAVES?
NO. I'M CREATING THEM. ECHO-LOCATION. META-MANIFESTATION ISN'T COMPLETELY RANDOM. IT MUST BE...PSYCHOLOGICALLY BASED? OR MAYBE SUBCONSCIOUS?
HOWEVER THIS VIRUS ACTUALLY WORKS OR WHATEVER IT WAS REALLY DESIGNED FOR, LUTHOR'S NOT TELLING US.
WE NEED TO GET PATIENT ZERO BACK TO LUTHOR.
HIS BLOOD MIGHT HOLD THE CURE TO THIS.
LUTHOR'S BEEN LYING TO US, DIANA...HIDING SOMETHING...WE SHOULDN'T TRUST...
...I HEAR A VOICE...
BRUCE?
BRUCE?!

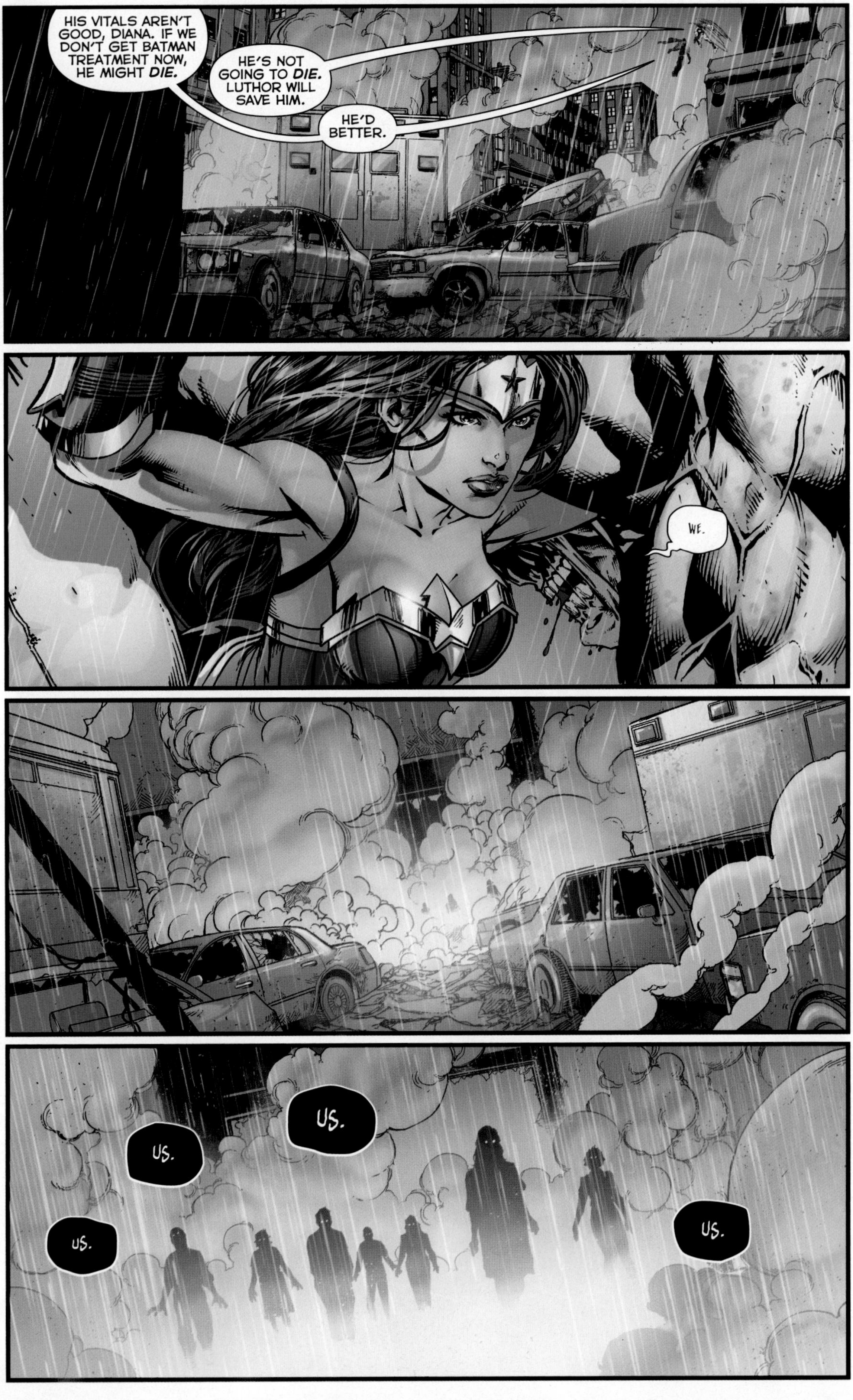
HIS VITALS AREN'T GOOD, DIANA. IF WE DON'T GET BATMAN TREATMENT NOW, HE MIGHT DIE.
HE'S NOT GOING TO DIE. LUTHOR WILL SAVE HIM.
HE'D BETTER.
WE.
US.
US.
US.
US.

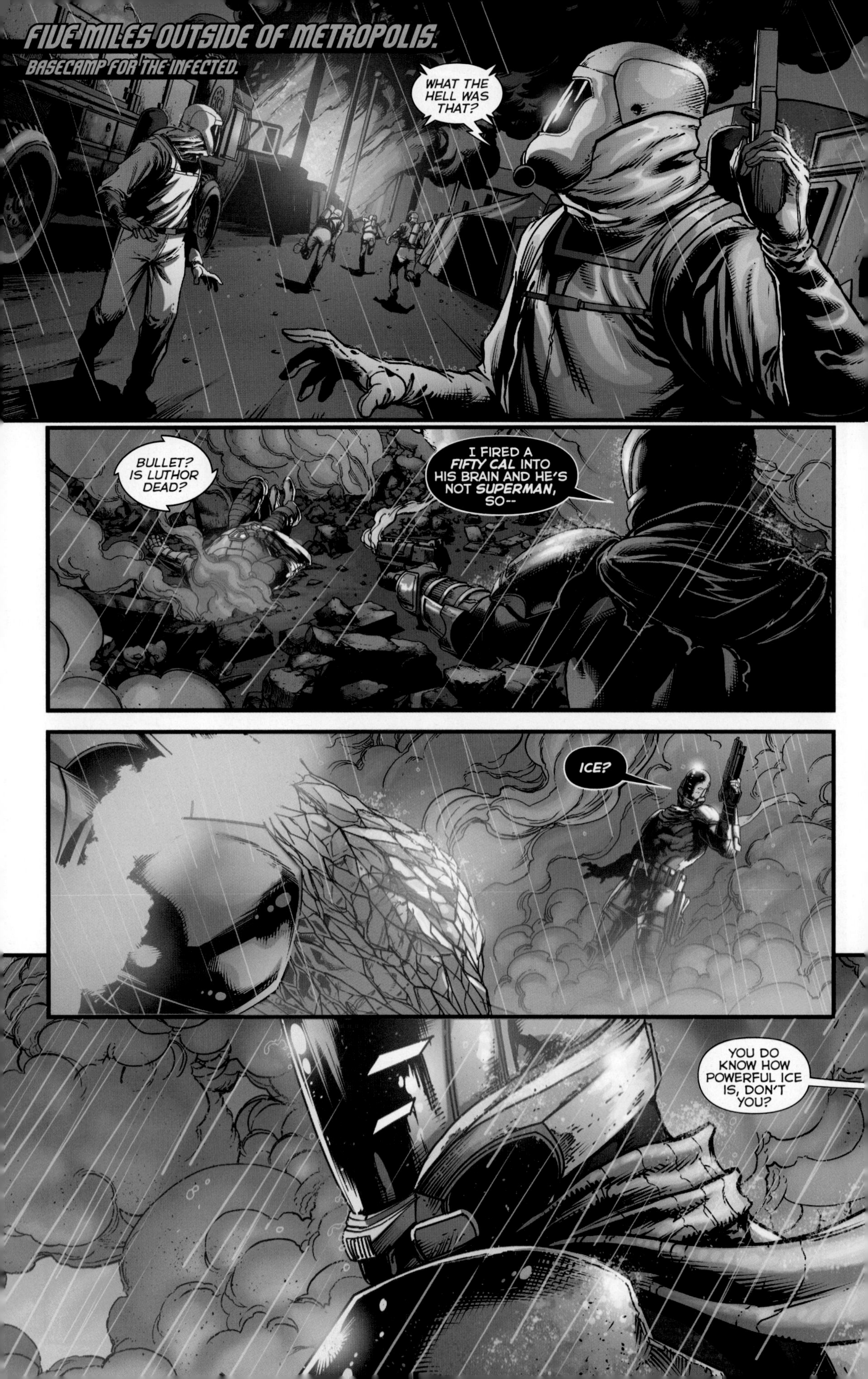
FIVE MILES OUTSIDE OF METROPOLIS.
BASECAMP FOR THE INFECTED.
WHAT THE HELL WAS THAT?
BULLET? IS LUTHOR DEAD?
I FIRED A FIFTY CAL INTO HIS BRAIN AND HE'S NOT SUPERMAN, SO--
ICE?
YOU DO KNOW HOW POWERFUL ICE IS, DON'T YOU?

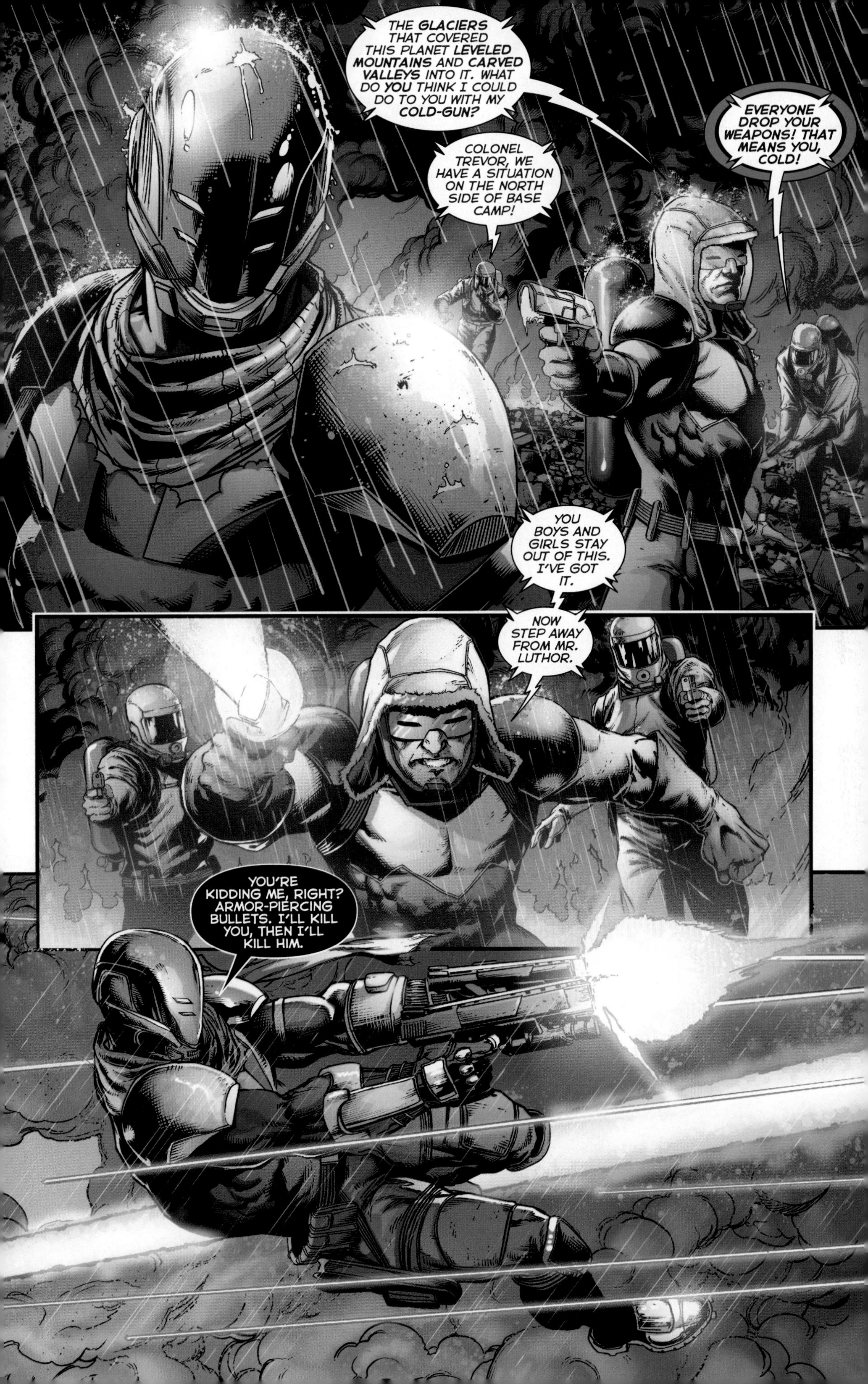
THE **GLACIERS** THAT COVERED THIS PLANET **LEVELED MOUNTAINS** AND **CARVED VALLEYS** INTO IT. WHAT DO **YOU** THINK I COULD DO TO YOU WITH MY **COLD-GUN?**
COLONEL TREVOR, WE HAVE A SITUATION ON THE NORTH SIDE OF BASE CAMP!
EVERYONE DROP YOUR WEAPONS! THAT MEANS YOU, COLD!
YOU BOYS AND GIRLS STAY OUT OF THIS. I'VE GOT IT.
NOW STEP AWAY FROM MR. LUTHOR.
YOU'RE KIDDING ME, RIGHT? ARMOR-PIERCING BULLETS. I'LL KILL YOU, THEN I'LL KILL HIM.

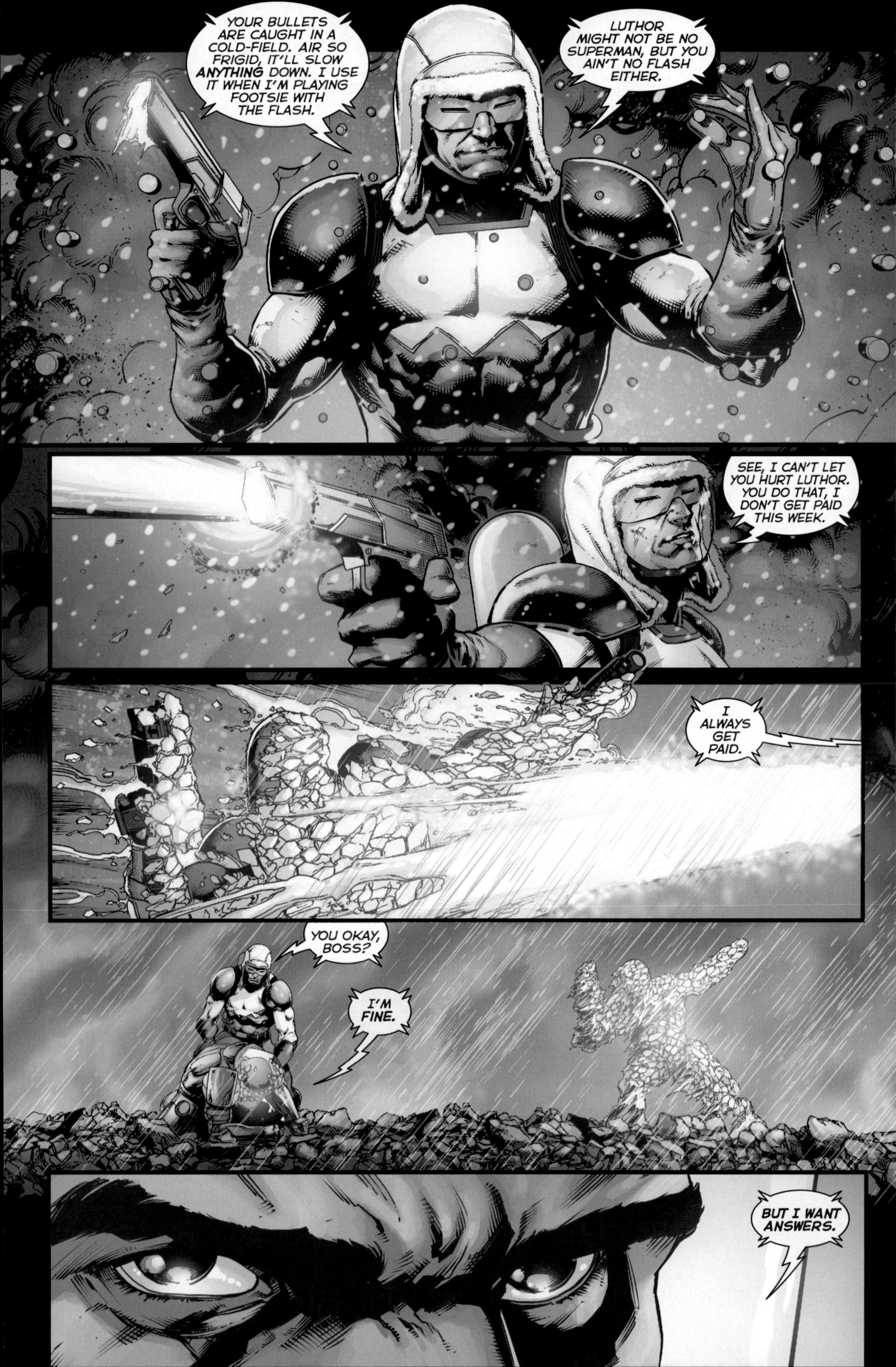
YOUR BULLETS ARE CAUGHT IN A COLD-FIELD. AIR SO FRIGID, IT'LL SLOW ANYTHING DOWN. I USE IT WHEN I'M PLAYING FOOTSIE WITH THE FLASH.
LUTHOR MIGHT NOT BE NO SUPERMAN, BUT YOU AIN'T NO FLASH EITHER.
SEE, I CAN'T LET YOU HURT LUTHOR. YOU DO THAT, I DON'T GET PAID THIS WEEK.
I ALWAYS GET PAID.
YOU OKAY, BOSS?
I'M FINE.
BUT I WANT ANSWERS.

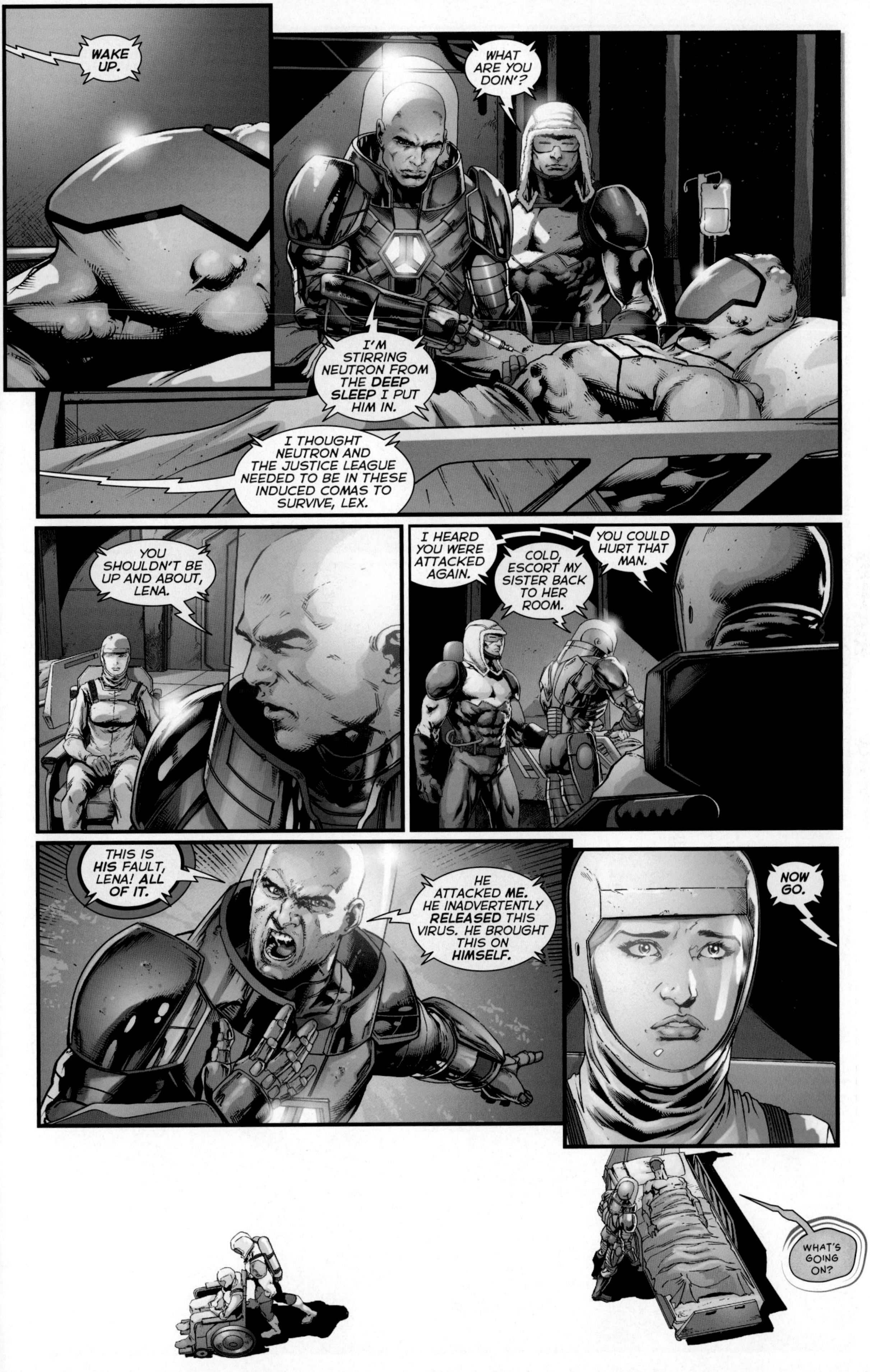
WAKE UP.
WHAT ARE YOU DOIN'?
I'M STIRRING NEUTRON FROM THE DEEP SLEEP I PUT HIM IN.
I THOUGHT NEUTRON AND THE JUSTICE LEAGUE NEEDED TO BE IN THESE INDUCED COMAS TO SURVIVE, LEX.
YOU SHOULDN'T BE UP AND ABOUT, LENA.
I HEARD YOU WERE ATTACKED AGAIN.
COLD, ESCORT MY SISTER BACK TO HER ROOM.
YOU COULD HURT THAT MAN.
THIS IS HIS FAULT, LENA! ALL OF IT.
HE ATTACKED ME. HE INADVERTENTLY RELEASED THIS VIRUS. HE BROUGHT THIS ON HIMSELF.
NOW GO.
WHAT'S GOING ON?

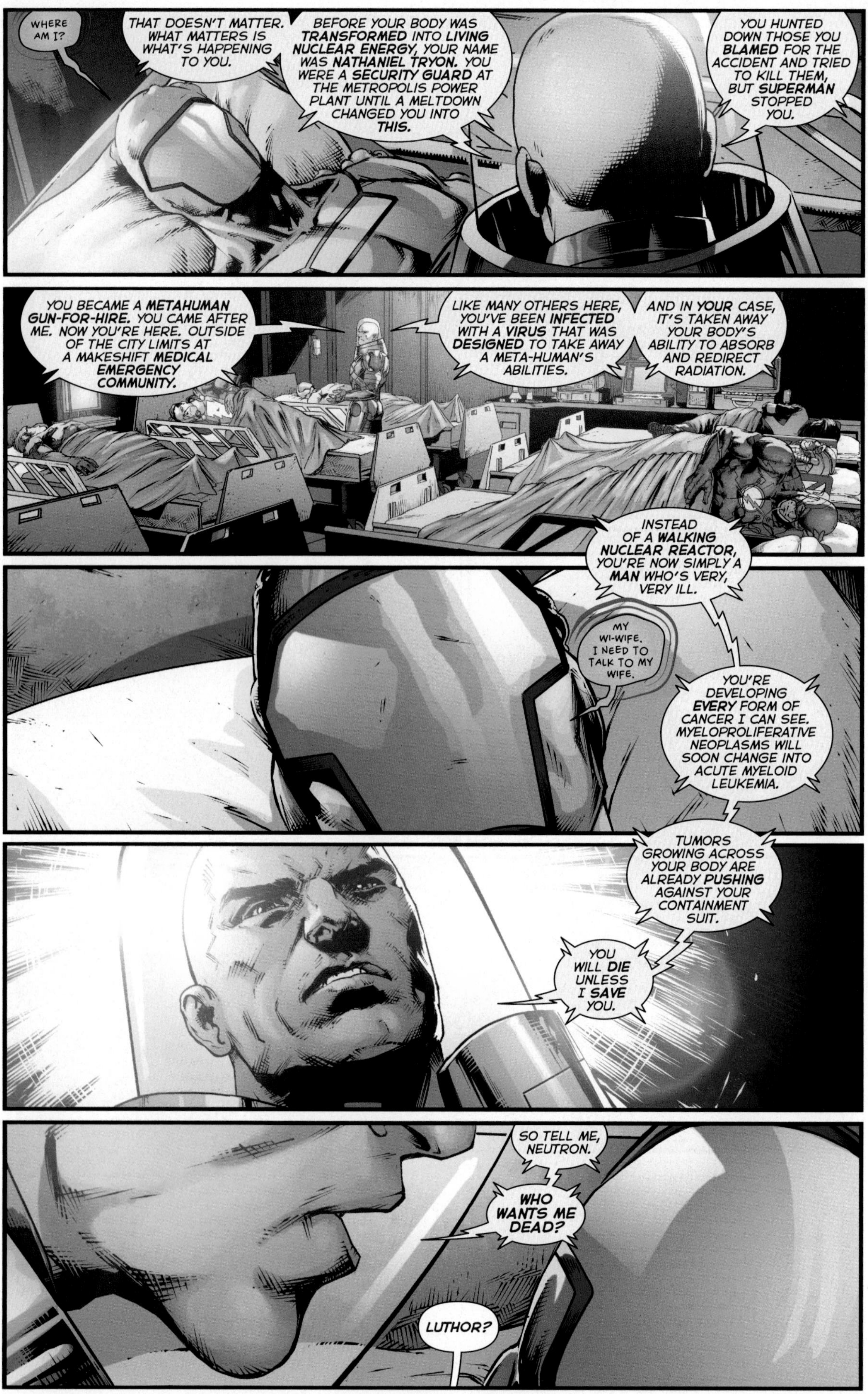

WHERE AM I?
THAT DOESN'T MATTER. WHAT MATTERS IS WHAT'S HAPPENING TO YOU.
BEFORE YOUR BODY WAS TRANSFORMED INTO LIVING NUCLEAR ENERGY, YOUR NAME WAS NATHANIEL TRYON. YOU WERE A SECURITY GUARD AT THE METROPOLIS POWER PLANT UNTIL A MELTDOWN CHANGED YOU INTO THIS.
YOU HUNTED DOWN THOSE YOU BLAMED FOR THE ACCIDENT AND TRIED TO KILL THEM, BUT SUPERMAN STOPPED YOU.
YOU BECAME A METAHUMAN GUN-FOR-HIRE. YOU CAME AFTER ME. NOW YOU'RE HERE. OUTSIDE OF THE CITY LIMITS AT A MAKESHIFT MEDICAL EMERGENCY COMMUNITY.
LIKE MANY OTHERS HERE, YOU'VE BEEN INFECTED WITH A VIRUS THAT WAS DESIGNED TO TAKE AWAY A META-HUMAN'S ABILITIES.
AND IN YOUR CASE, IT'S TAKEN AWAY YOUR BODY'S ABILITY TO ABSORB AND REDIRECT RADIATION.
INSTEAD OF A WALKING NUCLEAR REACTOR, YOU'RE NOW SIMPLY A MAN WHO'S VERY, VERY ILL.
MY WI-WIFE. I NEED TO TALK TO MY WIFE.
YOU'RE DEVELOPING EVERY FORM OF CANCER I CAN SEE. MYELOPROLIFERATIVE NEOPLASMS WILL SOON CHANGE INTO ACUTE MYELOID LEUKEMIA.
TUMORS GROWING ACROSS YOUR BODY ARE ALREADY PUSHING AGAINST YOUR CONTAINMENT SUIT.
YOU WILL DIE UNLESS I SAVE YOU.
SO TELL ME, NEUTRON.
WHO WANTS ME DEAD?
LUTHOR?

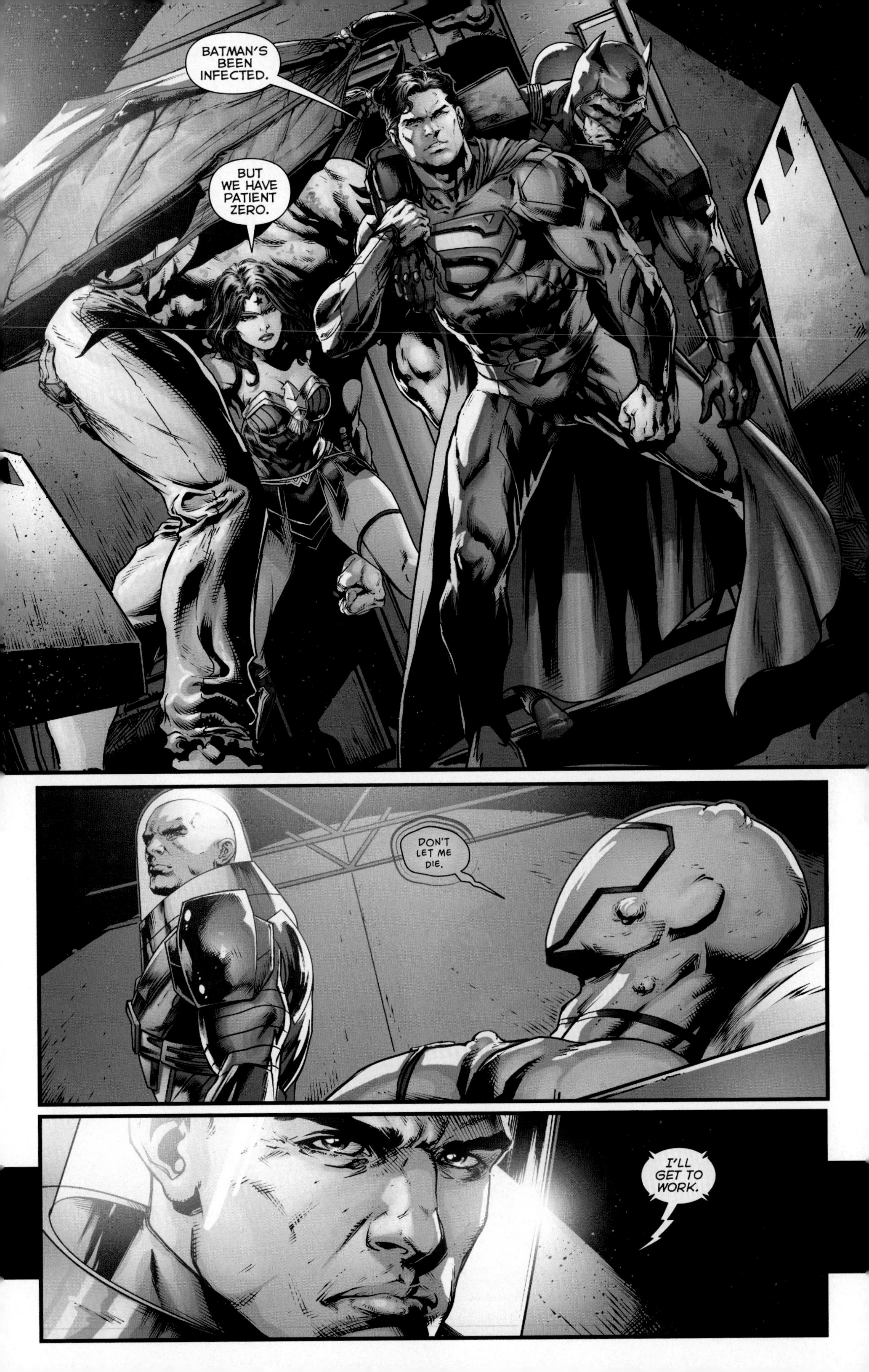
BATMAN'S BEEN INFECTED.
BUT WE HAVE PATIENT ZERO.
DON'T LET ME DIE.
I'LL GET TO WORK.

"COLONEL TREVOR?"

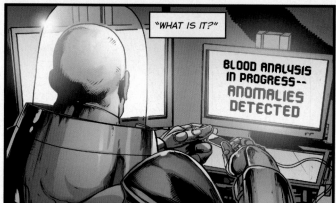

"WHAT IS IT?"

BLOOD ANALYSIS IN PROGRESS -- ANOMALIES DETECTED

US.

WE'RE GETTING MOVEMENT ALL AROUND BASECAMP. WHAT THE HELL'S GOING ON?

I DON'T KNOW.

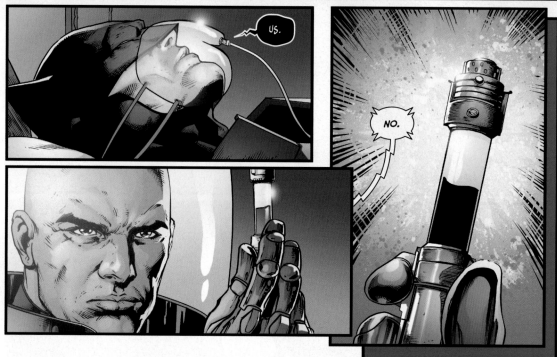

US.

NO.

HIS BLOOD CAN'T HELP US.

WHY NOT?

HE MAY HAVE THE ABILITY TO MIMIC ANYONE'S META-HUMAN POWERS ORGANICALLY, BUT HE'S AS SICK AS THE OTHERS. HIS ABILITIES JUST MANIFESTED DIFFERENTLY.

...I NEED A SAMPLE OF YOUR BLOOD SUPERMAN.

MINE?

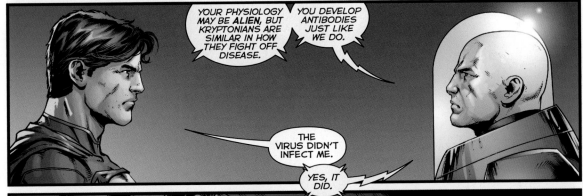

YOUR PHYSIOLOGY MAY BE ALIEN, BUT KRYPTONIANS ARE SIMILAR IN HOW THEY FIGHT OFF DISEASE.

YOU DEVELOP ANTIBODIES JUST LIKE WE DO.

THE VIRUS DIDN'T INFECT ME.

YES, IT DID.

WHAT ARE YOU TALKING ABOUT?

I EXPOSED YOU TO THE AMAZO VIRUS FOUR YEARS AGO.

YOU **WHAT?**

I TESTED IT ON YOU. IT FAILED. I PUT IT IN COLD STORAGE.

WHY?

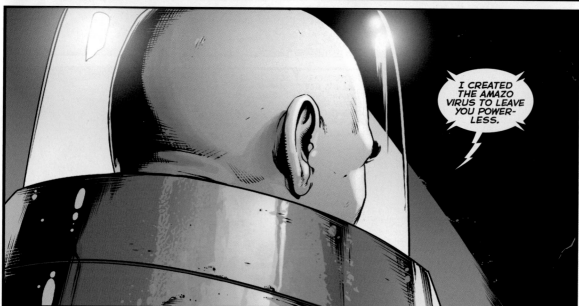

I CREATED THE AMAZO VIRUS TO LEAVE YOU POWER-LESS.

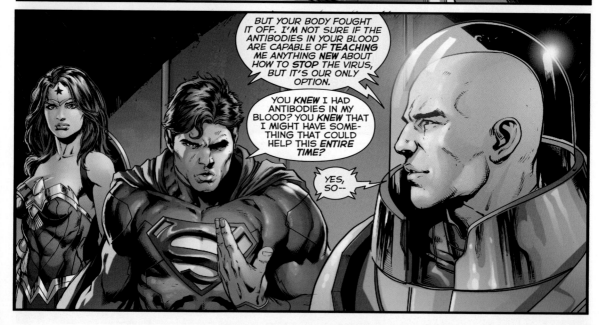

BUT YOUR BODY FOUGHT IT OFF. I'M NOT SURE IF THE ANTIBODIES IN YOUR BLOOD ARE CAPABLE OF *TEACHING* ME ANYTHING *NEW* ABOUT HOW TO *STOP THE VIRUS,* BUT IT'S OUR ONLY OPTION.

YOU *KNEW* I HAD ANTIBODIES IN MY BLOOD? YOU *KNEW* THAT I MIGHT HAVE SOME-THING THAT COULD HELP THIS *ENTIRE TIME?*

YES, SO--

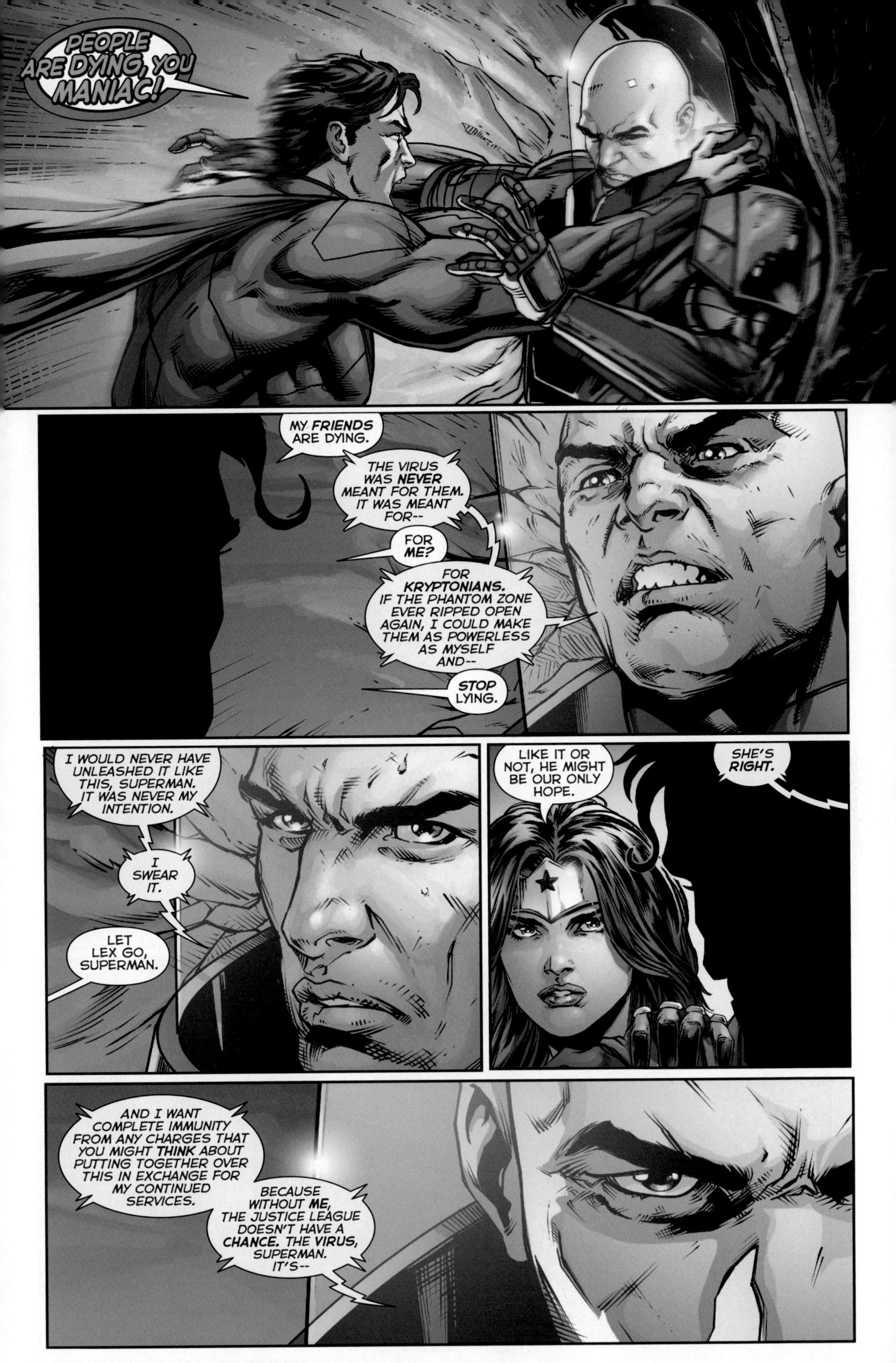
PEOPLE ARE DYING, YOU MANIAC!
MY FRIENDS ARE DYING.
THE VIRUS WAS NEVER MEANT FOR THEM. IT WAS MEANT FOR--
FOR ME?
FOR KRYPTONIANS. IF THE PHANTOM ZONE EVER RIPPED OPEN AGAIN, I COULD MAKE THEM AS POWERLESS AS MYSELF AND--
STOP LYING.
I WOULD NEVER HAVE UNLEASHED IT LIKE THIS, SUPERMAN. IT WAS NEVER MY INTENTION.
I SWEAR IT.
LET LEX GO, SUPERMAN.
LIKE IT OR NOT, HE MIGHT BE OUR ONLY HOPE.
SHE'S RIGHT.
AND I WANT COMPLETE IMMUNITY FROM ANY CHARGES THAT YOU MIGHT THINK ABOUT PUTTING TOGETHER OVER THIS IN EXCHANGE FOR MY CONTINUED SERVICES.
BECAUSE WITHOUT ME, THE JUSTICE LEAGUE DOESN'T HAVE A CHANCE. THE VIRUS, SUPERMAN. IT'S--

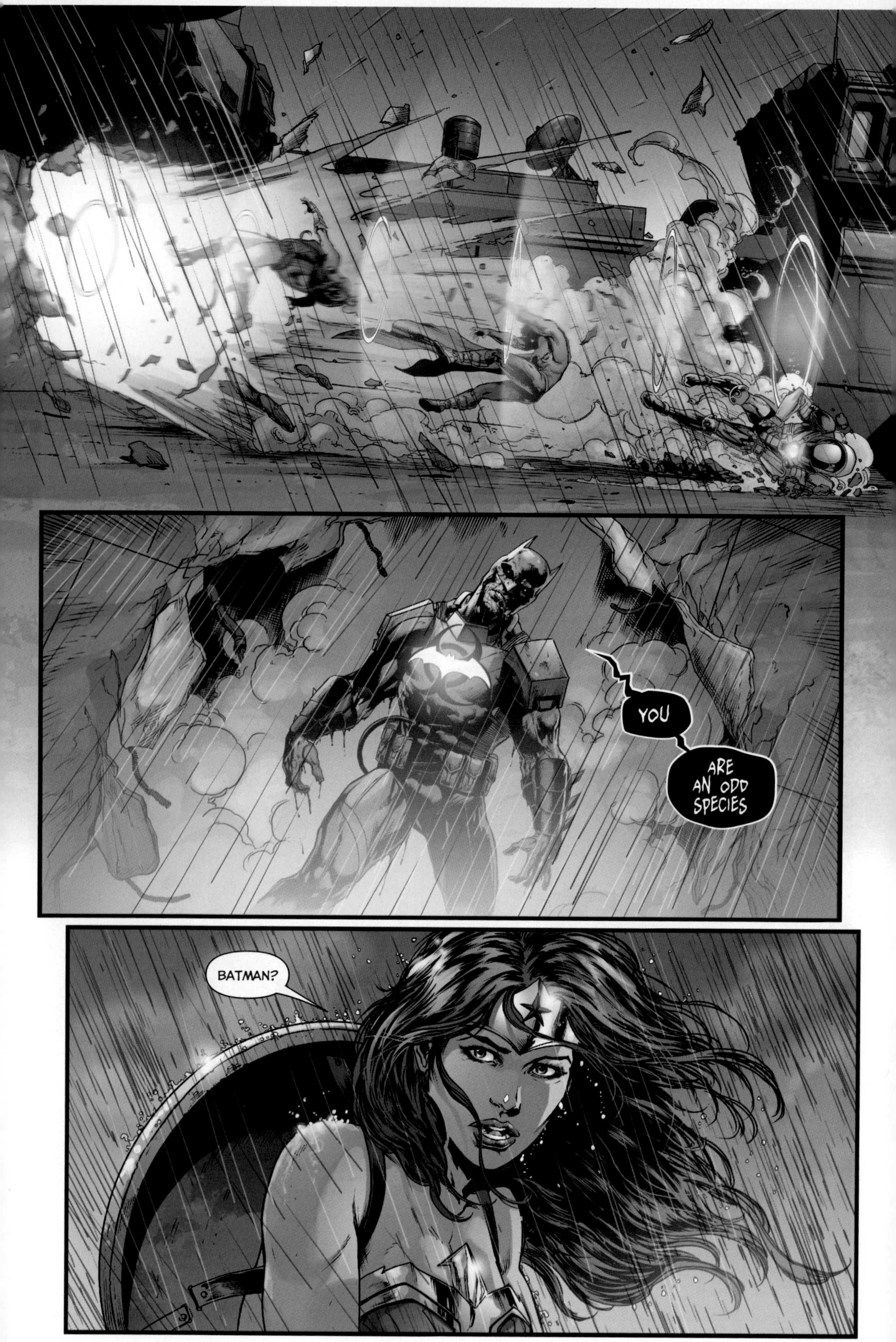
YOU
ARE AN ODD SPECIES
BATMAN?

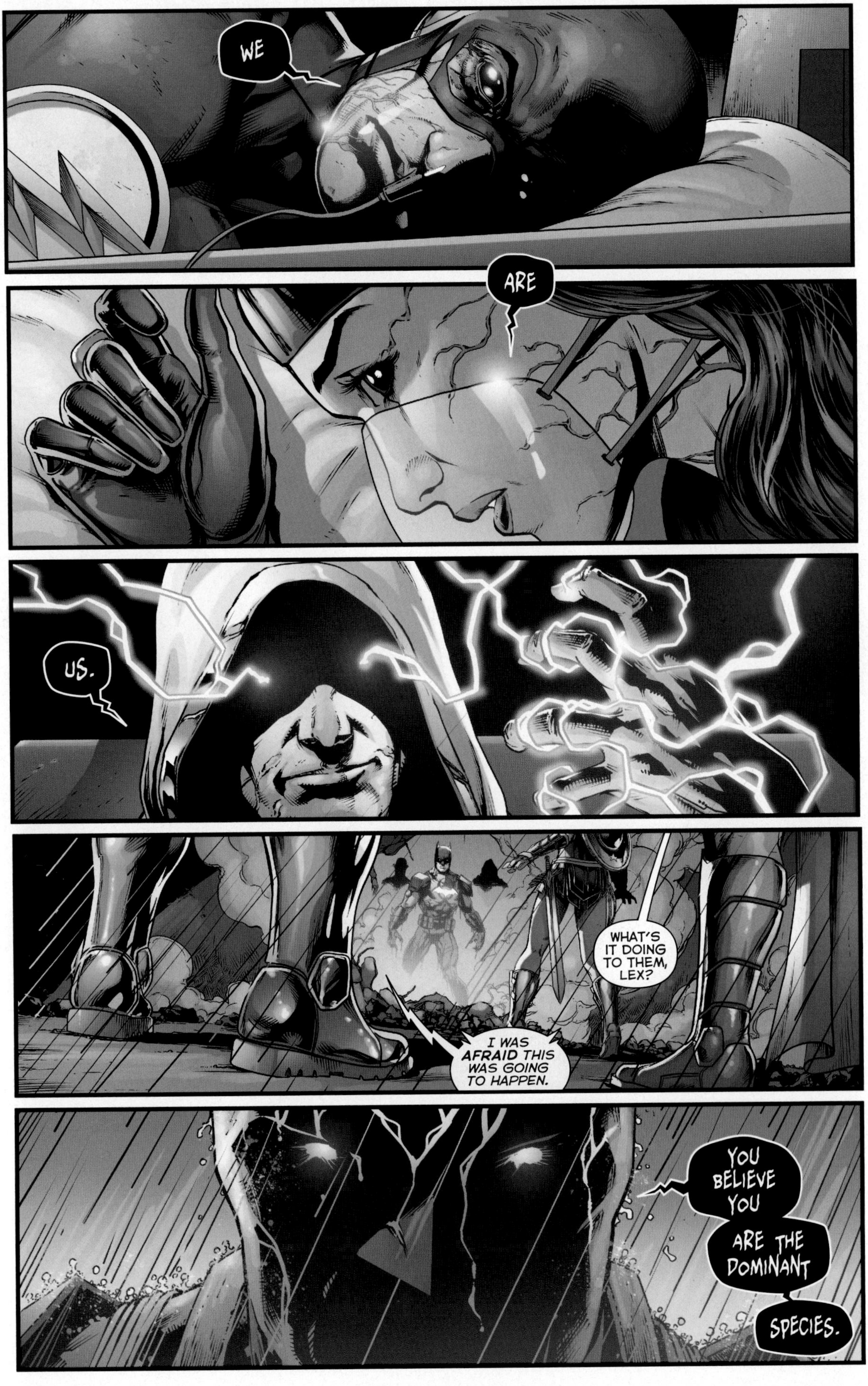
WE
ARE
US.
WHAT'S IT DOING TO THEM, LEX?
I WAS AFRAID THIS WAS GOING TO HAPPEN.
YOU BELIEVE YOU
ARE THE DOMINANT
SPECIES.

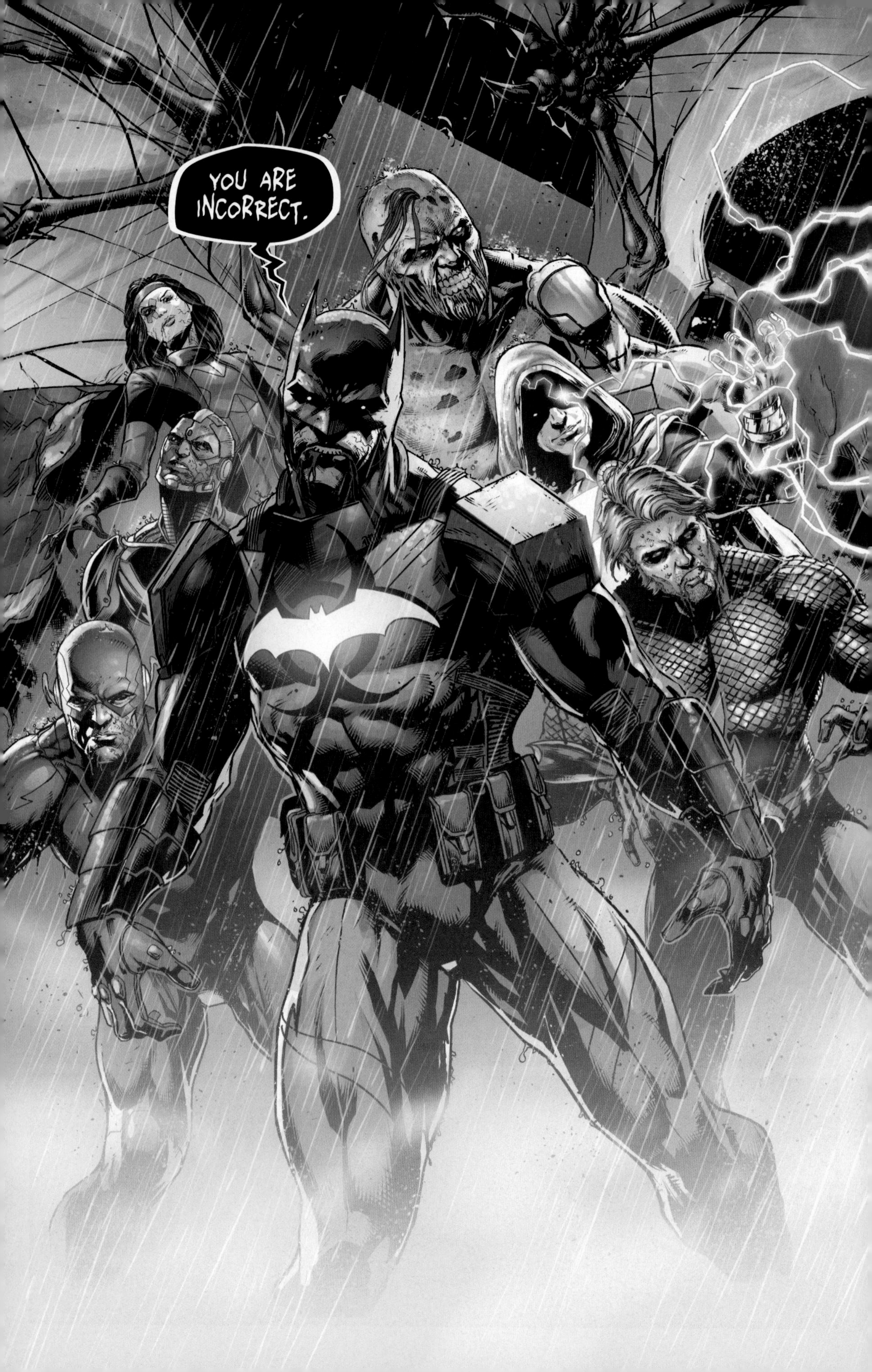
YOU ARE INCORRECT.

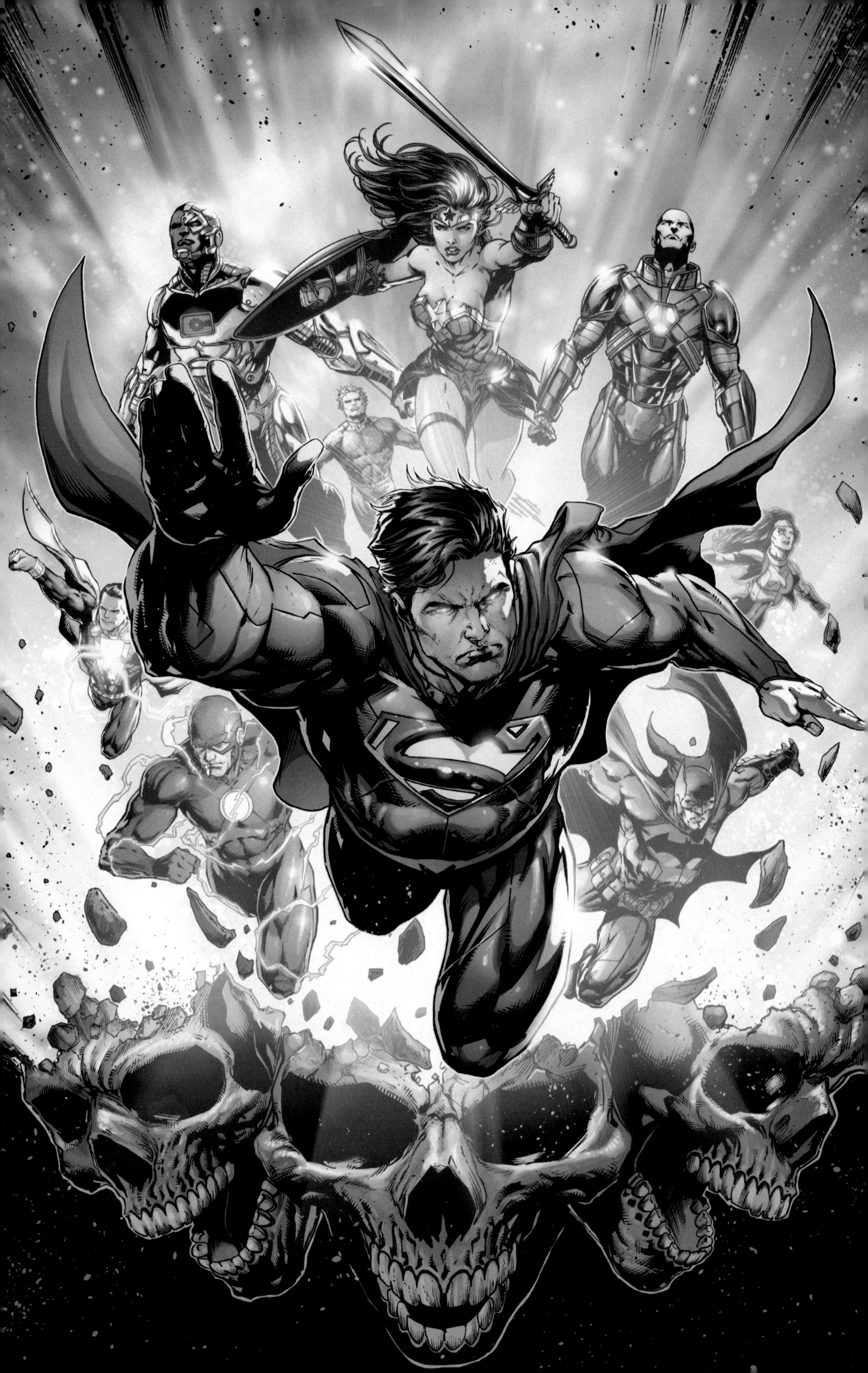

THE AMAZO VIRUS CHAPTER FOUR
THE INFECTED

GEOFF JOHNS writer **JASON FABOK** artist **BRAD ANDERSON** colorist
JASON FABOK & BRAD ANDERSON cover artists

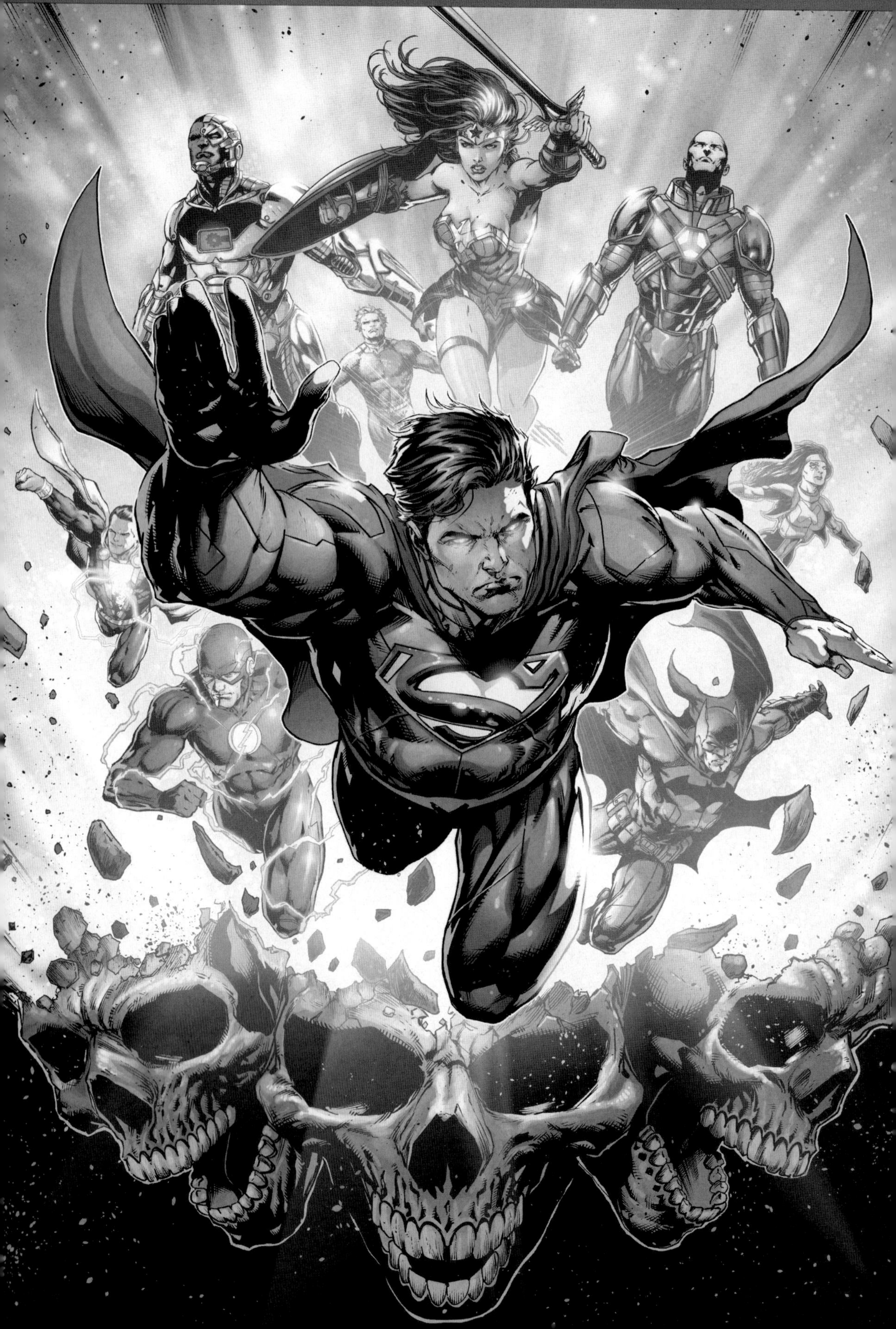

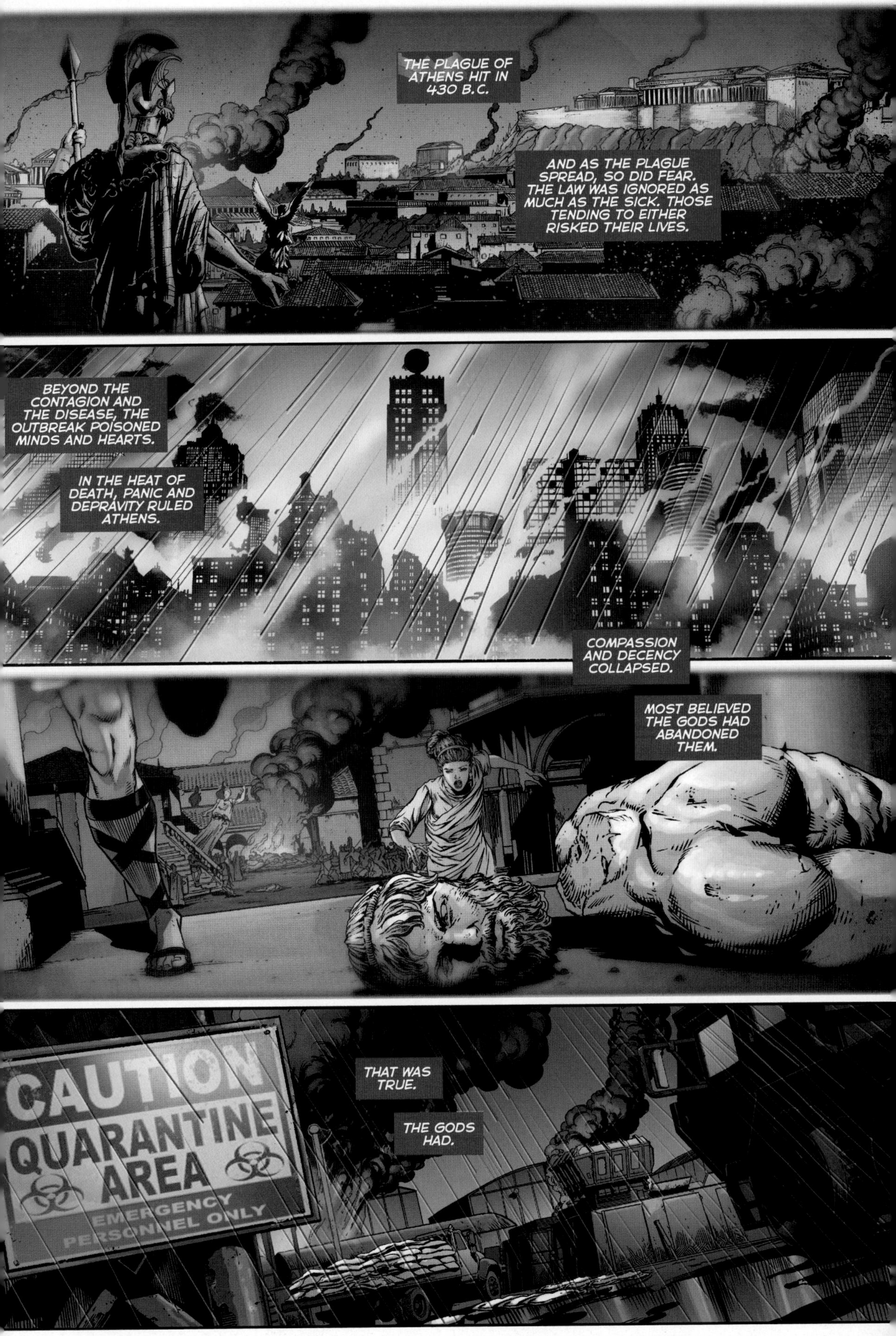
THE PLAGUE OF ATHENS HIT IN 430 B.C.
AND AS THE PLAGUE SPREAD, SO DID FEAR. THE LAW WAS IGNORED AS MUCH AS THE SICK. THOSE TENDING TO EITHER RISKED THEIR LIVES.
BEYOND THE CONTAGION AND THE DISEASE, THE OUTBREAK POISONED MINDS AND HEARTS.
IN THE HEAT OF DEATH, PANIC AND DEPRAVITY RULED ATHENS.
COMPASSION AND DECENCY COLLAPSED.
MOST BELIEVED THE GODS HAD ABANDONED THEM.
CAUTION
QUARANTINE AREA
EMERGENCY PERSONNEL ONLY
THAT WAS TRUE.
THE GODS HAD.

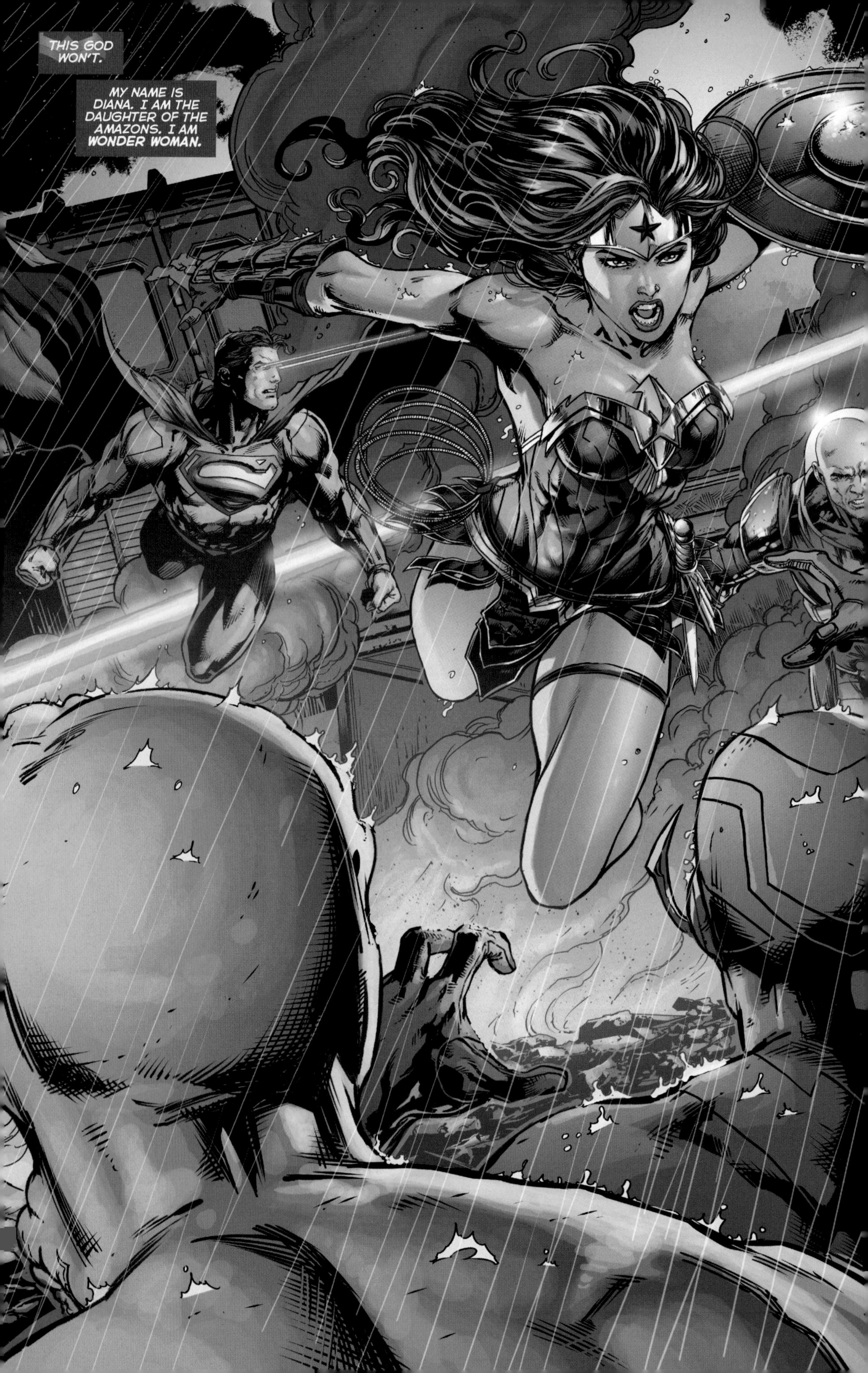
THIS GOD WON'T.
MY NAME IS DIANA. I AM THE DAUGHTER OF THE AMAZONS. I AM WONDER WOMAN.

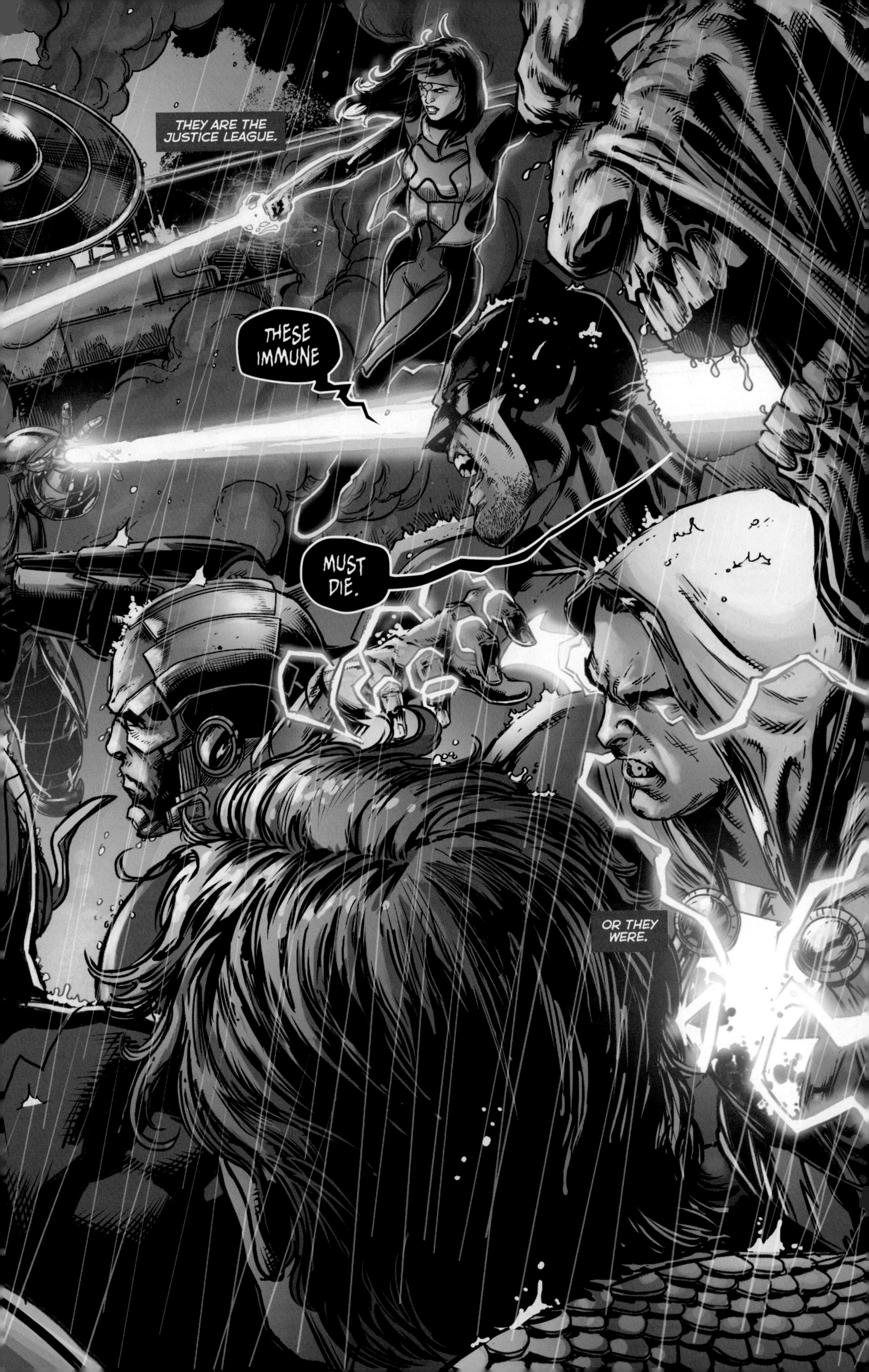
THEY ARE THE JUSTICE LEAGUE.
THESE IMMUNE
MUST DIE.
OR THEY WERE.

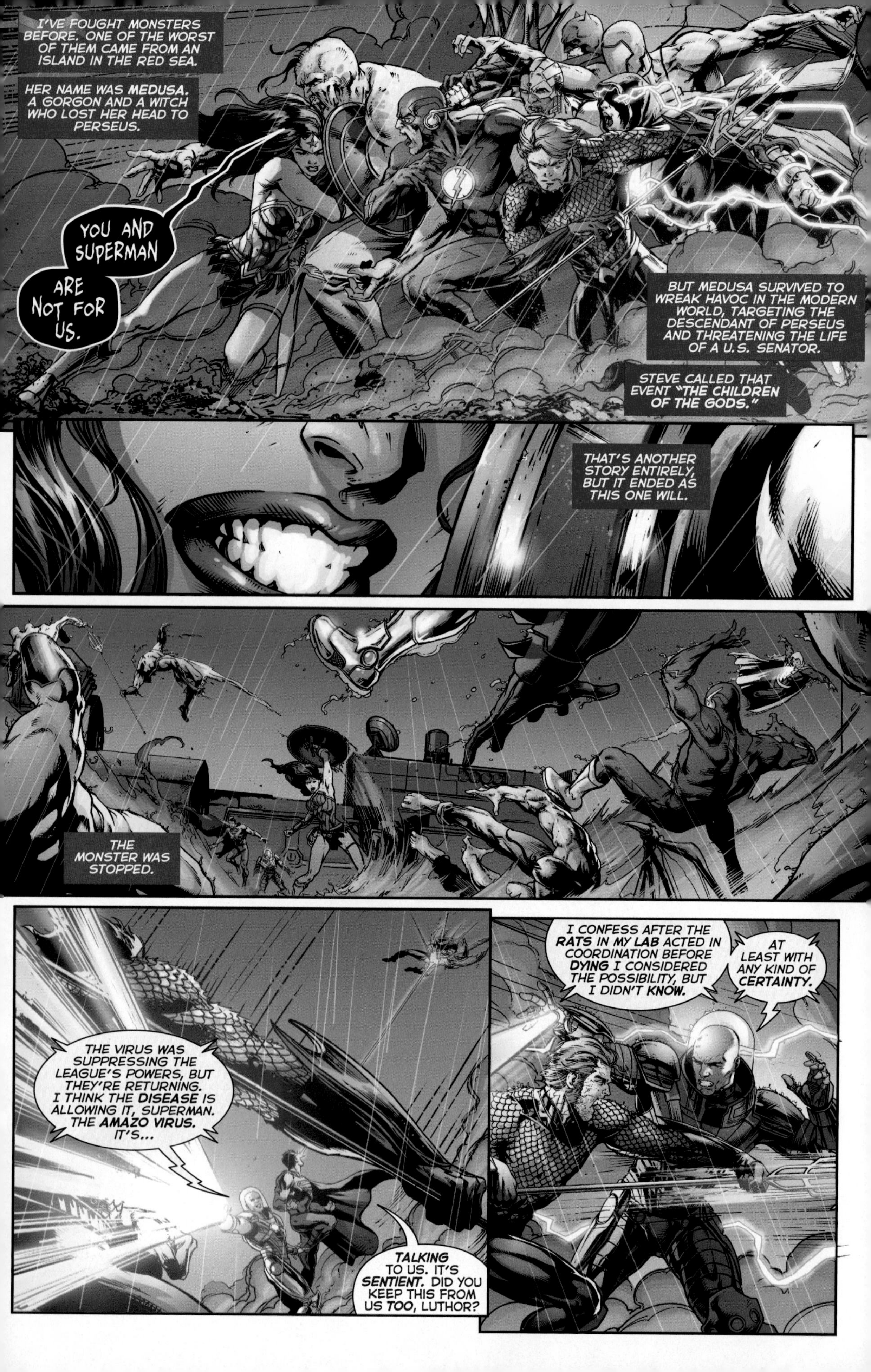
I'VE FOUGHT MONSTERS BEFORE. ONE OF THE WORST OF THEM CAME FROM AN ISLAND IN THE RED SEA.
HER NAME WAS MEDUSA. A GORGON AND A WITCH WHO LOST HER HEAD TO PERSEUS.
YOU AND SUPERMAN
ARE NOT FOR US.
BUT MEDUSA SURVIVED TO WREAK HAVOC IN THE MODERN WORLD, TARGETING THE DESCENDANT OF PERSEUS AND THREATENING THE LIFE OF A U.S. SENATOR.
STEVE CALLED THAT EVENT "THE CHILDREN OF THE GODS."
THAT'S ANOTHER STORY ENTIRELY, BUT IT ENDED AS THIS ONE WILL.
THE MONSTER WAS STOPPED.
THE VIRUS WAS SUPPRESSING THE LEAGUE'S POWERS, BUT THEY'RE RETURNING. I THINK THE DISEASE IS ALLOWING IT, SUPERMAN. THE AMAZO VIRUS. IT'S...
TALKING TO US. IT'S SENTIENT. DID YOU KEEP THIS FROM US TOO, LUTHOR?
I CONFESS AFTER THE RATS IN MY LAB ACTED IN COORDINATION BEFORE DYING I CONSIDERED THE POSSIBILITY, BUT I DIDN'T KNOW.
AT LEAST WITH ANY KIND OF CERTAINTY.

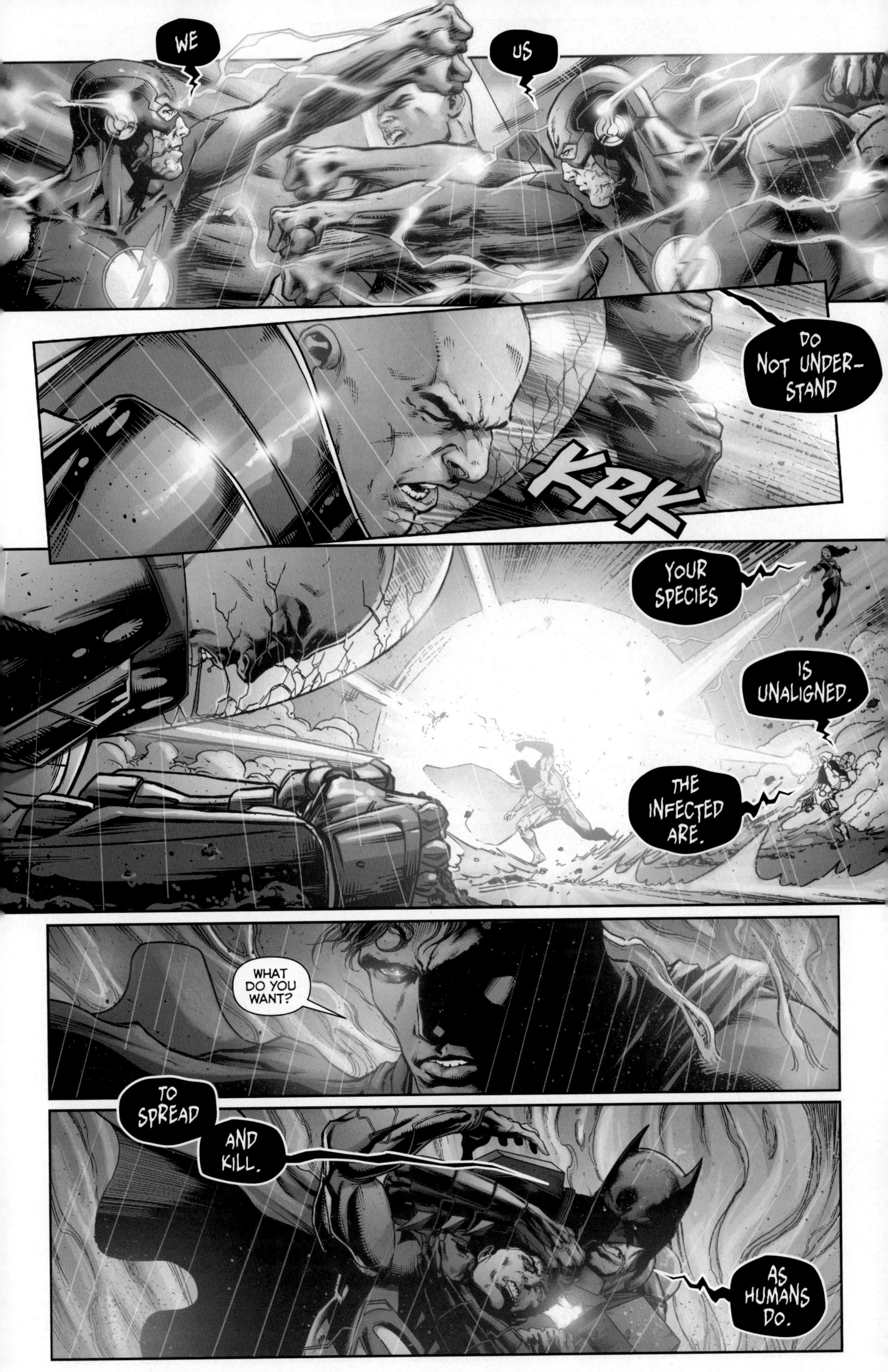
WE
US
DO NOT UNDER-STAND
KRK
YOUR SPECIES
IS UNALIGNED.
THE INFECTED ARE.
WHAT DO YOU WANT?
TO SPREAD
AND KILL.
AS HUMANS DO.

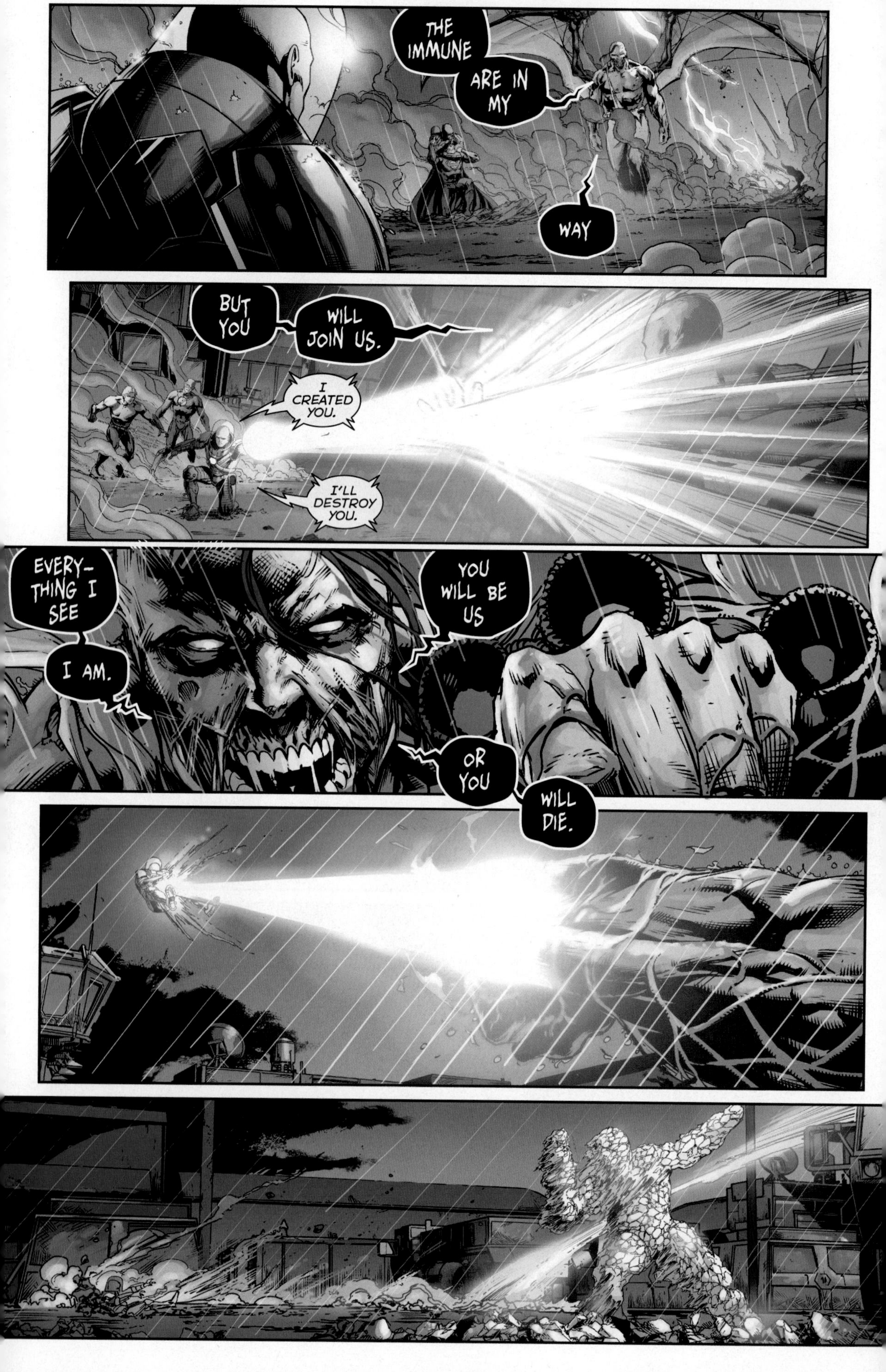
THE IMMUNE
ARE IN MY
WAY
BUT YOU
WILL JOIN US.
I CREATED YOU.
I'LL DESTROY YOU.
EVERY-THING I SEE
I AM.
YOU WILL BE US
OR YOU
WILL DIE.

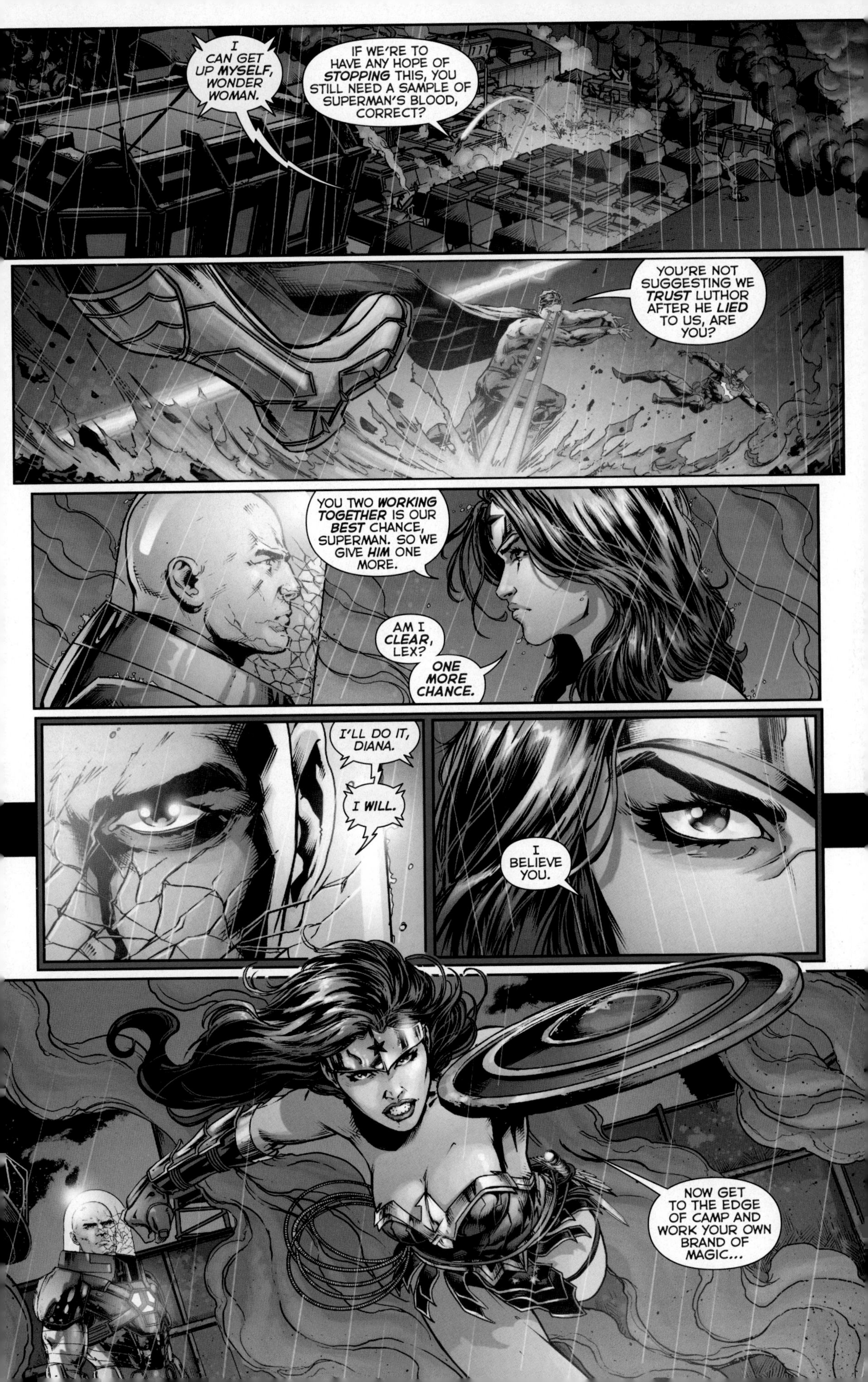
I CAN GET UP MYSELF, WONDER WOMAN.
IF WE'RE TO HAVE ANY HOPE OF STOPPING THIS, YOU STILL NEED A SAMPLE OF SUPERMAN'S BLOOD, CORRECT?
YOU'RE NOT SUGGESTING WE TRUST LUTHOR AFTER HE LIED TO US, ARE YOU?
YOU TWO WORKING TOGETHER IS OUR BEST CHANCE, SUPERMAN. SO WE GIVE HIM ONE MORE.
AM I CLEAR, LEX?
ONE MORE CHANCE.
I'LL DO IT, DIANA.
I WILL.
I BELIEVE YOU.
NOW GET TO THE EDGE OF CAMP AND WORK YOUR OWN BRAND OF MAGIC...

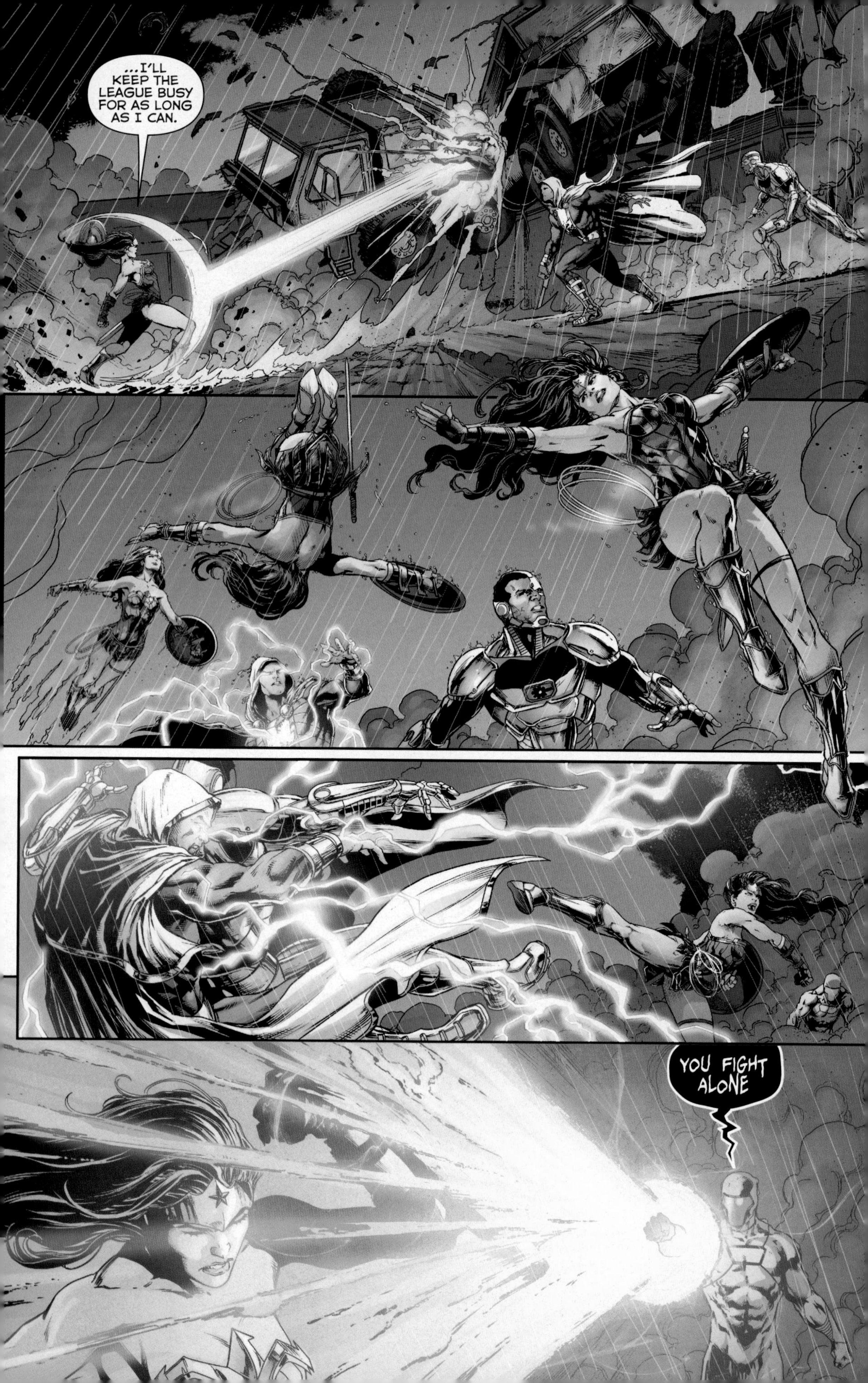
...I'LL KEEP THE LEAGUE BUSY FOR AS LONG AS I CAN.
YOU FIGHT ALONE

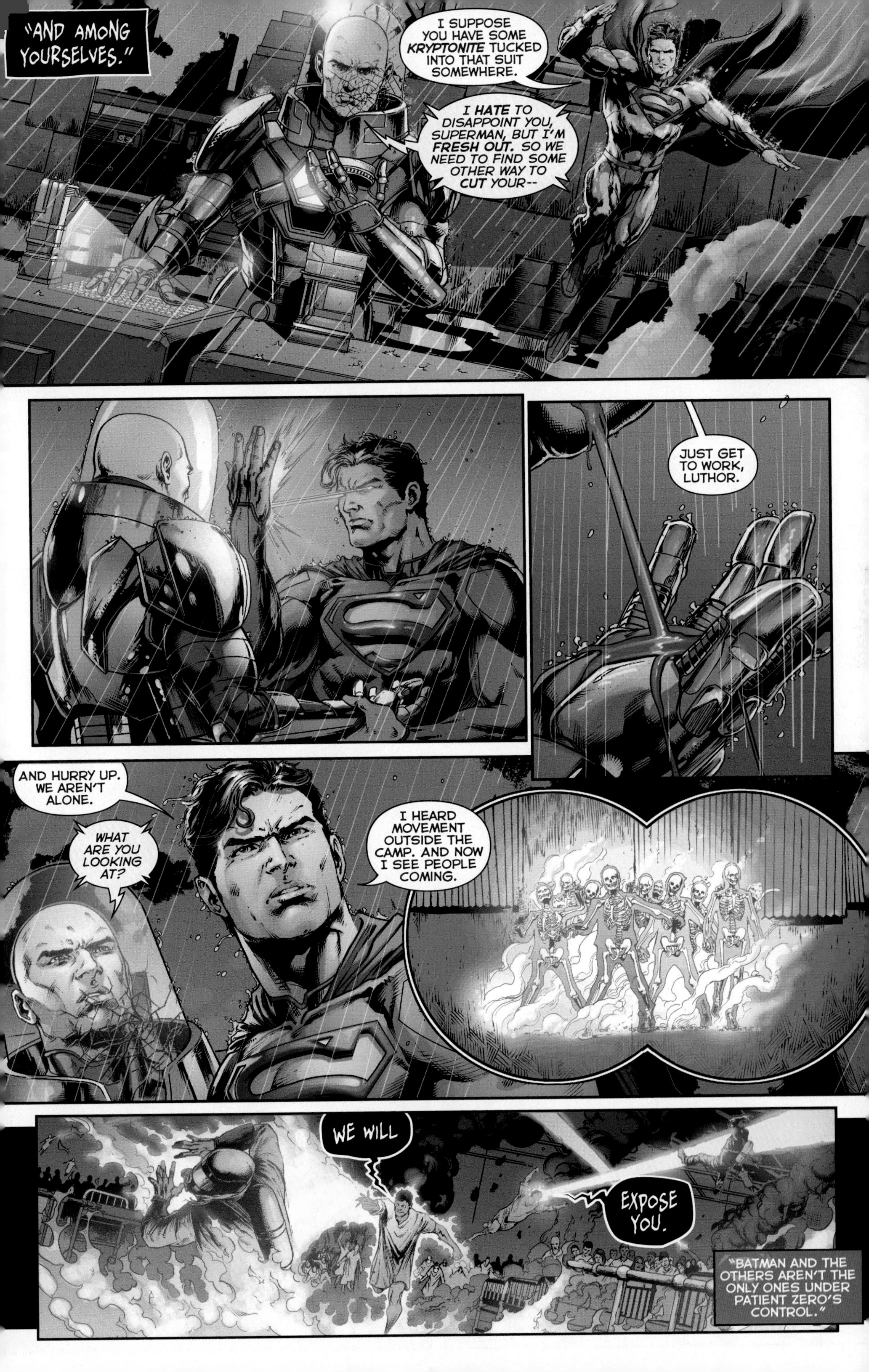
"AND AMONG YOURSELVES."
I SUPPOSE YOU HAVE SOME KRYPTONITE TUCKED INTO THAT SUIT SOMEWHERE.
I HATE TO DISAPPOINT YOU, SUPERMAN, BUT I'M FRESH OUT. SO WE NEED TO FIND SOME OTHER WAY TO CUT YOUR--
JUST GET TO WORK, LUTHOR.
AND HURRY UP. WE AREN'T ALONE.
WHAT ARE YOU LOOKING AT?
I HEARD MOVEMENT OUTSIDE THE CAMP. AND NOW I SEE PEOPLE COMING.
WE WILL
EXPOSE YOU.
"BATMAN AND THE OTHERS AREN'T THE ONLY ONES UNDER PATIENT ZERO'S CONTROL."

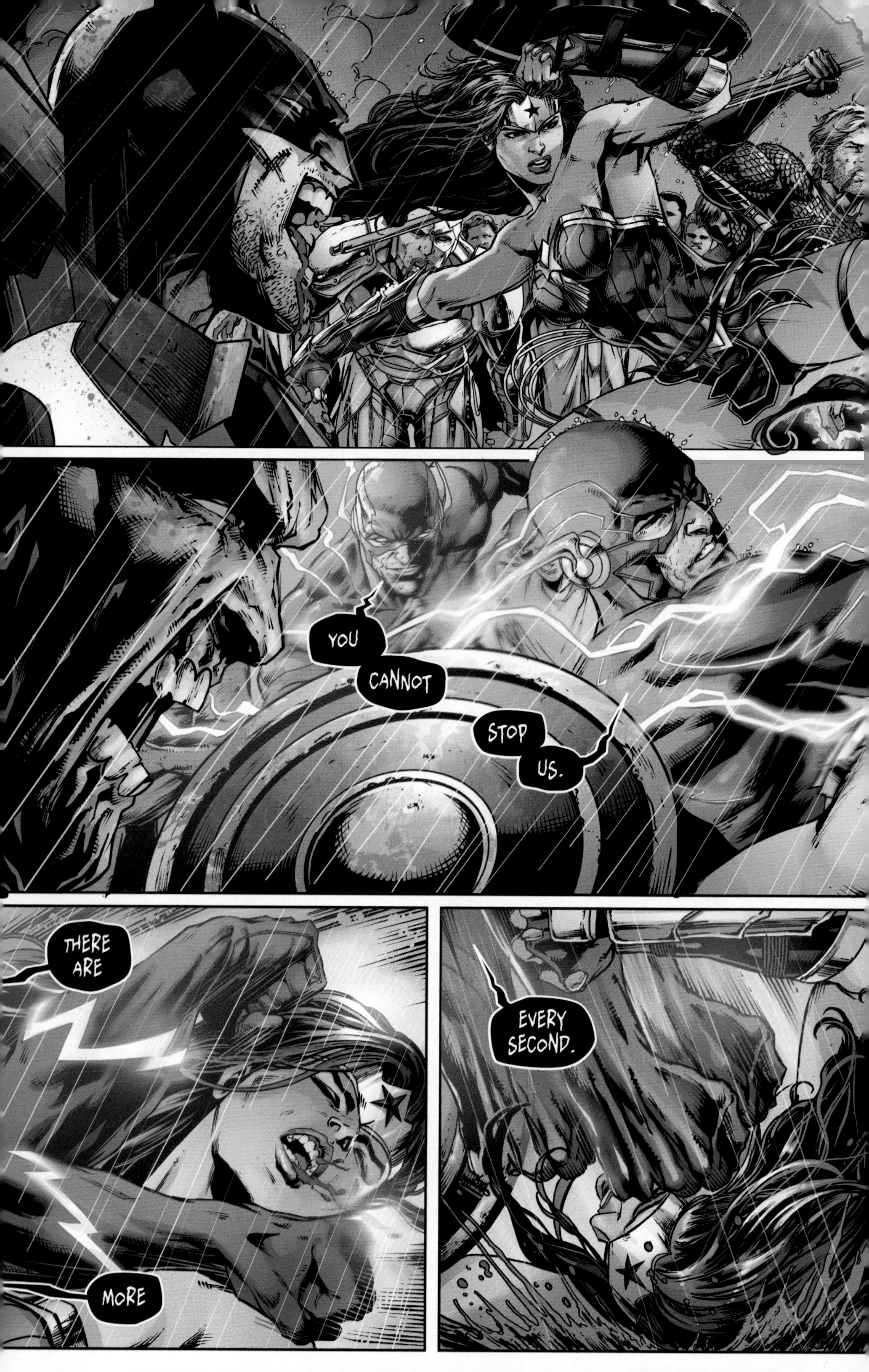
YOU
CANNOT
STOP
US.
THERE ARE
MORE
EVERY SECOND.

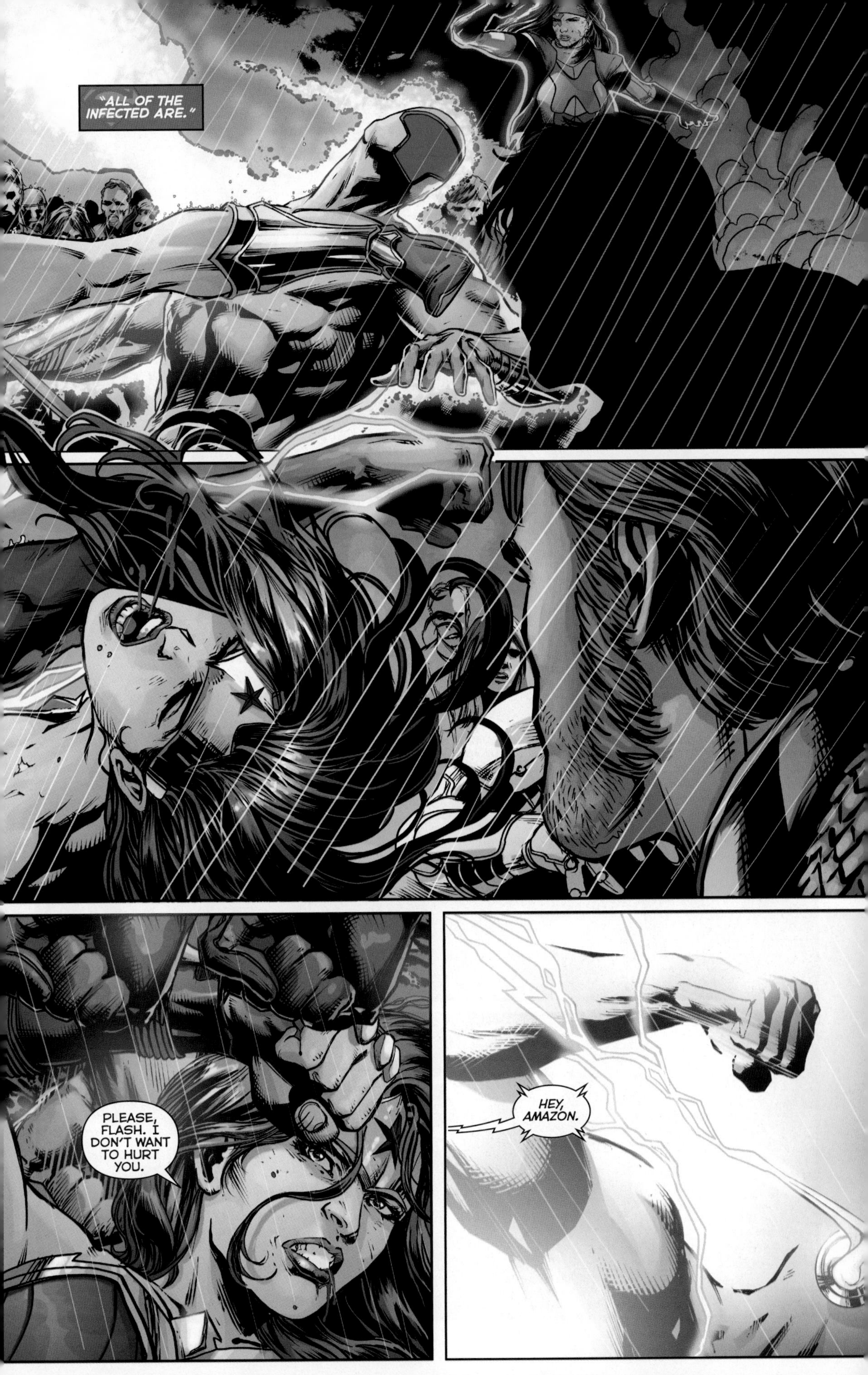
"ALL OF THE INFECTED ARE."
PLEASE, FLASH. I DON'T WANT TO HURT YOU.
HEY, AMAZON.

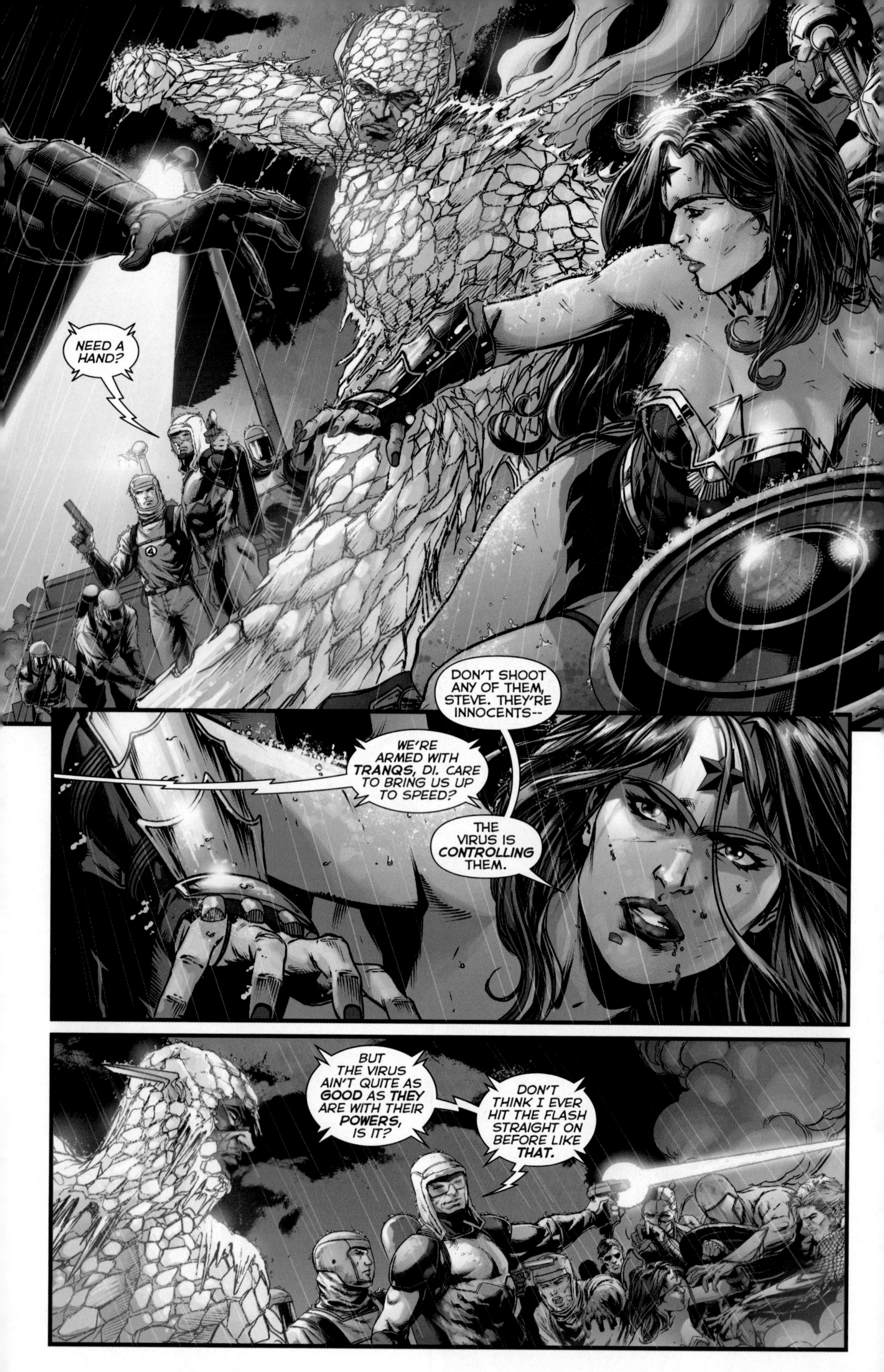
NEED A HAND?
DON'T SHOOT ANY OF THEM, STEVE. THEY'RE INNOCENTS--
WE'RE ARMED WITH TRANQS, DI. CARE TO BRING US UP TO SPEED?
THE VIRUS IS CONTROLLING THEM.
BUT THE VIRUS AIN'T QUITE AS GOOD AS THEY ARE WITH THEIR POWERS, IS IT?
DON'T THINK I EVER HIT THE FLASH STRAIGHT ON BEFORE LIKE THAT.

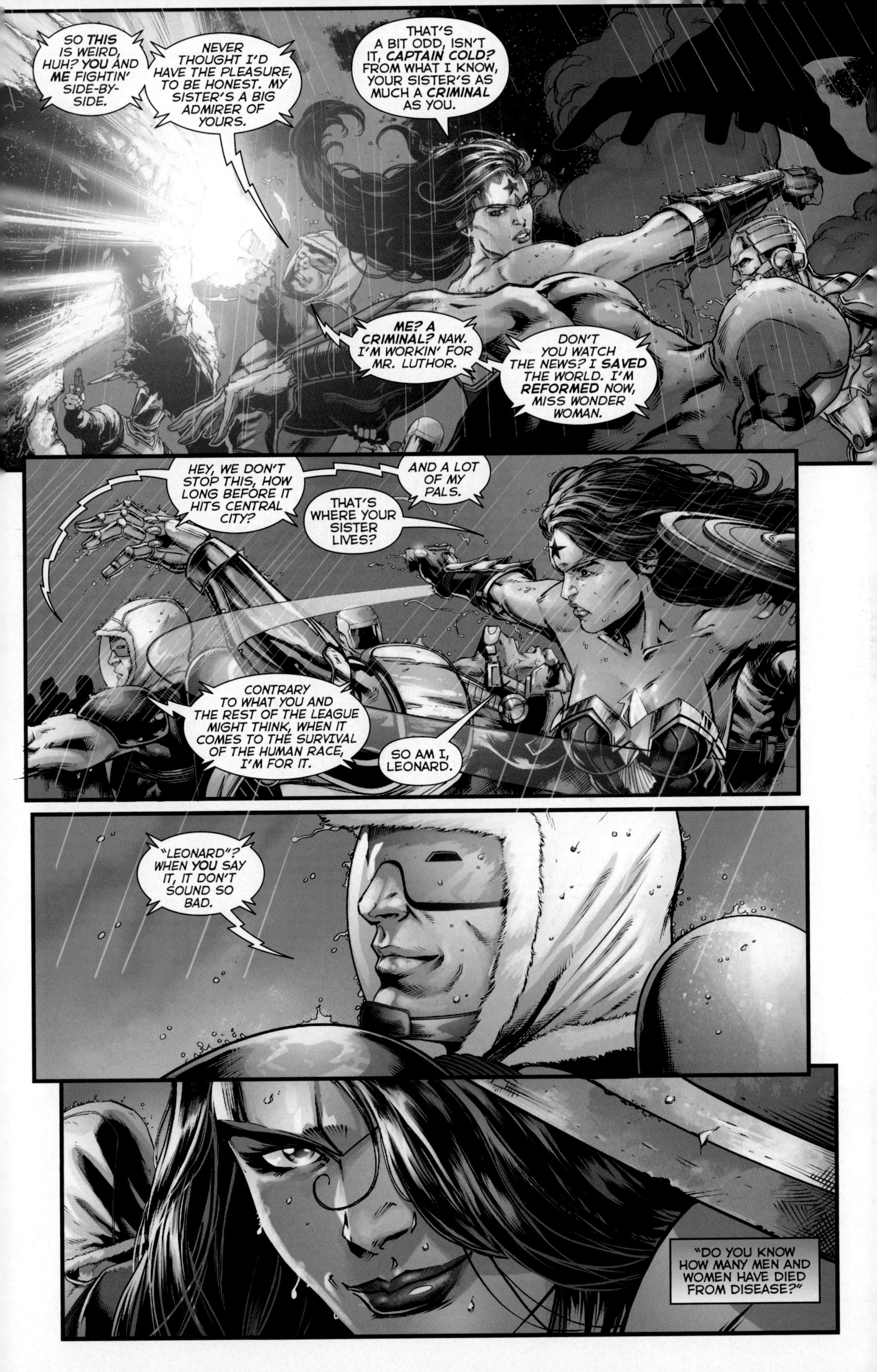

SO THIS IS WEIRD, HUH? YOU AND ME FIGHTIN' SIDE-BY-SIDE.
NEVER THOUGHT I'D HAVE THE PLEASURE, TO BE HONEST. MY SISTER'S A BIG ADMIRER OF YOURS.
THAT'S A BIT ODD, ISN'T IT, CAPTAIN COLD? FROM WHAT I KNOW, YOUR SISTER'S AS MUCH A CRIMINAL AS YOU.
ME? A CRIMINAL? NAW. I'M WORKIN' FOR MR. LUTHOR.
DON'T YOU WATCH THE NEWS? I SAVED THE WORLD. I'M REFORMED NOW, MISS WONDER WOMAN.
HEY, WE DON'T STOP THIS, HOW LONG BEFORE IT HITS CENTRAL CITY?
THAT'S WHERE YOUR SISTER LIVES?
AND A LOT OF MY PALS.
CONTRARY TO WHAT YOU AND THE REST OF THE LEAGUE MIGHT THINK, WHEN IT COMES TO THE SURVIVAL OF THE HUMAN RACE, I'M FOR IT.
SO AM I, LEONARD.
"LEONARD"? WHEN YOU SAY IT, IT DON'T SOUND SO BAD.
"DO YOU KNOW HOW MANY MEN AND WOMEN HAVE DIED FROM DISEASE?"

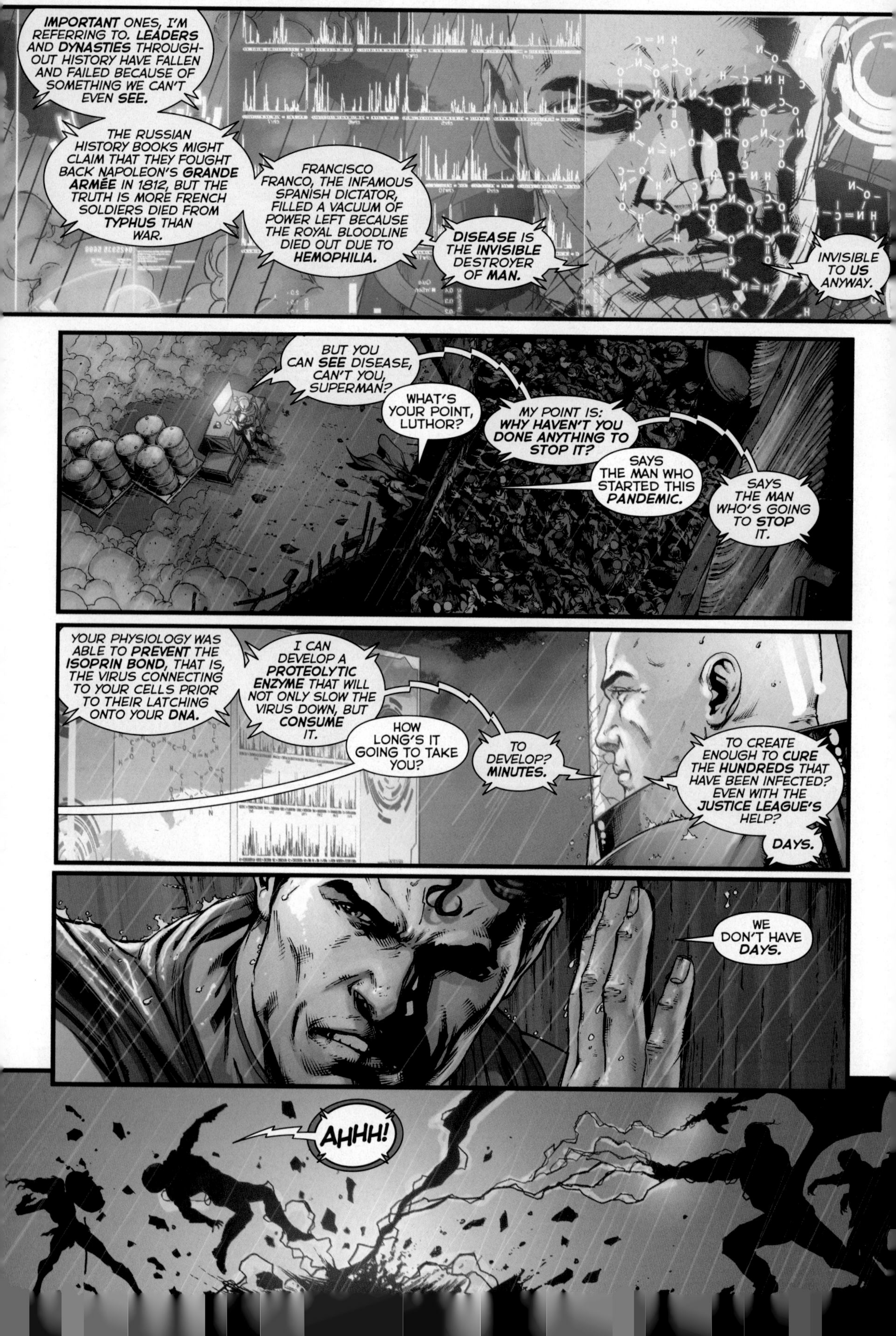

IMPORTANT ONES, I'M REFERRING TO. LEADERS AND DYNASTIES THROUGH-OUT HISTORY HAVE FALLEN AND FAILED BECAUSE OF SOMETHING WE CAN'T EVEN SEE.
THE RUSSIAN HISTORY BOOKS MIGHT CLAIM THAT THEY FOUGHT BACK NAPOLEON'S GRANDE ARMÉE IN 1812, BUT THE TRUTH IS MORE FRENCH SOLDIERS DIED FROM TYPHUS THAN WAR.
FRANCISCO FRANCO, THE INFAMOUS SPANISH DICTATOR, FILLED A VACUUM OF POWER LEFT BECAUSE THE ROYAL BLOODLINE DIED OUT DUE TO HEMOPHILIA.
DISEASE IS THE INVISIBLE DESTROYER OF MAN.
INVISIBLE TO US ANYWAY.
BUT YOU CAN SEE DISEASE, CAN'T YOU, SUPERMAN?
WHAT'S YOUR POINT, LUTHOR?
MY POINT IS: WHY HAVEN'T YOU DONE ANYTHING TO STOP IT?
SAYS THE MAN WHO STARTED THIS PANDEMIC.
SAYS THE MAN WHO'S GOING TO STOP IT.
YOUR PHYSIOLOGY WAS ABLE TO PREVENT THE ISOPRIN BOND, THAT IS, THE VIRUS CONNECTING TO YOUR CELLS PRIOR TO THEIR LATCHING ONTO YOUR DNA.
I CAN DEVELOP A PROTEOLYTIC ENZYME THAT WILL NOT ONLY SLOW THE VIRUS DOWN, BUT CONSUME IT.
HOW LONG'S IT GOING TO TAKE YOU?
TO DEVELOP? MINUTES.
TO CREATE ENOUGH TO CURE THE HUNDREDS THAT HAVE BEEN INFECTED? EVEN WITH THE JUSTICE LEAGUE'S HELP?
DAYS.
WE DON'T HAVE DAYS.
AHHH!

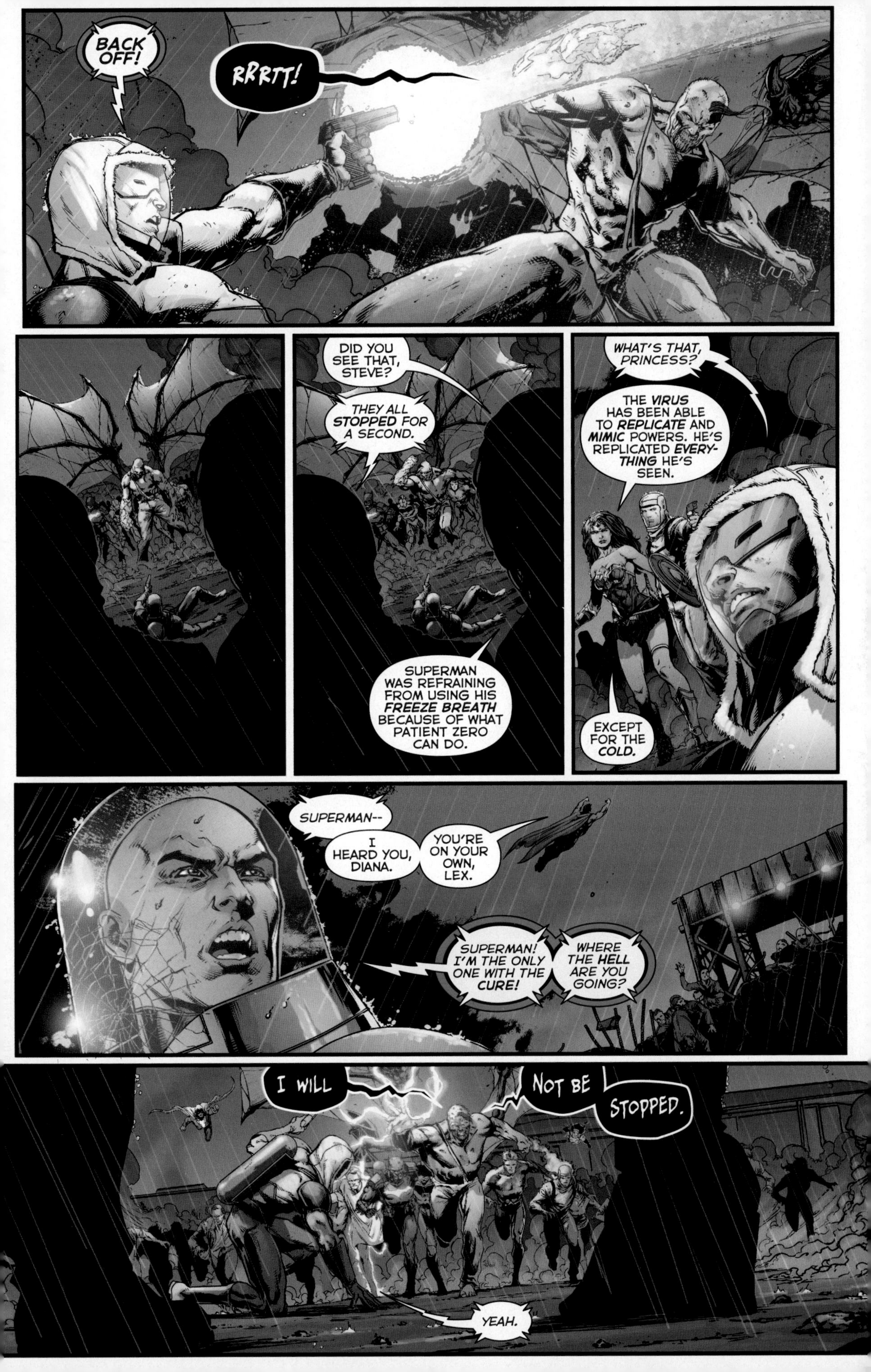
BACK OFF!
RRRTT!
DID YOU SEE THAT, STEVE?
THEY ALL STOPPED FOR A SECOND.
SUPERMAN WAS REFRAINING FROM USING HIS FREEZE BREATH BECAUSE OF WHAT PATIENT ZERO CAN DO.
WHAT'S THAT, PRINCESS?
THE VIRUS HAS BEEN ABLE TO REPLICATE AND MIMIC POWERS. HE'S REPLICATED EVERYTHING HE'S SEEN.
EXCEPT FOR THE COLD.
SUPERMAN--
I HEARD YOU, DIANA.
YOU'RE ON YOUR OWN, LEX.
SUPERMAN! I'M THE ONLY ONE WITH THE CURE!
WHERE THE HELL ARE YOU GOING?
I WILL
NOT BE
STOPPED.
YEAH.

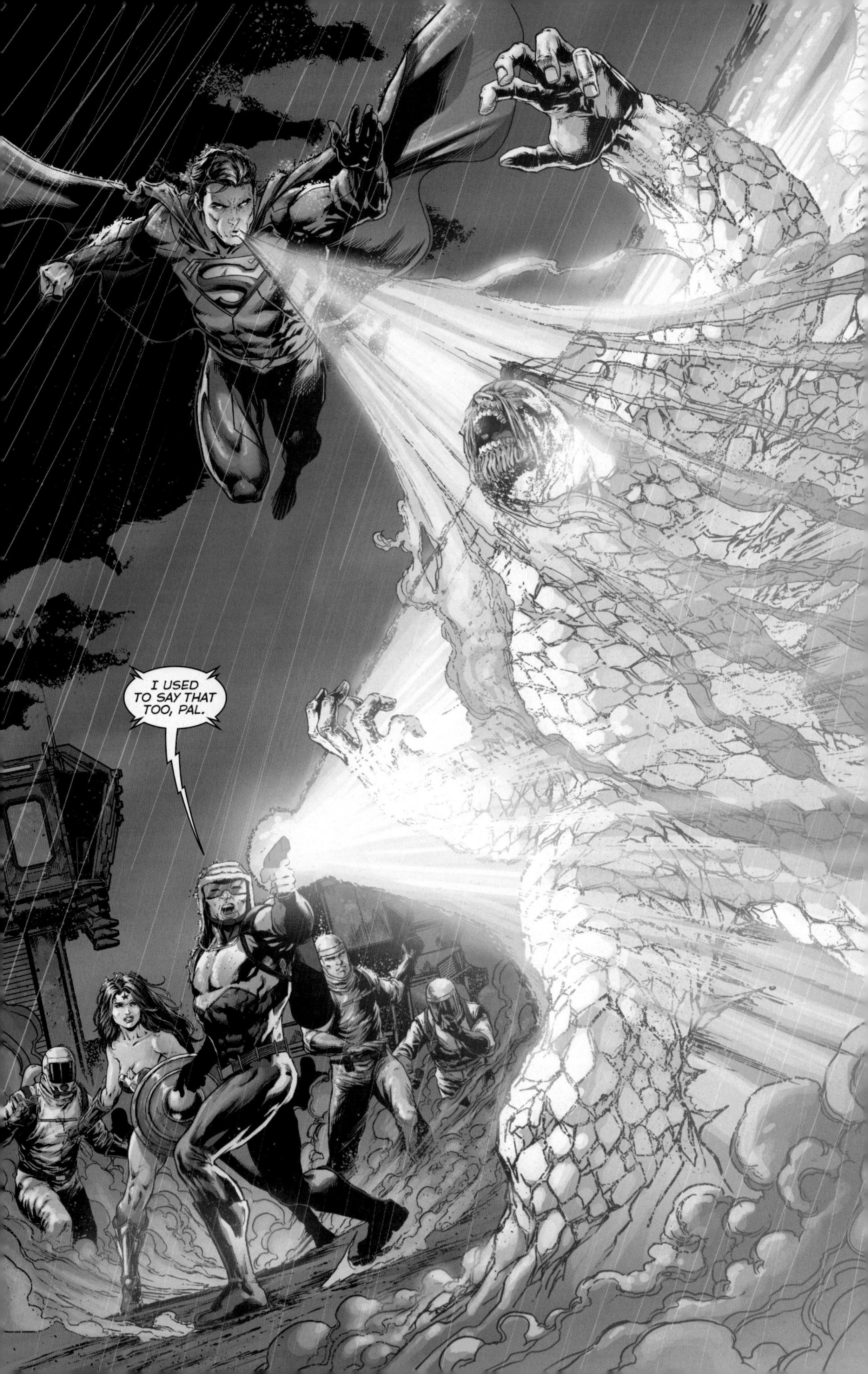
I USED TO SAY THAT TOO, PAL.

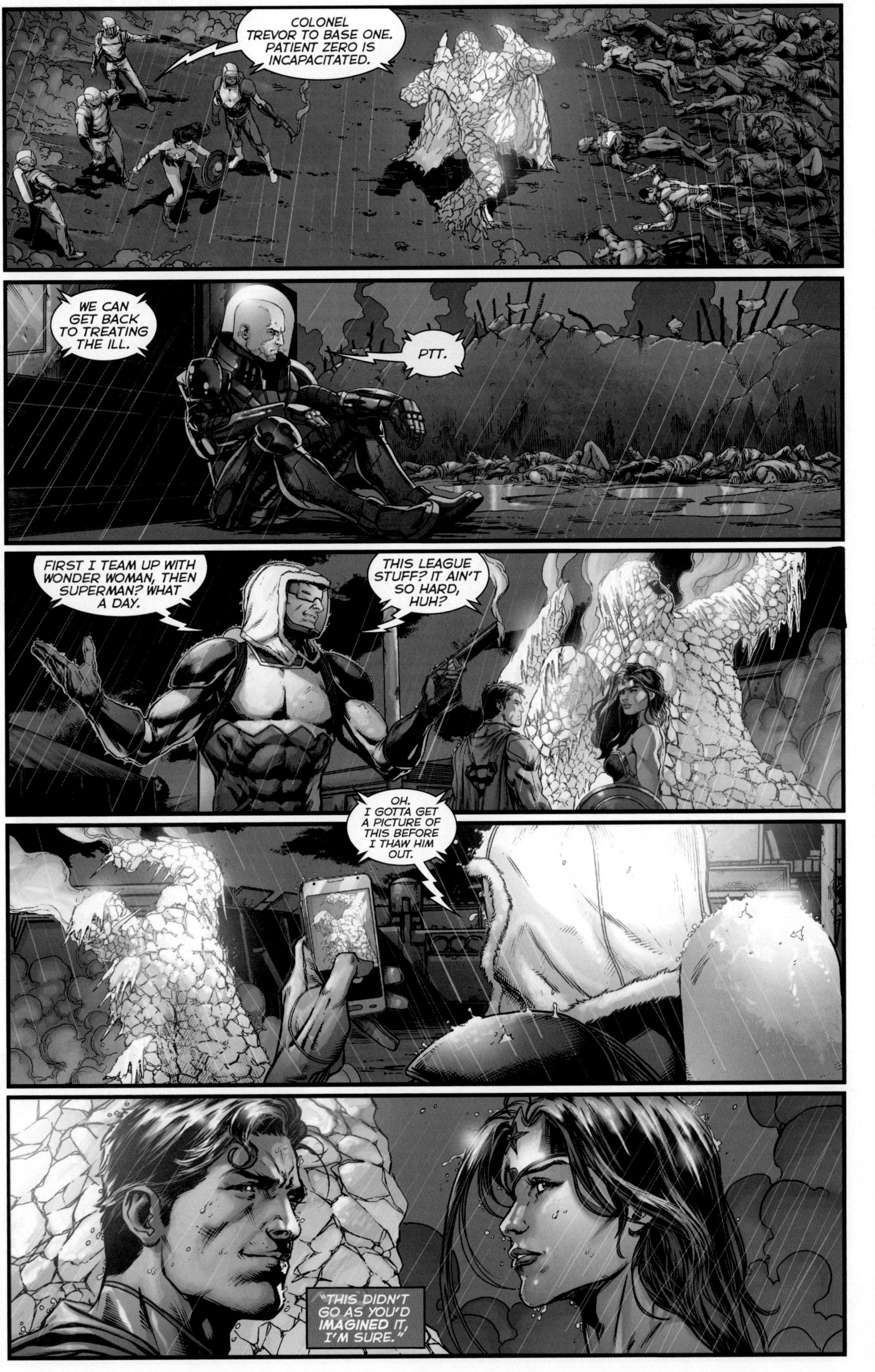
COLONEL TREVOR TO BASE ONE. PATIENT ZERO IS INCAPACITATED.
WE CAN GET BACK TO TREATING THE ILL.
PTT.
FIRST I TEAM UP WITH WONDER WOMAN, THEN SUPERMAN? WHAT A DAY.
THIS LEAGUE STUFF? IT AIN'T SO HARD, HUH?
OH. I GOTTA GET A PICTURE OF THIS BEFORE I THAW HIM OUT.
"THIS DIDN'T GO AS YOU'D IMAGINED IT, I'M SURE."

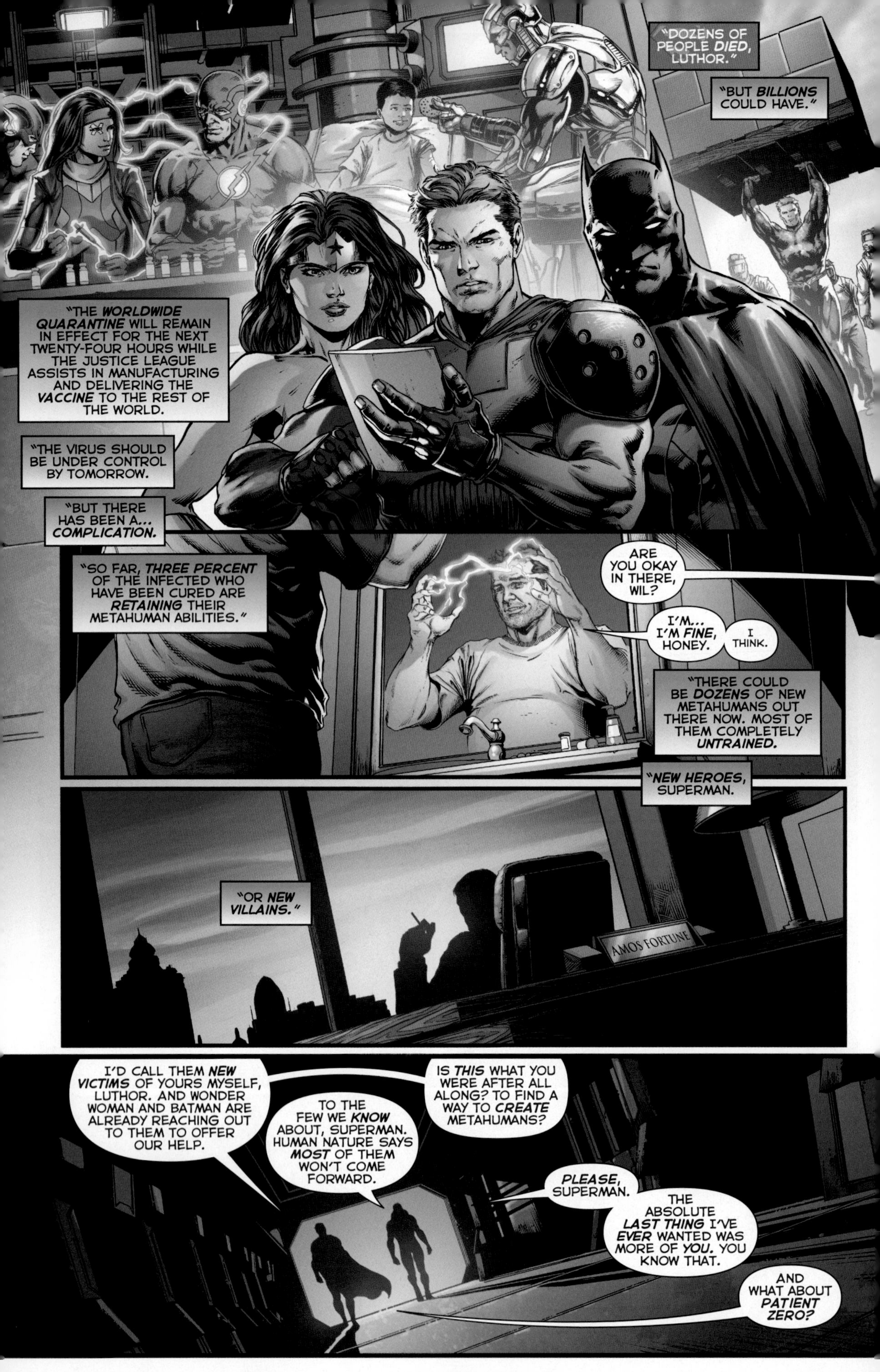
"DOZENS OF PEOPLE DIED, LUTHOR."
"BUT BILLIONS COULD HAVE."
"THE WORLDWIDE QUARANTINE WILL REMAIN IN EFFECT FOR THE NEXT TWENTY-FOUR HOURS WHILE THE JUSTICE LEAGUE ASSISTS IN MANUFACTURING AND DELIVERING THE VACCINE TO THE REST OF THE WORLD.
"THE VIRUS SHOULD BE UNDER CONTROL BY TOMORROW.
"BUT THERE HAS BEEN A... COMPLICATION.
"SO FAR, THREE PERCENT OF THE INFECTED WHO HAVE BEEN CURED ARE RETAINING THEIR METAHUMAN ABILITIES."
ARE YOU OKAY IN THERE, WIL?
I'M... I'M FINE, HONEY.
I THINK.
"THERE COULD BE DOZENS OF NEW METAHUMANS OUT THERE NOW. MOST OF THEM COMPLETELY UNTRAINED.
"NEW HEROES, SUPERMAN.
"OR NEW VILLAINS."
AMOS FORTUNE
I'D CALL THEM NEW VICTIMS OF YOURS MYSELF, LUTHOR. AND WONDER WOMAN AND BATMAN ARE ALREADY REACHING OUT TO THEM TO OFFER OUR HELP.
TO THE FEW WE KNOW ABOUT, SUPERMAN. HUMAN NATURE SAYS MOST OF THEM WON'T COME FORWARD.
IS THIS WHAT YOU WERE AFTER ALL ALONG? TO FIND A WAY TO CREATE METAHUMANS?
PLEASE, SUPERMAN.
THE ABSOLUTE LAST THING I'VE EVER WANTED WAS MORE OF YOU. YOU KNOW THAT.
AND WHAT ABOUT PATIENT ZERO?

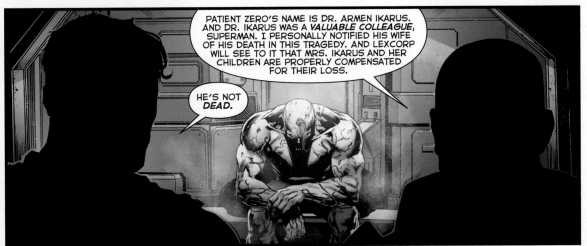

PATIENT ZERO'S NAME IS DR. ARMEN IKARUS. AND DR. IKARUS WAS A *VALUABLE COLLEAGUE*, SUPERMAN. I PERSONALLY NOTIFIED HIS WIFE OF HIS DEATH IN THIS TRAGEDY. AND LEXCORP WILL SEE TO IT THAT MRS. IKARUS AND HER CHILDREN ARE PROPERLY COMPENSATED FOR THEIR LOSS.

HE'S NOT *DEAD*.

OH, HE *IS*, SUPERMAN. HIS *BRAIN* IS.

AND UNLIKE THE OTHERS THAT WERE INFECTED, FOR SOME REASON I'LL DETERMINE SHORTLY, OUR "CURE" HAS BEEN UNABLE TO KILL THE VIRUS WITHIN HIM, THOUGH KEEPING HIM AT *LOW TEMPERATURES* IS HOLDING HIS *POWERS* IN CHECK.

BUT THERE *IS* A SILVER LINING. WE *CAN STUDY* THIS ONE. WE CAN PREPARE FOR ANY *FUTURE* META-OUTBREAKS IF THEY WERE TO OCCUR.

WHILE CONGRATULATING ME ON *SAVING* THE HUMAN RACE, THE PRESIDENT *HIMSELF* REQUESTED MY ASSISTANCE ON THIS. YOU CAN CHECK WITH STEVE TREVOR IF YOU WANT TO VERIFY THAT.

HE TOLD ME.

DON'T LOOK SO GLOOMY, SUPERMAN. IT DOESN'T SUIT YOU.

LOOK. WE DID THIS *TOGETHER*, I SUPPOSE.

WOULD YOU EVER IMAGINE IT?

WHATEVER'S BEEN ASKED OF YOU, LUTHOR, I'M NOT READY TO GIVE UP ON THIS MAN. IF THERE'S A CHANCE HE CAN STILL BE SAVED--

THERE IS NOT.

IT IS OUR FLESH.

OUR INCUBATOR.

YOU MISUNDERSTAND WHAT WE ARE.

WHAT I AM.

LEX LUTHOR.

EVEN NOW I AM MUTATING.

ONE DAY I WILL INFECT YOU, LUTHOR.

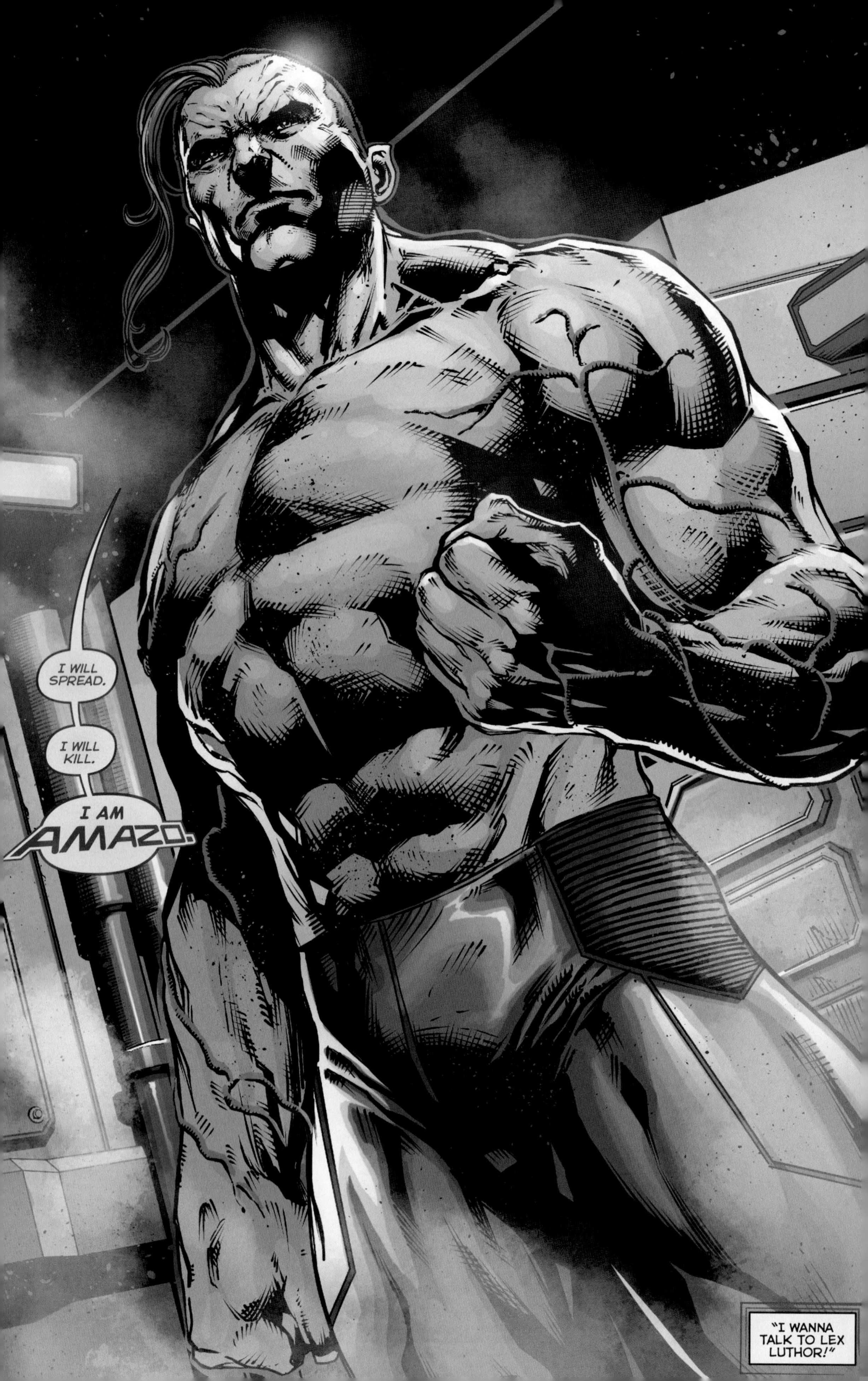
I WILL SPREAD.
I WILL KILL.
I AM AMAZO.
"I WANNA TALK TO LEX LUTHOR!"

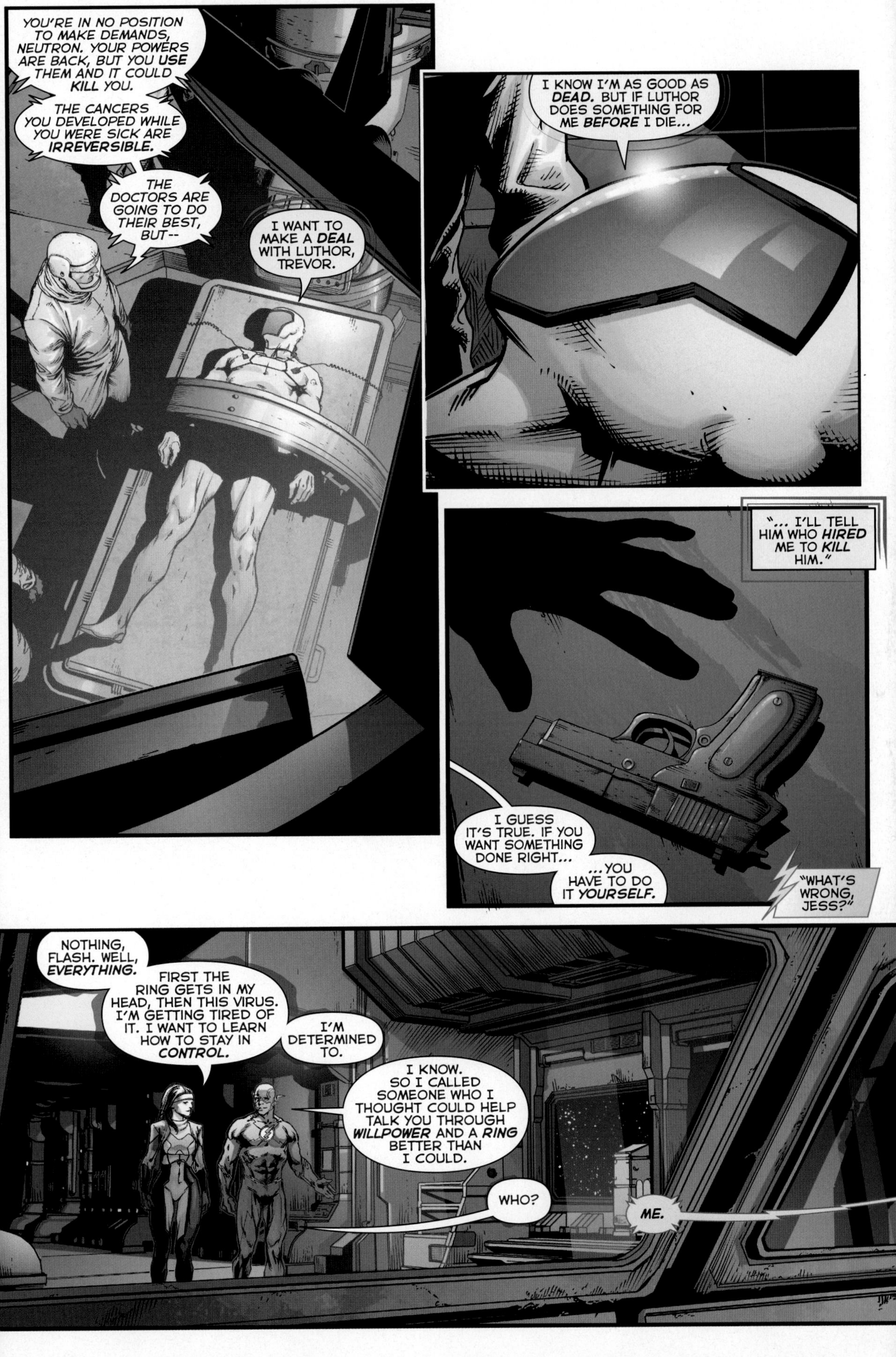

YOU'RE IN NO POSITION TO MAKE DEMANDS, NEUTRON. YOUR POWERS ARE BACK, BUT YOU USE THEM AND IT COULD KILL YOU.
THE CANCERS YOU DEVELOPED WHILE YOU WERE SICK ARE IRREVERSIBLE.
THE DOCTORS ARE GOING TO DO THEIR BEST, BUT--
I WANT TO MAKE A DEAL WITH LUTHOR, TREVOR.
I KNOW I'M AS GOOD AS DEAD. BUT IF LUTHOR DOES SOMETHING FOR ME BEFORE I DIE...
"... I'LL TELL HIM WHO HIRED ME TO KILL HIM."
I GUESS IT'S TRUE. IF YOU WANT SOMETHING DONE RIGHT...
...YOU HAVE TO DO IT YOURSELF.
"WHAT'S WRONG, JESS?"
NOTHING, FLASH. WELL, EVERYTHING.
FIRST THE RING GETS IN MY HEAD, THEN THIS VIRUS. I'M GETTING TIRED OF IT. I WANT TO LEARN HOW TO STAY IN CONTROL.
I'M DETERMINED TO.
I KNOW. SO I CALLED SOMEONE WHO I THOUGHT COULD HELP TALK YOU THROUGH WILLPOWER AND A RING BETTER THAN I COULD.
WHO?
ME.

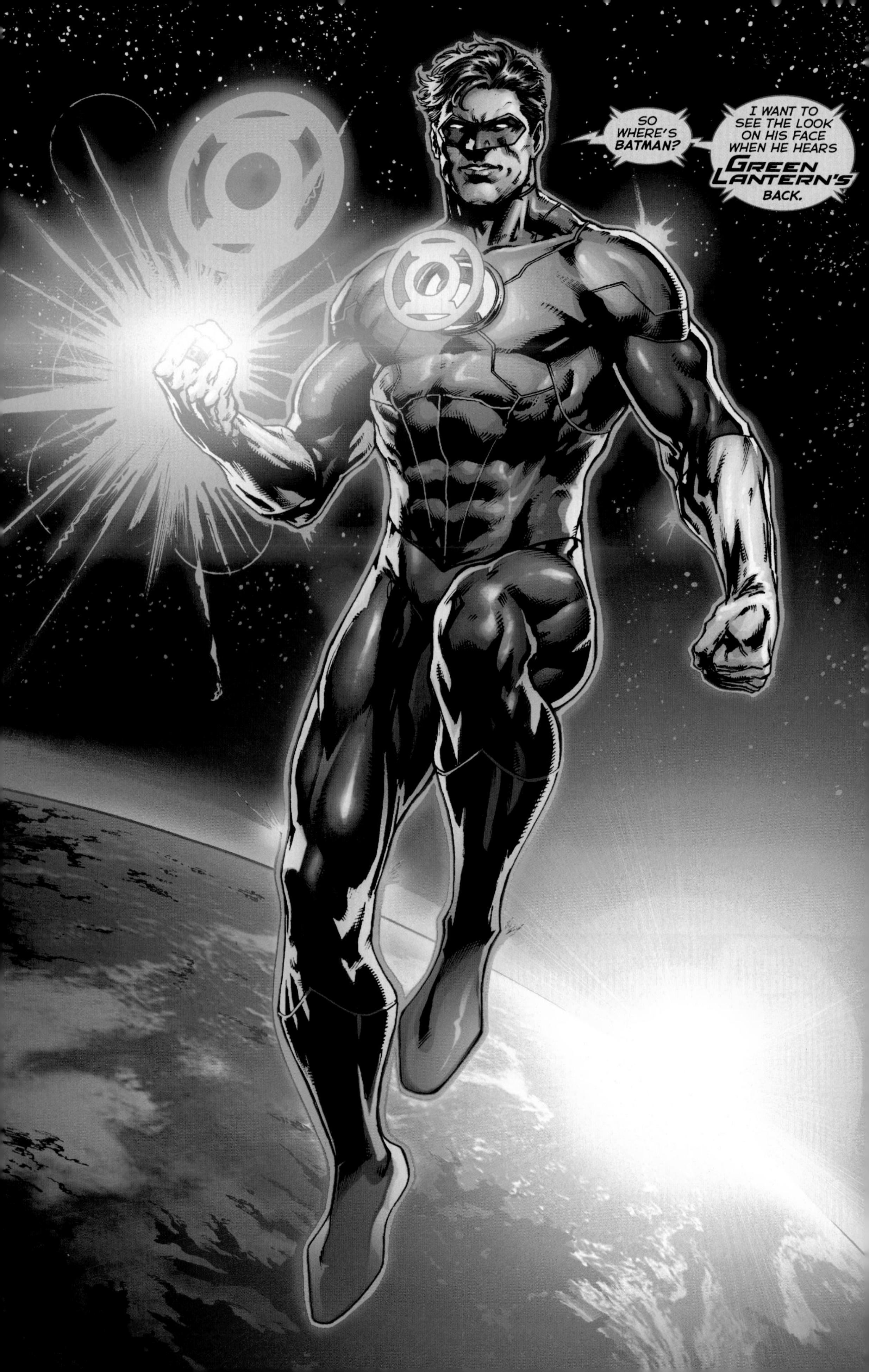
SO WHERE'S BATMAN?
I WANT TO SEE THE LOOK ON HIS FACE WHEN HE HEARS GREEN LANTERN'S BACK.

VARIANT COVER GALLERY

JUSTICE LEAGUE 30
MAD Magazine variant cover by Peter Kuper

JUSTICE LEAGUE 31
Batman '66 variant cover by Mike Allred

JUSTICE LEAGUE 32
Bombshell variant cover by Jim Fletcher

JUSTICE LEAGUE 32
Variant cover by Howard Porter & Hi-Fi

JUSTICE LEAGUE 33
Batman 75th anniversary variant cover by Darwyn Cooke

JUSTICE LEAGUE 33
Variant cover by Mikel Janin & Marcelo Maiolo

JUSTICE LEAGUE 34
Selfie variant cover by Dale Eaglesham & Alex Sinclair

JUSTICE LEAGUE 34
Variant cover by Rags Morales & Steve Buccellato

JUSTICE LEAGUE 35
Monster variant cover by Rafael Albuquerque

JUSTICE LEAGUE 35
Variant cover by Jerry Ordway & Alex Sinclair

JUSTICE LEAGUE 36
Lego variant cover

JUSTICE LEAGUE 36
Variant cover by Joshua Middleton

JUSTICE LEAGUE 37
Variant cover by Darwyn Cooke

JUSTICE LEAGUE 37
Variant cover by Szymon Kudranski

JUSTICE LEAGUE 38
Flash 75th anniversary cover by Tony Harris, after Mike Sekowsky & Murphy Anderson

JUSTICE LEAGUE 38
Variant cover by Andrew Robinson

JUSTICE LEAGUE 39
Harley Quinn variant cover by Dustin Nguyen

JUSTICE LEAGUE 39
Variant cover by Babs Tarr

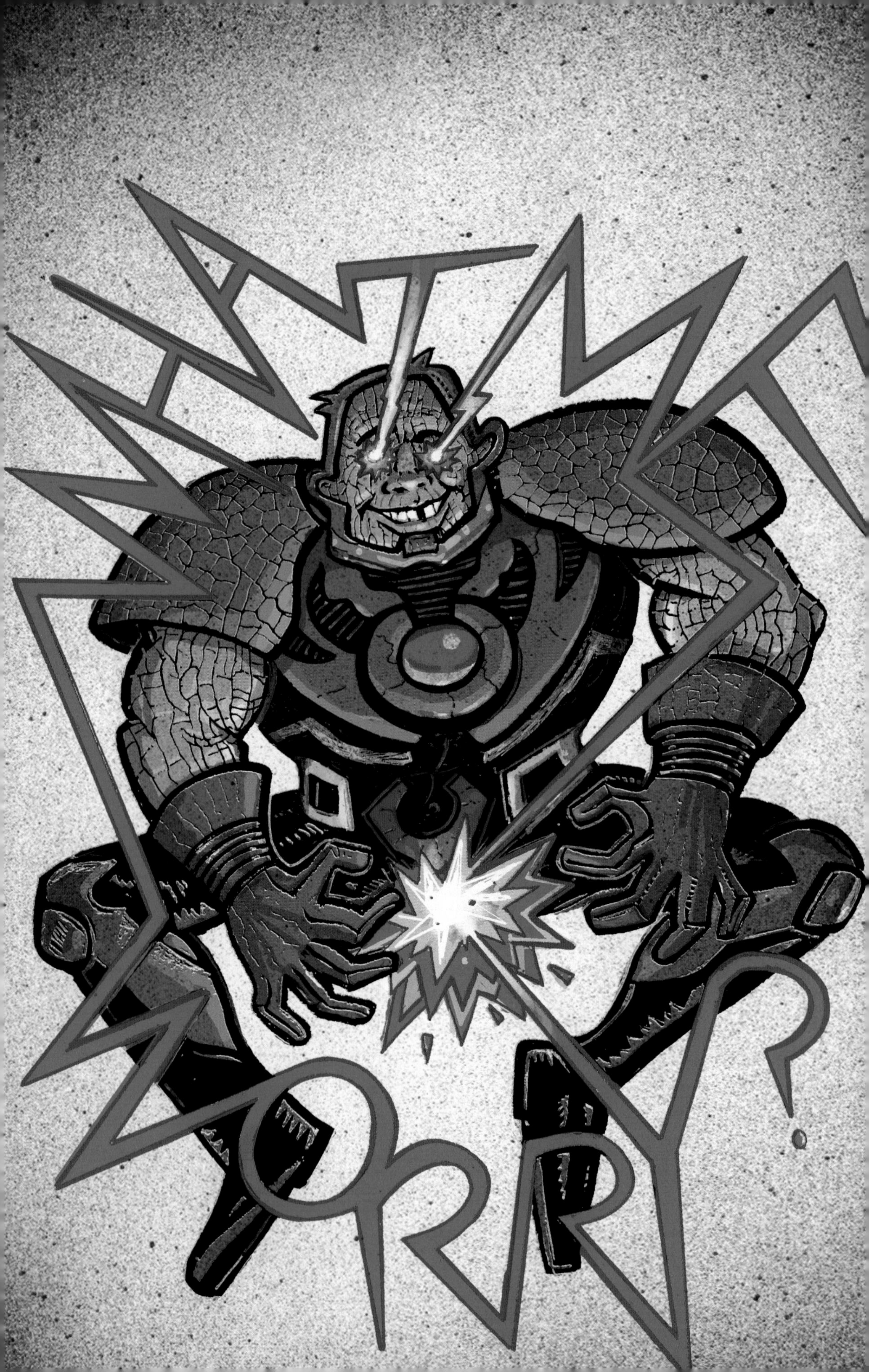
WHAT ME WORRY?

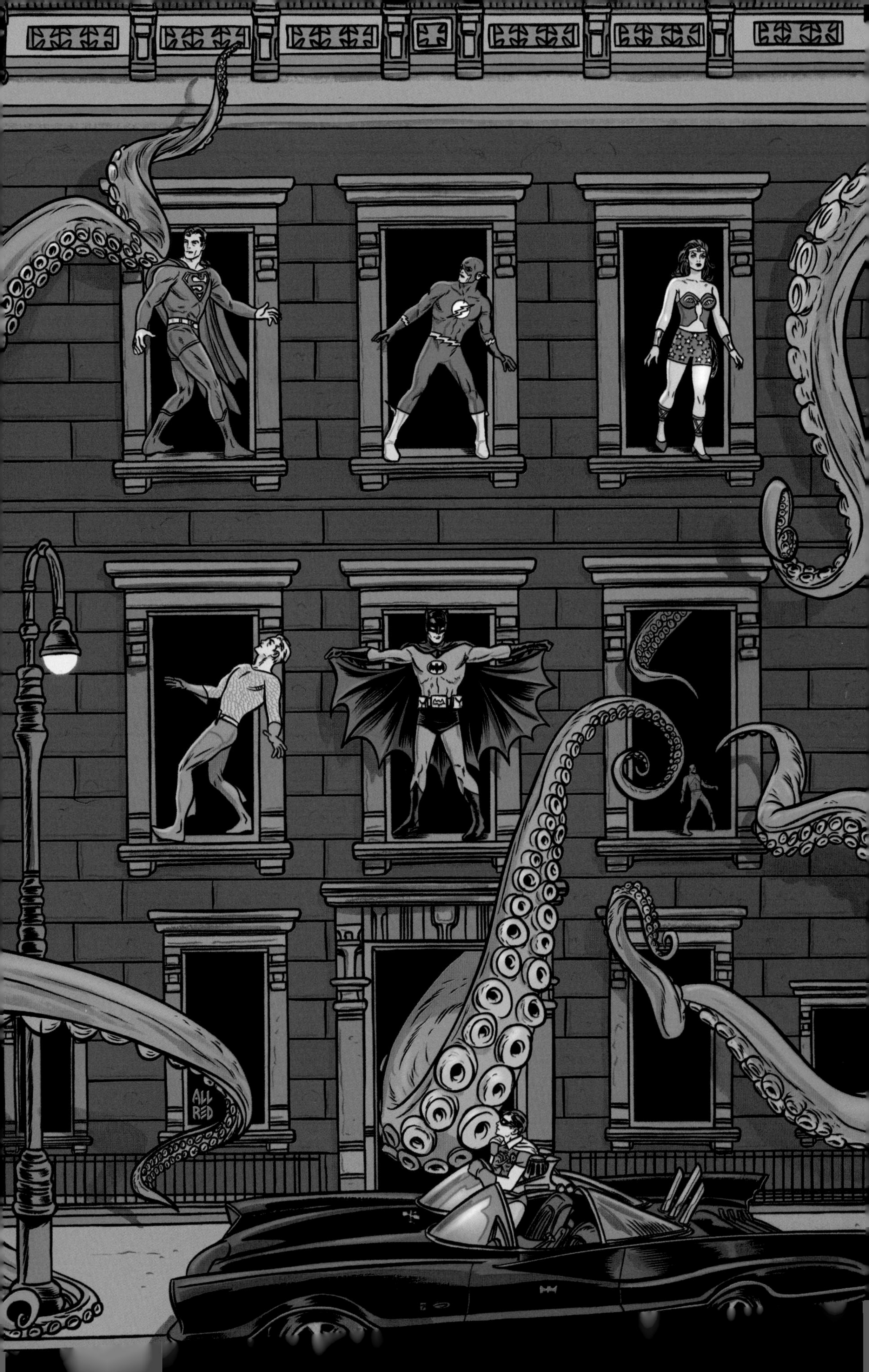
ALL RED

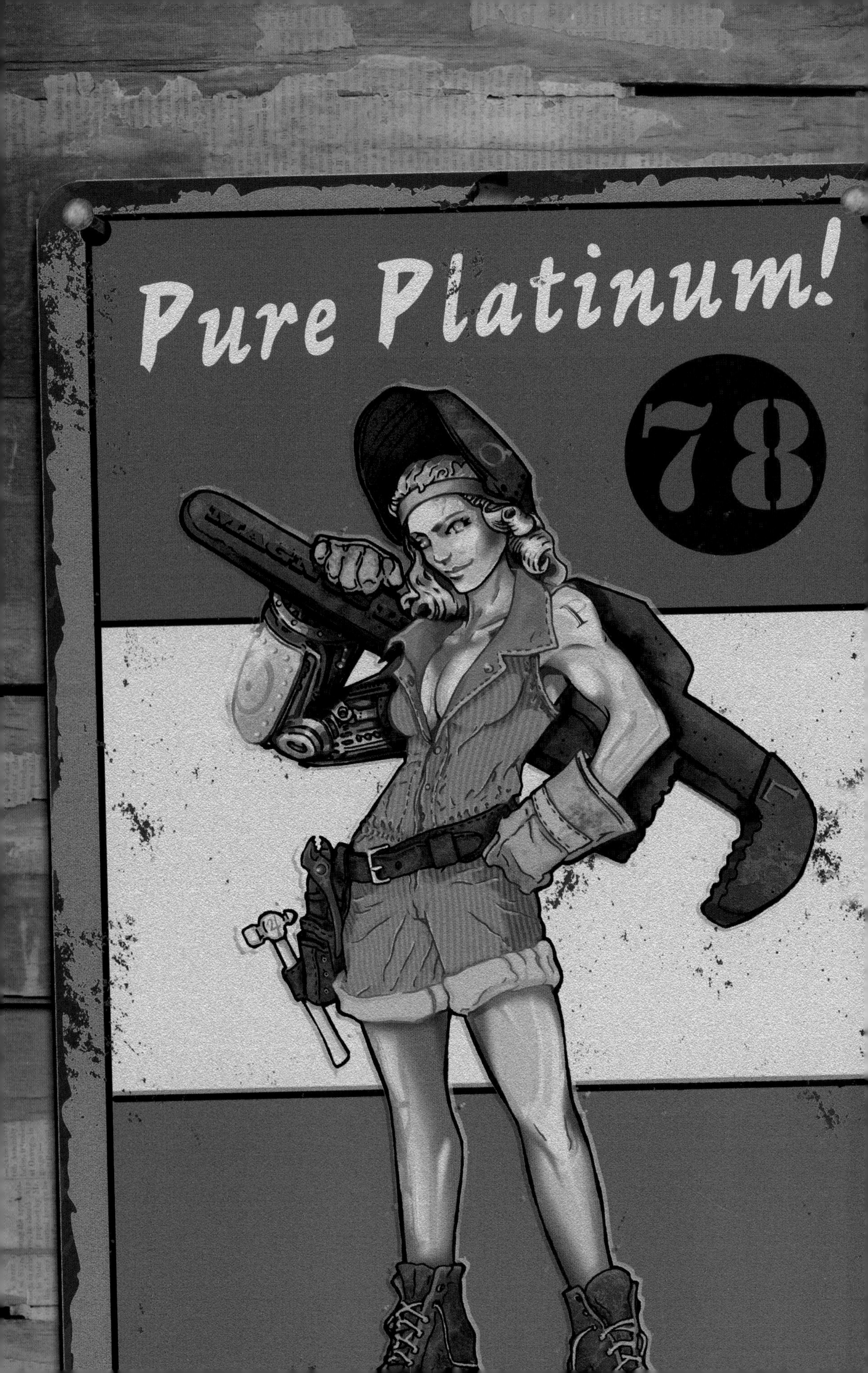
Pure Platinum!
78

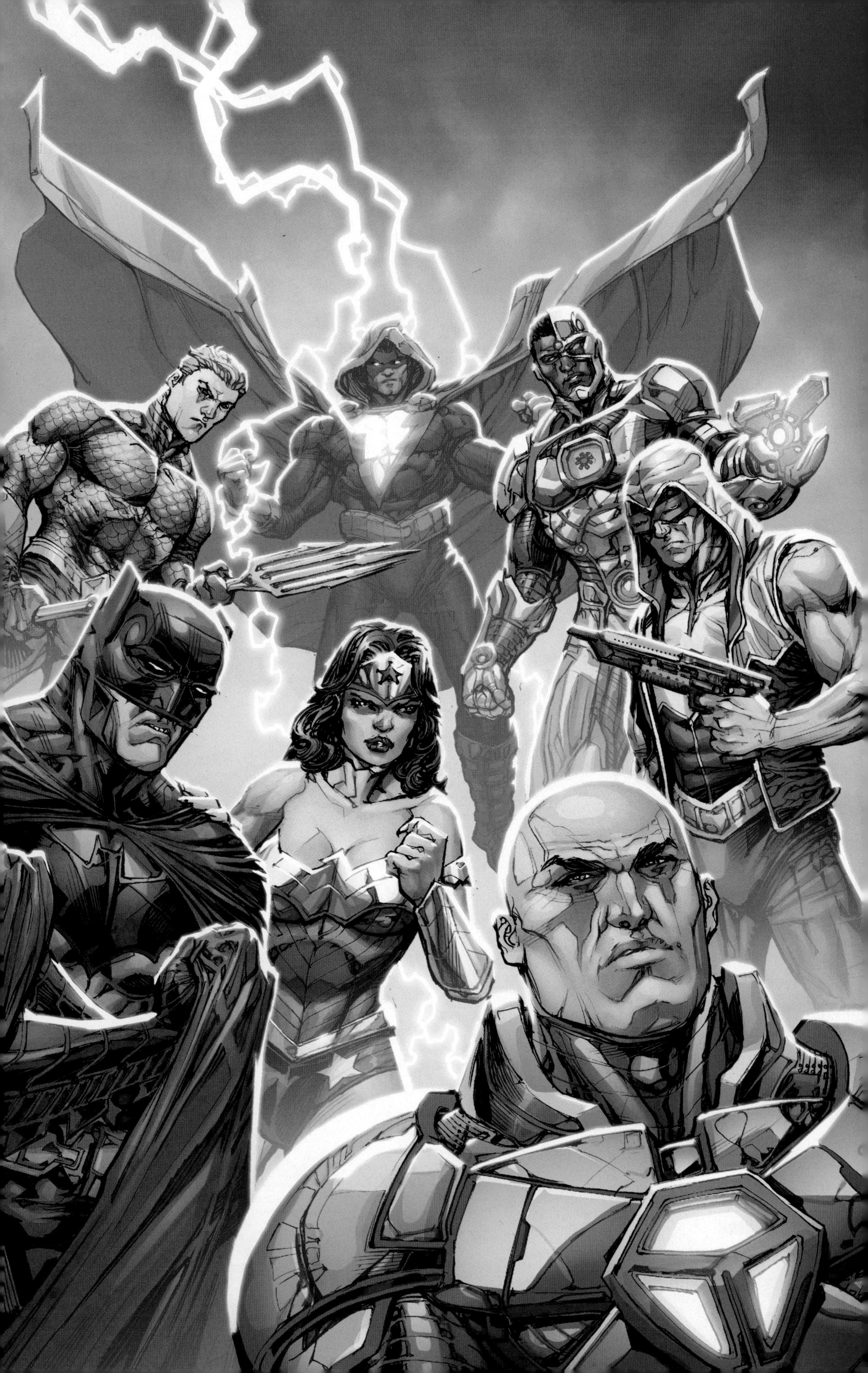

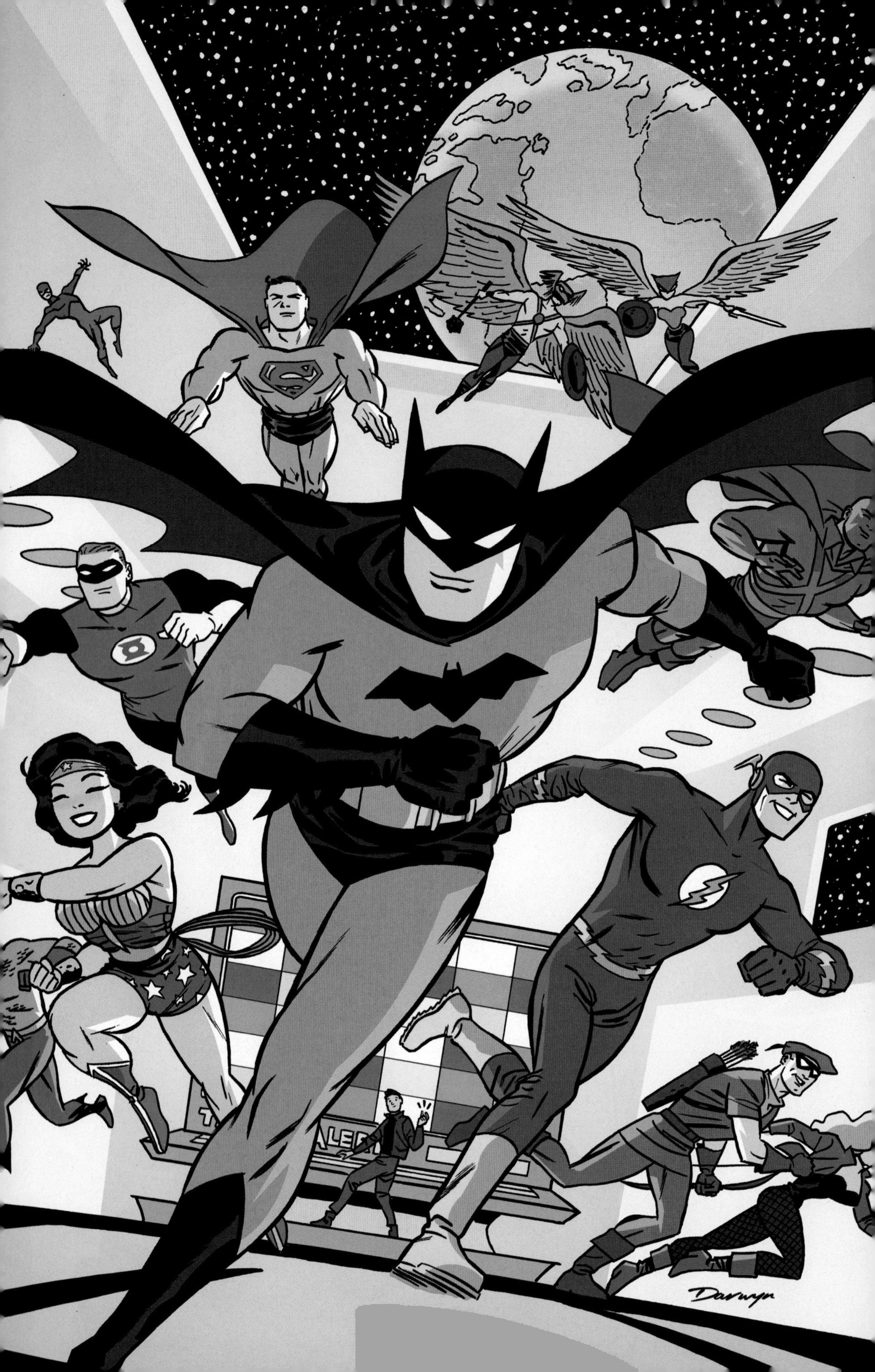
Darwyn

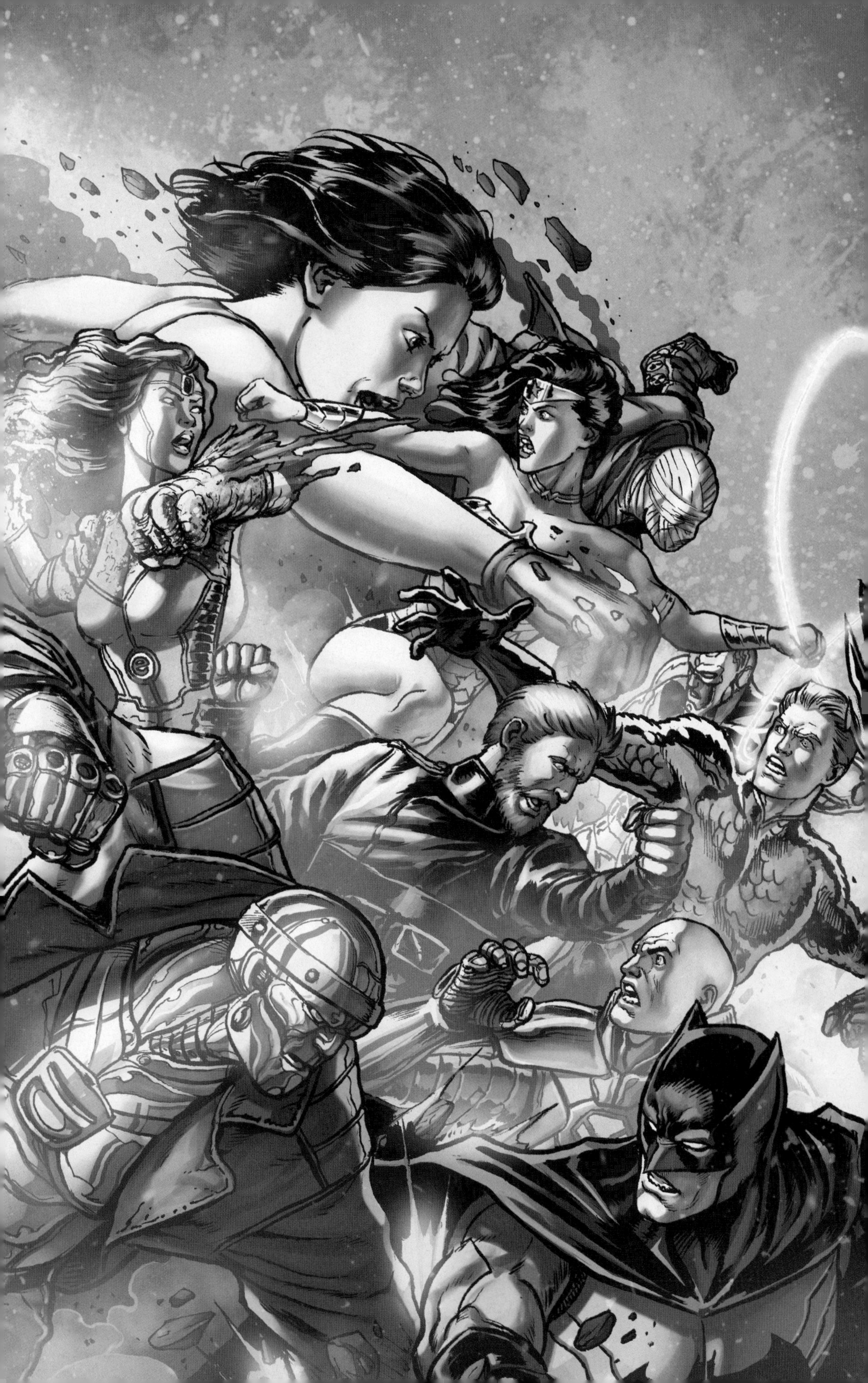

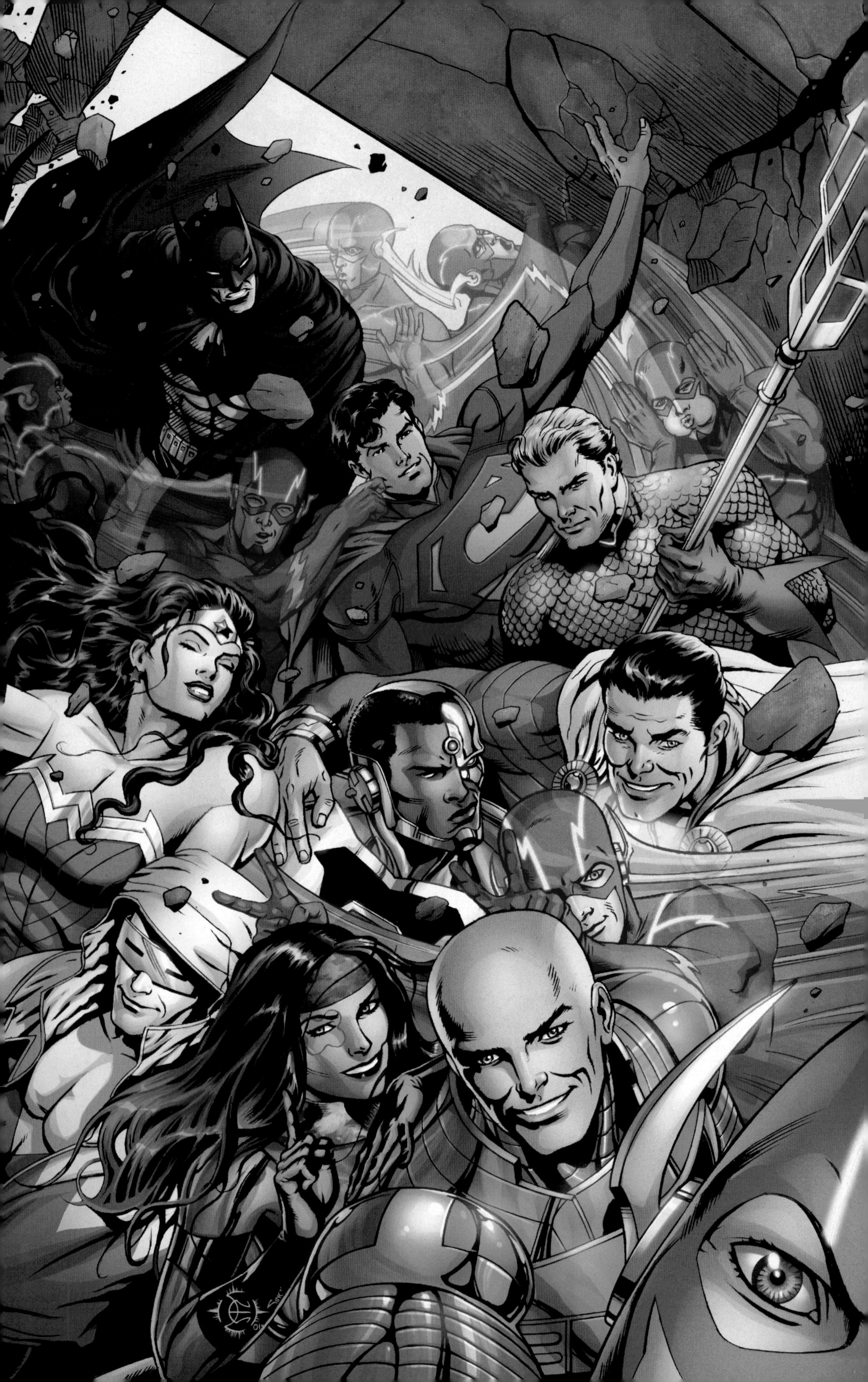

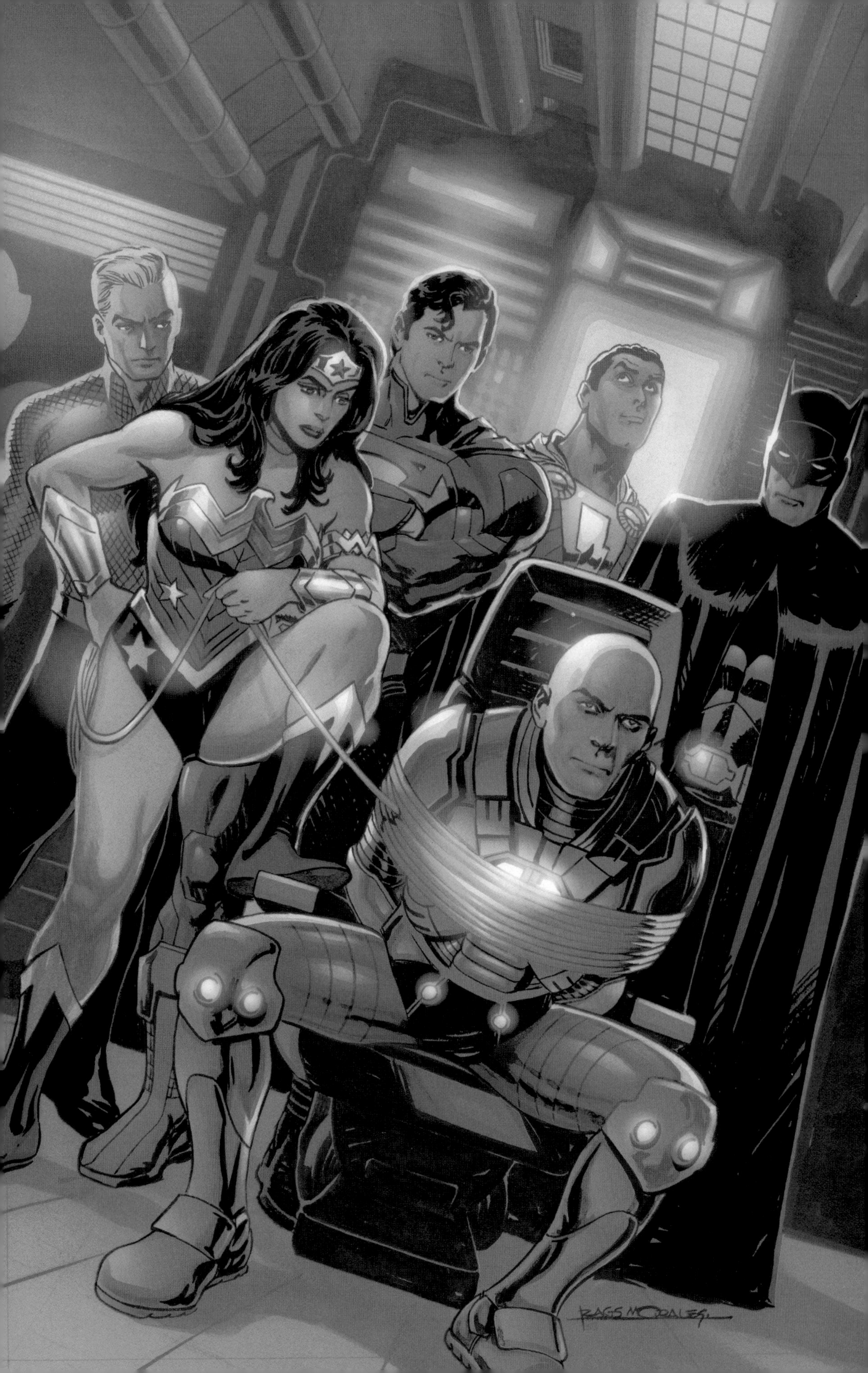
RAGS MORALES

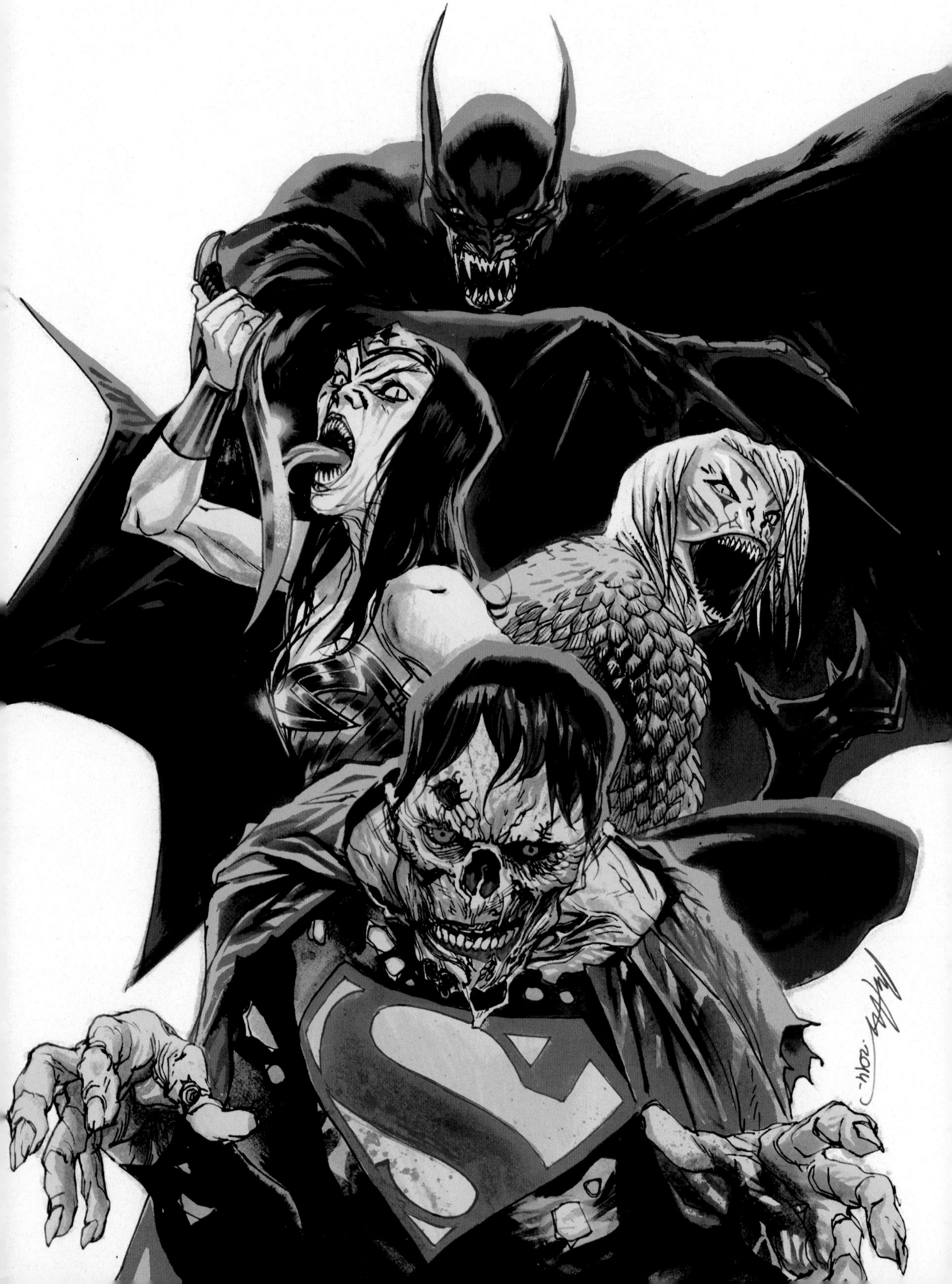

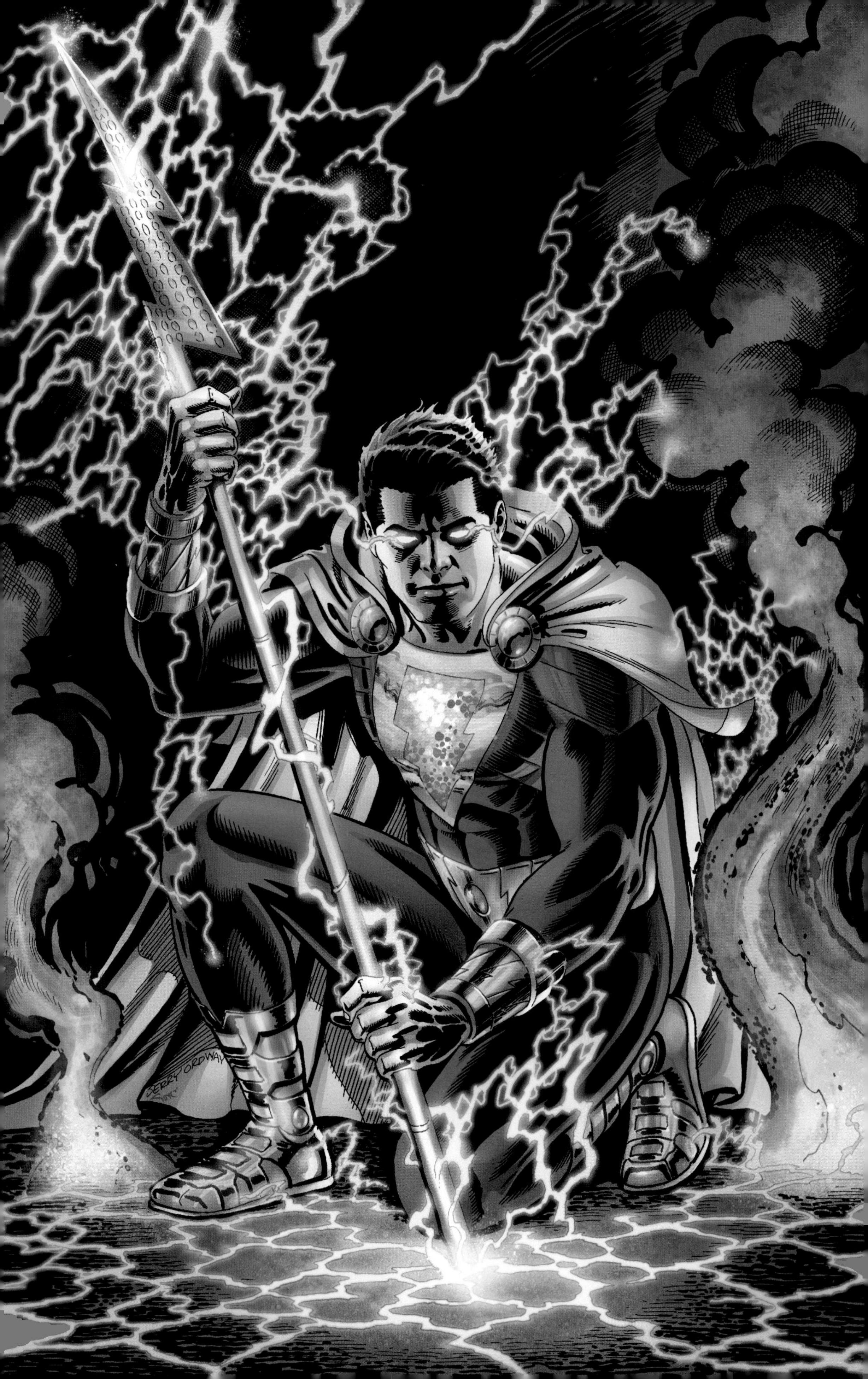
JERRY ORDWAY

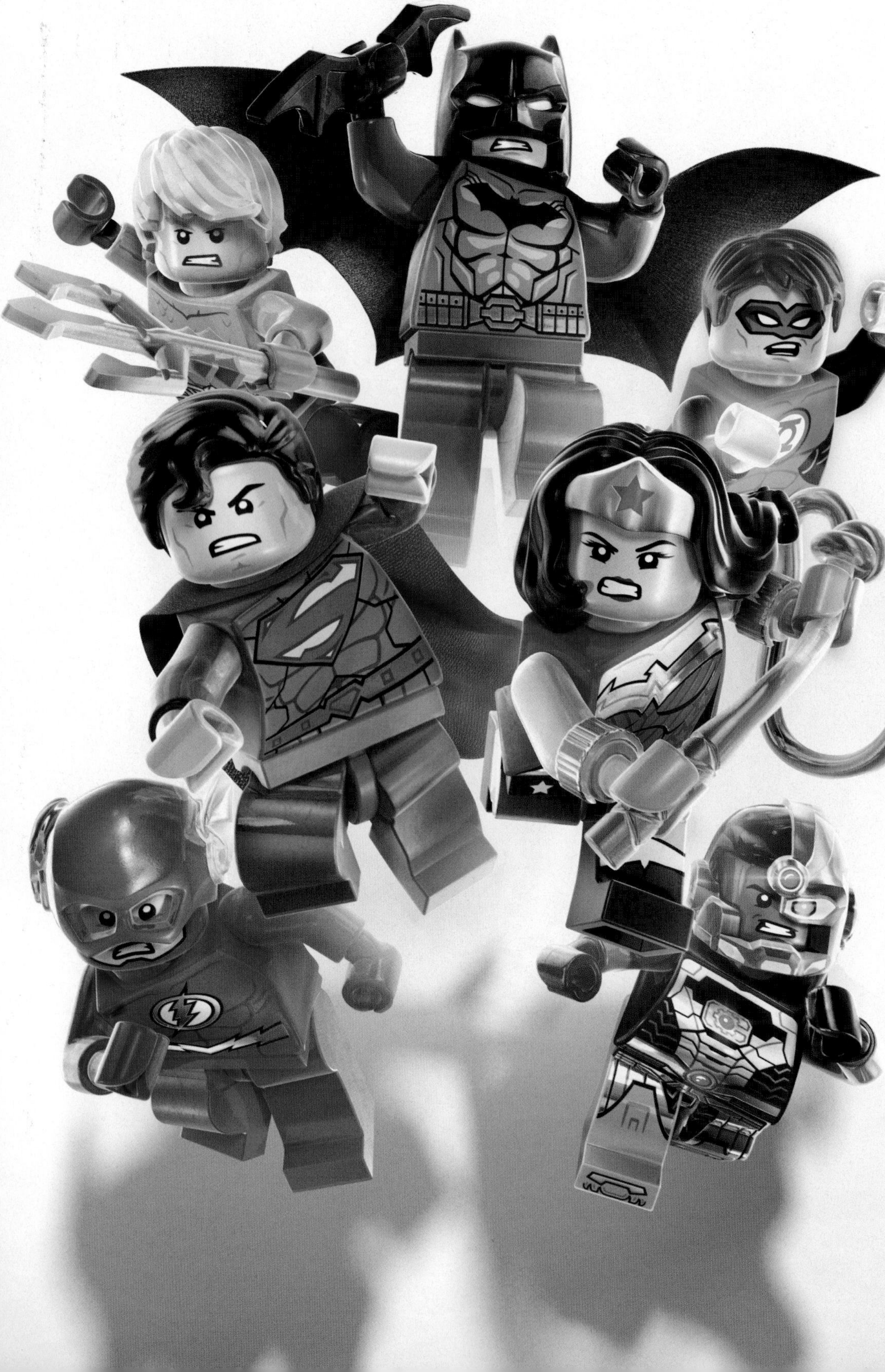

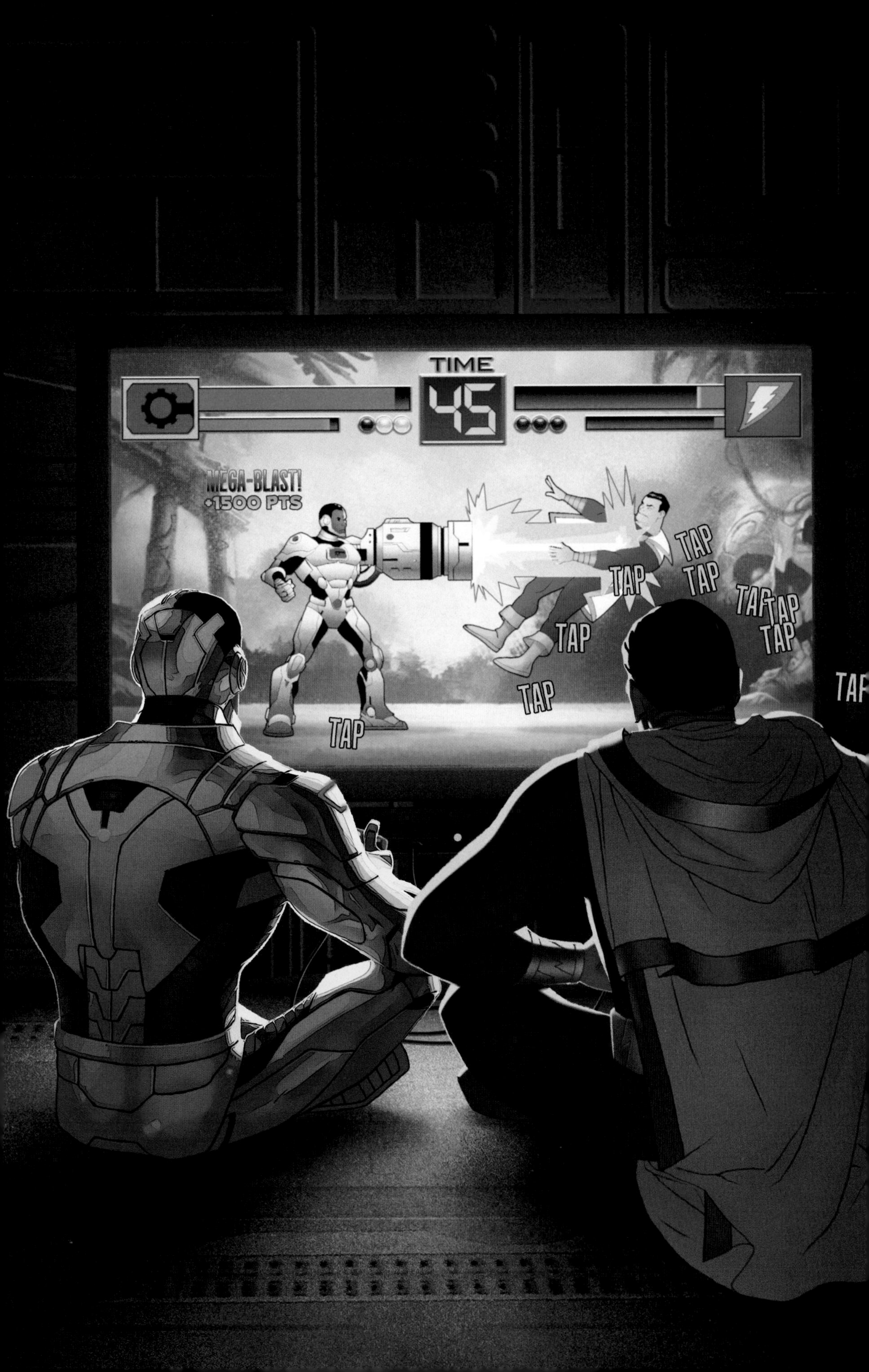
TIME
45
MEGA-BLAST!
+1500 PTS
TAP
TAP
TAP
TAP
TAP
TAP
TAP
TAP
TAP
TAP

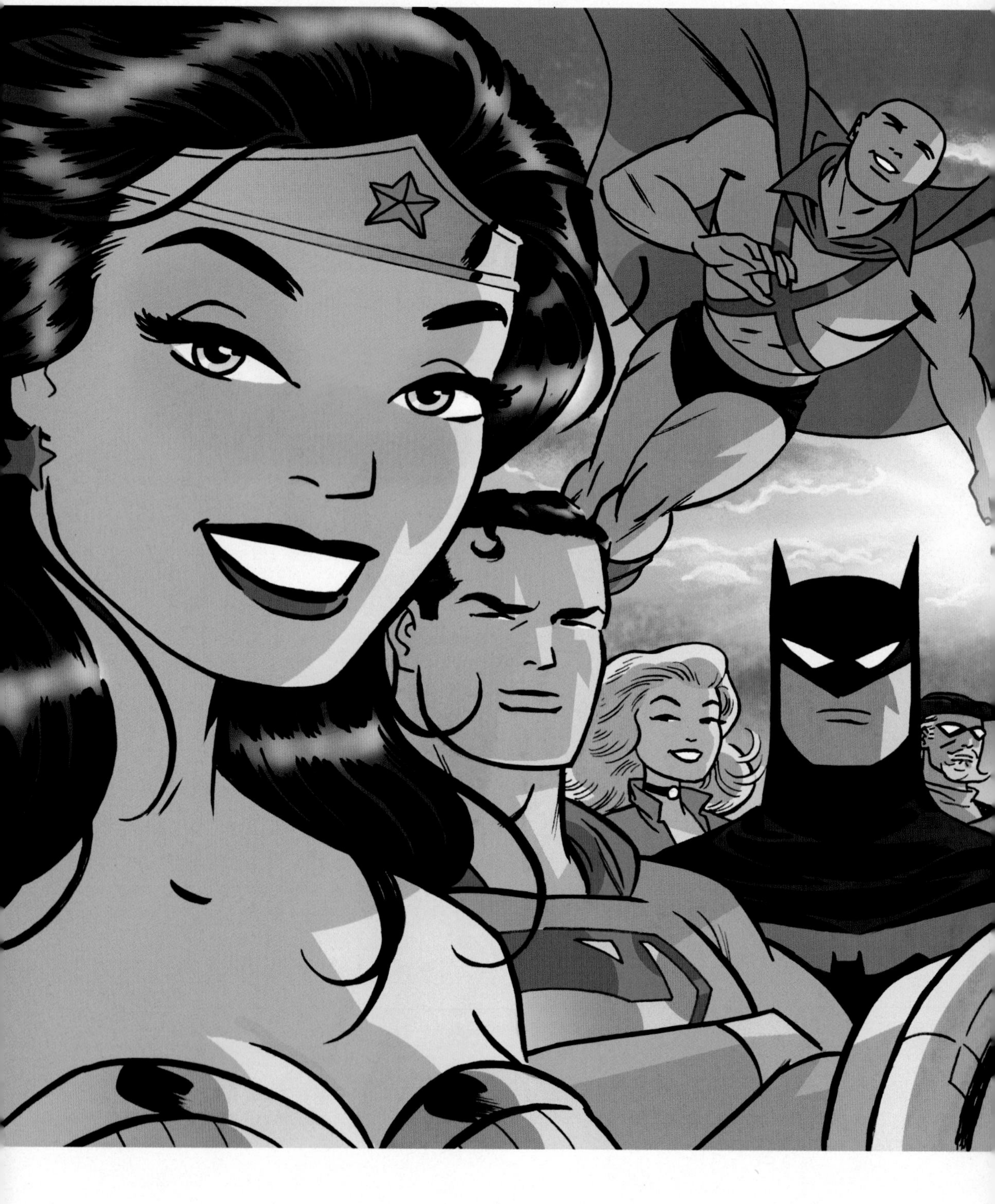

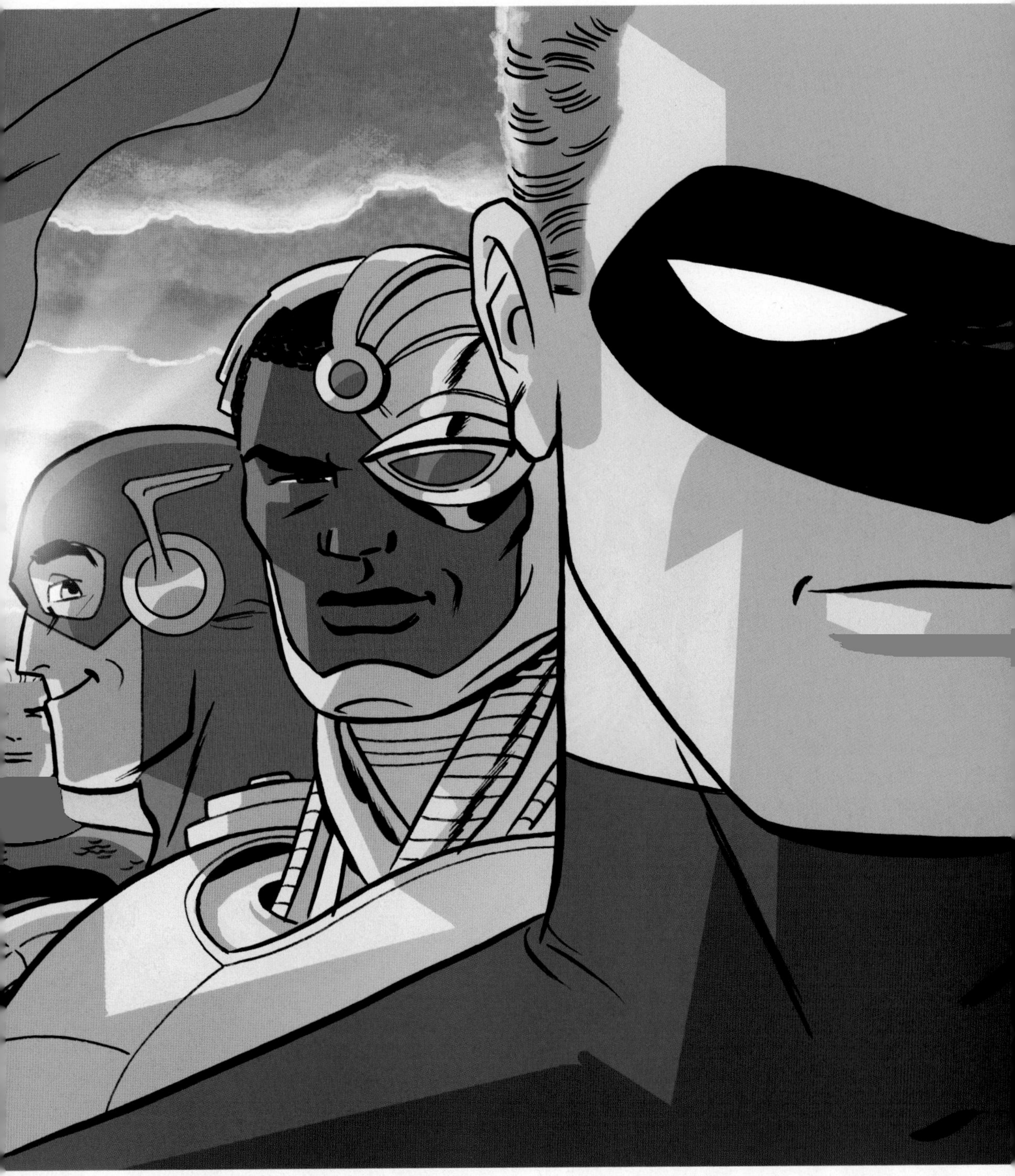

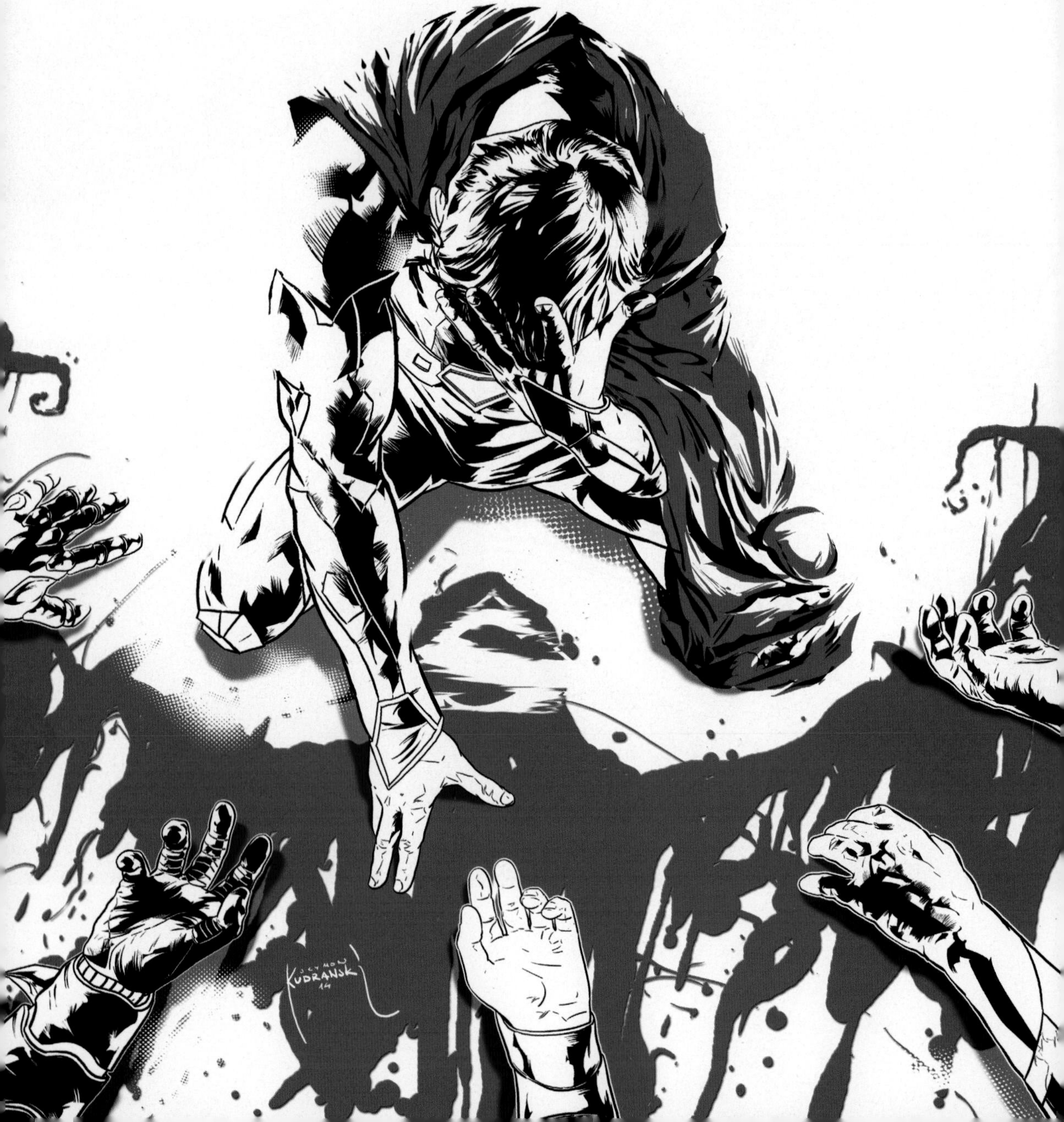
KUDRANSK
14

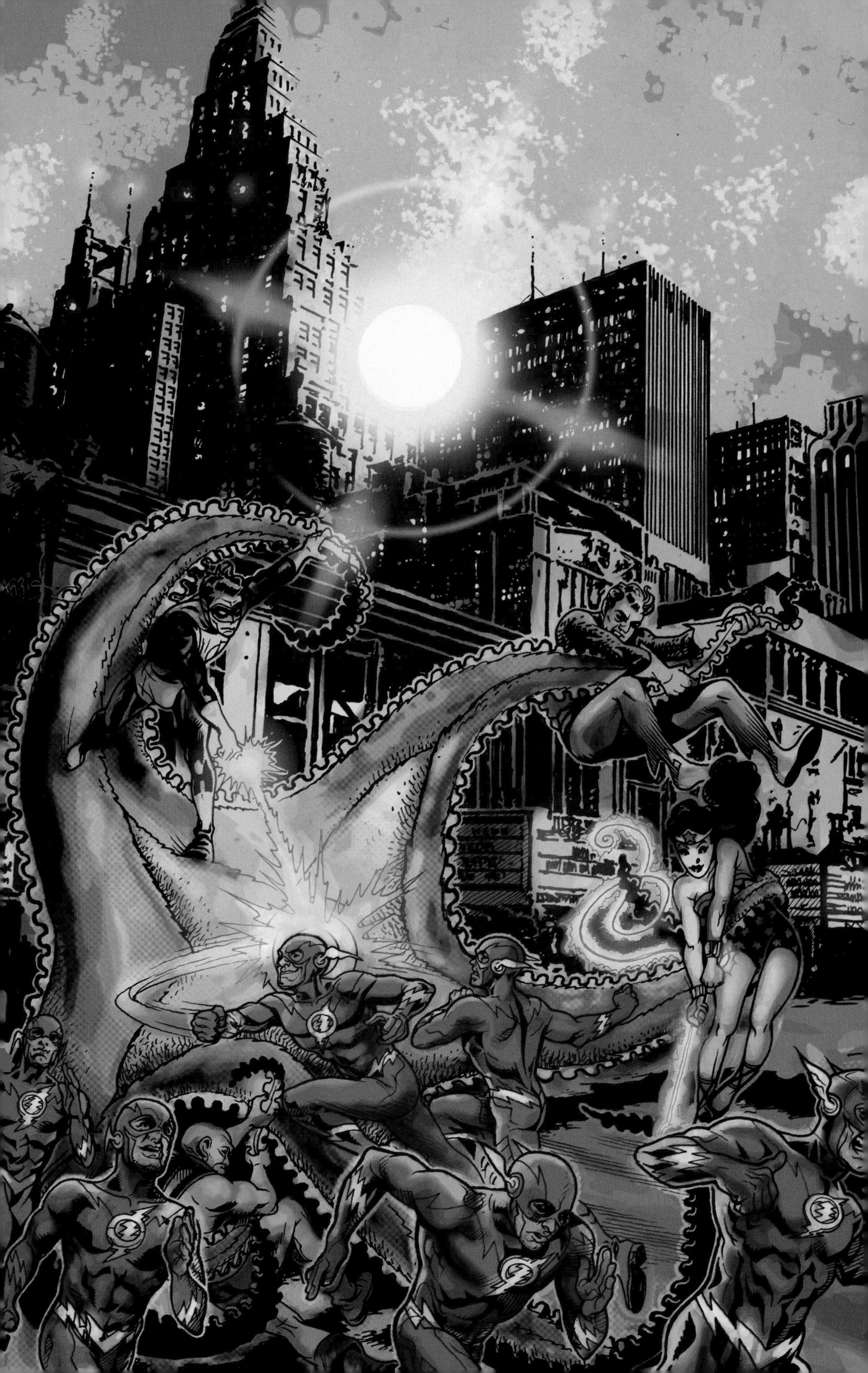

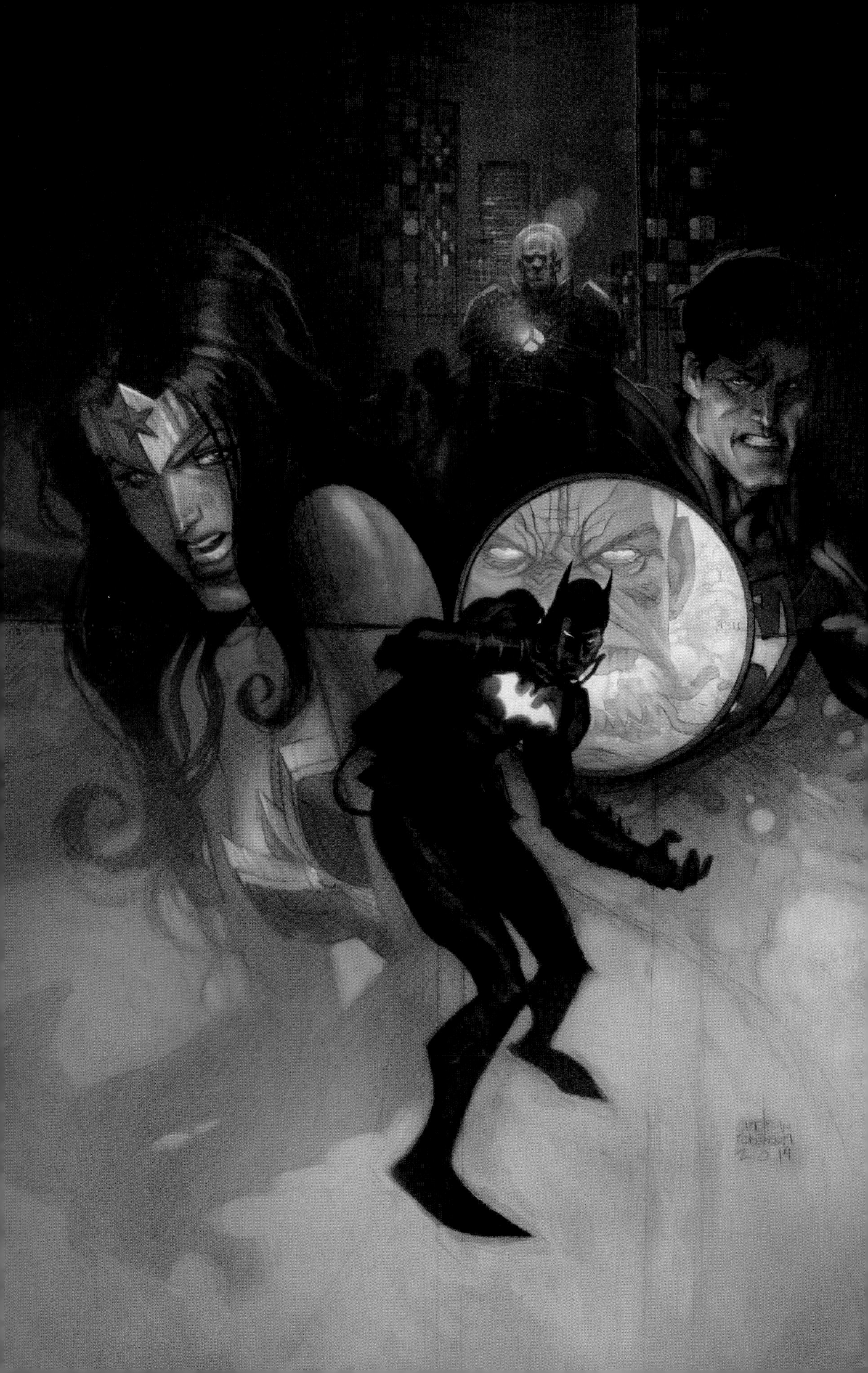

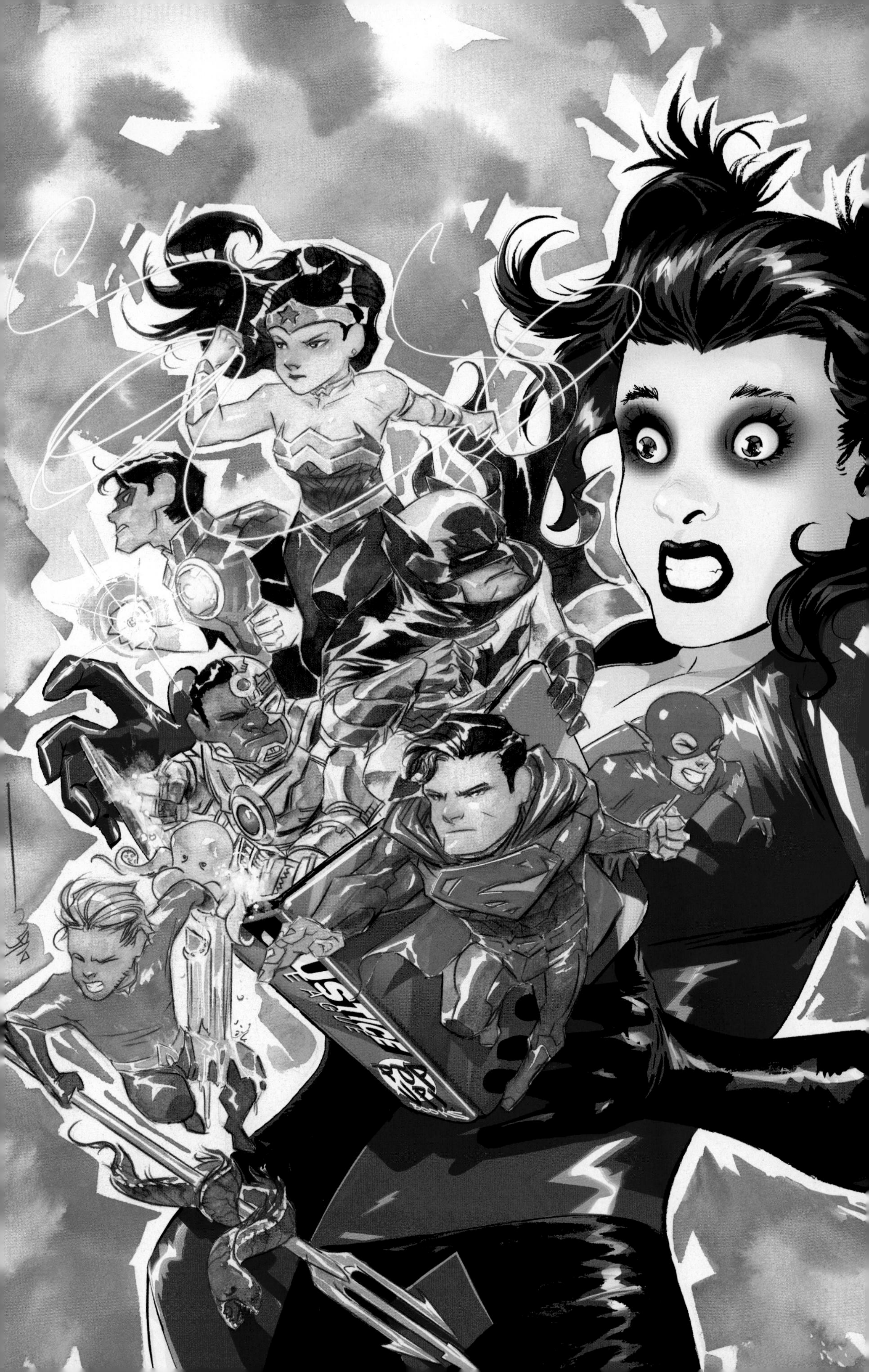
USTICE
EAGUE

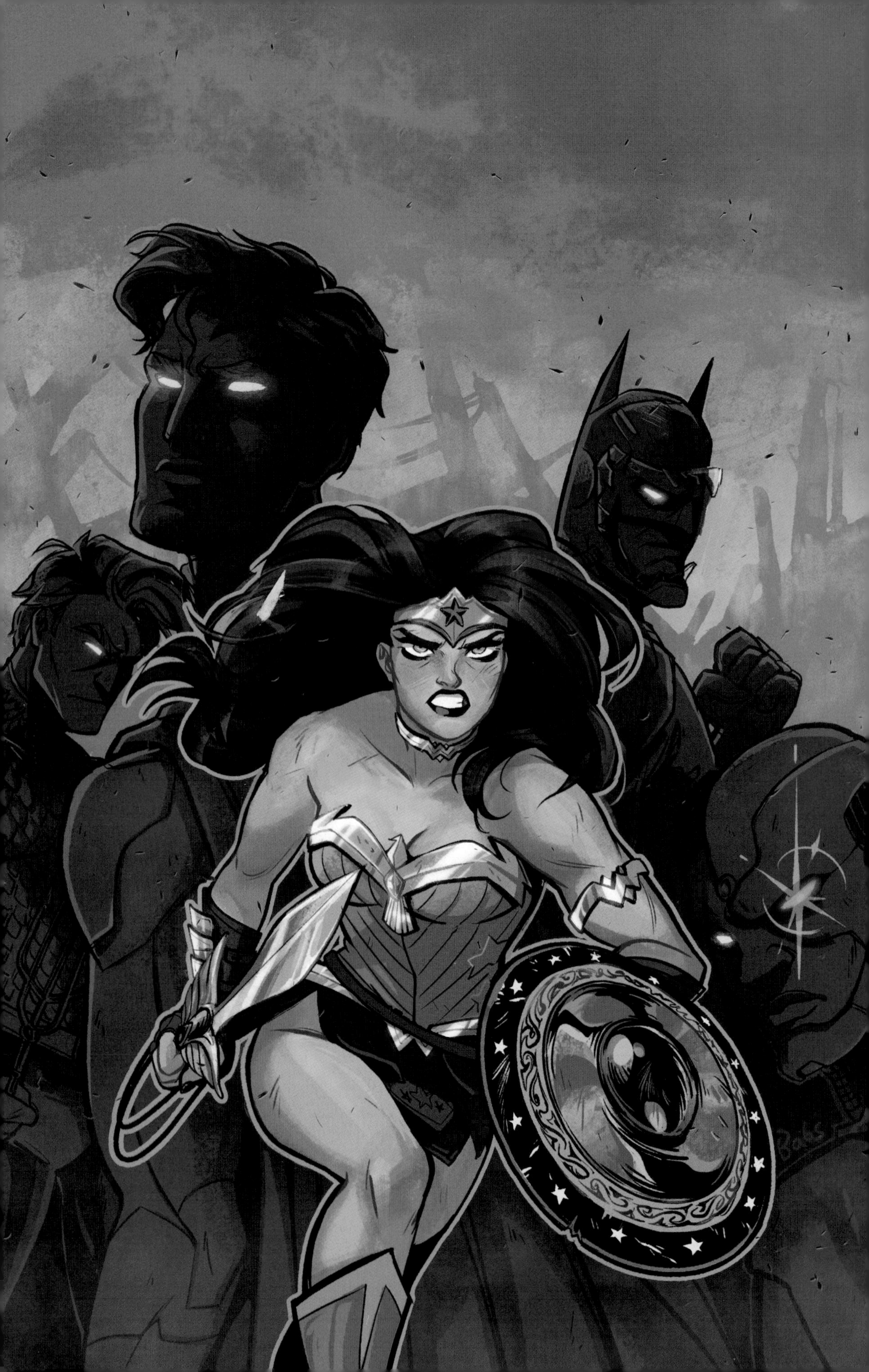

Unused early designs for Batman's contagion suit by Jason Fabok

BAT-ZMAT
SUIT
FORM FITTING FACEMASK
TANK
BAT-SYMBOL
GLOWS
CLASSIC
BAT-SYMBOL
CAPE?
FABOK
2014
JL

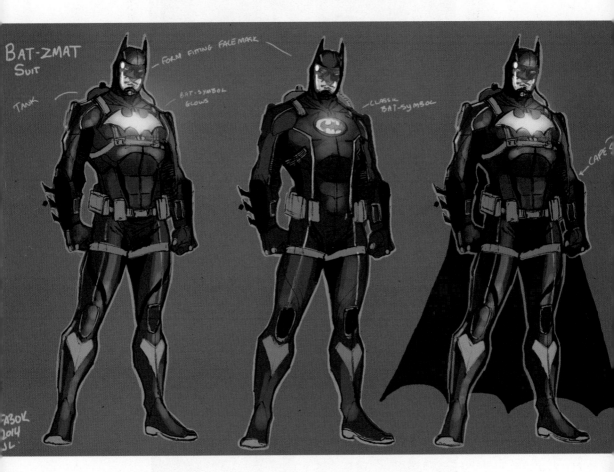

Final design for Batman's contagion suit

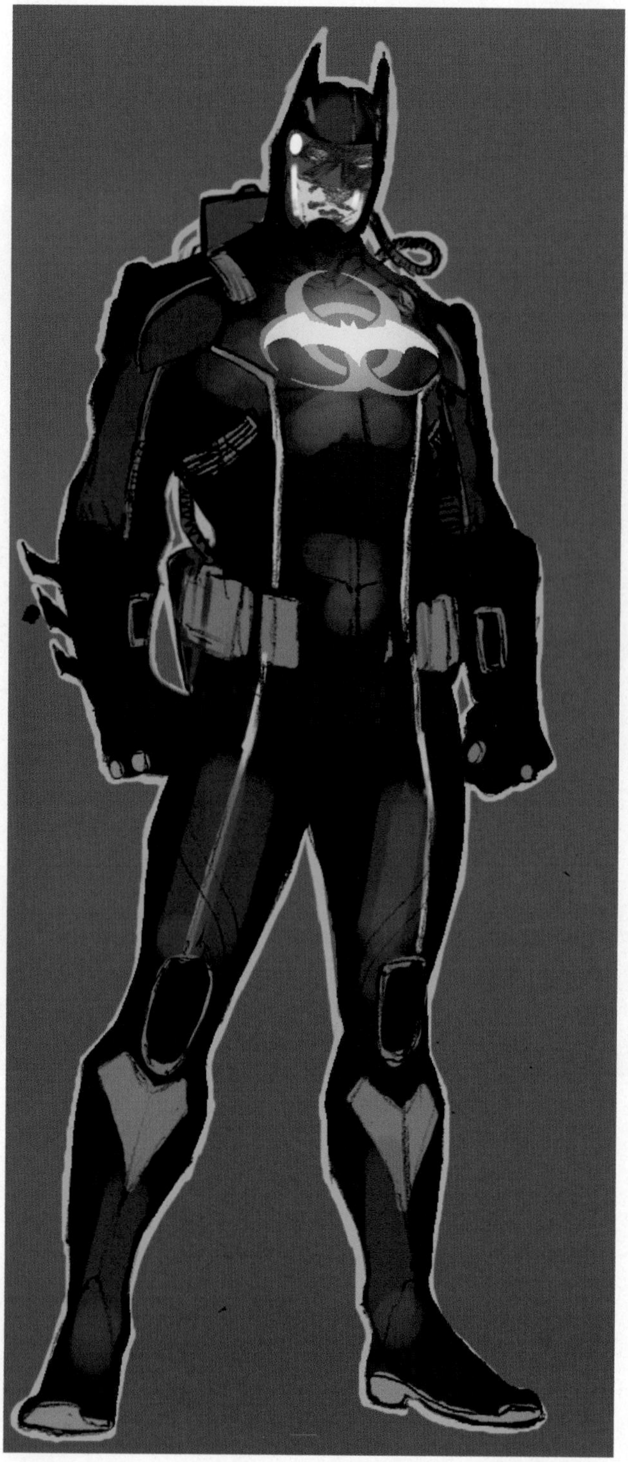

Cover sketches for JUSTICE LEAGUE #30 & 35 by Ivan Reis

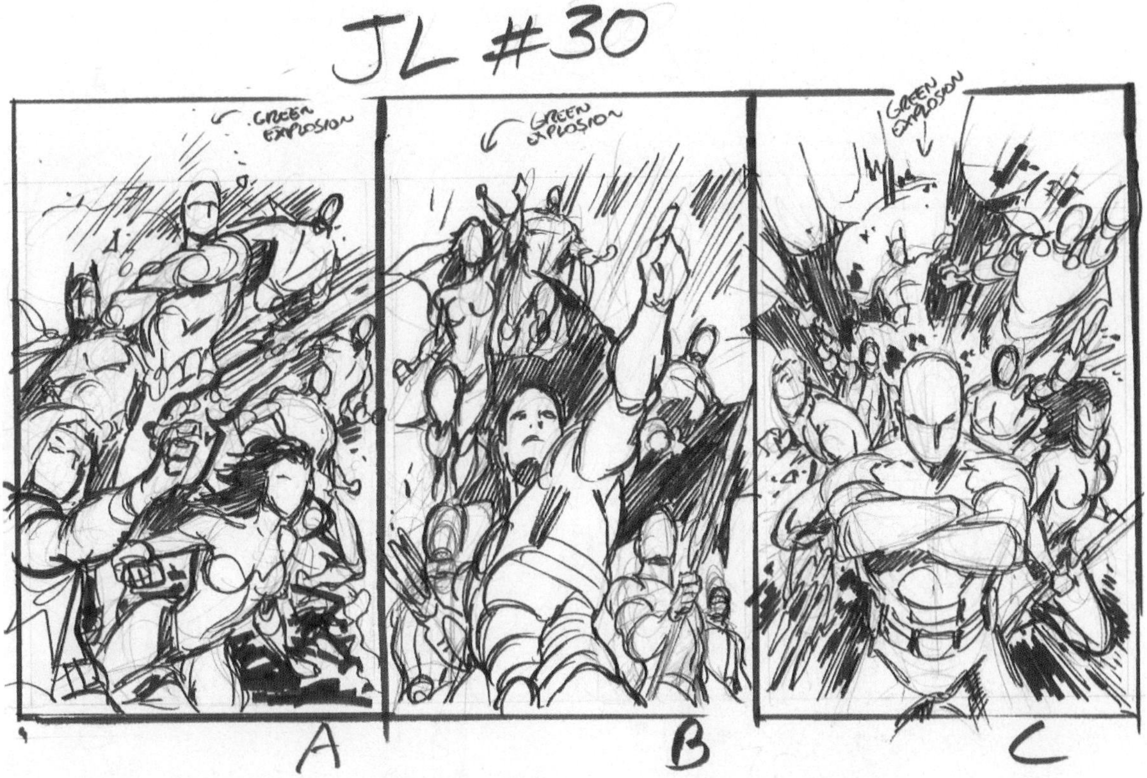
JL #30
GREEN EXPLOSION
GREEN EXPLOSION
GREEN EXPLOSION
A
B
C

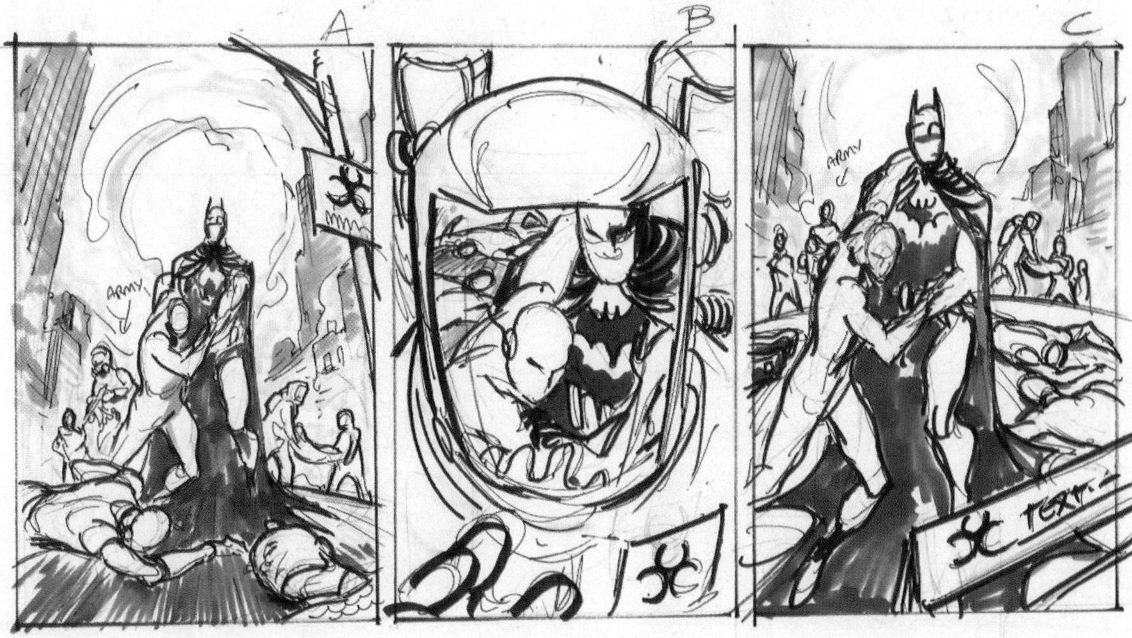
A
B
C
ARMY
ARMY
TEXT

Cover sketches for JUSTICE LEAGUE #32 by Ivan Reis

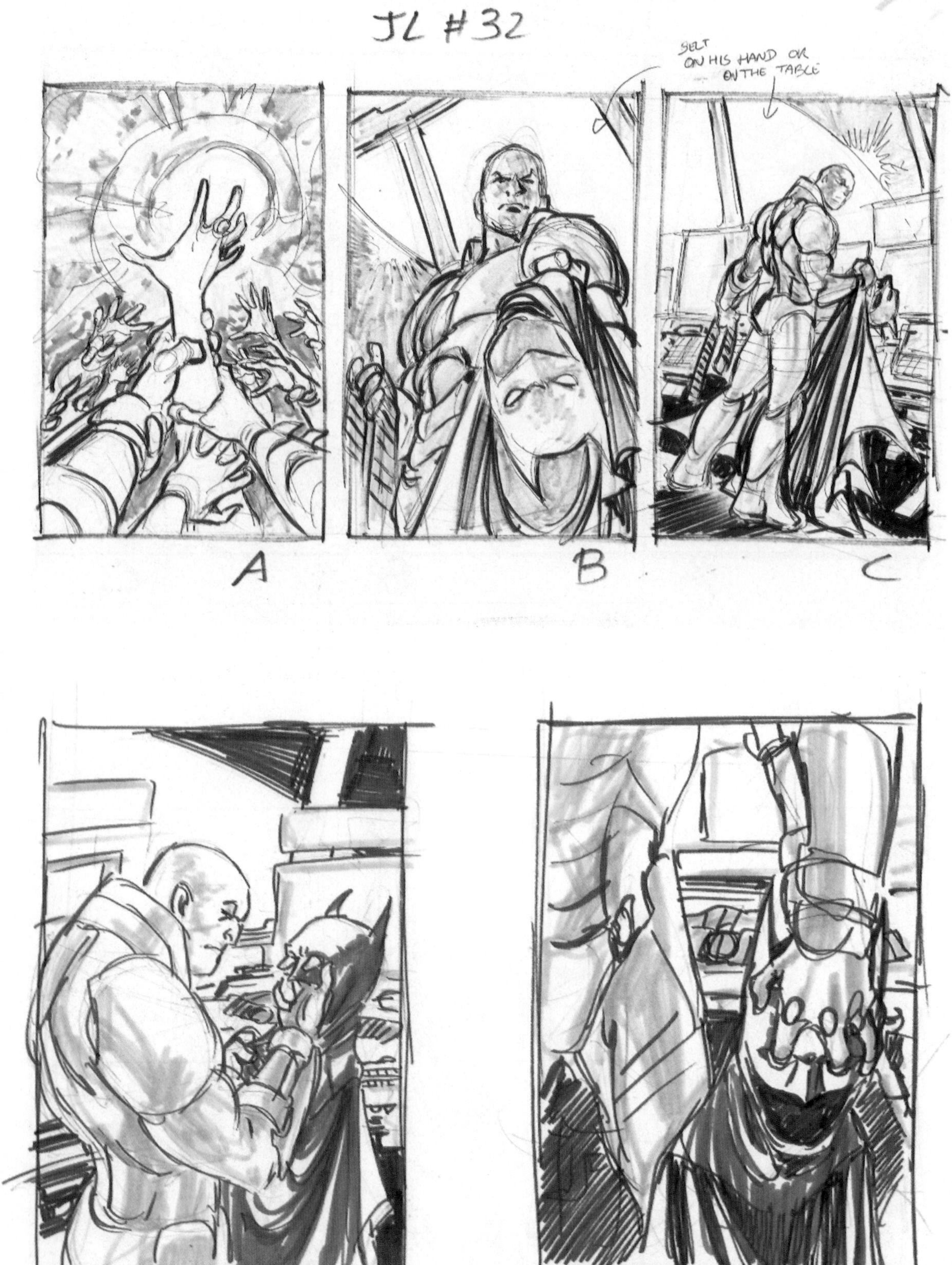
JL #32
BELT ON HIS HAND OR ON THE TABLE
A
B
C
D
E